Modern European Philosophers

Modern European Philosophers

Wayne P. Pomerleau

WILEY Blackwell

This edition first published 2023

© 2023 John Wiley & Sons, Inc.

All rights reserved. No part of this publication may be reproduced, stored in a retrieval system, or transmitted, in any form or by any means, electronic, mechanical, photocopying, recording or otherwise, except as permitted by law. Advice on how to obtain permission to reuse material from this title is available at http://www.wiley.com/go/permissions.

The right of Wayne P. Pomerleau to be identified as the author of the editorial material in this work has been asserted in accordance with law.

Registered Office
John Wiley & Sons, Inc., 111 River Street, Hoboken, NJ 07030, USA

Editorial Office
9600 Garsington Road, Oxford, OX4 2DQ, UK

For details of our global editorial offices, customer services, and more information about Wiley products visit us at www.wiley.com.

Wiley also publishes its books in a variety of electronic formats and by print-on-demand. Some content that appears in standard print versions of this book may not be available in other formats.

Limit of Liability/Disclaimer of Warranty
The contents of this work are intended to further general scientific research, understanding, and discussion only and are not intended and should not be relied upon as recommending or promoting scientific method, diagnosis, or treatment by physicians for any particular patient. In view of ongoing research, equipment modifications, changes in governmental regulations, and the constant flow of information relating to the use of medicines, equipment, and devices, the reader is urged to review and evaluate the information provided in the package insert or instructions for each medicine, equipment, or device for, among other things, any changes in the instructions or indication of usage and for added warnings and precautions. While the publisher and authors have used their best efforts in preparing this work, they make no representations or warranties with respect to the accuracy or completeness of the contents of this work and specifically disclaim all warranties, including without limitation any implied warranties of merchantability or fitness for a particular purpose. No warranty may be created or extended by sales representatives, written sales materials or promotional statements for this work. The fact that an organization, website, or product is referred to in this work as a citation and/or potential source of further information does not mean that the publisher and authors endorse the information or services the organization, website, or product may provide or recommendations it may make. This work is sold with the understanding that the publisher is not engaged in rendering professional services. The advice and strategies contained herein may not be suitable for your situation. You should consult with a specialist where appropriate. Further, readers should be aware that websites listed in this work may have changed or disappeared between when this work was written and when it is read. Neither the publisher nor authors shall be liable for any loss of profit or any other commercial damages, including but not limited to special, incidental, consequential, or other damages..

Library of Congress Cataloging-in-Publication Data
Names: Pomerleau, Wayne P., 1946– author. | Wiley-Blackwell (Firm),
    publisher.
Title: Modern European philosophers / Wayne P. Pomerleau.
Description: Hoboken, NJ : Wiley-Blackwell, 2023. | Includes
    bibliographical references and index.
Identifiers: LCCN 2022026425 (print) | LCCN 2022026426 (ebook) | ISBN
    9781119902355 (paperback) | ISBN 9781119902362 (adobe pdf) | ISBN
    9781119902379 (epub)
Subjects: LCSH: Philosophy, Modern–History. | Philosophy,
    European–History. | Philosophers–Europe.
Classification: LCC B791 .P64 2023 (print) | LCC B791 (ebook) | DDC
    190–dc23/eng/20220810
LC record available at https://lccn.loc.gov/2022026425
LC ebook record available at https://lccn.loc.gov/2022026426

Cover Design: Wiley
Cover Image: © Trifonov_Evgeniy/Getty Images

Set in 9.5/12.5pt STIXTwoText by Straive, Pondicherry, India

SKY10036192_092822

This book is respectfully dedicated to the thousands of undergraduate and graduate students I taught during my forty-four years of teaching philosophy at Gonzaga University and to my department colleagues during that entire time.

Contents

Acknowledgments   *xiii*

	Introduction	*1*
1	**Background**	*4*
1.1	Overview	*4*
1.2	Ancient Philosophy	*4*
	1.2.1 "Ancient"	*4*
	1.2.2 "Philosophy"	*5*
	1.2.3 The Pre-Socratics	*5*
	1.2.4 Socrates and Plato	*6*
	1.2.5 Aristotle	*8*
	1.2.6 Post-Aristotelians	*10*
	1.2.6.1 Epicurus	*10*
	1.2.6.2 Epictetus	*10*
	1.2.6.3 Sextus Empiricus	*11*
	1.2.6.4 Cicero	*11*
	1.2.6.5 Plotinus	*12*
1.3	Medieval Philosophy	*12*
	1.3.1 "Medieval"	*12*
	1.3.2 Augustine	*13*
	1.3.3 Boethius	*14*
	1.3.4 Anselm	*14*
	1.3.5 Aquinas	*15*
1.4	Renaissance Thinkers	*17*
	1.4.1 "Renaissance"	*17*
	1.4.2 Machiavelli	*17*
	1.4.3 Montaigne	*18*
	1.4.4 Bacon	*18*
	1.4.5 Galileo	*19*
1.5	Review	*20*
2	**René Descartes**	*21*
2.1	Overview	*21*
2.2	Biography	*22*
2.3	Knowledge	*23*
2.4	Reality	*25*
2.5	God	*26*
2.6	Humanity	*27*
2.7	Freedom	*30*

viii | *Contents*

2.8	Morality	*31*
2.9	Society	*32*
2.10	Review	*33*
2.11	Another Perspective	*33*

3	**Thomas Hobbes**	*36*
3.1	Overview	*36*
3.2	Biography	*37*
3.3	Knowledge	*38*
3.4	Reality	*40*
3.5	God	*41*
3.6	Humanity	*43*
3.7	Freedom	*45*
3.8	Morality	*46*
3.9	Society	*47*
3.10	Review	*48*
3.11	Another Perspective	*49*

4	**Blaise Pascal**	*51*
4.1	Overview	*51*
4.2	Biography	*52*
4.3	Knowledge	*53*
4.4	Reality	*55*
4.5	God	*55*
4.6	Humanity	*57*
4.7	Freedom	*58*
4.8	Morality	*59*
4.9	Society	*60*
4.10	Review	*61*

5	**Baruch Spinoza**	*62*
5.1	Overview	*62*
5.2	Biography	*63*
5.3	Knowledge	*64*
5.4	Reality	*66*
5.5	God	*69*
5.6	Humanity	*71*
5.7	Freedom	*73*
5.8	Morality	*74*
5.9	Society	*74*
5.10	Review	*77*
5.11	Another Perspective	*77*

6	**Nicolas Malebranche**	*79*
6.1	Overview	*79*
6.2	Biography	*80*
6.3	Knowledge	*81*
6.4	Reality	*84*
6.5	God	*87*
6.6	Humanity	*89*
6.7	Freedom	*90*
6.8	Morality	*91*

6.9	Society	92
6.10	Review	93

7	**John Locke**	94
7.1	Overview	94
7.2	Biography	95
7.3	Knowledge	97
7.4	Reality	101
7.5	God	103
7.6	Humanity	105
7.7	Freedom	106
7.8	Morality	107
7.9	Society	108
7.10	Review	111
7.11	Another Perspective	112

8	**G.W. Leibniz**	114
8.1	Overview	114
8.2	Biography	115
8.3	Knowledge	117
8.4	Reality	119
8.5	God	121
8.6	Humanity	124
8.7	Freedom	125
8.8	Morality	126
8.9	Society	126
8.10	Review	127
8.11	Another Perspective	127

9	**George Berkeley**	130
9.1	Overview	131
9.2	Biography	131
9.3	Knowledge	132
9.4	Reality	134
9.5	God	138
9.6	Humanity	140
9.7	Freedom	141
9.8	Morality	142
9.9	Society	143
9.10	Review	143

10	**Joseph Butler**	145
10.1	Overview	145
10.2	Biography	146
10.3	Knowledge	147
10.4	Reality	147
10.5	God	148
10.6	Humanity	149
10.7	Freedom	152
10.8	Morality	152
10.9	Society	153
10.10	Review	154

x | *Contents*

11	**David Hume**	*155*
11.1	Overview	*155*
11.2	Biography	*156*
11.3	Knowledge	*159*
11.4	Reality	*161*
11.5	God	*163*
11.6	Humanity	*167*
11.7	Freedom	*170*
11.8	Morality	*171*
11.9	Society	*175*
11.10	Review	*176*
11.11	Another Perspective	*177*

12	**Jean-Jacques Rousseau**	*179*
12.1	Overview	*179*
12.2	Biography	*180*
12.3	Knowledge	*185*
12.4	Reality	*185*
12.5	God	*186*
12.6	Humanity	*187*
12.7	Freedom	*190*
12.8	Morality	*191*
12.9	Society	*192*
12.10	Review	*196*
12.11	Another Perspective	*196*

13	**Immanuel Kant**	*198*
13.1	Overview	*198*
13.2	Biography	*199*
13.3	Knowledge	*202*
13.4	Reality	*206*
13.5	God	*207*
13.6	Humanity	*209*
13.7	Freedom	*211*
13.8	Morality	*212*
13.9	Society	*216*
13.10	Review	*221*
13.11	Another Perspective	*222*

14	**Jeremy Bentham**	*224*
14.1	Overview	*224*
14.2	Biography	*225*
14.3	Knowledge	*226*
14.4	Reality	*227*
14.5	God	*228*
14.6	Humanity	*229*
14.7	Freedom	*230*
14.8	Morality	*231*
14.9	Society	*234*
14.10	Review	*236*

15	**Johann Gottlieb Fichte**	237
15.1	Overview	237
15.2	Biography	238
15.3	Knowledge	239
15.4	Reality	242
15.5	God	244
15.6	Humanity	245
15.7	Freedom	246
15.8	Morality	247
15.9	Society	249
15.10	Review	251
16	**Georg Wilhelm Friedrich Hegel**	252
16.1	Overview	253
16.2	Biography	253
16.3	Knowledge	256
16.4	Reality	259
16.5	God	260
16.6	Humanity	263
16.7	Freedom	265
16.8	Morality	266
16.9	Society	267
16.10	Review	270
17	**Arthur Schopenhauer**	271
17.1	Overview	271
17.2	Biography	272
17.3	Knowledge	274
17.4	Reality	276
17.5	God	278
17.6	Humanity	279
17.7	Freedom	280
17.8	Morality	282
17.9	Society	283
17.10	Review	284
18	**Ludwig Feuerbach**	285
18.1	Overview	285
18.2	Biography	286
18.3	Knowledge	287
18.4	Reality	289
18.5	God	289
18.6	Humanity	292
18.7	Freedom	293
18.8	Morality	293
18.9	Society	294
18.10	Review	295
19	**Karl Marx**	296
19.1	Overview	296
19.2	Biography	297

xii | *Contents*

19.3	Knowledge	*300*
19.4	Reality	*301*
19.5	God	*302*
19.6	Humanity	*303*
19.7	Freedom	*304*
19.8	Morality	*305*
19.9	Society	*307*
19.10	Review	*308*

20	**John Stuart Mill**	*310*
20.1	Overview	*310*
20.2	Biography	*311*
20.3	Knowledge	*314*
20.4	Reality	*316*
20.5	God	*317*
20.6	Humanity	*319*
20.7	Freedom	*320*
20.8	Morality	*321*
20.9	Society	*325*
20.10	Review	*330*
20.11	Another Perspective	*330*

21	**Søren Kierkegaard**	*333*
21.1	Overview	*333*
21.2	Biography	*334*
21.3	Knowledge	*337*
21.4	Reality	*339*
21.5	God	*340*
21.6	Humanity	*342*
21.7	Freedom	*345*
21.8	Morality	*346*
21.9	Society	*347*
21.10	Review	*348*

22	**Friedrich Nietzsche**	*349*
22.1	Overview	*349*
22.2	Biography	*350*
22.3	Knowledge	*352*
22.4	Reality	*353*
22.5	God	*354*
22.6	Humanity	*355*
22.7	Freedom	*357*
22.8	Morality	*357*
22.9	Society	*359*
22.10	Review	*360*

Conclusion		*362*
Index		*363*

Acknowledgments

I am grateful to Gonzaga University for granting me several leaves of absence during the fifteen years I spent doing the research for and the writing of this book. I also thank the people at Wiley with whom I worked in the production of the book--especially Will Croft, Liz Wingett, copyeditor Giles Flitney, and Gopinath Anbalagan. Finally, my lack of computer skills is such that I could not have done this without the sort of technological assistance given me by Clark A. Pomerleau.

While I have been careful to avoid consulting other secondary sources in writing this book (not wanting to be commenting on the commentators), I have to acknowledge that, for more than half a century now, A History of Philosophy, by Frederick Copleston, S.J., has been my model of fair exposition and interpretation, striking an excellent balance between breadth and depth, meticulously supported by carefully documented primary-source references, and treating with respect even views to which the author was clearly opposed. I have tried to follow this example in my own work.

Introduction

This book is a history of modern European philosophy, focusing on the great philosophers of the seventeenth, eighteenth, and nineteenth centuries, from Descartes through Nietzsche, all of whom develop comprehensive systems of thought. Such a history can be seen as telling a story (indeed, the very word "story" comes from the Latin word *historia*). It has been traditionally understood since ancient times that a good story has a beginning, an end, and a middle that reasonably moves us from the beginning to its end. Although it may seem a bit artificial, we can think of the history of modern European philosophy as beginning in the 1620s, when Descartes was writing his *Rules for the Direction of the Mind*, and ending in 1900, with the death of Nietzsche. In some ways, the development from the former to the latter is a process of intellectual radicalization. Yet a focus that persists through this process is an emphasis on the individual thinker as the subject of experience, belief, knowledge, and action.

While the structure of our narrative will comprise major divisions of seventeenth-century (Descartes through Leibniz), eighteenth-century (Berkeley through Fichte), and nineteenth-century (Hegel through Nietzsche) philosophy, our study will comprise four great movements and the dynamic relations among them. These are (i) early modern rationalism (Descartes through Leibniz, if not also Rousseau), (ii) early modern empiricism (Hobbes through Hume), (iii) German idealism (Kant through Hegel), and (iv) anti-idealist alternatives (Schopenhauer through Nietzsche).

Perhaps it should be acknowledged from the outset that these great philosophers are not equally great and, hence, will not receive equal attention. More specifically, some of them (e.g. Descartes, Locke, Hume, Kant, Hegel, and Mill) have proved to be more influential than some others (e.g. Pascal, Spinoza, Malebranche, and Feuerbach). But, beyond this differential, some of them (e.g. Hume, Kant, Hegel, and Mill) developed more comprehensive philosophical systems, while others (e.g. Pascal and Feuerbach) produced less comprehensive ones. This difference has to do with areas of philosophy they seriously explored. Ever since ancient times, we have distinguished between theoretical or speculative philosophy and practical philosophy: the former comprises theory of knowledge or epistemology and various areas of metaphysics (especially philosophy of human nature, ontology or the study of being, and philosophy of religion), while the latter comprises ethics and sociopolitical philosophy. Philosophers vary in their efforts to work in some or all of these areas in building their systems, some confining their energies to a few, while others try to do it all.

It is easy to notice that all 21 of the modern systematic philosophers considered here are male. There were some female philosophers in Europe during these three centuries. Like many male philosophers, women philosophers typically did not construct comprehensive philosophical systems. Beyond that, their work was largely ignored or even lost. We shall briefly consider nine

---

Modern European Philosophers, First Edition. Wayne P. Pomerleau.
© 2023 John Wiley & Sons, Inc. Published 2023 by John Wiley & Sons, Inc.

women, each of whom will be included as a final section in chapters comprising ideas with which they become engaged. This will not only constitute recognition of their contributions, but will also provide some critical reflection on aspects of thought already considered.

Why should we study the history of philosophy, in general? First, it offers us a rich intellectual legacy that broadens our own thinking. Second, it gives us models of systematic, critical reflection that we can adapt for our own theorizing. Third, we can build on the accomplishments of our predecessors and try to avoid making their mistakes, if we can recognize them as such. Why should anyone study this period of modern philosophy, in particular? It is almost three hundred years of great and influential creators of philosophical systems – arguably more of them than in any other three-century period (even taking into account the "Golden Age" of ancient Greek philosophy). But also it is the modern period that contains the elements out of which (and often against which) contemporary philosophies will be constructed.

More than two millennia ago, Plato and Aristotle said that philosophy is born in our sense of wonder. Indeed, it is natural for us, as human beings, to wonder about many things. (One might say that the small child's incessant "Why?" questions provide a soil for philosophical theorizing.) Our wondering is typically expressed in the form of questions. Here are seven areas of theoretical questions that come naturally to us. (i) What does it mean to know something, as opposed to merely thinking or believing it, and what are the limits, if any, to human knowledge? (ii) What is the ultimate nature of reality, and what is our place in the realm of the real? (iii) Is there good reason to believe in a God or is it merely a matter of blind faith, and what should we believe about the divine nature? (iv) What is it that all humans essentially share in common that distinguishes them from nonhuman beings? (v) Why should we think that at least some of our actions are the product of free choice rather than that freedom is merely a happy illusion? (vi) How can we rationally differentiate between morally good and morally bad people and between morally right and morally wrong actions? (vii) What are characteristics of a good society, and what form of political government should it have? It is no accident and should not be too surprising that each of our comprehensive philosophical systems deals with issues in these seven areas of inquiry.

Every teacher and/or historian of modern philosophy might very well have his or her own preferred order for dealing with such matters. Here they will be dealt with in the order just presented. We shall begin with epistemology or the theory of knowledge, as that tends to be the starting-point of modern philosophy itself. Next we consider the larger metaphysical (or ontological) topic of reality. Third, we cover the subject of a supreme or divine reality. Fourth, there is the area examining our own human nature. Fifth, we grapple with the thorny topic of freedom versus determinism in human conduct. Sixth, we shall treat issues of ethical theory. And, seventh, there are the issues of society, including political society. To say that a theory that includes all this is a "system" is to indicate that the treatment of it all is coherent, that the parts fit together like the pieces of a jigsaw puzzle, collectively presenting an intelligible picture. Whether, and to what extent, we accept that picture as accurate will depend on how convincingly we think it is supported and how well it seems to illuminate our own experience. Some hints at evaluation, in the form of addressing strengths and weaknesses, will be given for these various philosophers. But, ultimately, each of us must draw his or her own conclusions about the adequacy of any theory.

Something should be said about the writings of great philosophers, such as the 21 highlighted here. Every one of these thinkers has at least one masterpiece for which he is famous. These works represent high-water marks of philosophical thought. Unfortunately, some of them, for all their greatness, are also notoriously difficult (e.g. Spinoza's *Ethics* or Kant's *Critique of Pure Reason*). This book will try to present their key ideas and arguments in a more "user friendly" sort of way. But our treatment will also consider less central primary source writings by each of the 21 philosophers in order to provide a more complete picture, topically organizing it all.

Every teacher of a history of philosophy course has to try to strike a balance between breadth and depth. In general, the more thinkers and works that get covered, the less depth is possible; likewise, the greater the depth of coverage, the smaller the number that can be included. Something similar is true for a history of philosophy. This one covers a fairly large number of philosophers and their writings, with the depth varying depending on what is needed to do justice to their treatment of our selected topics. This book has enough (brief) quotations from the primary source texts being covered that it can stand alone. Nevertheless, it is best used in conjunction with some primary source readings, the exposure to which is conducive to enlightenment. (There are several good anthologies of modern European philosophy, including Blackwell's *Modern Philosophy – From Descartes to Nietzsche: An Anthology*, edited by Steven M. Emmanuel and Patrick Gould.) At any rate, may you find this exploration of modern European philosophy, in the words of Hegel, a satisfying "voyage of discovery."

1
Background

Source: Soham Banerjee/Flickr/CC BY 2.0

1.1 Overview

While Descartes is commonly considered the "father" or founder of modern philosophy, even the most revolutionary of philosophers inherits and responds to an intellectual legacy from his past. While this study will focus on great thinkers from the seventeenth, eighteenth, and nineteenth centuries, they inevitably have to operate in some cultural context. By the time Descartes began his work, there was already a history of Western philosophy that was more than two thousand years old. Let us briefly review philosophies of the ancient Greeks and Romans, followed by medieval philosophies of Christian Europe. After that, we shall consider four thinkers who lived during the sixteenth-century Renaissance and laid some further foundations for early modern philosophy.

1.2 Ancient Philosophy

1.2.1 "Ancient"

For our purposes, ancient philosophy can be said to have originated in Greece in the sixth century BCE and to have run, in the Greek and Roman world, until sometime in the fourth century CE. We can analyze it, over the course of these (roughly) 10 centuries, as breaking down into the periods

Modern European Philosophers, First Edition. Wayne P. Pomerleau.
© 2023 John Wiley & Sons, Inc. Published 2023 by John Wiley & Sons, Inc.

of (i) the pre-Socratic philosophers, (ii) Socrates and Plato, (iii) Aristotle, and (iv) post-Aristotelian thinkers. Some of them, such as Plato and Aristotle, developed strikingly comprehensive systems, while others, such as most of the pre-Socratics and many of the post-Aristotelians, produced theories more limited in scope. The ancient Greeks and (even more so) Romans were very practical people, in general using the philosophical skills of critical reflection to try to determine answers to the question, "What is the good life for a human being?" Most of them did speculative as well as practical philosophy; but, generally, the former was oriented toward the latter. It may be the combination of their brilliant exploration of ideas and ideals, on the one hand, and their focus on issues of human value, on the other, that has allowed their philosophies to stand the test of time.

1.2.2 "Philosophy"

What does it mean to say they were distinctly philosophical, rather than being, say, natural scientists or religious speculators or psychologists or political theorists? The lines between philosophy and such other pursuits are not always clear. Many philosophers we shall study here also did some of these other things, often impressively well. Other disciplines, such as biology, physics, psychology, and political science, were originally part of philosophy and gradually declared their independence, establishing themselves as freestanding areas of study. So what is philosophy, as such? Well, this is a controversial issue, over which philosophers themselves have long disagreed. A working definition we can adopt is that it is systematic, critical reflection on basic concepts, assumptions, and principles of experience. But, then, "experience" covers an enormous amount of territory, does it not? This leads to the opening up of many areas of philosophy, since philosophers can philosophize about all sorts of experience. Thus metaphysics deals with ultimate reality, epistemology with knowledge and belief, ethics with moral values, sociopolitical philosophy with civic relations, and so forth. But different philosophers – despite their different approaches, commitments, and conclusions – share in common the activity of systematic, critical reflection on various dimensions of experience.

1.2.3 The Pre-Socratics

If the fifth and fourth centuries BCE, during which the great triumvirate of Socrates, Plato, and Aristotle lived, constitute the "Golden Age" of ancient Greece, the "pre-Socratics" did their work during the sixth and fifth centuries. They can be analyzed into two main sorts of philosophers.

First there were those who focused on a quasi-scientific cosmological speculation about the nature of reality, including human beings in the context of the universe. If we understand our own nature and place in the cosmos, it should be easier to determine how we ought to behave in hopes of achieving good lives. These thinkers, starting with Thales, who is commonly considered the first Western philosopher, were seeking a more rationally defensible alternative to the mythological explanations of reality of such writers as Hesiod and Homer, who explained things and events in terms of the sometimes less than reasonable actions of the gods (and goddesses) of ancient Greek polytheism. The first Greek philosophers, such as Thales and other Milesians who followed him, asked and tried to answer a new sort of question – what is the underlying common nature of all things real, including us? They realized that underlying reality does not always correspond to superficial appearances. Pythagoras and the Pythagoreans were dualistic, analyzing reality in terms of the two basic principles of the Limited and the Unlimited, and trying to understand things in terms of mathematical relationships. Heraclitus and his followers saw all reality as perpetually changing, with no enduring, permanent stability. By contrast, Parmenides and his followers argued

6 | *1 Background*

for the monistic view that all reality is one, for the stability of all genuine being, and that all change and becoming are essentially illusory. Empedocles, a pluralist, held that there are four eternal roots of all reality (earth, air, fire, and water), with Love and Strife being the forces or principles causing their changes of combination and separation. Atomists, such as Democritus, were mechanistic materialists, trying to account for everything in terms of an infinite number of invisible and indivisible constituent particles, moving through the void and interacting with one another through collisions, combinations, and separations. In contrast to most of these quasi-scientific theories that are inclined toward materialistic explanations, Anaxagoras tried to combine an infinite diversity of physical particles or "seeds" with the unifying principle of a cosmic Mind, although the precise nature of Mind and how, exactly, it is to be used as an explanatory principle remained quite obscure.

In contrast to this tradition of cosmological speculation, there arose a loose-knit band of philosophers called Sophists. They were professional teachers, often itinerant, who taught aristocratic and/or rich young men, throughout Greece, skills of rhetoric and argumentation that would be useful for gaining, exercising, and maintaining social influence and political power. Thus their goals were more obviously practical than were those of the cosmological speculators. But the Sophists also were keenly aware that people's views and values vary with different cultural conditions and that it is extremely difficult to establish our subjective beliefs as objective knowledge. This realization inclined the Sophists to relativism and skepticism. One of the most important of the early Sophists, Protagoras, famously expressed their relativism with his saying that human beings are the measure of everything. A later Sophist, Gorgias, famously expressed their skepticism by saying that nothing is real, that, even if there were something real, we could not know it, and that, even if something real were humanly knowable, we could never communicate it. Yet another important Sophist (the Greek word means "wise," and they tried to pass themselves off as wise men) was Antiphon, who sharply distinguished between custom (*nomos*) and nature (*physis*), claiming that we should understand and follow custom whenever we are likely to be observed by and accountable to other people but should follow the natural inclinations of self-interest when we think we can do so with impunity.

Socrates, Plato, and Aristotle (who disapproved of the Sophists) would try to synthesize the cosmological speculators' attempt to understand the nature of reality and the Sophists' emphasis on practical matters more directly related to our living successful lives. But, more broadly, the entire history of Western philosophy, including the modern period on which we shall focus, emerges out of this background and involves a dialectic between the speculative and the practical approaches represented by these two branches of pre-Socratic thinkers.

1.2.4 Socrates and Plato

Socrates, who died in 399 BCE, was one of the most original philosophical geniuses of any era; but, if he ever wrote down anything, it has not been preserved. A great deal of what we know of his teachings is represented in the writings of Plato (427–347), his most brilliant student. Their views significantly agree; however, it would be presumptuous to assume either that Socrates actually said all that Plato's dialogues attribute to him or that the historical Socrates would even easily have agreed with all of their content. Part of what has contributed to Socrates becoming a patron saint, so to speak, of Western philosophy is the dramatic ending of his life, as vividly narrated by Plato in a series of dialogues depicting his last days – in which he was charged with a couple of capital crimes, found guilty, sentenced to death, jailed until the day of his execution, and died. One of the suspicions he addresses during his trial is that he is either a shifty, deceptive Sophist or a quasi-scientific cosmological speculator meddling in inquiries that are (allegedly) none of our business.

It should not surprise us that he would be thought to be one or the other of these, as they were the dominant paradigms of the time. But the truth is that Socrates was a radically new sort of thinker (a "philosopher" in the literal Greek sense of a "lover of wisdom," wisdom being knowledge on which we can deliberately choose to act in a successful manner). Like the Sophists, and unlike the cosmological speculators, he was focused on value-laden issues relevant to the human condition; but, unlike the Sophists and like the cosmological speculators, he was neither a relativist nor a skeptic, committed as he was to the rational pursuit of knowledge of objective truth. His method for proceeding was also revolutionary – asking people thought-provoking questions about serious issues and subjecting their answers to critical analysis. He was particularly interested in the nature of human beings, adopting as his own the motto of the Delphic oracle, "know thyself," as well as in moral and sociopolitical values. Finally, he acutely appreciated the importance of clear and distinct concepts, often seeking increasingly precise and unproblematic definitions.[1] The spirit of Socrates has hovered over Western philosophy for more than 2400 years now.

Plato was the first thinker to write down a complete philosophical system, drawing on contributions from the pre-Socratics and Socrates, synthesizing them with his own ingenious ideas. The resulting theory, written in fresh and remarkably engaging dialogues, most featuring Socrates as their main character, addresses the inherited dichotomies of appearance and reality, change and stability, custom and nature. Let us briefly consider this with reference, first, to his speculative philosophy and, then, to his practical philosophy. Plato's great theoretical contribution to the history of philosophy was his theory of ideas. He is a dualist, maintaining that, in addition to the ever-changing, inferior physical world of appearances (symbolized by a subterranean cave occupied by shadows, echoes, illusions, and benighted people), there is an eternal, stable superior world of ultimate reality (symbolized by the Sun, as the source of light and life). The things of the physical world somehow participate in the Forms of the world of Ideas, deriving their characteristics from the Forms in which they participate. Thus what all maple, oak, pine, chestnut, and hemlock trees essentially have in common, despite their superficial differences, and what makes them all "trees," is that they all share in the eternal, immutable Form of a tree. While our access to a particular tree in the back yard is through our bodily senses, our only access to the Form of a tree is reason. Thus Plato is a great rationalist, thinking reason is our ultimate means to ultimate truth and reality, and a great idealist, holding that ideas are more valuable than physical things.

Plato also generated a very influential practical philosophy that connects to this (the other side of the coin of his philosophy, if you will). As the body belongs to the inferior physical world (of the cave), so the soul properly belongs to the superior ideal world (of the Sun). It is always a mistake to subordinate or sacrifice spiritual values of the soul to physical values of the body. In the area of ethics, the good life for a human is spent, as was that of Socrates, in pursuit of knowledge and virtue and not in pursuit of physical pleasures, luxuries, and creature comforts. Mere belief is inadequate, especially regarding things that concern the eternal soul, its origin, well-being, and destiny. Regarding such matters, we need beliefs which are true and which we are justified in holding; this is knowledge. Virtues are the excellences of the soul; while there are others as well, the pivotal virtues are wisdom, courage, temperance, and justice. In the practical area of sociopolitical philosophy, Plato holds that the community is even more valuable than individuals and that the order of a stable community must be maintained through the aristocratic rule of the rationally and morally best people, their inferiors obeying their orders. Some people are naturally superior and should

---

1 For a superb introduction to Socrates, see *Five Dialogues*, by Plato, trans. by G.M.A. Grube (Indianapolis: Hackett, 1981); the five dialogues are *Euthyphro*, *Apology*, *Crito*, *Meno*, and *Phaedo*.

8 | *1 Background*

rule, regardless what custom might dictate. Most people are not sufficiently rational or virtuous to be self-disciplined and must be kept in line for their own good as well as for that of society. Custom might indicate, for example, that we should do whatever we can to help our friends and hurt our enemies or to serve our own self-interests merely; but reason tells us that this is a violation of the spiritual nature of our true reality.[2] It has been famously maintained (by Alfred North Whitehead) that Western philosophy can be viewed as a series of footnotes to Plato; like so many truisms, it can be considered a hyperbolic statement of the truth.

1.2.5 Aristotle

Aristotle, the most brilliant of Plato's students, may arguably have left us the greatest set of "foot-notes" to Plato that we have. Having spent 20 years of his life working with Plato at the latter's Athenian Academy, Aristotle (384–322) was heavily influenced by his teacher. However, the younger man was too original a thinker to have been content to be anyone's follower. Whereas Plato was a visionary thinker, Aristotle was a natural scientist (arguably the greatest biologist of ancient times). This difference in orientation leads to the former being an idealist and a rationalist, while the latter is a naturalist and an empiricist. (To a great extent, the pre-Kantian history of Western philosophy represents a great debate between rationalism, generally following Plato, and empiricism, generally following Aristotle.) After leaving the Academy, Aristotle started his own important school of philosophy, called the Lyceum, in Athens, as an institutional competitor.

Aristotle's speculative philosophy strives for a more holistic view of reality – including human reality – than Plato's dualism can afford. Aristotle sees primary substances or things as the basic building blocks of reality. Qualities are characteristics of primary substances. Actions or events are those of primary substances. The most obvious relationships in the natural world are between or among primary substances. Individual human beings, for example, are primary substances. They have characteristics, such as baldness and being bearded; they perform actions, such as walking, and can be related to one another, as when talking together. In addition, they can be analyzed in terms of their genus and species (notice the biological categories), which he calls secondary substances and which are essential to defining their natures. Primary substances in our world are combinations of matter (*hule*) and form (*morphe*), the former being a principle of potentiality and the latter of actuality (a technical word for this view is "hylomorphism"). Thus, for example, a human being is a combination of body, the matter allowing for many potentialities, and soul, which actualizes the potentiality the body has for life and rational animal behavior (a human being a "rational animal"). One of the greatest services Aristotle rendered mankind was that he formally organized deductive logic into a scientific system, essentially teaching us the difference between effective and ineffective reasoning. Another extremely influential idea of his was that everything in our world can, at least in theory, be analyzed in terms of four explanatory principles (typically called the "four causes") – material, formal, efficient, and final, which answer the questions, respectively, (i) of what is it made? (e.g. the statue of bronze), (ii) what sort of thing is it? (e.g. a representation of a man in a sitting position), (iii) by what was it made? (e.g. a human sculptor), and (iv) for what was it made? (e.g. aesthetic satisfaction). Human beings are natural primary substances in an environment of other natural primary substances. They are animal organisms informed by a rational soul, giving them capacities of abstract thought and deliberate free action,

---

2 A magnificent place to start studying Plato's speculative and practical philosophy is his *Republic*, trans. by G.M.A. Grube (Indianapolis: Hackett, 1974).

but also needing their bodies to survive, communicate, and live good lives. So far, this sounds like one, single world (as opposed to the Platonic model of two worlds). But it turns out to be a bit more complex because, for Aristotle, the ultimate efficient cause of everything in our world is his god, called the "unmoved Mover" (or uncaused Cause), which is immaterial and, hence, not of this world. He uses a sort of causal argument (called cosmological) to establish the necessity of such an ultimate Being; refusing to think of it anthropomorphically, he depicts it as more a metaphysical principle than a personal god.[3]

Aristotle's practical philosophy coherently builds on this. In order to answer the question of how humans should best live in this world, it is necessary to understand their nature, in relation to their environment, including, especially, their final end. If everything in our world has a final end, what is that for a human being? His answer is deceptively simple – it is happiness or flourishing or well-being (in Greek, *eudaimonia*). But the analysis of this final end and its necessary conditions turns out to be quite complex, on account of our complex nature. In order to achieve a good life, one must be a good human being in good circumstances. More specifically, we need goods of the body, goods of the soul, and external goods, to some extent. How can we be happy, if our bodies are racked with pain and incapable of pleasure or activities of the mind pursued without major distractions? Yet Aristotle is not a hedonist: the goods of human life do not reduce to being pain-free and enjoying pleasures, including even those of the mind. We also need external goods of fortune, such as a sufficient amount of money, friends, and success. Yet this too is not sufficient. If we have all the physical goods of the body (good health, good looks, strength, coordination, etc.) we may desire, plus abundant blessings of external fortune, Aristotle thinks, we cannot have good lives without being morally good people. This also requires the spiritual goods of the soul that Socrates and Plato emphasized: knowledge and virtue. For Aristotle, the truly happy person must exercise the best part of the soul, what we call the mind, through contemplation. Also the virtues (or excellences) of the soul – both intellectual virtues of the mind and moral virtues of character – are essential. Wisdom and understanding are intellectually necessary; whatever else he may have going for him, the utterly ignorant, foolish man cannot be truly happy, although he might be content with multiple pleasures. The moral virtues, including courage, temperance, and justice, are rational mid-points (each is a "mean") between vicious extremes; they too are essential components of true happiness (*eudaimonia*). Given all this, it should not be surprising that not many of us enjoy the ultimate fulfillment of genuine well-being. But the matter is even more complex. For a human being is essentially not an isolated individual but a sociopolitical animal (*zoon politikon*) made for community living. In order to live good lives, we must be good people in good circumstances and living together in good communities. Aristotle analyzes various levels of community, from the nuclear family up to the political society or state, all of which are potentially important to our well-being. The internal relations of a family are defined with reference to an adult male citizen: wife subject to her husband, children to their father, and slaves to their master. Of the various sorts of state, the best one, under ordinary circumstances, seems to be a polity (as opposed to Plato's aristocracy), a government by all adult (male) citizens for the well-being of the entire society; like Plato, Aristotle considers democracy to be a bad form of government (although our sort of representative democracy had not yet been invented).[4]

---

3 Most of this material can be found in *Introductory Readings*, by Aristotle, trans. by Terence Irwin and Gail Fine (Indianapolis: Hackett, 1996).

4 Most of this material can be found in *Introductory Readings*.

1.2.6 Post-Aristotelians

In 323 BCE, Aristotle's most famous student, Alexander the Great, died. He had conquered all of the Greek world and included it in his massive Macedonian empire. When he unexpectedly died, his unified empire was fragmented, the ancient Greek city-states (including Athens) rebelled against Macedonian rule, and the "Golden Age" of Greece soon evaporated. Thus begins what is called the "Hellenistic" period, initially Greek, but then increasingly Roman. The philosophers of this period were attempting to develop practical philosophies that would help their followers cope with the trying circumstances of less glorious times. How can one best live in an environment in which the old order has broken down and given way to a precarious, rapidly changing future? We shall here briefly consider five sorts of answers, those of (i) hedonism, (ii) Stoicism, (iii) skepticism, (iv) eclecticism, and (v) neo-Platonism, focusing on one great thinker as representative of each, these being, respectively, Epicurus, Epictetus, Sextus Empiricus, Cicero, and Plotinus.

1.2.6.1 Epicurus

Even before Alexander the Great and Aristotle died, Epicurus was born (of Athenian parents). A few years after their deaths, he started the third great school of philosophy in Athens (after Plato's Academy and Aristotle's Lyceum), called the Garden. Epicurus (342/341–270 BCE) was a materialistic atomist and a hedonist. While he believed and taught that pleasure is our ultimate good and pain our ultimate evil, he was not the crude sensualist that he is often caricatured as having been. Like so many of the great Greeks, he advocated the virtue of temperance or moderation, even in the pursuit of pleasure. If we are reckless in pursuing pleasures and avoiding pains, we shall make mistakes of short-term decision-making that are likely to cost us dearly. What we should seek is to maintain an attitude of contentment (*ataraxia*, the tranquil imperturbability of mind), not allowing ourselves to be emotionally controlled by external circumstances, including superstitious anxieties regarding the gods and the fear of death. We should learn to distinguish between artificial, vain desires and natural ones, which should be preferred; of our natural desires, some are necessary, while others are not and are thus less important. Among the greatest pleasures in human life, he thinks (agreeing with Plato and Aristotle), are friendship and philosophical understanding.

1.2.6.2 Epictetus

Around the same time as Epicurus founded the Garden, a Greek named Zeno of Citium started a fourth school of philosophy in Athens, that of Stoicism. The Roman republic gave way to the Roman empire, which came to encircle the Mediterranean, including the conquered Greek world. Stoicism became the dominant philosophy of the Roman empire. Epictetus (c. 50–130 CE) was a Greek who was born into slavery to Romans. He was allowed to study with a Stoic teacher in Rome. Some time after the Emperor Nero died, in the year 68, he was freed from slavery and stayed in Rome to teach philosophy. Around the year 90, philosophers were expelled from Rome, and he returned to Greece, founding his own school of Stoic philosophy and practicing its rule of "bear and forbear" (*sustine et abstine*) until his death. Though suspicious of hedonism, like Epicurus, he taught that tranquility (or *ataraxia*) is the secret to the good life. We need to exercise reason, the best feature of our human nature, to understand our place in the universal order of the cosmos, to recognize our duty so that we can act rightly, and to control our desires. We should accept what is beyond our control, concentrating on those aspects of our inner life that are within our power, such as our own thoughts, feelings, choices, actions, and reactions. Through reason, we should learn to follow Nature, rather than fighting it. Like Plato, Epictetus considered Socrates a moral role model. Like Epicurus, he advised us to conquer our tendencies to fear death and the gods. But he warned against becoming slaves to the pursuit of pleasure. Finally, like many other Stoics, he advocated the "cosmopolitan" point of view, which holds that we are citizens of the cosmos, significantly related to all rational beings.

1.2.6.3 Sextus Empiricus

Another important Hellenistic philosophy was that of skepticism. Pyrrho of Elis, a contemporary of Epicurus and Zeno of Citium, is generally regarded as its founder, and a famous version of it is called Pyrrhonism in his honor. While Socrates ironically suggested that the only thing a wise man knows for certain is that we can know nothing for certain, the Pyrrhonists denied that we can know even that. Like Epicureanism and Stoicism, Skepticism became popular in the Roman world as well. Sextus Empiricus (who flourished around the year 200 CE), advocated the extreme skepticism of Pyrrhonism over other philosophies, including Epicureanism and Stoicism, which he condemned as "dogmatic." Employing the distinction between phenomenal appearances and noumenal reality, he maintained that we can know nothing of the latter and must settle for uncertain beliefs regarding the former. He called for a suspension of judgment (an *epoche*) regarding all metaphysical matters and a deliberate agnosticism about whether ethical customs can correspond to any laws of nature. Like Epicureanism and Stoicism, Skepticism should be considered a way of life aiming at *ataraxia* or inner peace but thinks the most effective means to that end is the avoidance of dogmatic claims to certainty.[5]

1.2.6.4 Cicero

Needless to say, it was possible to combine aspects of different philosophies, striving for a coherent synthesis. One of the most famous examples of such eclecticism was the Roman Cicero (106–43 BCE). As a youth, he studied with a once-famous Epicurean, as well as with a prominent skeptic, and then a famous Stoic. After practicing law successfully, in the days of the Roman republic, he went to Athens and studied with a head of the Academy. After returning to Rome and resuming the practice of law, he went into politics, climbing the political ladder but also making powerful enemies, including, especially, Julius Caesar and his followers. Recognizing the dangerous position into which he had gotten himself, he withdrew from politics and devoted himself to writing. After Caesar was assassinated (in 44 BCE), Cicero was proscribed for death by Caesar's followers and beheaded, while trying to escape. The most important of Cicero's philosophical writings concern values, especially moral, social, and political values. Like Aristotle, he thought that our chief good must be complex rather than something as simple as maximizing pleasure or achieving tranquility of mind (*ataraxia*). Using reason to determine our duty and exercising our will to do it represent the path of an honorable life. Like the Stoics, he advocated a cosmopolitan point of view, thinking each person, as a citizen of the entire world, to be related to every other. He argued for a republican government of laws rather than an aristocratic government of arbitrary human will (which was why he opposed Caesar). He believed in equal civil liberty under the law for all citizens (yet accepted slavery as permissible).[6]

---

5 Readings from Epicureanism, Stoicism, Skepticism, and Plotinus can be found in *Greek and Roman Philosophy*, ed. by Jason L. Saunders (New York: The Free Press, 1966).

6 The greatest philosophical writings by Cicero are, arguably, *On Obligations*, trans. by P.G. Walsh (Oxford: Oxford Univ. Press, 2001) and *The Republic* and *The Laws*, trans. by Niall Rudd (Oxford: Oxford Univ. Press, 1998).

12 | *1 Background*

1.2.6.5 Plotinus

In addition to these Hellenistic philosophies, there was also a kind of back-to-Plato movement. One of the greatest of all the neo-Platonists was the Roman Plotinus, who was born in Egypt (in 204 or 205 CE), educated in Alexandria, and later settled in Rome, where he started his own philosophical school. With him, Platonic philosophy took a distinctly mystical turn. He was a numerical monist, seeing all reality as ultimately one. The source of all being is the divine One and corresponds to the Good, the highest Form in Plato's world of ideas. Since it is all-encompassing, nothing can be separate from it, so that creation is impossible. Instead, Plotinus subscribes to a theory of emanation. Reality eternally and necessarily emanates from the One like rays of light from the Sun. The initial emanation is Mind, which grasps the One and itself and contains the Ideas. Then a cosmic Soul emanates from Mind and comprises all souls, including ours. The One, Mind, and Soul are all purely spiritual, a kind of divine Trinity. Soul emanates the phenomenal world of nature, comprising beings that are formed matter (as in Aristotle). Pure matter is utter darkness, the privation of light, and a principle of evil, the privation of good. But formed matter is partially illuminated, no longer purely evil. Human souls long to return to our divine Source. This requires self-purification, a renunciation of the body's base desires, and a spiritual conversion toward the Good. The achievement of this salvation, by self-discipline and the ongoing practice of a life of virtue, might require multiple reincarnations or a more rapid mystical union with the One.[7]

1.3 Medieval Philosophy

1.3.1 "Medieval"

As the ancient period in the history of Western philosophy was rather long but heavily dominated by the writings of Plato and Aristotle, so the medieval period lasted for about a millennium and was dominated by the writings of Augustine and Aquinas – but, again, with other important philosophers worthy of our consideration. The very word "medieval" helps us situate this period, as it means "middle ages," middle meaning between antiquity and modernity (it is controversial where to place the Renaissance in this schema – but more of that later). The boundaries here are imprecise. We have already said that, for our purposes, ancient Western philosophy can be seen as ending sometime in the fourth century CE. After the death of the Roman Emperor Constantine in 337, the empire was divided. From then on, the empire was torn by internal rebellions and fairly steady decline until the fall of Rome to "barbarians" in 410. The medieval period runs at least until the end of the fourteenth century, if not into the fifteenth. What is striking about this period, what sets it apart from the ancient period (and even from the Renaissance), is that, to such a great extent, philosophy begins with, is based on, and is guided by the doctrinal commitments of religious faith. This is true not only of the Christian philosophers we shall consider (because they are the ones who influenced the great modern philosophers), but also of medieval Islamic ones (such as Avicenna) and medieval Jewish ones (like Moses Maimonides). This entire period can be viewed as one, in the famous words of Anselm, of "faith seeking understanding," philosophy being regarded as the "handmaiden of religion." One last point of introduction: the great medieval philosophers tried to graft their religious beliefs onto the ancient theories we have just considered – especially those of Plato and/or Aristotle.

---

7 Many of these ancient philosophies are discussed at greater length in ch. I of *Twelve Great Philosophers*, by Wayne P. Pomerleau (New York: Ardsley House, 1997).

1.3.2 Augustine

By the fourth century, Christianity was becoming the official religion of the empire. Aurelius Augustine (354–430), both a Roman citizen and a Christian bishop, lived near the end of the Roman empire, when it was falling apart, and the beginning of medieval times; but his dominant influence clearly occurred during the Middle Ages. While his father was a pagan, his mother was a devout Christian (she was later canonized a saint, as was Augustine himself). A professional teacher of rhetoric before his conversion, Augustine was deeply influenced by neo-Platonism to renounce materialism and skepticism, converting to Christianity. He began writing works that used Plato's philosophy to articulate and argue for the Christian perspective, toward the end of the fourth century, including his dialogue *On Free Choice of the Will*.[8] He was ordained a priest in the Roman colony of North Africa and, later, consecrated as the Bishop of Hippo. He spent the last third of a century of his life largely combating theological heresies and died in Hippo at a time when the "barbarian" Vandals were besieging the city.

In many ways, Augustine created the perspective for all of Christian medieval philosophy. Advocating the Old Testament text, "Unless you believe, you will not understand" (Isaiah 7:9), he wholeheartedly embraces the idea that we must start with religious faith and use its doctrines as the basis for pursuing rational understanding. The final object of both religious faith and philosophical reason is God, the ultimate Source and the ultimate End of all the rest of reality. He adopts a neo-Platonic hierarchy of beings from God, the Creator, down to spiritual creatures, and, below that, to physical bodies. He holds that the two most important sorts of truth we should use philosophy to understand rationally concern God and the soul. Augustine is certain – against all the forces of skepticism – that, because he has beliefs, he can know that he exists; even if all his other beliefs are mistaken, he must exist in order even to be mistaken. So he knows at least that one truth for certain. This also indicates that he is a spiritual being, a soul, since he has rational knowledge. Being spiritual, the soul could not have been caused by purely physical forces. The soul has a hierarchy of powers, reason being its highest faculty. But truth is higher even than reason, and the soul did not invent objective truth. He uses this line of reasoning to establish the necessary existence of God. As truth is nonphysical, eternal, and immutable, either it is God or God is even higher than, and the source of, truth; but, either way, God must exist.

Like Plato, Augustine believes that knowledge and virtue are great goods of the soul – including, especially, the four "cardinal" virtues of prudence, fortitude, temperance, and justice. While we have bodies, our souls are more valuable, and we should always prefer spiritual goods of the soul to physical goods of the body. As we try to do right, avoid wrongdoing, and live lives of good will, we must try to be law-abiding, preferring God's eternal law over the temporal law of the state. Strictly speaking, if the temporal law conflicts with God's eternal law, it is not genuine law at all but a mere perversion of true law. Everything God created is good, evil being the privation of good. If we freely choose evil over good, that is a "sin," for which we are accountable. Like Plato, Augustine thought he could philosophically prove the immortality of the soul (actually, Plato, unlike Augustine, thought the soul is eternal, like the Forms, rather than merely immortal; for Augustine, only God is eternal). For Augustine, the most important thing is that we should choose to love God and other persons. And what is at stake in our making good or evil choices is, ultimately, the eternal salvation or damnation of our immortal souls. Sixteen centuries after he lived and worked, Augustine remains

---

8 *On Free Choice of the Will*, by Augustine, trans. by Thomas Williams (Indianapolis: Hackett, 1993), is a superb source for his Christian Platonism and is drawn on here.

1 Background

the best example of Christian Platonism. His philosophical influence in Western Europe went uncontested for eight centuries.

1.3.3 Boethius

About half a century after Augustine's death, Anicius Manlius Severinus Boethius (c. 480–524) was born into an ancient Roman family that had converted to Christianity. Rome had fallen to the "barbarians" and came to be governed by Theodoric, King of the Ostrogoths, who belonged to the heretical Arian sect of Christianity. Boethius was appointed Roman consul and one of his ministers. He was also an intellectual, who greatly admired Plato. Prior to the thirteenth century, he was the most influential medieval thinker after Augustine. He was the last of the great Roman philosophers. In time, he was falsely accused of treason (having disapproved of Theodoric's undermining of the power of the Senate), arrested, imprisoned, tortured, and executed by bludgeoning. While in prison, he composed *The Consolation of Philosophy*, which was a best seller in the Middle Ages, remaining much read and greatly admired even today; it is a dialogue between the imprisoned Boethius and a personification of philosophy.[9] We are cautioned against supposing that our final good consists in any combination of earthly goods, all of which are transitory, subject to the vicissitudes of fortune. Our ultimate happiness can only be legitimately achieved in relation to the highest Good, which is God, conceived of here in neo-Platonic terms. Like Augustine, Boethius wrestled with the problem of evil – how can so much evil exist and appear to go unpunished in a world created and governed by an infinitely perfect God? We are assured that our freedom requires the possibility of our making bad choices and that the good will ultimately be rewarded and evil ultimately punished. He also considered another problem of Christian philosophy – how can we be genuinely free when God infallibly knows from all eternity everything we shall ever do? But God's foreknowledge transcends time. You will commit a voluntary action because you will freely do it, not because God forces you to do it; God knows you will do it because you will choose to do it, and God knows all our future choices, but you will neither choose it nor do it because of what God knows.

1.3.4 Anselm

Some five and a half centuries after Boethius, Anselm (1033–1109) lived and worked. Born in northern Italy, he joined the Benedictine order at the monastery at Bec, in France. In time, he became prior of his abbey, later its abbot, and eventually the Archbishop of Canterbury. But he is mainly known today for a couple of his books that still stand as masterpieces of philosophical theology – *Monologion* (meaning "Soliloquy") and, especially, *Proslogion* ("Discourse"). He can be regarded as the beginning of "scholastic philosophy," the philosophy taught in Church schools during the Middle Ages, Renaissance, and early modern times in Europe. Scholasticism combined Christian doctrine with logical and philosophical teachings. A couple of centuries after Anselm, scholastic philosophy came to be identified with Aristotle and his commentators, in general, and with the notions of substance and accidents (substantial and accidental forms), in particular. Like Augustine, whom he follows, Anselm was a Christian Platonist. His slogan "Faith Seeking Understanding" is distinctly Augustinian. In the Prologue to *Monologion*, he expresses confidence that everything he wrote was consistent with Augustine's teachings. Religious faith and

---

9 *The Consolation of Philosophy*, by Boethius, trans. by V.E. Watts (Harmondsworth: Penguin Books, 1969).

1.3 Medieval Philosophy | 15

philosophical reason, while they may employ different methodological approaches, share truth as their common proper object, God being the supreme Truth. In that work, Anselm employs versions of the cosmological argument, trying to show that the ultimate causal source of all the goods we experience must be the supreme Good, God. A year or two later, he wrote his more famous *Proslogion*, which breaks new ground by inventing the approach of (what later came to be called) "ontological" argumentation. It is an arrestingly unique argument because it is a priori (or nonempirical), starting with an abstract idea in the mind and purporting to show that some Reality, corresponding to that idea, must exist outside the mind. Taking Augustine's idea of God as the greatest possible Reality, the supreme Being, Anselm reformulates it as the greatest conceivable Being. But as we analyze this definition of the idea of God, we recognize that if God exists only in our minds, then a supreme Being that also exists outside our minds, or in reality, would be greater still. But there cannot be anything greater than the greatest conceivable Being. Therefore God cannot only exist in our minds but must also exist in reality. This argument was criticized by another acute Benedictine monk named Gaunilo, and Anselm tried to rebut his criticisms; but we shall not go into that here.[10]

1.3.5 Aquinas

Arguably the greatest of all medieval philosophers was Thomas Aquinas (1224/1225–1274), who, like Augustine and Anselm before him, was also canonized a saint in the Christian Church. Aquinas was born and raised in southern Italy. As a young man at the University of Naples, he was first exposed to ideas of Aristotle and met members of the recently founded Dominican order. Against the wishes of his family, which wanted him to join the more prestigious Benedictines, he became a Dominican. In Paris, he studied theology with Albert the Great, who was a proponent of Aristotelian philosophy, accompanying him to Cologne. In time, he was ordained a priest, got the necessary education in theology and philosophy to qualify as a professor, and was granted a teaching chair at the University of Paris. Following the lead of his great teacher, Albert, Aquinas developed a powerful Christian Aristotelianism that would come to rival the Christian Platonism that had dominated European philosophy since Augustine. He did this in two remarkable multi-volume works, the *Summa contra Gentiles* ("Summary against the Gentiles") and the *Summa Theologica* ("Theological Summary").[11] In 1879, Pope Leo XIII wrote an encyclical called *Aeterni Patris*, recommending the study of Aquinas, calling him the prince of all scholastics, and praising his synthesis of faith and reason. Let us divide our consideration of his ideas here, as we did with those of Aristotle (whom he calls simply "the Philosopher"), into, first, his theoretical philosophy and, then, his practical philosophy.

Regarding his more theoretical philosophy, let us consider his philosophy of religion and his philosophy of human nature. Because all truth is coherent and, ultimately, truth is one, it is impossible for the truths of faith to be inconsistent with philosophical truths of reason. However, our human reason is limited, as we are finite creatures. Hence, in addition to truths in accordance with our reason, and, thus, in principle, understandable, some truths (such as mysteries of the faith) are beyond our capacities of rational understanding. Hence, religious faith and philosophical reason overlap and complement each other. Among the most pivotal of all truths of

---

10 Anselm, *Monologion and Proslogion, with the Replies of Gaunilo and Anselm*, trans. by Thomas Williams (Indianapolis: Hackett, 1995).

11 An old, but still very valuable, anthology, combining selections from these two great works, is *Introduction to St. Thomas Aquinas*, ed. by Anton C. Pegis (New York: Modern Library, 1948).

religious faith are those regarding the existence and nature of God, some of which are rationally demonstrable. While God's existence would be self-evident to anyone who could comprehend the divine essence, that is not the case for us in this life; therefore, Aquinas holds, Anselm's "ontological" argument fails to establish the existence of God outside the ideas in our minds. In answer to the question whether we can, nevertheless, prove God's existence, if we argue from the effects we experience in the world of creation to the necessary existence of God as their causal Creator, then we can. Next Aquinas produces his famous "five ways" of demonstrating God as (i) the unmoved Mover, (ii) the uncaused efficient Cause, (iii) the necessary Being, ultimately responsible for all contingent beings, (iv) the maximally perfect Being, and (v) the intelligent Governor of the world. Aquinas also believes human reason can prove some (but not all) important truths about God's nature, such as that God is simple, all-good, infinite, one, omniscient, and omnipotent. Some of God's creatures, including us humans, are animals; some, including us, are persons; we are allegedly unique in being both – personal animals. As such, we are (hylomorphic) combinations of body and soul, the body being organic matter of a particular animal species, the soul having the faculties essential to our being persons (rational intellect and free will) and created as immortal (like Augustine, he thinks he can prove this) and destined for a spiritual life after the death of the body.

Whether our souls achieve salvation depends on the choices we make and the actions we perform in this life. Like Augustine, Aquinas thinks that everyday experience confirms that we are free, in at least some of our actions. For (as the earlier thinker had already argued), otherwise, advice, encouragement, prohibitions, the prospects of rewards, and the threats of punishment would all be futile; however, in fact, they are effective. Like Plato, Aristotle, and Augustine, Aquinas advocates what we now call virtue ethics. For him, in addition to Aristotle's intellectual virtues of the mind and moral virtues of character, there are also the three supernatural (or theological) virtues of faith, hope, and charity. He agrees with Augustine's neo-Platonic notion that evil has no positive reality but is merely the privation of good that ought to be. We are morally responsible for the good and evil actions we perform as a result of deliberate choice. Because human nature is so complex, so is the moral evaluation of human actions. We must consider the sort of action being evaluated (its genus and species), as well as its circumstances and the purpose intended in choosing it. Contrary to moral relativists, Aquinas considers some freely chosen actions (such as deliberate lying and sex outside of marriage) to be always wrong (or "sinful"). Like Aristotle, he thinks we are naturally sociopolitical animals. We need law to regulate our actions. Everything in the world of creation is subject to God's eternal law. Personal creatures, like us humans, participate in God's eternal law through reason; this Aquinas calls "natural law" – it requires that we not destroy innocent human life, that we care for our own species, that we pursue knowledge of the truth, and that we try to get along with other members of our community. If we were rational and always obeyed natural law, this would suffice. But this is not the case. Hence, we need human laws, enforced by civil sanctions, to motivate us to behave rightly. Like Aristotle, Aquinas holds a traditional view of woman's place as in the household; like Plato, Aristotle, and Augustine, he accepts slavery as a fact of life. He agrees with Aristotle that there can be good or bad government by one person, by a few people, or by the many. Like Augustine, he believes in the possibility of a "just war," assuming certain conditions are met: it must be declared by someone in a proper position of authority; it must be waged for the sake of a just cause; and the warriors must intend good (for example, a just peace rather than vengeful bloodlust).[12]

---

12 For coverage of many of these medieval philosophers, see ch. II of *Twelve Great Philosophers*, and also ch. 1 of *Western Philosophies of Religion*, by Wayne P. Pomerleau (New York: Ardsley House, 1998).

1.4 Renaissance Thinkers

1.4.1 "Renaissance"

We have already seen a couple of good examples of how nonphilosophical historical events have triggered profound changes in philosophy: first, the death of Alexander the Great in 323 BCE precipitated the rapid decline of Greek influence, causing a shift from classical Hellenic culture to Hellenistic thought; and, second, the fall of Rome to the "barbarians" in 410 CE can be seen (if somewhat arbitrarily) as marking the end of antiquity (what a poet has called the glory that was Greece and the grandeur that was Rome) and the beginning of medievalism. Well, in 1453 another remarkable event occurred that would have repercussions beyond its time and place. That year the Ottoman Turks captured the great city of Constantinople, effectively ending the Byzantine Empire. Scholars and artists fled west toward Italy, taking with them that explosive burst of creative energy that would represent the "Renaissance" (a French word meaning "rebirth") of classical art and learning. As has already been indicated, a controversial issue is whether the Renaissance should be considered the last part of the middle ages or a separate period or the first part of modernity. The view advocated here is that it is a separate period, at least in philosophy, that it no longer involves a submission to religious faith in order to achieve rational understanding, and that it is not yet based on the epistemological methodologies of modern times. While we shall focus here on four important thinkers who lived in the sixteenth century, it must be admitted that the Renaissance produced no philosophers of the first rank, comparable, say, to Plato, Aristotle, Augustine, or Aquinas.

1.4.2 Machiavelli

Niccolo Machiavelli (1469–1527) was born in Florence, Italy, 13 years after the fall of Constantinople. While he admires some of the ancients, he did not think like the ancients; like other Renaissance thinkers, he used their ideas for his own purposes. While he lived in Christian Italy, he was not submissive to religious authority and was not even obviously a man of faith, like the great medieval philosophers. It can even be questioned whether he is a philosopher or a political historian – a dispute with which we need not struggle here. He was active in the political life of the Florentine Republic, serving as its defense minister and a diplomat until it collapsed and the Medici family was restored to autocratic power in 1512. He was dismissed from public office, arrested, imprisoned, and tortured on the rack because of unproved charges that he had conspired against the Medicis. On being released and banished from the city, he retired to his estate in the country, where he wrote his greatest works. So he encountered firsthand the vicious, pernicious, insidious, treacherous behaviors of cutthroat political life about which he would so knowledgeably write in his famous (and infamous) *The Prince*, which he dedicated to Lorenzo de' Medici. When the Republic was restored in 1527, because he had so obviously tried to ingratiate himself with the ousted Medici family, his fellow Florentines mistrusted him; never able to regain a desirable office, he died embittered. In many respects, *The Prince*, published in 1532 (five years after his death), is a revolutionary little handbook advising would-be leaders on how best to get, exercise, and maintain power over others. He seemed to advocate the view that sufficiently desirable ends can justify even immoral means. He advocated cruelty as necessary for effective leadership. While a prince will wish to be both feared and loved by the people, it is more important to be feared. On no account can a prince afford to be hated by the mass of the people. A prince need not keep his word when doing so would jeopardize his own interests. He should assign unpopular tasks to others to escape the people's hatred or

1 Background

contempt. Because people are naturally selfish and bad, a successful prince must be willing to do evil. It is better for him to appear virtuous than actually to be virtuous, because the people are shallow enough to settle for merely attractive appearances. Like other Renaissance thinkers, Machiavelli was struck by the unpredictable role of fortune in human affairs. But a shrewd leader will make the best of the circumstances life serves up.[13] While Machiavelli also wrote other works, such as *The Discourses* and *The Art of War*, it was the *realpolitik* of *The Prince* that made him notorious, that was condemned by the Church, and that is still much studied to this very day.

1.4.3 Montaigne

Born six years after Machiavelli died, Michel de Montaigne (1533–1592) is renowned as the French pioneer of the essay. (As was true of Machiavelli, it is difficult to say whether he should be considered a philosopher, strictly speaking; had he lived a couple of centuries later, the man of letters might have been classified as a *philosophe*.) He studied law, was a councillor in the Bordeaux parliament, and served as a mayor of Bordeaux. His first literary work, a translation of Raymond Sebond's *Natural Theology*, was published in 1569. But his reputation is chiefly based on his *Essays*, the longest of which is *In Defense of Raymond Sebond*. This is the primary source for his philosophical skepticism. While admitting that Sebond's reasons for holding his Catholic beliefs are faulty, he held that all attempts to justify doctrines of religious faith rationally are doomed to frustration and failure, that Christianity should rest on faith alone (this position came to be called "fideism"). He thought our alleged superiority over other animals (touted by Plato, Aristotle, Augustine, and Aquinas) is merely a presumption founded on conceit. It is our wide-ranging imagination that distinguishes us from other animals but is also the basis for our special problems. While our well-being consists in freedom from pain and suffering, we torture ourselves by imagining illusory ills and dreading possible future misfortunes. Like Sextus Empiricus, he thought that our interpretation of sense experience is unreliable, so that reason, trying to draw conclusions from this seminal source, has neither an indubitable criterion for certain knowledge nor any assurance that it can ever be achieved. He adopted as his personal motto, *Que sais-je?* ("What do I know?"), implying that the answer to that rhetorical question is, nothing substantive. When we sleep, our dreams sometimes seem more real than ordinary waking experiences. Since we and all we experience are constantly changing, things seem quite relative. Even our notion of an abiding self is an unverifiable product of the imagination. So what does he recommend? Well, a good skeptic will suspend all judgment about that which transcends experience, will regard the interpretation of experience itself as fallible and tentative, and will try to follow the rules and customs of his own society. This is the most likely path to the calm tranquility of *ataraxia*.[14] Thus, in his own way, Montaigne broke from medieval philosophy, as had Machiavelli, in his way.

1.4.4 Bacon

Francis Bacon was an English thinker who straddled the sixteenth and seventeenth centuries (1561–1626). Like Montaigne, he was an early essayist; but, unlike him, he was a philosopher of science. Like Montaigne, he was in public life for a while as a Member of Parliament, rising to the level of Lord Chancellor of England. He was knighted but quit politics in 1621, when he had to

---

13 Niccolo Machiavelli, *The Prince*, trans. by N.H. Thomson (New York: Dover Publications, 1992).
14 Michel de Montaigne, *In Defense of Raymond Sebond*, trans. by Arthur H. Beattie (New York: Frederick Ungar, 1959).

confess to bribery as a judge. He did not think that the traditional method of deductive logic was productive of scientific knowledge. While he too was an empiricist, the very title of Bacon's book *The New Organon* (1620) was a deliberate critique of the *Organon*, which is the collective name for the methodological and logical writings of Aristotle (the Greek word *organon* means "tool" or "instrument"). Like Galileo and later seventeenth-century European thinkers, he was reluctant to conform his thinking to that sanctioned by religious authority, he despised scholastic learning, and he found Aristotelian reasoning in terms of final causes to be useless. He advocated inductive logic as more practically productive than deduction, since it reasons from concrete experience rather than from abstract principles. Arguably, his most famous contribution to philosophy was his discussion of four sorts of misleading opinions or prejudices, which he called "idols," that are subjective impediments to our achieving objective knowledge. The first of these, Idols of the Tribe, represent our natural tendency to assume that the way we humans generally see things is determinative of the way they are. The second, Idols of the Cave, are inclinations individual persons have to form opinions based on their own experience. The third, Idols of the Market Place, represent our tendency to be misled by language. And the fourth, Idols of the Theater, are prejudices generated by the various theories we have received from others and tend to swallow uncritically.[15] Probably the only thing that prevents Bacon from being a modern philosopher is that he does not place much emphasis on the centrality of the individual subject of experience and knowledge.

1.4.5 Galileo

Like Bacon, the Italian mathematician and scientist Galileo Galilei (1564–1642) worked into the seventeenth century. While he was appointed "Chief Philosopher and Mathematician" to the Medici court in Florence (in 1610) and would exert the powerful influence of a role model on later philosophers of that century, he was not so much a philosopher as a mathematical physicist. Because he publicly supported the Copernican model of the universe as heliocentric (or sun-centered) rather than geocentric (earth-centered), he was denounced by the Roman Catholic Inquisition (in 1615), being severely warned against publicly denying Church views. After his *Dialogues Concerning the Two Chief World Systems* (in 1632) favorably presented the Copernican point of view, he was summoned to Rome (1633), forced to recant his view that our planet revolves around the Sun, and placed under permanent house arrest near Florence. There is an anecdote to the effect that, as he was leaving the Inquisition's proceedings against him, he muttered, "Nevertheless, it does move!" Among his scientific feats, he developed the telescope from a Dutch child's toy into a scientific instrument, using it to discover four of Jupiter's natural satellites, the mountains of the moon, sunspots, and vast reaches of our galaxy, the Milky Way. In his book *The Assayer* (1623), he declared that the book of the physical universe was written by God in the language of mathematics. He distinguished between primary and secondary qualities of bodies, the former being real properties of things and the latter merely representing the way we humans experience them. He advocated a form of atomism called corpuscularianism, seeing all bodies as composed of minute corpuscles, each having its own shape, size, and motion.[16] As an alternative to the Aristotelian-scholastic notion that events in the natural world occur as they do because of final ends, Galileo depicts the physical universe as a complex machine, operating according to purely mechanical principles.

---

15 *The New Organon and Related Writings*, by Francis Bacon, ed. by Fulton H. Anderson (Indianapolis: Bobbs-Merrill, 1960).
16 Galileo, *The Essential Galileo*, ed. and trans. by Maurice A. Finocchiaro (Indianapolis: Hackett, 2008).

1.5 Review

These thinkers, from Thales through Galileo, represent high-water marks of ancient, medieval, and Renaissance thought. Needless to say, the intellectual legacy of this period of more than two millennia of Western learning was remarkably rich, with a few of these philosophers (Plato, Aristotle, Augustine, and Aquinas) being giants, comparable in breadth and depth to the greatest philosophers of modern times. But what none of them does yet (making them premodern, rather than modern, philosophers) is shift the epistemological focus to the experiencing, thinking, believing individual subject, away from external reality, whether of the natural world or social relations or God. We shall see how modern philosophers could tap into and build on the intellectual legacy of their predecessors in such a way as to revolutionize the way we philosophically think today. As we study these dynamic developments, we shall encounter achievements on which we can build and mistakes we can learn to avoid committing ourselves. This fascinating story begins with Descartes, a genius worthy of comparison with the best of his predecessors, and ends with Nietzsche, an iconoclast who would radically challenge the entire project of modern philosophy.

2

René Descartes

Source: Georgios Kollidas/Adobe Stock

2.1 Overview

While this coverage of Descartes will include aspects of his philosophy that are revolutionary and original enough to qualify him as the first great modern philosopher – especially his decisive focus on the knowing subject as the legitimate starting point of philosophical reflection – nevertheless, it will also attempt to connect his thought with that of his predecessors and, subsequently, with that of great thinkers who inherit, criticize, and build on it. As a rationalist, he argued that we can use reason to know a great deal, but not everything, about reality, including God, human nature, and its freedom; and he offers us less developed ideas regarding morality

Modern European Philosophers, First Edition. Wayne P. Pomerleau.
© 2023 John Wiley & Sons, Inc. Published 2023 by John Wiley & Sons, Inc.

2 René Descartes

and society. He invited objections from would-be critics; and, as we shall see, he got them from followers and opponents alike.

2.2 Biography

Like all four of the Renaissance thinkers we have briefly considered, René Descartes lived at least part of his life in the sixteenth century. More specifically, he was born on March 31, 1596, in northern France, the son of a lawyer[1]; his mother died, when he was a baby, of a lung disease which he thought he had inherited, which disease might, in fact, have led to an early death for himself. He does not seem to have been close to his father, who subsequently remarried. At about the age of 10, the boy entered the Jesuit college of La Flèche, where a relative, Fr. Charlet, a theologian, looked out for him with paternal care. Even though his partially autobiographical *Discourse on Method* is critical of the education he received, it is clear that he regarded the school as being as good a place to study philosophy as any other of his time. Like so many of the great thinkers of the seventeenth century, he had little use for the Aristotelian–Thomistic scholasticism then taught in the schools of Europe. Some nine years after being sent there, he left La Flèche to travel and earn law degrees from the University of Poitiers. Then he amused himself in Paris for a while, before joining an army near the beginning of the Thirty Years' War (which lasted from 1618 to 1648). On the evening of 10 November 1619, while stationed in Germany, he had a series of three dreams, which would change his life. For he interpreted them as revealing God's will that he should dedicate the remainder of his life to rationally seeking indubitable truth. After leaving the army, he returned to Paris and began pursuing this vocation. He developed a mathematical method and resolved to reform philosophy. He wrote his *Rules for the Direction of the Mind* (never completed and unpublished until 1701), as an attempt at working out a reliable method for doing philosophy. But the social life in Paris was too much of a distraction, and he moved to Holland in 1628. He would live there for more than 20 years, finding it quiet, peaceful, tolerant, and comfortable. In 1629, he started writing a scientific treatise on *The World* but, four years later, abandoned it after receiving news of the Inquisition's condemnation of Galileo's geocentric theory of the universe, with which he agreed; it was only published, posthumously, in 1677. Descartes never married, but he had a daughter, named Francine, born in 1635, who died in childhood (in 1640) and whose loss he grieved (III, 250–251, 240–241, 123–124, 236, 4, 30–32, 40–45, 167).

In 1637, he anonymously published (in French) his *Discourse on Method*, as a simpler statement of rules of philosophical methodology than his abandoned *Rules* had turned out to be. He briefly applied the method of reasoning recommended there to show how the basic building blocks of a philosophical system can be developed. But this was done more fully, more cogently, and more systematically in his masterpiece, *Meditations on First Philosophy*, published in Latin in 1641, using geometrical deduction as a model of reasoning. (He was also a distinguished mathematician, the founder of analytic geometry; the system of Cartesian coordinates is named after him, Cartesius being the Latin version of his French name.) Descartes had a friend, Fr. Mersenne, invite scholars to respond to his work, publishing six sets of their objections, along with Descartes's own replies to them; later a seventh set, plus his replies, was added. During the last decade of his life, his

---

1 References will be to *The Philosophical Writings of Descartes*, in three volumes, trans. by John Cottingham, Robert Stoothoff, Dugald Murdoch, and Anthony Kenny (Cambridge: Cambridge Univ. Press, 1984–1991); they will be made in text by volume and page numbers.

philosophy became famous and controversial. In 1644, he published his *Principles of Philosophy*, dedicated to Princess Elizabeth of Bohemia, a very astute critic of his earlier work. A little later, he wrote *The Passions of the Soul* and began a correspondence with Queen Christina of Sweden, sending her a manuscript copy of that book. She invited him to come to her court to instruct her in philosophy. After getting that last book published, he accepted her offer and left for Stockholm in September of 1649. His correspondence soon bore witness to his unhappiness there (III, 383–384). Within months of his arrival, the combination of bitterly cold weather and the queen's expecting him to tutor her in her library at an extremely early hour led to his getting pneumonia. He died on February 11, 1650, and was buried in Stockholm; his body was subsequently transferred to France, where he was buried in Paris. The Catholic Church placed writings of his on its Index of Forbidden Books in 1663. His *Treatise on Man* was posthumously published the following year, and an uncompleted dialogue called *The Search for Truth* was published in 1701 (as were his *Rules*).

2.3   Knowledge

In the wake of the scientific revolution of Galileo (and others), using the inductive reasoning of Bacon, modernism placed knowledge at the very foundation of philosophical pursuits. The two great pioneers of early modern philosophy do precisely that: Descartes advocating rationalism and Thomas Hobbes advocating a radical empiricism. Let us begin our consideration of Descartes's epistemology where he did – with his *Rules*. There he holds that all the sciences are interconnected and that a philosopher should pursue scientific knowledge using "the natural light of his reason." He espouses the deductive pursuit of factual knowledge, which is reliable, over an empirical approach, which can be erroneous, with mathematics providing his paradigm models. Typical of modern thinkers, he thinks we should not appeal to the authority of other thinkers, including Plato and Aristotle, as the basis for our cognitive claims. Instead, we should rely on the two basic operations of reason – namely, "intuition" and "deduction." We should note that, by "intuition," he does not mean a vague hunch or any conclusion based on external sense experience or the imagination. It is, rather, the direct apprehension of an idea that is so clearly and distinctly grasped as to be certain. By contrast, deduction is a logical operation of reason, whereby truths are logically inferred from other truths that are known to be certain, so that the inferences themselves are necessarily true. Intuition and deduction, he emphasizes, are the only two approaches we can trust – not those of external sensibility or the imagination, which can lead only to belief or fancy (I, 10–15).

Why has so little philosophical progress, on which thinkers can agree, been made since ancient times – despite the genius of such men as Plato, Aristotle, Augustine, and Aquinas – as contrasted with the precision and certainty achieved in mathematics? Well, the latter, unlike the former, employs a methodology designed to achieve indubitable knowledge on which agreement is readily forthcoming. So Descartes tries to develop a set of rules which collectively constitute a method of reasoning that would likewise yield knowledge. Nor does reason have to start from nothing or from the uncertain findings of external sense experience (and imagination), since it already encompasses innate ideas and principles. It is important that we try to canvass, at least once in our lives, ideas we can grasp and to determine what can be known regarding them. While the understanding is the only faculty of the mind that can achieve rational knowledge, it can be either assisted or hindered by three other faculties, memory, sensibility, and the imagination. But Descartes, the rationalist, like other rationalists going back to pre-Socratic times (e.g. to Parmenides), maintains that reason must be in charge and not cede its authority to any combination of the other three faculties (I, 15–17, 30–32, 39).

In the very important second part of his *Discourse*, he resolves, at least temporarily, to suspend belief in all of his old opinions, in order either to replace them with sounder ones or to establish them as rationally justified. He sets forth the four methodological principles which he would try to follow in seeking philosophical knowledge. The first is one of clarity and distinctness: he should, for philosophical purposes, accept nothing as true, unless it can be "so clearly and so distinctly" conceived that its truth cannot rationally be doubted. The second is one of analysis or division: he should analyze matters and divide them into parts so that they need not be comprehended all at once. The third is a principle of "order": he should start by understanding the simplest parts, gradually working his way up to increasingly complex ones. And the fourth is a principle of review, making sure that he has not made any errors or left out anything significant. Like skeptics such as Montaigne, he would doubt whatever can be reasonably doubted; but, unlike them, the goal he is confident he can achieve is that of vanquishing radical doubt and arriving at indubitably certain knowledge. This, he affirms, unlike the abstract, speculative scholastic philosophy, would bear practical fruits that may prove "very useful in life" and be conducive to "the general welfare of mankind." In a memorable simile (from a preface to the French translation of his *Principles of Philosophy*), Descartes compares all of philosophy to a tree, whose roots are metaphysics, whose trunk is physics, and whose major branches are medicine, mechanics, and morals. On that view, it seems legitimate to hope that, by coming to understand the theoretical foundations of all human knowledge, we can increase the chances of our being able to apply it for useful purposes – even to the point (as he wrote in the *Discourse*) where we might become "the lords and masters of nature" (I, 117, 120, 125, 127, 142, 186, 142–143). As Bacon had already famously said, "Knowledge is power." For Descartes, too, a legitimate goal of understanding is control.

The *Meditations*, his masterpiece, most obviously used his four principles of method. The first of the *Meditations* dramatically utilized a process of systematic doubt that would seem to be influenced by Montaigne's skepticism. Descartes wants to doubt all that can be reasonably doubted, in order to get down to undeniable bedrock, on which he can establish secure foundations for an unshakeable system of knowledge. Because we have been deceived by our senses, he cannot trust anything based on sense experience, unless and until it can be firmly justified. Second, he is worried about our lacking any solid criterion for distinguishing the false appearances of dreams, which can seem very real, from waking realities. One might think that this leaves mathematical truths, at least, as indubitable. But, now, third, suppose that, instead of the infinitely perfect and all-good God of Christianity, "some malicious demon," just as powerful and intelligent, but wickedly deceitful, exists and is bent on fooling Descartes? Now what can he claim to know with certainty? At the beginning of the second of his *Meditations*, he employs the powerful metaphor of feeling as if he is epistemologically drowning: he has gotten into a pool of skepticism so deep that he cannot touch bottom; but neither does he know how to swim or stay afloat in such treacherous waters. So of what can he now be certain? He begrudgingly gives the depressing answer of the skeptic: "Perhaps just the one fact that nothing is certain." As we shall see, he will manage to find his epistemological feet by using rational intuition to establish the certain fact of his own mental existence and then employing deductive logic to prove the existence of an infinitely perfect God. These two ideas – of his own mental reality and of God's infinite reality (the same two chief objects of philosophical knowledge as for Augustine) – could not have been derived from sense experience or from the imagination (whose components must themselves be derived from sense experience); thus, since there are only three types of ideas, by a deductive process of elimination, he concluded they must be innate or inborn in the mind. And the ultimate guarantee of their truth is allegedly their clarity and distinctness (II, 12–16, 24, 26). But here lie two related problems for Descartes: first, how, exactly, are we to understand these innate ideas, and what evidence can we secure that there are any? And, second, what precise criteria do (can) we have for the alleged clarity and distinctness of ideas we can accept as indubitably true? While aware of these problems, he did not succeed in adequately solving them.

2.4 Reality

For traditional philosophers – and, in this respect, at least, that includes Descartes – the proper object of knowledge is reality. Despite his rebellion against Aristotelian–Thomistic scholasticism, he accepts a substance-based metaphysics (without the business about substantial forms) and the idea that all substances in our world, at least, must have been caused. So here we need to explore his analyses of substance and causality. In the first of his *Meditations*, he defines a substance as "a thing capable of existing independently" (II, 30; see also 10, 114, 157). This is more fully developed later, in his *Principles of Philosophy*, where he says that a substance not only is real but needs nothing else in order to exist. He realizes that, strictly speaking, this definition applies only to God. But, in a looser sense, things are substances if they exist and need nothing other than God to do so. By contrast, attributes necessarily have to be attributes of substances. A substance must have one principal attribute, which is to be distinguished from its other qualities and modifications. For example, a living human body is a substance (in the looser sense). Its principal attribute is that it is extended, that is, taking up space and having spatial dimensions. Its being muscular, bearded, bald-headed, and bowlegged are nonessential qualities; and its being bruised is a modification. For Descartes, there are three different sorts of substances: God, whose principal attribute is infinity, (created) minds or spirits, whose principal attribute is thought, and bodies, whose principal attribute is extension. All of reality comprises these three types of substances and their interrelationships. All actions must be performed by substances. Descartes is confident that we can have "clear and distinct" ideas of all three kinds of substances, so that at least some limited knowledge of each is humanly possible (I, 201–211). Thus, for Descartes, as surely as for the Aristotelians, metaphysics has to be substance-based. But, while we (allegedly) can know something of each sort of substance, a problem arises as to whether we can know any substance as substance (substantially) or whether our knowledge of any substance is limited to its attributes, qualities, modifications, actions, and relationships – in other words, its appearances rather than its essence.

God, the absolutely infinite and independent Substance, must be uncaused. And God, the Creator, is the creative Cause of all creatures. As a typical modern thinker, Descartes thinks of causality as efficient causality, not bothering with Aristotle's three other sorts of causes. In the third of his *Meditations*, Descartes states his very important causal principle, which he considers to be rationally self-evident (so that he does not even try to argue for it), holding that in every cause–effect relationship, the efficient cause must have at least as much reality or perfection as its effect. Descartes is confident that the principle that everything that can be discovered in any effect must also exist in its cause, in either a similar or a higher form, is a "primary notion," as intuitively certain as the old maxim that nothing can come from nothing (II, 28, 97, 116). Again, a problem is lurking here. If a serious, thoughtful critic were to call into doubt Descartes's views on causality (which, as we are about to see, he desperately needs to make systematic progress), all he can say is that they are rationally self-evident. If the critic then responds that it is not rationally self-evident to her, Descartes has no place to go. This is an inherent danger in all appeals to alleged self-evidence. Hume will exploit this vulnerability relentlessly, casting doubt on whether we can certainly know anything at all about the alleged necessary connection between a cause and its effects.

2.5 God

The ultimate uncaused Cause of every substance other than God is the infinite Substance, God. While the Christian Descartes does not claim thoroughly to comprehend the divine nature, he does claim "clear and distinct" knowledge of God's existence and at least some understanding of God's essence. He pursues his method of systematic doubt so powerfully that, if his demonstrations of God all fail, all he will be able to claim to know is his own reality as a mind or thinking being and his own mental states (a severely impoverished philosophical position called solipsism). In other words, because he has doubted everything based on sense experience, God is his necessary bridge between his own mind and external finite reality (we shall soon see how that bridgework functions in his system). Let us immediately proceed to the *Meditations*, which contain his most famous (and infamous) attempts to deal with God.

In order to demonstrate God's existence, in the third of his *Meditations*, Descartes needed a starting point to which he could apply his causal principle. All he had that he could use, at that point, were the reality of his own mind and his own mental states. How does he allegedly know that he exists as a mind or thinking thing with mental states? Well, he has intuitive experience of his own mental states. It is rationally self-evident that, even if he is deceived (as by his hypothetical "malicious demon"), he would have to exist in order to be deceived. Thus he can be certain of his own existence as a thinking thing whenever he experiences his own thinking, including doubting whether or not he is being deceived in his thinking. As one of his most astute contemporary critics (theologian Antoine Arnauld, in the fourth set of objections) pointed out, this is essentially the move Augustine made (e.g. in *On Free Choice of the Will*) to show that radical (Pyrrhonian) skepticism is mistaken in denying that we can know anything. Now, by combining his own mental existence and one particular idea he mentally experiences with the causal principle, he thinks he can demonstrate God's existence as an infinitely perfect Being. He has an idea of God as an infinitely perfect Being. But the causal principle allegedly requires that the ultimate cause of the idea of infinite perfection must itself be infinitely perfect; that, whatever else is the case about its nature, must be God. He also anticipates the empiricist's rejoinder – that he does not really have a true idea of an infinitely perfect Being but only supposes such as the negation of finite reality, such as himself, which he does experience. His claim is that the very idea of anything as finite itself presupposes the idea of the infinite. It would be difficult to prove whether the finite or the infinite is more basic. The other strand of this causal argument inquires into the only adequate ultimate cause of his own mind, which has that unique idea of an infinitely perfect Being. It is illogical to suppose that his mind is self-caused, since it would have to exist already in order to cause itself to exist. While his parents and other ancestors might be causes of his being, they were all finite, contingent beings, whose own existence must be ultimately caused by a necessary Being, that must also be infinite in order adequately to account for his mind's idea of infinity; and that is God. (We note that these causal arguments bear some resemblance to the cosmological ones among the "five ways" of Aquinas.) Let us observe one more important point here: if Descartes has, indeed, succeeded in establishing God's existence as an infinitely perfect Being, that rules out God's being a deceiver, since deception is an *im*perfection. Thus either we can dispel the concern about a "malicious demon" or, at least, see that it would be finite and imperfect and, therefore, inferior to God. We can also now understand what sort of idea our idea of God as an infinitely perfect Being is. It could not be an "adventitious" idea, such as that of a tree, which comes into the mind through sense experience, because any object of sense experience would be limited rather than infinitely perfect, and we never have sense experience of a nonphysical object. Second, it could not be a product of the imagination, since ideas of the imagination compound ideas derived from sensation. But, since these are the only three sorts of ideas that are available to us, by a process of elimination, we can deduce that it must be an "innate" idea of pure reason (like the idea of the mind as an immaterial substance). Descartes used an arresting figure of speech, comparing this idea in the mind to the mark the divine Artist stamps on a masterpiece, signing it to make obvious its authorship (II, 26–35).

After explaining, in the fourth of his *Meditations*, how the evil of error could come to be in a world created by an infinitely perfect God in such a way that God clearly is not to blame (and divine perfection is not compromised), in the fifth, Descartes develops a radically different (though not entirely original) argument to demonstrate God's existence. Why? Well, it is not clear. The answer may have to do with the enormous importance of rationally establishing the necessary reality of an infinitely perfect Being. Given the anti-empirical way in which he has set things up, he needs God to overcome the unwelcome position of solipsism – the view that all he has reason to suppose as real are his own mind and its mental states. So why not settle for the causal reasoning for God that we have just considered? Perhaps it is because it rests on that causal principle, which he claims to be self-evident and innate. What of readers who might not necessarily agree with it? What is striking about the "new" argument for God is that it does not use the causal principle at all. This argument purports to analyze the mind's idea of God as "a supremely perfect being" in such a way as to render it evident that God must also exist independently of the human mind. The argument can be formulated thus: God, by definition, is "the supremely perfect being." A "supremely perfect being," by definition, must have all perfections. But "existence" is "a perfection." Therefore God must have the perfection of existence; or, in other words, God necessarily exists. It also follows that there cannot be more than one God, since two supremely perfect Beings would limit each other, and that God must be eternal, since having come to be would be a limitation. At the end of this meditation, Descartes claims that the reality of this perfect, non-deceiving God serves as a warrant for the reliability of all truths that have ever been demonstrated, that, without such a God, we could never have any "perfect knowledge about anything else." We may note that this "new" argument for God is a version of the old argument Anselm invented in the eleventh century (and which Kant, in the eighteenth century, would name "ontological"). Thomas Hobbes objects that we cannot have any genuine idea of soul or substance or any nonphysical object, since an idea is a mental image, and we can only have mental images of objects of sensibility. Further, there can be no innate ideas. In reply, Descartes defends innate ideas as not involving mental images. Descartes is also accused, by Arnauld, of creating a "circle" of reasoning. The alleged circular reasoning goes like this: our knowledge of everything other than God depends on our knowing God, but our knowledge of God depends on our knowing about our own minds and their idea of infinite perfection. In reply, Descartes explains that the "perfect knowledge" that requires God as a warrant is that which depends on our memory of past clear and distinct understanding, at times when we are not attending to its foundation (II, 45–49, 130–132, 150, 171). Finally, although Descartes has enormous confidence in the power of human reason and is rightly regarded as one of the great rationalists of Western philosophy, he is keenly aware that human reason is limited. Also, as he makes obvious in his *Principles of Philosophy*, he readily admits that we should have faith in truths God has revealed, such as religious mysteries, that are beyond the range of human comprehension, that we should submit our reason to divine authority in matters of revelation, being ruled by reason in all other areas (I, 201, 221–222).

2.6 Humanity

As we shift from Descartes's views on what we can know of divine reality to those regarding what we can know of human reality, we need to say something about his metaphysical dualism. Not all dualists are identical in their dualisms, and his is significantly different from the two-worlds dualism of Plato; although Descartes also could be said to distinguish between the supernatural realm and the natural order, it is his theory of dualism applied to this world that is differently significant and controversial. His is a substance dualism, in that he thinks there are two sorts of substance, the material substance of bodies and the spiritual substance of minds, which are mutually irreducible. All bodies are extended, nonthinking, physical created substances. All finite minds are non-extended, thinking, nonphysical created substances. But things get more complex and interesting in human nature, which represents some sort of convergence of the two kinds of substance. Descartes thinks that human beings are the only creatures who are some kind of combination of body and mind. Given his methodology, including, especially, his first principle (of clarity and distinctness) and his view that only rational intuition and logical deduction are (at least initially) to be trusted, he cannot affirm any physical substance, including even that of his own body, until later. The *cogito* (the claim that "I am thinking, therefore I exist") allegedly yields indubitably certain knowledge of his own mind as a thinking substance whenever he experiences his own thinking (I, 127, 195). Thus far, he could draw no reliable conclusions regarding any physical or bodily implications; therefore he had no justification for the common belief that he was a rational animal, as he makes clear in the second of his *Meditations*. So, at that point, what could he know himself to be? "A thing that thinks" is his answer. In explaining what that means, he employs a functional definition – namely, a substance "that doubts, understands, affirms, denies, is willing, is unwilling, and also imagines and has sensory perceptions." This is allegedly self-evident intuition so "clear and distinct" that it cannot be reasonably doubted. It also provides him with his first example of an (allegedly) innate idea, a model for future ones. One thing that was painfully clear to him was that his mind, now proved to exist, is fallible and makes mistakes, unlike God, who is infinitely perfect. This introduces a new problem, which is the inverse of the initial one he had to solve. In the first meditation, the problem was how he could know anything for certain; by halfway through his *Meditations*, he was sure he had solved that. But now, at the beginning of the fourth meditation, he has to wonder how he could make mistakes if he was created by an infinitely perfect God, who is so far removed from a "malicious demon." (In our next section, on freedom, we shall see how he solves it; but, for now, let us observe that this problem of error is the intellectual version of the moral problem of evil.) In moving toward an answer, he must analyze more deeply two key mental faculties of human nature. Like medieval Christian philosophers, such as Augustine and Aquinas, he must explain how things go wrong in a world created by God and governed by divine providence without pointing the accusatory finger of blame at God. But, unlike them, he is not satisfied with the privation theory, which too glibly answers that evil is not any positive reality, for which God is responsible, but merely a privation of good in something God has created. To his credit, Descartes felt a need to dig deeper. This requires more careful analysis of two most important dimensions of the human mind – "the intellect" or "faculty of knowledge" and "the will" or "faculty of choice." He was acutely aware of how limited the intellect is and how much we do not understand. Yet, despite this limitation, he saw it as a great and good gift from God, setting us apart from other animals. By contrast, the human will, another great and good gift of human nature, is virtually unlimited, in that we can choose anything of which our minds can conceive; he is so impressed with the extensive reach of free will, another faculty allegedly separating us from all other animals, as to indicate that it is the respect in which our human nature is most godlike (II, 17–19, and 38–40). Before we proceed to discuss what he says about the body and its relation to mind, let us briefly consider what he says in the fifth part of his *Discourse*. The human body, assuming that it exists, like every living body in the universe, is merely "a machine," operating mechanically, all of its actions being necessarily determined by external causes. But human nature, on account of the rational mind, has two capacities which already distinguish it from all other animals (again, assuming that there are any). These are the capacities for abstract language usage and for deliberately chosen action. He held that these two would allow us, clearly and distinctly, to distinguish a human person from any other sort of animal or any possible mere machine (I, 139–141).

Now, returning to the *Meditations*, we can see, first, how all bodies are radically different sorts of created substances from minds, second, how we allegedly can establish that bodies are real, and, third, how the human body is related to the human mind in a living human being. In the second meditation, after establishing the existence of the mind as a thinking thing, Descartes considers the essential nature of a commonplace object such as a "piece of wax," if, indeed, such a thing were to exist. Our initial inclination is to try to define it in terms of qualities we seem to perceive through sensation – color, texture, sound, shape, hardness, smell, taste, and so forth. But when we place a piece of wax too close to an open fire, it seems that all these qualities change, although it is the same piece of wax. The conclusion must be that those are only accidental qualities. So what qualities, if any, endure from before to during to after the fire experiment? The answer is that the object remains "something extended, flexible and changeable." But these essential qualities – the most fundamental of which is extension – can only be apprehended by reason and not by sensation or imagination (II, 20–22). Thus every body, including the human body, is an extended finite substance, which is subject to the determinations of mechanical forces and the physical laws of nature – unlike the human mind, which, while also a finite substance, is thinking and indivisible, rather than extended and divisible.

Now, second, how do I know that an external, physical world of bodies, including my own, is real rather than a mere figment of the imagination? We need another argument to deduce this. The one Descartes employs (in his sixth meditation) involves the infinitely perfect nature of God he has already demonstrated and can be formulated thus: if God created me such that I cannot help believing in an external world of bodies, then either God is a deceiver or an external world of bodies must actually exist; but, in fact, I cannot help believing in such a world, and, as we have already proved, God, a being infinitely perfect, cannot be a deceiver; therefore, such a world must be real. Among all the bodies in the external world, one in particular seems most intimately related to me – that is, to my mind – so that I possess it as my own body. Notice he is saying that I – my mind – have a body rather than that I am a body; after all, I am essentially a mind, and his dualism has committed him to saying that it must be essentially different from any body. Now, third, how is my body related to the mind that is me? It has to be a special relationship since such everyday experiences as "pain, hunger, thirst," and so forth repeatedly drive home the point that the one body that I identify as my own is somehow so "very closely joined and, as it were, intermingled" with my mind that the two, while being irreducibly different from each other, somehow "form a unit." Other bodies are located in relation to my own, many of them being either useful or dangerous to it. In pointing to "the union and, as it were, intermingling of the mind with the body" in human nature, Descartes is maintaining that, somehow, they interact, the mind affecting the body and vice versa. Thus his position can be called one of dualistic interactionism. Although the mind is related to every part of the living body, it is intimately conjoined to a particular "small part of the brain" (II, 55–59). In his *Treatise on Man* and his *Passions of the Soul*, he identifies this as the pineal gland, located in the middle of the brain (I, 100, 340). In that latter work, he writes of human emotions or passions, which attest to the special relationship between the living human body and the mind or rational soul (for him these are the same).

There are problems with this position. First of all, today we know what Descartes did not know, that the function of the pineal gland is to secrete melatonin, a hormone that controls a person's body clock. Not knowing its function and believing that God would not create anything that did

30 | *2 René Descartes*

not serve some purpose, he jumped to the conclusion that it must be the special meeting place between the physical brain and the nonphysical mind. Second, as Princess Elizabeth shrewdly objected (in 1643), it seems mysterious how there can be any contact (in the pineal gland or anywhere else) between the extended, physical brain and an unextended immaterial mind, contact in any literal sense being incompatible with the latter. Further, she objects, how could the mind (not being physical) move the body in any way, and how can the body, including the brain, possibly affect the mind, given Descartes's dualism? His replies to her are quite unconvincing, spawning the mind–body problem that would haunt modern philosophy for more than a century to come. Third, and most radically, can Descartes ever convincingly argue that the functions of human nature that he attributes to mind alone cannot be met by the human body, including its brain (and central nervous system)? Thomas Hobbes, the materialist, poses this problem in his third set of objections – why cannot the thinking thing be material rather than an immaterial substance, thought being a product of brain activity? Again, Descartes's replies are disappointing.

2.7 Freedom

Among the issues that modern philosophers regard as most important concerning humanity is that of freedom versus determinism: are all actions in our world, including all human actions, causally determined as necessary, or are at least some human actions freely chosen by us? It seems obvious that some of the things we do are not freely chosen, as when we involuntarily twitch or sneeze. But the issue is whether *any* of them are truly free. In an age of science, such as that represented by all three centuries of modern philosophy, there are pressures to view all actions and events as causally determined, to eliminate the role of miracles in our world, and, thus, to compromise free choice. After all, if the only reason a person performs an action is that she freely chooses to do it, then the action is spontaneous and seems a matter of arbitrary chance and, hence, defies scientific comprehension. On the other hand, if every human action is causally determined as is the falling of a book toward the center of our planet when it is no longer supported in space, then it could not be avoided, given antecedent circumstances. But, then, the agent – if it even still makes sense to designate her such – cannot fairly be blamed or morally praised for it, in which case rewards and punishment are rendered morally inappropriate (remember, this was, essentially, the argument for human freedom used by such medieval philosophers as Augustine and Aquinas). So there would seem to be a dilemma here, with a good deal at stake, theoretically speaking.

As was indicated in our previous section, Descartes comes down on the side of freedom. Yet, as a man of science, he wants to affirm rather than deny causal necessity. Can he have it both ways? He obviously believes that his dualism allows him to do so. Every material substance operates in a mechanical, thoroughly deterministic manner – including the human body. But every mental (immaterial) substance is capable of free choice regarding at least some of its actions. As we have seen, he thinks that human freedom is virtually unlimited, in that the mind can choose in accordance with any ideas it can conceive. Thus, while I cannot actually become an immortal emperor of the universe, because I can imagine such an outlandish idea, I could always choose to try to do so (at risk of being dismissed as a lunatic or condemned as a megalomaniac). In the fourth meditation, he defines the freedom of the will as "our ability to do or not do something (that is, to affirm or deny, to pursue or avoid)." The explanation Descartes offers of how we commit error is that we neglect to restrict the will, which has a more extensive range than the understanding, to making judgments within the limits of clear and distinct understanding. When we do this, we risk falling into error and sin – for which we, and not God, are responsible, for, in such cases, we fail to make proper use of the good gift of freedom God gave us. Conversely, the secret to avoiding error and sin is limiting our judgments of will within the bounds of clear and distinct understanding. But, in the very last sentence of the final meditation, Descartes admits that, because of the practical exigencies of actual circumstances, this is more easily said than done. Hobbes typically offers a trenchant criticism (in the third set of objections), that "the freedom of the will is assumed without proof" by Descartes. In reply, the latter asserts that it is rationally self-evident, in which case, it would not require a deductive argument. Here Descartes was typically disrespectful toward, and dismissive of, Hobbes, the materialist (II, 40–43, 62, 133–134).

We also find important additions in *The Principles of Philosophy*, which (passing over passages that would repeat what we have already considered) can be briefly surveyed. He distinguishes "desire, aversion, assertion, denial, and doubt" as "various modes of willing," all of which we directly and immediately experience. He maintains that this capacity for free choice is our "supreme perfection," allowing us to be responsible for (at least some of) our actions, helping to distinguish us from "automatons." As if replying to Hobbes's objection several years after it was raised, he holds that our freedom is "evident" and should be recognized as "among the first and most common notions that are innate in us." Finally, he does provide a sort of argument that goes beyond mere assertion: in the very act of doubting what is not clear and distinct, we experience our freedom to believe or to suspend belief. But now comes another problem. As a Christian, Descartes believed that God created our whole world and governs it with "divine preordination." But if all our actions are preordained by God, how can any of them be freely chosen and possibly otherwise? In other words, how can we reconcile these two apparently conflicting claims? Disappointingly, he does not even try to resolve the problem, avoiding doing so by reminding us that our finite minds should not presume to comprehend God's infinite power (I, 204–206). While this may be the best Descartes can do, it is philosophically unimpressive.

2.8 Morality

At any rate, another claim he makes about human reality is that we can know that it involves the capacity for free choice. This, of course, is relevant to what he will have to say about morality (which is fairly slight but worth considering). Recall that "morals" was held to be one of the important "branches" of the "tree" of philosophy. Without a doubt, his most valuable treatment of morality is in the third part of his *Discourse* (interestingly, he offers no parallel in later works he published); there he presents "a provisional moral code consisting of just three or four maxims." First, he should obey the laws and customs of his own country, follow the religion in which he was raised, and otherwise act with moderation in all things. The conservatism of this position is striking relative to his bold, revolutionary epistemology. Second, he should staunchly stay on the course of action he has chosen, even when it seems dubious. This practical rule is in tension with his recommendation, in the fourth meditation, as to how we can best minimize the risk of error. Third, whenever his own desires conflict with the established way of the world, he should change his own desires rather than fruitlessly trying to change the world, knowing that, in general, he can control little other than his own thoughts. Here we see the clear-cut influence of Stoicism, which promotes a defensive sort of resignation. Finally, he considers the various ways he could live his life and, convinced that the one he was following was the best one for him, resolves to continue along that course, without necessarily suggesting that anyone else should follow his example (I, 122–124). Here, as with the previous three "maxims," or rules for living, it is not clear whether and to what extent he thinks others ought to follow his example. This all seems so uninspired as to seem almost unworthy of so great a thinker as Descartes. But another reason it is problematic and disappointing is that it goes against the entire spirit of his own relentless and untrammeled rational quest for truth.

In *The Passions of the Soul*, he maintained that "the chief utility of morality" is that it helps us to control our passionate desires. The latter are good when they accord with genuine knowledge but bad when infected with error. Like the Stoics, he held that we are dangerously susceptible to failing to distinguish between things within our control and those beyond it. We open ourselves to being miserable by pursuing things beyond our control. What we can control and that to which we should commit ourselves is "the pursuit of virtue," leading to our choosing to do the good we can do. There is satisfaction in becoming virtuous, which points us in the direction of happiness. This all sounds quite Platonic. And, somewhat like Plato, he thought that "vice usually proceeds from ignorance." The virtues, he wrote, are habits that dispose us to think in certain ways (I, 379, 387). We cannot help wondering why Descartes settled for so little regarding what he himself considers one of the most important "branches" of philosophy. Well, there is a clue to be found in his correspondence. In a letter, written near the end of his life, he explained that he had refrained from discussing morality much in writing because doing so would provide opponents with ammunition to use against him and because he thought that only those in positions of authority have the right to dictate others' morals (III, 326).

2.9 Society

As thin and devoid of argumentation as his views on morality are, those on society are even more scattered and impressionistic. In *The Passions of the Soul*, he discussed various kinds of love (including friendship) which help to establish social relationships. Love is, generally, an emotion that draws us toward a bond with attractive objects (as opposed to hatred, an emotion which motivates us to avoid objects that repel us). What he called "concupiscent love" is selfish desire, while what he called "benevolent love" seeks the well-being of the beloved. He drew another interesting threefold distinction among "simple affection" for something we esteem as lower than ourselves, such as a house or a dog, "friendship" for others we esteem as roughly on the same level as ourselves, such as other humans, and "devotion" for things we esteem as higher than ourselves, such as God, king, and country. Generosity is an interpersonal inclination that is valuable for establishing and maintaining good social relationships. The good member of society tries to do "whatever he judges to be best." The generous person avoids contempt for others by trying to assume that they too are trying to do their best rather than assuming ill will of them. The generous person is also inclined toward humility in not supposing himself morally superior to others. Such people aim at "doing good to others," even at cost to their own self-interest, at always being "courteous, gracious, and obliging to everyone" (I, 356–357, 384–385). To the extent that they can achieve this ideal, they render themselves good members of society.

In some of his correspondence, Descartes discussed love and friendship further, though what he has to say is no more novel than what we have just considered. He held that love creates an emotional bond and identity between the one who loves and the object loved, so that self-interest becomes expanded to include the beloved. In a letter to Princess Elizabeth, he made the striking claim that "the chief good of life is friendship." In another, he maintained that a devoted member of community "delights in doing good to everyone," even at the risk of his own life, if necessary. Indeed, if our connections to society are sufficiently genuine, in striving on behalf of our own legitimate interests, we also benefit society (III, 311, 323, 266, 273).

In an important letter (of 1646) to Princess Elizabeth, Descartes reported that he had read Machiavelli's *The Prince*, sharing with her some of his reactions, in effect giving her political advice regarding how to deal with "subjects, friends or allies, and enemies." Alarmingly, he thought a ruler can legitimately claim "a virtual license" to treat enemies in any way desirable, so long as it seems likely to benefit the ruler or the ruler's subjects. And the word "enemies" includes everyone who is neither friend nor ally. The one exception he draws that distinguishes him here from Machiavelli has to do with trying to deceive enemies into thinking they are friends. He held that a ruler should honor commitments to allies, even when doing so is to the ruler's disadvantage, so long as the consequences will not be catastrophic. Prudent rulers should try to remain "on friendly terms" with most neighbors but should only form alliances with less powerful sovereigns who would not be tempted to betray them. He divides political subjects into "great people," strong enough to form threatening alliances against a ruler, and the "common people," who lack such power. A ruler needs to be assured of the loyalty of great people or cut them down like enemies if they threaten "to rock the ship of state." Regarding more common subjects, a monarch must, above all, be sure to "avoid their hatred and contempt." The best way to manage this is to rule justly in accordance with familiar customs and laws, being neither too quick to pardon nor too harsh in punishing. The key is the appearance of justice – persuading the people that they are being justly ruled (III, 292–295). It may be surprising that Descartes expressed as much sympathy for Machiavelli's amoral perspective as he does; but the two, no doubt, shared a desire for a productive society and a stable political order.

2.10 Review

It seems that Descartes was most impressive when dealing with such (relatively) abstract, theoretical issues as knowledge, reality, God, and humanity; that he was less thorough when dealing with the more practically oriented topic of freedom; and that he was most sketchy when dealing with the even more practical areas of morality and society. But, throughout, he emphasized the individual thinking subject as the proper starting point, having some difficulty getting convincingly beyond it. For Descartes, everything in our world was material and functioned with mechanical determinism, with the one exception of the human mind. We shall soon turn to Hobbes, his greatest contemporary critic, who thought that was essentially correct except for that one exception.[2]

2.11 Another Perspective

Princess Elisabeth of Bohemia (1618–1680) was the oldest daughter of Frederick V, King of Bohemia, and Elisabeth Stuart, a child of King Charles I of England. Frederick lost his throne a couple of years after she was born, and the family moved to The Hague. As a royal, the princess was educated, learning the classical languages of Greek and Latin, as well as French, English, and

---

2 For more on Descartes, see ch. III of *Twelve Great Philosophers*, by Wayne P. Pomerleau (New York: Ardsley House, 1997), and ch. 2 of *Western Philosophies of Religion*, by Wayne P. Pomerleau (New York: Ardsley House, 1998).

2 René Descartes

German. After their correspondence had begun, Descartes dedicated his *Principles of Philosophy* to her (in 1644). At her request, Descartes developed his theory of human emotions, leading to *The Passions of the Soul*, the last book he published. As far as we know, she never wrote a philosophical treatise; her correspondence with Descartes, in the 1640s,[3] contains her most important contributions to philosophy. In 1660, she entered a Lutheran convent in Germany, becoming its abbess in 1667.

The most famous part of the correspondence is their exchange about the mind–body relation in 1643. Puzzled about how a purely physical substance, such as the human body, can interact with a purely spiritual substance, such as the human mind, and calling Descartes "the best doctor for my soul," she requests an explanation, signing her letter, "Your affectionate friend." Descartes regards this as an incisive query that he has not sufficiently addressed. He claims that "the power with which the soul acts on the body" is radically different from "the power with which one body acts on another" body. In her reply, Elisabeth suggests that she still cannot understand how this distinction explains interaction between mind and body, adding that she would find it easier to consider the soul physical than to comprehend how "an immaterial thing" could possibly move and be moved by a body. Descartes does not do a good job of responding, instead claiming that the ideas we have of body, of mind, and of their union are all different from each other. He admits that it is difficult, if not impossible, to grasp distinctly "and at the same time, the distinction between the soul and the body and their union" (62–63, 65–66, 68–72). It might be noted that he is far more open to her thinking of the mind as material than he was when the materialist Hobbes made the same suggestion. At any rate, the way she pinpoints the problem with dualistic interactionism was excellent, and he would never succeed in solving it adequately.

The other part of their correspondence that is noteworthy here is her successful urging of Descartes to develop his views on moral psychology, on ethics, and on political philosophy. This represents a significant contribution to students of Cartesian philosophy, in general, and to Descartes scholars, in particular. Descartes had recommended that she read "Seneca's *De vita beata*" (*On the Happy Life*). She did so and asked him how we can achieve "true happiness" without being blessed with the sort of good fortune which is independent of our will. She correctly observes that there are physical diseases that either impair or "destroy altogether the power of reasoning." He has to grant her point that our happiness can be contingent on circumstances, such as illness, over which we have little, or no, control, leaving us unable to direct our passions rationally. Descartes further holds that mental contentment, rather than happiness, is the highest good, although the former presupposes the latter. He agrees with Stoics (such as Zeno and Seneca) that virtue should be the goal of our free choices. Mental contentment presupposes both happiness and virtue. A virtuous life requires that we "have a firm and constant will to execute all that we judge to be the best and to apply all the force of our understanding to judge well." She observes that not all passions disturb the mind but that some actually promote reasonable choices. She is correct. Descartes maintains that rational action requires knowledge of what is truly most useful to us and being guided by this knowledge, when circumstances call for it. Still, he does not seem to trust passions enough to allow our judgments to be guided by them, and he tries to distinguish between emotional passions and mental actions, the former being physiologically explicable. She politely expresses her doubt that passions can be both excessive and subject to reason, as he had suggested, as well as that we can have free will when everything is subject to God's will. He answers that when we focus only on this world, the will seems independent; but when we consider

---

3 References in this section will be to *The Correspondence between Princess Elisabeth of Bohemia and René Descartes*, ed. and trans. by Lisa Shapiro (Chicago: Univ. of Chicago Press, 2007).

God, we should see that it does depend on the will of the Creator. He admits that there are good passions that can be both excessive and subject to reason (97, 100, 103–107, 110–111, 113, 118–120, 123, 125). So here we see her successfully urging him to develop his views on ethics and moral psychology.

Having done that in 1645, the following year, she asked him to move from discussing reason's role in "private life" to reason's proper role in "civil life," although she adds that, because the latter so often depends on dealing with people who do not act rationally, she has often found it preferable to rely on experience rather than on reason. In reply, he says that it would be "impertinent" of him to presume to advise a royal princess regarding civil affairs. She apparently asked him (in person) to read Machiavelli's *The Prince* and tell her his reactions. He tells her that he thinks some of its precepts seem "very good" to him, while he "cannot approve" of others. Details of these reactions have already been given in the "Society" section above; but, again, we note that it is thanks to her gentle probing that he develops his ideas regarding political philosophy. He particularly disapproves of the advice to a ruler that, in order to be effective and maintain power, one must learn to be wicked (134, 137, 139–142, 149). In concluding, we should notice that, while their correspondence was consistently friendly and mutually respectful, Princess Elisabeth exhibited a keen critical mind in challenging Descartes on some points and a persistent knack for eliciting his previously undeveloped views.

3

Thomas Hobbes

Source: Georgios Kollidas/Adobe Stock

3.1 Overview

It is difficult to think of another modern philosopher who is a better point-counterpoint intellectual contrast with Descartes than Thomas Hobbes. While the former is the first great Continental rationalist, the latter is the first great modern British empiricist; while the former is one of the greatest of all philosophical dualists, the latter is one of the greatest philosophical monists; while the former develops a system that critically needs God, the latter develops one that does not; while the former sees humans as essentially spiritual substances that are contingently related to bodies, the latter views us as merely sophisticated bodies, ruling out any and all immaterial substances; while the former is thoroughly committed to human freedom, the latter is a thoroughgoing determinist; while the former would not reduce all moral values to products of human agreement, the latter does precisely that; and, while the former considers us essentially social beings, the latter regards society as an artificial, egoistically useful construct. Both of them are first-rate thinkers with well-developed philosophical systems.

3.2 Biography

Whereas Descartes left us no autobiography, as such, Hobbes left us two of them, both written during the last decade of his long life, one in prose, the other in verse.[1] He was born on April 5, 1588 (during the reign of Queen Elizabeth I), in Malmesbury, England, the second son of a quarrelsome vicar, after whom he was named. In one of his autobiographies, more than eight decades later, he joked that his mother was so terrified of the invasion launched against England by the Spanish Armada that she prematurely gave birth to twins – himself and fear. We know almost nothing of his mother. But his hot-headed father lost his temper, hit a parson in front of the church, ran off into hiding, and died in obscurity. His uncle, who was rather successful, paid for his education; and, at the age of 14, the boy was sent to Oxford, which was then administered by Puritans. He got a good education; but, like Descartes, he reacted negatively to the Aristotelian scholasticism that was dominant in colleges at that time. After completing his Bachelor's degree in 1608, he went into service as a tutor to the aristocratic Cavendish family. This position provided him access to influential people, a fine library, and foreign travel. He became associated with Francis Bacon, translating some of his essays into Latin; they shared a rejection of Aristotelian scholasticism, preferring the methodology of modern science. In 1628, Hobbes published his English translation of Thucydides's *History*, agreeing with the Greek's distrust of democracy. In 1636, while on one of his trips to the continent, he visited Galileo near Florence. After leaving Italy, he passed through Paris, where he met Mersenne, whom he liked and admired; he claims that, from then on, he was considered a philosopher. It was through Mersenne that his contact with Descartes would be established. After returning to England, he wrote *The Elements of Law*; though it would not be published for another decade, manuscript copies were circulated. Civil war was brewing between the royalists, who supported the sovereign authority of King Charles I, and parliamentarians, who wanted the authority of the monarch checked. Hobbes sided with the royal prerogative and fled to France near the end of 1640, remaining there for about 11 years. He was cordially received by Mersenne, who, acting on behalf of Descartes, invited Hobbes to compose what would become the third set of objections, to be published with the *Meditations*. This would help solidify the reputation of Hobbes as a serious philosopher (*Elements*, 245–247, 254–258).

In 1642, Hobbes published (in Latin) his book *De Cive* (*On the Citizen*). After Charles, the Prince of Wales, arrived in Paris, where he would be safe from the parliamentarians, Hobbes became his tutor. In 1649, King Charles I, who had lost the civil war and been arrested, was tried and executed (beheaded). The following year, the two parts of *Elements of Law* (*Human Nature* and *De Corpore*

---

1 These are contained in a collection of his writings that also includes his *Elements of Law* (his *Human Nature* and his *De Corpore Politico*); references to *The Elements of Law* (hereafter called *Elements*), by Thomas Hobbes, ed. by J.C.A. Gaskin (Oxford: Oxford Univ. Press, 1994), will be made in text with appropriate page numbers. Other primary source materials to be used (and referenced in the same way) are *Leviathan*, by Thomas Hobbes, ed. by Edwin Curley (Indianapolis: Hackett, 1994), *Body, Man, and Citizen* (henceforth called *Body*), by Thomas Hobbes, ed. by Richard S. Peters (New York: Collier Books, 1962), *Man and Citizen*, by Thomas Hobbes (henceforth called *Man*), ed. by Bernard Gert (Indianapolis: Hackett, 1991), and *The English Works of Thomas Hobbes* (henceforth called *Works*), ed. by Sir William Molesworth, Vol. IV (London: John Bohn, 1840).

Politico) were published; in 1651, Hobbes published both his English translation of *De Cive* and, in English, *Leviathan*, his masterpiece. These published works antagonized royalists in France, because of their political slant and his attacks on the Catholic papacy; his friend Mersenne had died (in 1648); Hobbes was isolated and on the defensive. So he returned to England in the winter of 1651–1652. He came to terms with the anti-royalist government and was pardoned, settling into a quiet, private life and writing *De Corpore*. While engaged in that important work, he got embroiled in a nasty controversy with a Bishop Bramhall because of his denial of free will. His work *Of Liberty and Necessity* was published, without his consent, in 1654, developing his problematic position of determinism. Although this controversy represented a serious distraction, he finished and published *De Corpore* (*On the Body*) in 1655, with an English version published the following year. (Notice how, thanks to the invention of the printing press, by the middle third of the seventeenth century, it had become relatively easy for scholars like Descartes and Hobbes to publish their works in both the vernacular – e.g. French or English – and the academic language of Latin, broadening their potential audiences considerably.) In 1658, his *De Homine* (*On Man*) was published, arguably his last great philosophy book. In 1660, the monarchy was restored, the Prince of Wales returning to England from voluntary exile, his coronation as King Charles II occurring in 1661. Even though Hobbes had made more than his share of political and religious enemies, the new king invited him to join his royal court and granted him an annual pension. In 1665–1666, when London was devastated by the Great Plague and the Great Fire, his enemies identified Hobbes as their scapegoat, maintaining that these miseries were visited on England by God as punishment for his ideas. Some of the bishops apparently went so far as to demand that he be burned at the stake, and a parliamentary bill was introduced to investigate him as an atheist. Luckily, however, he was under the royal protection of the king, so that these hateful initiatives fizzled. Nevertheless, Charles did refuse to give permission for Hobbes to publish his *Behemoth*, written in 1668, because it would prove too politically inflammatory, and it was only published posthumously. When he was in his mid-eighties, Hobbes translated Homer's *Iliad* and *Odyssey* into English verse (for lack of anything better to do, as he said), publishing them in 1675. In late 1679, he became paralyzed and died, on December 4, at the age of 91. He had committed approximately half of his life to producing the philosophical work for which he remains famous – especially in the area of politics – and to practicing what he preached. As he wrote near the end of his verse autobiography, "My Life and Writings speak one Congruous Sense; Justice I Teach and Justice Reverence" (*Elements*, 247–253, 258–264). In 1683, two of his most important political works (*De Cive* and *Leviathan*) were condemned and burned at Oxford.

3.3 Knowledge

For Hobbes, the direct, immediate objects of experience are mental images derived from sensation. We should notice how this position of radical empiricism, from the outset, differs from the epistemology of Descartes. For the earlier philosopher, as we have seen, there are three sorts of ideas – the innate ones of reason, the adventitious ones of sensation, and the fictitious ones of the imagination. Hobbes, spurning any notion of innate ideas not derived from sense and not adding any new candidate to replace ideas of pure reason, must make sensory ideas and those of imagination do all the work. (By the way, the reason this position is being called "radical" empiricism is to distinguish it from that of more moderate empiricists, like Aristotle and Aquinas, who hold that, while all knowledge is ultimately derived from experience, we can use reason to go beyond what we experience to achieve knowledge that transcends it; a "radical" empiricist, like Hobbes, tends to say that all knowledge is both derived from sense experience and limited within its bounds.) In the very first chapter of *Leviathan*, called "Of Sense," he makes it quite clear how unstinting he is about insisting that the ultimate source of all ideas whatsoever must be sensory: "For there is no conception in a man's mind which hath not at first, totally or by parts, been begotten upon the organs of sense." The objects of sense experience put pressure on our bodily organs, in an utterly mechanistic manner, so as to produce mental images in us. In this way, those objects appear to us as they do by means of those mental images. Those images become stored in the brain as memories and can be mentally manipulated in the imagination. But memory and imagination are ultimately two different ways of thinking about the same faculty of the brain; both of them are, to use his memorable phrase, "decaying sense," for, with time, our memories fade and the products of our imagination become further removed from the original sense experience. What we call "*experience*" is the accumulation of memories. When images stored in our memories constitute a sequence or "train of thoughts," this is what Hobbes calls "mental discourse," which can be either random ("*unguided*") or ordered ("*regulated*"). And we use speech to help us better to recall our mental discourse, as well as to communicate it to others. While all of our experiences are particular and of particular objects, it is valuable to us that our speech involves general names; but there is "nothing in the world universal but names" (this is called "nominalism"). Truth itself is nothing abstract or mysterious, but only the agreement between spoken and/or contemplated language and its objects; and the person who is sloppy in the use of language can not only miss grasping the truth but can "find himself entangled in words, as a bird in lime twigs," so that precise definition can be very valuable. Thus, for example, because Descartes fails to grasp the concept of substance adequately, he imagines that a soul or mind might be "an *incorporeal substance*," when, in fact, this is an oxymoron like "an *incorporeal body*," getting himself entangled in the insoluble problem of how that mind is related to the body. When speech causes a person's ideas to be true, "he is said to understand." So far, all of this applies to nonhuman animals ("beasts") as well as to humans, differences being quantitative ones of degree, rather than qualitative ones of kind. If we imagine that this changes once we start talking about human reason, we would be mistaken. Reasoning is nothing more than the brain's capacity for calculating ("*reckoning*") the consequences of relating words or names. There is no reason why a dog or chimpanzee cannot have this capacity as well as we do, even if to a lesser extent. So what we notice Hobbes doing here is undermining the idea that humans are radically unique in their capacity for cognitive experience: there is no such thing as a mental substance, all cognition is grounded in images derived from sense experience, our images can form mental discourse that can be cast into speech, reason is a function of speech, and, hence, we are not as cognitively special as we like to suppose. (As we shall see, free will, being a mere illusion, also cannot distinguish us.) All "absolute knowledge of fact" can only come from sense and memory, and "science" can never be more than "conditional knowledge," philosophy being a science, whose knowledge can only be conditional, never absolute. Elsewhere, he endorses a Cartesian "tree of philosophy," whose major branches are geometry, physics, and morals (*Leviathan*, 6–9, 12–13, 16–17, 19, 21–24, 35–36, 47; *Man*, 91) – all sciences but only yielding conditional (not absolute) knowledge.

Let us now move from the greatest book of Hobbes to what is arguably his most underappreciated one, *De Corpore*. There he defines the conditional knowledge of philosophy in terms of causal reasoning – either from causes to effects or vice versa – where the starting point of the reasoning is supposed to be cause or effect, so that the generation of any absolute knowledge of fact is never possible. Nevertheless, it is a kind of knowledge and, hence, valuable; for, Hobbes reminds us, "The end of knowledge is power" (a point his patron Bacon had already famously made). The power of even conditional knowledge stems from its helping us better to understand our experience and, hence, our world, ourselves, and our natural and social environment. He uses an example of knowing the evils that result from war, as well as what tends to cause the wars that produce those evils;

this provides us with ample motivation to try to reduce the dangers of war in critically practical ways. Philosophy should only deal with the reality of the world of bodies, since, as we shall see, material reality is all there is. Like Descartes, he holds that a fruitful methodology is crucial to the development of conditional knowledge, as going beyond the direct experience of sensation, memory, and imagination; this method must be inductively "analytical" and/or deductively "synthetical," both of which are valuable. When we analyze the concept of a human being as "*a body, animated, sentient, rational*," and so forth, and experience Socrates as being that sort of body, then we know that Socrates is a man; and, in order to know that Socrates meets these requirements of the definition, we must synthesize different aspects of our experience of that body we refer to as Socrates. Hence, in philosophy, as in geometry, definition is foundationally important. As all knowledge requires ideas ultimately derived from sensation, the five senses – "namely, *sight, hearing, smell, taste,* and *touch*" – are crucial, as are their proper objects in our experience. In *Human Nature*, he makes a move that is important in modern philosophy, claiming that the objects of our senses are mere appearances, while physical reality, independent of our experience of it, comprises matter moving in space, rather than, say, brown, smooth, flat desks. "And this is the *great deception of sense*, which is also by sense *corrected*." We should recognize the implications of this. The ultimate touchstone of all our experience is sensation, which only reveals to us the way objects *appear* to us; we are deceived in supposing that those appearances correspond to reality as it is independent of human experience. Remember that Descartes worried about how we could ever protect ourselves from the deceptions of sense and offered innate ideas and deductive reasoning from them as his solution to the problem. This solution is not available to Hobbes, forcing him to the conclusion that deceptive sensation can only be checked by other sensations, which are themselves deceptive. While Hobbes himself does not overtly embrace skepticism, here he is dangerously close to Sextus Empiricus. The implications of this position, which Hobbes himself does not explicitly draw, will lead us inevitably to the powerful challenge of Hume's skepticism. As we have seen, Hobbes distinguishes between absolute factual knowledge, based on sense, memory, and imagination, and the conditional knowledge of science. Knowledge requires evidence on the part of the knowing subject and truth on the part of the object known (*Body*, 24, 27–31, 72–75, 83–85, 156–158, 188, 203–204; see also 376–377). While an obvious opponent of Cartesian rationalism and its doctrine of innate ideas, Hobbes too places the spotlight of epistemology on the individual experiencing, believing, knowing subject.

3.4 Reality

Like Descartes (and virtually all other philosophers after Aristotle and up to that time), Hobbes conceives of substances as the basic building blocks of reality. However, unlike the dualist, who considers mind (or soul) and body as two distinct and irreducible substances, Hobbes is a monist. He is a generic monist, seeing all reality as of the same sort of substance (as opposed to Spinoza, who, as we shall see, is a numerical monist, maintaining that only one, single substance is real). For Hobbes, there are innumerable substances, but all of them are of the same nature – physical, material, bodily, corporeal. He puts the point so lucidly in *Leviathan* that it would be difficult for us to miss it: "For the *universe*, being the aggregate of all bodies, there is no real part thereof that is not also *body*, nor anything properly a *body* that is not also part of (that aggregate of all *bodies*) the *universe*." This will have serious negative implications for spiritual reality; and, as we proceed, we should wonder, how will this affect the spiritual dimension of human nature, and what will happen to God? But, for now, let us allow Hobbes to make his point even more emphatically, maintaining that "*substance* and *body* signify the same thing," so that the Cartesian idea of incorporeal substance is as much an oxymoron as "*incorporeal body*." Every substance, as a body, is quantitatively analyzable (as Galileo might have observed) in terms of "the dimensions of magnitude (namely, length, breadth, and depth)." As we explore the ideas of Hobbes more deeply, we must try to appreciate the seriousness and the radical consistency of his materialism: "And consequently, every part of the universe is body, and that which is not body is no part of the universe. And because the universe is all, that which is no part of it is nothing." Given that he will remain relentlessly consistent in his radical materialism, he will have two logical options regarding spirit – he can deny it or analyze it as material. Now what do bodies do? They move, in accordance with the mechanical laws of natural science. In living bodies, like us (as opposed to inanimate ones like rocks), there are two sorts of motions; the "*vital*" ones (blood flow, breathing, heartbeat, etc.) are necessary for the maintenance of life, while the "*voluntary*" ones (walking, talking, reading, etc.) are not and arise from the will (more about that later). Both sorts of animal motion, in theory, are as scientifically explicable as – though, of course, more complex than – the movements of inanimate bodies (*Leviathan*, 261–262, 459, 8, 27). This view militates against the sort of mystery that a theory such as that of Descartes would inevitably leave beyond the parameters of any possible human understanding.

In *De Corpore*, we find supplementary details. All change is, ultimately, bodily change and is caused in some way or other by motion. A cause of change is any motion or set of motions that is sufficient or necessary to bring it about. We experience bodies as changing, moving in time and through space, interacting with other bodies. But we should remember that all of this is experienced through the filters of images in our minds (or "phantasms") rather than directly and immediately. Through these filters, we experience the accidents of bodies and never their essence. There are enduring accidents, such as a body's extension and figure, and transitory ones, such as its motion and rest. Hobbes, unlike the Aristotelians, thinks that motion, rather than rest, is the natural state of a body. Moving bodies will continue to move unless and until they are stopped by other bodies. (Later that century, Newton would develop his scientific theory of the laws of motion.) Of the four old Aristotelian causes, Hobbes spurns the formal and final, retaining only material and efficient causality, which is typical of modern thinkers. No two bodies can occupy exactly the same place at the same time, so that any two bodies will always be distinguishable at least spatially. The problem of the enduring identity of a body through time is difficult. In order for a body to remain the same through time, it must not physically change. He offers us an apt example, "whether a man grown old be the same man he was whilst he was young, or another man." Legally and psychologically, he may be the same; but since his body has changed over time, he cannot be physically the same. But then, we might observe, every body will always be different at any moment in time from what it was or will be at any other moment (as if Heraclitus was correct about all substantial reality constantly changing). Physical science, then, must study the constantly changing appearances of material phenomena (*Body*, 75, 80, 95–96, 101–103, 106–107, 111, 115–116, 124–125, 127–129, 146). Are we to imagine that nothing remains constant in science other than its laws explaining that constant change? But, then, are not those laws governing the changing phenomenal appearances perceived by the senses themselves the conditional constructs of reason? Hobbes does not clearly answer this, yet we are exploring some of the implications of his materialistic monism.

3.5 God

Unlike Descartes, with his innate ideas of pure reason, Hobbes holds that all human ideas are mental images ultimately derived from sense experience. This epistemological commitment logically compels him to deny that we have, or even can have, any idea of divine infinity. In *Leviathan* he writes, "Whatsoever we imagine is *finite*. Therefore there is no idea or conception of anything we call *infinite*." He purportedly believes in a deity and does not object to our calling God "infinite," so long as we realize that this is merely an honorific term that indicates that we cannot imagine in what way the deity could be limited. But, he maintains, the most honest adjective we can use to describe God, from our human perspective, is *"incomprehensible"*; we simply cannot understand the divine nature and should get past pretending we do. It does not seem that our reverence for God and religious rituals could benefit God in any way. Indeed, Hobbes defines religion humanistically in terms of our natural fear of the unknown, distinguishing between the illegitimate fear of "Superstition" and the legitimate fear of "True Religion"; unfortunately, he gives us no solid criterion for distinguishing between the two. A simple path whereby reason leads us to a God stems from our experience of the world as intelligently designed, so that, "by the visible things of this world and their admirable order, a man may conceive there is a cause of them, which men call God, and yet not have an idea or image of him in his mind." Our natural intellectual curiosity regarding the causal origin of our world has the bad side effect of causing anxiety regarding our future, as we fear the power of the deity to which reason leads us. Having given us this simple argument from design for God, in the chapter "Of Religion," he offers us a more technical one (a version of what is called cosmological argumentation, as it seeks the only adequate cause of the cosmos) such as was used by Aristotle, Aquinas, and others. Everything we experience in our world, including ourselves, is an effect of something else; but its cause, in turn, is also caused by something or other which, in turn, was the effect of something else. But there must be some ultimate cause in the chain of causes and effects, which itself is uncaused and the ultimate explanation of everything else; whatever the nature of this uncaused cause, that is God. But, again, people should not leap from this reasoning to the existence of God to thinking they can know anything of God's essence, as the divine nature "is incomprehensible, and above their understanding." Our best approach to religious doctrine is that of faith in "supernatural revelation" rather than that of logical argumentation. Worship of God can be either public or private. In worshipping God, when we attribute desirable qualities to the divine nature, this merely serves the function of honoring God, not that of expressing any real understanding. The person of genuine faith should try to obey God's law, to the extent that that is revealed (*Leviathan*, 15, 31, 62–66, 234–235, 237–242, 263, 407; cf. *Elements*, 64–67). In his own lifetime, Hobbes was accused of atheism, and some may still suspect him of that. But, given how directly he commits himself to claiming that there is a deity, even to the point of proving it, it is difficult to consider him an atheist without also indicting him for hypocrisy.

In *De Cive*, Hobbes holds that the natural law and the moral law coincide and are products of God's will. (Presumably this is a statement of belief, rather than a knowledge claim, on his part.) He quotes both the Old Testament of the Bible and its New Testament to support his point through divine revelation. Again, if he really did subscribe to atheism, these textual citations would expose him as a hypocrite. But, further, he actually writes, "I am so much an enemy to atheists" as to "show them to be enemies of God" and "justly punished" by both God and the state. He reminds us that everyone can use reason to come to know of God's existence, even apart from revelation, so that there is little or no excuse for atheism. As to the divine nature, here again he warns us against the (Cartesian) illusion that we can have any rational knowledge of the Infinite. He is warning us against the sort of anthropomorphism that would presumptuously reduce God to finite human qualities. In *De Homine*, he writes that true religion involves both faith and worship. The pragmatic point of loving God is trying to obey the divine law; and the pragmatic edge of fearing God should be effort not to disobey it. Religious faith is defined as "opinion which ariseth from the authority" of, for example, prophets and Church leaders. While Christianity advocates the three theological virtues of "*faith, hope,* and *charity*," Hobbes maintains that, even without the teachings of authority, reason can use the Golden Rule to determine our duty. But, since we can be confronted with conflicting interpretations of revelation and conflicting claims to religious authority regarding God's will, what are we to do? His answer is that "the will of God is not known save through the state" (*Man*, 153–154, 284–285n., 298–299, 71–73, 85). So, far from advocating anything like our separation of Church and state, Hobbes seems to favor their conjunction.

In the most obscure work of his we are considering here, we see how, probably against his better judgment, he let himself be goaded into applying his thoroughgoing materialism to God. In criticizing *Leviathan*, Bishop Bramhall accused him of "atheism, blasphemy, impiety, subversion of religion," and so forth. Hobbes was in a bind here. As we have seen, he had claimed that everything that is substantially real must be materialistic. So what of God? If Hobbes is not going to back down from this claim or contradict himself (and he is not about to do either), then he has only two options. He can *either* embrace atheism, admitting there is no God (which, itself, would land him in inconsistency), *or* he can accept the conclusion that God must be a material reality. This last option is the one he adopts, calling God both "*corporeal* and *infinite*." Since all substantial reality is physical, that must include the infinite substance, God, who is "a most pure, and most simple corporeal spirit." We can point out here what Descartes might have objected, that the notion of an infinite "corporeal spirit" is so problematic as to suggest an oxymoron. What he is forced to do is define spirit in materialistic terms: "Spirit is thin, fluid, transparent, invisible body." Even if this conception of God as "a most pure, simple, invisible spirit corporeal" is coherent, it could not help but land Hobbes in extreme trouble in seventeenth-century Christian England. He would have been better off *either* standing by his claim that we can know nothing about God's nature, despite the fact that materialism would seem to point to its being corporeal, *or* making God an exception to the general rule that all substances (in the universe) are material (as Aristotle's God is an exception to the rule that everything is a combination of matter and form). Finally, Hobbes holds that the ultimate arbiter regarding how to interpret the Scriptures and God's law must be the civil authority of the state (*Works*, 281, 306, 309, 313, 339). This will make sense in the context of the social stability and political order that, as we shall see, he regards as paramount.

3.6   Humanity

His materialistic monism also lands him in trouble regarding his theory of the human person, as it leaves no room for any mental or spiritual substance. While he does not deny the human mind or spirit (any more than he denies the existence of God), it can only be a function or by-product of the body, since that is all we substantially could be. This becomes as clear as the light of day from the very first paragraph of the Introduction of *Leviathan*, where he writes that all "life is but a motion of limbs," comparing a human being to a functioning clock that works mechanically. As our vital motions are materialistically explained, so are our voluntary motions (as we shall see, he is a determinist, who denies any free will), being caused by imperceptible bodily forces, which he calls endeavors. We should notice the physical language he uses to distinguish the two sorts of endeavors – appetites or desires, which attract us toward objects, and aversions, which repel us away from them. Our appetites and aversions relate to objects we imagine will please or displease us, the basic meanings of "good" and "evil" having to do with the former and the latter, respectively (and not signifying any objective, absolute moral values at all). Thus, for example, the elementary emotions of love and hatred refer to our feelings regarding objects of attraction and repulsion, while contempt refers to our not much caring about something one way or the other. Other less fundamental emotions are based on these. Often we experience our own emotions as in conflict – either because

3 Thomas Hobbes

something we desire involves something we would like to avoid or because we cannot satisfy two (or more) desires. Then we are said to "deliberate," the final appetite or aversion in that deliberation process being called by Hobbes "the Will." Every "*voluntary act*," as opposed to vital actions, "is that which proceedeth from the *will*." If we imagine that this will lead away from determinism to a position of free choice, we shall be disappointed. Indeed, everything said in this paragraph thus far, he thinks, applies to "beasts" as well as to humans. We naturally will to pursue what seems subjectively good to us and to avoid what subjectively seems bad to us. Human happiness, then, is simply a life mostly satisfying our desires and avoiding what we dislike (*Leviathan*, 3, 28–34). While many of our preferences are natural rather than artificial, our basic values are all relative to our preferences (not far, in this respect, from the ancient Sophists).

Hobbes is not squeamish about the value of power. Like Machiavelli, he sees it as good because it is the means whereby we can get what we want. He defines a person's "*value* or Worth" in terms of what might be "given for the use of his power" and his "Dignity" in terms of his public worth in political society, honor (and dishonor) having to do with respecting (or not) his dignity. In our quest for power and respect, we naturally are competitive. Unlike most of the ancient Greeks, Hobbes also thinks that we are, on balance, naturally about equal, leading us to dare to confront one another in an antagonistic way when our interests conflict. Next, human nature is (again contrary to the great Greeks) antisocial outside of artificial social structures, for "men have no pleasure, but on the contrary a great deal of grief, in keeping company when there is no power to over-awe them" and restrain their dangerous tendencies. But this is not all we find controversial here. For Hobbes is a psychological egoist, holding that "of the voluntary acts of every man the object is some *good to himself*." In other words, naturally speaking (i.e. apart from social conditioning), the motivation behind every act of the human will is self-interest, pure and simple. To call someone a "person," for Hobbes, is to attribute to him responsibility for (at least some of) his words and deeds. Also, while it is less important for our purposes, we might observe that, whereas the substance dualism of Descartes renders it easy to believe that the death of the body will not terminate the life of the mind (or soul), the philosophical anthropology of Hobbes renders belief in immortality quite problematic, since all there is must be physical substance, which is doomed to be nonliving. But Hobbes is clever enough not to get himself into more trouble on this point. He can appeal to his radical empiricism to say that we just cannot know about life after death, so that it must remain a matter of faith. While he has to insist that all life must be bodily, he can appeal to the old Christian doctrine of the resurrection of the body, which is a matter of faith rather than of reason, as a basis for belief in life after death (*Leviathan*, 41, 50–52, 58, 74–78, 82, 101, 429).

Let us now supplement these views on human nature to be found in his masterpiece with those in another of his great works. In *De Cive*, he considers the ancient Greek assumption that a human being is naturally a social animal (*zoon politikon*), "a creature born fit for society." This is a false assumption, allegedly derived from an excessively superficial study of humanity. If we naturally seek out others, it is only for some good we imagine associating with them might do us: "We do not therefore by nature seek society for its own sake, but that we may receive some honour or profit from it." What we naturally desire is what we think best for ourselves, especially our own self-preservation; what we naturally avoid is what seems bad for us, especially our own death. Other people are naturally significant to us only as means to our own selfish ends; and, Hobbes adds, it is rational and right for people to do whatever they judge best for avoiding pain and death and for achieving self-preservation and self-satisfaction, including using others as they see fit. Thus the motions of hope and fear motivate the will to employ some voluntary actions and avoid others. And, as we shall see, we must learn rationally to restrain our selfish desires, fears, and hopes for our own selfish good. By the way, we should note that he denies that *any* of this implies "that men are evil by nature." He is analyzing what he considers natural (and dangerous), but without casting any moral judgment on it. Four sorts of human faculties – "bodily strength, experience, reason, passion" – represent nothing intrinsically good or evil, from a moral perspective (*Man*, 110–111, 115–116, 165, 167, 100, 109). If it seems that too much is being made of this here, we must wait to see the profound impact this will have on moral obligation and the interpersonal relations of political society.

3.7 Freedom

We have already seen reason to think that Hobbes was a determinist. Of any proponent of free will (such as Descartes), he said in *Leviathan*, "I should not say he were in an error, but that his words were without meaning, that is to say, absurd." We have seen that will is merely the prevailing endeavor in a process of deliberation and, hence, not itself any body. But all substances (allegedly) are bodies, and only a substance *could* be free. So, on this view, the notion of a "free will" is nonsense. So what would it mean to say that something is free? Here we must distinguish between natural (or metaphysical) liberty, which we shall discuss here, and civil (or political) liberty, which we shall discuss later. Natural liberty is nothing more than "the absence of external impediments"; it applies to nonhuman animals, nonanimal living things, and inanimate objects, as well as to humans. When a person acts freely, he acts according to his will rather than having that will checked by external forces. His act can still be free, if his will is motivated by fear. "*Liberty* and *necessity* are consistent" as well – for example, "in the water, that hath not only *liberty*, but a *necessity* of descending by the channel," unless it be blocked from its natural flow. But no action in the world can be free of all causal determination, even if we cannot discern what it is or how it operates (*Leviathan*, 24, 79, 136–137). In *De Homine*, Hobbes added an interesting observation: while a person may "be free *to act*" on his desires, this does not mean that he is "free *to desire*"; if I am on a diet, I may be free to satisfy my hunger or not but cannot control my desire for food (*Man*, 46).

Let us now turn to *De Corpore* to see how serious Hobbes is in his commitment to determinism, beginning with his universal claim that "all the effects that have been, or shall be, produced have their necessity in things antecedent." In other words, nothing ever occurs without some causal explanation, whether or not we understand it. When we think of something as contingent (e.g. it may or may not rain tomorrow), this merely reflects our inadequate grasp of the cluster of causal conditions that will inevitably lead to its raining or not; but, despite our ignorance, for example, "*it will rain tomorrow*" is "either necessarily true, or necessarily false." This determinism applies to all actions in the universe, human as well as nonhuman. Whereas tomorrow's rainfall is not determined by human will but by other forces, my taking an umbrella to work is determined, but by my will. This view that human freedom, properly conceived, is a special sort of determinism is nowadays called "compatibilism." But, further, the freedom to act according to the will, far from being a unique prerogative of humans, is also characteristic of "beasts." As on previous points, here we see Hobbes breaking down the supposed radical qualitative difference of kind between humans and other animals. The most sustained writing on human freedom in the works of Hobbes was a long letter, *Of Liberty and Necessity*, which originated in his dispute with Bishop Bramhall. Here, again, human freedom was defined as the capacity "to do a thing" in accordance with one's will or to forbear doing it. But if the willing itself is necessary, then the free act must be determined. Every act of voluntary will, though determined, arises from a process of deliberation. Laws prohibiting and punishing are not unjust, even if our will to disobey them were determined by circumstances and desire, because injustice only results from "the *will* to break the law," and laws and their sanctions reinforce justice by deterring such ill will. Second, determinism does not necessarily nullify all consultations and admonitions, because they are themselves effective causal determinants of our future behavior. Third, praise, blame, reward, and punishment are not rendered morally useless without free will (as Augustine and Aquinas feared) because, in fact, they are effective influences society uses to "conform the will to good and evil." Fourth, the same response is offered to the objection that books, teachings, and courses of study would be fruitless. Fifth, this deterministic theory does not eliminate sin, because sin consists in voluntary action contrary to law, whether or not the will has been determined. Given a proper understanding of motivating forces, he says, "we acknowledge *necessity*; but when we see not, or mark not the force that moves us, we then think there is none, and that it is not *causes* but *liberty* that produceth the action." Thus an empty word is used to camouflage our ignorance (*Body*, 117, 123, 161, 245–246, 248–251, 254–257, 260, 264, 269–274). The whole point of this long letter was to argue not only that determinism is not dangerous but also that it is more easily supportable than belief in undetermined freedom.

3.8 Morality

Given what we have already considered of his philosophical theory, it should not be surprising that Hobbes is a moral relativist, denying all objective, absolute values and treating all values as person-relative. In *Leviathan*, he makes this clear when he writes that anything a person desires he naturally tends to call "good," and anything he wants to avoid he naturally tends to call "evil," there being "nothing simply and absolutely so" and no objective criterion of moral evaluation naturally available. Indeed, he goes on to write that, from a natural (e.g. nonconventional) perspective, it is better to speak of "*apparent* or *seeming good*" and "*apparent* or *seeming evil*." All those selfish, greedy desires that are natural to humanity, he assures us, "are in themselves no sin," only becoming morally wrong in the context of laws forbidding the behaviors to which they give rise. Apart from the conventional agreements of civil society, as there is no authority to enforce any law, so there can be no law generating a common morality. "The notions of right and wrong, justice and injustice, have there no place." When he spoke of natural law that is always binding on us, he did not mean anything like the natural law of Aquinas, but only a set of prudential maxims we should follow if we know what is good for us (*Leviathan*, 28–29, 34, 77–79, and 174; cf. *Man*, 42–43, 47–49, 68–70).

In *De Cive*, Hobbes introduces a trichotomy of types of duties – natural duties we have as humans, civic duties we have as subjects, and religious duties we have as Christians. It is telling that he listed them in that order. We have a natural "right," he holds, "in the bare state of nature" (as opposed to in civil society) to whatever we desire and judge for ourselves we might gain. The most we can say about right and wrong in the state of nature is that we ought (for our own selfish good) to act in accordance with reason and to try to avoid irrational behavior (which might hurt us). In this vague sense, we can say that the natural law is a moral law, but it cannot yet specify which sorts of behaviors are to be prescribed and which proscribed. Unless and until we achieve a social context, the moral relativism of subjectivism would seem to prevail (*Man*, 95, 116–117, 122–123, 150–152, 282–283). In *De Corpore Politico*, he recommends the Golden Rule as a device for moderating our dangerous egoistic tendencies, as well as trying to use our imaginations to put ourselves in the place of others with whom we are dealing. He focuses on the cardinal virtues of temperance and prudence, analyzing the former in terms of abstaining from what is likely to hurt us and identifying the latter "with virtue in general." Finally, he maintains, if all of nature stems from God, then nothing natural to us can be contrary to the divine law (*Body*, 298–301, 304–305). Before we move on, we should notice how great a challenge this theory poses to explaining how the peaceful interpersonal relations of civil society can ever be achieved, given our natural egoism, antisocial tendencies, mutual distrust, grasping competitiveness, ease of being provoked to hostility, and lack of any objective, absolute, substantive moral standards.

3.9 Society

As did the ancient Greeks, Hobbes thinks that the primary function of philosophy ought to be to instruct us how to maximize our chances of living good lives, which, for better and for worse, have to be lived in society. But, if anything, he is even more tough-minded than they were in facing the arduous task of explaining how that could even be possible. We have already seen his characterization of our natural condition and his portrayal of the state of nature as one of "a war as is of every man against every man," as he wrote in *Leviathan*. It is as if he were trying to paint so alarming a picture as to motivate us to appreciate civil society and to make the best of it we can, since the only credible alternative is a life that is "solitary, poor, nasty, brutish, and short" – a hell on earth, in which we are all likely to die young and to be miserable until we do. So the intelligent person, who knows what is good for him, will seek a way out. Motivated by fear (especially of death), desire (for a pleasant, comfortable life), and hope (that there might be some way to get it), he employs reason to try to find it. Thus he discovers those prudential laws of nature, which will illuminate his exit. The first (in the sense of most basic) of these has two parts to it: the positive one says that a person should do what he reasonably can to achieve peace with others; the negative one says that, where they will not make peace with him, he should do whatever it takes to defend himself against them. The second one, assuming that all of us are egoists, who will do nothing except for self-interest, says that we should be willing to give up something, if others will do likewise. What we have a great deal of in the state of nature is freedom or liberty; what we hardly have any of and desperately need is security. We must find a way to give up some of our liberty (such as the freedom to threaten and hurt others) in return for the security we could derive from their giving up either the same or some comparable liberty. Here we have the first beginnings of the sort of agreement that will constitute a pact or covenant, the social contract, whereby civil society can come to be. The signs of such an agreement can be explicit and/or implicitly assumed. But we should notice that our motivation can be purely selfish, with no presuppositions regarding our basic concern for others or allegiance to any abstract, non-egoistic principles. Once we have gotten this far, for the first time we can meaningfully speak of justice, which has no meaning except in the context of agreement. But, given social agreement, then we can say, "Injustice is no other than *the not performance of covenant*. And whatsoever is not unjust, is *just*." In other words, having entered into a social contract, we have given up some of our freedom but remain at liberty to do anything we reasonably wish, so long as it does not violate our explicit or implicit agreements, which forever bind us. But there remains a practical problem: having given you my word, why should I try to keep it when I think I can get away with not doing so? Or, perhaps even more problematic, how can I trust you to keep your word to me when you could probably get away with breaking it? Our giving one another our word does not dissolve our natural egoism. "For no man giveth but with intention of good to himself, because gift is voluntary, and of all voluntary acts the object is to every man his own good." Our agreements without coercive force are hollow and useless. As Hobbes concisely put the point, "And covenants without the sword are but words, and of no strength to secure a man at all." What is needed is "Sovereign Power" with adequate enforcement authority to render it unreasonable for any of us subjects to succumb to the temptation to violate the laws established under the social contract. Only thus can arise a true commonwealth with a chance of achieving social stability. If one objects that this invests too much authority in the Sovereign, at

3 Thomas Hobbes

the expense of the subjects' liberty, Hobbes replies that this is at least preferable to the horrors of civil war and political anarchy. How extensive a subject's civil liberties will be is relative to "the silence of the law," in that he is free to do what the law does not forbid. Notice here (against Augustine and Aquinas) that, for Hobbes, no law of the political Sovereign can be unjust. Of course, a just law can be either good or bad, depending on whether it is or is not sufficiently necessary and clear to be conducive to the general welfare of the people (*Leviathan*, 76, 78–82, 89, 95, 106, 109, 117, 143, 229). The material represented in this paragraph, by the way, is that for which Hobbes is most famous.

We have seen that Hobbes openly acknowledges the valuable importance of power as a means to an individual's greater satisfaction of desire. Now we must recognize the crucial significance of power to a political society that is to preserve order and its autonomy. In *De Cive*, he speaks of a need for "*the sword of justice*" to punish wrongdoers and preserve the fabric of law, as well as for "*the sword of war*" to defend its people against foreign aggressors. Thus power is needed to deal with both internal and external threats to peace and security. Because the Sovereign must be absolute, it makes no contract with its subjects, is not itself subject to the law, and cannot rightly be punished. Hobbes holds that there are three types of government. A people, at the initial contract, tends to be democratic, ruled by the many involved in the contract. Aristocracy – the rule of the best (however that be defined) – tends to emerge from that. This, in turn, often evolves into monarchy, the rule of a single person. Notice that he maintains that anarchy, oligarchy, and tyranny are merely disapproving words used of the very same three sorts of government, respectfully. Subjects can only be freed from political obligation to their Sovereigns if the latter abdicate their authority or if a kingdom falls under the power of an enemy or (in the case of a monarchy) if there is no legitimate successor. In comparing the three sorts of government, Hobbes favors monarchy as having the most advantages and the fewest disadvantages. The latter tend to be due to the failings of the individual monarch rather than to the form of government itself. Democracy tends to be a hotbed for demagogues and their toadies, all of whom want to feed at the public trough. While a democracy might feature more arbitrary license, Hobbes denied that it offers more genuine liberty than most monarchies. The process of decision-making is considerably more efficient in a monarchy, as opposed to democracies, which get bogged down in long-winded rhetoric, become distracted by the in-fighting of divisive factions, and incessantly leak information that should be kept confidential. For all these reasons, monarchy is preferable to democracy (*Man*, 177, 180–183, 192–199, 203–204, 221–232), with aristocracy being better than the latter but not as effective as the former.[2]

3.10 Review

Hobbes is a worthy alternative to Descartes. As the latter built a philosophical system using pure reason, the former relentlessly pursued the implications of his radical empiricism. It logically pushed him to espouse unpopular positions – monistic materialism, egoism, determinism, and moral relativism. All of this necessitated the dramatic *tour de force* that is his sociopolitical theory. While this is an admirably consistent philosophy, it may shave off too much in wielding Ockham's razor – universal and necessary factual knowledge, truly spiritual humanity and a spiritual God, human freedom in the sense of self-determination, any objective and absolute value, and a political society whose laws must be limited by a respect for human rights. While Hobbes establishes an empirical tradition to challenge the rationalistic one of Descartes, rendering them the two progenitors of modern philosophy (with its

---

2 For more on Hobbes, see ch. III of *Twelve Great Philosophers*, by Wayne P. Pomerleau (New York: Ardsley House, 1997).

focus on the individual human subject), neither of these two antitheses would prove sufficient. Nevertheless, a hard-won synthesis would only emerge after another century of interim developments.

3.11 Another Perspective

Margaret Lucas Cavendish, the Duchess of Newcastle (1623–1673), during the English Civil War, was a lady-in-waiting of Queen Henrietta Maria and went with her into exile (in 1644) in Paris. There she met and married William Cavendish (for whose family Hobbes worked), a fellow royalist, who later became the Duke of Newcastle. She and her husband established a salon there, called the Newcastle circle. Its visitors included Descartes and Hobbes, both of whom she critically discusses in her *Philosophical Letters* of 1664. She and her husband (she had no children) returned to England after the Restoration of Charles II as King of England. Like Hobbes, she is a materialistic monist, so that she clearly disagrees with the dualism of Descartes. But she is also critical of a number of explanations by Hobbes. For example, she was not a mechanist but held a position of vitalism, according to which all natural objects consist of animate, self-moving matter.[3] In 1667, she was honored to receive an invitation to join a meeting of the Royal Society, despite her gender.

In a letter discussing the philosophy of Hobbes, she maintains that "all things, and therefore outward objects as well as sensitive organs, have both sense and reason," though neither external objects nor sense organs cause either sensation or reason. It is allegedly the motions of sense and reason that cause perception. She rejects Hobbes's notion that perception is caused by pressure of an external object on sense organs, because we see and hear things that are too far away for such pressure to occur, and sometimes we sense objects although other bodies are between them and us. She claims, against Hobbes (and Descartes) that "life and knowledge, which I name rational and sensitive matter, are in every creature, and in all parts of every creature." Understanding is the product of "rational matter" and cannot be explained adequately by perception or external objects that are perceived. The idea that everything has both "sensitive matter" and "rational matter" and thus is alive and has knowledge would strike most of us as strange. She also criticizes Hobbes's view that dreams are simply workings of the imagination while we sleep, using images derived from prior sense perception since "rational matter" itself can produce dreams (*Early*, 195–197).

In agreement with Hobbes, she even more radically disagrees with the dualism of Descartes, in general, and with his idea that there is immaterial substance or a substantial mind, in particular. She regards motion as essentially identical to the body moving and not "only a mode of a thing." For if motion were merely a mode of a body, how could it be transferred to another body? Since every creature allegedly comprises a combination "of animate and inanimate matter," it must have both "life and knowledge, sense and reason." She not only rejects the Cartesian notion of mind as substantial and separable from body, but she also pokes fun at the idea that its seat is in the pineal gland of the brain. Sense and knowledge, rather, purportedly occur throughout the entire body. Further agreeing with Hobbes against Descartes, she sees no reason to suppose that all nonhuman animals are lacking in reason, considering it a "conceited" notion based on one's inability or unwillingness to recognize it (*Modern*, 143–144, 148–149, 153).

---

3 References in this section will be to *Early Modern Philosophy: An Anthology* (hereafter called *Early*), ed. by Lisa Shapiro and Marcy P. Lascano (Peterborough, Canada: Broadview Press, 2022), and *Modern Philosophy: An Anthology of Primary Sources*, third edition (hereafter called *Modern*), ed. by Roger Ariew and Eric Watkins (Indianapolis: Hackett, 2019).

She believes in a deity but, like Hobbes, thinks that "God's actions are incomprehensible" (*Modern*, 147). Elsewhere (in her *Observations upon Experimental Philosophy*), she writes that "there is a God above nature, on which nature depends, and from whose immutable and eternal decree it has its eternal being . . .; but what God is in his essence, neither nature nor any of her parts or creatures is able to conceive." She seems dubious regarding God's miraculously changing the course of nature without destroying it first and replacing it with a new natural order. She considers "conscience" to be a product of our beliefs concerning God's will and advocates a respectful "liberty of conscience" (*Early*, 208, 227–228). In conclusion, we can see that Margaret Cavendish represents an alternative voice in the wake of the dialogue between Descartes and Hobbes, arguably managing to be more controversial than either of them – thanks to such beliefs as that all natural objects (presumably including even rocks) have "rational matter" as well as "sensitive matter" and are therefore alive and having knowledge.

4

Blaise Pascal

Source: G. Edelinck after F. Quesnel, junior. / Wellcome Collection/Public Domain

4.1 Overview

For well over a century (from Descartes through Hume), modern philosophy revolved around a clash between rationalists, like Descartes, and empiricists, like Hobbes. But Blaise Pascal was a significant thinker who was subversive in not fitting comfortably in either category. Instead, he was a fideist, in that he thought neither reason nor natural experience can serve as an adequate basis for our most important beliefs. However, this is a controversial label, in that it is sometimes

Modern European Philosophers, First Edition. Wayne P. Pomerleau.
© 2023 John Wiley & Sons, Inc. Published 2023 by John Wiley & Sons, Inc.

52 | *4 Blaise Pascal*

taken to mean an irrationalist, which might typify extreme or radical fideism. Pascal, a moderate fideist, was, in many ways, a man of reason; his reservations about it have to do, rather, with its limitations. Indeed, as was the case with Montaigne (and others), it is even problematic whether Pascal should be called a philosopher at all. He was a great mathematician, a scientist and an inventor, and, especially, an apologist for (Catholic) Christianity. Unlike Descartes and Hobbes, he never attempted to develop a rationally demonstrated philosophical system. Yet he was a philosophical man of letters in that he was committed to arguing for a particular worldview. Like Kant, a century later, he sought a preferable middle ground between the undesirable extremes of skepticism and dogmatism.

4.2 Biography

Whether he is called a philosopher in the strict sense or only in a loose sense, Pascal was a polymath whose work in various areas had implications for the philosophical dialectic of the seventeenth century. He was born in Clermont (now Clermont-Ferrand), France, on June 19, 1623, the second of three surviving children of Étienne Pascal, a lawyer who educated him at home. (His mother died in 1626.) In 1631, his father moved the family to Paris, where he introduced Blaise to Marin Mersenne's circle of intellectuals. The boy was a prodigy, whose genius was evident. At the age of 12, he is said to have independently worked out for himself the first 32 propositions of Euclid's geometrical system. In 1639, he wrote a treatise on conic sections, which was published the following year. In the early 1640s, he designed a calculating machine to help make easier his father's work in the public tax department. He designed experiments to verify Torricelli's view that Aristotelians are wrong to assume that "Nature abhors a vacuum." He suffered from a frail and sickly constitution almost all his life. He studied the writings of Montaigne and Descartes; he met the latter, in 1647, in Paris, where they discussed mathematics (they did not seem to get along any better than Descartes and Hobbes did). In 1646, Étienne fell on ice, seriously injuring a leg. Two kind men, who were Jansenist Christians, nursed him, exposing him, his son, and his younger daughter, Jacqueline, to their stringent religious beliefs (the elder daughter, Gilberte, had already married and left home). Jacqueline wanted to join the Port-Royal convent as a nun, but her father forbade it. Five years later the father died; Jacqueline was determined to enter Port-Royal, and, despite her brother's objections, she did so. Following the death of their father, Pascal entered the worldliest period of his short life, associating with libertines. This would suddenly end with what would be the most dramatic and puzzling experience of his life.

"From about half past ten in the evening until half past midnight," starting on November 23, 1654, he had a religious experience that burned like "Fire" and must have been mystical and/or ecstatic in nature. He wrote a "Memorial" of the experience and had it sewn into his jacket, apparently wearing it every day for the rest of his life. He seems to have experienced the "'God of Abraham, God of Isaac, God of Jacob,' not of philosophers and scholars" (a distinction which would prove quite germane to his later approach to writing about God). He emerged with a profound sense of "certainty," of "joy," of "peace," prepared to forget the world "and everything except God."[1] He never got over this life-altering experience, abandoning his worldly ways and focusing on his Christian religion for the last eight years of his life. He associated with the Jansenists at

---

1 Unless otherwise noted, references in this chapter will be to *Pensées*, by Pascal, trans. by A.J. Krailsheimer (London: Penguin Books, 1966). Otherwise, references will be to *Pascal Selections* (henceforth called *Selections*), ed. by Richard H. Popkin (New York: Macmillan, 1989).

Port-Royal, although he denied that he was ever one of their "solitaries." While we have neither the time nor the space to explore deeply the story of Jansenism, it is so pertinent to these last few years of Pascal's life that a bit of attention is warranted. It is a sect of Catholic Christianity, which stems from the teachings of a Dutch theologian named Jansen (who died in 1638). Its most controversial doctrine maintains that we are not able to obey God's law without God's grace, which is irresistible, when extended – leading to a version of determinism that would seem to rule out moral freedom. In 1653, the Roman Catholic Church condemned five allegedly Jansenist propositions. Antoine Arnauld, a distinguished Catholic theologian at the Sorbonne (and one of the most acute contemporary critics of Descartes), subscribed to and advocated Jansenism. In 1655, he was condemned for his purported heterodoxy, being expelled from the Sorbonne in 1656. In 1656 and 1657, Pascal wrote a series of *Provincial Letters* defending Arnauld's strict views (and attacking the Jesuits for what he saw as their lax casuistry). These writings of Pascal, which are not particularly philosophical in nature, were condemned by the Church in 1657. He staunchly denied that he or Port-Royal held any heretical views at all: "You say I am a Jansenist, that Port Royal maintains the Five Propositions, and that I maintain them: three lies" (309, 334). About that time, Pascal conceived a plan to write an *Apology for the Christian Religion*. But in 1659, he became so ill that he was unable to concentrate for long. Thus his *Apology* (in the old-fashioned sense of a defense) was never finished and, at his death, comprised nothing more than brilliant fragments that were only partially organized and came to be published under the title of *Pensées* (*Thoughts*). He had become very committed to works of charity and invented a large carriage to provide bus service in Paris, with the proceeds to go to finance public hospitals. In 1661, the year in which Port-Royal was closed down, Pascal withdrew from all public controversy. The following year, urgently needing care, he had to move in with his older sister. He died on August 19, 1662, his last words allegedly being, "May God never forsake me!" He was buried in Paris. His unfinished masterpiece, *Pensées*, was first edited and published in 1670 and has remained a provocative classic ever since.

4.3 Knowledge

Like other members of Mersenne's circle, Pascal eschewed submission to authority in areas of natural and mathematical science. In defending his position that Aristotelians are wrong in holding that "Nature abhors a vacuum," he maintained that scientific hypotheses are never conclusively demonstrable but can be refuted if they can be shown to imply logical contradictions and/or to be incompatible with any empirically observable facts. Among competing hypotheses that *could* be correct, one should tentatively adopt the one that best explains phenomena observable at that time (*Selections*, 53–54). This nondogmatic approach is characteristic of modern science in being experimental, open to criticism, and progressive. Notice how this stance connects with Pascal's wish to find a more acceptable middle ground between the extremes of, say, Montaigne and Descartes. It avoids skepticism by being able, with certainty, to rule out views that have been falsified; and it avoids dogmatic claims regarding which hypotheses necessarily correspond to reality as it is in itself. This constitutes the edge of the wedge of a starting point for Pascal's epistemological views on belief and knowledge. It might also be mentioned here that, like Descartes and Hobbes, he employs a deductive method and regards geometry as his epistemological paradigm.

Perhaps this is an appropriate place to discuss the controversial category of "fideism" that is being applied here to Pascal. Let us initially acknowledge five key points. First, while the term is generally intended to apply to the use of faith over reason, especially in inquiries concerning religious truth, when we try to get more specific about its meaning, it becomes notoriously difficult to generate general agreement. Second, the word seems to date from around the middle of the nineteenth century, so that the writings of Pascal (and Hume, as well as most of those of Kierkegaard) pre-date its use. Third, it is difficult to find any great philosophers (such as those included in this book) who apply the term to themselves. Fourth, the term has usually been employed in a pejorative sense, to imply a general irrationalism. And, fifth, if it is taken to mean the forsaking of reason altogether in favor of a universal, blindly arbitrary faith, then the term does not apply to great philosophers. Having now acknowledged those five points, what shall we mean by the term? It is a commitment to faith, especially regarding religious belief, in the absence of, or even against, evidence, where "evidence" refers to epistemic, and not merely pragmatic, justification. Believing that some significant truths are beyond the possible grasp of reason (as Descartes does) will not suffice to make a thinker a fideist. Also, a fideist can hold (as Pascal does) that some truths (such as those of mathematical and natural science) are within the bounds of reason. Also, a fideist need not hold that any truths are against reason, only (like Pascal) that some of the most important ones, such as those of religion, are above it. Finally, a fideist can assert that a believer can have good reason for religious faith, in the sense of pragmatic justification that is not epistemically warranted through logical cognition applied to natural experience. Whereas neither Descartes nor Hobbes can be plausibly designated a fideist in this sense, this chapter will attempt to show that Pascal can be.

In doing so, we shall turn to his *Pensées* and try to construct a systematic theory from its often aphoristic fragments. Like Descartes, Pascal favors a deductive mathematical method of reasoning where that applies. Yet he is closer to the skepticism of Montaigne regarding certain knowledge in areas concerning human nature, God, and values (religious, moral, and sociopolitical). From his perspective, it is a mistake to apply the deductive methods of mathematics in such areas. Perhaps this is (part of) the reason he condemns his great predecessor, writing, "Descartes useless and uncertain." The results of our reasoning in these areas, despite Descartes, are doomed to remain "uncertain"; and it is "useless" to try to deduce conclusions by applying a method where it does not legitimately apply. These are areas of belief and not of logical deduction. "But this faith is in our hearts, and makes us say not 'I know' but 'I believe,'" to the extent that we are careful. Unsupported and insupportable extravagant knowledge claims tend to move people to skeptical *dis*belief. When philosophers such as Descartes overreach, they actually undermine, rather than bolster, the sort of faith that people legitimately care about. Perhaps this is (at least part of) what Pascal means by his infamous claim that "we do not think that the whole of philosophy would be worth an hour's effort." He is not an enemy of reason but wants to limit it within reasonable bounds. It is important to try to understand what he means by "the heart" when he makes such claims as, "We know the truth not only through our reason but also through our heart." If "reason" here refers to deductive, demonstrative reason, such as works well in geometry, "the heart" does not refer to sentimental emotions. He is not saying that strong passionate feelings suffice to establish the truth of any conclusions. Rather, if reason is the engine of logical argumentation (or deductive reasoning), "the heart" is the means whereby we achieve intuitive "knowledge of first principles," from which we can rationally derive conclusions. But there is no logical proof possible of any "first principles" intuited by "the heart." Skeptics like Montaigne are correct on that point. It is only by means of "some natural intuition" that "the heart" can know the truth of first principles. This is the knowledge of faith rather than that of reason. Yet "dogmatists" like Descartes are correct that, once we have encountered such first principles, they become certain truths that cannot be honestly doubted. We should notice here how Pascal is trying to find a middle ground between the unacceptable extremes of skeptics like Montaigne and dogmatists like Descartes. Like the former, he holds that we cannot know first principles regarding God, humanity, and values through deductive reasoning; but, like the latter, he thinks we can achieve such knowledge through intuition. There are areas of legitimate doubt in which the skeptics' denial of indubitable certainty is inappropriate; there are other areas, such as mathematics, where it is appropriate to affirm deductive certainty; and there are others still in which it is appropriate to submit our beliefs to authority. Skeptics go too far in denying the power of reason, while dogmatists grant it more power than is warranted. It is reasonable to acknowledge the limited power of reason. In this respect, Pascal anticipates Kant by writing, "There is nothing so consistent with reason as this denial of reason." We can now understand one of Pascal's most famous aphorisms: "The heart has its reasons of which reason knows nothing." It is through intuition only that we can gain knowledge of first principles that vitally affect our lives; logical reason has no access to such knowledge but must accept it in order to build upon it (300, 34, 37, 52, 58, 62–64, 83, 85, 147, 154, 214, 216, 257). This is the epistemological approach to be applied in the pursuit of knowledge in areas of metaphysics, human nature, and values.

4.4 Reality

We can cover Pascal's treatment of reality more briefly. What is striking here is the extent to which it is discussed, beyond the areas of mathematics and theology, in relation to infinity. We and everything we can perceive or imagine are mere specks in the incalculable context of reality. Reality involves not only the infinitely large (durations of time, extensions of space, and motions approaching incalculable speeds), but also the infinitesimal (infinitely small durations of time, extensions in space, and speeds approaching absolute rest). Everything real in our world, including ourselves, is situated between the "two abysses" of infinite immensity and nothingness. Thus, in relation to reality thus conceived, what do we find our own nature to be? "A nothing compared to the infinite, a whole compared to the nothing, a middle point between all and nothing," unable to gain rational certainty regarding either our ultimate source or our destiny. Reality never definitely answers our ultimate questions but leaves us terrified by insuperable doubt. "The eternal silence of these infinite spaces fills me with dread," he autobiographically comments. I find myself inhabiting a tiny dot in infinite space. The span of my earthly life, between womb and tomb, is a few years swallowed up in infinite time or eternity. My feeble, pathetic activities are lost in the awesome motions of the universe. I had no control over my birth and cannot indefinitely avoid my death. Nature gives me no knowledge as to where I ultimately came from or where I am ultimately going. All of reality constantly threatens to engulf me in its infinite void with no certainty given regarding my origin or my destiny, generating profound insecurity (89–90, 95, 158).

4.5 God

The two dimensions of reality in which Pascal was most philosophically interested were God and humanity; the two topics to which he most eagerly wanted to apply his theory of knowledge during the last eight years of his life (i.e. after his religious experience of 1654) were belief in God and the analysis of human nature. His God is the infinitely perfect Creator of Catholic Christianity, and no alternative would be seriously considered. This God was allegedly knowable by us, but only by "the heart" and not by logical reason. Thus the attempts by Descartes (and Hobbes, as well as many of their predecessors) to prove God by means of logical demonstration were considered "useless and uncertain." But God should also be regarded as abidingly central to the entire philosophical enterprise rather than used merely to serve the function of explaining how we and our world could have come to be in the first place. This may be what Pascal had in mind when he wrote, "I cannot forgive Descartes: in his whole philosophy he would like to do without God; but he could not help allowing him a flick of the fingers to set the world in motion; after that he had no more use for God." Whether or not this indictment is fair to Descartes, it is true for Hobbes. Pascal liked to speak of God as "hidden," while maintaining that human experience provides us with signs that allow us to find God. He held that we know God through faith and not through reason (the dichotomy that anchors his fideism), and that faith is a gift from God rather than anything we can achieve on our own. Another dichotomy that may be disturbing is between God and our world, where he held that "we must love him alone and not transitory creatures." He saw our love of the things of this world as an impediment to our loving God appropriately. Because of the evil of our sinful nature, he would have us "hate ourselves" and all the things of this world that might divert us from God. If we ask for evidence that might lead us to follow him here, what he has to offer us is scriptural testimony regarding miracles and the fulfillment of prophecies, particularly the former (300, 355, 359, 227, 234–235, 264, 286, 291). Of course, this evidence is not scientific and requires the subjective commitment of faith. (Later we shall see how this sets up the devastating critique of this approach to religious faith that would be developed by David Hume.)

While we shall focus on Pascal's analysis of humanity in our next section, for now we should observe that the fulfillment of human nature allegedly cannot be achieved in this world apart from God and that therefore our quest for God is of paramount importance. And, as we have seen, there are "signs" that point us to God. In connection with this all-important mandate, Pascal distinguishes "only three sorts of people": (i) those who are both reasonable and happy are those who have found and serve God; (ii) those who are unhappy but reasonable are seeking but have not yet found God; and (iii) those who are both unhappy and unreasonable have not found and are not seeking God. In this quest for God, we must neither violate reason nor expect reason to establish religious truth; if we go to the former extreme, "our religion will be absurd and ridiculous," but, if we go to the latter extreme, we shall forfeit everything "mysterious or supernatural." While our belief in God must transcend reason, it must not violate it, being above but not against it. The "metaphysical proofs" of thinkers like Descartes and Hobbes are too abstract to be anything more than intellectual gymnastics. If they establish anything, it is only abstract principles, and never the God of Abraham, Isaac, and Jacob, never the personal God of Christianity. Intentionally or not, Pascal thought, they tend to lead us to deism or agnosticism or even atheism (81–83, 85–86, 103, 146, 169–170).

Though we cannot prove God by means of logical demonstration, he thought we can at least show why it is reasonable for a person to believe in God. This takes us to the most famous philosophical passage in his writings, usually called his "wager argument," which can acknowledge that God is incomprehensible to and radically other than us. Logic tells us that a particular God either does or does not exist. But abstract reason cannot determine which is the case or even which is more probable. So, to cast this in the terminology of gambling, the odds each way are incalculable. We might therefore say that we refuse to bet. But nonbelief is itself a bet – against God. Thus, whether we wish to bet or not, we all "must wager." Since we have no clue regarding the odds, all we can consider are the stakes in the bet: what do we have to gain, and what do we stand to lose if we do or do not believe? Since God is infinite goodness, such as would perfectly fulfill us and establish our happiness, believing in God, if God exists, offers an outcome of infinite reward (first scenario). If we believe and there is no God, then we have made a mistake which costs us the trivial, insignificant selfish indulgences of this world (second scenario). If we do not believe in God and God does not exist, then we have bet correctly and might enjoy the petty gains of transient pleasures (third scenario).

But if we do not believe in God and God exists, then there may be hell to pay, eternal damnation constituting the consequences (fourth scenario). Let us now cast this into argument form. First premise: If it is impossible to determine whether or not God exists, and if it is more advantageous for us to believe in God (given this impossibility), then it is rational for us to believe in God. Second premise: It is impossible to determine whether or not God exists. Third premise: It is more advantageous for us to believe in God (given this impossibility). Intermediate conclusion: Therefore it is rational for us to believe in God. Fourth premise: But if it is rational for us to believe in God, then we should do so. Final conclusion: Thus we should believe in God. Let us begin our assessment by acknowledging that it is a valid argument, as thus constructed, and then evaluate its four premises. Using the principle of charity, we have deliberately cast the argument into a valid form; that is, the conclusion logically follows IF all four premises are true. But are they? Let us initially notice that Pascal has not established them as true on the basis of evidence. Are they so intuitively obvious that "the heart" should embrace them without evidence, or does analysis show them to be problematic? Let us take them one at a time. (i) It is not obvious that it is "rational" for us to believe a falsehood that we do not know to be such merely because it seems personally advantageous to engage in that sort of wishful thinking. (ii) Descartes and Hobbes (and many other great philosophers) try to show that God's existence can be demonstrated; and there may be evidence, such as the fact of massive evil in the world, which counts against (perhaps even decisively) Pascal's sort of infinitely perfect Creator. (iii) What is advantageous to us, as intelligent beings, is to believe the truth and not in fantasies; and, in believing in Pascal's God, we may be failing to believe in some other God that does exist and will condemn us to eternal damnation for getting it wrong. (iv) Even if it were rational for us to believe in Pascal's God, in the sense of more likely to lead to our being significantly rewarded than significantly punished, it seems somewhat immoral for us to try to force ourselves to believe what we do not honestly believe or to pretend to do so and, thus, something we should *not* do. So, all of his premises seem dubious. Even though Pascal is giving us a reason to believe in his God, from a philosophical perspective, it is a poor one. He wrote, "It is the heart which perceives God and not the reason. That is what faith is: God perceived by the heart, not by the reason" (150–154). Not everyone need approach belief in God philosophically. But, to the extent that we do, the "heart"-based approach, divorced from rational evidence, which constitutes fideism, leaves a great deal to be desired.

4.6 Humanity

The subject other than God with which Pascal was most concerned after his religious experience was human nature. His view of humanity – more dramatically asserted than cogently argued – was distinctly dualistic. He was particularly interested in how corrupt and unavoidably wretched we are apart from God and how blessed and happy we would be with God. Our selfish pursuit of pleasures, creature comforts, and distractions can all be used to divert our own attention from our natural misery. Without God, humans are incorrigibly fickle, anxiety-ridden, egoistic, vain, and inclined to boredom. Without God, our lives are ultimately inexplicable and pointless, so that nervousness and fear are natural. Our actions tend to be driven by irrational desire within and powerful forces without. Our dignity is not a function of our physical nature, which is miserable, but of our conscious reflection whereby we understand that we are miserable, even though that understanding adds to our misery: "Thus it is wretched to know that one is wretched, but there is greatness in knowing one is wretched." It is a dangerous mistake to exaggerate our similarity to other animals and to angels, as it is a mistake to exaggerate our differences from other animals and angels. We are

58 | *4 Blaise Pascal*

between the brutes and pure spirits. We must learn to accept "the duality of human nature," which renders us uniquely paradoxical creatures. The danger of knowing our wretchedness without knowing God is despair; the danger of knowing God without knowing our own wretchedness is pride. We must learn to accept both in order to achieve a healthy balance. Pascal agrees with Descartes (against Hobbes) on the dualism of "soul and body." If we were purely material, we could not reason our way to self-knowledge; so we must also be "spiritual" beings. He offers us a now famous metaphor to capture both the glory and the pettiness of our dual nature: "Man is only a reed, the weakest in nature, but he is a thinking reed." It is the spiritual principle that enables us to engage in reflection that sets us apart from the rest of the natural world. "Thus all our dignity consists in thought." And, again (despite Hobbes), such reflective thought could not be the product of our bodies alone. And it is this spiritual dimension of human nature (again, as Descartes believed) that opens up the possibility of immortality and salvation. Here lies the greatness of humanity, establishing its "most excellent" status among all earthly creatures (33–34, 36–37, 48, 54, 59–60, 64–65, 87–88, 94–95, 125, 156, 163).

Yet we find our souls corrupted by sin and shackled to wretched, mortal bodies that we know are destined to expire. Pascal offered us a haunting image of the awful misery of our lot apart from God: "Imagine a number of men in chains, all under sentences of death, some of whom are each day butchered in the sight of the others." Our awareness of what lies in store for us is properly disturbing; for "those remaining see their own condition in that of their fellows, and looking at each other with grief and despair await their turn. This is the image of the human condition." Constant change is the hallmark of our way of being, as it is of everything else in our world. That juggernaut of change hurtles us toward dysfunction, death, and decay. Making matters worse, in a way, is the fact that we know it. Unlike the angels, we die; unlike the beasts, we know we must die. How can we bear the horror of our fate? We can know that distractions are temporarily possible and passionately throw ourselves into their pursuit. Or we can know that salvation is possible and passionately throw ourselves into its pursuit. If we know of our misery but not of God, we shall despair of making any effort at all. If we know only our greatness and not our wretchedness, pride will undermine our effort. "Four kinds of person: zeal without knowledge, knowledge without zeal, neither knowledge nor zeal, both zeal and knowledge." The first three are bad options; the fourth can be good, if the zeal and the knowledge are directed to right ends. We need both rational thought and passionate zeal, although they can be misplaced and can conflict. Like Socrates more than two millennia earlier, Pascal endorsed the permanent value of the Delphic Oracle's injunction, "Know yourself." If we do not, we squander this life, and lose salvation in the next. The body-soul relation is such that the body needs the soul to live, but the soul will survive the death of the body, which will result from their separation. Without faith in and commitment to God, we are so driven by self-love that our sinful faults will seem invincible (165, 213–214, 230, 235, 242, 258, 268, 336, 347–348). Without God's grace and the proper use of our own will, we are doomed. This is a credible enough analysis of human nature, particularly if we assume the perspective of Christian thought. But a philosopher wants to ask what external reason can be given to support our believing it. Pascal offers none – which is, once again, symptomatic of his fideism.

4.7 Freedom

His position becomes even more problematic when we try to untangle his conflicted position on divine grace and human freedom. If our salvation and happiness can only result from our use of reflective thought to know and seek God, and if our misery is insuperable as long as we remain absorbed in sinful self-love, then it matters incalculably whether or not we maintain a selfish commitment to this world or devote ourselves to loving God. But to what extent is that a matter of our own voluntary choice? This raises the critically important issue of freedom versus determinism. While Pascal denied that he was, himself, a Jansenist, he frequented Port-Royal, was sympathetic to Jansenism, and defended Arnauld when he was condemned by the Church. Near the end of the first of Pascal's *Provincial Letters* (which, themselves, were placed on the Church's Index of Forbidden Books), he asserts four doctrines as "undisputed" throughout this controversy: "*First*, That grace is not given to all men"; God can grant it or not as God sees fit. "*Second*, That all the righteous have always the power of obeying the divine commandments" by virtue of the grace God has granted them. "*Third*, That they require, nevertheless, in order to obey them, and even to pray, an efficacious grace, which invincibly determines their will," so that it is irresistible. "*Fourth*, That this efficacious grace is not always granted to all the righteous, and that it depends on the pure mercy of God" (*Selections*, 97). The upshot of these four theses is that it is God's grace or the lack thereof that necessarily determines moral conversion and, hence, salvation. It is this denial of salvific free choice that led to the Church's condemnation of Jansenism, of Arnauld, and of Pascal's *Provincial Letters*. Of course, philosophically, that does not suffice to show that it is wrong. And, indeed, pushing the commitment to free choice too far can lead to a dismissal of the need for divine grace, which lands us in an opposite heresy of Pelagianism (which had been vigorously denounced by Augustine). There are problems in Christian philosophy regarding how a robust acceptance of human freedom can be reconciled with God's omnipotence, omniscient foreknowledge, and lack of any moral responsibility for the sins of humans. Pascal avoids these problems, but at the steep price of denying or severely compromising our moral freedom.

There is remarkably little explicit discussion of this topic in *Pensées*. The first striking relevant statement is a puzzling aphorism – "It is not good to be too free." Traditionally, a dangerous, excessive freedom might be identified with license (as, for example, by Plato). But Pascal's claim may also involve a concern about its negative implications regarding God. At any rate, it ties in with his tendency to lean toward determinism. Much later he writes that people who believe in and love God do so because of irresistible divine grace: "We shall never believe, with an effective belief and faith, unless God inclines our hearts, and we shall believe as soon as he does so" – clearly a form of theological determinism. Yet he goes on to say that the will – which he does not call free – can influence our mental perspective and, thus, what we tend to consider true and false, so that it is "one of the chief organs of belief." But if that influential human will is itself determined by divine grace, then it would seem we are not responsible for where it does and does not take us. Finally, Pascal maintains that, as the mind must have some object(s) of belief, so that, if deprived of true ones, it will embrace false ones, so "the will naturally loves" and, if deprived of good and worthy objects, will "necessarily become attached to false ones" (45, 138, 218, 241). It is not clear that Pascal thinks that this deterministic denial of freedom undermines morality and social responsibility. But we shall now consider its sobering repercussions in those two areas.

4.8 Morality

Given that what Pascal says about freedom and determinism does not concern petty, trivial choices but only those that are significant in having to do with religious, moral, and sociopolitical values, let us see the implications for morality now. As we learn in the first of his *Provincial Letters*, the moral obligation of all persons is to obey God's commandments, as best they understand them. But, when the righteous do so, is the "proximate power" for so doing already theirs, or is it the

60 | *4 Blaise Pascal*

result of divine grace? Now we can say that it is the result of God's grace, which is given them in response to their requesting it in prayer. But this merely pushes the issue back a step. Do they need God's "efficacious grace" as a necessary condition for requesting the proximate power, or can they freely and independently request it? Pascal embraces the former alternative: God's efficacious grace is a necessary condition of their being able to pray to do the right thing; and, furthermore, it "determines" their doing so (*Selections*, 92–96). How does this analysis leave any room for moral responsibility?

This serious problem aside, granting that we should obey God's commandments, how are we to know what they are, and by what measure(s) should we interpret them? Pascal's answer relies on authority. Those with sufficient authority can tell us what are God's commandments and establish the norms we should follow. In *Pensées*, he makes it clear that he believes in God's natural laws regarding moral action; but our nature is so corrupted (by sin) that agreement regarding them is problematic. We cannot even agree as to what is our greatest good. We all seek happiness; yet we disagree as to what it is and how to achieve it. And, whatever it is, we cannot permanently achieve it on our own. Pascal is confident that our greatest good, God, cannot be achieved without divine grace. Indeed, at one point, he says that "the whole of morality" consists in being given God's grace so that we overcome the selfish, sinful desire of "concupiscence." What, then, is the secret to moral goodness? "We must love God alone and hate ourselves alone." Indeed, our morally good life allegedly must consist in knowing and loving Christ. "Apart from him there is only vice, wretchedness, error, darkness, death, despair." He also disagrees with Montaigne that the reason to follow moral custom is that it is reasonable and just, for we cannot know this. "The only reason for following custom is that it is custom," although people are motivated to follow it by believing that it is reasonable and just. Notice how this attitude establishes a severe, uncritical moral conservatism and even a campaign to convince people of what we do not know to be true. It is best that moral custom adopt Christ as a role model, whose example we should follow (46, 49, 74–75, 100, 136, 148, 214, 222, 297, 305, 321). What we have here is a remarkably narrow ethical perspective with little or no room for moral nonconformism or reform.

4.9 Society

Things are no better in the area of sociopolitical values, in which force and custom must rule. Social and political values may be couched in terms of ideals like justice. But we have no independent rational criteria for establishing these ideals and must resort to faith in authority. For, given the corruption of their sinful nature, people are weak and foolish. As a means to preserving social order, "each man should follow the customs of his own country" (remember we saw the same sort of views in Descartes and Hobbes). Those in positions of influence and authority will try to pass off the values they favor as being just. "Justice," however, turns out, on analysis, to be merely "a matter of fashion." People must be led to believe their values are "just," in order to decrease the chances of their violating them. We wish to pretend that right makes might, that justice has its own force; but, in reality, might determines right, and force has its own powerful justification. Like Hobbes, Pascal subscribed to "the right of the sword"; but, unlike his predecessor, Pascal offered no social contract as foundation. The two agreed that civil war, which would threaten the very order of society, is the greatest sociopolitical evil to be avoided. Pascal also curiously agreed with Hobbes that we humans are driven by selfish desire ("concupiscence"), "naturally hate each other," and hypocritically speak of promoting "the common good." What is advisable, for our own welfare, is conformity – we should obey the laws of the land and follow established customs. Thus we submit to the opinions that spring from power. If we follow the opinions of the majority, it is because they are stronger, rather than because they are right. What about the noble ideal of "mutual respect"? That is more hypocrisy, founded on social necessity. There is no need to go on multiplying illustrations of Pascal's misanthropic cynicism regarding human interpersonal relations. It is all deceptive pretense. We not only continuously deceive others, when doing so seems to our advantage, but we tend to avoid admitting the truth even to ourselves (36, 45–48, 51–52, 54, 56, 97–98, 215, 220, 241, 249, 277–278, 347, 349–350). This seems to be the upshot of denying reason a fundamental role in determining values and, instead, of embracing that of faith without rationally or experientially justifiable evidence.

4.10 Review

There are problems with the rationalism of Descartes – e.g. with his theory of allegedly clear and distinct innate ideas, with his attempts at deductive proofs of metaphysical conclusions, and with his dualistic interactionism. There are problems with the empiricism of Hobbes – e.g. with his dogmatically assumed materialistic monism, with his atomistic, egoistic, deterministic psychology, and with his relativism of values and subsequent desperate need for a social contract. Pascal's fideism offers us another alternative, but it is no improvement. Faith is a precious value, indeed. But it is philosophically suspect to give up on the quest for rational support for faith in the areas that most vitally affect our lives and values. Indeed, fideism seems contrary to the very spirit of philosophy, in threatening to discourage, if not suppress, critical inquiry in the face of already established views – whether those be the Catholic God and religion, Christian ethics, or the social order of seventeenth-century France. While *Pensées* is a great book, in that it is provocative, controversial, and (despite its fragmentary nature) arrestingly well written, it does not bear close critical scrutiny.[2] It represents an approach which we shall encounter again, and perhaps that will prove to be a stronger version. But, for now at least, let us see if we can do better.

---

2 For a discussion of Pascal's approach to religious faith in relation to that of the great American philosopher William James, see *Western Philosophies of Religion*, by Wayne P. Pomerleau (New York: Ardsley House, 1998), 464–469.

5

Baruch Spinoza

Source: C. F. Riedel./Wellcome Collection/Public Domain

5.1 Overview

Spinoza was every bit as infamous as Hobbes – both during his lifetime and for several generations after his death. Although it may seem a negative approach, we can quickly grasp why by summarizing what his philosophy turns out to deny: that more than a single substance exists, that

Modern European Philosophers, First Edition. Wayne P. Pomerleau.
© 2023 John Wiley & Sons, Inc. Published 2023 by John Wiley & Sons, Inc.

God is any different from Nature, that God ever created anything for any purpose, that the human body and the human mind are substantially different, that there is any free will or personal immortality, that our motivations can ever extinguish self-interest, that there is any absolute, objective morality, or that there is any natural law or natural right beyond sheer desire and power. He was heavily influenced by Descartes and generally adopted his rationalistic methodology; yet their divergent theories of substance deeply divided them. He spurned the empiricism of Hobbes and developed an alternative sort of monism; yet he shared that predecessor's egoism, determinism, naturalism, moral relativism, social contractarianism, and cynicism about organized religion. Like both Descartes and Hobbes, Spinoza constructed a logically argued, comprehensive philosophical system.

5.2 Biography

Even in the case of creative geniuses such as the four considered in the last three chapters and this one, no matter how original their thinking may have been, their cultural history mattered. As Descartes and Pascal were products of their French Catholicism and Hobbes of the English Protestant civil war, so was Spinoza a product of his background, which was Dutch and Jewish. Bento (meaning "blessed," which is Baruch in Hebrew) Spinoza was born and raised in Amsterdam's Portuguese Jewish community. Near the end of the sixteenth or beginning of the seventeenth century, the Espinoza family had emigrated from the Iberian Peninsula (Spain and Portugal) into Holland, seeking refuge from the persecution of the Roman Catholic Inquisition. The Jews had thrived in the Peninsula under the rule of the Muslim Moors. But, when Catholic King Ferdinand conquered Granada in 1492, expelling the Moors from leadership positions, the Jews were deprived of rights and liberties and forced to choose between converting to Catholic Christianity, on the one hand, and suffering harsh punishment at the hands of the Inquisition, on the other. Many of them fled the Peninsula, seeking freedom elsewhere. In 1565, the Dutch began a war of independence against the tyranny of Spain. Fourteen years later, the Union of Utrecht created the United Provinces and decreed religious tolerance in the Calvinist Northern Provinces. This attracted refugee Jews to the Netherlands, in 1593. They were, indeed, tolerated by the dominant Calvinist authorities so long as they did not cause trouble and bring attention to themselves. Miguel (Michael) d'Espinoza had probably come to Amsterdam as a child, becoming a successful merchant in the Jewish community. In 1598, the Jews were granted permission to build the first synagogue in Amsterdam.

Baruch d'Espinoza was born in Amsterdam on November 24, 1632; his mother, the second of his father's three wives, died in 1638, probably of consumption. The boy, who grew up speaking Portuguese and Spanish, was intellectually gifted and sent to rabbinical school, where he learned Hebrew and studied the Jewish Scriptures and theology. Some, probably including his father, expected him to become a rabbi. But, for whatever reason(s), he left the school at the age of 17 and went to work in his father's business. Still, his acute probing and critical mind was such that he wanted to broaden his knowledge. Realizing that this required that he learn Latin, he started studying under the tutelage of Francis Van den Ende, a former Jesuit, democrat, and radical doctor of medicine, who also taught him mathematics and the Cartesian philosophy. Spinoza himself became intellectually radical, especially after 1654, when his father died and he started meeting with the "Collegiants," a group of churchless Christians in Amsterdam. His views became progressively heterodox, and he may have become lax in observing Jewish law. At any rate, in July of 1656, he was formally excommunicated from the Jewish community, the writ of expulsion (or *cherem*)

64 | *5 Baruch Spinoza*

harshly accusing him of unspecified "abominable heresies" and "monstrous deeds," calling him "cursed" for all time, and forbidding all Jews from ever having anything to do with him. That same year, the teaching of Cartesianism was banned in Holland. Spinoza started using the Latin form of his given name, Benedict (still meaning "blessed"). A few years later, in 1660, he left Amsterdam, temporarily settling in Rijnsburg (near Leiden), where he started writing his epistemological essay *On the Improvement of the Understanding*,[1] which was never finished, and his *Short Treatise on God, Man, and His Well-Being*, which was also left unfinished. There he may have associated with local "Collegiants," who tended to republicanism and freethinking, as well as being very interested in Cartesianism. In 1662, he started writing his *Principles of Cartesian Philosophy*, which was published the next year (II, 287–288), soon after he moved to Voorburg (near The Hague), along with an appendix of *Metaphysical Thoughts*; this was the only book published under his own name during his lifetime.

While in Voorburg, he began work on his masterpiece, *The Ethics*. By 1665, significant chunks of it were circulating, in manuscript form, among his friends. But he deferred completing it, in order to write his *Theologico-Political Treatise*, whose publication (anonymously) in 1670, provoked a flood of furious protests. Around that time, he moved to The Hague and resumed work on *The Ethics*. He was helping to support himself by grinding and polishing optical lenses, a skill he had learned as a boy. In 1673, he was offered and declined a chair in philosophy at Heidelberg; although he was assured that his academic freedom would be respected, so long as he did not abuse it by stirring up controversy, he did not see how he could honestly do philosophy without running the risk of disturbing the peace. That same year, his *Theologico-Political Treatise* was formally condemned in Holland, along with various "other heretical and atheistic writings," including some by Hobbes. In 1675, Spinoza finished *The Ethics*, circulating it privately but prudently deciding against publishing it. He also started writing his *Political Treatise*. He was in poor physical health, suffering from phthisis or consumption, a tubercular lung disease, no doubt aggravated by years of inhaling finely ground up glass from his optical work. In 1676, he was visited by G.W. Leibniz, with whom he had briefly corresponded about optics some five years earlier (II, 373–375, 296, 370–373, 405). Spinoza died at home on February 21, 1677, leaving his *Political Treatise* unfinished. Friends arranged for the posthumous publication of his writings, including *The Ethics* and some of his correspondence. However, in 1678, these writings were condemned and banned in Holland.

5.3 Knowledge

We have two important works of epistemology by Spinoza, and they are quite different from each other. The first is his essay *On the Improvement of the Understanding*. Though it was left unfinished and only published posthumously, the fact that it was his first philosophical work may help mark him as a modern. The second is the second part of *The Ethics*. The two are very different in style. The earlier work used an "analytic" method, comparable to that of Descartes's *Meditations*, which starts with immediate experience (such as cognitive doubting) and progressively uncovers its conditions (e.g. the existence of the mind with its various kinds of ideas, the special idea of a supremely perfect Being, the necessary existence of that God, the reality of the physical world outside the mind, and the experience of one particular body that is uniquely related to the thinking mind). By contrast, *The Ethics* employs a "synthetic" geometrical method, which starts with

---

1 References to Spinoza's writings will be to *Works of Spinoza*, in two volumes, trans. by R.H.M. Elwes (New York: Dover Publications, 1951 and 1955); they will be made in text by volume and page numbers.

the most basic concepts and axiomatic truths, on the basis of which the broadest propositions are demonstrated, which propositions can then be used to demonstrate more particular truths. Spinoza shared Descartes's admiration for Euclidean geometry as involving great precision and generating absolutely certain conclusions. Indeed, Descartes himself experimented with doing philosophy in the geometrical way in a brief (about seven pages) appendix to his replies to the second set of objections (compiled by Mersenne). Well, Spinoza also used this methodological approach throughout almost all of his masterpiece, the complete title of which is *The Ethics Demonstrated in Geometrical Order*. It may be that the reason he abandoned the earlier work was that he came to think the Cartesian approach inadequate. In an early letter, having been asked to criticize the Cartesian philosophy, he responded that, while he did not normally like to criticize other thinkers, he had identified three key problems: first (and worst), it did not adequately focus on our "knowledge of the first cause and origin of all things" (God); second, it failed to grasp "the true nature of the human mind"; and, third, it had a distorted, erroneous understanding of "the true cause of error" (II, 278). At any rate, we shall consider what he says about human knowledge in both works.

To use a phrase that has recently become fashionable (but was not yet invented in the seventeenth century), Spinoza constructed a "moral epistemology." That is to say, the theory of knowledge, for him, was not merely abstract but involved more and less virtuous ways of thinking and was ultimately oriented toward our genuine good or well-being. In the very opening paragraphs of *Improvement* (say, the first four pages or so), he inquired into the "real good" that would constitute our "continuous, supreme, and unending happiness." We live in permanent danger of squandering our lives pursuing the false and illusory ends of "Riches, Fame, and the Pleasures of Sense," instead of our genuine good, which is the ultimate happiness that can only spring from our "knowledge of the union existing between the mind and the whole of nature" or God. He would have us distinguish four different degrees of awareness. "Perception arising from hearsay" is the lowest, least reliable level; as examples, he gives the date of his birth, his parentage, and other objects of belief based on what he had heard from others. "Perception which arises from mere experience," which generalizes from empirical observations, is next to worst; as examples, he gives his belief that he will die, since other people have done so, that oil feeds a fire while water can extinguish it, and virtually all the practical knowledge of everyday life. "Perception arising when the essence of one thing is inferred from another thing, but not adequately" is next to the best; for example, we reason, on the basis of physical sensations we feel, that there is some intimate relation between our minds and our bodies, yet we fail to understand the nature of that relation. "Lastly, there is the perception arising when a thing is perceived solely through its essence, or through the knowledge of its proximate cause"; for example, by reflecting on my knowing anything, I can know what it is to know and that the fact of knowing requires a knowing mind. Spinoza adds that this highest level of awareness does not yet extend very far. Reliable knowledge requires true ideas adequately understood. Spinoza adopts a correspondence theory of truth: in order for an idea or belief to be true, it must "correspond to its correlate in the world of reality." A false idea is one that does not so correspond but is mentally believed in (unlike the fictional, in which we do not really believe). Like Descartes, Spinoza pursued clarity and distinctness, since "ideas which are clear and distinct can never be false." The lack of clarity and distinctness, like the lack of an orderly method of thinking, can lead to doubt, a suspension of belief, as well as to error. Careful definitions are valuable means to clarity and distinctness (II, 3–15, 25, 27, 30–31, 35–36; cf. 282, 395, from the Correspondence). Curiously, this treatment is not itself based on careful definitions of key concepts. Realizing this could have led Spinoza to abandon this "analytic" approach to epistemology in favor of the "synthetic" approach of *The Ethics*, to which we now turn.

5 Baruch Spinoza

In the second part of *The Ethics*, using the geometrical method, he lays down key definitions and axioms. He defines an *"idea"* as "the mental conception which is formed by the mind as a thinking thing" and *"an adequate idea"* as one which, considered in itself (as opposed to being considered in relation to external objects), bears the hallmarks of truth. Among the axioms, we might cite the first three: (i) the essence of a human being does not require necessary existence (as opposed to the divine essence, which does); (ii) a human being thinks (the foundation of Descartes's *cogito*); and (iii) all modes of thinking presuppose some idea(s) thought. On this basis, he could logically proceed. As God is "an infinite thinking being" and the only existing Substance, Thought must be a divine attribute. Because God is one and the divine nature is ontologically indivisible, there must be an identity between ideas as objects of divine Thought and all beings that can be their objects. In one of the most famous statements of philosophical rationalism, Spinoza writes, "*The order and connection of ideas is the same as the order and connection of things.*" This signifies that the ideas employed by rational thought somehow relate to reality and thus are capable of having some adequacy. Because Spinoza's God is infinite and the divine nature is all-encompassing, the divine essence must comprise an infinite number of attributes. Of these, we can know only Thought and Extension, because they are the only ones evident in the world of our experience. Because God is the only Substance, God "constitutes the essence of the human mind," which can only know itself through ideas that are ultimately rooted in experiences of the body. Spinoza next proposes the radical and problematic notion that the mind is itself the idea of some particular existing thing and that that turns out to be the body; in other words, your mind is allegedly the idea of your body, so that it is an idea of the body that is somehow thinking ideas. The ideas drawn from bodily experiences, lacking clarity and distinctness, are not themselves "adequate" but can rationally lead to adequate knowledge – such as that we are thinking and must, therefore, be mental beings. Falsehood is nothing positive, as is truth, but merely "*the privation of knowledge which inadequate, fragmentary, or confused ideas involve*" (II, 82–83, 86–87, 90, 92, 103–106, 108).

We are now ready for Spinoza's revised analysis of levels of mental awareness, which are three, rather than four, those of hearsay and empirical observations being collapsed into the first of these. He chooses to call all of them degrees of "knowledge," despite the fact that the first is "inadequate and confused," being "the only source of falsity." So, he identifies "*knowledge of the first kind*" with "*opinion, or imagination.*" Next comes rational "*knowledge of the second kind.*" It is "*necessarily true*" as far as it goes but piecemeal rather than comprehensive. Finally, there is "a third kind of knowledge, which we will call intuition." It is not only necessarily true but also comprehensively adequate, seeing all objects as united in God. "It is in the nature of reason to perceive things under a certain form of eternity (*sub quadam aeternitatis specie*)." From this ultimate perspective, we allegedly come to know not only what is but also that everything must be as it is. "From the third kind of knowledge necessarily arises the intellectual love of God" (*amor Dei intellectualis*) that purportedly will constitute our blessedness (II, 113–114, 117, 263). This will be crucial to Spinoza's view of how we can achieve fulfillment. Unfortunately, he gives us little specific insight into how we can achieve such all-encompassing intuitive knowledge.

5.4 Reality

Like Hobbes, Spinoza responded to the problems of interactionism involved in the substance dualism of Descartes by proposing a monistic alternative. But, while Hobbes advocates a generic monism, Spinoza argues for numerical monism. That is to say, for Hobbes, there is only one sort of reality (which is materialistic), whereas, for Spinoza, reality comprises one and only one, single

5.4 Reality | 67

Substance (which, as we shall see, is ultimately God). Again, he did this by using a "synthetic" geometric method, starting by defining key concepts and laying down basic axioms, then proceeding to demonstrate the most fundamental propositions, from which he subsequently deduced less fundamental ones that logically follow. Of his initial eight definitions, those of "*substance*," "*attribute*," "*mode*," and "*God*" will concern us now. His ultimate foundation was the concept of "*substance*," which he defined as "that which is in itself, and is conceived through itself: in other words, that of which a conception can be formed independently of any other conception." So a substance needs nothing else to exist and can be conceptualized independently of anything else. We might recall that Descartes had essentially the same sense of substance but then used a more relaxed interpretation so that a substance could be and be conceived independently of everything else except God. Spinoza adopted that same initial understanding but consistently applied it more stringently. This gets us into his reasoning (in the first part of *The Ethics*) for his monism, which is arguably the most controversial and most often studied portion of his philosophical system. An "*attribute*" constitutes the essence of some substance, he says, while a "*mode*" refers to what "exists in, and is conceived through" a substance as one of its "modifications." Like Descartes, Spinoza defines "*God*" as "a being absolutely infinite" but then adds that God must be "a substance consisting in infinite attributes," each expressing infinite essence. A couple of axioms that will be important are the fourth, that knowledge of any effect requires knowledge of its cause, and the fifth, that things with nothing in common cannot be conceived or understood in terms of one another (II, 45–46). Now we are ready to track his reasoning for God as the only Substance.

By definition, a substance must be logically prior to its attributes and modifications (Prop. I); and, since attributes define the essence of a substance, by definition, no two substances whose attributes are different can have anything in common (Prop. II). But, then, having nothing in common, they neither can be understood in terms of one another (by Axiom V) nor can either cause the other (by Axiom IV) (Prop. III). Any two separate substances must be distinguishable in terms of their attributes and/or their modifications. So far, it would seem, so innocuous. But things start becoming more obviously controversial, beginning with the fifth proposition: "*There cannot exist in the universe two or more substances having the same nature or attribute.*" If this is correct, there cannot be two or more dogs, existing as substances and sharing a canine nature. But, worse than that, on this view, no two people can exist as substances sharing the attribute of thought. That strikes us as, at least, counterintuitive. So how does Spinoza argue for this claim? Well, if there were two (or more) substances, they would have to be distinguished from each other by their attributes and/or their modifications. It could not be by their modifications, which are not essential to substances, the latter being "naturally prior to" all their modifications. But neither could it be by their attributes, since, he claims, if this were the case, then they could not share any identical attributes. (This premise is neither well supported nor entirely plausible.) Therefore, no two (or more) substances could have the same nature or share any identical attribute. (Spinoza concludes his argument with the geometrical abbreviation Q.E.D., which stands for *quod erat demonstrandum*, meaning "as was to be demonstrated.") From this it follows (by Prop. III) that no substances can be causally produced by any other (Prop. VI). Thus every substance not only exists but must exist by its very nature – "that is, its essence necessarily involves existence" (Prop. VII). But a necessarily existing substance cannot be finite, as it could only be limited by something else of its own kind (this is a dubious premise), and it has already been argued that no two substances can share a nature or attribute – which would be necessary if they were of the same kind – so that every substance must be infinite or absolutely unlimited (Prop. VIII). Spinoza's rationalism allows him to claim, "There is necessarily for each individual existent thing a cause why it should exist." (We shall speak of a more famous version of this as Leibniz's "principle of sufficient reason.") In other words, there has to be some rational explanation, even if we do not know what it is, for every real thing's existing and being as it is. The next proposition (IX) is also dubious, claiming that the more reality a substance has, the greater its number of attributes must be; he claims that this is true by virtue of the very definition of an attribute, though one might well question this claim. If we grant him this, then we must admit that God, who, by definition, is "an absolutely infinite being," must have an infinite number of attributes, each expressing the divine essence. But, if all the preceding is accepted, we have, in effect, already proved the necessary reality of God, an absolutely infinite being, whose very "essence necessarily involves existence" (Prop. XI) – however, we shall go into the proofs of this proposition more thoroughly in our next section on "God." Every substance must be ontologically indivisible (Prop. XIII). For, if a substance were divisible, its parts would *either* retain the nature of the substance and thus be infinite, producing "several substances of the same nature, which (by Prop. v.) is absurd," *or* the infinite substance would be reduced to parts that were not themselves infinite substances, so that "(by Prop. vii.) substance absolutely infinite could cease to exist, which (by Prop. xi.) is also absurd." So any substance must be utterly indivisible, in addition to being infinite and necessarily existing. Finally, we reach the crucial proposition (XIV) establishing his numerical monism: "*Besides God no substance can be granted or conceived.*" This follows nicely from the preceding. We have established that God, "an absolutely infinite being," necessarily exists and must have all attributes. So, if there were any other substance than God, it would have to have at least one attribute, which it would share with God. But we have already argued (Prop. V) that no two substances can share any attribute. Thus, reality comprises only one substance, and that is God. So, we might wonder, what about you, me, and the trashcan? Well, as he observes in Prop. xv, such things are not substances at all but exist merely as part of God: "Whatsoever is, is in God, and without God nothing can be, or be conceived." The technical term for this theory of reality is *panentheism* (meaning, literally, all things in God); as Spinoza points out in a letter (II, 46–51, 54–55, 298), he is here agreeing with St. Paul, who wrote (Acts 17:28), speaking of God, "For in him we live, and move, and have our being." What he does not say, however, is that Paul meant this metaphorically enough that, unlike Spinoza, he was not denying divine transcendence.

Well, what are we critically to make of this? Since so much of what follows is based on this position of panentheistic monism, it is probably best that we try to answer this question now. First, let us admit that the previous paragraph is both long and a difficult slog. Although it is a simplified summary of the first few (i.e. 11) pages of *The Ethics*, it focuses on Spinoza's reasoning, which is remarkably careful and thick. Second, as has already been indicated, if we go along with the content of these first 11 foundational pages, we shall subsequently find ourselves logically forced to swallow some unwelcome implications. Third, connecting this metaphysical theory to his epistemology, we should note that the approach is distinctly nonempirical, avoiding appeals to opinion, imagination, and ordinary sense experience, and that it is relentlessly rational in its approach. Fourth, we have already pointed out a few premises in Spinoza's reasoning that seem unsupported and importantly dubious. Fifth, and finally, we might question three of his most basic definitions, which are stipulated, not necessarily conventional, and, hence, problematic. To start with the most important one, his definition of "*substance*" pretty well predetermines his monistic conclusions. A less slanted conception would hold that a substance is something that has attributes, is capable of action, or is a thing in relation to other things. An attribute is normally conceived of as a quality of a substance – an essential attribute being a quality without which it would not be that sort of substance, and an accidental attribute being removable without the substance ceasing to be that sort of thing. Thus, we would say (as Spinoza would not) that a tree is a substance, green, capable of growth, and living in a grove with other trees; "wooden" is an essential attribute of a tree, while "mature" is an accidental quality. A modification is a change, either essential or accidental, in a substance: if a tree is pruned of a couple of branches (accidental), it remains a tree; but if it burns up so as to be reduced to ashes (essential), it has ceased to be a tree at all. But, with these more normal interpretations of "substance," "attribute," and "modification," Spinoza's startling conclusions could not readily be deduced. So he stacks the deck by defining these key concepts in his own idiosyncratic manner, favorable to generating a remarkably unusual philosophical position.

5.5 God

We have already seen both Spinoza's definition of God and, generally, how the preliminary logical moves of his system allegedly mandate God's necessary existence as "an absolutely infinite being." But now we shall probe more deeply into the cluster of arguments, comprising the very important eleventh proposition, allegedly demonstrating divine existence, as well as (after that) Spinoza's conclusions about the implications of his theory of God for appropriate versus inappropriate approaches to religion – which conclusions have turned out to be considerably more acceptable for our culture than for his seventeenth-century European culture. His first proof is a *reductio ad absurdum*, reducing to absurdity the idea that God might *not* exist: on that hypothesis, God's "essence does not involve existence. But this (by Prop. VII) is absurd. Therefore God necessarily exists." This is a form of the ontological argument, nonempirically (and noncausally) deducing from the idea of the essence of God the necessary existence of a Being corresponding to that idea. The argument fails to be cogent to the extent that the seventh proposition is dubiously established. The second proof does employ causality, starting with the idea that there must be an adequate cause to account for everything (something like what Leibniz would call the principle of sufficient reason). That cause must either be inherent in the thing's essence or external to it. Spinoza then posits a negative form of that principle, which is even more questionable, maintaining that "a thing necessarily exists, if no cause or reason be granted which prevents its existence." So, on this view, there is a presumption of existence for everything, the burden of evidence falling on the denial of existence. Well, if there were any sufficient reason to prevent God's existence, it would have to be either within God's nature or outside it. Now if there were any substance external to God, it could not have anything in common with God (by Prop. II), and thus could not causally affect God (Prop. III). But the idea that God, "a being absolutely infinite and supremely perfect," would or could prevent God's existence "is absurd." Hence, nothing could possibly cause God not to exist, and, thus, "God necessarily exists." Spinoza next shifts from these a priori proofs to one that is a posteriori. If God did not exist and any finite being(s) did exist, then the finite being(s) would be "more powerful than a being absolutely infinite," since the potentiality of nonexistence is a limitation indicative of a lack of power. But we at least do exist as finite. However, that we or any other finite beings could be more powerful than an absolutely infinite being "is obviously absurd." Therefore "God (Def. VI) necessarily exists. Q.E.D." This is a posteriori in that it has an empirical premise – that we do exist as finite. But is there not something suspicious about comparing the lack of power in something nonexistent to the power of something existent? If God does not exist, then we are comparing the alleged lack of power of an idea or concept to the supposed power of an existent thing. Is that not peculiar? It is this unsupported a priori premise, in an a posteriori proof, that seems problematic (II, 51–53). Because of its relevance to Spinoza's system, to metaphysics, and to his philosophy of religion, this eleventh proposition could represent the most famous part of his reasoning.

So God is allegedly the only Substance, and everything else that is real, including every person, is an aspect of God. There can be no creation of us or our natural world, since God is not transcendent and nothing else can be ontologically separate from God. Nevertheless, without being a Creator,

God is "the efficient cause" of our world and everything in it. God is the only "free cause," in Spinoza's sense of freedom as acting solely according to the necessity of one's own nature and not being determined by anything else (as there is nothing else external to God). Spinoza warns us against anthropomorphically thinking and talking of the infinite God in terms only appropriate to finite humans, saying, for example, that "neither intellect nor will appertain to God's nature." Proposition XVIII tells us that God is an immanent rather than a transcendent cause of everything, which follows from everything else being "in God." Spinoza's monistic panentheism leads him to the striking claim that God and Nature are identical, the same divine reality viewed from two different perspectives. God's "nature viewed as active (*natura naturans*)" is the divine substance and attributes; God's "nature viewed as passive (*natura naturata*)" is the sum total of modifications. For Spinoza, there are no final causes, and nothing God does is done for any purpose, final causality being nothing more than a philosopher's fanciful myth. (To use a word that became current much later, Spinoza is trying to "demythologize" our thinking about God.) In the Appendix to the first part of *The Ethics* (called "Concerning God"), temporarily abandoning the rigorous geometric method in favor of the more readable treatise style, Spinoza develops this and other controversial points. This, of course, undercuts the argument from design: if there is no design in our world, we have no grounds to claim for it a designer. Conventional religion claims not only that God has purposes for us but also that it knows what they are, thus manipulating gullible followers for its own self-serving purposes. Against such superstition, Spinoza writes that "nature has no particular goal in view, and that final causes are mere human figments." After all, if God acted to achieve certain ends, then God was seeking to rectify something that was lacking – which undermines perfection, since God is everything. One might detect some autobiographical bitterness in his writing that the person who tries to understand the true nature of alleged "miracles," rather than gaping "at them like a fool, is set down and denounced as an impious heretic" by those so brainwashed by religious leaders who maintain authority by keeping them ignorant. Nor does Spinoza fear that evil exists in such a way as to compromise the infinite perfection of the divine nature, since good and evil are relative to our limited ways of viewing things – relative, that is, to what we happen to suppose "pleasing" or displeasing to ourselves. Because we get carried away by our own extravagant imagination, we rashly and wrongly suppose that evil exists outside and contrary to God. But we are not arbiters of such matters (II, 56, 59–60, 46, 62, 68, 75, 77–81, 347). As we have seen, nothing is external to God; thus nothing, properly understood, can be truly contrary to God.

We have already questioned Spinoza's ninth proposition, which maintains that "an absolutely infinite being" must have an infinite number of attributes. But, let us ask, what are the infinite number of attributes allegedly expressing the divine essence? Well, it turns out that we can only know two of them – Thought and Extension. Why can we only know these two? Because they are the only ones that are modified in the world of our experience – as minds and bodies. Well, what of God's moral attributes? Does God not love good people and hate evildoers, as organized religion preaches? No, that too is sheer superstitious mythology, foisted on us by religious leaders to maintain their authority over us (II, 83–84, 256, 298–299). All of this exposure of orthodox doctrines of God as superstition undermines the authority of organized religion, as is clear from Spinoza's Preface to his *Theologico-Political Treatise*, the remainder of which we shall only touch upon here. The Scriptures tell us so much about God which is unverifiable by natural experience, and Spinoza asserts that the most important thing is that a person "has right opinions and a true plan of life." In other words, one's moral values and conduct are more important than the theological doctrines in which one believes. As opposed to any particular faith, Spinoza advocates what he calls "universal religion." It holds that one perfect God exists and that the best way to worship this "Supreme Being" is by practicing love and justice toward other people. Against the mainstream view of

Christian philosophy of religion, he asserts that "there is no connection" between philosophy, on the one hand, and theology or religious faith, on the other; the former aims at the rational understanding of truth, while the latter aims at obedience and piety (I, 3–11, 77–79, 183–187, 189–190, 194, 198–199). It should be fairly easy to see how these iconoclastic views regarding God and religion might threaten, disturb, and antagonize the orthodox authorities of organized Judaism and Christianity.

5.6 Humanity

It should come as no surprise that Spinoza's philosophy of human nature is stranger than any other we have considered thus far, since it holds that no human being can be substantially real and that every human being is a small part of God/Nature, the only actual Substance. On this view, our ontological individuality turns out to be an illusion; and every human being turns out to be connected not only to every other human being but to all of Nature. (It was probably this emphasis on the oneness of things and this respect for all of Nature as a whole that would later endear Spinoza to the Romantics.) We might consider how different this is from Descartes, who wanted to emphasize the radical distinction between human beings and all other sorts of beings in our world and who thought that a legitimate goal of philosophical knowledge is to conquer and dominate nature. We shall also consider how Spinoza developed a creative alternative to the substance dualism of Descartes, which generated problems of interaction.

To start with an apparently noncontroversial claim (with which Descartes, Hobbes, and Pascal might all agree), we can say that, for Spinoza, human beings are bodies living in an environment of bodies. But his definition is much more difficult to accept: "By *body* I mean a mode which expresses in a certain determinate manner the essence of God, in so far as he is considered as an extended thing." In other words, every body, including yours, is a particular modification of God's attribute of extension. "The essence of man does not involve necessary existence," since a human being is finite – as are all modes (*natura naturata*), in contrast to Substance and the divine attributes (*natura naturans*). The only objects of our experience are physical (bodies) and mental (ideas), and our perception of our own body is uniquely direct and immediate, in contrast to that of all other bodies. "Man thinks," and all modes of human thought are ideas in a broad sense, emotions "such as love, desire, or any of the other passions" being ideas (in a broad sense) or presupposing ideas as their objects. Neither our bodies nor our minds are substances, the only Substance being God. Hence, Spinoza can say, "substance thinking and substance extended are one and the same substance, comprehended now through one attribute, now through the other." This lays the foundation for Spinoza's "dual aspect" solution to the mind–body problem: rather than being ontologically separable, our mind and our body are merely two different aspects of the same reality (like two sides of the same coin). This radical claim is associated with Spinoza's ultimate statement of extreme rationalism: "*The order and connection of ideas is the same as the order and connection of things.*" Notice that this does not merely assert a correlation (parallelism) between the mental and the physical, but an *identity* between them. On this view, there is nothing cognitive that is not identical to something physical. That is one of the most spectacularly bold claims in the entire history of Western philosophy! But here follows an equally bold claim: not only does the human mind *have* ideas, but it "*is the idea of some particular thing actually existing.*" Of what could the human mind be the idea? His answer is that, for example, your mind is the idea of your body! Not only are they not separable, but they are *definable* in terms of one another – your mind being the idea of your body and your body being the object of your mind. He adds, "We thus comprehend, not only that the human mind is united to the body, but also the nature of the union." All of this occurs in the first few (about 10) pages of the second part of *The Ethics*. (Between the thirteenth and fourteenth propositions of that Part II, he offers us a number of axioms, lemmas, and postulates regarding bodies, which are of some interest but which we have not time and space to consider here.) Despite their "union" and identity, the human mind has no adequate knowledge of the body, all of its ideas of the body being drawn from sense experience and imagination, representing the lowest level of epistemological awareness, being insuperably inadequate (II, 82–83, 86, 89–90, 92–97, 102–105).

Let us now consider Spinoza's theory of human psychology. Like Descartes, he considers understanding and will to be two most important aspects of the mind. But, unlike his predecessor, he does not consider them different faculties of the mind; they are the same and not faculties at all, since only a substance could have faculties, and the mind is not a substance. As he succinctly puts it, "Will and understanding are nothing beyond the individual volitions and ideas" of the human mind. In Part III of *The Ethics*, he starts explicitly dealing with our emotions. All of our "passions of hatred, anger, envy, and so on" have particular causes through which they are determined and in terms of which they can be understood. In other words, they are not mysterious and can, at least in principle, be scientifically explained. Let us examine his definition: "By *emotion* I mean the modifications of the body, whereby the active power of the said body is increased or decreased, aided or constrained, and also the ideas of such modifications." Thus, the definition indicates both physical and psychic dimensions to emotions in keeping with his "dual aspect" theory: on the one hand, they are modifications of the modification that is the body; on the other, they are ideas of those modifications in the mind. If the person who has an emotion is its "adequate cause," then it is "an activity"; but, otherwise, it is "a passion, or state wherein the mind is passive." So, strictly speaking, a passion is one sort of emotion, namely one whose cause is external to the person experiencing it. (There is a problem here, which we can just mention in passing – strictly speaking, everything in our world is extrinsically caused by God, the divine Substance, which is at least distinguishable from humans and their minds and bodies, so that all emotions would seem to be passions.) It is the nature of minds to think; and bodies are either in motion or at rest. But there is no causal interaction between them, since that would imply that they are distinct: "*Body cannot determine mind to think, neither can mind determine body to motion or rest.*" Next we encounter Spinoza's famous theory of essential "*endeavours*" (or *conatus*), which ought to remind us of Hobbes. Going beyond his predecessor's notion that endeavors are the motivating forces behind all voluntary action, Spinoza holds that everything "*endeavours to persist in its own being*" and that this endeavor for its own self-preservation just "*is nothing else but the actual essence of the thing in question.*" So, on this view, not only does a rock, as an extended thing, endeavor to maintain its existence as a rock, but, further, that endeavor to maintain its own existence actually *is* the essence of the rock. This is, at least, counterintuitive, is it not? This endeavor for survival, when predicated of a mind, is its "*will*, when referred to the mind and body in conjunction it is called *appetite*," and appetite of which the mind is conscious is called "*desire.*" Every emotion can increase or decrease a person's power – "*the power of activity in our body*" and "*the power of thought in our mind.*" Desire is one of the three basic emotions, the other two being pleasure, which increases power, and pain, which decreases it; and "all other emotions arise from these three," including love and hatred. Also, depending on circumstances, in theory, anything can provoke desire, pleasure, or pain, as well as other emotions, such as love and hatred. Despite our natural self-interest, we can also feel compassion for others, benevolence being a desire, arising from comparison, for the well-being of another. We naturally desire to pursue pleasure, which increases our power, and to avoid pain, which decreases it; through pleasure, he says, we move "from a less to a greater perfection" and, through pain, "from a greater to a less perfection" – perfection translating here into power. Hope, sympathy, and joy are kinds of pleasure, and fear, disappointment, and pity kinds of pain. The ideas involved in passions, as passive emotion, are always confused and, therefore, also dangerous. Spinoza considered our inability or unwillingness to control our passions to represent a kind of psychological "bondage," which became the focus of Part IV of *The Ethics*. As long as we can maintain rational impulse control, he favored (contrary to Dutch Calvinism, perhaps), rather than condemning, our enjoyment of the simple pleasures of food, drink, music, even sports. (We know that he personally enjoyed both his pipe tobacco and watching spiders at work!) But rational self-control is crucial to our liberation from bondage, to our achieving such freedom as is possible, and to human "blessedness." The best means to this end is our reaching the intuitive third kind of knowledge, becoming able to see things from the perspective of eternity, and achieving "the intellectual love of God." To the extent that we can accomplish this task, we shall not only be able to control our passions, but we shall enjoy the "blessedness" of liberation from psychological bondage. (Remember that the Spanish, Hebrew, and Christian versions of Spinoza's given name all mean "blessed.") This is the apotheosis of human virtue and represents true "salvation." He honestly acknowledges that the achievement of this is "exceedingly hard." But, in the famous final sentence of *The Ethics*, he reminds us, "But all things excellent are as difficult as they are rare" (II, 121, 129–132, 136–138, 140, 149, 174–178, 185, 187, 219, 260–263, 270–271). Since there is no personal immortality (our essence, God, being eternal, of course), this is the ultimate salvation and blessedness possible for us human beings.

5.7 Freedom

Spinoza was a determinist, maintaining that there is no free will and that everything that happens is causally determined to happen just as it does. When something's "existence would imply a contradiction," it is called "*impossible*"; and when something exists, whose "non-existence would imply a contradiction," it is said to be "*necessary*." There is no truly contingent reality; but we call something "*possible*" when, because of our ignorance of determining causes, we suppose that "neither its existence nor its non-existence imply a contradiction." For Spinoza, genuine freedom is self-determination: "That thing is called free, which exists solely by the necessity of its own nature, and of which the action is determined by itself alone." So everything real is necessary, and freedom is itself a special form of determinism. By contrast, something that is extrinsically determined is said to be "constrained." Spinoza maintains that only God is free, and that is only in his deterministic sense of the word. Nothing that happens in our world (of *natura naturata*) occurs contingently, but everything is determined by the divine Substance (*natura naturans*). Spinoza does not try to camouflage his determinism: "*Nothing in the universe is contingent, but all things are conditioned to exist and operate in a particular manner by the necessity of the divine nature.*" The will is not a substance but "only a particular mode of thinking, like intellect"; it cannot freely cause anything. Even God, who is free in Spinoza's sense of the word, has no free will and acts as the divine nature makes necessary. "*Things could not have been brought into being by God in any manner or in any order different from that which has in fact obtained.*" We like to think of ourselves as independent individuals; and, in our "ignorance of any cause" of our actions, we enjoy supposing that we are free. Now there is a sort of freedom, which we have discussed, which is a liberation from the "bondage" of our passions. In this condition, we are allegedly free of confused, inadequate ideas and the "fear" that inevitably attends a life that lacks rational impulse control (II, 19, 46, 68, 70–71, 75, 108–109, 116, 232; cf., from the Correspondence, 279, 366, 390–391). Like Hobbes, Spinoza did not want entirely to give up using the language of freedom or liberty, but was clearly a causal determinist. (Is it a mere coincidence that, of the four modern thinkers we have considered thus far, the two Catholics – Descartes and Pascal – believe in human freedom, while the two non-Catholics – Hobbes and Spinoza – do not?)

5.8 Morality

It might strike readers as odd that the first four pages of Spinoza's *On the Improvement of the Understanding* are devoted to the moral value of correcting our way of thinking and achieving ultimate knowledge (as if he were doing what today is called moral epistemology). But his theoretical work is motivated by moral objectives. This is why he makes a point of insisting that our "true happiness" – that is, "continuous, supreme, and unending happiness" – cannot be the result of "Riches, Fame, and the Pleasures of Sense" but can only be achieved by the sort of knowledge that will banish fear, hatred, and other "disturbances of the mind." There are virtues of mind and character that can lead us to this knowledge that will generate "the intellectual love of God" we have considered. While we usually think of *The Ethics* as a metaphysical masterpiece, its title indicates that its ultimate concern is moral, having to do with how we should live. While good and evil are relative to pleasure, pain, and desire (the three basic emotions), what is good for us (as bringing joy and satisfying legitimate desire) is what will fulfill our human nature, and what is bad for us (as bringing discontent and satisfying only perverse desire) is what will thwart that fulfillment. From that perspective, Spinoza's definitions near the beginning of Part IV make sense. "By *good* I mean that which we certainly know to be useful to us." This is not riches, fame, and extravagant physical pleasures. "By *evil* I mean that which we certainly know to be a hindrance to us in the attainment of any good," as a life of "bondage" to our passions would surely be. By "*virtue*" Spinoza means "the same thing" as "*power*" – specifically, the power to fulfill our natures, to liberate ourselves from the "bondage" of the passions, and, thus, to achieve what salvation is possible for us. What is truly good serves the endeavor (*conatus*) to preserve and perfect our being; what is genuinely evil frustrates that endeavor, preventing our achieving the power (or "virtue") needed to be truly happy. We should note, perhaps, that Spinoza was not an ascetic or anti-pleasure and wrote, "*Pleasure in itself is not bad but good.*" It is the unreasonable indulgence in immoderate pleasure that is dangerous and bad, because it leads to greater pain. While this ideal represents a difficult challenge, it appears that Spinoza himself achieved this sort of fulfillment and happiness in his own life, indicating that it is at least possible (II, 3–6, 189–191, 195, 201–205, 211–213, 217, 224, 231, 237–238, 244, 247–248, 250, 255, 266, 270–271, 337).

5.9 Society

A striking feature of Spinoza's theory of society is the extent to which it agreed with that of Hobbes. We know that he owned and studied a copy of, at least, *De Cive*, so that influence is plausible. (One can also track similarities with Machiavelli's *Prince*, though those will not be highlighted here.) Like Hobbes, Spinoza was a naturalist, a monist (though of a different sort), an egoist, a determinist, an advocate of the fundamental significance of endeavors, power, and self-preservation, a secularist, a moral relativist, and a social contractarian. This, of course, is not to say that their social theories were identical. Recall his theory of endeavor (*conatus*) as our ultimate motivation: "*Everything . . . endeavours to persist in its own being.*" This is a statement of psychological egoism,

5.9 Society | **75**

descriptively claiming that we all, as a matter of fact, are thus motivated. But later he wrote that it is rational and natural that everyone should love himself, should seek what is truly useful to him, and should "endeavour as far as he can to preserve his own being." This is a statement of ethical egoism, prescriptively claiming that we all ought to be so motivated. Rather than arguing for the claim, he indicated that it is intuitively evident: "This is as necessarily true, as that a whole is greater than its part." So Spinoza is both a psychological and an ethical egoist. He also holds that in "the state of nature" there is no general agreement regarding "good and evil," and a person is "bound by no law to anyone besides himself." In the state of nature, there is no private property and no place for "justice and injustice." Obviously, this poses problems of insecurity and constant danger, and it is useful to people to establish stable, mutually supportive relationships. This clearly sounds a lot like Hobbes. When asked about this, Spinoza replied, in a letter, that, unlike Hobbes, he always preserved "natural right intact," only acknowledging in rulers as much right to rule as they had power in excess over that of their subjects (II, 136, 201, 214–215, 238, 369). We have already seen that, for Spinoza, virtue is synonymous with power; now we see that he thought that natural right is also equivalent to power – might makes right, as we say. His view of the state of nature is similar to that of Hobbes, but they have different theories of civil society.

Arguably Spinoza's most important writing on political society is the sixteenth chapter of his *Theologico-Political Treatise*. Remembering that God is identified with all of Nature, we notice that natural right is "coextensive" with the power of nature and also that "every individual has sovereign right to do all that he can," that the limits of a person's rights are the "limits of his power." Thus a person naturally has the "right" to seek and do whatever he thinks will serve his own self-interest – and to acquire whatever he wants by any means that seem likely to prove effective, including brute force. But acting according to the "laws of nature as a whole" is not necessarily following the "dictates of reason," so that interpersonal hostility and dreadful insecurity loom as awful problems. We must learn to follow the "dictates of reason" and to cooperate peacefully with other people. Here, for Spinoza (as for Hobbes), is where the social contract becomes important. We agree to respect others, to refrain from injuring them, and even to help protect them from harm. Such a "compact" is the foundation of political society. But it is only as validly binding as it proves to be useful. If a person can do himself more good than harm by breaking his word, it is rational for him to do so: "Everyone has by nature a right to act deceitfully, and to break his compacts, unless he be restrained by the hope of some greater good, or the fear of some greater evil." As a member of political society, a citizen transfers some of his right to the sovereign – whether that be a monarch or an assembly or the whole of the electorate – or, in other words, a portion of the use of his power. The sovereign can then use that transferred power as leverage to force members of society to obey the law, with criminal sanctions and the threat of punishment for disobedience. Thus lawful order can be established, as well as the societal security normally accompanying it. When the sovereign authority is the whole of the citizenry, it is a democracy. Spinoza exhibits a more positive attitude toward democracy than anyone else we have considered – or, for that matter, than any great philosopher of ancient, medieval, or Renaissance times. He said of it, "I believe it to be of all forms of government the most natural, and the most consonant with individual liberty"; it also comes the closest to maintaining the equality of the state of nature. While there was no justice or injustice in the state of nature, in a civil society, under the rule of law, "Justice consists in the habitual rendering to every man his lawful due," while "injustice consists in depriving a man . . . of what the laws, rightly interpreted, would allow him." The power of the state to enforce the laws is the ultimate warrant of sociopolitical justice. But, notice, the rule of law and rules of justice are only as strong as is the power to enforce them. If a citizen has the power to defy the sovereign, to break the laws, and to violate the social contract, then he also has the "right" to do so. Thus social stability should assure that people do not suppose they have so much power. Spinoza's twentieth chapter, advocating freedom of speech, was far ahead of its time (Kant would develop the ideas in the eighteenth century, and Mill in the nineteenth). He argued that government cannot effectively control its citizens' thinking, and trying to do so will only get it condemned as "tyrannical." Every person has a "natural right" to freedom of thought, "which he cannot abdicate even with his own consent." But, since free speech is a necessary condition of freedom of thought, it too cannot be denied citizens "without disastrous results." Indeed, that would violate a basic objective of good government, which is to enable (rather than forbid) citizens to develop their own minds securely and unmolested. While citizens should be free to criticize the established order, they nevertheless are obliged to obey the laws in their physical actions. Next, he argues that freedom of thought and free speech will never, in the long run, prove injurious "to the rights and authority of the sovereign power." In short, he holds that legal restrictions, backed up by penal sanctions, "should merely have to do with actions, but that every man should think what he likes and say what he thinks" (I, 200–208, 247, 257–265). This is a splendid articulation of the value of preserving free speech (but one with which Hobbes would disagree).

Spinoza was writing his *Political Treatise* when he died; although it was unfinished, it contained some provocative ideas. He makes it clear in its opening paragraph that he was writing like a political scientist and not like the idealists who "conceive of men, not as they are, but as they themselves would like them to be." (Here, we might note, he is in agreement with Machiavelli as well as with Hobbes.) He more fully develops the theory of "natural right" as power here than we have already considered. He argues that people associate to form political societies in order to combine their power and, thus, to reinforce their rights. There could be no wrongdoing "in the state of nature," but only unreasonable, potentially counterproductive actions. There are, essentially, three different forms of sovereign government, according to Spinoza – "democracy, aristocracy, and monarchy" – all of which he meant to analyze. Whatever form may be adopted, its rightful authority – for example, to lay down, interpret, and enforce laws or to wage war and make peace – extends only as far as its power. But the rightful exercise of authority is not the same as "the best way" of exercising it, which is relative to serving the chief end of the state, "which end is nothing else but peace and security of life." People are "not born fit for citizenship," but must be educated for it. Otherwise, they must be forced to obey or allowed to behave in ways that threaten a reversion to the dangers of the state of nature. Spinoza mentions Machiavelli as a theorist who explained how a monarch can manipulate the people and, thus, consolidate his power. But this sort of autocracy generates a kind of civic slavery, which is both undesirable and unstable. Because of the checks and balances among the rulers of aristocracies and, thus, a lesser likelihood of the abuse of power, Spinoza (unlike Hobbes) seemed to favor them over monarchies. Moreover, a decentralized aristocracy was deemed "preferable" to a centralized one for, basically, the same reasons. He had only written very few paragraphs on democracy when he died. In this form of government, freeborn citizens have a prima facie right to vote and hold public office. He did say that this right only extends to freeborn citizens "who are independent," thus excluding women and children. Children, of course, will normally mature and grow into such responsibilities. He admits that if women were capable of achieving independence, then, in theory, such civil rights could be extended to them; but he believed that, in fact, they are not (I, 287, 291–292, 296–301, 309, 311–315, 317, 377, 385–387). What Spinoza did not live long enough to develop was argumentation regarding the advantages and disadvantages of democracy. But, even so, when we combine his *Theologico-Political Treatise* with his unfinished *Political Treatise*, we get a remarkably progressive sociopolitical theory.

5.10 Review

This is clearly the strangest philosophy we have considered in depth here thus far. Like Hobbes, Spinoza was decried and vilified during his lifetime and for generations thereafter. His monistic panentheism – whether it strikes us as attractive or as unattractive – is wildly counterintuitive; while this does not prove that it is wrong, it is difficult to accept a view that flies in the face of common experience. The same can be said about his unusual "dual aspect" theory of humanity. There is a tension between his general determinism and his notion that we can, nevertheless, achieve a kind of freedom to the extent that we control our passions and follow a life of reason (there is considerable similarity to the Stoics here, by the way). But the determinism also undercuts his advice regarding a morally good life and a good society: if, ultimately, we have no free choice over how we are going to behave and interact, what is the point? Finally, if all values are merely a function of desire and all right reduces to power, then it would seem that we shall and should do whatever we rationally calculate is most likely to serve our own selfish interests. His progressive advocacy of democracy and tolerance is a fine contribution to intellectual history. But, overall, his philosophy leaves a great deal to be desired. Let us, then, consider another radical alternative.[2]

5.11 Another Perspective

Lady Anne Finch Conway (1631–1679) married the third Viscount Conway in 1651, and they had one child, who died of smallpox in infancy. She was instructed in philosophy by Henry More, a prominent Cambridge Platonist. She is best known for her book on *The Principles of the Most Ancient and Modern Philosophy*, written in English in the early 1670s and translated into Latin and published posthumously and anonymously in 1690.[3] She converted to Quakerism in 1677. Her philosophy is opposed to the panentheistic monism of Spinoza, as well as to the dualism of Descartes and Hobbes's mechanistic materialism. Leibniz owned a copy of her book and seems to have regarded it favorably.

Conway's only surviving treatise might be described as Platonic vitalism and exhibits the influence of Henry More. Like Spinoza, she starts with God, from whom all creatures are derived. Her God is pure spirit, non-composite, and eternal, "infinitely wise, good, just, mighty, omniscient, omnipotent, creator and maker of all things visible and invisible" in the realm of creation. God is infinite, immutable substance, "distinct from his creatures," such that none of them is a part of God or can become divine. This immediately sets her metaphysics in opposition to Spinozism. God is allegedly "most free," though not characterized by "indifference of will," since that would render God "changeable," which would defy divine perfection. So, even though she calls God "the most free agent, yet he is also above all the most necessary agent" (*Early*, 232–233, 235–236), his free action being necessitated by the divine nature (which sounds similar to Spinoza).

As God and creatures represent two distinct forms of substance – the former immutable and the latter mutable – Christ represents the third sort, "a middle being"; as both immutable and mutable, she avers, Christ is "a medium between God and the creatures." So, instead of Descartes's two types of substances or Hobbes's one sort of substance or Spinoza's single substance, Conway posits three

---

2 For more on Spinoza, see *Twelve Great Philosophers*, by Wayne P. Pomerleau (New York: Ardsley House, 1997), 174.

3 All references in this section will be to *Early Modern Philosophy: An Anthology*, ed. by Lisa Shapiro and Marcy P. Lascano (Peterborough, Canada: Broadview Press, 2022).

distinct kinds of substance. She explicitly rejects the panentheistic view that "there is but one being of which the creatures are real and proper parts" as absurd. She also believes in the "transmutation" of creatures into other creatures over the course of successive lifetimes and even of such "transmutation of things from one species into another" (as did Plato). Every substantial creature comprises "a body," which is the "more passive principle," and "a spirit," which is its "more active" principle (she compares this to the relation between female and male in a marriage). But there is no inert or "dead" matter, so that all bodies are characterized by spirit and are alive; this is a form of vitalism (239–240, 243–244, 246–251).

All creatures are more or less like God, whose "divine attributes are commonly and rightly distinguished into communicable and incommunicable" properties. Among the former are spirituality, life, goodness, justice, and wisdom; among the latter are independence, immutability, infinity, and absolute perfection. Unlike Hobbes, Conway sees God as pure spirit devoid of matter. Christ, as a "medium between God and creatures," does have a body, though she claims that "his body is of another substance than the bodies of all other creatures." Just as every creature's body is comprised of innumerable bodily parts, likewise every creature's spirit is comprised of innumerable spirits. No human soul can be transmuted into another individual, so that God's justice can insure that each gets rewards or punishments it deserves. Ultimately, body and spirit are substantially one in creatures (not radically opposed, as for Descartes), the former being grosser, more "condensed spirit" and the latter being more "subtle" and refined body (252, 254–255, 258–259, 262).

Conway is explicit in declaring her opposition to "the Cartesian philosophy" with its dualism that sees mere bodies as inert or "dead," but even more so "to Hobbes's opinion" that every real substance is material, and even more than that to the monism "of Spinoza," which "confounds God and the creatures" in its panentheistic metaphysics. She denounces the view "that God and creatures are one substance," the former being infinite and immutable and the latter finite and mutable (263–265). But she does not merely take issue with all three of these modern philosophers whose systems we have explored. She also develops her own imaginative alternative, which, though it may strike us as strange in its vitalistic notion that everything is alive, in some ways anticipates the far more influential system of Leibniz, which we shall soon consider.

6

Nicolas Malebranche

Source: Jean-Jacques MILAN/Wikimedia Commons/Public Domain

6.1 Overview

The influence of Descartes on seventeenth-century philosophy was so great that it is not surprising that Hobbes, Pascal, and Spinoza all reacted to his ideas before Malebranche, as would Locke and Leibniz after him. But, of these six who worked in the wake of Descartes, Malebranche was the one most fittingly called a Cartesian. Descartes was his primary philosophical source, although his departures from the master are both radical and fascinating. Thus, in covering his thought, especially in the areas of epistemology and metaphysics, we shall periodically refer to Descartes. More specifically, the influence of the earlier rationalist on this later one was greatest on the topics of knowledge, reality, God, and humanity, somewhat less on that of freedom, and

Modern European Philosophers, First Edition. Wayne P. Pomerleau.
© 2023 John Wiley & Sons, Inc. Published 2023 by John Wiley & Sons, Inc.

weakest on those of morality and society (where Descartes had rather little to say). Because Anglophone philosophy neglected Malebranche's thought for more than a couple of centuries, it may be difficult for us to believe that, for longer than a decade, he was arguably the most famous living philosopher.

6.2 Biography

Nicolas Malebranche was born in Paris on August 5, 1638, and died in Paris[1] on October 13, 1715 (so that the span of his life almost exactly coincided with that of King Louis XIV, France's "Sun King"). The factual details of his external life are less than exciting; as a philosopher-priest, he led the interior life of mind and spirit. He was the youngest of 13 children in a prosperous family. His father, also named Nicolas Malebranche, was a secretary to King Louis XIII; and his mother, Catherine, was a sister of a French Viceroy of Canada. He was a frail and sickly child, with a curvature of the spine and a sunken chest that caused him health problems. Thus he was privately educated until, when he was 16, he enrolled in the Collège de La Marche, where he studied scholastic philosophy and from which he graduated. His family hoped he would become a lawyer, but he went on to study theology at the Sorbonne. Like so many gifted seventeenth-century thinkers, he had a distinct distaste for the Aristotelian scholasticism that dominated European higher education at that time. After leaving the Sorbonne, in 1660, he entered the Oratory, a religious order founded earlier that century by Cardinal Bérulle (a friend of Descartes), studying Church history, linguistics, the Bible, and the works of Augustine, to whom the order was devoted. While Oratorians were allowed to study Descartes, they were forbidden to teach him (after all, some of his writings were placed on the Church's Index of Forbidden Books in 1663). Malebranche was ordained an Oratorian priest on September 14, 1664. That same year, he had a life-changing experience that would launch him on a new philosophical path. According to his first biographer (a Jesuit named Yves André), he visited a bookstall in Paris and saw a copy of the recently published posthumous work of Descartes, the *Treatise on Man*; he started reading it and became so overexcited with heart palpitations that he allegedly had to put it down in order to catch his breath. Our best guess is that what thrilled him was a sense of a correct scientific alternative to the stale Aristotelian scholasticism he had come to despise. At any rate, he spent the next decade of his life studying natural philosophy, in general, and the works of Descartes, in particular. He saw his scholarly vocation as being to synthesize Cartesianism and Augustinianism. He seems to have been a modest, conscientious, and pious man, quite kindly and gentle, except that he could be fierce in dealing with controversial polemics raised by his critics, such as Antoine Arnauld. He experienced frequent bouts of fever and suffered from chronic back pain. He chewed tobacco and was among the first coffee drinkers in Paris; and he was allegedly adept at billiards. He amassed a library of over a thousand volumes, almost half of which were works in science. In 1699, he was elected to the Royal Academy of Sciences, his inaugural address being a defense of Descartes's theory of color and the frequency of light (*Search*, vii–x).

---

1 References to Malebranche's work will be to *The Search after Truth*, by Nicolas Malebranche (hereafter called *Search*), trans. and ed. by Thomas M. Lennon and Paul J. Olscamp (Cambridge: Cambridge Univ. Press, 1997), to *Dialogues on Metaphysics and Religion*, by Nicolas Malebranche (hereafter called *Dialogues*), ed. by Nicholas Jolley and trans. by David Scott (Cambridge: Cambridge Univ. Press, 1997), to *Treatise on Ethics*, by Nicolas Malebranche (hereafter called *Ethics*), trans. by Craig Walton (Dordrecht: Kluwer, 1993), and to *Treatise on Nature and Grace*, by Nicolas Malebranche (hereafter called *Grace*), trans. by Patrick Riley (Oxford: Oxford Univ. Press, 1992).

In 1674, Malebranche published the first three books of *The Search after Truth*, his *magnum opus*, followed a year later by Books 4–6. This work, which went through several editions during his lifetime, established him as a significant Christian philosopher. In 1675, Leibniz, whom he may have previously met, visited him at the Oratory; in their brief subsequent correspondence, in 1679, Leibniz expressed admiration for Malebranche's two most distinctive doctrines, that we see all things in God and that bodies (including our own) cannot directly act upon our minds, while admitting that he could not agree with all of his views. Following the example of Descartes, Malebranche invited scholars to submit written responses to his work, and in 1678, he appended to the third edition a set of "Elucidations," partly triggered by criticisms. Arnauld was initially sympathetic to Malebranche, as a fellow Cartesian. But in 1680, Malebranche published his *Treatise on Nature and Grace*, which took issue with Arnauld's Jansenist views on grace and salvation. Arnauld, ever the sharp polemicist, denounced Malebranche. A fierce controversy between them developed, extending beyond Arnauld's death (in 1694). In 1684, Malebranche published his *Treatise on Ethics*, and then, in 1688, his masterful *Dialogues on Metaphysics and Religion*, in which the character Theodore explains his views to Aristes, often arguing for them and defending them against the objections of Malebranche's critics, represented by Aristes. Malebranche's *Dialogues* went through four editions in his lifetime. In 1690, Arnauld and his supporters had his *Treatise on Nature and Grace* put on the Church's Index of Forbidden Books, followed by his *Search after Truth*, in 1709. In June of 1715, Malebranche became ill while visiting a friend; he died in Paris, at the Oratory, on October 13, 1715. Hume exaggerated when he said that appreciation for the importance of his work was limited to his own country and his own age. It has persisted continuously (to this very day) in France. It was evident in British philosophy for about a century (Locke writing a book against him, Berkeley being accused of being a Malebranchean, and Hume himself mentioning Malebranche as a thinker to study as background for his own philosophy). It is true that Malebranche was largely neglected by Anglophone philosophers in the nineteenth and for most of the twentieth centuries; but in the 1990s, a revival got underway. Historically, for a few years in the 1670s and 1680s, between the death of Descartes and the publication of Locke's great works, he was arguably the most famous living philosopher. He has remained the most studied proponent of occasionalism (*Search*, xvi–xxiii).

6.3   Knowledge

At the very outset of his *Dialogues*, Malebranche has his primary spokesman, Theodore, declare that the method to be adopted in the pursuit of knowledge is that of philosophical rationalism, saying that they must not appeal to sense experience or the imagination but must utilize "universal Reason." This is not to deny the authority of faith in other areas but only to say that reason is the proper path to philosophical knowledge. As an Augustinian, Malebranche is committed to the reality of ideas. As objects of the mind, they exist (*Dialogues*, 3, 5, 8). But here he makes his first departure from Descartes[2] that we shall consider. (Because Malebranche is a Cartesian, a historical account of his thought must make frequent references to Descartes' writings.) Descartes had a representationalist theory of ideas, maintaining that ideas in our minds represent realities outside our minds; also, as we have seen, he believed we have three sorts of ideas, the innate ones of

---

2 As in our Descartes chapter earlier, references will be to *The Philosophical Writings of Descartes*, in three volumes, trans. by John Cottingham, Robert Stoothoff, Dugald Murdoch, and Anthony Kenny (Cambridge: Cambridge Univ. Press, 1984–1991); they will be made in text by volume and page numbers.

6 Nicolas Malebranche

reason, the adventitious ones of sensation, and the fanciful ones of imagination (II, 29, 26). For Malebranche, by contrast, all ideas, including those we think of as ours, are in God rather than in us, have a reality of their own, rather than being merely representative of other realities, and do not include ideas innate in humans. His most famous epistemological doctrine is arguably that of Vision in God: "For in terms of their intelligible reality all our clear ideas are in God. It is only in Him that we see them." He traces this notion back to Augustine and argues for it thus: we have ideas that are "eternal, immutable, and necessary"; but such ideas could only be found in an "eternal, immutable, and necessary" being, unlike our own, which is God. Aristes (the student) resists the strange notion that our ideas are located in God rather than in our minds, thinking that all of our general ideas must be formed by us from the more particular ideas derived from sense experience. Theodore distinguishes between "our perceptions," which are finite and limited, and infinite, unlimited ideas, which, as such, have "more reality." Malebranche seems to be using Augustine's theory of divine illumination as his inspiration here: how could our finite, time-bound, changeable minds ever grasp infinite, eternal, immutable ideas except by means of God's illuminating them? "They know nothing except by the light of the universal Reason which enlightens all minds," Theodore says. We see truths by means of light we cannot create. Malebranche takes this a step further, saying that the ideas whereby we see such truths are in God rather than, as Descartes thought, in us. The nature of such knowledge should make it obvious that epistemological empiricism's approach – based on sensation and imagination rather than on pure reason – is misguided and futile. The senses seem to tell us that fire is hot, ice is cold, sugar is sweet, hammers pounding metal are loud, and so forth; but reason tells us that such secondary qualities are not in the things themselves but are merely products of our perception of them. And, if anything, "our imagination and passions" are even less helpful in revealing the truth about reality (as Descartes also taught). Theodore distinguishes between two sorts of sciences – those, such as mathematical ones, that consider the relations among ideas and can lead to evident certainty, on the one hand, and those, on the other, such as meteorology, that consider the relations among things by means of their ideas, which cannot be clearly and distinctly certain, because they must presume "that things are similar to the ideas we have of them." (This is a distinction which, in the eighteenth century, Hume used to great effect, as we shall see.) The sorts of beings of which we can gain some knowledge are the same three as for Descartes: "God, or the infinitely perfect Being who is the principle or cause of all things; minds, which we know only through the inner feeling we have of our nature; and bodies, of the existence of which we are assured by the revelation we have of them" (more on each of these in later sections). We can achieve some metaphysical knowledge through reason, though some truths can be known only through faith; and, like Augustine, Malebranche accepts religious faith as a guide to philosophizing (*Dialogues*, 11, 16–17, 25–29, 32–33, 54, 68, 85–86, 91, 93, 154, 157, 265, 268, 283–284; cf. *Ethics*, 75, 83). Thus far, we have seen Malebranche developing a Cartesian, rationalistic epistemology, without appealing to any innate ideas and featuring that distinctive Vision in God theory.

In now turning to his longer, more demanding *Search after Truth*, let us start by noticing its subtitle: *Wherein Are Treated the Nature of Man's Mind and the Use He Must Make of It to Avoid Error in the Sciences*. Again these two epistemological topics are distinctly Cartesian. In the Preface, he comes out decisively against the empirical approach to philosophical knowledge. In his first chapter, he does a good job of indicating why, like Descartes, he thought it so important that we try to minimize error, explaining that he considers it "the cause of man's misery" and an obstacle to our well-being. The understanding is "that passive faculty of the soul" or mind that allows it to receive both rational perceptions and sensible ones. Unlike ideas, which are in God, our "perceptions of ideas" are in our own minds and can be distorted and erroneous. So how can we allegedly avoid error? "*We should never give complete consent except to propositions which seem so evidently true that we cannot refuse it of them without feeling . . . the surest reproaches of reason.*" This first rule of method corresponds to the Cartesian principle of clarity and distinctness. His second one sounds more Augustinian: "*We should never absolutely love some good if we can without remorse refuse to love it.*" The upshot of this second rule is that we should reserve our unqualified love for God, the greatest Good. He also cautions us against committing ourselves to accepting any philosopher's views – whether they be those of Aristotle, whose principles he dismissed as obsolete and useless, or those of Descartes, whose principles he thought were generally accurate and fruitful – uncritically and merely on authority. Thus a third rule is "*that one must never give complete consent, except to things seen with evidence*" except, of course, in matters of religious faith, which have their own sort of evidence. In some matters, including in practical areas such as ethics, medicine, and politics, we must settle for mere probability. But, like Descartes, he holds that, when we rashly and unnecessarily make judgments of the will beyond the bounds of the understanding, that is a "misuse of freedom" that opens up possibilities of error. Our perceptions are through three faculties of the soul – "by the pure *understanding*, by the *imagination*, and by the *senses*." And we are constantly subject to the undue influence of "our *inclinations* and *passions*." Thus we must beware of five sorts of errors: those of the senses, of the imagination, of the inclinations, of the passions, and of the understanding. In every case, as Descartes maintained, our wills are the agents of erroneous judgments, for which we are responsible. We must be particularly vigilant not to assume that things are as they appear or as we would wish them to be. Malebranche, while generally mistrusting the senses as avenues to the truth about reality, distinguishes between our judgments regarding what would come to be called (by Locke) primary qualities, such as those "concerning extension, figure, and motion of bodies," which bear "some measure of truth," and secondary qualities, such as those "concerning light, colors, tastes, odors," and so forth, which do not. Thus, for example, the table can rightly be judged to be oblong in shape but not to be intrinsically brown, though we perceive it as both oblong and brown. This partial skepticism might sound a bit like Montaigne; but, in fact, Malebranche condemned this French predecessor as "dangerous," in that his entertaining style might seduce a reader to accept his general skepticism as to the possibility of our ever knowing any truth at all; whereas Descartes used doubt as a pathway to certain knowledge, Montaigne ends up embracing doubt in a pernicious way (*Search*, xxxviii, xlii–xliii, 1–3, 10, 13–17, 23, 29, 32, 48, 184, 189–198). Thus far, Malebranche clearly is trying to help us avoid error and generalized doubt, to achieve the knowledge of truth, using the approach of pure reason.

Now let us dig more deeply into his theory of ideas and knowledge. First, what is an idea, as opposed to our perception of it? He wrote that, "by the word *idea*, I mean here nothing other than the immediate object, or the object closest to the mind, when it perceives something." Thus, when I perceive the table, the direct, immediate object of my mind is not the table itself but the idea of a table. I can perceive ideas, such as that of "a golden mountain," to which nothing outside the realm of ideas corresponds in fact. Our thoughts or perceptions are in our own minds and may or may not correspond to things outside our minds; but, in either case, the ideas that are the direct, immediate objects of our thoughts or perceptions are allegedly in God alone. What is the causal source of our thinking of or perceiving those ideas? He considers five possible answers, the first four of which he denied are correct. First, our ideas could come from the objects of which they are ideas, such as that table, with those objects mysteriously transmitting intelligible species into our minds, as the scholastics held; but how could a body, such as a table, actively transmit anything into our minds, including some mythological intelligible species that mysteriously "resemble them"? Second, some might imagine that our souls produce the ideas in some creative manner, as they do the fictitious notions of imagination, such as that of "a golden mountain"; but we want to deny that it is arbitrary to imagine that "a moving ball which strikes another" in some sense actually is involved in the communication of motion to that other ball, and to aver that we do not simply make it up. Third, some might suppose that God invents the idea in an ad hoc manner when creating the soul that thinks it or at the moment the soul thinks it; but it is implausible that all of us were born with a common set of "innate" ideas or that God plants ideas in our minds at the moment we shall think them, as this would violate the simplicity of divine activity. Fourth, it could be supposed that our souls acquire ideas by reflecting on their own perfections; but, as the soul cannot be oblong or brown, it could not derive those ideas from self-awareness alone. Hence, fifth, by a process of elimination, we can conclude that the remaining option is correct – "*That we see all things in God*" (indeed, this is the title of one of Malebranche's most famous chapters). On this view of Vision in God, our minds are directly linked to God, in whom they see or perceive all their ideas. But our minds' seeing ideas in God does not imply that they can see the divine essence, for it is infinite, while they are merely finite. Because the ideas are in the eternal, immutable mind of God, they "are real" rather than imaginary, even when (as in the case of "a golden mountain") nothing extramental corresponds to them. Our minds or souls are most intimately linked to God, and Malebranche endorses St. Paul's claim that "in Him we live and move and have our being" (though not in the literal, panentheistic sense of Spinoza). There are four different ways of knowing: first, we can know something in itself, as when we know God; second, we can know through ideas, as when we know bodies; third, we can know through the "inner sensation" of our own consciousness, as when we know our own souls or minds; and, fourth, we can "know" things "through conjecture," as when we "know" the minds or souls of other humans. (We might compare these to Spinoza's various ways of knowing.) We cannot know nothing, since knowledge always intends some object(s) or other. Knowledge is always objective, as are ideas, as opposed to our subjective perceptions; thus neither knowledge nor ideas should be identified with mere perception. Likewise, truth is objective, "a real relation, whether of equality or inequality," falsehood being nothing but the negation of truth. There are three sorts of truths: (i) those relating ideas to other ideas, (ii) those relating ideas to things, and (iii) those relating things to other things; examples, respectively, are (i) "that twice two is four," (ii) that something exists corresponding to the idea of the sun, and (iii) "that the earth is larger than the moon," rather than their being equal in size. Of the three, only truths regarding the relations among ideas are eternal and immutably necessary. Truths perceived directly and immediately are clear and distinct and indubitable even on the hyperbolic assumption of a Cartesian "evil genius"; by contrast, such a hypothetical scenario could put at risk beliefs requiring the use of memory, which require the warrant of a perfect, non-deceiving Creator. The mind knows some things, such as mathematical truth, "through illumination" (Augustine's influence is evident here) and others, such as its own existence and that of bodies, "through sensation": the latter sort of knowledge is more or less "confused," as opposed to the former, which is clear and distinct. In conclusion, the mind is oriented toward knowledge of the truth, its direct immediate objects being ideas rather than things, all of which it perceives "in God" rather than in the objects themselves (*Search*, 217–232, 234–240, 320, 322–323, 433–434, 480–481, 621, 628). This Vision in God doctrine is distinctly rationalistic (nonempirical).

6.4 Reality

Ultimately, the knowledge the mind seeks to achieve is of the metaphysical truth regarding reality. Early in the *Dialogues*, Theodore embraced the Cartesian substance theory of reality: "Everything that exists either can be conceived to exist on its own, or it cannot be conceived on its own"; the

6.4 Reality | 85

former is a substance, while the latter is some sort of modification of substance – think of a table and roundness, respectively, as examples. As we have seen, for Malebranche, ideas are importantly real; they are not substances but modifications of God's mind. As a good Cartesian, he is a dualist, believing in "a material world," inhabited by bodies, and "an intelligible world," inhabited by minds and spirits. Among the most important ideas, real but not comprehensible by us, is that of infinite intelligible extension, which, in the mind of God, is like the archetype of finite, sensible extension, which is a substance. Unlike Descartes, Malebranche does not believe we can rationally develop "an exact demonstration" of the material world of extended bodies, as God did not have to create it; so our knowledge of it must be based on supernatural revelation. Since it is not self-sufficient, it must have been freely created by God; and, like Descartes, Malebranche maintained that God's ongoing "conservation" of it amounts to its "continued creation." As the Vision in God doctrine is his most distinctive contribution to epistemology, so his "occasionalism," though not utterly original, is, arguably, his most distinctive contribution to metaphysics. Refusing to embrace the Cartesian theory of causal interaction among bodies, he holds that what appears to be a body causing an effect in another body is not what it seems. For example, when one rolling ball "strikes another ball at rest," he claims, the impact is not the direct, immediate cause of the second one's subsequent motion; rather, God is the direct, immediate Cause, using the impact as the "occasion" for moving the second ball. "Therefore bodies cannot move each other, and their encounter or impact is only an occasional cause of the distribution of their motion." God is the only true Cause of all effects in the world. Why would he make such a counterintuitive claim? Bodies are extended bits of matter, having figure and passively capable of being moved, but with no active powers of their own, so that there is no "necessary connection" between one body's being moved and the motions of any other body. But neither can our minds directly and immediately cause bodily motion; again, there is no "necessary connection," for example, between your wanting to raise your arm and the arm actually rising. So not only is all created reality utterly dependent on God, but all events in the world are as well: "All creatures are united only to God in an immediate union. They depend essentially and directly only on Him." Although Descartes's poor account of how two substances as different as body and mind could interact may have led Malebranche to abandon interactionism, it is a mistake to think that his occasionalism is merely an ad hoc solution to the mind–body problem; in fact, it functions here as a general, all-purpose account of causality. All causal relations among created substances (body to body, body to mind, mind to body, and mind to mind) go through God, who functions here as a central switchboard through whom all transacted calls must pass. Every created substance "is united immediately and directly simply to God alone" and not to any other created substance. This is, admittedly, a strange doctrine, whose strangeness tempts Aristes to draw the Spinozistic conclusion that we are all just part of God, who is nothing more than "the aggregate of all that is." Theodore sharply repudiates and rejects this panentheistic view of God as monstrous. For how could the Infinite be comprised of finite parts? He denounces the idea as "an appalling and ridiculous chimera!" This concern to dissociate himself from Spinozism shadowed Malebranche, who regarded it as a form of atheism (*Dialogues*, 7, 9, 15, 40, 94–96, 100, 112, 115–124, 150, 138; cf. *Ethics*, 45–48, and *Grace*, 197, 201–202). Let us, before moving on, quickly consider three observations. First, in his *Treatise on Man*, Descartes said that an event in our brain can serve as an "occasion" for our minds experiencing certain feelings and sensations (I, 103), though he did not develop this as a theocentric general theory of causation, as Malebranche did. Second, even if it is true that we cannot see any "necessary connection" between any event and any other (a crucial point that Hume would later exploit), it does not logically follow that there is none. And, third, we shall have to discuss how Malebranche handles the problem of human freedom this theory poses; for, if God is the only true Cause of everything, how can we, then, be responsible for anything?

6 Nicolas Malebranche

In the very first paragraph of the Preface to his *Search after Truth*, Malebranche subscribes to an Augustinian hierarchical theory of reality: "The mind of man is by its nature situated, as it were, between its Creator and corporeal creatures." (Curiously, there is no mention here of pure created spirits, such as angels, perhaps because we don't experience them.) He claims that it is the mind's special "union" with God that renders it superior to all bodies and the mind's "union with the body" that "debases man" and is the source of "all his errors and miseries." The two essential properties of extended matter are both passive – the capacity to be differently shaped and "the capacity for being moved." This is true of the human body as it is of a piece of wax. The human mind, as a spiritual substance, analogously comprises two faculties, those of "the *understanding*" and "the *will*." All of this, of course, is strikingly Cartesian. But, again, things get more complicated when we try to analyze the relationship between mind and body. They *seem* to interact; yet it is problematic how two created substances, so essentially different, could actually do so – a problem that drove Spinoza to deny that they are separate substances at all. Consider, for instance, an experience so common as (probably) to be universal: "I feel pain, for example, when a thorn pricks my finger; but the hole it makes is not the pain. The hole is in the finger . . . and the pain is in the soul." One can *say* that the (physical) pricking of the finger causes the mental feeling of pain. But how can one improve on the feeble Cartesian attempts to explain how this could possibly be? The answer, as we have seen, comes out of Malebranche's (in)famous theory of occasionalism. The thorn pricking the finger is, allegedly, the "*occasional*" cause of the mind's feeling pain, but God is the "true" (i.e. direct and immediate) Cause. Likewise, when you will to raise your hand, that is (allegedly) only the occasional cause of its rising, God being the true Cause. There is never "any necessary connection" to be found between the human "will and the motion of any body whatsoever." Even though we can say that a moving ball hitting a stationary one is the "natural cause" of the latter's subsequent motion, we should realize that a "natural cause" is "occasional," not "true." Because we cannot understand everything that would be involved in our raising our hand by our own will alone, he thinks, we cannot possibly be the true cause of any such action. He explains, "A true cause as I understand it is one such that the mind perceives a necessary connection between it and its effect." We can perceive such a "necessary connection" between God's infinite, omnipotent will and any such effect as a hand rising or a ball at rest being set in motion – but not between our will, sadly limited as it is, and any physical effect, or between any natural, physical cause and its effect. Therefore, it is God who is the "true cause and who truly has the power to move bodies" – not other bodies or the human will. Granting that this is a counterintuitive theory, where does it go wrong? Even the existence of bodies, contrary to what Descartes maintained, cannot be established as rationally indubitable, but is known through faith in divine revelation. Assuming that bodies do exist, our own is the one of which we can be most certain, on account of its special relationship to our soul. But since we commonly attribute such properties as color, odor, and taste to bodies (what would come to be called their "secondary qualities"), which reason tells us are in perceiving subjects rather than in perceived objects, how can we claim to know even that bodies, including our own, exist "merely on the testimony of the senses"? (Here Malebranche anticipated a key move that would later be made by Bishop Berkeley, as we shall see.) No, Malebranche concludes, we must settle for our knowledge of bodies being a matter of faith rather than of reason and for their being causally connected both to minds and to other bodies only through God. Meanwhile, if the reality of bodies is rationally problematic, that of "eternal, immutable" ideas, he asserts, is not, and to deny it is to invite skeptical Pyrrhonism and "the most dangerous error" of relativism. Likewise, any empirical philosophy based on sense experience, such as "the philosophy of Aristotle," dangerously leads to God's being regarded as superfluous, he feared, feeding the prejudices of everyday natural perception. Philosophy, at which Descartes was a master, should not be confused with experimental science, at which Newton was a master (*Search*, xxxiii, 2, 49, 448–450, 569–574, 620, 658, 660–662, 664, 668, 673, 676, 689, 716, 733). Experimental science can only reveal natural ("occasional") causes, while Cartesian philosophy can lead us rationally to discover the "true" cause of things, which, purportedly, is God. (Notice, before we turn to that topic, how Malebranche has made a couple of key, unjustified assumptions: that bodies, being passive, could never cause anything and that our minds could not cause anything without understanding how they do so.)

6.5 God

What Malebranche has to say about God, humanity, freedom, morality, and society is interesting enough, but flows out of his more distinctive theory of knowledge and reality. The second of his *Dialogues* is focused on the topic of God. It starts out with Aristes asserting that, since we "see all things in Him" and "nothing finite," including merely finite ideas, could adequately "represent Him," all we need do is think of God in order "to know that He exists." He then gives an argument purporting to show that God must necessarily exist: we have an idea of infinite intelligible extension – an idea which is "immutable, eternal, and necessary"; but a finite mind, such as ours – contingent, ever changing, and time-bound – could never be the ultimate causal source of such an idea, which could only be found in infinite Reason, which is God (notice the similarity between this argument and the reasoning of the third of Descartes's *Meditations*). Theodore observes that this idea of "infinite intelligible extension," which is "the archetype" not only of our actual world of material substances but of "an infinity of other possible worlds," helps us to know God's existence (*that* God is) but not to comprehend God's essence (*what* God is). It might suffice to let us know some of God's metaphysical attributes, such as omniscience, omnipotence, unity, and simplicity; but these attributes do not characterize even infinite intelligible extension, which is not itself a substance but is an idea in God. Thus the divine Substance, "the infinitely infinite infinite" is not to be reduced to that archetype idea, though encompassing it. While infinite intelligible extension is the archetype of all bodies, God, the infinite Being, "has no archetype" and thus cannot be adequately represented by any combination of finite ideas. Also, in creating us, God communicated some divine perfections but not the divine substance, so that our knowledge of God's essence must remain limited. Being infinite and eternal, God cannot be quite like us; for example, God's knowledge—having no past, present, and future—cannot be the result of discursive thought as is so much of ours; also, being perfect and immutable, God "cannot change His thoughts, His plans, His volitions" to improve them in any way. Also, despite the fact that the idea of infinite intelligible extension is in God, there is nothing "corporeal" about the divine nature; thus, God is omnipresent, though transcendent, which would be a contradiction if God were material. (This should suffice to show that Malebranche is not a Spinozistic panentheist, as he was accused of being.) Even though God transcends the world, created it, and could have chosen not to do so, in some sense, all of creation "is in God," in Whom, in the words of St. Paul, "we live, and move, and are" (Acts 17:28); this should be interpreted metaphorically, as God is transcendent and not reducible to the created world (avoiding panentheism). Ultimately, all the divine attributes, however, "are incomprehensible to the human mind" (a point on which, remember, Hobbes also insisted). We must be careful not to reduce God to the natural world, as Spinoza did, which Malebranche insists would be tantamount to atheism. Because God is perfect, we can know that God knows all truth and wills the good; but we should not presume to comprehend divine knowing or willing, particularly as we have limited understanding of our own. And the same is true of God's moral qualities – e.g. justice, goodness, mercy, and so forth. In the area of theodicy or the problem of evil, we must admit that this world of God's creation contains "many disorders." But God was free not to create any world at all. Also, in theory, God could have created another of the many possible worlds. But God could not act contrary to the divine nature, which is simple, so that, in practice, the world of God's creation had to be characterized by "simplicity and uniformity," which ours allegedly maximally is (this is a dubious claim). It must be an orderly world, operating in accordance with rational, general laws (*Dialogues*, 19–25, 128–133, 135–138, 140, 143, 145, 160–161, 163–164; cf. *Grace*, 116–120, 139, 158, 195) and not chaotic. This view, we might note, renders miracles problematic (though Malebranche wants to preserve their possibility), getting him into trouble with the Jansenists and, more importantly, with the Church.

In *The Search after Truth*, Malebranche embraces the traditional Cartesian and Christian conception of God as the unlimited, infinite Being. Like Descartes (II, 28–31), he thinks that our idea of the finite stems from that of the infinite (empiricists would argue for the other way around) and tries to prove the reality of infinite Being on the basis of our finite minds having an idea of the infinite. And, again, he proves the existence of God on the basis that only infinite Being could be the source of the idea of the infinite we (allegedly) have. He seems implicitly to employ an abbreviated version of the "ontological" argument (of the fifth of Descartes's *Meditations*) when he writes that "necessary existence is included in the idea of the infinite." Being infinitely perfect, it follows "that God is not a deceiver," as the will to deceive is an imperfection. But, then, we can rationally conclude that we must have a body and be surrounded by other bodies, as we cannot reasonably help believing that (notice how very Cartesian all this is). Still, we should not assume that any bodies necessarily are exactly as we perceive them to be through sensation and/or imagination, since these are often pathways to correctable errors. Because we rationally know eternal, necessary, immutable truths, such as those of mathematics, but are ourselves finite (contingent, changeable, and time-bound), our limited minds must (somehow) participate in universal Reason. But since "only the infinite and universal being" could contain "an infinite and universal reason," and since all creatures are finite, particular beings, there must be an infinite, universal Being; and that, of course, is God. Since the archetype idea of infinite intelligible extension could only be in infinite universal Reason, "God, then, contains bodies within Him." Here Malebranche unwittingly invites charges of Spinozistic panentheism, though he almost surely does not mean that any material objects are literally in God. For a Christian philosopher, committed to a rational approach to an infinitely perfect Creator, the problem of evil is serious: how could the world of God's creation contain so much evil, given the omniscience, omnipotence, and infinite goodness of the Creator? While God could, in principle, have created some other logically possible world lacking some of the things we consider evil, Malebranche thinks that this world (somehow) reflects the simplicity, uniformity, and lawful order that God's nature requires (two problems with this are that it is dogmatically asserted rather than compellingly argued and that, if taken seriously, it militates against miraculous exceptions to the laws of nature, as Malebranche did not wish to do.) Also, he claims, when we sin, it is our own doing, responsibility, and fault, never God's. (Again, this is problematic, given his tendency to make God the only true agent; we shall see his slick solution to this problem soon.) The "general laws" of the universe (*Search*, 241, 232, 481–482, 613–614, 624–626, 665–666, 668, 746; cf. *Ethics*, 47, 50), as God created it, are such that our moral actions are our responsibilities, not God's. Malebranche is walking a bit of a philosophical tightrope here between the logic of his position and the orthodoxy of Christian doctrine.

6.6 Humanity

Near the beginning of the *Dialogues*, Theodore seems to channel the *cogito* passage from Descartes (II, 17–19) in saying that I know that I exist as a mind or thinking thing whenever I experience myself thinking, but do not know that I exist as "a body" or as "a human being" comprised of body and mind. After all, it is not at all apparent that a body, which is essentially extended matter, could carry out the mental act of thinking. For I can conceive of thinking and states of consciousness without any necessary reference to matter or physical states. The thinking thing must be a non-extended mind or rational soul. "Thus my soul is not material." And if it is importantly related to a body, that will lead us to a dualistic philosophy of human nature. Also, if the mind or soul is, indeed, a separate substance, independent of bodies, then it would be reasonable to believe in its immortality. But this, thus far, only scratches the surface of human nature's essence, or "what I am," given that I am. Once the reality of the human body has been established, we have Cartesian dualism, and the issue of how it is related to the mind or soul comes into focus. Granting that, at times, your mind and body seem to interact, Malebranche has no better way to explain *how* this could happen than Descartes had, given substance dualism. If your best friend stabs your body and your mind feels pain and then suffers a sense of betrayal, there seems to be no "necessary connection" between what we call the cause and what we call the effect – at least we cannot find one. If only God is adequate for causing any effect, then the appearance of interaction is misleading in the mind–body relation. But, given the customary conjunction, the parallelism must be rationally explicable. So what better theory than that of occasionalism, that God causes you (i.e. your mind) to feel pain and a sense of betrayal on the *occasion* of the physical stabbing. (Of course, as we have seen, it is even more complex than that in that God is also the mediating causal link between the physical movements of the stabber and the physical result of a knife penetrating your body.) It all happens in accordance with the general laws of creation and divine providence, maintaining "a perfect uniformity" of phenomenal events in the world. "God never performs miracles, He never acts against His own laws by means of particular volitions, unless order either requires or permits it." This preserves the possibility of miracles, while minimizing their actual occurrences. But it is allegedly always the case that the natural cause is only an "occasional cause," as opposed to the ultimate true cause, which is God. In speaking of purely physical interaction – as opposed to that between body and mind – at least, Descartes did say that "*God is the primary cause of motion*," that is, its "general cause," as opposed to a "particular cause," such as a stabbing (I, 240). So Malebranche embraces Cartesian substance dualism in his theory of humanity: "Humans are composed of two substances, mind and body." But he rejects causal interactionism, subscribing, instead, to occasionalism. Whatever may be the actual relation between your mind and your body, each of them is more directly related to God than to the other. It appears that, through your body, your mind is related to your physical environment; but, in point of fact, your mind is related both to your body and to other bodies through God (*Dialogues*, 6–8, 34, 56–60, 66–67, 105–106, 108–109, 226; cf. *Ethics*, 114, 152, 170). So what are we, critically, to make of this? First, philosophically speaking, it is no worse a theory than the Cartesian pineal gland account. But, second, it is counterintuitive and, unlike the theory of interactionism, flies in the face of common sense. Third, it is difficult to see how it does not make God a deceiver, if God is the Creator that engineered this systematic illusion – and for what conceivable reason? And, fourth, would it not be preferable to accept dualistic interactionism while admitting that we do not understand how, exactly, mind and body interact in human nature?

We can now do a brief survey of what Malebranche says about humanity in *The Search after Truth*. On its second page, he endorses the Cartesian analysis of mind in terms of the primary faculties of "the *understanding* and the *will*." Through the former, we encounter ideas and pursue knowledge of the truth; by means of the latter, we experience free choices. Despite the distinct independence of body and mind, the former can indirectly influence the activities of both understanding and will. For certain "traces in the brain" establish habits or inclinations, some of which are "natural" and "very deep," while others are "acquired" and normally "not as deep." Thus, the desire for sexual intimacy might be an example of the former, while a desire for a good reputation might be an instance of the latter. Such habits or inclinations can tempt us to make bad choices (we shall discuss freedom in our next section). But, counterbalancing these is our natural "inclination for the good in general." Second, we also have a natural inclination for self-preservation. "Thirdly, we all have an inclination toward other creatures useful either to us or to those whom we love." These are all valuable to us in establishing and following moral and social values. As our understanding is oriented toward knowledge of the truth, our will is oriented toward choosing of the good. Likewise, our passions involve the inclination to preserve and satisfy our own bodies; and they can get us into trouble, when out of the control of reason. While the body and its passions are good, as God created us, because of sin, our minds can be "subjugated" to them in ways that defy proper order. "The soul is superior to the body, and, according to the light of reason, its happiness or unhappiness should not depend on the body." Here we see a negative attitude toward the body, which has a history in the tradition of Platonism, including Augustine's Christian version of it. Just as we cannot rationally demonstrate the existence of any body, including our own, so "we have no *clear idea* of our soul, but only *consciousness* or inner sensation of it," so that (contrary to Descartes) Malebranche thinks that "we know it much less perfectly than we do extension" (*Search*, 2, 102, 121, 268–269, 338, 341–342, 345, 559, 613, 633; cf. *Grace*, 153, 171). We experience the activities and operations of our own minds through inner sense, yet we have no adequate idea of the soul's or mind's essence. Curiously, as we shall see, this later led other modern philosophers to an increasing skepticism regarding knowledge of mind or soul.

6.7 Freedom

We should now confront the problem that occasionalism poses for freedom of choice. If God is the only true, real cause of any action relating anything to anything else in our world (whether both are bodies or both are minds or one is physical and the other mental), how can the human will be truly free in any way? And, if it cannot be, if human freedom is an illusion, then how can there be any place for human responsibility? That is the problem. Remember that the will is that faculty of the mind whereby it is oriented toward choosing the good. Freedom is *"the power that the mind has"* of turning the will from particular apparent goods to the ultimate universal Good, which is God. Without freedom, we would "always be deceived" into pursuing our passions and selfish inclinations. We must use our freedom to pursue the ultimate Good rather than settling for inferior, apparent goods. "We must try to make as much use of it as we can, that is never to consent to anything until we are forced to do so, as it were, by the inward reproaches of our reason." Now it may seem a bit peculiar to define freedom in terms of what "we are forced to do"; but this should not be taken literally and should be interpreted as being rationally convinced or persuaded. But the key word for solving our problem is "consent." No two substances can directly interact. But the will is not a substance (but a faculty of mind), and neither are its acts of consent and rejection themselves substantial. "In short, it is of the greatest importance to make good use of our freedom by always refraining from consenting to things and loving them until forced to do so by the powerful voice of the Author of Nature, which till now I have called the reproaches of our reason and the remorse of our conscience." Here we have direct control, and only here: we can choose to accept or reject any goods we conceive, and we can choose some goods over others. And, since sin is a matter of wrongful choice rather than of physical action, we (and not God) are responsible for our own sins. This is not to say that we can do without God's grace "as the Pelagians would have it"; but neither is it to say that God's grace irresistibly determines our choices, as the Jansenists suppose. The sins and errors resulting from our bad choices are nothing positive, but the privation of good (as Augustine taught). Free choice is a necessary condition of moral responsibility: "If we had no freedom, there would be no punishment or future reward, for without freedom there are no good or bad actions" (*Search*, 5, 10–11, 548–549, 553, 555, 669, 679; cf. *Ethics*, 83–85, 87, 89). This attenuated conception of free choice at least provides a platform for moral character and conduct.

6.8 Morality

Malebranche's theory of Christian ethics was about as conventional as his views on knowledge and reality were distinctive. Although, as we have seen, he worried about the body's potentially corrupting influence on the soul, he was not a puritanical ascetic. As he wrote in *The Search after Truth*, "Now, it cannot be doubted that pleasure is good and pain bad; of this we are inwardly convinced, and, consequently, the objects of our passions are genuine goods to which we should be dedicated in order to be happy." The danger, of course, is the immoderate pursuit of personal pleasure and the unreasonable avoidance of pain at all costs. Reason should inform us that God is our greatest Good and that the spiritual pleasures of the afterlife vastly outweigh the temporary physical ones of this life. This conviction should lead us to develop virtuous characters and to pursue right conduct. Thus, we can overcome our tendencies to selfishness and become compassionate. As Jesus of Nazareth preached a gospel of love, so Malebranche thought the moral life should be motivated by love. There is always a dangerous tension between our love of things of the physical world and the love of spiritual goods, so that we must be careful to use our sensible experiences to draw us closer to eternal Truth. God always draws us toward the love of our ultimate Good; but we must consent to God's grace, despite the distracting temptations of lesser goods. In principle, the choice between the love and pursuit of God and the love and pursuit of physical goods should be easy; but, because we have been corrupted by sin, we find it an ongoing struggle. We all naturally want to be happy. Yet, in our weakness, we too often misuse our freedom to choose inferior goods over our ultimate Good, which is God (*Search*, 76–77, 114, 349, 364, 367, 415, 418, 547, 579–580, 593–594, 657, 681–685; cf. *Grace*, 151, 157).

In his *Treatise on Ethics*, Malebranche gets more specific. Again, there is little new there, but let us briefly consider some highlights. Striving for moral perfection increases our sense of dignity, makes us more like God, and renders us worthy of happiness. We must strive to know our true Good, to love it above all else, and to feel enjoyment therein. This is our primary moral duty and the root of virtue, the principal moral virtue being the love for rational order. This will lead us to exercise our freedom properly by consenting to the best choices against the temptations of selfish, sensual concupiscence, moderating our passions, rather than foolishly indulging them. This requires "*strength*" of mind to seek the truth and "*freedom*" of mind to consent to it alone. Our moral duties ultimately stem from God and relate to divine wisdom, divine power, and divine love. We have moral duties to God, to others, and to ourselves; they are duties of love and respect (*Ethics*, 48–51, 53, 85–86, 89, 111–112, 137–139, 143–145, 171, 220–222). Like the rest of Malebranche's philosophy, his ethics is theocentric (except for that fact, it bears a resemblance to that of Kant, as we shall see, without the carefully argued development) and quite Augustinian in character.

6.9 Society

As Malebranche had little to say about morality that was either new or impressively well argued (as was true of Descartes), the same tends to be true on the topic of society (again, as was true of Descartes). But, in his *Treatise on Ethics*, he did discuss our duties to other members of society. As a Christian, he asserted that God created us to associate with other humans in society under the rule of Reason. We were made for both temporary society in this life and eternal society in the afterlife; the former is oriented toward mutual comfort and interpersonal relationships in the physical world of bodies, while the latter is oriented toward the eternal communion of blessedness with God. (We might notice here the inspiration of Augustine's notion of the secular city of man versus the spiritual city of God.) Our duty "to love one another" practically involves a willingness to try to help other people. The love we owe other members of society is that of benevolence – wishing them "happiness and perfection" and being willing to try to help them achieve those goods. The honor or respect we owe other people is a matter of valuing their excellence as persons or the moral perfection, actual and potential, of their characters. Membership in civil society can, of course, involve risks as well as benefits – e.g. risks of corruption. Nevertheless, very few people are self-sufficient and "can stand a life of solitude." The desire to associate with good people is natural and healthy. "Hence we need to live with others. But we need to choose those who are reasonable, or at least capable of hearing Reason" and responding appropriately. The esteem we owe others is relative to their "excellence and perfection." But contemptuously to withhold esteem from a person is hurtful, and only nothingness should be held in contempt, so that some degree of "esteem is a duty we ought to render to all men." While we are under no obligation to be personally involved with all members of society, we should make ourselves worthy of being loved and respected by others. "What then are the qualities which make us lovable?" They are not the superficial, shallow qualities of celebrities, such as seeming erudite, sophisticated, wealthy, upper class, and physically attractive. It is, rather, a matter of being (or, at least, seeming to be) a good person. Thus, one who is dishonest or cruel in relation to other members of society is not likely to be seen as lovable or to be loved. Someone who is rich and powerful, though feared by others, is not necessarily lovable – but may become so by using wealth and power generously, to help and protect others, trying to make them happy. With Jesus of Nazareth as a role model, we can strive to be good members of society by maintaining a "constant and true friendship" with others. In the area of political society, citizens owe their rulers respect and obedience, to the extent that their authority is legitimate. What, exactly, this entails in the way of specific behaviors will "depend on laws and customs observed in a state." The two sorts of sovereign powers in this world, to whom respect and obedience are normally owed, are civil authorities, like the king, and ecclesiastical ones, like a bishop. A prince's duty is to establish and maintain peace for a state and the people's welfare; that of a bishop is to enlighten and serve the people in his Church. It is the duty of good political and religious authorities, normally, to consider and follow established rules of state and Church, respectively, rather than arbitrarily disregarding them. Subjects "ought to obey blindly" what Church and state authorities dictate, so long as only their own self-interest is at stake. Where civil and ecclesiastical authorities disagree, we must follow our informed consciences. The same is true, to varying degrees, of the respect and obedience we owe lesser authorities, such as local magistrates and parish priests (*Ethics*, 168–173, 214–218, 187–191). Again, we see nothing particularly new or well argued here, and it is generally quite compatible with the views of Augustine and Descartes. There is no sense of civil or human rights to be found. It seems that, so long as we try to love and respect other members of society and obey lawful authorities, details of social structures do not much matter.

6.10 Review

Given the commitments of Malebranche's intellectual biography, it should not be surprising that his own philosophy involves an attempted synthesis of Augustinian and Cartesian elements. His two distinctive contributions are the Vision in God doctrine in epistemology and his occasionalist theory of causation. The former, inspired by Augustinian illumination, is an attempt to answer a key Cartesian problem – how can the finite human mind contain ideas of the infinite? The latter addresses the Cartesian problem of how two independent created substances can possibly interact. Neither contribution has garnered much support or offered cogent argumentation. (Hobbes avoided both problems by denying that we have any positive idea of infinity and that any substantial soul is real, reducing ideas to empirical sources and reality to material substance.) So why, we might wonder, even consider Malebranche? There are three reasons. First, his ideas were historically influential – especially on Locke, Leibniz, Berkeley, and Hume. Second, he serves as an example of how logic, divorced from common sense experience, can lead us to strange destinations. And, third, to the extent that his thought is unconvincing, we can learn not to accept it but, rather, to seek for a more adequate system elsewhere – as we are now about to do.

7

John Locke

Source: J. Chapman, 1811, after Sir G. Kneller, 1697./Wellcome Collection/Public Domain

7.1 Overview

It would be difficult (though, of course, possible) to exaggerate the importance of John Locke in the history of modern European philosophy. Indeed, after Descartes, he was probably the most important of seventeenth-century philosophers, the most influential Christian common-sense

Modern European Philosophers, First Edition. Wayne P. Pomerleau.
© 2023 John Wiley & Sons, Inc. Published 2023 by John Wiley & Sons, Inc.

empirical realist of that century. His *Essay Concerning Human Understanding* was the first great work of comprehensive, systematic empirical epistemology, which would dominate the field for almost a century, leading to the profound reactions of Berkeley and Hume, which would, in turn, precipitate the work of Kant. His published letters on toleration became the standard for Enlightenment thought on that key issue in the eighteenth century. His *Two Treatises of Government*, especially the second one, became a manifesto of Whig liberalism, massively influential on English, American, and French political thought. No other thinker of that time so successfully challenged Cartesianism and shifted the philosophical agenda away from its dominance.

7.2 Biography

Locke was born in the Somerset village of Wrington, near Bristol, England, on August 29, 1632 (the same year as Spinoza), the first of two sons. His parents, John and Agnes Locke, were landed gentry and Puritans. His father, a county lawyer, served as a cavalry captain in the parliamentary army during the civil war against King Charles I. Thanks to the influence of his father's commander (who was a Member of Parliament), he was admitted to the prestigious Westminster School in London in 1646. There he learned Greek, Latin, and Hebrew under strict Puritan tutelage; his father was also very strict with him when he was a boy, although he relaxed his discipline as the boy approached manhood, until they actually became friends (Locke admired the fact that his father once apologized to him for having struck him once when angry). In 1652, Locke left Westminster for Oxford University, where he experienced the same useless, tedious decadent Aristotelian scholasticism that Hobbes had experienced there – and with the same reaction of distaste. He got a Bachelor's degree there in 1656, and a Master's degree in 1658, being elected to a senior studentship (like a fellowship) that same year. He became a lecturer in Greek there in 1660 and in Rhetoric in 1663. Around this time, he wrote his *Essays on the Law of Nature*. It was not clear what career he wanted to pursue. There was, no doubt, some thought given to his taking holy orders; but he decided to study medicine. He worked with the great experimental scientist Sir Robert Boyle. Always in delicate health himself (like Descartes, Pascal, and Malebranche in that respect), while still in his twenties he had lost all the members of his immediate family – first his mother, whom he described as pious and affectionate, then his father, and then his younger brother. Though elected a fellow of the Royal Society in 1668, he was unable to get his medical degree until 1674 and then chose neither to practice medicine publicly nor to teach it.

By then he had happened to meet Lord Ashley (who, in 1672, became the first Earl of Shaftesbury) at Oxford. They hit it off extremely well, becoming close friends. In 1667, Locke joined Ashley's household as private physician, gradually becoming his researcher, secretary, and advisor, as well as tutor to his son. Ashley, one of the richest men in England, was also rapidly gaining political influence. Locke helped Ashley write a constitution for the Carolina colony in America, calling for religious toleration. In 1672, Ashley became Lord Chancellor of England, under King Charles II. But, by 1675, Locke's health had so deteriorated that he needed to go to France to recuperate. Staying there until 1679, he seriously encountered Cartesianism, as well as anti-Cartesianism. While never becoming a Cartesian himself, he found the approach of Descartes far more fruitful than the barren Aristotelianism he had rejected at Oxford. After returning to England, he reentered Shaftesbury's service. But the latter's political intrigues were already dangerous. Shaftesbury conspired to pass a bill that would exclude Catholics from the throne. Because Charles II had no legitimate heir, his Catholic brother, James, was next in line to succeed him. The bill failed; Shaftesbury was arrested in 1681 and imprisoned in the tower on charges of treason, but acquitted by the grand jury. A plot to assassinate Charles and James also failed, and Shaftesbury fled for his life to Holland in 1682, dying there early in

1683. Locke stayed in England a few more months until the plot was discovered, when he also fled to exile in Holland (in the summer of 1683). The king had Locke's studentship at Oxford revoked. Locke was denounced as a traitor. The government demanded that the Dutch extradite him to England, but the Dutch ignored the demand. For a while Locke lived in hiding under the pseudonym of Dr. van der Linden. While in Holland, Locke met and befriended Prince William and Princess Mary of Orange.

In 1685, Charles II died and was succeeded by his brother, the Catholic James II. Rebels united around the Duke of Monmouth, the illegitimate but Protestant son of Charles. Thanks to the efficiency of the king's spies, Monmouth's rebellion failed, and Monmouth himself was executed for treason. There is no evidence that Locke himself was actively involved in any of these conspiracies, though we can safely assume that he was opposed to having a Catholic on the throne, who might be sympathetic to Catholic France. At any rate, James was so unpopular that he alienated his supporters. Parliament rose up against him in the so-called Glorious Revolution of 1688, which was allegedly "bloodless" (at least in England), James abdicating and fleeing for his life into France without any fight. Parliament invited Prince William of Orange to become King of England. While in Holland, Locke completed his great *Essay Concerning Human Understanding* (begun in the previous decade) and wrote and published a *Letter Concerning Toleration* (1689), as well as writing his *Two Treatises of Government*. William accepted the invitation to become King of England, and Locke subsequently accompanied the Princess of Orange, soon to become Queen Mary, on her voyage to England. In 1690, Locke's *Essay* and *Two Treatises* were published. Locke was offered an ambassadorship; but, mindful of his delicate health, he prudently declined, instead accepting less demanding offices at home. While living in London, he often visited Oates, the country estate of Sir Francis and Lady Masham. The latter had been Damaris Cudworth before marrying. She was the well-educated, philosophically capable daughter of Ralph Cudworth, one of the most prominent of the Cambridge Platonists, who favored rationalism and liberal Christianity and were opposed to Hobbes, to materialism, and to any mechanistic account of nature. Despite the fact that Locke was a generation older than she and the fact that she was often critical of Locke's philosophical views (for example, on innate ideas), they seem to have been in love – exchanging love letters and romantic verses. But, while Locke was in exile in Holland, she married the widowed Sir Francis, becoming Lady Masham and taking up residence at Oates. In 1691, at her invitation, Locke made Oates his primary residence for the rest of his life, being occasionally visited by such prominent friends as Isaac Newton, whose work he greatly admired. Locke published two more letters on toleration (1690 and 1692), wrote *Some Thoughts Concerning Education*, published in 1693, published a second edition of the *Essay* (in 1694), and wrote *The Reasonableness of Christianity*, published anonymously in 1695. He carried on a controversial exchange with Edward Stillingfleet, the Bishop of Worcester, who attacked his ideas. Two more editions of the successful *Essay* were published during his lifetime. In 1700, in poor health, Locke retired from all offices, remaining in retirement at Oates until October 28, 1704, when he died, while Lady Masham was reading to him from the Psalms. An incomplete fourth letter on toleration, his critique of Malebranche, and the unfinished *Conduct of the Understanding* were all published anonymously.[1] By the time of his death, he was quite famous, and his reputation would only grow.

---

1 References to Locke will be to the following works: *An Essay Concerning Human Understanding*, by John Locke, in two volumes (hereafter called *Essay*), with references by volume and page numbers (New York: Dover, 1959), *Two Treatises of Government*, by John Locke (hereafter called *Treatises*), ed. by Thomas I. Cook (New York: Hafner, 1947), *Locke on Politics, Religion, and Education* (hereafter called *Politics*), ed. by Maurice Cranston (New York: Collier Books, 1965), *Political Essays* (hereafter called *Essays*), by John Locke, ed. by Mark Goldie (Cambridge: Cambridge Univ. Press, 1997), and *Works of John Locke*, Vol. IX (hereafter called *Works*), in 10 volumes (Germany: Scientia Verlag Aalen, 1963).

7.3 Knowledge

If one can fairly distinguish between an epistemologist and a philosopher who does epistemology, Locke is arguably the first great epistemologist; if one can distinguish between a great work of epistemology and a great work that includes some epistemology, his *Essay Concerning Human Understanding* is arguably the first great work of epistemology. In covering it here, after a brief consideration of its "Epistle to the Reader" and "Introduction," we shall focus on key elements of each of its four books, dealing, respectively with (i) his critique of innatism, (ii) his own empirical theory of ideas, (iii) his views on language, and (iv) his treatment of certain knowledge and judgments of probability. In the "Epistle," Locke indicates that the occasion leading to his writing the *Essay* was a discussion with "five or six friends" that reached a dead end due to their perplexity over human knowledge and its limits. (One of those friends tells us that the subject of the discussion was the "principles of morality and revealed religion.") Locke wrote the book over a long period of time and realized that it was extremely long and needed editing, commenting, "But to confess the truth, I am now too lazy, or too busy, to make it shorter." He modestly disclaims any pretense of being one of the "master-builders" of knowledge, such as Boyle or "the incomparable Mr. Newton" but expresses the hope that he might function "as an under-labourer in clearing the ground a little and removing some of the rubbish that lies in the way to knowledge." In the "Introduction," he writes that this must be acknowledged to be a worthwhile topic, as it is human understanding that elevates us above the beasts. In setting forth his own purpose, he gives us an excellent definition of epistemology – "to inquire into the original, certainty, and extent of *human knowledge,* together with the grounds and degrees of *belief, opinion,* and *assent*" – adding that he intends to employ a "historical, plain method," as opposed to one that is abstract and technical, and indicating the steps he would use. He warns that he will use "the word *idea*" in a broad sense, referring to "whatsoever is the *object* of the understanding when a man thinks," expressing his confidence that we all experience ideas for ourselves before he begins considering their origin (*Essay*, I, 9–10, 14, 25–28, 32–33).

In Book I, he develops a critique of the theory of innate ideas and principles we have seen in Descartes and shall see again in Leibniz. Rationalists (including, by the way, Ralph Cudworth and other Cambridge Platonists) often employed the doctrine of innate ideas and innate principles. The latter can be either speculative – such as the Law of Identity, that everything is what it is, and the Law of Non-Contradiction, that the same thing cannot be and not be in the same respect at the same time, which are two axioms of Aristotelian logic – or practical. If speculative principles were universal, he argues, then all humans would be aware of them, so that they had "universal assent." But such is not the case, as "children and idiots" are not aware of them. Hence such fundamental principles cannot be innate. Nor does it suffice to evade this argument by objecting that our knowledge of such principles is *"implicit."* For what meaning could we attach to this except that the human mind can somehow potentially acquire such knowledge; for that indicates that it is not innately actual. Nor does the case for practical innate principles fare any better, since they also fall "short of an universal reception" by all humans. Even so basic a one as that we should honor our commitments and fulfill our contracts is not "universally received"; and where it is practiced, it is often regarded merely as a matter of useful social convenience, motivated by the carrot of hopes for rewards and the stick of fear of punishment. Locke refers to a typical "Hobbist" as one who might confess to such motivation. Also, in order for there to be innate principles, they would need to involve innate ideas. But why should we imagine that we are born with even the most basic of ideas, such as those of *"impossibility* and *identity"*? What idea is more seminal than "the idea of *God"*? In order for that idea to be innate, it would need to be universal in all human minds. But people in different cultures have different ideas of God and some none at all (*Essay*, I, 38–42, 56, 58–59, 64, 66, 69, 92–93, 95, 98, 103, 105–106, 114; nor will Malebranche's theory suffice – that we perceive ideas in God rather than in our own minds – for Locke's extended critique of this view, see *Works*, 211–255). No, we must seek the origin of our ideas elsewhere.

As we directly and immediately experience the ideas in our own minds and have (presumably) ruled out the possibility of any of them being innate, it must be the case that all are somehow acquired. But if the mind is initially like "white paper, void of all characters, without any ideas" (the *tabula rasa* theory), then where do we get the ideas we have? Locke's answer is, "in one word, from experience." This must be the source of all of our ideas. But what sort of experience, then? The empirical answer is that of external sensation and internal reflection. Through the former, we get the idea, for example, of yellow; through the latter, we derive that of doubting. These are the only sources of our ideas. We can also distinguish between "simple" ideas, such as "softness and warmth," and "complex" ones, such as a "piece of wax," which are comprised of simple ones in combination. In addition to such simple and complex ideas of sensation, there are also simple and complex ideas of reflection, such as those of anger and of the mind itself. There are four sorts of simple ideas: (i) those acquired by a single sense, such as the ideas of red and loud; (ii) those acquired by more than one sense, such as those of shape and motion; (iii) those acquired from reflection alone, such as those of remembering and envy; and (iv) those acquired by a combination of sensation and reflection, such as those of unity and existence. A most important idea of the first sort is that of solidity, which we rightly see as constituting the essence of bodies. We all experience this idea on account of our feeling bodies. If anyone doubts that he grasps this idea, Locke challenges him to "put a flint or a football between his hands, and then endeavour to join them, and he will know." Simple ideas of the second sort that are basic to our experience of bodies are those "of *space* or *extension, figure, rest,* and *motion*." Simple ideas of the third sort arise from our reflecting on the operations of our own minds; these include, in particular, the ideas of the "thinking" power of the Understanding and the power of "volition" of the will. Simple ideas of the fourth sort include those of "*pleasure*," "*pain*," "*power*," "*existence*," and "*unity*." Every complex idea must be comprised of simple ideas. Through our senses, we experience three aspects of physical objects: (i) "*primary qualities*," which exist in bodies themselves; (ii) "*secondary qualities*" that are in perceivers of a body, due to its power to affect them; and (iii) the "powers" that bodies have to affect other bodies. Examples of these three, respectively, are the shape of a piece of wax, its color, and its capacity to stick to surfaces. It is important that we recognize the primacy of perception in the acquisition of ideas: since all reflection is stimulated as a result of external and/or internal sensation, "perception is the first operation of all our intellectual faculties, and the inlet of all knowledge in our minds." Once we have experienced perception, memory, "the storehouse of our ideas," is crucial to our ability to process the ideas thus acquired. But, of course, memory has its shortcomings and limitations; for example, sometimes it fails us, and at other times it operates very slowly. Thus far, we have focused on the mind as passive. But the mind can also compare and contrast ideas, as well as combining them. Also, as a result of perceiving similarities among ideas, the mind can abstract those similar features, ignoring their differences, forming "general" ideas that can represent the more particular ones. Thus, after perceiving bulldogs and boxers, collies and terriers, beagles, and so forth, your mind can abstract their common features, not focusing on their specific differences, to form the general idea of a dog. Such "general ideas" are crucially important for our reasoning and result from an active operation of the understanding. So prior to experience, the human mind is like a "*dark room*" or an unlit "closet" with the senses being like "windows" through which light may enter. We can form complex ideas of substances, such as pencils and pieces of paper, modes, such as writing, and relations, such as that between writing and reading.

Some ideas, such as that of infinity, are so remote from concrete experience as to be difficult to comprehend; that one is best analyzed as a negation of limits rather than as a positive idea. The idea of power is another challenging complex idea; the "billiard-stick" has the active power to move the billiard ball, and the ball has the passive power to be moved – both involving "some kind of *relation*." Two basic powers of the human mind are the power of the Understanding to think and the power of volition in the Will. Understanding and will are sometimes called "*faculties* of the mind." Particularly problematic are our complex ideas of substances. Not being able to imagine how the qualities and powers we perceive could possibly "subsist by themselves," we suppose that they subsist in something substantial, such as a table or a mind. But as we experience only the qualities and powers and not the substance itself, therefore we can only know the former and should admit that the latter is never directly experienced and that "we do not know what it is." (This is going to turn out to be a devastating move in modern epistemology, leading to increasingly dramatic conclusions on the parts of Berkeley, Hume, and Kant.) For Locke, this is as true of the spiritual substance of mind as of the physical substance of body. Other important ideas are those of "*identity* and *diversity*," which the mind acquires by the process of comparing and contrasting. In analyzing our various ideas, like Descartes, Locke holds that "some are *clear* and others *obscure*; some *distinct* and others *confused*." In addition, ideas can be "real or fantastical," "adequate or inadequate," and either "true or false." But all of our simple ideas must be real and adequate, he added. Locke adopts a correspondence theory of truth: ideas are "true" when they conform to the objects they supposedly represent (*Essay*, I, 121–124, 141, 144–146, 148, 151, 156–160, 164, 169–174, 191, 193, 198, 204–207, 211–217, 276, 289, 308–314, 390–397, 439, 486, 497–498, 502, 515).

As ideas can more or less accurately represent objects, so words can more or less adequately express ideas. In Book III of his *Essay*, Locke develops a theory of language as part of his epistemology. In order to communicate our thoughts to one another effectively, we need verbal language (body language and facial expressions not getting us very far). But verbal language is also very useful to us as a memory aid, most of us finding it easier to recall something we can put into words. All the objects of our perceptual experience are particulars. Yet, as we have seen, it serves our purposes to have general ideas. Likewise, it is helpful to us to have general terms, such as "school" and "running" to communicate with one another. "Words become general by being made the signs of general ideas: and ideas become general, by separating them from the circumstances of time and place, and any other ideas that may determine them to this or that particular." General terms (and universals) are creations of the understanding rather than realities existing outside the mind. We have seen how the understanding forms abstract ideas. "And when general names have any connexion with particular beings, these abstract ideas are the medium that unites them." A "*nominal essence*" is an abstract idea of similar qualities shared by particulars of a certain sort. For example, the nominal essence of a tree, in general, is the abstract idea of a plant, with roots typically set in soil, with a trunk leading to branches that can have leaves or needles; these qualities are shared by pines, firs, maples, hawthorns, chestnuts, oaks, and so forth. Thus the nominal essence defines what a class of particulars has in common. Now the name of a thing and its nominal essence tend to be so closely associated that, for example, we would not ordinarily (e.g., unless we were speaking metaphorically) call a particular object a "tree" unless it met the requirements of that nominal essence. By contrast, "*real essences*" are whatever account for particulars sharing those similar qualities – for example, what is it about trees themselves (not merely our concept of them), as existing particulars outside the mind, that accounts for their having those perceptible qualities comprising the nominal essence? Locke's bold (non-Aristotelian) claim is that we cannot experience, and thus cannot know, the real essences of things. This claim fits with his denial that we can know substances as they are in themselves – all of which will entail dramatic conclusions regarding our ability to know reality. Nothing is essential to an individual's being some sort of particular or other; for example, when a tree is chopped down and cut into twigs and firewood, though no longer a tree, it has been rendered into various forms of wooden particulars. We should now acknowledge that not all words name ideas in the understanding. There are also words that relate ideas and propositions. For example, "my cat is a mammal" uses a form of the verb "to be" to relate the subject (a word representing a particular) to "a mammal," which is a general term; when I say "my dog is not an amphibian," the negative form of that verb relates the subject (a word representing a particular) by negation to another general term. Locke calls such relational words "particles." While language is quite valuable to us for the twin purposes of remembering our thoughts and communicating them to others, for both social purposes and in the quest for true knowledge, Locke admits that it is an imperfect tool that can obscure, distort, and deceive if we are not careful (*Essay*, II, 8–9, 14–17, 21–22, 24, 27–29, 56, 58–60, 98, 104–105). Still, despite its limitations, we have no ready, preferable substitute for language.

In Book IV, Locke develops his theory of certain knowledge and probable judgments. As most of our ideas can be linguistically represented by words, many of our concepts can be interrelated to constitute judgments of knowledge and/or probability. As a modern empiricist, Locke is committed to the notion that we can only know what we experience. But, since the only direct, immediate objects of the mind are its own ideas, it follows that they serve as limits to what we can know. Indeed, he defines knowledge as "nothing but the *perception of the connexion and agreement, or disagreement and repugnancy, of any of our ideas.*" While he was not the first to hold such a view, the bold way in which he explicitly stated it proved to be historically decisive. To the extent that he was consistent here, what follows is that Locke could not directly know any body, including his own, any mind, including his own, or any deity, including his own – but only his own ideas of them. Locke is no friend of skepticism; yet unwillingly – and, probably, unwittingly – he paves the road to Hume (as we shall see in the course of this narrative). Locke goes on to show that there are "four sorts" of knowable "agreement or disagreement" among our ideas: "I. *Identity*, or *diversity*. II. *Relation*. III. *Co-existence*, or *necessary connexion*. IV. *Real existence*." The most basic of these is the first, without which, he suspected, no knowledge would be possible at all. Indeed, the very Aristotelian laws of identity and noncontradiction require them. Thus one white thing is identical in color to another, as one round thing is in shape to another; but no white thing is identical in color to any red thing, nor is any round thing identical in shape to any square one. Second, any perceived body comprises some color in relation to some shape, and white is closer to beige than to red, as a square thing is closer to a rectangle in shape than to a circle. Third, when we think of, say, gold, we think of certain qualities, such as a certain color, weight, and malleability, as coexisting in the golden substance. And, fourth, we cannot help believing in the real existence of our own minds, as many of us are likewise committed to believing in some sort of God. We can also distinguish between "*actual knowledge*" the mind has when focused on its own known ideas and "*habitual knowledge*," which is "lodged" in a person's memory even when not the object of attention. Sometimes, habitual knowledge is remembered, even though we cannot remember how we once justified it, as when one knows the Pythagorean Theorem while no longer remembering the demonstration understood in the past. Our memories generally "more or less decay" over time (as Hobbes observed), which is why Locke insisted that "*demonstrative* knowledge," which requires them, is "more imperfect than *intuitive*" knowledge, which does not. This takes us to the famous chapter on the degrees of human knowledge. In a remarkably Cartesian passage, Locke holds that our "*intuitive knowledge*" is most certain and basic, all other sorts being built on it, and that the "*demonstrative*" sort can also be certain but is never as fundamental, because it builds on intuitions, rationally linking them together in a discursive manner that can go wrong and lead to error.

Next, he makes a bold (Cartesian) claim, which, as an empiricist, he has to abandon almost as soon as he has made it: "These two, viz. intuition and demonstration, are the degrees of our *knowledge*; whatever comes short of one of these, with what assurance soever embraced, is but *faith* or *opinion*, but not knowledge, at least in all general truths." Then, in the very next sentence, he takes it back, mentioning that our perception of "*the particular existence of finite beings without us*" through sensation "goes beyond base probability," and begrudgingly grants that it "passes under the name of *knowledge*." It is as if he immediately realized that he was an empiricist rather than a Cartesian rationalist. So, however reluctantly, he concludes that we humans have "three degrees of knowledge, viz. *intuitive, demonstrative,* and *sensitive*," each with its own appropriate types of evidence and levels of certainty. Our intuitive knowledge must be limited within the parameters of our experienced ideas and cannot reach even that far. Our demonstrative knowledge is limited by our intuitive knowledge and cannot reach even that far. And, finally, our sensitive knowledge is even more limited, not reaching beyond "the existence of things actually present to our senses." So, we conclude, the "*extent of our knowledge*" falls short of both the extent of our ideas and the reality of things that could be known. (We might wonder, at this point, what room this leaves for scientific knowledge, as of the size of the Sun, and historical knowledge, as of the assassination of Julius Caesar.) In establishing such limits, Locke is trying to avoid the dogmatism of the rationalists; yet he does not wish to slide into skepticism. What of truth, then? "Truth," Locke explains, pertains to mental and verbal "propositions," rather than to substantial objects or to isolated ideas or words. When you say, "The cat is on the mat," what is true (or false) is the proposition, depending on whether what it asserts corresponds to the real situation described (or not). Given the limits of human knowledge, we would be in dire straits if we had to rely on what we can certainly know. Luckily, we are capable of broader judgment regarding what is probable or improbable; and this suffices for our ordinary practical purposes. Two areas where this is crucial for our purposes involve cases where a new experience is similar to an old one already known and where we base our belief on the testimony of others whom we have reason to trust. The degrees of our assent, of course, reasonably vary with circumstances (*Essay*, II, 167–183, 185–186, 188, 190–191, 195, 244, 360–366, 369, 371, 373; Leibniz severely criticized this empirical epistemology, and, although his critique was not published in their lifetimes, Locke saw at least part of it and did not find it at all impressive – see *Works*, 407, 417). Surely, certain knowledge is intellectually desirable; yet it is rarely necessary.

7.4 Reality

While Locke's theory of reality is less impressive than was his epistemology, as we explore it, notice how he erected an essentially Cartesian metaphysical superstructure atop his empirical infrastructure. To begin, we return to Book II of his great *Essay*. Through sensitive knowledge, we become aware of bodies or physical substances. But we experience them only through their "primary qualities," their "secondary qualities," and their "active and passive powers," and not as they substantially are in themselves. Likewise, through intuitive knowledge, we are aware of the reality of our own minds, by experiencing their powers of "thinking, and moving a body, being as clear and distinct ideas as the ideas of extension, solidity, and being moved" in bodies. But we should quickly admit that "our idea of substance is equally obscure, or none at all, in both: it is but a supposed I know not what to support those ideas we call accidents" and that we do experience. So in the cases of our own bodies (physical substances) and our own minds (spiritual substances), we experience properties of a permanently unknown substance – real but humanly unknowable by us. Third, what about God (to be dealt with more thoroughly in our next section)? Our idea of a Supreme Being is comprised of simple ideas from reflection – such as existence, duration, knowledge, power, and bliss – indefinitely enlarged by means of "our idea of infinity" and combined to constitute the complex idea of God. Thus, as Hobbes liked to say, God is forever "incomprehensible." When we engage in any sort of factual reasoning, including concerning metaphysical reality, as empiricists, it is important to be able to understand the relationship between "*cause* and *effect*." Given Locke's rejection of innatism, the idea of causality cannot be innate; nor can any causal principle. "*That which produces any simple or complex idea* we denote by the general name, *cause*, and *that which is produced, effect*." Notice two points: first, this does not commit Locke to viewing either causes or effects as anything real outside the mind; and, second, it is rather circular, defining a cause as what is productive and an effect as what is produced (Hume later denounced such circularity in his critique of causal knowledge). Our ideas of three sorts of realities – "1. *God*. 2. *Finite intelligences*. 3. *Bodies*" – can, of course, be causally interrelated. Thus what produces a watch is a watchmaker, and what causes his handiwork to be and to function like a watch is its organization of parts designed for the purpose of keeping time. What about a human being (again, more of this follows below)? It is the effect of an organization of dynamically interrelated parts – including a particular organic body and a particular rational soul. If only the identity of soul or mind sufficed to cause the same human to persist, then a soul that transmigrated into other bodies, including that of a "hog," would be the same human being, a problem for certain strands of Platonism (*Essay*, I, 399–401, 406, 415–422, 433, 440, 444–445, 448).

In Book IV of the *Essay*, Locke clearly states that we have three types of knowledge "of the *real actual existence of things*"; these are "an intuitive knowledge of *our own existence*, and a demonstrative knowledge of the existence of a *God*: of the existence of *anything else*, we have no other but a sensitive knowledge; which extends not beyond the objects present to our senses." Given his earlier reluctance to attribute knowledge to sensibility, we might wonder whether that third sort is merely a set of probable judgments (again not that distant from Cartesianism). In a chapter entitled "Of the Reality of Knowledge," Locke tries to distinguish between judgments reliable enough to constitute knowledge and those that might amount to little more than "dreams and fancies." Given that our knowledge is nothing but our perception of the agreements and disagreements among our ideas, does it all end up being subjective, or is objectivity to be found here? Here again Locke appeals to the correspondence theory of truth: "Our knowledge, therefore, is real only so far as there is a *conformity* between our ideas and the reality of things." In other words, the subjective ideas in our minds must correspond to the objects they are supposed to represent. At this point, Locke asks one of the most penetrating questions in all of seventeenth-century philosophy: "But what shall be here the criterion?" With these seven words, Locke challenged more than two millennia of Western philosophy. "How shall the mind," he asked, "when it perceives nothing but its own ideas, know that they agree with things themselves?" Unfortunately, Locke never does as good a job answering the query as he did posing it. He does say that all simple ideas must correspond to the things they represent and that, among complex ideas, the truly problematic ones are those that concern substances – not, for example, mathematical or moral ideas. But, of course, it is precisely ideas about substantial realities that most interest us. Thus, Locke's lack of a better answer is frustrating. It would be left to geniuses of the eighteenth century (such as Berkeley, Hume, and Kant) to wrestle further with the issue. Even Locke's (Cartesian) knowledge of the reality of our own minds, allegedly based on self-evident intuition, amounts only to "an internal perception that we are," based on our immediate experience of thinking, but (unlike for Descartes) nothing of *what* our minds are substantially. Can we, on these terms, even claim to have grounds for assuming that our minds are substantial, rather than merely a by-product of our brains and central nervous systems? But now, remembering that our only access to other finite beings than our own minds is through sensation, which seems somewhat uncertain as a warrant of substances existing in our physical environment, we might wonder about our knowledge of other "finite spirits," including the people in our lives we most cherish. Of course, we believe that their bodies are animated by personalities comparable to our own. But, in truth, this is a matter of probable judgment rather than one of certain knowledge (*Essay*, II, 212, 227–232, 237, 242–243, 304–305, 325–328, 337). Locke, trying to be careful here, seems unaware that he is sowing seeds of doubt that, in the next century, would become hardy weeds of skepticism.

7.5   God

Locke's *Essay* includes a couple of classic chapters to which we now turn – one on "Our Knowledge of the Existence of a God," the other on "Enthusiasm," in the sense of excessive zeal or religious fanaticism. Despite our having no innate idea of God, Locke assures us that we have another path to theological knowledge. We can start with the self-evident intuition of our own minds. As they are neither eternal nor self-sufficient, they must have some external, eternal Cause that produced them, which is God. This God must be the causal Source of all dependent power and, hence, "most powerful." Also, since we (our minds) are knowing beings, God, who produced them, must be "most knowing." Thus, God, as the uncaused original Cause, must exist as "*an eternal, most powerful, and most knowing Being.*" Locke adds that we could proceed to deduce other divine attributes from this if we like. He goes so far as to assert that "we more certainly know that there is a God than that there is anything without us," thanks to that sort of demonstration. Locke considers this truth of God's necessary existence to be "fundamental" to "all religion and genuine morality." He also uses a simple version of the argument from design to show that the first Cause could not be material (as Hobbes thought) on account of the thought and unity to be found in the natural order. Even if a "*material*" Force were the uncaused first Cause of us and our world, that would still lead us to "an eternal, omniscient, omnipotent Being." Thus we have allegedly demonstrated the existence and something of the essence of God, though we should not presume to imagine that we could ever comprehend the divine nature (*Essay*, II, 306–312, 315–316, 324; cf. *Essays*, 103–105). Before we move on to consider Locke's views on "enthusiasm," what can we say about this demonstration? First, we see that, while he does not want to admit that the divine nature might be material rather than spiritual, it seems he must begrudgingly acknowledge the possibility. Second, notice how he quietly slips from calling God "most powerful" and "most knowing" to "omnipotent" and "omniscient"; God could be the most powerful and the most knowing of all beings without having *all* power or *all* conceivable knowledge. Third, why must the first Cause that produced us and our world, even if itself uncaused, necessarily be "eternal"? Why could it not have been from all time prior to designing or creating our world but then subsequently have ceased to be? And, fourth, if we were to accept this line of argumentation, it would only give us a metaphysical ultimate principle (what Pascal called the god of philosophers) and not necessarily the personal God of religion. Locke simply glides over too much for the demonstration to function as intended.

Enthusiasm, the fanatical, irrational commitment to a belief or set of beliefs at all costs, threatens to obstruct the open-minded pursuit of truth. Locke tells us that the sure criterion of a genuine truth-seeker is the "not entertaining any proposition with greater assurance than the proofs it is built upon will warrant." A practical problem with dogmatic, partisan belief is that it slips readily into the will to dictate it to others. Embracing alleged private revelations, "*enthusiasm*" shirks both reason and traditional revelation "and substitutes in the room of them the ungrounded fancies of a man's own brain, and assumes them for a foundation both of opinion and conduct." Reason and traditional revelation are both valuable and complementary. "*Reason* is *natural revelation*," according to Locke, and "*revelation* is *natural reason enlarged*" by the communication of truths to us by God. We should never imagine that they are at loggerheads or that we should deny either for the other. "So that he that takes away reason to make room for revelation, puts out the light of both, and does muchwhat the same as if he would persuade a man to put out his eyes, the better to receive the remote light of an invisible star by a telescope." But the enthusiast succumbs to the temptation to be seen as receiving and being able to communicate a private revelation from God. And what evidence to the contrary might reasonably dissuade such a person? Such a person can easily interpret passionate inclinations as missions ordered by God. When such "conceits of a warmed or overweening brain" become translated into action, they become socially dangerous, operating beyond the legitimate bounds of rational restraint. How can anyone reason with such people? "Reason is lost upon them, they are above it." No counterevidence can succeed against their zealotry; "they are sure because they are sure: and their persuasions are right, because they are strong in them." No matter how passionately we may "*take*" a proposition to be true, that is no assurance that we "*know*" it to be true or, indeed, that it actually *is* true. What evidence is there, or could there be, that a private revelation actually comes from God, rather than from diabolical forces or the fevers of a frenzied imagination? But, for such enthusiasts, none of this matters. "*It is a revelation, because they firmly believe it*; and *they believe it, because it is a revelation*." Even when we are sincere in such cases, we are notoriously prone to error. So what must we do to protect ourselves from both our own enthusiasm and that of others? "Reason must be our *last judge and guide in everything*" (*Essay*, II, 429–440). These are superb cautions from Locke. The problem is that they would seem to screen out religious doctrines valuable to Locke – i.e. matters of revelation that defy reason – including his own favorite, the doctrine of the Incarnation of Jesus of Nazareth as the God-man.

In another great work of Locke's, *A Letter Concerning Toleration*, he develops principles and guidelines for dealing with people with alternative sets of religious beliefs. (Remember that Locke's seventeenth century was one of religious intolerance, hatred, persecution, and warfare – particularly among the Christians.) Given our natural tendencies toward dogmatic "enthusiasm," it would at least be salutary if we could learn to tolerate those of other persuasions. Locke maintains that the proper practical function of "true religion" is "the regulating of men's lives according to the rules of virtue and piety." So genuine religion should make us morally better people. Surely we should try to tolerate alternative belief-systems on the part of other people who are also seeking to live good lives. Legislation and public magistrates should only concern such civil matters as "life, liberty, health, and indolency of body" and "the possession of outward things, such as money, lands, houses, furniture, and the like." Obviously, this does not include religious doctrines and rituals. We are not born members of churches but should be free to join one of our own choosing or not. "A church," Locke writes, is "a voluntary society of men, joining themselves together of their own accord, in order to the public worshiping of God, in such a manner as they may judge acceptable to him, and effectual to the salvation of their souls." Without calling for a (Jeffersonian) separation of Church and state, Locke stands opposed to any member of civil society depriving another of his civil rights because of their religious differences. As we should not force a person to be prosperous or healthy, so we should not try to force another to be pious or devout. There are multiple religious paths to God. Even if only one of them is correct, who is to say which one that is? Under the influence of enthusiasm, of course, "zealots" will claim to know that their own path has a monopoly on truth and, if allowed to do so, be tempted to impose it on others. Let people privately worship as they think best. Likewise for "the articles of faith" to which a person of conscience is committed. Yet this does not mean that anything goes. Opinions that are counter to social order and public safety are not to be allowed. Likewise for religious commitments that, if followed, would render adherents traitors against the state, as serving – openly or secretly – a foreign power against its national interests. This provision, in Locke's mind, rules out Roman Catholics, whose fundamental loyalty, he thinks, is to Rome. Finally, atheists are not to be tolerated, because, lacking any supernatural sanction for morality, they (purportedly) cannot be trusted to keep their word, including when under oath and under contract (*Politics*, 104–105, 107–108, 110–111, 113–115, 119–121, 124–125, 131, 133–140; cf. *Essays*, 136–137, 139, 151–152). We balk at some of the exceptions Locke draws; however, for a seventeenth-century Christian, he establishes a refreshingly liberal perspective on religious toleration. He takes God seriously but, within limits, wants others to be free to do so in their own ways.

7.6 Humanity

As a dualist, Locke regards human beings as dynamically interacting minds and bodies. The body has various natural capacities (e.g. for seeing, walking, eating, growing, and so forth); and the mind has its own natural capacities, including, especially, "the *intellectual faculty*, or the understanding" and "the *elective faculty*, or the will." So far, so Cartesian! We have already seen that the identity of a human being is constituted by the dynamic interrelationships between a particular living body and a particular mind or rational soul. In the course of a normal human lifetime, both the body and the mind change considerably. What establishes the selfsame identity of the body, throughout its development over the decades, is a continuity of changes through time, as when the body of an infant grows into childhood, then adolescence, then young adulthood, then maturity, and finally old age. Now what constitutes "personal identity" in the sense of the identity of the "*person*"? Locke's answer is in terms of the continuity of "consciousness," for which memory is crucial. An interesting aspect of this theory is that it indicates that one's identity as a person only reaches back as far as memory goes. And it is in these very terms that Locke defined one's sense of self: "*Self* is that conscious thinking thing . . . which is sensible or conscious of pleasure and pain, capable of happiness or misery, and so is concerned for itself, as far as that consciousness extends." He is not as dogmatic as Descartes was in ruling out the Hobbesian theory that this consciousness might be rooted in the body rather than in some spiritual substance. Nevertheless, he clearly tells us where he stands: "I agree, the more probable opinion is, that this consciousness is annexed to, and the affection of, one individual immaterial substance." Thus the Cartesians were probably correct (against the materialists) that a substantial mind is the source of personality or selfhood. Surely, it is theoretically possible that God *could* have made matter capable of thinking. It is, perhaps, best to admit that we cannot be certain "of what *kind* of being" the mind is, steering clear of dogmatic claims to such substantial knowledge. At any rate, it is "*reason*," which is "the faculty which finds out the means, and rightly applies them, to discover certainty . . . and probability," that definitively distinguishes humans "from beasts" and establishes the superiority of the former over the latter. The mind of humans is capable of "*intuitive knowledge*" as well as of the discursive knowledge "*of reasoning*." And, in addition to intuitive and rational knowledge, the human mind has an even broader capacity for probable "judgment" that falls short of certainty but so often suffices for our practical purposes. Truth is the object of the understanding's judgments, which can be "according to" reason (as that dairy products are nutritious, while hemlock poison can be lethal) or "above" reason (as that God literally became human in the person of Jesus of Nazareth) or "contrary to reason" (as that the president might be a married bachelor). In a justly famous chapter "Of

Faith and Reason," Locke distinguishes between the two, arguing that truths that are "*above reason*" and revealed by God are "*the proper matter of faith,*" that we should never believe anything that is "*contrary to*" reason, and that only "reason is the proper judge" of whether an alleged truth is credible or not (*Essay*, I, 324, 448–450, 458–459, 465–466; II, 193, 197, 386–387, 407, 409, 412–413, 415–427; this discussion of alleged truths we should reject as irrational raises the tricky – for a devout Christian – issue of miracles, which Locke cautiously discusses in his *Discourse of Miracles*, in *Works*, 256–264). Thus far, in this section, we have focused on the mind.

In *Some Thoughts Concerning Education*, Locke emphasizes the importance of psycho-physical balance. "A sound mind in a sound body" is an ancient Roman (from Juvenal) slogan Locke embraces. We shall not deeply probe his ideas here. But he offers advice on how to raise healthy, well-balanced children. They should be disciplined to become self-disciplined, educated to teach themselves, and made to obey in order to become morally autonomous. A well-raised child will acquire "virtue, wisdom, breeding, and learning" on the path to fulfilling his human nature, the most important of the four being the first. In *The Reasonableness of Christianity*, while avoiding the collective guilt associated with the doctrine of original sin, Locke represents the life of Jesus as penetrating humanity's natural "state of darkness and error" and revealing the path to moral virtue, as well as serving as a role model for us. In *The Conduct of the Understanding*, Locke warns us against (i) unthinkingly going along with the choices of others, (ii) allowing passion rather than reason to determine our choices, and (iii) using insufficiently informed reason for making choices. He is confident that if we learn to use reason effectively and then take the time and make the effort to do so, we shall do our best. It is important that we develop and exercise good habits. We should learn to use language to reveal the truth rather than to camouflage our own ignorance. Some truths will be recognizable as more "fundamental" than others. An example in the area of physical science "is that admirable discovery of Mr. Newton that all bodies gravitate to one another"; another, in the area of interpersonal relations, is the rule of Jesus that "*we should love our neighbor as ourselves*" (*Politics*, 149, 159–160, 169, 182–183, 188–189, 205, 210–211, 213–226, 233–235, 262, 276). At any rate, we can best fulfill our humanity by living intelligently.

7.7 Freedom

A long chapter, "Of Power," in Book II of the *Essay,* deals with the issue of human "*liberty and necessity*." For Locke, as for so many seventeenth-century philosophers (pulled one way by modern science and the other by religious beliefs), this is an important issue. He tries to be clear as to what it would mean for us to act freely, writing that, "so far as a man has power to think or not to think, to move or not to move, according to the preference or direction of his own mind, so far is a man *free*." Thus, without yet committing himself to whether we actually are so, he presents the conditions of mind requisite to our being so. The idea of freedom or liberty is that of "a power in any agent to do or forbear any particular action, according to the determination or thought of the mind." Thus freedom requires thought, which, in turn, requires a thinking mind. If beasts have no minds, they cannot be free; if we do have minds, they may or may not be free. An act would need to arise from volition to be free. Most actions in the physical universe are acts of necessity, disconnected from "the direction of thought." If an agent were forced to do something against his will, that would be an act of "compulsion"; and if another agent were prevented from acting according to her will, that would be a case of "restraint." Like Hobbes, Locke rejects the notion of free will; since will is a power of the mind and freedom is a power of action, freedom of will would be a power of a power, while every power should presumably be of a substance. So the question, properly posed, is not whether the will is free, but whether a person or the mind or soul or human being is ever free or not. We act on our volitions in performing voluntary actions. But our volitions, determined by desires, are not themselves free, as we are not free to choose our desires. So it would *seem* that, even in our voluntary actions, we cannot be genuinely free. Yet, assuming we are not free to will something or not, are we ever free to choose whether or not to *act* on what we will? For Locke, that is the key issue, and he needs to find a path to an affirmative answer, for the sake of moral accountability. Suppose that you imagine a peppermint ice cream cone and cannot help desiring one. You cannot help the fact that you have the will to enjoy a peppermint ice cream cone. You know how to act in order to satisfy that desire. But suppose you also desire excellent health and have a volition to avoid high-fat, high-cholesterol food. Are you free to indulge your wish for the ice cream or to refrain from doing so? Locke's answer is in the affirmative. Your mind can determine on which of these conflicting volitions you will act. We are motivated by the natural desire for "satisfaction" and the natural aversion to "uneasiness." But, contrary to determinists (such as Hobbes), Locke holds that this fact nevertheless allows room for our sometimes freely choosing whether to act in certain ways or not. This is not to say that the prospect of "satisfaction" cannot be overpowering or that acute "uneasiness" cannot overwhelm our freedom, which, after all, is limited rather than absolute. After all, the desire for happiness and aversion to misery are natural and healthy. Understanding what is in our long-term interests expands, rather than limiting, our freedom, liberating us from the shackles of base desire. Although the desires may remain psychic realities, they need not determine how we shall act (*Essay*, I, 315–321, 323–331, 334, 339–340, 367). This is, arguably, the most subtle, most sophisticated, most satisfactory theory of human freedom or liberty of the seventeenth century (including that of Leibniz, whom we shall discuss next). It takes seriously the powerful influences of desire over all acts of human volition; yet, where volitions conflict, it leaves room for free choice and moral responsibility. We, perhaps, should note, however, before moving on, that, like Descartes, as an orthodox Christian, Locke is committed to both God's all-knowing, omnipotent preordination and genuine human freedom, sees a conflict between the two beliefs, but throws up his hands in frustration as to how to resolve it (*Works*, 305). This is as philosophically unimpressive here as it was in Descartes; yet this disappointment need not detract from the strength of his general theory of freedom.

7.8 Morality

Locke is not among the great ethicists of modern times, and what he has to say about morality tends to be unoriginal or inadequately supported (or both). Like Hobbes, he adopts a kind of hedonism, making "*good*" relative to what we think will "increase pleasure, or diminish pain in us" and "*evil*" relative to what we think will "produce or increase any pain, or diminish any pleasure in us." He immediately clarifies the fact that he is not merely talking about physical, sensual pleasures and pains. Nevertheless, he calls pleasure and pain and their sources "the hinges on which our passions turn." Then he proceeds to discuss the passions of love, hatred, desire, joy, sorrow, hope, fear, despair, anger, envy, and so forth in those terms. The ultimate object of human desire is happiness, and the ultimate object of human aversion is misery – both of which can be analyzed in terms of pleasure and pain, "good and evil" being relative to that. So far, this may sound like ordinary (e.g. Hobbesian) hedonism. But Locke goes on to speak of "*moral good and evil*," as opposed to generic good and evil. These moral values involve "*the conformity or disagreement of our voluntary actions to some law, whereby good or evil is drawn on us, from the will and power of the lawmaker.*" There are three different sorts of such laws: "1. The *divine* law. 2. The *civil*

7 John Locke

law. 3. The law of *opinion* or *reputation*." Relative to the first are sins; relative to the second are crimes; relative to the third are vices. Offenses against all these sorts of laws are subject to appropriate forms of punishment. Locke boldly claims that the rules of morality are rationally demonstrable, as are the truths of mathematics, yielding knowledge as clear and certain. He gave one example of a moral principle (and one of a political principle): "Where there is no property, there is no injustice," since injustice is a violation of right, and having a right to anything is to be able to claim it as one's property (the political principle is "No government allows absolute liberty," as the latter involves an absence of enforced rules or laws, which entails a lack of government). While these are all well and good as examples of how some principles are matters of definition, Locke never actually produces a system of ethics, whether demonstrated or otherwise. He expresses admiration for Cicero's book on moral duties and maintains that "*morality* is *the proper science and business of mankind in general*" (*Essay*, I, 303–307, 340–341, 467, 474–476, 480–481; II, 156–157, 208–209, 233–234, 347, 351; we know that a dear friend named William Molyneux repeatedly entreated Locke to produce a treatise on morality, but Locke put him off, claiming that the Gospels offer us a sufficiently perfect ethical system – *Works*, 291, 294–295, 329, 377). Still Locke never developed his own mature ethical system. The word "mature" was used because when Locke was in his early thirties, as a Censor of Moral Philosophy at Oxford, he wrote a series of *Essays on the Law of Nature*, which he delivered as lectures and never published during his lifetime, though urged to do so. These do represent a fairly systematic Christian theory of natural law, more comparable to that of Aquinas than to the laws of nature of Hobbes. While Locke never renounced these early essays later on, they do not represent the approach of his philosophical maturity and will not be further explored here (*Essays*, 81–133). In general, Locke's ethical view held that we ought to obey the rules of law, the just reward for our so doing being happiness.

7.9 Society

It is interesting how sharply Locke's views on political society changed from when he was working at Oxford before joining Lord Ashley's service (in 1667) and thereafter. His "First Tract on Government" clearly marks him as an advocate of authority who condemns liberty in the sense of doing as we please and stirring up discord, saying that "a general freedom is but a general bondage." Indeed, he declares himself in favor of the sort of "absolute and arbitrary power" he later famously decried. By the time he writes "An Essay on Toleration" (1667), he is calling for the tolerating of a broad range of views and values, as long as they are not "destructive to human society." Here he has shifted to denying that government should enforce morality, except where the secular welfare of society would be threatened. In what he wrote of "The Fundamental Constitutions of Carolina" (1669), he advocated tolerating a variety of religions, so long as they teach that there is a God, call for public worship, and provide for bearing witness to the truth before God. While Locke accepted slavery in Carolina, he maintains that even slaves should enjoy freedom of religion; he condemns anyone's interfering with any adult's religious beliefs or forms of worship (*Essays*, 7–9, 140–144, 178–180). By the time Locke writes his *Two Treatises of Government*, he has become a champion of liberty.

While the second *Treatise* is his political masterpiece, it is a companion piece to the first, which, in turn, is a critique of the divine right of kings theory, as developed by Sir Robert Filmer in his *Patriarcha*, published posthumously (in 1680). Filmer argued that "the greatest liberty in the world" requires monarchy and that any other form of government involves "slavery." He also maintained that legitimate "regal authority" is ultimately ordained by God and stems from the parental power that fathers have inherited from (the Old Testament) Adam. Even though Locke started writing his *Two Treatises* long before the Glorious Revolution of 1688, his Preface expresses the hope that they will help establish the legitimacy of King William's rule, as derived from "the consent of the people" and as having saved England from "slavery and ruin" under the Stuarts. Even though Locke accepted slavery in some circumstances, he considered it "so vile and miserable an estate" as to be inappropriate for a good and civilized people. Yet the absolute monarchy advocated by Filmer and divine right of kings theorists is political slavery. Their position goes something like this: human beings are born subject to authority and never escape that subjection to achieve the liberty to choose their own government and rulers. Since God gave Adam absolute authority over everyone and political rulers inherited that authority, their power should be considered "absolute and by divine right." More specifically, the God-given authority inherited by every prince, king, and emperor, on this view, is "an absolute, arbitrary, unlimited, and unlimitable power over the lives, liberties, and estates of his children and subjects." Without exploring all the details of Locke's critique here, we can observe that almost every element of this crude argument is defective. Adam's parental authority over his children was neither political nor absolute. Human beings, though temporarily subject to their parents, are born to develop into free subjects. They must be educated (by good parents) to exercise their freedom rationally and responsibly, including giving reasonable consent to the political structures under which they will live. But even if God had given Adam absolute political authority over everyone else, there would be no way of determining which subsequent claimants to political power legitimately inherited it, breeding "endless contention and disorder" (*Treatises*, 253, 255, 3, 7–9, 17, 78), with no hope of resolution other than the "might makes right" approach that is nothing short of an immoral fiasco. So what is the alternative?

Locke carefully develops his famous answer in his *Second Treatise*. The short version of that answer is that legitimate political power is derived from the consent of the governed. "Political power," as he defines it, is the "right of making laws with penalties of death and, consequently, all less penalties for the regulating and preserving of property, and of employing the force of the community in the execution of such laws, and in the defence of the commonwealth from foreign injury, and all this only for the public good." Like Hobbes, Locke believes in a pre-political "state of nature" in which people were free and equal. But, unlike Hobbes, he thinks that, in this natural state, they were morally bound by the "law of nature" to respect one another's "property" in the broad sense that they should not harm anyone else with respect to his "life, health, liberty, or possessions." Therefore this natural "state of liberty," according to Locke, should *not* be construed as "a state of licence" to do whatever a person can get away with doing. Thus, at no time does any human being have any natural "absolute or arbitrary power" over any other. A practical problem with this situation, Locke proclaimed, was that everyone must enforce his own rights against all others, creating a situation both unstable and dangerous. Thus it was desirable to find a vehicle into civil society, which would protect the rights of all, that vehicle being a social contract. For Locke (unlike for Hobbes), "the state of nature" was not necessarily a "state of war"; but he does agree that it would be problematic and better replaced by civil society. Every human being is naturally free from all subjection to "absolute, arbitrary power"; the only way a person can forfeit this right is by his own wrongdoing (e.g. a reprehensible crime or an unjust act of aggressive, violent warfare). In the state of nature, presumably, all people originally held everything in common. But, since people own their own bodies, they were able to appropriate part of what had been held in common by mixing their own labor with it. Consider an example of this labor theory of property: in the original state of nature, the apples growing on trees are owned in common by all. But when a person takes the time and makes the effort to gather up a dozen of them, as a result of this labor, they then belong to him. Yet there are reasonable limits to how much he can thus appropriate – not so much that there is none left for others or that it will spoil unused. The same holds true for appropriating land – it can be claimed by being worked, so long as there is some left for others and what is appropriated does not go to waste. Prior to the introduction of money, bartering was a way of exchanging property with others. But once people started owning durable goods, such as shells and metals, things became more complex. And even more so with the use of money, which allowed for significant extensions of legitimate acquisitions. In the state of nature, of course, not everyone was equal to everyone else in all respects. There was parental (both paternal and maternal, by the way) power over children. But it is a condition of trust and responsibility, with parents caring for their children until they are capable of caring for themselves. Even with children who will sadly never develop self-determination ("lunatics and idiots"), this is never tantamount to "absolute arbitrary dominion," but merely the limited authority of guardianship. And, it should be clear, this is never political power, nor is the latter ever legitimately derived from it. Far from being naturally antisocial (as Hobbes suggested), human beings are naturally social, the family being a basic natural social unit. Authority structures are needed in any society, including that of the family; but they should be limited. Civil or "political society," which should also never be absolute, is set up to remedy the defects of the state of nature, having to do with the protection of property (in Locke's broad sense), the enforcement of established rules, and the punishment of transgressors (*Treatises*, 121–148, 150–153, 155, 159–164).

Through a voluntary social contract, people could join together to form a civil union under a common government, leaving the state of nature, transferring their own power to that government. The form of government can vary; but an "absolute monarchy" would be so destructive of liberty as to be contrary to the very purposes of civil society. By contrast, in a civil society ruled by law, subjects could appeal to the law for justice, with no subject above the law. People must give their consent – whether express or tacit – in order to subscribe to the social contract. In doing so, they agree to abide by the will of the majority of citizens, the end being the well-being of all. Nobody can legitimately make this commitment for another – including a father binding his son – forever; though inheriting land does render us subject to its government, once we have reached maturity, we can leave both of them. Also, merely being an inhabitant of a country does not automatically imply political consent. In joining political society, of course, we give up some of our natural freedom. What we gain is the "mutual preservation" of our "property," meaning our "lives, liberties, and estates." There are various forms of government possible: democracy, oligarchy, monarchy (whether hereditary or elective), and mixed. It is the legislative authority, which has the right to make the laws, that is "supreme." Nevertheless, it must not be arbitrary but must serve the "public good." It is also bound to serve the interests of society justly, avoiding corruption and attempts to grab "absolute arbitrary power." Also, it cannot legitimately confiscate citizens' property without popular consent, taxation requiring "the consent of the majority." The legislature must not shirk or alienate its fundamental responsibility to make the laws. In order to avoid tyranny, Locke called for a distinction of government powers. In addition to a legislature meeting at times to make laws, an executive power must always be at work enforcing those laws and coordinating government functions. A third power, the "federative," having to do with "war and peace, leagues and alliances," is normally associated with the executive (as would be the judiciary, which is not a separate power). The legislative is "a fiduciary power" granted by the people and subject to being recalled by them. While the executive might call the legislature into session, it should not prevent it from meeting to do its job. The use of unauthorized force by the executive against the people or its legislature is an act of war. The executive does need a certain amount of discretionary authority, or "prerogative," to act for the common good in circumstances "where the law was silent." When someone illegitimately seizes power, without changing the form of government, that is usurpation; when someone exercises political power beyond the limits allowed by law, that is tyranny. In the face of usurpation or tyranny, the people have a right to disobey and rebel, even to the point of dissolving the government (which is not equivalent to dissolving the society). When government officials "act contrary to their trust," violating the property rights of citizens (that is, "the lives, liberties, or fortunes of the people"), the latter can rightfully protect themselves. Locke is sensitive to the charge that this would provide a license for disgruntled citizens to revolt against their government. In reply, he protests that people are naturally conservative, not inclined to dissolve their governments lightly or frivolously. When the people do rise up in self-defense against usurpation or tyranny, it is those who illegitimately seize power who "are guilty of rebellion" against the rule of law, as a result of using "force without authority." The public welfare is the ultimate purpose of government; when rulers subvert that for their own good, they are the rebels, not the people who defend their rights. If it be asked who is the proper judge of whether there is just cause for their rising up, Locke's answer is, "The people shall be judge." They alone constitute "the proper umpire" in such a case (*Treatises*, 164–171, 179–200, 203–207, 221–222, 224–225, 228–239, 245–247).

Locke deserves to be regarded as the great pioneer of modern liberalism because of a convergence of five aspects of his theory of political society. (i) Most important is that he is a champion of personal rights and individual liberty. (ii) Next is his clear-cut insistence that any government, whatever its form, can only be legitimate if based on popular consent. (iii) Then there is his consistent repudiation of "absolute arbitrary power" as incompatible with civil society. (iv) Next is his call for a separation of the powers of government, particularly between legislative and executive branches, as a check against abuses. And (v) there is the people's right to revolt against usurpation or tyranny. The democratic republic that would be born as the United States of America, a few decades after Locke's death, would be significantly influenced by his political liberalism.

7.10   Review

To a great extent, Locke's greatness is a function of his capacity to work out a reasonable balance between extreme points of view; but, at times, that attempt to have things both ways sinks him into the muddle of the middle. The most obvious example is his epistemology. In avoiding the dogmatic rationalism of some predecessors, he modestly limits our ideas within the parameters of sensation and reflection, limits knowledge to relationships among our ideas, and denies that we can experience or know any substance in itself. But he thus opens the door to the very skepticism he considers so unwelcome. He tries to build a Cartesian metaphysical theory of reality on his empirical epistemology, ending up with no adequate basis for some of his claims. His views on God are nothing new, and his proof of God is unconvincing.[2] But his views on religious toleration have proved remarkably progressive, even if his own prejudices (against atheists and Catholics) were obstacles to their broader application. His theory of human nature is quite Cartesian but fails to solve the Cartesian problem of the mind–body relation. His theory of human freedom works well, taking seriously the role of influential forces on all our actions, while carving out space for choosing among motivating desires. His views on morality are derivative, and he never manages to show how it might be presented as a demonstrative science. And, finally, his work on legitimate government is a most valuable gift contributing to the development of modern political liberalism. His epistemological and metaphysical theories would come under attack by British philosophers of the next generation (as we shall see). But first he would serve as a foil for the last of the great seventeenth-century rationalists, Leibniz.

---

2 For more on Locke, see ch. 3 of *Western Philosophies of Religion*, by Wayne P. Pomerleau (New York: Ardsley House, 1998).

7.11 Another Perspective

Catharine Trotter Cockburn (1679–1749), daughter of a captain in the royal navy and his wife, who was a member of the Scottish aristocracy, was educated in Latin and logic. Early in life, she wrote several plays that were performed on the stage. She anonymously published a *Defense of Mr. Locke's Essay of Human Understanding* (in 1702) against an anonymous critique of Locke (by a student of the prominent Cambridge Platonist Ralph Cudworth); Locke was so favorably impressed by it that, having found out the identity of its author, he sent her a gift of several books. Having been raised as a Protestant, she first converted to Catholicism and then reconverted to Protestantism in 1607. In 1608, she married the Reverend Patrick Cockburn, who had been ordained in the Church of England, after which she spent many years focusing on her roles as wife and mother (of four children). In 1726, she mounted another defense of Locke, this time against charges of heresy. She was particularly interested in religion and moral theory and admired the work of Bishop Joseph Butler (whom we shall consider later), with whom she generally agreed. A two-volume collection of her writings was posthumously published in 1751.[3]

Cockburn's defense (of 1702) of Locke's great *Essay* will nicely illustrate her interest in the relationship between philosophy, on the one hand, and religion and morality, on the other. More specifically, she avers, it has been "objected against Mr. Locke's principles, that they give us no certainty regarding the immortality of the soul without revelation," reason merely being able to argue for its probability. Not only does this concern relate to Christian doctrine, but it also has to do with just punishments and rewards after death, a motive for morally virtuous conduct in this life. As Locke said, personhood requires a continuity of self-consciousness, while a human being is a unity of soul and body. When that unity is severed by the death of the body, if the soul's self-consciousness continues, then the life of the soul also continues. Cockburn somewhat harshly accuses Locke's critic of not understanding what he criticizes. There are so many things about the soul we can reasonably believe without completely understanding its nature and activities. Otherwise, we risk sinking into skepticism. But empiricism need not condemn us to this (*Women*, 128, 131–133).

Although our very idea of the soul is drawn from our experience of its operations, that does not logically mean that it exists only when it actively operates. Suppose that in certain phases of sleep, the soul is not thinking. Is it logical to conclude that it does not then exist but subsequently comes back into existence when sleep has ended, even though, after awaking, the soul retains and can think about the previous day's experiences? That seems absurd. Locke is more reasonable in holding that "it is not necessary to the existence of the soul that it should be always in action." Nobody can prove that the soul is always thinking; but that is not necessary in order for it to have a life after death. To base the doctrine of immortality of the soul on such a dubious claim as that the soul is always thinking, she charges, is to render religion pitifully small service (*Women*, 137–140).

The same would be the case if we attempted to demonstrate immortality based on the claim that the human soul "is *immaterial*," since (i) immateriality of the soul cannot itself be proved, (ii) even if it were immaterial, that would not assure its continued existence after the death of the body, and (iii) even if the soul is material (as Hobbes thought), God might resurrect it and its operations for an afterlife. Cockburn quotes Locke as writing that God could "give to certain systems of matter a

---

3 References in this section will be to *Women Philosophers of the Early Modern Period* (hereafter called *Women*), ed. by Margaret Atherton (Indianapolis: Hackett Publishing Co., 1994).

power to perceive and think, though it be most highly probable that the soul is immaterial." But even without our being able to achieve "demonstrative certainty" in this matter, she agrees with Locke that "all the ends of morality and religion are well enough secured" by the dualistic distinction between soul and body. As a just God made us "capable of *happiness* and *misery*," with the ability to choose "*good* or *evil*," it is reasonable to believe in an afterlife in which persons receive their just deserts, as they so often do not in this life (*Women*, 140, 143–146). This, at any rate, is a good example of Cockburn's forceful advocacy.

8

G.W. Leibniz

Gottfried Wilhelm Leibniz.

Source: orion_eff/Adobe Stock

8.1 Overview

Gottfried Wilhelm Leibniz was the first great German philosopher of modern times. It is customary to label him a "rationalist"; and, to be sure, he shared with Descartes, Spinoza, and Malebranche a sanguine confidence in the power of human reason to know the truth about reality; like them, he used mathematics as his a priori model for deducing knowledge. Yet he was as interested in empirical truth as Hobbes and Locke, and as technologically inventive as Pascal. He was a polymath and a universal genius. He was one of the most innovative metaphysicians in all of Western philosophy, not merely of his own times. And his philosophical theology – his theory of God and God's relation to our world – was, arguably, more ingenious than that of any modern we have considered thus far.

Modern European Philosophers, First Edition. Wayne P. Pomerleau.
© 2023 John Wiley & Sons, Inc. Published 2023 by John Wiley & Sons, Inc.

8.2 Biography

Leibniz was born on July 1, 1646 (near the end of the Thirty Years' War), in Leipzig, the son of Friedrich Leibniz, a professor of moral philosophy at the university there, and his third wife, Catharina, the daughter of a law professor there. His father owned an extensive private library and, by the time he died, when the boy was six years old, had already instilled in him a love of learning. With his father's passing, his mother took charge of the boy's education. He started school at the age of seven and allegedly taught himself Latin at the age of seven or eight, after which he was given access to his father's library. He entered the University of Leipzig in 1661, at the age of 14, soon completing a Bachelor's degree in philosophy.[1] While encountering the thought of moderns such as Bacon, Galileo, Descartes, and even Hobbes there, most of the philosophy he was taught was the old medieval Aristotelian scholasticism – to which he did not react as negatively as had many of his predecessors. He said that, by the age of 15, he had chosen to follow the modern way of thought, while continuing to appreciate premodern contributions, and denied that he was a Cartesian (*Papers*, 654–655, 94). Nevertheless, he admired Descartes's work, the absorbing of which required a great deal of serious reflection; by being "self-taught," he could avoid accepting what he studied "on the authority of teachers" and getting uncritically carried away with any thinkers' revolutionary innovations (*Essays*, 2–3, 6, 138–141). After earning a Master's degree in philosophy in 1664, he spent a year studying law, getting a Bachelor's degree in law in 1665. By 1666, he had completed the requirements for a doctorate in law; but the University of Leipzig refused to grant him the degree – purportedly because he was too young! So he left the university (never again living in his native city) and transferred to the University of Altdorf, where his dissertation "On Perplexing Cases in Law" not only got him the doctorate in law by the end of 1666, but also was deemed so brilliant that, despite his youth, he was offered a professor's chair. He declined the offer, aspiring to a more active life than academia could afford him. Instead, he went into public service, working for a baron who was a minister to the Elector of Mainz. Germany, devastated by the Thirty Years' War, was easy prey for Louis XIV of France's geopolitical ambitions. Leibniz concocted a scheme to try to convince France to turn its military initiatives to the conquest of Egypt instead. Leibniz was sent to Paris, the intellectual center of Europe, to try to promote his scheme. While nothing came of this, the four years he spent in Paris (1672–1676) represented a philosophical turning point for the young man, because he seriously encountered and deeply took in modern thought. He gained access to unpublished manuscripts of Descartes and Pascal; he met with Malebranche and Arnauld; he was sent to London, where he met with Robert Boyle and so impressed the Royal Society with the calculating machine he had invented (improving on Pascal's earlier design) that it elected him an external (foreign) member. At about this time, he was working out his discovery of the infinitesimal calculus (although he did not publish it until 1684). On his way back to Germany, he passed through Holland, where he met with Spinoza. By the time he got back to Germany, his employer and the Elector of Mainz had both died, so that he needed to find new employment.

---

1 References to Leibniz will be to the following works: *Philosophical Essays*, by G.W. Leibniz (hereafter called *Essays*), ed. and trans. by Roger Ariew and Daniel Garber (Indianapolis: Hackett, 1989), *Philosophical Papers and Letters*, by Gottfried Wilhelm Leibniz (hereafter called *Papers*), trans. and ed. by Leroy E. Loemker, second edition (Dordrecht: D. Reidel Publishing Co., 1969), *Philosophical Writings*, by Leibniz (hereafter called *Writings*), ed. by G.H.R. Parkinson and trans. by Mary Morris and G.H.R. Parkinson (London: J.M. Dent & Sons, 1973), *The Shorter Leibniz Texts*, by Leibniz (hereafter called *Texts*), ed. and trans. by Lloyd Strickland (London: Continuum, 2006), and *Theodicy*, by G.W. Leibniz, ed. by Austin Farrer, trans. by E.M. Huggard (La Salle, IL: Open Court, 1985).

He was offered a position by Johann Friedrich, the Duke of Brunswick, at Hanover, as head librarian and diplomatic advisor. He worked on a project to reconcile Lutheranism (which he followed) and Catholicism (to which the Duke had converted). He worked for the House of Brunswick for the last four decades of his life. When Johann Friedrich died in 1680, his brother, Ernst August, became Duke of Brunswick and Leibniz's employer. Leibniz was close to the new Duke's wife, Sophie, who was both the younger sister of Princess Elizabeth of Bohemia (with whom Descartes had corresponded) and related to the English monarchy. He was also fond of her daughter, Sophie Charlotte, the Queen of Prussia. In 1682, he participated in founding a scholarly journal, in which he published several important papers. In 1686, Leibniz was assigned to write a history of the House of Brunswick, a massive task he never completed. He traveled around Germany and to Italy, doing research for this history, returning to Hanover in 1690. After Ernst August died, his son, the Elector George Ludwig, became head of the House of Brunswick and Leibniz's employer. In the 1690s, Leibniz was accused of plagiarizing his discovery of the calculus from Sir Isaac Newton, some of whose unpublished manuscripts Leibniz was said to have seen while he was visiting England a couple of decades earlier. Scholars believe that they had discovered it independently, Newton working it out first, but Leibniz publishing it first. Leibniz appealed to the Royal Society for assistance in the dispute, but it took the side of the Newtonians against him. In 1700, with the support of Sophie Charlotte, he founded the Berlin Academy of Sciences. In 1711, Peter the Great, Tsar of Russia, stopped over in Hanover and met with Leibniz. But in 1714, when Queen Anne of England died childless, Elector George Ludwig became King George I of Great Britain. He forbade Leibniz to join the royal court in the move – ostensibly leaving him in Hanover to work on the history of the House of Brunswick, but, in reality, his presence in England would have generated unwelcome friction, given the controversy over priority in the discovery of the calculus. His last couple of years were dismal and lonely. His protectress Sophie died in 1714, her daughter, the Queen of Prussia, another dear friend, having preceded her in death. Leibniz died in his bed in Hanover on November 14, 1716. No member of the court attended his funeral. Neither the Royal Society nor the Berlin Academy of Sciences, of each of which he was a member, honored his death. Only the Academy of the Sciences in Paris, which had also accepted him as a member, chose to do so, with a eulogy by Fontanelle.

The would-be Leibniz scholar has a formidable task, because he never wrote a systematic, definitive *magnum opus*. He wrote two book-length works. *Theodicy* was the only one published during his lifetime (in 1710). The other, *New Essays on Human Understanding*, was a critique of Locke, which Leibniz refrained from publishing because Locke had died (and could no longer defend his own views); it was only published posthumously in 1765. He wrote hundreds, if not thousands, of short works, many still not published, let alone translated. He was himself aware of the scattered nature of his work, which continued to stand in need of organization and further reasoning (*Papers*, 12–13). He corresponded with hundreds of people, perhaps a thousand, their letters often containing discussions of serious ideas. These included Christian Wolff, who developed some of his ideas and whose career he helped promote (and who became the most important German link between Leibniz and Kant). Among Leibniz's most important writings, other than those two book-length works, are "Meditations on Knowledge, Truth, and Ideas" (1684), "Primary Truths" (1686?), *Discourse on Metaphysics* (1686), correspondence with Arnauld (1686–1690), "On Freedom" (1689?), "New System of Nature" (1695), "On the Ultimate Origination of Things" (1697), "On Nature Itself" (1698), "The Theodicy: Abridgement of the Argument Reduced to Syllogistic Form" (1710), "The Principles of Nature and of Grace, Based on Reason" (1714), "The Principles of Philosophy, or, the Monadology" (1714), and correspondence with Clarke (1715–1716).

8.3 Knowledge

We can begin our analysis of Leibniz's epistemology by considering his rationalistic theory of ideas and knowledge. In an early (before the 1680s) paper, "What Is an Idea?," he offers us a broad, Cartesian definition of an *"idea"* as "something which is in our mind," making it explicitly clear that he does not mean events, or traces of events, in the brain. Some contents of the mind, such as thoughts, affections, and perceptions, are not themselves ideas but presuppose ideas. And we can have an idea in our mind even when not actively thinking about it, so long as we can retrieve it and think about it. Some ideas are more conducive to knowledge than others. Sensible ideas, in particular, such as those of green and horses, while often pragmatically useful in relation to helpful beliefs, do not lead us to certainty about how things are in themselves. "To seek any other truth or reality than what this contains is vain, and skeptics ought not to demand any other, nor dogmatists promise it." (Here, by the way, Leibniz is foreshadowing a perspective Kant would carefully develop.) Also, Leibniz sees no constructive value in the Cartesian approach to knowledge through a process of systematic doubt (*Papers*, 207, 384). We combine ideas to constitute propositions, which can be true or false, true ones expressing what might be knowable. "A true proposition is one whose predicate is contained in its subject," he writes in "The Nature of Truth" (c. 1686). This conceptual containment principle would turn out to be both important and controversial, as we shall see. It is easy to see how it is true of necessary propositions, such as that no bachelors are married, but far more difficult in the case of contingent ones, such as that most bachelors tend to be frivolous. The subject term, "bachelors," conceptually contains the idea of being unmarried; but we do not think of it as conceptually indicating anything about frivolity. Another way to put the point is to say that, while the idea of a married bachelor violates the principle of noncontradiction, it does not seem the same can be said of the idea of totally serious bachelors. Assuming it were true that most bachelors are frivolous, it would be a contingent, rather than a conceptually necessary, truth. Thus it would need to be governed by some principle other than that of noncontradiction. This would turn out to be the famous Leibnizian principle of sufficient reason (*Writings*, 93–94). Elsewhere, he indicates that both principles – that of noncontradiction and that of sufficient reason, are mandated by the very "definition of the true and the false" (*Theodicy*, 419). What we already see here is the start of a distinctively rationalistic epistemology.

The first mature philosophical article Leibniz published was his "Meditations on Knowledge, Truth, and Ideas." It draws the usual Cartesian distinctions between clear and obscure cognition: clear cognition can be either confused or distinct; distinct cognition can be either inadequate or adequate; and adequate cognition can be either symbolic or intuitive. He holds that adequate cognition which is intuitive is "absolutely perfect." So rational intuition is epistemologically foundational here (as it was for Descartes). Another important paper from the 1680s is "Primary Truths." Two of the most basic of these are that everything is what it is (the principle of identity) and that nothing can both be something and not be it in the same respect at the same time (the principle of noncontradiction). Here again the conceptual containment principle is presented as foundational to a proper understanding of truth. Another primary truth is "that *nothing is without reason,* or *there is no effect without a cause,*" an early version of the principle of sufficient reason. Another is that any two things that differ numerically must also differ qualitatively; this later becomes the principle of the identity of indiscernibles. Another is that every created substance must mirror the universe from its own unique perspective. Another is that no created substance can directly and immediately causally interact with any other. Another is that God has established a parallelism between acts of the body and acts of the soul; he called this "the hypothesis of concomitance," though it later acquired the more popular name of a principle of preestablished harmony. Another was that material substance never comes to be or ceases to be except as a result of divine creation or annihilation; this would later be used to characterize his concept of monads. There are others; but this will suffice for our present purposes. Then there was this puzzling but tantalizing statement: "Extension and motion, as well as bodies themselves (insofar as only motion and extension are placed in bodies) are not substances, but true phenomena, like rainbows" (*Essays*, 23–25, 30–34). Unlike Descartes, Hobbes, and Malebranche, who considered bodies to be substances, and unlike Spinoza, who thought God the only substance, Leibniz held that bodies are mere "phenomena," comprised of "many substances" – which would later lead to his theory of monads.

In his *Discourse on Metaphysics* (sections 24–29), Leibniz discusses epistemology, distinguishing between clear and obscure cognition, clear cognition as distinct or confused, distinct cognition as adequate or inadequate, and adequate cognition as intuitive or not. Like Locke, he distinguishes between "nominal" definitions, where it is doubtful whether the notion defined is possible, and "real definitions," where it is clearly possible. Our knowledge of truth requires real ones; because mere names can be arbitrary, he does not agree with Hobbes that it could ever be based on mere nominal definitions. We can never adequately grasp an impossible idea, so that understanding a notion presupposes knowing that it is at least possible. Like Descartes (and against Locke and other empiricists), Leibniz believes that some ideas are innate and "always in us," whether or not we consciously think of them. Ideas of which we are expressly aware can be called "*notions*" or "*concepts*." Here he is disagreeing with Locke's assumption that, if there were any innate ideas, we humans would universally be aware of them. He acknowledges that the empirical *tabula rasa* approach of Aristotle and his followers is more popular but insists that the Platonic tradition "goes deeper" and aligns himself with it. Examples of such innate ideas that are not derived from the senses are "being, substance, action, identity, and many others." He agrees with Malebranche that God is the only "immediate external object" of our perceptions "and that we see all things by him"; but he disagrees with him that our "ideas are in God and not at all in us." When we think, the ideas thought are truly and uniquely our own. In a letter (of 1702) to Queen Sophie Charlotte, Leibniz analyzes our notions at three levels: the lowest are purely sensible ones, which are imaginable; even if clear, they are confused rather than distinct; the middle level are both sensible and intelligible; they are also imaginable but distinct; and the highest, being purely intelligible, are clear and distinct and "above the imagination." Our notions of "*being* and *truth*," for example, are purely intelligible (non-sensible and beyond the imagination), accessible only to "the *natural light*" of reason. When we use inductive reasoning to derive conclusions based on sense experience alone (as when we generalize), we can never reach universal and necessary conclusions, only particular, contingent ones (a point Kant would later argue against empiricism as well). There are two sorts of truths, according to "The Monadology": truths of reasoning, which are necessary and governed by the principle of noncontradiction, and truths of fact, which are contingent and governed by the principle of sufficient reason. If there were no innate ideas and principles, everything would have to be derived from sensibility and imagination (the *tabula rasa* theory of empiricists like Hobbes and Locke). But then we could never reason our way to universal and necessary truths of fact. Thus, while Locke has the advantage of presenting the "more popular" view and Leibniz the disadvantage of advocating one that is "more esoteric and abstract," innate principles, such as we have been considering, and such innate ideas as "being, unity, substance, duration, change, action," and so forth, allow for the universally necessary factual knowledge that separates us from the beasts. But, again, Locke was mistaken in assuming as a premise of his argument that, if there were innate ideas and principles, we would all be consciously aware of them. For there are ideas that are not yet consciously perceived; those are "tiny perceptions [*petites perceptions*]," too easily drowned out by the ideas of sensibility and imagination but nevertheless of great intellectual importance

(*Essays*, 56–60, 188–189, 191, 217, 284–285, 287, 291–298). This concept, anticipating the theory of the subconscious, seems opposed to Descartes's suggestion that all of our ideas are or can be objects of conscious thought.

8.4 Reality

Leibniz wrote three great metaphysical works, all of which we should consider here: the *Discourse on Metaphysics*, the "Monadology," and his "Principles of Nature and Grace" (1714). The *Discourse* begins with his Cartesian conception of God as the "absolutely perfect being." Given that definition, God could only act "in the most perfect manner" possible. Thus, it is not possible that God could have created in such a way that, overall, the world of creation could conceivably have been better. Thus the "ends or effects" of God's creation are rich in varied abundance, while the means employed for rationally ordering them are marvelously simple. The architecture of the universe is so harmoniously designed that every substance in it uniquely reflects or expresses the whole in its own unique way, mirroring God and the universe itself. Nothing is alien to the whole or a misfit. In section 13 of the *Discourse*, Leibniz presents his predicate-in-subject containment theory (that would incur the hostile fire of Arnauld and whose problematic implications for freedom we shall consider later), which maintains that "the notion of an individual substance includes once and for all everything that can ever happen to it." This is held to apply to all true propositions, whether "absolutely necessary" or "contingent." His example is Julius Caesar. On this view, the notion (or essence) of Caesar at least implicitly involves everything that would ever be true of him – not only that he was a Roman born before Christ but that he had to defy the orders of the Senate, leading his army across the Rubicon, precipitating civil war, and becoming a perpetual dictator. In other words, God's creating this world required the inclusion of that particular man, who had to be who he was and to do everything that he did do. (When the matter is put like that, the problem of Caesar's free choice and responsibility ought to become obvious.) While we may not know why it was best that God create this world with that man in it, the principle of sufficient reason allegedly assures us that there must be an adequate reason, and the divine nature assures us that, in this matter, as in all things, God has acted for the best. God not only created every aspect of our world but also conserves every substance in existence, each created substance being independent of every other and dependent on God alone. We might recall, at this point, that the great seventeenth-century philosophers have tended to despise the scholastic philosophy taught in colleges and universities of their day and, in particular, to repudiate all appeals to final causality, as unscientific. Though only half-hearted in his acknowledgment of scholastic philosophers, whom he says should not be altogether disdained, Leibniz does see value in the use of final causes, in addition to the efficient causes favored by the moderns. Efficient causes work best in explaining events in the physical realm of nature, while final causes are particularly valuable in accounting for mental purposes in the realm of spirit (*Essays*, 35–42, 44–47, 43, 52–55, 64; see also 28–30, 87).

In "A New System" (published anonymously in 1695), Leibniz maintains that, while a soul provides substantial unity to a living thing, a body is merely a collection of "*atoms of substance*" with no intrinsic unity. Three years later, he published a paper, "On Nature Itself," in which he introduces the term "monads" to refer to those atomic substances and maintains that the apparent "*interaction*" among created monads is actually the result of God's coordinating them to act in harmonious order. He writes that this also explains the relation between "*the soul and the body*" – they seem to interact because they are so harmoniously designed in the system of God's creation. Here he appears to adopt something like a position of Aristotelian hylomorphism, analyzing things in terms of a combination of matter and a unifying substantial principle, "called *the soul* in living things and *the substantial form* in other things." Every monad seems to be capable of "something like perception and appetite." The "Monadology" is probably his most studied piece, being a very condensed summary of his mature system. It begins with an argument for the reality of monads: we experience things that are composite aggregates of parts; these simpler parts either are themselves comprised of yet simpler parts or are themselves ultimate, indivisible (this is what atomic means) atoms, the basic building blocks of reality; but, either way, monads, "the true atoms of nature," must exist. Because these monads are not composed of simpler parts, they cannot be taken apart. This is why Leibniz claims that finite monads could only come into existence by divine creation and could only cease to exist as a result of God's annihilating them. They are impervious to the causal influence of any other created monads, which is why they are so independent and why he considers them windowless (to invoke his marvelous metaphor, which may be a takeoff on Locke's comparing the soul to a dark closet, whose windows are the senses). Unfortunately, he does not give us a particularly sharp definition of a monad. But, based on what he does say, we can cobble together a definition of a monad as a simple, indivisible, substantial unit of psychic force. Those last two words are particularly significant in understanding physical reality. A body is a conglomeration of monads, whose essence is neither physical nor extension. Every monad is essentially force, rather than extension, and spiritual, rather than physical. But, from a critical point of view, this poses a problem: how can the basic building blocks of a physical object, such as a chair, which is extended in space, themselves be neither physical nor extended? Leibniz does not provide a compelling answer to this problem. Monads, being spiritual, have perception and appetition, and he used the scholastic word, describing all created monads as "entelechies," meaning systems organized (by God) and oriented toward their own sort of perfection. Apart from God, the infinite Monad, there are three levels of created monads: the lowest level, called "bare monads" (like a rock), have utterly dormant perception but, in their own primitive way, do mirror the universe; the dominant, organizing monad of a living thing is a soul; in a plant, it has no memory, while in animals it does; finally, rational animals like us have dominant monads called "minds" or spirits and have not only perception but "apperception" (that is, self-awareness in perceiving and desiring), so that they are uniquely created in the image and likeness of the infinite Mind or divine Spirit. Also no created monads can be altogether separate from bodies, so that only God is entirely bodiless. Because Descartes and his closest followers thought all souls capable of apperception and were unaware of subconscious "tiny perceptions," they made the mistake of holding that only minds or spirits are souls, so that no nonhuman animals had souls, all of them being merely living machines. The relation between every body, which is physical, and its dominant monad, which is spiritual, is one of a "pre-established harmony," engineered by God in creating the world, and not one of direct, causal interaction. In an imaginative letter (of 1696), Leibniz explains three possible solutions to the mind–body relation, using as his illustration "two clocks" so synchronized as to keep exactly the same time. One explanation might be that the clocks (symbolizing body and mind) are two distinct, separate substances, which causally interact to maintain their synchronicity; this is, essentially, "the common" solution of Descartes and his closest followers, and it fails to explain how such separate realities could affect each other causally. The second explanation is that, while both clocks are "faulty," the clockmaker is constantly readjusting them to ensure that they keep time together; this is, essentially, the solution of Malebranche and the occasionalists, and it requires God (the clockmaker) to be constantly intervening with miraculous activity. The third explanation is that the clocks have been so constructed by the clockmaker as to be constantly synchronized; this is Leibniz's own solution of *"pre-established harmony"* (*Essays*, 142, 161–163, 213–217, 221–223, 147–148). We might observe that two shortcomings of this theory (both of which applied to occasionalism as well) were that it is intractably counterintuitive and that it portrays God as having established a cosmic illusion, of which we are the helpless victims.

Turning now to the "Principles of Nature and Grace," we find an alternative presentation of the same theory. It too begins with the logical observation that the composite substances we constantly experience must be made up of "simple substances" or monads. "*Monas* is a Greek word signifying unity, or what is one." The idea of a "*composite substance*" suggests that a body, such as a rock or a chair, might be substantial rather than mere phenomenon. The internal actions of any monad are "its *perceptions* . . . and its *appetitions.*" Every composite substance, or body, in addition to comprising a multiplicity of simple monads, must have a "central monad," which is "the principle of its unity." Here Leibniz holds that "a living substance" must be a combination of its dominant monad, or soul, and its body, an aggregate of simple monads. Minds, or spiritual monads, Leibniz maintains, experience both "*perceptions*" of external reality and *apperception*, or internal, reflective self-consciousness (could this be a rough parallel to Locke's distinction between sensation and reflection?). While disagreeing that souls can transmigrate from body to body in Plato's sense, he thinks they can undergo transformative change over time. After stating his principle of sufficient reason, that nothing happens without an adequate explanatory cause, he poses what may be the most profound question in the entire history of metaphysics – "*why is there something rather than nothing?*" The ultimate sufficient reason for all contingent reality must be self-sufficient or uncaused, "a necessary being" or God. Because this God must be infinitely perfect (more of this in our next section), everything God does, including the generation of our universe, must be in accordance with the most rational plan, so that ours is "the best possible" world – meaning that it combines "the greatest variety" of phenomena "with the greatest order" relating everything to everything else. This is not only "the best" for us rational souls, but "the best possible" overall, for the infinitely perfect God could do no less. While "the Kingdom of Nature" is governed by natural laws, "the Kingdom of Grace" is governed by the moral law. Against the Newtonians, Leibniz (anticipating Kant) argues that time and space are not objects in themselves, that "*space* is only the order of existing for possibles that exist simultaneously just as *time* is the order of existing for possibles that exist successively." Likewise (contrary to what Cartesians supposed), extension is nothing absolute but is merely relative to phenomenal appearances. At least at times, Leibniz treats bodies as collections of substances rather than as substances, sometimes referring to a body as a "well-founded phenomenon" and not merely a figment of the imagination. (In our next chapter, we shall see Berkeley maintaining that the reality of bodies is phenomenal rather than substantial. Toward the end of his life, Leibniz was aware of Berkeley's ideas and tried to dissociate himself from them.) The realm of nature, "a kingdom of efficient causes," and the realm of grace, "a kingdom of final causes," are separate and independent, yet marvelously well coordinated "*through a harmony pre-established by God*," the entire system of monads and phenomena constituting the best of all possible worlds (*Essays*, 207–211, 170–171, 179, 181–182, 198–200, 306–307, 319; cf. 177; see also *Writings*, 145–147, 172–178, and *Papers*, 363–365, 614) – a view Voltaire later mercilessly satirizes in his *Candide*.

8.5 God

In his "Meditations on Knowledge, Truth, and Ideas," Leibniz utilizes a version of (what later is called) the ontological argument for God (which we have seen used by Descartes, Spinoza, and Malebranche): whatever a thing's essence requires can be predicated of it, as it is; but, because God is, by definition, "the most perfect being" and a "most perfect being" must include "all perfections," one of which is existence, God must exist. So far, so standard. But Leibniz adds a provision to the proof, maintaining that it logically works, but only if God's existence is possible. After all, nothing self-contradictory – such as a square circle or a married bachelor – could possibly exist. If the definition of God is merely "*nominal,*" we are not assured of God's possibility; on the other hand, if it is "*real,*" as Leibniz maintains, then its possibility is guaranteed, and the proof allegedly works. In his *Discourse on Metaphysics*, Leibniz defines God as "an absolutely perfect being," a perfection being a desirable quality. On this view, God has all possible moral and metaphysical perfections and would only act in the best way possible. Here, again, Leibniz employs the ontological argument, again with his distinctive addition to it. In "On the Ultimate Origination of Things," he uses his own distinctive "sufficient reason" version of the cosmological argument for God: we cannot find in any individual objects of our experience or "even in the entire collection" of phenomena any "sufficient reason for why they exist." Yet the metaphysical principle requires that there must be a sufficient reason for everything's being and being as it is. Therefore there must be a sufficient reason for every object of experience and for the world of phenomena as a whole. But the ultimate sufficient reason for the entire "chain" of phenomenal objects and states must, itself, lie beyond the world to be explained, and that is God, "the Author of the World" and the ultimate causal explanation for "both essences and existences" of all contingent beings whatsoever (*Essays*, 25–26, 35–37, 56, 149–152; earlier, more complex arguments for God can be found in *Texts*, 183–184, and *Papers*, 73–74, while an earlier version of the ontological argument is in *Papers*, 231). This argumentation for God is one of the two most important of Leibniz's contributions to philosophical theology.

The other one is his theodicy (from the Greek, meaning "the justice of God"), a word that may have been coined by Leibniz, referring to our attempts to vindicate divine justice in the face of the problem of evil. He uses it in the title of the only book-length work he published during his lifetime, which seems to have developed out of discussions he had with Sophie Charlotte. He begins with a confident affirmation "of the *conformity of faith with reason,*" such that philosophical theology is a legitimate undertaking. The "truths of reason," he claims, are of two sorts: (i) "the 'Eternal Verities,' which are altogether necessary, so that the opposite implies contradiction," and (ii) "*positive*" ones, which hinge on the laws God assigned to the world of creation. No truths of any sort can contradict those of divine revelation. Mysteries of religious faith, while above reason, cannot be contrary to it. So what of evil? We sometimes speak of it as a mystery, but Leibniz thinks it can be rationally explained and sets out to do so in this book. He provides another version of his argument for God from sufficient reason. The "infinite" and "absolutely perfect" God this allegedly demonstrated would be so unlimited "in *power,* in *wisdom* and in *goodness*" that divine action other than that for the best, while theoretically possible, would be practically impossible, so that God could have only chosen to create "the best (*optimum*) among all possible worlds," in its balance of rich multiplicity of phenomena and the orderly simplicity whereby they are interrelated, even if we rashly imagine that we see how it might be better. This doctrine earned Leibniz the title of "philosopher of optimism" and garnered him the scorn of mockery found in Voltaire's *Candide*, whose character Dr. Pangloss is a deliberate caricature of Leibniz. Like Augustine, he adopts a "privation" theory, viewing evil as not any sort of positive reality but only the negation of good that ought to be. He distinguishes among three types of evil: "*Metaphysical evil* consists in mere imperfection, *physical evil* in suffering, and *moral evil* in sin." God could never directly cause moral evil, since that would be counter to divine perfection. God wills the physical evil of suffering only as a just consequence of the moral evil that personal creatures, such as us, choose to do. All creatures, being dependent on God for their very being, are, to that extent, at least, imperfect or metaphysical "evil"; the only way God could have avoided imperfection altogether was not to create at all. But, Leibniz staunchly maintains, *"the rule of the best"* must prevail, and, somehow, it was best that God create this world (*Theodicy*, 73–76, 88, 127–129, 136–138, 187, 264, 267–268).

The same year in which he published *Theodicy*, he wrote an "Abridgement of the Argument Reduced to Syllogistic Form," a brief *tour de force* in which he summarizes eight arguments against belief in an infinitely perfect God, formally presented, each logically refuted by Leibniz himself. Let us consider them one by one. The first objects that God must be imperfect, since only an imperfect being would choose less than the best, as God does. The last premise is supported by the fact that there is evil in the world and the claim that evil in God's world shows that the world is not the best possible. Leibniz denies this last premise because the evil in the world is justified by being "accompanied by a greater good." He seems correct that, in some cases at least, evil can be justified by being accompanied by a yet greater good. The second objection argues that there must be more evil than good in all of God's creation, since there is more evil than good in God's intelligent creatures like us. But there are two problems here: first, it illicitly generalizes from the intelligent part of creation to its whole; and, second, there is no evidence to support even the claim about all intelligent creatures. Once again, he seems to be correct. The third objection argues that since all sin is necessary rather than freely chosen, it is unjust of God to punish the sinners. The reason all sins are called necessary is that they are all predetermined; and the reason for this last premise is that every event is foreseen by God, making it predetermined. Here what he denies is that "everything predetermined is necessary," in the sense of absolute necessity that "destroys" moral responsibility, yielding only an allegedly innocuous "conditional or hypothetical" necessity that is not problematic. Here Leibniz is unconvincing, and we shall discuss his problem with freedom and necessity in a later section. The fourth objection argues that God must be at least an accessory to sin, since God could prevent intelligent creatures from sinning but fails to do so. Leibniz denies that this makes God an accessory to sin. After all, we do not become accessories to evil merely because we allow undesirable evils simply as means to some greater good. But there are two problems here: first, his God is infinitely perfect, as we are not, so that he employs a shaky analogy; and, second, we can easily imagine certain types of evil in our world so heinous as to be morally intolerable, even for the sake of bringing about some greater good. The fifth objection argues that God must actually be "the cause of" (and not merely an accessory to) sin, since "God produces all that is real in sin." Here he points to an ambiguity in the word "real." If it refers to positive reality alone, then he denies that one becomes the cause of something merely by producing all that is real in it; on the other hand, if it refers to the negative reality of privation as well, then he denies that "God produces all that is real in sin." But, on either interpretation, the argument allegedly fails. On this traditional (Augustinian) view, it is we, and not God, who produce the privative reality of sin by misusing the good faculties God gave us. But there is a problem here, since his God has presumably known from all eternity that we would abuse them and caused us to have them anyhow. The sixth objection argues that God must be unjust, since God punishes people who have done their best. But he denies that God ever punishes people who have done their best. The problem here is with his theory of freedom, stemming from his claim that what we do is determined by our natures, as God created us. The seventh objection argues that God is insufficiently good, since God only gives some people, and not all people, the means necessary to save themselves. While admitting that God does give some more grace than others and could overcome human resistance, he denies that God's not giving everyone enough grace to overcome all resistance means that God is insufficiently good. For God has adequate reasons which we humans cannot comprehend. This response (which is comparable to something we have seen in Descartes) disappointingly renders the problem mysterious and rationally inexplicable. The eighth objection argues that God cannot be truly free, since it is necessary that God will always "choose the best," which God (presumably) cannot fail to see and bring about. But Leibniz holds that God's is the ultimate sort of freedom – that which cannot choose wrongly, not as a result of external compulsion, but rather as determined by a perfect nature (*Theodicy*, 377–388; cf. *Texts*, 207–208). It is difficult to say whether one's nature determining one's always choosing the best is a form of necessity or some higher sort of freedom. Even though we may seem to have been picking and choosing where to agree and where to disagree with Leibniz, overall, this is a splendid piece of theodicy, whose ideas are essentially Augustinian, but whose logical form is arguably the most impressive in Christian thought up to that time.

8.6 Humanity

Among created monads, as we have seen, the mind or rational soul is especially like unto God and made for some sort of special relationship with God. This dominant monad in a human is uniquely fit for personal immortality and impervious to bodily changes, including those brought about by physical death, as he maintains in the *Discourse*. Still, we might recall, the monads comprising the body are also immortal, barring divine annihilation, as they too are spiritual in nature. While the soul is a single, simple monad, the body is a vast assemblage of monads. Although "the connection between the soul and the body" appears to be that of interaction (as Descartes thought), how this could possibly occur defies rational explanation. But this does not mean that the mind and the body are insubstantial and merely two dimensions of the same supernatural substance (as Spinoza thought). Nor should we deny the substantial reality of soul, reducing it to an epiphenomenon of the body (as Hobbes thought). But to hold that God is constantly intervening in the natural order in order to produce parallel events between the mental and the physical (as Malebranche did) is clumsy and does not give God sufficient credit for working out the system of parallelism from the outset. What is left is the system of preestablished harmony (which Leibniz advocates). Minds or rational souls have conscious self-awareness, "discover necessary and universal truths," and are capable of free choice and moral responsibility. In short, they are suited for interpersonal society with their Creator in "the City of God," conceived of as "the most perfect republic" of spirits (Kant would later develop this idea of a "kingdom of ends," as we shall see). In "A New System of Nature," Leibniz compares God's governance of this "moral republic" to that of a loving, caring Father. Because created spirits, like ours, are designed to follow higher laws, they are specially fit for "being citizens of the society of minds." In a letter to the Queen of Prussia, Leibniz compares humans "in a small way" to God, because we not only understand order but, to some extent, can impose order. In his "Principles of Nature and Grace," he maintains that we are citizens or members of the moral republic, while God is its monarch (again, anticipating Kant). In humanity "the kingdoms of nature and grace" seem to converge. As we establish our worthiness of this society with God, while we may never achieve "complete joy," as there may always be further perfection to be desired, we can and should embark on the path of "perpetual progress." Toward the end of "The Monadology," Leibniz reminds us that, as we represent a "pre-established harmony" between body and mind, so the order of efficient causes and that of final causes correspond to and complement each other in the relation between the realm of nature and that of grace, in each of which we participate (*Essays*, 64–68, 140–141, 144, 173, 192, 212–213, 223–224; cf. 305–306; see, also, *Texts*, 79–85).

8.7 Freedom

As our last section could be relatively brief because we had been introduced to the pertinent ideas in our "Reality" section, so the same should be the case for this section. Let us begin by recalling the striking claim from the *Discourse* that "the notion of an individual substance includes once and for all everything that can ever happen to it." Leibniz admitted that a critic might object that this view requires that all truths should be necessary and none contingent so "that there would be no place for human freedom, and that an absolute fatalism" would be inevitable. In response, he tries to distinguish between what is "absolutely necessary" and, hence, incompatible with freedom, and that which is only contingently necessary and, hence, compatible with freedom. Using the historical example of Julius Caesar, given his essential nature, as God created it in this best of all possible worlds, the very concept of Caesar required that he defy the orders of the Senate, lead his troops across the Rubicon, precipitate a civil war, and "become perpetual dictator" of Rome. Nevertheless, there is no *logical* contradiction in the idea of Caesar obeying the Senate and not causing such trouble. It is just that that peaceful, acquiescent man would not have been the same Caesar. Given his essential nature, it was contingently necessary that Caesar do what he did; for, "otherwise he would not be this man." And, yet, presumably, Caesar was morally responsible for his actions. Arnauld strenuously objected to this position on the grounds that it hopelessly undermined human freedom and responsibility. Given the world God created, including the historical Caesar, the actions that Caesar performed *had* to occur. In a very interesting letter to Arnauld (from May of 1686), Leibniz defends his view. He does not renounce his predicate-in-subject containment theory but, rather, tones it down, maintaining that "each individual substance always contains traces of what has ever happened to it and marks of what will ever happen to it." Their exchange goes on. But Leibniz never successfully meets Arnauld's challenge, despite his clever subtleties. Yet it was an important issue for Leibniz, as for all modern Christian philosophers, whether all human actions are necessary or some are truly free. It was a topic to which he kept returning both before and after 1686. In the early 1680s, in a paper, "On Freedom and Possibility," he introduces that suspicious distinction between "hypothetical" or contingent necessity, on the one hand, and the "absolutely necessary," on the other. In another paper, "On Contingency," written around 1686, he explicitly espouses the predicate-in-subject containment theory. In another paper, "On Freedom," written around 1689, he calls the problem of freedom and necessity one of the "two labyrinths of the human mind" in which we can easily lose ourselves. In "The Source of Contingent Truths," written in the late 1680s, he clearly and explicitly tries to dissociate himself from the determinism of Hobbes and Spinoza. Toward the end of his life, he writes a letter (December 19, 1707) on human freedom, in which he is still trying to use the dubious distinction between "hypothetical" or contingent necessity and "the absolute necessity" that would "destroy" all freedom and contingency. Though all our voluntary actions be influenced by circumstances and inclinations which determine them and render them certain (at least to God), he tries to insist that this is not tantamount to the sort of "absolute necessity" that would destroy our freedom and responsibility (*Essays*, 44–46, 60–62, 69–76, 19–23, 28–30, 94–98, 100, 193–195; cf. *Writings*, 96–105, and *Texts*, 91–113). Leibniz is a classic example of an early modern Christian philosopher trying to have it both ways: on the one hand, he wants to be in line with the new science, which views every event in our world as causally determined by antecedent conditions; on the other hand, he wants to preserve a zone of freedom from causal necessity, of genuine choice, and of moral responsibility. Despite his brilliance and frequent efforts, he finds no adequate solution.

8.8 Morality

His writings in ethics were rather few and far between. Corresponding to the three sorts of evil, there are three kinds of good: "*metaphysical*" good has to do with the degree of perfection of anything real; "*moral good*" consists of virtue, which is more or less perfectly achieved; and "*physical good*" is identified with pleasure (*Theodicy*, 258). We are obliged to strive for greater moral perfection, to the extent that we are metaphysically capable of it and given our natural desire for pleasure. In the *Discourse*, he indicates that a substance "passes to a greater degree of perfection" when it "exercises its power and *acts*," while it "passes to a lesser degree" of perfection and "shows its weakness" whenever it is merely passive or "*acted*" upon" and that moving to a greater degree of perfection "involves some *pleasure*," while losing perfection and becoming more passive involves "some *pain*." So, on this view, it would seem reasonable that we ought to seek the pleasure involved in being more active and to want to avoid the pain involved in being more passive. In "The Monadology," the "pre-established harmony" between our bodies and our minds connects with that between efficient and final causality. We naturally desire ends that will give us pleasure and the means thereto; and we naturally shy away from final ends and efficient means thereto that will likely cause us pain of any sort (*Essays*, 49, 223). Of course, in the real world of moral psychology, these relationships often get far more complicated than this suggests. In order to achieve the peace and contentment that make this life "happy," we need to cultivate the virtuous habits called for by "right reason." Like the Stoics, who also advocated the life of reason, Leibniz identifies happiness with tranquility, with "*wisdom*" being "the science of happiness" and a "*virtue*" being "the habit of acting in accordance with wisdom." A most important virtue is justice, the habit of trying to promote others' welfare, in proportion to their "needs and merits." Our ultimate happiness is a function of knowing and loving God, the ultimate Good; but this, in turn, involves our having charity for one another, charity being "the touchstone of true virtue" (*Texts*, 166–170). This is fairly standard Christian ethics of the sort that can be traced back at least to Augustine. In some "Reflections on the Common Concept of Justice" (1702?), Leibniz considers Plato's Euthyphro problem – whether God wills what is good and just because it is good and just *or* whether it is good and just merely because God wills it. He is convinced that the former must be the case, as the latter option would render goodness and justice relative to arbitrary, subjective will. He likewise criticizes the Hobbesian view that justice is relative to power, since it confuses the "*fact*" of what one "*can*" enforce with the matter of "*right*" regarding what "*ought* to be." He anticipates at least a portion of Kant's moral argument for personal immortality: God's "perfect government" requires that people be rewarded or punished proportional to their deserts; but, since that obviously does not occur in this life, there must be another in which it will do so (*Papers*, 561–564). Though these views on morality are respectable enough, they are not particularly well developed.

8.9 Society

In some notes Leibniz wrote "On Natural Law," he defines a "*society*" as "a union of different men for a common purpose," leaving open the issue of what sort of purpose, so that even a gang of thieves might qualify as a (bad) society (serving an immoral purpose). Artificial societies, such as a gang of thieves, presumably operate according to their own (written or unwritten) rules. But he also analyzes six sorts of "*natural* society" that are allegedly required by our human nature: (i) that between man and woman; (ii) that between parents and their children; (iii) that between master and servant; (iv) that of the household; (v) that of civil society; and (vi) that of a Church. The first five of these, at least, are quite Aristotelian. To the extent that a society is good, its purpose is universal happiness. "*Natural* law is that which preserves and furthers natural societies," as opposed to human law that maintains or promotes some artificial society. Now every society is more or less "equal or unequal." Also "limited" societies serve certain specified purposes, while "unlimited" ones attend to "the whole life and the common good" of the people involved. True friendship is an example of an unlimited equal society; the relation between rulers and their subjects is unequal and unlimited. And, of course, a society can be restricted to a few (even two) people or open to a vast number. Ideally, husbands and wives, parents and their children, and other relatives should be bound together by ties of friendship as well. Shifting back to Leibniz's reflections on justice, we find him maintaining that confusion regarding the rights of sovereigns and nations tends to stem from a lack of common agreement about the understanding of justice. A definition he proposed was that "justice is a constant will to act in such a way that no person has reason to complain of us." If you have a complaint against your neighbor, it may or may not be reasonable. But if your neighbor has consistently treated you justly, then any complaint against him you may have should be unreasonable (even if you honestly believe otherwise). The Golden Rule – negatively formulated as not doing to others what you would not have done to you – is a useful way of measuring justice more objectively and requires that we sometimes help others, as opposed merely to refraining from harming them. Matters of "*strict Right*" require our not doing to others what we would not want them to do to us, while "*equity*" requires that we sometimes do for others what we would want them to do for us (a positive formulation of the Golden Rule). Against Hobbes, Leibniz denies that obligations of justice are merely functions of social agreement rooted in self-interest (*Papers*, 428–430, 566–569; cf. 421–424). Like his views on morality, Leibniz's perspective on society is not very dramatic, given his background and cultural influences.

8.10 Review

Like the other seventeenth-century philosophers we have studied, Leibniz offers us a comprehensive system which was stronger in some areas (in his case, epistemology, metaphysics, and philosophy of religion) and sketchier in others (e.g. ethics and sociopolitical thought). Like the others, he can be seen as being motivated to improve on Descartes. On one hand, he was the first great modern philosopher in Germany; on the other, he was the last great seventeenth-century rationalist. Unlike earlier rationalists, he has the advantage of familiarity with not only Hobbes's radical empiricism, but also Locke's moderate empiricism. But, like other early modern rationalists after Descartes, he presents us with a worldview that has an air of unreality to it – e.g. his noninteracting dualism. His suggestion that bodies are not substances seems counterintuitive. His predicate-in-subject containment theory runs at loggerheads with his advocacy of human freedom and moral responsibility. As we shall see, his influence on Kant proved to be profound. But first we should consider the developments of early modern empiricism.[2]

8.11 Another Perspective

Damaris Cudworth, Lady Masham (1659–1708), was the daughter of Ralph Cudworth, a leading Cambridge Platonist. She met John Locke when she was 23 years old and corresponded with him until he returned from Holland to England (in 1688). In 1685, she married Sir Francis Masham,

---

2 For more on Leibniz, see ch. 4 of *Western Philosophies of Religion*, by Wayne P. Pomerleau (New York: Ardsley House, 1998).

with whom she had a son. When her father died (in 1688), he left her books of her choosing from his library. Locke frequently visited Oates, her country home. In 1691, he made it his own home, bringing with him his library of almost two thousand books; he continued living there until he died in 1704. He left half of his estate to her son. She wrote a biography of Locke. Some of her best philosophy can be found in her correspondence with Leibniz, which we shall now consider.[3]

The correspondence between Masham and Leibniz (like the earlier one between Descartes and Princess Elisabeth) is very polite, Masham being deferential and even, at times, self-effacing. Their exchanges of 1704 and 1705 seem to begin with her sending Leibniz a volume of her father's work, a letter she wrote ending by communicating Locke's best wishes to Leibniz. She asks there for an explanation of forms that Leibniz refers to sometimes as "primitive forces," sometimes as "souls," and sometimes as "substances," while classifying them as "neither spirit nor matter." In reply, he says they are the principles of action and perception in a thing and can "be called forms, entelechies, souls, or minds." He also claims that no minds, other than the divine mind, can be "entirely separate from matter." Wrestling with the problem of how minds and bodies can affect one another led him, he says, to his explanation based on a preestablished harmony that he tries to distinguish from the theory of occasionalists like Malebranche, which would have God constantly intervening miraculously in events in the natural world (591–593).

This opens the gate to her courteous but probing critique. She points out that his assertion that there is, in us, a simple principle of action and perception seems without supporting argumentation, as is his view that all such spiritual principles except God have "organic bodies." As for his system of preestablished harmony, it strikes her as not yet any "more than a hypothesis." It does not seem that there is a significant difference between Leibniz's theory and Malebranche's theory of "occasional causes" other than the timing of when God operates. She ends this letter by saying that Locke was honored that Leibniz was reading and critically considering his *Essay* and that it does not appear he has long to live, given his bad lungs. In reply, Leibniz claims that if all competing theories but one can be shown to be impossible, then it is "extremely probable" that the one that is possible "is the true one." We might object that we cannot be sure we have considered all competing theories. But Leibniz thinks he can establish more than the high probability of his theory since, he claims, it is the one that is "most in conformity with God's wisdom and the order of things." It is not clear how he imagines he can know that, however. He claims that the advantage of his theory over occasionalism is that the latter, unlike his, has to resort to a constant complex of miracles. He holds that this is also the problem with supposing that "God could give to matter the power of thinking," since only miraculous intervention by God would allow for something whose nature is nonthinking to think (594–597). But this is less than convincing, as God might have created at least some bodies (such as the human brain) such that they can think.

In reply to Leibniz, she cannot see how basing a theory on its seemingly being "the most agreeable one" to God's wisdom can yield a convincing conclusion, since we cannot presume to understand how God's "infinite wisdom" operates. She agrees that extension is inseparable from all created substance but finds his idea of "an infinite substance" to be inconceivable. Why should we believe that God creates unextended substances and unites them with extended substances? Like Hobbes before her, she cannot see why God could not give the power of thought to some bodies. Then she introduces a new problem (which we have considered above) regarding human free will: if God has ordered all of creation according to a providential preestablished harmony, how are we genuinely free to generate our own actions. She is confident that she exercises freedom of choice

---

3 References in this section will be to *Early Modern Philosophy: An Anthology*, ed. by Lisa Shapiro and Marcy P. Lascano (Peterborough, Canada: Broadview Press, 2022).

8.11 Another Perspective | **129**

and that it is a prerequisite for moral accountability. Again she concludes by expressing her concern for Locke's ill health (598–600).

One place in their correspondence where Leibniz seems to get a bit sharp with her is when he warns her against falling into skepticism: "We must guard against a clever Pyrrhonism which, disguised by false modesty, takes too far the truth that we do not properly understand God's ways." His argument for unextended substance is that God must be unextended; but we have already seen Hobbes deny that. Leibniz grants that she has no idea in the sense of a mental "image of a nonextended substance" but holds that she can nevertheless have "a notion of one" (using a distinction we shall see again in Berkeley). Toward the end, he gets rather dogmatic – merely asserting that souls without bodies would be incomplete, that the same substance has both thought and extension, so long as that substance is a "composite of a soul and a body," that his system has no more of a problem with free will than any other, and that his system emphasizes "our spontaneity, and does not detract from our choice." In subsequent letters, she tells Leibniz of Locke's death, of his generous legacy of money and books left to her son, of her hope that one day she might visit Hanover and meet with him in person, and of her regret that Locke's death might prevent him from publishing his reflections on Locke's *Essay* (600–602). What we see here (as we did with Princess Elisabeth's correspondence with Descartes) is a woman with a keen intellect not only understanding a great philosopher better than courtesy allows her to reveal, but also developing acute criticisms of essentials of his theory.

9
George Berkeley

Source: Wellcome Collection/Public Domain

9.1 Overview

To say that George Berkeley was the most critical philosophical link, in British empiricism, between John Locke and David Hume is accurate enough but fails to do justice to his importance in his own right as, perhaps, the only significant empirical idealist in the history of Western philosophy. (To call him an "idealist" is already to invite misleading comparisons. Schopenhauer, whom we shall study later, calls him, indeed, the father of idealism. Maybe he should have said *modern* idealism, since Plato surely deserves the unqualified title. But Berkeley was not only an idealist; unlike Plato and his closest idealist followers, Berkeley espoused an idealism that did not revolve around mind-independent eternal ideas, any more than would that of the greatest examples of German idealism, which we shall also study.) His most striking philosophical contributions, in epistemology and metaphysics, were theocentric and opposed to skepticism. Yet Hume, who later acknowledged his own skepticism and who praised Berkeley's critique of abstract ideas as among the greatest philosophical achievements of the time, was probably correct in observing that, despite himself, Berkeley (like Locke before him) unwittingly sowed seeds of skepticism. He is our first example of an Enlightenment thinker, the Enlightenment being that eighteenth-century intellectual movement, in Europe and America, committed to such ideals as reason, experience, science, nature, liberty, education, progress, and human welfare.

9.2 Biography

Berkeley was born near Kilkenny, Ireland, on March 12, 1685, of Anglo-Irish descent, the eldest of the six sons of William and Elisabeth Berkeley. In 1696, at the age of 11, he entered Kilkenny College, a boarding school; and, in 1700, at the age of 15, he entered Trinity College in Dublin, from which he graduated with a BA in 1704. In 1707, he got an MA from Trinity and was elected a Junior Fellow there, writing minor works on mathematics. In 1707–1708, he was keeping notebooks, which he never intended for publication, but which were first published in 1871; they subsequently came to be called his *Philosophical Commentaries* (to be referred to here as *Commentaries*) and are quite valuable aids to tracking the development of his ideas. In 1709, he was ordained a deacon in the Anglican Church of Ireland and published his first important work, his *Essay towards a New Theory of Vision* (to be referred to here as his *Essay*). The following year, he was ordained an Anglican priest and published the first part of his *Treatise concerning the Principles of Human Knowledge* (to be referred to here as the *Principles*), which initially elicited little response. In 1712, he published *Passive Obedience* (here called *Obedience*), his chief work on morality and political society, using what later came to be called rule-utilitarianism, and became a junior lecturer in Greek at Trinity. The following year, he made his first visit to England, where he published his *Three Dialogues between Hylas and Philonous* (here called the *Dialogues*), which was immediately more popular than the *Principles*; its content was largely the same as that of the *Principles*, though the earlier work had an important critique of abstract ideas not included in the later work, while the *Dialogues* placed more explicit emphasis on attacking skepticism. Thus in a brief five-year period, from 1709 through 1713, he published his four greatest works.[1] In 1713–1714, he accompanied the Earl of Peterborough, appointed ambassador to the King of Sicily, to the continent as his chaplain. There he

---

1 References to Berkeley will be to the following two anthologies: *Philosophical Works*, by George Berkeley (hereafter called *Works*), ed. by Michael R. Ayers (London: Everyman, 1975), and *Berkeley Selections* (hereafter called *Selections*), ed. by Mary W. Calkins (New York: Charles Scribner's Sons, 1957).

132 | 9 George Berkeley

probably met with an ill (with a lung infection) Malebranche, at that time arguably the most famous living philosopher on the planet. There is an intriguing story (going all the way back to the eighteenth century) that they had such a violent row that the Catholic priest got so agitated that he died a few days later; but this anecdote has to be false, since Malebranche did not actually die until late in 1715. By the end of the summer of 1714, Berkeley was back in London, where he stayed until 1716. Then he went to France and Italy as a traveling tutor to a son of the Bishop of Clogher. He worked on a second part of his *Principles* but lost the manuscript in Italy (*Works*, 425); he wrote *De Motu*, a work of natural science, while in France, and witnessed the 1717 eruption of Mt. Vesuvius, his account of which was published by the Royal Society. In 1721, having returned to London, he published *De Motu*; then he went back to Trinity, took a Doctor of Divinity degree, and lectured on Divinity Studies, as a Senior Fellow. In 1722, he was appointed Dean of Dromore. The following year, he inherited half of a lady's estate, which was surprising as he hardly knew her. In 1724, he was appointed Dean of Derry and, now financially secure, resigned his fellowship at Trinity.

That same year, he returned to London, this time to promote an ambitious project of his, to create a college for native Americans and the sons of American colonists in Bermuda. Thinking that Europe was in a state of spiritual decay, he wrote a poem to America as the land of future progress; its most famous line is, "Westward the course of empire takes its way" (*Selections,* viii). In 1726, he secured a royal charter for the founding of St. Paul's College in Bermuda, and the Parliament promised a fairly generous grant for its funding. Two years later, Berkeley married Anne Forster, daughter of a speaker of the House of Commons in Ireland; the next month, they sailed for America. In 1729, Berkeley bought a farm near Newport, Rhode Island; it was run by Anne for the period of more than two and a half years that they were there. While in Rhode Island, he befriended Samuel Johnson, an American philosopher, who became his first known disciple, the author of the first philosophy textbook in America, and the first President of King's College (now Columbia University). In 1731, when he was informed that the promised grant money would not be forthcoming, the family returned to London. (Berkeley had given his Rhode Island property to Yale University and donated books to Harvard and Yale.) There he sought advancement within the Church. In 1732, he published *Alciphron*, his major work in the philosophy of religion, mostly written while he was in America. The following year, he published his *Theory of Vision Vindicated and Explained*. In 1734, he published *The Analyst* and, appointed Bishop of Cloyne, returned to Ireland. From 1735 to 1737, he published *The Querist*, dealing with economics, in three parts. In 1744, he published *Siris*, promoting the medicinal value of tar-water, made from a vegetable extract distilled from pine resin steeped in water, regarded as a panacea (*Selections*, 406–408). In 1745, he declined an offer to be appointed Bishop of Clogher. Mostly during these 18 years (1734–1752), he worked as a conscientious, devoted bishop. He and Anne had seven children; three died in infancy, and his oldest son, William, died (in 1751) at the age of 14. In the summer of 1752, he and Anne went to Oxford, where his second son, George, was a student at Christ Church. On January 14, 1753, Bishop Berkeley died in Oxford. In accordance with his will, five days were allowed to elapse before he was buried (in Christ Church Chapel), for fear of his being interred while still alive. The city of Berkeley, California was named after him (although the pronunciation was Americanized) by a man who admired some of his work.

9.3 Knowledge

Epistemologically, Berkeley generally follows Locke's empiricism, though, metaphysically, he rejects his predecessor's dualism. In his Preface to the *Principles*, Berkeley identifies "skepticism" as his target. In its Introduction, while doing the same, he defines philosophy as "the study of

9.3 *Knowledge* | 133

wisdom and truth." Any theory that leads us into "a forlorn skepticism" is a foolish path to error, he thinks. His stated goal is to expose and counter the "absurdities" that lead us into ways of thinking filling our minds with doubt – so that we have "raised a dust, and then complain we cannot see." As the complete title of his *Principles* indicates, it is analyzing "Human Knowledge" as the means to accomplishing this. As an empiricist, following Hobbes and Locke, he sees language as significant in both leading us to truth and misleading us. Indeed, he quotes Locke (in the Introduction) in his attack on the view that we have, or even can have, any "*abstract general ideas.*" All objects of experience outside our minds are particulars. Thus, for example, we experience those individual humans "Peter, James, and John." But then we can "abstract" from their individual distinguishing features to arrive at "the abstract idea of *man* or, if you please, humanity or human nature." Nevertheless, when we think of a human being, the mental image must be particular and cannot be general. So there are no general ideas in the sense of mental images; but the only things that are general are words, such as "man," "tree," "horse," and so forth, which represent a range of particulars that resemble each other in certain respects. This view that only words are truly general is called "nominalism." The importance of this to Berkeley is that it renders futile the quest for mysterious entities, corresponding to general words, that can never be objects of experience. The abstractions of scholasticism and the innate ideas of rationalism, on this theory, can be dismissed. Berkeley also denies that "the communicating of ideas" is the only significant use of language, as it can also serve the important functions of eliciting emotions, encouraging and discouraging action, and influencing attitudes, for example. By understanding the role of language and its possible abuses, we can learn to protect ourselves from the "delusion of words" and thus increase our chances of achieving knowledge and avoiding skepticism (*Works*, 73–88).

Berkeley is a typical modern philosopher in that he sees ideas (in a broad sense of the word) as the direct, immediate objects of the mind: "It is evident to anyone who takes a survey of the objects of human knowledge, that they are either ideas actually imprinted on the senses, or else such as are perceived by attending to the passions and operations of the mind, or lastly ideas formed by help of memory and imagination, either compounding, dividing, or barely representing those originally perceived in the aforesaid ways." The ultimate origin of ideas, on this empirical view, is external and/or internal sensation. So far this sounds like Locke: ideas are the passive objects of minds, which are active subjects. But, unlike Locke, he does not believe that mental ideas represent or copy material substances such as tables and chairs, because the latter are not substantially real (this is Berkeley's "immaterialism" on which we shall focus in our next section). Rather, the essence of an idea consists in its being perceived by some mind(s). "Their *esse* is *percipi*, nor is it possible they should have any existence, out of the minds or thinking things which perceive them." Dualists, such as Descartes and Locke, are mistaken if they suppose that there are mind-independent material substances. Rather, Berkeley claims, "extension, figure and motion are only ideas existing in the mind." The idea of a body in the mind cannot resemble a body existing independently of any mind, since "an idea can be like nothing but another idea." This will turn out to be a critical premise in his argument for immaterialism; and we shall question it soon. Since matter would have to be mind-independent to be a substance and since matter is only an idea in the mind, "the very notion" of "*corporeal substance*" is impossibly contradictory. As ideas, by their very nature, are perceived by minds, the former are "inactive," passive, and inert. By contrast, minds, by their very nature, are thinking substances and, hence, naturally active (*Works*, 89–92, 98–99). Thus ideas, by their very nature, are essentially different sorts of realities from the minds that are aware of them. Before proceeding, it might be timely to ask a few critical questions, even though this may not yet be the time to try to answer all of them. First, why should we not agree with philosophers (such as Descartes and Locke) who believe that ideas in the mind can more or less adequately represent material objects outside the mind? This is because an idea can allegedly resemble only an idea, not a physical object, and because there allegedly are no substantial material objects for any ideas to resemble. We shall have to wait until the next section to see Berkeley's argumentation for immaterialism before we can assess its merit. But, for now, why should we agree that "an idea can be like nothing but another idea"? Berkeley presents the claim without any argued support, as if it were self-evident. But, far from being self-evident, is it even true? Suppose that yesterday you fell into a ravine, injuring yourself a bit and frightening yourself a great deal. Then, last night, after finally falling asleep, you dreamed of doing it again, waking up in a cold sweat, remembering the stream of ideas constituting your nightmare. Why can that set of ideas constituting your bad dream not be like the actual earlier event of falling? One last critical consideration: strictly speaking, all our knowledge must be of our perceived ideas; but no idea is of a substance, and, therefore, strictly speaking, we cannot know any substance. While being overtly opposed to skepticism, does Berkeley not thus, unwillingly and unwittingly, prove to be its accomplice?

So all knowledge requires a foundation in sensing; yet it cannot be reduced to sensing. As Berkeley writes in *Siris*, "We know a thing when we understand it; and we understand it when we can interpret or tell what it signifies. Strictly, the sense knows nothing. We perceive indeed sounds by hearing, and characters by sight. But we are not therefore said to understand them." So, while knowledge must be grounded in sensible experience, it is reason which must achieve it. The mind has no innate ideas but must derive all its ideas from sense experience; nevertheless, it has rational acts capable of generating useful "notions" (*Selections*, 413–416, 420, 422; more about this later). We can know our own ideas regarding phenomenal objects of sense experience but mistakenly imagine that they represent qualities of substances that are mind-independent. Remember that Locke thought we can know the secondary qualities of bodies, perceived by a single sense, as in our perceptions rather than in the object itself; for example, we see the grass as green but should not assume it is green in itself. By contrast, Locke thought we can know primary qualities of bodies, perceived by more than one sense, as in the objects themselves; for example, we see and feel the cubical shape of a body, which in itself allegedly has that figure. But a friend of Locke's named William Molyneux had a problem with this, to which Berkeley refers in his *Essay*: if a man born blind had learned to differentiate by touch between a cubical shape and a spherical one and then gained his sight through a surgical operation, would he immediately be able to differentiate, by sight alone, between the two shapes, which, of course, he could distinguish by touch? Molyneux and, later, Berkeley thought that he could not. In 1728, such a medical case actually occurred, showing that they were correct. The point is that visible shape and tangible shape are not identical. This will lead Berkeley to deny any significant difference between secondary and primary qualities, so that the latter also should be considered in the mind of a perceiver rather than in the material object – which will lead him to the denial of material substance. Berkeley returned to "Molyneux's problem" in *The Theory of Vision Vindicated and Explained*, at the end of which he mentions the medical case that proved him correct against Locke (*Works*, 20, 25, 51, 54–55, 293–295, 304; the *Commentaries* also contain scattered relevant material – see *Works*, 311, 313–314, 339, 344, 352, 363, 371, 373, 375, 384–386, 391, 410). The reason this is important, as we shall see, is that it will help him to dismiss the substance dualism of Locke (and also Descartes) and to argue for his "immaterialism."

9.4 Reality

Berkeley is most famous for his denial of material substance and view that only spirits or minds are substantial. He called his view "immaterialism," which represents the negative side of his metaphysical theory; the positive side, that only ideas and the minds that think them are real, can be called idealism. The theory turns out to be as strange a version of empiricism as were Spinoza's, Malebranche's, and Leibniz's versions of rationalism. As Spinoza, Malebranche, and Leibniz all simplified the system of Descartes in order to eliminate the problem of interaction, creating their own stranger theories, so Berkeley simplifies Locke's metaphysics in order to eliminate dualism's problems with substance, creating his own stranger theory. While Descartes and Locke were dualists, Spinoza and Berkeley were monists. But, whereas Spinoza was a numerical monist, claiming that there is only one reality, Berkeley was (like Hobbes) a generic monist, claiming that there is only one *kind* of reality, and that that is mind or spirit (as opposed to bodies, for Hobbes). Even though, in its own way, Berkeley's metaphysical theory is as odd and counterintuitive as Spinoza's, his arguments for it are as carefully considered. Thus, as we did with that earlier thinker, here we shall need to analyze his supporting arguments, lest he appear as crazy as some of his contemporaries thought him to be.

As we saw in our last section, his motive for attacking abstract general ideas was that he thought them conducive to the sort of materialism that leads to atheism, agnosticism, skepticism, determinism, and deism, which threaten to undermine his core philosophical and religious values. In the *Principles*, he presents an argument, which can be formulated as a syllogism: All objects of experience are things perceived by sense; all things perceived are ideas or sensations; therefore all objects of experience are ideas or sensations. Immediately we can suspect a problem here: while only ideas or sensations may be the direct, immediate objects of mental experience, we might (with Descartes and Locke) want to insist that they represent things outside the mind, which are its indirect, mediate objects, so that there would be a sort of equivocation on the phrase "objects of experience." Here is a second deductive argument: External things (e.g. outside the mind) are either perceivable or they are not; if they are, then they must be ideas; but if they are not, they cannot resemble ideas (which must, by their very nature, be perceivable); so either they are ideas (as Berkeley holds) or they are unlike ideas (and, hence, useless and inconceivable). This is called a dilemma, the problems being that physical objects, such as tables and chairs, might be at least indirectly perceivable and that, as argued above, it is not obvious that something that is not directly perceivable might not resemble directly perceivable ideas. Here is a third argument, a syllogism: Qualities of things are only ideas in the mind; but "an idea can be like nothing but another idea"; thus, since ideas can only exist in the mind, qualities of things cannot exist outside the mind. Whether the first premise is adequately supported depends on whether Berkeley has shown (against Locke) that primary qualities are as restricted to the mind as secondary ones; and we have already given a counterexample to refute the second premise. The fourth argument, against dualists, can be framed as a syllogism: All solidity is a function of extension, and there can be no extension "in an unthinking substance"; so there can be no solidity in "an unthinking substance." Granting the first (Cartesian and Lockean) premise for the sake of argument, the second one begs the question, in that this entire web of arguments is designed to explode the idea of "an unthinking substance" as a myth of philosophers. A fifth argument is another dilemma: We could only know material substance (assuming it were real) by sense or by reason; but by sense we only know our own perceptions (e.g. sensations and ideas), and reason cannot discover any necessary connection between our perceptions and any external bodies; therefore we cannot know material substance (if there were any) at all. The second premise is ambiguous regarding our immediate knowledge of our own perceptions and our mediate knowledge of external realities; the third one (which will be an important thesis of Hume's) is just dogmatically stated rather than supported. A sixth deductive argument (neither a syllogism nor a dilemma this time) can be formulated thus: There must be some active cause of our ideas; only a substance could be an active cause (and all ideas are passive); but there can be no "material substance"; hence there must be some immaterial "active substance or spirit." The problematic premise here is the third one, since the impossibility of "material substance" (immaterialism) is precisely what has been in question here. Finally, a seventh argument takes the form of a syllogism specifying the transcendent nature of that spirit and represents the edge of the wedge of reasoning that will lead us to God: My ideas do not all depend on me or even on us humans (as I experience some despite all human will); yet ideas must depend on some (mental) spirit; consequently, there must be some (mental) spirit other than me or us on whom such ideas depend. But this argument only works if there are no material substances on which depend those ideas of mine that do not originate in us, and, again, that is precisely the point of contention. Berkeley goes on to say, "The ideas imprinted on the senses by the Author of Nature" (God), as opposed to the imaginary ideas that depend on us, "are called *real things*," as opposed to figments of our imagination. This may be the greatest problem with his brand of idealism. It is not just that there are holes in his arguments but that his position itself renders it difficult to distinguish clearly between reality and imagination. What he claims is that reality, as grasped through the "ideas of sense," will always be "more strong, orderly, and coherent than the creatures of the mind" (*Works*, 90–93, 95, 98–101). But, again, we have an assertion without argued support; and it is doubtful whether the assertion is even universally and necessarily true. (These seven arguments, by the way, appear in sections 4, 8, 9, 11, 18, 26, and 29 of the *Principles*.)

To his credit, Berkeley considers and tries to answer many objections to his philosophy, 13 of them philosophical (*Works,* 101–121), followed by a couple of religious ones (*Works*, 121–122). While we do not have time to go through all these, let us do a bit of critical cherry-picking. At the end of the first one, he claims that his theory, far from promoting skepticism, opposes it; while that was, no doubt, his intention, history has proved otherwise. The second objection holds that his immaterialist theory undermines the clear distinction between reality and imagination, which, despite his claims to the contrary, seems well founded. The fourth one holds that his theory only maintains the continued reality of things while we are perceiving them; in answering this, as we shall see, he argues that God exists as the permanent Perceiver of all reality. Another objection is that his theory confuses "ideas" in our minds and "things" outside our minds. He admits that popular discourse makes such a distinction and that it is usually prudent to talk that way so long as we are not misled by that popular mode of talk; as he put it, "in such things we ought to *think with the learned, and speak with the vulgar*." Finally, the twelfth objection asks why not simply accept the occasionalist view (of, for example, Malebranche) of matter? But, then, matter would become superfluous for explanatory purposes, as it and our minds cannot directly affect each other; and to hold that a material event serves as "an *occasion*" for our experiencing mental events is only a convoluted way of saying that it is an occasion for God's giving us ideas; but then God does not need matter to occasion "exciting ideas in us" (*Works*, 103–105, 108, 115–118). So, on the occasionalist view, matter is useless and misleading. It would allegedly be better to do away with it, as immaterialism tries to do.

Let us now turn to the last few pages of the *Principles* for Berkeley's analysis of "*spirit*," the only sort of substance that he considers real. After all, even if we were to agree that there is no material substance, there could still exist spiritual substance – namely, the reality of God, or infinite Spirit, and of finite human minds. And, given that there are ideas (unless one is a Platonist, believing in mind-independent ideas, which Berkeley clearly does not), there must be minds to think them. Since we immediately and directly perceive ideas, we must exist as thinking minds or spirits. Ideas are passive, while spirits thinking them must be active; therefore spirits cannot be ideas. And "by the word *spirit* we mean only that which thinks, wills, and perceives." Whereas the reality of an idea consists in its "being perceived," that of a spirit or mind consists "in perceiving ideas and thinking." But now comes another problem. "*Spirits* and *ideas* are things so wholly different," the former being active substances and the latter being passive objects of experience, that no idea can adequately represent any spirit. Thus "it is evident there can be no idea of a spirit." But then, it would seem, there can be no knowledge of spirit, which is "the only substance," since knowledge requires ideas. But, surely, that is skepticism. Berkeley tries to evade the problem by saying that we do have some "notion of *spirit*," without clearly explaining the difference between a "notion" of an active reality and an "idea" of a passive one *or* how a "notion" can substitute for ideas in the acquisition of knowledge. It seems that notional knowledge is conceptual, having to do with grasping "the meaning of the word" "soul" or "mind" or "spirit" or whatever: "I have some knowledge or notion of my mind, and its acts about ideas, inasmuch as I know or understand what is meant by those words." It seems that I can have only a notional knowledge of other spirits, based on my rational interpretation of what I experience of their actions. "Hence the knowledge I have of other spirits is not immediate, as is the knowledge of my ideas; but depending on the intervention of ideas, by me referred to agents or spirits distinct from myself, as effects or concomitant signs." Through interpersonal communication, we conclude that we have similar experiences and similar ideas, inferring that others are spirits rather like us. In our next section, we shall consider Berkeley's discussion of God. But for now we can observe that our knowledge of God, like our knowledge of other humans, is notional or indirect but that he claims "that the existence of God is far more evidently perceived than the existence of men" (*Works*, 144–150). Even apart from the fact that God is not "perceived" by us at all, this is clearly inadequate. If the objects of knowledge are ideas, and we have no idea of spirit, and spirit is the only sort of substantial reality, then we cannot know any substantial reality. Berkeley thus unwillingly and unwittingly leads us into the very skepticism he means to destroy. It does not seem that his murky, shady use of "notions" can help him evade the issue. Is it any wonder that Hume, the self-professed skeptic, considers Berkeley a skeptic despite himself? Of course, it must be admitted that Berkeley, the idealist, was as free of substance dualism's problem of interaction as was Hobbes, the materialist; but, as Hobbes's metaphysical theory had problems adequately accounting for all the rich dimensions of human experience, so Berkeley's theory of reality is as counterintuitive as was Spinoza's without sufficiently cogent argumentation to establish its alleged truth.

It can be easily observed that we have been focusing on the *Principles* as our source for Berkeley's epistemology and metaphysics. Most of the key points emphasized here, however, could also find textual support in his *Dialogues*. Indeed, let us now briefly consider some contributions made there. The *Dialogues* (even more than the *Principles*) aim at attacking skepticism; in fact, the subtitle included the words "in opposition to Sceptics and Atheists." Its two characters are Hylas and Philonous. In Greek *hylas* means "matter," and this character represents a materialist such as Hobbes; *philonous*, in Greek, means "lover of mind," and that character represents Berkeley's own immaterialism. Philonous not only argues for immaterialism but tries to show that materialism leads to skepticism and irreligion. Hylas originally defines "a *sceptic*" as "one that doubts of everything"; under cross-examination, he adds to that definition the words "or who denies the reality and truth of things." As we have seen, through the senses, the mind perceives ideas, as when we see a "picture of Julius Caesar" and read, below it, a caption identifying him. But the senses cannot perceive the truth that what we see is supposed to be a picture of Julius Caesar. That truth can only be meaningful and understandable to the mind through "reason and memory," the truth having to do not with the ideas sensed so much as with the "archetypes of our ideas." Thus the truth that this is supposed to be a depiction of Julius Caesar does not depend on us who are aware of it. In the second dialogue, Philonous uses the idealistic theory of reality as a basis for a typically Berkeleyan proof of God that might be formulated thus: Sensible things that do not depend on me or any other humans for their existence obviously exist; but, since they exist as ideas, they must depend on some "infinite, omnipresent Spirit," which is God. Here is how Philonous himself neatly argues the point syllogistically: "*sensible things do really exist: and if they really exist, they are necessarily perceived by an infinite mind: therefore there is an infinite mind, or God.*" He claims that this argument will defeat the irreligion (unfairly called "atheism") of both Hobbes and Spinoza and is at odds with the extravagant, far-fetched "enthusiasm of Malebranche," whom Berkeley was often thought to follow. But we must critically consider whether the argument works and must, regrettably, conclude that it is a non sequitur. First, we have already called into question the upshot of Berkeley's metaphysical theory that all sensible things such as table and chairs, which continue to exist when no humans perceive them, really are essentially ideas. But, second, even if, for the sake of argument, we were to let that pass, notice what a huge leap Berkeley makes from the long-term nonhuman mind to which this would lead us to the "infinite, omnipresent Spirit" that is the God of Christianity. Berkeley does not justify this leap; and it is doubtful that he could do so. The argument, though defective, has inspired a couple of anonymously composed limericks, the first of which poses the problem: There was a young man who said, "God/Must think it exceedingly odd/ To find that the tree/Continues to be/When there's no one about in the Quad." In reply, the second offers Berkeley's solution: "Dear sir, your astonishment's odd./I am always about in the Quad./And that's why the tree/Continues to be,/Since perceived by, yours faithfully, God." In the third dialogue, Philonous admits that, strictly speaking, we have "no idea, either of God or any other spirit," for reasons we have already considered. But our conceptual notion of "mind, spirit or soul" is of an "indivisible unextended thing, which thinks, acts, and perceives." We infer this notion from self-reflection. By analogy, we infer that it applies to other humans as well as to ourselves. And our notion of God is similarly, but not identically, derived. "For all the notion I have of God, is obtained by reflecting on my own soul, heightening its powers, and removing its imperfections." This is a reasonable empirical account of our idea of God, except that, again, the distinction between an idea and a "notion" is never clarified, though Philonous insists, "I have a notion of spirit, though I have not, strictly speaking, an idea of it. I do not perceive it as an idea or by means of an idea, but know it by reflexion." What Berkeley's theory of reality represents is a partial phenomenalism. That is to say, material objects are nothing but collections of ideas or phenomenal appearances and not substantial, while minds or spirits are supposed to be substances (and not mere clusters of phenomenal appearances). But Hylas raises an extremely acute, critical point: Why should we not regard the mind phenomenally as well, as "only a system of floating ideas, without any substance to support them"? This is the critical point that Hume later presses against Berkeley. As Hylas puts it, "And as there is no more meaning in spiritual substance than in material substance, the one is to be exploded as well as the other." Unfortunately, Philonous (and thus Berkeley) offers us no cogent response, so that the specter of skepticism is left hovering. By the way, it is near the end of the *Dialogues* that Berkeley uses the word "*immaterialism*" and contrasts it with "*materialism*"; however, he does not call his theory "idealism." In his *Commentaries*, he calls his theory "the immaterial hypothesis" and offers us his most famous succinct summary: "Existere is percipi or percipere," meaning "To exist is to be perceived or to perceive" (*Works*, 155, 163, 193–194, 201–205, 221–223, 246–249, 308, 354), the former being the reality of ideas and the latter that of spirits.

9.5 God

We have already considered Berkeley's views on God to some extent, in the context of his theocentric theory of reality. But there is more, to which we now turn. So let us build on the distinctive Berkeleyan proof of God and empirical account of our "notion" of God that we have already seen in the *Dialogues*. As God is the ultimate Cause in this metaphysical system, it would be good to consider Berkeley's theory of causes as signs. In the *Principles*, he asserts that "the connexion of ideas does not imply the relation of *cause* and *effect*, but only of a mark or *sign* with the thing *signified*." It is not that there is any substantial causality between my mind and my body when I feel pain in my hand. Rather, my feeling pain is a *sign* that I need to attend to a sort of identifiable business. Understanding such a system of signs is the business of science, given the intimate relation of the human spirit to the "*infinitely wise, good, and powerful*" Spirit "*in whom we live, move, and have our being*" (*Acts* 17:28). Berkeley next offers us his classical version of the cosmological argument for God, followed immediately by an indication of the argument from design. The former runs like this: Most of our ideas and sensations are not ultimately caused by us at all; yet it is absurd that (passive) ideas "should subsist by themselves"; there must, therefore, be "some other Spirit that causes them," the ultimate Cause being God. The latter argument runs like this: The complex "constant regularity, order, and concatenation of natural things, the surprising magnificence, beauty, and perfection" of the world of our experience, could not have arisen by chance but must have been the design of "one, eternal, infinitely wise, good, and perfect" Spirit, God. These arguments are as implausible as earlier ones we have examined: the cause of our ideas could be material reality (an option already denied) or some lesser spirit, short of God; the design we perceive could be in our imaginations or the product of a spirit greater than human but less than divine. Near the end of his *Principles*, Berkeley considers the problem of evil. But his solution (God has reasons we cannot comprehend, a certain amount of what we consider "evils" is "necessary" and "not without their use," and we have such a narrow and biased perspective on things) adds nothing new to what Leibniz gave us (and without his impressive logical structure of argumentation). The *Principles* conclude by linking our awareness of God to moral "*virtue*" and "our *duty*." This would-be linkage is typical of a Christian cleric of that time but seems unconvincing from our later perspective. As we have seen, in the *Dialogues*, given the alleged permanence of ideas to which we humans are sometimes not attending, their warrant is held to be God, "the Author of them," a Being "*wise, powerful, and good beyond comprehension*." We have already called into question this argument, which would represent God as the necessary "Supreme and Universal Cause of all things" and, later, as the "omnipresent eternal Mind." Hylas accuses Philonous of making God responsible for all of creation, and hence, for all evil. In reply, the latter answers that moral evil is not a matter of external physical action but of internal, deliberate will, that God is not the only agent, but that we are free and responsible for our own acts of will. Hylas objects that, if God is the ultimate causal Source of all ideas, the absurd conclusion should follow that "God suffers pain." But Philonous explains that God can actively comprehend all ideas without passively suffering anything. God's ideas are "archetypal and eternal," while ours are merely "ectypal and natural . . . created in time." On Berkeley's view that all natural "*phenomena* are nothing else but *ideas*," the ultimate mind experiencing them eternally must be divine; thus, "God is a *spirit*, but matter is unintelligent, unperceiving being" (*Works*, 114–115, 117, 148–149, 151–153, 205, 220, 226, 229–231, 244, 247; in the *Commentaries*, Berkeley spurns all attempts, such as those of the ontological argument, to prove God on the basis of the Idea of God, as we have none – 400). This might be regarded as the most radical opposite extreme from Hobbes, for whom all substantial reality was reduced to the material.

A key place to seek Berkeley's mature philosophical treatment of God is *Alciphron*, the work of Christian apologetics he wrote while in Rhode Island, although it is uneven, and we shall focus on its two most important philosophical dialogues (IV and VII). By the way, for whatever reason(s), this work does not contain his doctrine of immaterialism. Its target is "free-thinkers" (skeptics, deists, agnostics, and atheists). Two of the characters, Alciphron and Lysicles, are such "free-thinkers,"

9 George Berkeley

while Euphranor and his friend Crito speak for the author. Euphranor's task, with help from his friend, is to make a convincing case for God. But Alciphron first lays down three ground rules: (i) no abstract "metaphysical arguments," such as those drawn from the idea of an infinitely perfect Being; (ii) no appeals to authority as a cheap substitute for serious evidence; and (iii) no proofs based on mere "utility or convenience." He observes that, if God existed, there would surely be "evident, sensible, plain proof of it." He is willing to accept the reality of an unexperienced God so long as God's "effects and operations" are obvious, the latter being the "signs, or sensible tokens" of the former. Euphranor, in response, points to the obvious unified "design" of the natural order governed by "fixed and immovable" laws that apply universally (think of Newton's laws of motion). But all of this, Euphranor holds, indicates an intelligent designer behind the intelligent design and should "demonstrate an invisible God." But this is too facile for Alciphron, who insists, "I have found that nothing so much convinces me of the existence of another person as *his speaking to me*." This seems fair enough, if we interpret those last three words broadly enough to mean "communicating." So, remarkably, Euphranor undertakes to convince him "that God really speaks to man" by means of "outward, sensible signs, having no resemblance or necessary connexion with the things they stand for" – comparable to the words we use to communicate with each other. Euphranor tries to convince him that the natural order is a visual language God uses to communicate with us, a planetary "Language of Vision." This far-fetched analogy gains no immediate traction, though it is not altogether clear how it could be refuted. Crito supports Euphranor in endorsing "this Optic Language" as indicative of "not a Creator merely, but a provident Governor." Lysicles (anticipating Hume) maintains that it matters little whether this be thought an argument for some sort of being; what is crucial is its nature; after all, if it turns out to be the "God" of Hobbes or Spinoza, what would that be worth? Crito, employing the medieval (e.g. Thomistic) "doctrine, therefore, of analogical perfection in God," thinks we can intelligibly describe God's nature by attributing our perfections, such as they are, to God, but without any restrictions or limits. Thus, God could be characterized as wise, knowledgeable, powerful, and "good," but infinitely so and thus worthy of worship. Once divine goodness is invoked, Alciphron pounces on the problem of evil. Euphranor's answer was weak – that the good vastly outweighs the bad. Without our being able to defend any divine moral attributes, Alciphron reasonably objects, there would be little point to "Religion or Divine worship" (*Selections*, 351–352, 354–361, 366–374, 377, 385–388, 390; see also 414). While Berkeley clearly intends his spokesmen to get the better of the "free-thinkers," from a dispassionate point of view, it is doubtful that they did so.

9.6 Humanity

As was true for the previous section, some of what needs to be said regarding Berkeley's theory of human nature has already been discussed in our section on Reality. But, again, there is more. Given the immaterial hypothesis, a human being, experiencing passive ideas, must be an active spirit. In the *Principles*, he writes, "A spirit is one simple, undivided, active being: as it perceives ideas it is called the *understanding*, and as it produces or otherwise operates about them, it is called the *will*." This analysis essentially corresponds to the Cartesian theory of mind. As we have seen, we allegedly have some "notion of *spirit*," in that we have some understanding of the concept as it applies to us but, strictly speaking, no idea of it, because an idea is essentially passive, a spirit essentially active, and the two are hopelessly different sorts of reality. We suppose there are other spirits than our own based on communicative behaviors, so that we have reason to believe in our own spirits, other humans, and God, the infinite Spirit. Since every spirit is essentially "indivisible, incorporeal, unextended" reality, it must be naturally "incorruptible," so as to live forever unless God chooses to annihilate it; thus, *the soul of man is naturally immortal.*" In his *Essay*, Berkeley observes that human spirits were so created by God as naturally to seek what is conducive to "the preservation and well-being" of their bodies and "to avoid whatever may be hurtful and destructive of them" (*Works*, 99, 146–147, 61–62; while we do not have time to discuss them here, the *Commentaries* contain many relevant passages: see, for example, entries 194a, 200, 478a, 650–652, 708, 738, 791, 820–821, 828, 841–842, 849). Elsewhere (*Selections*, 472), in his advertisement for *The Querist*, he writes that, since the happy fulfillment of human nature requires "goods of mind, body, and fortune," he has devoted his studies to helping mankind secure all three. But, despite this, the main problem with this philosophy of human nature is that, like ancient Platonism, it seems to discount the body and our physical environment.

9.7 Freedom

Curiously, his two greatest philosophical writings (the *Principles* and the *Dialogues*) offer us very little of interest regarding his views on human freedom. For that we must search scattered passages in his *Commentaries* and about seven pages of the seventh dialogue of *Alciphron*. In the former, he holds that it is the same thing to consider the Will a power as to regard Volition as an act. He does not hesitate to affirm that man is free; but what is tricky is to determine exactly what that means. It would probably be fruitless to try to get to the bottom of "what determines the Will" when the Will freely acts. We might wish to say, for example, "Uneasiness." But that is merely an idea and, thus, must be inactive and incapable of being anything at all (*Works*, 380–381, 383–384). We must turn to *Alciphron* for his most sustained treatment of this topic, and even it is rather brief. The title character opens up this part of the discussion by simply denying that "there is any such thing as freedom of the will." His argument goes like this: Since the will is never completely indifferent (e.g. uninclined) in its actions, "it is evident the will cannot be free" (as every inclination brings its own necessity to determine its actions). Before Euphranor can respond, he piles on a second argument: God has eternal foreknowledge of all things; all actions are therefore "necessary," and, hence, our freedom is impossible. On cross-examination from Euphranor, Alciphron admits that it is theoretically possible that God could have made humans free; but then he retracts that concession as incompatible with an eternally omniscient God such as Euphranor embraces. But the latter could then appeal to our ignorance of how eternal omniscience works to advance the weak claim that it could, conceivably, be compatible with the free actions of creatures. Then the focus shifts to Alciphron's first argument. Euphranor tries to distinguish between certainty and necessity: the fact that God is "certain" regarding the choices we shall make does not render our actions "necessary." He appeals to introspective self-evidence that some of our actions are freely chosen by us, also maintaining that "any plain untutored man" would heartily concur, in an obvious "appeal to the Common Sense of mankind." Euphranor has not yet convinced Alciphron, any more than Berkeley would have convinced Hobbes. Appeals to popular opinion are philosophically problematic in modern times (e.g. since Galileo); indeed, as we have seen, Alciphron lays down a ground rule against them. Nor will the distinction between certainty and necessity obviously suffice, slick though it be: if it is certain that I shall stand, then it is necessary that I must do so (indeed, this is even less convincing than Leibniz's distinction between "absolute" necessity, which destroys freedom, and "contingent" necessity, which does not). Euphranor plausibly claims that people are "free" to the extent they can act as they will and correctly holds that human accountability hinges on it, with such morally and socially important "notions" as those of "guilt and merit, justice and reward" (*Selections*, 393–399). While engaging enough, this is not Berkeley at his best.

9.8 Morality

While it should not be surprising that the *Dialogues* has a practical goal of undermining "*atheism and skepticism*," it is curious that the very first sentence of its Preface (*Works*, 157–158) asserts that "the end of speculation" should "be practice, or the improvement and regulation of our lives and actions." Yet neither of his philosophical masterpieces (the *Principles* or the *Dialogues*) had much to offer us regarding his views on morality; for that we must turn to his *Commentaries* and his "Passive Obedience." In an entry of his *Commentaries* (*Works,* 365), Berkeley makes it clear that this topic should be viewed in relation to two topics we have recently considered: "The 2 great Principles of morality, the Being of a God & the Freedom of Man"; he writes that he intends to deal with these in the second part of his *Principles* (he lost the manuscript for this part in Italy).

In "Passive Obedience," he points to our self-love as universal and fundamental to human nature, to such an extent that we tend to consider "good" whatever seems conducive to "our own happiness" and "evil" whatever tends to "impair our own happiness." So far this sounds like psychological egoism (such as we saw in Hobbes). But, as we morally develop, we learn to defer satisfaction for the realization of "a greater future good." We also learn that there are some goods that are "far more excellent than those which affect the senses" alone. Thus, with practice, we learn to prioritize in making our choices. More specifically, we come to recognize that our happiness depends on "a sovereign omniscient Spirit," to whose will our choices must conform, according to duty. Since this is a God "of infinite goodness," the divine will is only for the good. But since God, being perfect, cannot benefit, the good willed by God must be that of us creatures – yet not of any one or few, as opposed to the rest: "It is not therefore the private good of this or that man, nation, or age, but the general well-being of all men, of all nations, of all ages of the world, which God designs should be procured by the concurring actions of each individual." It is this "general well-being of all" – the ideal we shall come to identify with classical utilitarianism – that provides the rationale for all moral obligations. Either we must pursue this ultimate end, without any universal moral rules, each person judging what seems most conducive in any given set of circumstances, or we must adopt and respect some moral rules which, "if universally practised," would tend to "the well-being of mankind," even though, taken in isolation, they might sometimes generate undesirable results. Berkeley argues against the first of these alternatives: it would cause too much confusion and uncertainty and leave us devoid of any moral objectivity. Hence we should seek out and follow universal moral rules, "called *Laws of nature*," which will tend to human well-being, if generally followed, despite any troubling consequences that might flow from our following them in isolation from the entire system of rules. (This is, arguably, the first known expression of what later comes to be called "rule-utilitarianism.") We should adhere to such rules for the sake of their overall utility; "no private interest, no love of friends, no regard to the public good, should make us depart from them." This defines the right as we must try to do it, even though, in particular, isolated cases, more good might be accomplished by breaking them. Thus morality becomes a matter of long-term rational good: "the Law of Nature is a system of such rules or precepts as that, if they be all of them, at all times, in all places, and by all men observed, they will necessarily promote the well-being of mankind, so far as it is attainable by human actions." This moral law contains some absolute prohibitions, to be unfailingly observed, no matter what. Such "negative precepts," such as one forbidding the deliberate killing of innocent persons, are to take precedence over "positive" ones, such as those promoting an increase in the standard of living. Ultimately, a precept (negative or positive) is part of the moral law because it is commanded by divine will; and God wills it because it is good, and it is good in that it tends to the general well-being of creation. While self-love is natural, we must not prefer our own temporal good, or even our own physical life, "to the observation of any one moral duty." Berkeley approvingly invokes the Pauline principle

(*Romans* 3:8), used by such medieval Christians as Aquinas, that "evil is never to be committed, to the end good may come of it." We might notice here what a powerful contrast this is to the moral philosophy of Hobbes. Indeed, Berkeley may remind us of Locke, in writing, "In morality the eternal rules of action have the same immutable universal truth with propositions in geometry" (*Selections*, 432–439, 448–449, 451, 454, 467), although he has made a stronger case for the view than did his predecessor. His adoption of what later comes to be called rule-utility is quite interesting. But, from a critical perspective, can we ever know, before the fact, what will produce the happiest consequences for humanity? And, even if we could, would this fact alone suffice to establish right and wrong, or why should moral duty be reduced to merely a matter of the good of human happiness?

9.9 Society

In "Passive Obedience," Berkeley applies this theory of (what is now called) rule-utilitarianism, against Locke, to the alleged "Christian Duty of not resisting the supreme Power" of civil government. He considers the duty of passive obedience, the duty not to resist the head of state, to be an absolute negative precept, even in cases where the immediate consequences of compliance are undesirable. Every civil community, to avoid anarchy, must involve some "Supreme Power" in the making and enforcing of laws. When the citizens respect and obey such laws, they are loyal; when they flout them (especially by "making use of force and open violence"), then they are in "*rebellion*." Now loyalty is "a natural or moral duty," while the disloyalty of rebellion is "a vice" and violation of the natural law. The consequences of a breakdown of lawful authority would be dire: disorder, war, misery, and confusion. It is our moral duty to try to act in such a way as to avoid them. Lawful order and effective government are necessary for our social well-being. Indeed, they are so important that the morality of nonresistance cannot be left to the whims of individual discretion. Whether or not political society was originally "founded in a contract," as Locke thought, he was wrong to conclude that sovereign legislators have only a "conditional and limited" authority over their subjects. The end toward which that dangerous view must tend is that of political instability. While we have a universal "natural tendency or disposition to a social life," that must be bolstered by a general respect for law. As it is a violation of the law of nature for any subject "to lift up his hand against the supreme power," so it would also be for sovereigns to abuse their power "to the ruin and destruction of the people committed to their charge." Yet their doing that would not justify subjects violating "the doctrine of passive obedience." However, this is not to deny them the right to judge matters for themselves and to do what they legally can to protect their own interests, so long as they regard "non-resistance as an absolute, unconditioned, unlimited duty" (*Selections*, 429–431, 439–448, 460, 464–469; while we cannot afford to consider Berkeley's economic ideas for social well-being here, see *Selections*, 473, especially the first three sections of *The Querist*). Needless to say, Berkeley has proved to be on the wrong side of history (against Locke) in this debate regarding a right to rebellion in Western political philosophy. Democracy can only flourish to the extent that, like Locke, we trust people to judge for themselves what is and is not in their own interest, educating them to the point where they can do so responsibly.

9.10 Review

Berkeley is an eccentric thinker, who is important both philosophically and historically. While empiricism traditionally tends toward materialism, he steers his toward immaterialism. Where other idealists rely on the a priori, he was committed to foundations in sensibility. At his best, he marshaled batteries of arguments to support his conclusions; yet those conclusions were so bizarre that we are sure that something must be wrong. As Locke tried to subvert skepticism with his common-sense dualism but unintentionally abetted its cause, so does Berkeley with his curious empirical idealism. For a full three centuries now he has continued to beguile us while rarely converting anyone to his point of view. As he radicalizes Locke, so Hume would radicalize him, drawing conclusions from his inspiration which, surely, would have repelled the good Bishop. The history of philosophy often functions in accordance with a law of unintended consequences. Yet there seems, in retrospect, an intellectual inevitability to the crisis of Humean skepticism that Berkeley helped precipitate and, beyond that, to the cataclysmic revolution subsequently perpetrated by Kant in response to that crisis. But, before we can see how all that plays out, we need to consider yet another early eighteenth-century philosophical bishop of the Church of England; and to him we now turn our consideration.

10

Joseph Butler

Source: Magnus Manske/Wikimedia Commons/Public Domain

10.1 Overview

Even though Joseph Butler's philosophical light has been eclipsed by his older contemporary George Berkeley and his younger contemporary David Hume, there was a time when he was a prominent British thinker – especially in the areas of moral philosophy, philosophy of human nature, and the philosophy of religion. It should not be considered shocking that Hume, who so radically differed with his views, nevertheless listed him among a handful of recent English thinkers who have started putting the science of human nature on a more solid foundation. Unlike most of the philosophers we have considered thus far, Butler was not much interested in such study for its own sake as epistemology and abstract metaphysics. He rather did philosophy as a committed Christian. Thus it was appropriate that his two greatest works were a collection of

Modern European Philosophers, First Edition. Wayne P. Pomerleau.
© 2023 John Wiley & Sons, Inc. Published 2023 by John Wiley & Sons, Inc.

146 | *10 Joseph Butler*

philosophical sermons and a work of philosophical apologetics. Although he has been eclipsed by others (especially Hume), there is still much we could learn from his judicious analysis of men, morals, and religion.

10.2 Biography

Joseph Butler was born at Wantage, England, the youngest of eight children, on May 18, 1692. His father, Thomas Butler, a respectable Presbyterian retired linen-draper, intended him to become a Presbyterian minister, sending him to an academy at Gloucester with that end in view. One of Butler's dearest friends there, Thomas Secker, later became Archbishop of Canterbury. Butler converted to the Church of England, against his father's wishes, and, in 1714, went to Oxford. There he established a friendship with Edward Talbot, the son of a Dr. William Talbot, the Bishop of Oxford, who later became Bishop of Durham. Having studied the philosophical theology of Samuel Clarke, at the age of 22, Butler anonymously entered into a critical correspondence with Clarke, who was so impressed with his critique that he published it in later editions of his own work; the young Butler claimed to have been persuaded by Clarke. He was dissatisfied with the lightweight lectures and useless disputations at Oxford, from which he received his Bachelor's degree, protesting against the unwillingness to entertain any doubts regarding dogmatically held orthodox opinions. In 1718, he was ordained a deacon and a priest in the Church of England. Through the influence of Dr. Talbot and Dr. Clarke, he was appointed Preacher at the Rolls Chapel in London. There, for eight years, he preached sermons, including the 15 that were his first writings published under his own name (in 1726). His friend Secker, who had also converted to the Church of England and was a royal chaplain, recommended him to Queen Caroline, who took a keen interest in theology. Butler was appointed chaplain to Edward Talbot's brother, who was Lord Chancellor of England, in 1733. On his way to London, he stopped at Oxford to get a Doctor of Law degree. He then became one of the queen's chaplains, meeting with her on a regular basis. Meanwhile, he had been writing *The Analogy of Religion*, a critique of deism, which was published in 1736, along with two dissertations – "Of Personal Identity" and on "the Nature of Virtue."[1] He presented a copy of it to the queen. When she was dying, the following year, she recommended him to her husband, King George II.

Butler was appointed Bishop of Bristol in 1738 and became one of the king's chaplains in 1746. There is an apocryphal story (almost surely false) that he was offered and declined the primacy at Canterbury the following year. In 1750, he was appointed Bishop of Durham, an ecclesiastical office he held until his death, on June 16, 1752, at Bath. He was buried in Bristol Cathedral. He seems to have been a kindly, modest, conscientious cleric, who never married and was forthright and plain spoken (the source for some of this biography is the "Life of Butler," by Joseph Angus, in *Fifteen*, vii–xii). He was intellectually inclined, avoiding emotionalism and the evangelical fervor of "enthusiasm." Indeed, as Bishop of Bristol, he met with John Wesley, the founder of Methodism, scolding him for "horrid" claims to personal revelations. Although he was famously accused of living in a metaphysical cloud, the truth is that usually his interests were practically relevant to people's living good Christian lives.

---

1 References to Butler will be to *Five Sermons and A Dissertation upon the Nature of Virtue* (hereafter called *Sermons*), by Joseph Butler, ed. by Stephen L. Darwall (Indianapolis: Hackett, 1983), to *The Analogy of Religion* (hereafter called *Religion*), by Joseph Butler (New York: Frederick Ungar, 1961), and to *The Analogy of Religion, also Fifteen Sermons* (hereafter called *Fifteen*), by Joseph Butler (London: The Religious Tract Society, 1865).

10.3 Knowledge

As has been indicated, Butler did not seem to be very interested in developing an epistemological theory, except to the extent that he thought it needed for the views on religion and man as a moral agent that were his focus. Still, he does offer us a few scattered comments worth considering. In the Preface to his *Sermons*, he laments the loss of the pursuit of truth as practically oriented toward how we should live. He wants to discuss "morals, considered as a science," from an empirical perspective, conceding that the subject is theoretical but wanting his sermons to discuss it without getting "very abstruse and difficult" (*Sermons*, 11–12). Arguably his most important contribution in this area is his shifting away from the quest for demonstrative certainty to the attempt at establishing probable evidence to support our beliefs; he explains that "probability is the very guide of life," apart from abstract theorizing. We function at two levels – at the level of sensation and appetite, where probability must suffice, and at that of reason and reflection (*Religion*, 1–2, 23), where certain knowledge is sometimes possible. We must take experience as life allows us to do, accepting its findings as more or less likely, given the evidence. "Things and actions are what they are, and the consequences of them will be what they will be," however disappointed we may be at the inability to achieve certainty. Regardless of how intense "the delight of knowledge is," we should be mindful that "it cannot be the chief good of man," for our essential good is moral "goodness" (*Fifteen*, 432–433, 514–515), which is not typically the result of demonstrative knowledge at all.

10.4 Reality

While Butler was very interested in the parts of metaphysics having to do with God and human nature, he spent little time discussing a general theory of reality. But, as with our previous topic, let us briefly consider what he did say, most of which is to be found in his *Analogy of Religion*. His main emphasis is on the reality of the world of our experience as having been created by God and subject to the order of God's "natural government" and "moral government," which he thinks analogous to each other. Ultimately, he thinks, both of these elude our limited comprehension. Nevertheless, he is confident that "the natural and moral constitution and government of the world are so connected as to make up together but one scheme." And he thinks it "highly probable" that the former serves the purposes of "the latter, as the vegetable world is for the animal, and organized bodies for minds." All ends that are achievable in our world require instrumental means, some of which are often "very undesirable" except as means to desirable ends, the connection being established by experience. Just as the "natural government of the world" operates according to "general laws," so its "moral government" must operate according to general moral laws. Although God's providential "scheme" for our world is, ultimately, "incomprehensible" to us, Butler is confident that it is dynamic rather than static, "not a fixed but a progressive one" (this commitment to progress was typical of Enlightenment thinkers). When we deem the natural order and/or the moral order to be defective, that is due to our limited understanding. Even though we may partially grasp their laws, both orders are "so complicated" that we should not expect complete understanding of them (*Religion*, 62, 70, 108–109, 111–113, 117, 167–171, 194; cf. *Fifteen*, 519–520).

10.5 God

By contrast with the topics of knowledge and reality, Butler has a great deal to say concerning God. When we experience the order of the world, we are led to consider God as "the author and cause of all things," whom we should love, apart from selfish motives of "hope of rewards or fear of punishments." Also, he thinks, apart from a religious devotion to God, our sense of fulfillment would devolve to the pursuit of "riches, honors, sensual gratifications" (*Sermons*, 22, 32), and other such transitory, shallow goods. Much of what Butler has to say about God is in his *Analogy of Religion*. In keeping with his shift away from demonstrative certainty toward probability reasoning, unlike almost all the modern thinkers we have considered thus far (Pascal being an exception), he does not try to develop a deductive argument for God, "taking for proved" the reality of "an intelligent Author of nature," viewed as perfect without argumentation, but suggested by "the manifold appearances of design" in the world of our experience. Needless to say, it will be difficult to critically evaluate his argumentation to the extent that he did not offer us any. To be sure, Butler's views on God are not devoid of reasoning; but it is problematic because based on dubious presumptions. He thinks he sees a "natural government" of the world, whereby "virtue *as such* is actually rewarded, and vice *as such* punished" and that, as "moral government" is analogous, there ought to be an extrapolation of such justice, under God, beyond this life (*Religion*, 5–6, 39–40, 45, 59, 114–115, 121–122). One need not already have studied Hume to be able to detect holes here: the natural government of the world is presumed, as is its rewarding of virtue and punishing of vice, as is the extension of this alleged moral government into the hereafter.

It is the second part of *Religion* in which Butler explicitly targets deism. The term "deism" is a broad umbrella concept used to cover a range of religious views, particularly popular among eighteenth-century intellectuals (on both sides of the Atlantic), which deviated from orthodox Judeo-Christian doctrine. Clarke had already recognized several different varieties of it: (i) far removed from orthodoxy were those deists who believed in a God, who created or designed our world but is no longer involved with it in any meaningful way; (ii) less far removed were those who believed God is involved but unconcerned about our moral conduct; (iii) even less further removed were those who believed in a God that cares about our moral conduct but did not believe in human immortality or an afterlife of eternal rewards and punishments; and (iv) least removed were those who believed that God rewards and punishes us after death for our conduct but who rejected revelation, taking seriously only rationally justifiable truth-claims. We should notice that none of these is atheistic or even agnostic, so that Butler did not need to try to demonstrate a God, on whose existence he and the deists already agree. He is, then, at pains to try to defend revelation, an afterlife for humans, and a God who will see to it that they will experience the morally appropriate consequences for the ways in which they have lived in this world. These are all important doctrines, from the perspective of orthodox Judeo-Christian teachings. Some of the teachings of Christianity are purely matters of revelation and not justifiable by natural reason, while others, though not easily proved, are "a republication" of what can be rationally established. Butler distinguishes between "positive *precepts*" and "*duties*," arising from divine command and not justifiable by natural reason alone, and "moral" precepts and "*duties*," which arise out of the nature of things and are thus justifiable by natural reason alone. Both are important. Miracles, in particular, are supported by revelation and transcend the powers and scope of natural reason. While not impossible, miracles, by their very nature, are "extraordinary phenomena" contrary to the normal course of nature. Indeed, our understanding is so limited that, Butler maintains, "The constitution of the world, and God's natural government over it, is all mystery," in the last resort. We should note here that this attempt to collapse these two sets of beliefs is so ad hoc and dubious that no self-respecting deist would feel rationally compelled to go along with it. But, as we blur the line between the natural world and the mysterious, the analogy between one sort of belief and the other becomes stronger. Thus, if the first sort is rational, why should we deny that the second can be as well? But, if belief in revelation need not be irrational, "what positive evidence" can "we have for the truth of it"? Here Butler makes another problematic move, maintaining that the teaching of scriptural revelation (e.g. that of the Judeo-Christian tradition) "is to be admitted as an authentic genuine history, till somewhat positive be alleged sufficient to invalidate it." Again, no deist with any intellectual backbone would allow Butler to get away unchallenged with this attempt to place the burden of proof on him. Indeed, the appeal to ignorance (we should accept a belief unless we know for certain that it is false) is a traditional logical fallacy. Even on his own terms, Butler needs to be careful here. He is an opponent of "enthusiasm" as well as of deism, making that clear. But, in combating the latter, he is inviting the former, since he could provide us with no criterion for distinguishing between genuine and bogus claims to revelation (including those regarding prophecy as well as those regarding miracles). He recognizes some problems here but, nevertheless, is pleading a partisan cause. Indeed, at one point, we might wonder whether he does not realize his vulnerability here when, near the end of the book, he writes, "It is most readily acknowledged, that the foregoing treatise is by no means satisfactory; very far indeed from it." By his last paragraph, all he can honestly claim to have shown is that the Christian "religion is throughout credible," neither demonstrably certain nor to be rejected as irrational (*Religion*, 125–128, 137–138, 145–146, 149, 186–189, 198, 207, 209–210, 213–219, 232, 247, 258–259). The book had considerable influence in its day but seemed less problematic before than after Hume. On the other hand, to the extent that Butler's reasoning is convincing, deism should seem inadequate, and religion legitimately calls for attitudes of "love, reverence, fear, desire for approbation," and so forth, in relation to God, as well as our resignation to God's will that is definitive of piety. Nor does Butler think we should be deterred from such devotion by "the appearances of evil" in the world, as "our ignorance" of how things are and why is allegedly too extensive for them to be serious barriers (*Fifteen*, 506–508, 521, 523–524). This perfunctory dismissal of the problem of evil would not pass uncriticized by Hume.

10.6 Humanity

The first three of Butler's *Fifteen Sermons*, plus their Preface, philosophize "Upon Human Nature"; while less philosophically respected in his day than *The Analogy of Religion*, they have stood the test of time better than that later work. Perhaps the two greatest features of this earlier work are his powerful alternative to the egoistic hedonism of Hobbes and his analysis of human nature as fundamentally moral. Regarding every natural and artificial thing as an organized system of parts, he draws an analogy between an organic human being and a mechanical watch, neither of which can be properly understood in terms of its parts alone; in both cases, we need a conception of how those parts are interconnected so that the thing can function as a whole. As the watch is designed for the purpose of telling time, there must be some purpose for a human being. (Notice that what Butler goes on to argue, in his theory of human nature, would build on this dubious analogy between an artificial thing like a watch and a natural and organic, living thing like a human being.) "Appetites, passions, affections, and the principles of reflection" are among the "several parts" of a human, "the chief of which is the authority of reflection or conscience." Of course, he rejects Hobbes's materialistic view of humans as merely complicated machines: "A machine is inanimate and passive, but we are agents," with rational intelligence and a capacity for free action. Like "brutes," we have instincts that prompt behaviors oriented toward our own (or society's) perceived good. Like so many Christian philosophers before him (starting with Augustine), he adopts a hierarchical theory of human nature. At the bottom of the hierarchy is the body and its animal instincts. Then there are other particular passions and affections, such as feelings of friendship and a love of fairness. Above particular passions are the principles of self-love and benevolence. Finally, he indicates that "the principle of conscience or reflection" rightly claims "authority over all the rest" of the components of human nature (although he was not entirely consistent about this), carrying with it a natural source of moral obligation. He takes Hobbes to task by name for imagining that all human motivation ultimately issues from and reduces to self-love and for denying natural feelings of benevolence that could rationally conflict with that. By confusing self-love with selfishness, Hobbes was led to regard the latter as the ultimate ground of everything we do, so that any "benevolent" actions inconsistent with our own perceived self-interest would be irrational – either impossible or crazy. Our "happiness consists in this that an appetite or affection enjoys its object," as Hobbes argued. But self-love cannot be the only ultimate object of our concern. It must be involved with specific desires, such as those for friendship, success, and honor. "Take away these affections and you leave self-love absolutely nothing at all to employ itself about; no end or object for it to pursue except only that of avoiding pain." This is the egoistic paradox that bedevils the theory of Hobbes and renders it implausible. While benevolence is a different principle from that of self-love, they are equally genuine and not necessarily opposed to each other. "Everything is what it is, and not another thing." Benevolence is not identical to self-love; yet the two can be so associated with each other that a person's happiness can depend on the well-being of others he cares about. That caring is neither egoistic nor reducible to physical pleasures and pains; yet it can determine choices we morally should make at the highest level of "reflection or conscience" (*Sermons*, 14–20). This seems more plausible than the Hobbesian claim that all our voluntary actions are ultimately motivated by our own self-interest in pursuing our own pleasures and avoiding our prospective pain.

Turning now from the Preface to the first three sermons, we find Butler developing further details, some of which we shall now consider. Even apart from revelation, we can allegedly rationally determine that we are creatures of God, whose reflective consciences leave us subject to "the natural law," as well as that we are part of the social organism of community analogous to the physical body, comprised of its various parts. Against Hobbes, Butler (rashly and without cogent argumentation) claims that our own well-being and the welfare of society "are so far from being inconsistent that they mutually promote each other" naturally. Against Hobbes, he maintains that benevolence is "a natural principle" in us, and not merely an artificial one. It "is a mere question of fact" whether or not we are sometimes benevolent, even against our own self-interest. The facts in this matter seem to be on Butler's side against Hobbes. Very small children, before they are old enough to calculate the most likely means to their own selfish satisfaction, already exhibit sympathetic attitudes toward others. People who appear to be perfectly rational sacrifice not only their own pleasure for the sake of others, but even their own lives. In some cases, their altruism is such that they care more for those others' interests than for their own; in other cases, they are subordinating their own self-interest for the sake of moral principle, doing as they feel morally obliged to do. This is not to deny that we sometimes "do evil to others," when we are guided by our selfish "ungoverned passions," rather than by conscience. Yet we are generally directed by "good-will" and not, without some cause, by general "ill-will." When St. Paul said that even people who have not been taught the moral law act in accordance with it because they "are a law unto themselves" (Romans 2:14), Butler thinks that he was referring to "the highest principles" in human nature, our reflective conscience. Shame is a natural reaction to our doing something we consider wrong, and it can serve as a deterrent to wrongdoing. An impetuous, hasty self-love may often be in conflict with conscience, but not a "reasonable and cool self-love." There is no reason, in principle, why all people should not live according to a mature and muscular reflective conscience. "Had it strength, as it has right; had it power, as it has manifest authority, it would absolutely govern the world." As there is a natural order to the external world, so human nature has its own natural order, to which we have been alluding. At one point (near the end of the third sermon), Butler places reasonable "self-love and conscience" on the same level as "the chief or superior principles in the nature of man," a claim which seems inconsistent with the view that conscience is supreme. Even more problematic is his claim, without any supportive argumentation, that "conscience and self-love, if we understand our true happiness, always lead us the same way. Duty and interest are perfectly coincident, for the most part in this world." Even those of us who want to believe this might be on our guard against wishful thinking. In the first of his two sermons "Upon the Love of Our Neighbor," Butler develops even more carefully the paradox of (Hobbesian) egoistic hedonism. He writes, "Happiness does not consist in self-love." If we were so self-absorbed as to care only for ourselves, we could not enjoy anything else that might give us satisfaction. Thus, true egoism would be counterproductive as regards giving us pleasure: "Immoderate self-love does very ill consult its own interest; and how much soever a paradox it may appear, it is certainly true that even from self-love we should endeavor to get over all inordinate regard to and consideration of ourselves." This seems a psychologically compelling refutation of at least a crude sort of egoistic hedonism that would try to set up a conflict between self-love and an altruistic concern for others or what St. Paul (Romans 13:9) called the love of our neighbor (*Sermons*, 25–41, 45, 47–50). At the same time, a more subtle form might prove less vulnerable – for example, one that always involves some sense of pleasure we might enjoy (and/or pain we might avoid) in relation to some of a wide range of possible objects, including things, other people, ideals, and relationships.

In his dissertation "Of Personal Identity" (an appendix to *The Analogy of Religion*), Butler critically considers an issue Locke had tried to solve, as to what constitutes the identity of a person. As we experience our own consciousness functioning over time, we intuitively grasp the idea of a person temporally enduring through those experiences. Locke had held that personal identity is a function of the continuity of consciousness, as retrievable by one's memory. But this is problematic, in that it denies that the past that a person cannot remember can be part of his personal identity. "And one should really think it self-evident, that consciousness of personal identity presupposes and therefore cannot constitute personal identity." Rather, the person enduring through time "must either be a substance or the property of some substance." In either case, our remembered consciousness of the self continuing to function through time requires the enduring substantial reality of a person. Butler admits that this requires memory of our conscious past and that a skeptic could easily challenge the reliability of memory. (In just a few years, Hume would question whether we have any reason to suppose the self to be substantial at all.) Butler's theory of human nature emphasizes our natural moral agency at least as much as anyone we have studied thus far. Our reason allows us to put ourselves imaginatively in the place of others. Our sympathy motivates us to do so. Our reflective conscience leads us to practice the Golden Rule in the way we treat them. Because we are naturally moral agents (rather than only artificially so, as Hobbes thought), conscience is available to us as "the guide of life." This is why we naturally approve of virtuous character in other people, even when it does not personally benefit us. If any being were to have infinitely good character, that would inspire our love, admiration, and devotion. But, of course, for Butler, there is such a morally perfect being – God (*Fifteen*, 313–316, 319–320, 466–467, 502–505).

10.7 Freedom

In the Preface to his *Sermons*, after distinguishing between "inanimate and passive" machines and human beings, who are living agents, Butler writes, "Our constitution is put in our own power. We are charged with it; and therefore are accountable for any disorder or violation of it." It is clear that, like all orthodox Christians, he needs to clear space for a commitment to human freedom. And this commitment is connected to his allegiance to St. Paul's idea (Romans 2:14) that a human person "is by his very nature a law to himself," autonomous, rather than merely the recipient of rules from without, and having a moral conscience. While we are governed by authority figures, including God and the head of state, our "moral nature" renders us also "capable of moral government" (this is a theme which would be developed by Rousseau and Kant). Here we see why it was so important that Butler's philosophy of human nature emphasized man's "moral nature" (*Sermons*, 15, 18, 42, 69).

This gives us at least partial control over our own lives, including, as he explains in *The Analogy of Religion*, our own "happiness and misery," both in this life and in the afterlife. The most extended discussion of freedom he provides is in the sixth chapter of Part I of that later book; but it also tends to complicate the picture considerably. He admits that determinism, the theory of "universal necessity," can be compatible with religion, even though he considers it "so absurd a supposition" as to be easily rejected. After all, there could still be a God who created or designed the world and is still involved as its "moral Governor," worthy of our devotion and reverence. The objection, of course, would be that we then would have no choice, that our devotion and reverence would be determined for us rather than by us. Butler seems mistaken in maintaining that the deterministic doctrine of universal "Necessity does not exclude deliberation, choice, preference, and acting from certain principles, and to certain ends." He holds that agency can be either "Necessary" or "Free." But a "Necessary Agent," if that phrase is not an oxymoron, would have no genuine choice and would "act" in the manner of a robot, devoid of true moral responsibility. In trying to argue that even a thoroughgoing determinist ought to maintain a commitment to choice, accountability, and religion, Butler seems confused and confusing. Just a few pages later, he seems to flip-flop and admit that just "rewards and punishments" require "that we are Free and not Necessary Agents." It seems that he is attempting to have it both ways and lands himself in inconsistency. In trying to represent "the principles of the Fatalists" fairly, while not believing them to be true, he is playing devil's advocate (*Religion*, 62, 92–99, 104–106, 249–250). But this muddles up the theory of freedom he has clearly developed in his *Sermons*.

10.8 Morality

In the Preface to his *Sermons*, Butler distinguishes two possible approaches to morality – a rationalistic one starting from abstract relations and an empirical one based on our observation of facts. It is the latter approach he adopts. The facts that are relevant are those of our experience and behavior associated with human nature and human freedom, which we have now considered. These include the facts that we act both out of regard for our own interests (self-love) and out of concern for others (benevolence), both of which are natural and good. What is bad is that we too often do so impetuously and unreasonably rather than on the basis of reflective conscience. Unbridled passion clouds our judgment and is always dangerous. Even when our passions are natural, we should follow our higher nature of rational, reflective conscience rather than recklessly "acting as we please." Butler is no moral relativist but holds "some actions to be in themselves just, right, good; others to be in themselves evil, wrong, unjust," regardless of our preferences or desired consequences. He reveals an optimistic confidence that "any plain honest man" could use his rational, reflective conscience to discern what is right and good. The "authority" of our reflective conscience is such that we have "an obligation" to use our freedom responsibly and "obey" it. Another strikingly optimistic claim he makes is that our true self-interest usually accords with our moral duty. As a follower of Christian ethics, Butler adopts the view of Jesus of Nazareth (Matthew 22:37–40) that our most fundamental moral obligation is that of love – the love of our neighbor, to which he dedicates two of his 15 sermons, and the love of God, to which he devotes another two. Indeed, he identifies the fulfillment of our human nature and our true happiness with that, rather than merely with material goods and creature comforts, such as "riches, honors, and the gratification of sensual appetites." The virtuous pursuit of "what is right and good" (Deuteronomy 12:28) is essential to our genuine well-being, as we can see "when we sit down in a cool hour," beyond the throes of morally blinding passion. Butler thinks that happiness is the only good to which every person has a natural "right," so that love of others requires that we behave in such a manner as to respect that right. However, while Butler suggests that happiness is what God most wants for us, he is not a utilitarian, in that he could not justify violating moral absolutes in order to bring about happy consequences. In his "Dissertation upon the Nature of Virtue," Butler analyzes the functioning of our "moral faculty, whether called conscience, moral reason, moral sense," or whatever. It naturally leads us to pursue "justice, veracity and regard to common good," in driving us to feel "guilt" when we violate it. Interestingly, Butler thinks we have duties toward ourselves, respecting our own legitimate interests and well-being, as well as toward other people and God. He associates the traditional virtue of prudence with those duties. Again, it should be emphasized that, while human happiness is very valuable, morality should not be reduced to "promoting the happiness of mankind" (*Sermons*, 13, 21–22, 32, 36–38, 41–46, 52–53, 56, 64–67, 69–74; cf. *Religion,* 49, 87; we do not have the time and space to deal with them here, but Butler's discussions of resentment, forgiveness, and self-deceit in sermons 8, 9, and 10 are impressive examples of early modern Christian moral psychology – see *Fifteen*, 434–467). At any rate, Butler is not a utilitarian.

10.9 Society

He thinks that, while we sometimes do evil and harm to one another, our "benevolence or good-will" is so natural that we normally value the happiness of others and deliberately mistreat them only out of uncontrolled greed or personal animosity, but that we normally have no "love of injustice, oppression, treachery, ingratitude," cruelty, etc., as such. Of course, that last adverb ("normally") leaves room for the occasional psychopath. We naturally seek the fellowship of society with at least some other people. Just as there is a natural order in an individual human being (passions, self-love, benevolence, reflective conscience), so society needs to be based on an organizational structure of some sort, with the "united strength" of its members founded on "a civil constitution" establishing "various subordinations under one direction" provided by a "supreme authority" acting for the common good. Just as there is no true contrariety between benevolence and self-love, properly understood, according to Butler, so, he believes, there is no necessary contrariety between the public good and one's own "private good," properly understood. Butler compares happiness to air and sunlight, in that one person's enjoying it does not, in itself, diminish the ability of others to enjoy it as well. It is not like money or land, which are in limited supply, so that some people getting more will entail others getting less. Thus, it should be possible to wish all persons well, so that love of neighbor can refer to all "mankind," even if, in fact, we tend to be more concerned about people with whom we interact and with whom we have more in common. Beyond following the laws to which our membership in society commits us, Butler thinks that we should practice the Golden Rule toward all other people: "Whatsoever ye would that men should do to you, do ye even so to them" (Matthew 7:12). Yet, Butler warns, anticipating Kant, we must not expect or demand of people more than they can deliver, as "moral obligations can extend no further than to natural possibilities" (*Sermons*, 31, 35, 41, 46, 51–52, 54–55, 57–59, 62).

In *The Analogy of Religion*, Butler imagines a good political community, whose members are so well united that there are no factions and the handling of public affairs for the common good is willingly shared. All would contribute, even if they were not equipped to contribute equally. There would be no injustice, force, or fraud in their treatment of one another. He imagines that the good example of such a blessed society would spread, so that others would try to follow its path. Ideally, the end result might be a peaceful cosmopolitan society under a "universal" sovereign authority. Butler admits that this ideal is not likely ever to be fully realized in this life but thinks it a worthy goal to try to approximate (*Religion*, 56–57; cf. *Fifteen*, 405, 417, 448).

10.10   Review

It must be admitted that Butler was a lesser philosopher than Berkeley before him or Hume after him, that some of what he was famous for writing seems dated and less relevant today, and that he too often bases his reasoning on controversial but unjustified assumptions. However, he also represents a solid, sensible, respectable position of Christian moderation. He should be given credit for helping to shift modern philosophy away from the seventeenth-century fixation on deductive demonstration to inductive reasoning. His philosophy of religion, for which he was so highly regarded during his lifetime, has not worn well over the centuries. The five philosophical sermons which are most read today, plus the Preface to his *Sermons*, and his little dissertation on virtue, by contrast, have stood the test of time quite well – particularly his emphasis on human beings as essentially moral agents and his defense of altruism against the egoistic hedonism of thinkers like Hobbes. His views on human freedom are undeveloped in the *Sermons*; and, unfortunately, his development of them in *The Analogy of Religion* leaves his theory murkier (perhaps opening the door to the determinism of Hume). He offers us a very attractive philosophical theory of Christian ethics, although not argued sufficiently to convert anyone who did not already follow it. And his views on society, while scattered and idealistic, present us with a nice vision of what could and should be, if not an accurate analysis of whatever has actually been. All in all, it is regrettable that nowadays his work tends to fall through the cracks between that of the more eccentric Berkeley and that of the more disturbing Hume.

11

David Hume

Source: Georgios Kollidas/Adobe Stock

11.1 Overview

If we want to use labels to identify Hume philosophically, he was a radical empiricist who tended toward phenomenalism, a naturalist, a skeptic, a determinist, an ethical emotivist, and a deist. It is not too great an exaggeration to say that his skepticism represents the culmination of a hundred years of philosophy (from 1637, when Descartes started publishing, to the late 1730s). None of the thinkers to whom chapter-length treatments have been devoted here thus far was as clear-cut a skeptic as Hume (and most of them were archenemies of skepticism); indeed, never in the history of Western philosophy before him had there appeared a skeptic with his astonishing intellectual firepower. His empiricism (which was radical like that of Hobbes rather than moderate like Locke's) led him to an anti-metaphysical phenomenalism, which, in turn, in combination with his naturalism, generated his skepticism. His skepticism regarding human freedom rendered him a determinist; that regarding the capacity of reason to motivate action rendered him an ethical

Modern European Philosophers, First Edition. Wayne P. Pomerleau.
© 2023 John Wiley & Sons, Inc. Published 2023 by John Wiley & Sons, Inc.

156 | 11 David Hume

emotivist; and that regarding any infinitely perfect God rendered him a deist. As he assembled these pieces to form his philosophical system, he precipitated one of the most serious crises ever in Western philosophy.

11.2 Biography

David Hume was born in Scotland on April 26, 1711, the youngest of three children of Joseph Home, a lawyer and landowner, and Katherine Falconer Home, the daughter of a president of the College of Justice. Since the English and Scottish crowns had been united in 1603, Scotland was part of Great Britain, with some seats representing it in both houses of the Parliament. In 1701, the Act of Settlement determined that, when Queen Anne, the (childless) last of the Stuart monarchs, died (which occurred some 13 years later), the German Elector of Hanover (by whom Leibniz was employed) would succeed her. In 1714, George I became king; and, with the defeat of the French (under Louis XIV) and the Peace of Utrecht going into effect, Great Britain embarked on a quarter of a century of peace, the years of Hume's childhood and early adulthood. But, internally, there was still a power struggle between conservative Tories, who believed in absolute divine-right monarchy, and liberal Whigs, who were committed to representative government.

Hume grew up on the modest family estate of Ninewells. His father died in 1713, but his mother did a fine job of raising her three children by herself, as well as managing the estate. The family was Presbyterian, strict Calvinists, and David seems to have been a pious little boy. He was privately educated at home until 1723, when, at about the age of 12, he followed his older brother, John, to the University of Edinburgh. As a younger brother, David could not expect to inherit the family estate; and, since the family was financially comfortable but not wealthy, he would have to earn a living.[1] In addition to the splendid seven-page autobiographical piece called "My Own Life," which he wrote some four months before he died, we have a valuable six-page letter he wrote shortly before his twenty-third birthday, most of which constitutes what he called "a kind of History of my Life." There he writes that, from "earliest Infancy," he had had "a strong Inclination to Books & Letters." At the university, he added a fascination with philosophy to his love of literature. There he was probably exposed to the writings of such modern thinkers as Newton and Locke and started to lose his orthodox Christian faith. He left the university (without getting a degree) at about the age of 14, pursuing his studies privately at Ninewells from 1725 to 1734. His family had encouraged him to follow in his father's footsteps and become a lawyer, which he (halfheartedly) tried to study. But he had become obsessed with the contemplation of ideas. As he wrote, "The Law, which was the Business I design'd to follow, appear'd nauseous to me, & I cou'd think of no other way of pushing my Fortune in the World, but that of a Scholar & Philosopher." But in 1729 something or other punctured the balloon of his enthusiasm; he lost his

---

1 Most references to Hume's writings will be to *Essential Works of David Hume* (hereafter called *Essential*), ed. by Ralph Cohen (New York: Bantam Books, 1965), to *A Treatise of Human Nature*, by David Hume (hereafter called *Treatise*), ed. by L.A. Selby-Bigge (London: Oxford Univ. Press, 1967), and to *Essays Moral, Political, and Literary*, by David Hume (hereafter called *Essays*), revised edition, ed. by Eugene F. Miller (Indianapolis: LibertyClassics, 1987). Other references will be to *The Letters of David Hume*, 2 vols. (hereafter called *Letters*, followed by volume and page numbers), ed. by J.Y.T. Grieg (Oxford: Oxford Univ. Press, 1932), to *New Letters of David Hume* (hereafter called *New*), ed. by Raymond Klibansky and Ernest C. Mossner (Oxford: Oxford Univ. Press, 1954), to *The Natural History of Religion*, by David Hume (hereafter called *Religion*), ed. by H.E. Root (Stanford: Stanford Univ. Press, 1956), and to *The History of England*, by David Hume (hereafter called *History*, followed by volume and page numbers) (Indianapolis: Liberty Fund, 1983).

energy and good spirits, becoming listless and depressed. His recovery was slow and gradual. He decided "to seek out a more active Life," going to England to work as a clerk for a merchant in Bristol (*Letters*, I, 13–18). But he hated the job, quarreled with his supervisor, and quit. (During this time in Bristol he changed the spelling of his surname from "Home" to "Hume" so it would conform to its proper pronunciation.) In the summer of 1734, he went to France to resume scholarly work.

He was in France for three years, composing *A Treatise of Human Nature*. It is ironic that the greatest English-language philosophy book, such a trenchant critique of earlier modern philosophy, should have been written at the Jesuit college of La Flèche, where Descartes, its founder, had studied during the previous century. Between 1737 and 1739, he was in London, preparing his *Treatise* for publication; he found a publisher in 1738. Books I and II of the *Treatise* were published together anonymously in 1739. Then he anonymously published an *Abstract* of the work, followed, in 1740, by Book III. He had decided to remove "some Reasonings concerning Miracles," prior to publishing, for fear of offending, among others, "Dr Butler," whom he unsuccessfully tried to meet. He was obviously ashamed of this "Piece of Cowardice" on his part, which he colorfully described as "castrating" his work, "that is, cutting off its noble Parts" (*New*, 2–3). Let us now turn to Hume's diagnosis of the poor reaction his book received anyhow, from "My Own Life," where he writes, "Never literary attempt was more unfortunate than my Treatise of Human Nature. It fell *dead-born from the press*, without reaching such distinction, as even to excite a murmur among the zealots." It is easy to imagine that his disappointment may have left him at a crossroads: should he persist in his scholarly-literary efforts or give them up as hopeless? Luckily, from 1739 to 1745, he was at Ninewells writing. In 1741, he anonymously published the first volume of his *Essays, Moral and Political*, followed the next year by the second volume. As he writes, "the work was favourably received, and soon made me entirely forget my former disappointment." This gave him renewed hope that his philosophical efforts might yet prove successful. In 1744, he applied for a chair of ethics and spiritual philosophy at Edinburgh, a position that would have required instructing students in Christianity. Accused of skepticism, deism, and even atheism, in 1745, his application was decisively rejected. So he took a job as private traveling tutor (actually caretaker) in England for the Marquess of Annandale, who turned out to be insane. The job paid well but was quite taxing, as the mad marquess exhibited erratic and sometimes violent behavior. (That same year, Hume's beloved mother died in Scotland.) Hume was dismissed from his position and quickly accepted another as secretary to General James St. Clair, a distant relative, who was planning a military expedition against the French in Canada. The project never materialized. Instead they unsuccessfully tried to invade the coast of France. In 1747, Hume accompanied the general on a secret mission to the courts of Vienna and Turin. Although this was a two-year break from the scholarly-literary work to which he was committed, Hume seems to have generally enjoyed this period of his life (eating well and becoming rather corpulent). He had determined that the failure of his *Treatise* was due to style rather than content and to try to recast its first book (at least) into a shorter, more readable work, being encouraged by the success of his *Essays*. In 1748, his *Enquiry concerning Human Understanding* (his "first *Enquiry*") was published. It contained the essay on miracles that he had earlier declined to publish, for fear of giving offense. At first the book was not much more successful than the *Treatise*. In 1749, he left Italy, returning to Ninewells, where he lived with his brother until John married. In 1751, he published his *Enquiry concerning the Principles of Morals* (his "second *Enquiry*"), which was a revised version of the third book of his *Treatise* and, in his own opinion, the best of all his writings. From 1751 to 1763, he lived in Edinburgh with his sister, Katherine, who also had never married. In 1751, he was elected secretary of Edinburgh's Philosophical Society. In 1752, he applied for a

11 David Hume

chair in logic at Glasgow University and was rejected (as he had previously been by Edinburgh). That same year, he published his *Political Discourses*, which he said was the only one of his books that was successful immediately on publication (*Essential*, 3–5).

In 1752, he was appointed Keeper of the Advocates' Library in Edinburgh, a position that was valuable not only for its salary but also because it gave him access to a fine collection of thousands of works, of use in the writing of his *History of England*, which he published, in six volumes, between 1754 and 1762. At first the work did not do well, and he was vilified for exhibiting sympathy for the Stuart monarchy. As he wrote, "I was assailed by one cry of reproach, disapprobation, and even detestation; English, Scotch, and Irish; Whig and Tory, churchman and sectary, free-thinker and religionist; patriot and courtier, united in their rage against the man, who had presumed to shed a generous tear for the fate of Charles I." He sardonically says that he was so "discouraged" that he considered leaving the country forever, retiring to some provincial town in France, and changing his name. But, as Great Britain and France were at war, he did no such thing. (Later, in 1764, Voltaire called it possibly the best history ever written in any language.) In 1757, he published *Four Dissertations*, one of which was his *Natural History of Religion*, which orthodox Christians hated, as they earlier had hated his essay on miracles. In 1763, having become prosperous enough, through his writings, to resign his librarian's job, he accepted a position as personal secretary to the British ambassador to France. He was in Paris for some three years and seems to have been taken aback by his popularity with the French, especially the *philosophes*, including d'Alembert and Diderot, the coeditors of the great *Encyclopedia*. He fell in love with a considerably younger Madame de Boufflers, who was estranged from her husband and the mistress of a prince. She seems to have led him on; and, when her husband died, she set about trying to marry her prince. In 1765, Hume was appointed official secretary to the British embassy in Paris. At the beginning of 1766, Hume resigned his position and left for London, accompanied by Jean-Jacques Rousseau, who was being persecuted in France. Although he had been warned about Rousseau's volatile, paranoid personality, he helped him get settled in England. Their relationship, however, quickly disintegrated when Rousseau got to accusing Hume of hypocritically plotting against him. Hume then returned to Edinburgh (*Essential*, 5–7).

Between 1767 and 1769, however, he was in London as Under-Secretary of State for the Northern Department. It was an honor, though he had ceased to want to live in England, his political sympathies being suspect there. In August of 1769, he retired to Edinburgh, where he spent the remainder of his life. He was living once more with his sister, as well as his dog, Foxey. He was close to his brother's family, being particularly fond of his nephew, David, named after him. In 1775, he was struck with a bowel disorder (perhaps intestinal cancer), which would prove fatal. Nevertheless, he maintained his typical good attitude, revising his *Dialogues concerning Natural Religion*, which he had begun in the early 1750s and on which he worked, off and on, for about a quarter of a century. Friends dissuaded him from publishing them during his lifetime as they were certain to prove extremely controversial. His good friend Adam Smith, the great economist, refused to have anything to do with publishing them. In a codicil to his will, he specified that if they were not published within two and a half years after his death, his nephew, David, should see to it that they were. Hume died on August 25, 1776; he was buried four days later, a large crowd gathering in the rain to see his coffin pass. Near the end of his autobiography, he gives us an apparently accurate self-analysis: "I was, I say, a man of mild dispositions, of command of temper, of an open, social, and cheerful humour, capable of attachment, but little susceptible of enmity, and of great moderation in all my passions. Even my love of literary fame, my ruling passion, never soured my humour, notwithstanding my frequent disappointments" (*Essential*, 7–8). In a letter, written a few weeks later, Adam Smith memorably concludes, "Upon the whole, I have always considered him, both in his lifetime, and since his death, as approaching as nearly to the idea of a perfectly wise and virtuous man, as perhaps the nature of human frailty will permit" (*Letters*, II, 452). In 1777, Hume's autobiographical *My Own Life* was published, as were his controversial essays "On Suicide" and "On the Immortality of the Soul." In 1779, his beloved *Dialogues concerning Natural Religion* were published, proving to be as inflammatory as had been predicted.

11.3 Knowledge

As background for his epistemology, Hume recommends some familiarity with Malebranche, Berkeley, and Descartes. In both the Introduction to the *Treatise*, widely recognized as a very important book, and in his *Abstract*, which is largely ignored, he mentions Locke and Butler as helping to "put the science of man" on a firm empirical foundation. He even praises Leibniz for moving away from earlier rationalists' fixation on demonstrative deduction to acknowledge the value of inductive reasoning and probability calculation. In the *Abstract*, he embraces Locke's empiricism and rejects the rationalism of Malebranche. He explains that he focuses on "the science of human nature" because it is seminal to all other scientific knowledge. He holds that all of our perceptions comprise impressions and ideas, the latter being weaker and somehow derived from the former. He seems particularly proud of his account of "the association of ideas," as involving resemblance, contiguity in time and space, and causal relations. Since every idea must be somehow derived from impressions, he recommends that every idea that cannot be so derived should be rejected as "altogether insignificant." He claims that all human reasonings regarding matters of fact "are founded on the relation of cause and effect," which he analyzes as involving spatiotemporal contiguity, temporal priority of the cause to the effect, and a customary conjunction between the two. But this does not seem sufficient, and the question arises as to whether we can detect any "necessary connection betwixt the cause and effect," as is commonly supposed. The problem is that this would assume the uniformity of nature – "that the future must be conformable to the past" – which is indemonstrable. The closest he could come to any necessary connection was linkage in the human mind – our expectations based on custom, which is the product of habitual past experience. So the necessary connection, such as it is, must be in the perceiving mind rather than in external objects perceived. This was the root of Hume's skepticism regarding reasoned knowledge concerning matters of fact and existence. He concludes the *Abstract* by acknowledging that the upshot of his phenomenalism is that our perceptions are "the only links that bind the parts of the universe together," that they alone, as far as we can know, constitute "the cement of the universe" (*Essential*, 535–547). We may regard this as the overture to the symphony of his epistemology.

Let us now consider these elements more carefully, as well as how they are logically related in the *Treatise* and the first *Enquiry*. Let us track this logic by starting with the most basic elements and then gradually working our way up. First, the direct and immediate objects of our experience are nothing but the perceptions of our own minds, all other objects being filtered through them. You encounter that bench through the filters of your own perceptions. This was not a radically new notion but has at least been implicit through modern philosophy going all the way back to Descartes (it is sometimes called his "subjective turn"). What is remarkable about Hume is how he would pursue the logic of his position to generate his avowed form of skepticism. Second, the two sorts of perceptions of the human mind are impressions and ideas somehow derived from them. Impressions of sensation (e.g. of brown) and of reflection (e.g. of anger) are relatively vivid, forceful, and lively, while ideas (e.g. those of brown or anger) are relatively less so. Third, they are related by virtue of the facts that they resemble each other and that "all our ideas or more feeble perceptions are copies of our impressions or more lively ones." Fourth, this indicates that there can be no innate ideas, such as Descartes and Leibniz advocated; Hume deals with innate ideas only briefly because Locke

160 | *11 David Hume*

and Berkeley (each of whom he calls "a great philosopher") had "already refuted" that notion. Instead, all ideas must be "derived from sensation and reflexion." Fifth, but how does this work? More specifically, what, exactly, is the relation (apart from resemblance) between our impressions (of sensation and reflection) and our ideas, which somehow copy them? It is temptingly simple to say that there is a one-to-one correspondence, such that every idea is derived from and a copy of a corresponding impression. But Hume sees at once that this will not do. This is the point of his own counterexample of "a golden mountain": we all have (or can get) an idea of a golden mountain. Yet no one has ever experienced one as anything but an idea in the human imagination. There is no mountain made of solid gold. So, sixth, a more complicated solution is needed. We must distinguish between "Simple and Complex" perceptions (both impressions and ideas), such that complex ones are compounded of relatively simpler ones. Now, seventh, we are in a position to say that every simple idea is derived from a corresponding simple impression, that every complex idea is made up of relatively simple ones (for example, the idea of a golden mountain of the ideas of gold and mountain). This is certainly a better explanation, though Hume is self-critical enough (and honest enough) to admit that he can think of a counterexample. This is the point of his missing shade of blue passage: if a person has experienced a range of shades of blue but never an impression of a particular shade within that range, the person can nevertheless form an idea of it. Hume's reaction is less than adequate: he refuses to change his theory for the sake of such a "singular," bizarre phenomenon. A far better response would have been for him to say that the idea of the missing shade is a product of the imagination, which can conjure up an idea of a shade a bit darker than one shade of which impressions have been experienced but a bit lighter than another – a process of interpolation. Eighth, this leads us to what we might call "Hume's empirical test": whenever we have an idea which does not seem to be grounded in any impression(s), we should reject it as spurious and not waste time on it any further. Ninth, there are three principles of association interconnecting our ideas – "*Resemblance, Contiguity* in time or place, and *Cause* or *Effect*." We naturally tend to associate with each other ideas related in any combination of these three ways. Tenth, all human reasoning regarding associated ideas is of two sorts: "*Relations of Ideas*" such as mathematical truths can be absolutely certain but tell us nothing about the facts of reality outside our own minds. "*Matters of Fact*," by contrast, purport to inform us about reality existing independently of us. Eleventh, "All reasonings concerning matter of fact seem to be founded on the relation of *Cause and Effect*. By means of that relation alone we can go beyond the evidence of our memory and senses." And, twelfth, no causal reasoning can ever yield certain conclusions; and, thus, all reasoning about matters of fact can only be more or less probable (*Essential*, 52–57, 62–63, and *Treatise*, 1–20, 35, 158). This is the foundation of Hume's epistemology, systematically (if somewhat artificially) analyzed, which will ineluctably lead us to his notorious skepticism.

We need to say more about Hume's theory of belief, his account of certain knowledge and probability, and his resulting skepticism. Building on this theory of ideas, Hume writes, in the *Treatise*, "The idea of an object is an essential part of the belief of it, but not the whole. We conceive many things, which we do not believe." Those of us, for example, who are "Star Wars" fans conceive of a fictional creature called a "wookie"; yet we do not believe that any being like Chewbacca ever actually existed outside the human imagination. The difference between a fiction conceived but not believed in and that same idea believed in is not one of content but one of "the *manner*" in which it is apprehended by the mind. An idea in which we believe is livelier than one fancied *and* more closely associated with our impressions of sensation and memory. Our beliefs are particularly important psychic aspects of our lives, in that most "of our reasonings, with all our actions and passions," stem from them. Hume admits that this analysis is somewhat lacking in clarity but thinks that our everyday experience renders it sufficiently intelligible. Let us turn to certain knowledge versus probable belief. So much of modern philosophy from Descartes through Berkeley was a quest for certain knowledge. From Hume's perspective, what can be certainly known? First, relations of ideas, such as "seven plus five equals twelve" or the Pythagorean Theorem in (Euclidean) geometry. Second, all matters of fact as they are being sensed; I know I see what I take to be a green rectangle when I am looking at it. And, third, all matters of fact, where previous sensations are clearly and distinctly remembered, such as the fact that I drank several cups of tea this morning. Hume may or may not have realized how murky this third sort is, due to our lack of an adequate standard of clarity and distinctness (which was also a problem Descartes had). He distinguishes, as did Locke, between reasoning that leads to demonstrative knowledge, as of relations of ideas, on the one hand, and reasoning leading to empirical proofs and probability calculations, on the other. No human reasoning regarding matters of fact can lead to conclusions demonstratively knowable. This renders empirical proofs (e.g. that Martin Luther King's death was caused by a gunshot wound) and probability calculations (e.g. that a higher percentage of philosophy majors enjoy studying Hume than of business majors) all the more important in our lives. Of the "seven different kinds of philosophical relation," three (identity, spatiotemporal relations, and causation) can never be objects of certain knowledge. Only the other four ("*resemblance, contrariety, degrees in quality, and proportions in quantity or number*") can be so. We should appreciate how narrowly this assigns the bounds of certain knowledge. Empirical proofs, in particular, depend on causal relationships, which are merely probable. Thus, whenever we reason regarding matters of fact, "all knowledge degenerates into probability." Here is the epistemological basis of Hume's notorious skepticism. "Since therefore all knowledge," apart from the intuitions of sense and memory and the demonstrations of relations of ideas, "resolves itself into probability," skepticism ought to prevail. In the last section of the first *Enquiry*, he distinguishes among three sorts of skepticism. First, he identifies "*antecedent*" skepticism with Descartes, who started off trying to doubt everything but allegedly overcame doubt and discovered certain truth. Hume rejects this approach as either a game of theatricals or as "entirely incurable." Second, another sort is that which is "*consequent* to science and enquiry." Hume rejects this sort (sometimes called Pyrrhonism) as "*excessive*," in that we could not practically function in accordance with it: "The great subverter of *Pyrrhonism* or the excessive principles of skepticism, is action, and employment, and the occupations of common life." Third, the sort Hume embraces is "a more *mitigated*" skepticism, moderated "by common sense and reflection." This is a healthy corrective to the sort of dogmatism that can lead to fanaticism, "haughtiness and obstinacy"; yet its practitioners can lead a normal life. (In the *Treatise*, he speaks of "moderate scepticism.") Hume's skepticism aims at the elimination of metaphysics, including theology, as a science. At the end of his first *Enquiry*, he urges us to ask and answer two questions about such work. First, is it "*abstract reasoning concerning quantity or number*" or mathematics? And, second, is it a work of empirical science, featuring "*experimental reasoning concerning matter of fact and existence*"? The answer to both questions is obviously, "No." But these are allegedly the only two types of human reasoning that are legitimate. "Commit it then to the flames: For it can contain nothing but sophistry and illusion" (*Treatise*, 94–96, 101, 103, 629, 118–119, 629, 124, 69–70, 180–181, 224; *Essential*, 79–81, 85n., 155–156, 162–164, 167). We shall now see how this skepticism plays out in more specific areas we have been considering all along.

11.4 Reality

Hume's radical empiricism leads him to become even more skeptical about substance than Locke, a more extreme phenomenalist than Berkeley, and arguably the most powerful critic of causal knowledge in the history of Western philosophy up to his time. We have already seen how Locke compromises substance metaphysics by identifying substance as intrinsically unknowable; yet he clings to his (Cartesian) belief in the divine Substance (God), spiritual substance (the mind), and physical substance (bodies). He seems not to appreciate any tension there or to realize how this might open the door to skepticism. Berkeley, we now know, accentuates the problem by denying that there is any physical substance at all and embracing a phenomenalism regarding material objects. Hume, applying his empirical test, is more radical than either of them. He asks, point blank, "whether the idea of *substance* be deriv'd from the impressions of sensation or reflexion?" His answer is neither. We never see, hear, smell, touch, or taste substance; we only sense its qualities, movements, and relations. Nor can we even feel the substance of our own minds; all we experience through "our passions and emotions" are our own states of consciousness. Yet, since these are the only two sorts of impressions (of sensation and of reflection) and since all legitimate ideas must be derived from impressions, the startling conclusion follows and can be expressed syllogistically: All of our ideas are perceptions, grounded in impressions. "A substance is entirely different from a perception. We have, therefore, no idea of a substance." This reduces all objects of our experience to phenomenal appearances and represents a full-blown phenomenalism. Our supposed idea of substance thus fails Hume's empirical test. But the idea of existence fares no better, as "the idea of existence is not deriv'd from any particular impression." There is no difference between perceiving a teacup and perceiving it as existing – at least not in the object perceived. "The idea of existence, then, is the very same with the idea of what we conceive to be existent." So here another crucial metaphysical concept fails Hume's empirical test. But Hume's most famous critique of a key metaphysical concept is that of causation (*Treatise*, 15–16, 234, 66).

As we have seen, he maintains that all human reasoning about factual matters must involve causal reasoning, which will never yield certain knowledge. But now we should explore how he reaches that conclusion. Once more, his empirical test comes into play. Using Malebranche's example of the billiard balls, Hume could say that we have a visual impression of, say, the cue ball moving toward the stationary eight ball, the auditory impression of their impact, and a subsequent visual impression of the eight ball moving toward the corner pocket. But what impression do we have of the cue ball communicating motion to the eight ball upon impact? It would seem that we have no sense impression whatsoever of that. Yet we think and say that the cue ball's hitting the eight ball is the *cause* that produces the *effect* of the eight ball's starting to move. What can we actually experience of the relation between those two distinct events? First, they are contiguous or spatially near one another at some particular time(s). Second, the event we consider the cause must be temporally prior to the event we consider the effect. And, third, there is a "customary conjunction" between events like those two (Hume sometimes uses the phrase "constant conjunction" between events like those two, which constitutes a needless exaggeration). But that does not seem sufficient. Suppose that I customarily get up out of bed immediately after sunrise on my part of our planet. While the sunrise may be the *occasion* of my rising, we would not normally say that the former is the cause that produced the effect of the latter. For what "necessary connection" between the two can we locate in the realm of our impressions? It would seem that the answer is none at all, which would tar the alleged idea of causation with the brush of illegitimacy. "All events seem entirely loose and separate. One event follows another; but we never can observe any tye between them. They seem *conjoined* but never *connected*." Thus the conclusion "*seems* to be" that the idea of causation is bogus. This would be a drastic conclusion to draw about one of the most practically useful of all human concepts. But perhaps we have been looking for our impression in the wrong "place": maybe it is not outside the mind, in the world of billiard balls, at all. Maybe it is to be located in the mind itself. Let us consider this. It is as a result of repeated experiences of a similar nature in the past that we get into the habit of expecting like associations in the future.

Thus we assume that, in broad outline at least, nature is uniform, so that the future will (roughly) cohere with the past. This natural tendency is the psychological result of habitual experience, and not of logical reason. "Custom, then, is the great guide of human life." There is nothing absolutely necessary about it; yet we have found the impression that gives rise to the idea of causal connection. "This connexion, therefore, which we *feel* in the mind, this customary transition of the imagination from one object to its usual attendance, is the sentiment or impression from which we form the idea" of causation (*Essential*, 63–101). Given that there are no innate ideas (or principles), the only way the idea of causation could pass Hume's empirical test would be if an impression or set of impressions could be found from which it might be derived. Unlike the ideas of substance and existence, this one has passed muster. However, it is merely the subjective impression of a feeling in the imagination rather than any objective determination of reason. So we need not dispense with the idea of causation but can hardly suppose that it could ever lead to certain knowledge. What Hume has done here is undermine the cognitive credibility of three of the most crucial concepts for doing metaphysics – those of substance, existence, and causality. This would precipitate a crisis that would require a response from a younger contemporary, a German professor of metaphysics, named Immanuel Kant.

11.5 God

Hume's skepticism is arguably no more apparent in any other part of his works than in his writings on God and religion (only a portion of which we shall be able to explore here). From his own time until today, he has been accused of being an atheist and irreligious. If that characterization were accurate, he was also a hypocrite, as in work after work he claims to believe in some sort of deity. So the claim that he was an atheist will be rejected here. Rather we shall treat him as a deist in his views on God, a fideist regarding religious belief, and an enemy of popular (as opposed to philosophical) religion. Not only does Hume not deny the existence of a deity, but he repeatedly asserts it. Both the introduction and the concluding chapter of his *Natural History of Religion* affirm that the world of nature involves the sort of natural order that points to an intelligent designer (*Religion*, 21, 74–76). His *Dialogues*, which were every bit as inflammatory and never published during his lifetime, make it clear that the point of contention among the three major characters has nothing to do with "the being of a God," the truth of which is called "obvious," but only with what reason can establish regarding "the nature of that divine Being." Even Philo, the character whose skepticism comes closest to Hume's own position, never doubts the reality of a deity and clearly affirms it in the final part of the book. The first *Enquiry*, in addition to the scandalous essay on miracles, contains an equally controversial critique of argumentation for God (equally offensive to orthodox Christians); both essays (sections X and XI), far from advocating atheism, merely lodge protests against the illegitimate uses to which miracle stories and the argument from design are put by proponents of orthodox Christianity. To characterize Hume as a deist, who did not subscribe to the theism of his culture, is to indicate that he believed in a finite, limited deity who designed (or, possibly, created) our world but is no longer involved with it, who cares little nor nothing how we humans behave, communicates nothing through revelation, and probably, as far as we can tell, has no moral qualities whatsoever. Let us examine the skeptical philosophical theology developed so artfully in his *Dialogues*. Of the three major characters, Demea represents the sort of rationalism we saw in Leibniz, Cleanthes the kind of moderate theism we saw in Locke, and Philo Hume's own skeptical deism. Pamphilus, the narrator, condemns both "the careless skepticism of Philo" and "the rigid inflexible orthodoxy of Demea," favoring "the accurate philosophical turn of Cleanthes."

164 | *11 David Hume*

But this is a dodge: Pamphilus, as the "pupil" of Cleanthes, is prejudiced (*Essential*, 304, 379, 145–146, 150–154, 305); yet Philo "wins" round after round in his skirmishes with the other characters. And we know that, in 1751, Hume implored his good friend Gilbert Elliot to help him strengthen the reasoning of Cleanthes (*Letters*, I, 155); he needed no such help in representing the skeptical position of Philo, which comes naturally to him.

Let us consider how Hume deals with traditional arguments purporting to prove God's existence. In *The Natural History of Religion*, he attacks the argument from general consensus, which can be formulated like this: If there is a general consensus among human beings that God exists (or that gods exist), then it must be so. There is such a general consensus. So God (or gods) must exist. Hume was not as hard as we might expect on the first premise in this (admittedly valid) argument, whose consequent in no way follows from its antecedent. It is false that all people in all cultures at all times agree, if that is what the second premise means to claim. But even if we interpret it to mean only that the vast majority of people agree, all the historical evidence supports is that the vast majority have believed in some "invisible, intelligent power" or other – not necessarily infinitely perfect and possibly many (polytheism) rather than one (monotheism). The argument fails to do the work that ethical theists want of it (*Religion*, 31, 44). Second, it should come as no surprise that Hume does not take seriously the ontological argument, which is utterly nonempirical. As we have seen, he maintains that there is no difference between the idea of anything (including God) and the idea of it as existing. On this view, rationalists (such as Descartes) are simply wrong in thinking that existence is a perfection that might be required by the very idea of a thing: "When I think of God, when I think of him as existent, and when I believe him to be existent, my idea of him neither encreases nor diminishes" (*Treatise*, 66–67, 94). Hume took somewhat more seriously the cosmological argument, used by so many philosophical theologians (including Leibniz), having Demea advocate it in part IX of the *Dialogues*. It can be formulated thus: Everything that exists must have a cause or sufficient reason; either the chain of causes and effects goes on to infinity or there must be "some ultimate cause, that is *necessarily* existent"; the first of these alternatives is "absurd," as the causal chain would never get started; so there must be some necessarily existent Being that caused everything else, and that is God. From Hume's perspective, the argument (though valid) is utterly disreputable: (i) why could something that does not necessarily exist not just happen (contingently) to exist, thus far, from all eternity, causing every thing else without being divine? (ii) Cleanthes observed that in order for the existence of anything (including God) to be demonstrable, its nonexistence would have to be self-contradictory and thus inconceivable, but the nonexistence of anything (including God) is at least conceivable; (iii) the phrase "necessary existence" is ungrounded, if not meaningless, because it cannot pass Hume's empirical test; (iv) if we could overlook all this, why could "the natural universe" itself not be the necessarily existent cause of everything it comprises? (v) the very idea of the whole world, as allegedly requiring causal explanation, is deeply problematic, probably also failing Hume's empirical test (*Essential*, 354–356). It is curious that Hume assigns the task of demolishing this argument to Cleanthes (who is like Locke, who himself used such a causal argument) rather than to Philo (the Humean skeptic).

The argument for God for which Hume exhibits the most respect is the argument from design. In his Introduction to *The Natural History of Religion*, he writes, "The whole frame of nature bespeaks an intelligent author" (*Religion*, 21; see, also, 74). In his Appendix to the *Treatise*, he says, "the order of the universe proves an omnipotent mind" (*Treatise*, 633n.); he later drops any attachment to divine omnipotence. In section XI of his first *Enquiry*, Hume presents a thinly disguised "friend who loves sceptical paradoxes" to criticize the argument from design. This skeptical "friend" comes to the conclusion that it is "both uncertain and useless. It is uncertain; because the subject lies entirely beyond the reach of human experience," requiring us to draw an analogy

11.5 God | 165

between causes and effects we experience, where the causes produced the effects by intelligent design, and causes (e.g. God) and effects (e.g. the world as a whole) which we never can experience. "It is useless" because, even if we accept it, it gives us only an intelligent and powerful designer, providing no practical guidance regarding human "conduct and behavior" that would be appropriate (*Essential*, 142–154).

But it is in the *Dialogues* that Hume presents his most masterful analysis of the argument from design, having Cleanthes advocate it as a logical argument from analogy in part II: The world of our experience is both a very complex and an extremely well designed "machine" comprising "an infinite number of lesser machines," which are themselves well ordered, resembling the results of human intelligent design. But since the world and products of human design are so strikingly similar, "the Author of Nature is somewhat similar to the mind of man," though, of course, greater. Demea's reaction is one of rejection of a merely empirical proof rather than an a priori rationalistic demonstration. Philo, by contrast, favors an empirical approach but attacks the logic of the argument. This is an argument from analogy; as such, it is inductive rather than deductive, establishing, at best, a probable conclusion rather than a certain one. But, among inductive arguments, those from analogy are relatively weak, because they require concluding that, because two things that are not identical are similar in some observed respects, they must be similar in other (unobserved) respects which the argument aims to establish. But, even among arguments from analogy, those comparing objects of human experience to things we cannot experience are particularly untrustworthy. Cleanthes tries, in the face of this critique, to shift the argument from a logical proof to psychologically suggestive reasoning (starting in part III). Philo maintains his assault. Among other points, he considers the fact of evil in the world as empirical evidence of bad design indicative of (if anything) a limited designer. By part XI, Cleanthes has retreated to the weak position of "supposing the Author of Nature to be finitely perfect, though far exceeding mankind." Part XII is the most puzzling portion of the *Dialogues*. Philo, who has been consistently critical of the argument from design, here (with the departure of the dogmatic Demea) executes a partial reversal, concluding "*That the cause or causes of order in the universe probably bear some remote analogy to human intelligence*" (*Essential*, 316–326, 366–367, 379, 388). While this may be a surprising turnaround, as we analyze it closely, we realize that it is very carefully hedged as a probability statement regarding one or more designers of the universe that are remotely similar to humans – no certainty, not necessarily a single, unique Designer, no indication of infinite perfection, and nothing to suggest any likely moral qualities or ongoing relations with anything in our world, including us. This is deism, of the sort that was so popular among eighteenth-century Enlightenment thinkers.

Some believers, such as Pascal, who are themselves skeptical of logical arguments for God, prefer to appeal to stories of miracles (and prophecies) as offering us supporting reasons to believe. But in the infamous Section X of his first *Enquiry*, Hume makes it evident that this approach is doomed to frustration and failure. How can we know that there is any literal truth to these scriptural stories? We have to rely on the testimony of strangers, transmitted to us over the course of generations. But, remember, Hume was a serious, accomplished historian. As such, he knew about sources and evidence. "A miracle is a violation of the laws of nature," which are supported by a great mass of human experience. For example, "once dead, forever dead" is a principle drawn from the laws of nature, supported by thousands of years of cross-cultural human experience. While it may be conceivable that someone, such as Jesus of Nazareth, might be truly dead and then return to life, it seems highly unlikely, given the findings of natural experience. Why should we believe that it literally happened? Because the Scriptures (in this case, the New Testament) report it, allegedly based on eyewitness testimony. Thousands of years of human testimony support the laws of nature. "A miracle may be accurately defined, *a transgression of a law of nature by a particular volition of the Deity, or by the interposition of some invisible agent*," such as an angel. There are at least four reasons to be suspicious of miracle stories: (i) we fail to find enough intelligible, reliable witnesses testifying to exactly the same account, interpreted in exactly the same way; (ii) people enjoy telling tall tales that amaze and fascinate others; (iii) miracle stories prevail among relatively primitive people, who are generally ignorant of scientific explanations; and (iv) the miracle stories of different religious traditions purport to support conflicting systems of belief. Hume's conclusion stops short of ruling out miracles as impossible: "Upon the whole, then, it appears, that no testimony for any kind of miracle has ever amounted to a probability, much less to a proof." He adds that everything he wrote about miracles applies equally well to prophecies. He draws the conclusion of fideism: "Our most holy religion is founded on *Faith*, not on reason" (*Essential*, 128–133, 139, 141–142). Hume does not explicitly apply his empirical test to the idea of a miracle; but, if he had done so, his conclusion would have been that we have no way of establishing that it was based on veridical impressions rather than being mere fancies of the imagination. And what if he had applied his test to the idea of God? It would be an idea of the imagination. The deistic version of a designer who was more intelligent and powerful than we, but not infinitely perfect or even necessarily good, could simply represent an extrapolation of our experience of ourselves. But the theistic version of an infinitely perfect, eternal, omniscient, omnipotent, absolutely good supernatural Being could not possibly pass the test.

Contributing to Hume's belief in a limited, finite Deity is his sensitivity to the problem of evil, discussed in Parts X and XI of his *Dialogues*. Probably every human being who is at all thoughtfully aware of our world could see that it is infested and infected by the evil of pain, suffering, misery, cruelty, disease, treachery, and so forth. To put the problem bluntly, how is the fact of evil in the world compatible with the belief that the causal Source of the world was an infinitely perfect God – all-knowing, all-powerful, and absolutely good. Hume has Philo ask three pointed questions regarding this alleged God: "Is he willing to prevent evil, but not able? Then is he impotent. Is he able, but not willing? Then is he malevolent. Is he both able and willing? Whence then is evil?" Demea gives a traditional Christian response, that our world represents only a small part of reality and that the "present evil phenomena" we experience will be "rectified in other regions, and in some future period of existence." Cleanthes objects, in a way probably representative of Hume himself – these are "arbitrary suppositions" of wishful thinking. Yet his own initial solution to the problem of evil is even worse. He suggests that the best approach is to deny evil altogether. But this denial of everyday reality is an outrageous move for an avowed empiricist to make, and he quickly moderates his position to maintain that the good in the world significantly outweighs the evil. Still, as Philo observes, this is a shuffling evasion of the challenge that confronts belief in an infinitely perfect Creator of the world: "Why is there any misery at all in the world?" He is willing to grant, for the sake of argument, the possibility that the evil of the world might be compatible with an infinitely perfect God. Still, the former surely counts against the likelihood of the latter. Hume's own solution to the problem of evil (assuming that Philo speaks for him) must have struck eighteenth-century Christians as shocking. He conceives of "*four* hypotheses" regarding the moral nature of gods (or God): (i) that they are perfectly good, (ii) that they are perfectly evil, (iii) that they are a mixture of good and evil, and (iv) that they are neither good nor evil. The phenomena of our world are so mixed as to provide evidence against the first two options, and the uniformity and coherence of the world count against the third. Thus, by a logical process of elimination, we are left with the fourth, that the gods (or God) are (or is) neither good nor evil, having no moral qualities, as far as any evidence would indicate (*Essential*, 358–359, 362–367, 374). From a critical perspective, Hume is hasty here: if God's power and/or knowledge were limited, God could be perfectly good and entirely benevolent. For that matter, Hume too rashly dismisses the positions of Demea and Cleanthes: while we may have no evidence that the suffering of this life will be rectified in an afterlife, it is not irrational to think that it might be and hope that it will; and a perfectly good God could allow evil as a necessary condition for the great good of having personal creatures with free will.

Was Hume irreligious? He was clearly no orthodox ethical monotheist. He was opposed to the popular religion of orthodox theism, because it is based on "*superstition* and *enthusiasm*, the corruptions of true religion." So much of reality is unknown to us, which naturally worries and terrifies us. "Weakness, fear, melancholy, together with ignorance, are, therefore, the true sources of Superstition," which takes the form of childish religious fancies. As we become fanatically devoted to these fancies, we imagine that we are better than people who are not so committed, favored over them by the Deity. "Hope, pride, presumption, a warm imagination, together with ignorance, are therefore the true sources of Enthusiasm" (*Essays*, 73–74). Superstition undermines rational thought, and the fanaticism of enthusiasm breeds intolerance and hatred of those who do not share our beliefs. Both are characteristic of popular religion and dangerous obstacles to open-minded critical thought. The final disagreement between Cleanthes and Philo (after the departure of Demea), in Part XII of the *Dialogues*, concerns whether religion is beneficial or detrimental. Cleanthes emphasizes its salutary effects, while Philo highlights the harm that it has caused. The popular religions of the masses (Christianity included) tend to foster dogmatism, hostility, persecution, and oppression. "True religion," by contrast, is "the philosophical and rational kind" associated with deism. It sanctions no superstitious religious practices and encourages open-minded critical reflection. Finally, unlike the theism of Cleanthes, the deism of Philo could avoid the foolish anthropomorphism of thinking and speaking of the Deity as if it were a superhuman, respecting the idea that, whatever its nature, it must be quite different from us and the things of our world. Near the beginning of the *Dialogues*, Cleanthes sarcastically states that Philo seemed to be trying "to erect religious faith on philosophical scepticism." But, mockery aside, this seems to be an apt account of Hume's project. For, at the end of the *Dialogues*, he has Philo say, "To be a philosophical Sceptic is, in a man of letters, the first and most essential step towards being a sound, believing Christian" (*Essential*, 381–387, 307, 388). While it would not be appropriate to conclude that Hume himself was a Christian, his skepticism leads him to fideism. As we shall see, a similar path is taken in the next century by Kierkegaard, one of the most committed Christians in modern philosophy.

11.6 Humanity

As Hume's skepticism radically reduces the range of what we can certainly know, reduces reality to a complex mass of phenomenal appearances, and reduces God to a limited object of faith that is neither experienced nor knowable, it also reduces the human person to a psycho-physical natural being. Because of his aversion to metaphysics, he does not make it easy for us to characterize his analysis of human nature. He is not a dualist like Descartes or Locke or a monistic immaterialist like Berkeley or a dual aspect theorist like Spinoza; but neither is he obviously a materialist like Hobbes. After all, as we have seen, he does not even trust the concept of substance, which fails his empirical test. That said, however, for all his skepticism, he accepts the reality of the body as a necessary condition of our everyday sense experience, saying that "'tis in vain to ask, *Whether there be body or not? That is a point, which we must take for granted in all our reasonings.*" (We might note how he here put considerable distance between himself and Descartes.) Yet our belief that bodies, including our own, have a continuing existence independent of our perceptual experience of them can neither itself be sensed (that would be a contradiction in terms) nor conclusively established by reason. "That opinion must be entirely owing to the imagination" (*Treatise*, 187–193). The belief pragmatically works for us but cannot otherwise be proved. Like Descartes and Hobbes, he conceives of "the human body" as "a mighty complicated machine." Its matter is a construct of the imagination, inaccessible in itself. He sounds rather like Locke, when he writes, "Bereave matter of all its intelligible qualities, both primary and secondary, you in a manner annihilate it, and leave only a certain unknown, inexplicable *something*, as the cause of our perceptions." The phenomenalism here is epistemological, having to do with what we can know, rather than ontological, having to do with what is. He is working to construct a "science of human nature" (*Essential*, 108, 159, 44). This "science of man" is to be utterly empirical rather than metaphysically speculative, an "experimental philosophy" based entirely "on experience and observation" (*Treatise*, xx), perhaps modeled on Newton's physical science. In the first section of his first *Enquiry*, Hume analyzes human nature as comprising at least three dimensions. A human being is naturally "a reasonable being," as well as "a sociable" being and "also an active being" (*Essential*, 46). The first book of his *Treatise* and his first *Enquiry* focus on humans as reasonable; the second and third books of the *Treatise* and his second *Enquiry* focus on humans as active; and his political essays, especially, focus on them as sociable.

Like Hobbes, he has no qualms about acknowledging that a human being is an animal, differing from other animals only quantitatively (in degree of capacities) and not qualitatively (radically in kind). Philosophers (and theologians) had long tried to show that humans are unique in using reason rather than merely acting on instinct. But in a section of the *Treatise* entitled "Of the reason of animals," he agrees with Hobbes that beasts "reason as well as men, . . . adapting means to ends" to fulfill their desires. Indeed, he avers, our much vaunted "reason is nothing but a wonderful and unintelligible instinct" reinforced by experience. But, we might wonder, what about the mind or self or soul? Here Hume stretches the phenomenalism that Berkeley applied to bodies into the realm of spirit, where the good Bishop was unwilling to apply it. Even if there were a human spiritual substance, we would have no good experiential reason to affirm it, as all we can experience of our own minds are its thoughts, feelings, desires, and other states of consciousness. Here we encounter his notorious phenomenalistic theory of the mind as a mere bundle of perceptions. He writes that "what we call a *mind*, is nothing but a heap or collection of different perceptions," which we like to imagine has a continuing identity. This view clearly runs contrary to the spiritual view that dominated Western philosophy up to that point, as well as to that of Christianity. Applying Hume's empirical test, the idea of mind (or self or soul or person), as having an enduring identity over time, is derived from no impression at all. We may imagine that we can experience such an impression. But, putting the point quite personally, Hume writes, "For my part, when I enter most intimately into what I call *myself*, I always stumble on some particular perception or other, of heat or cold, light or shade, love or hatred, pain or pleasure. I never can catch *myself* at any time without a perception, and never can observe any thing but the perception." (It might prove to be an interesting experiment for us to try this for ourselves.) He admits that "some metaphysician" (we might think of Descartes here) may fancy he can do better. But, he ventures to assert sarcastically, apart from a few such people, we might best think of the mind as "a bundle or collection of different perceptions which succeed each other with an inconceivable rapidity and are in a perpetual flux and movement" with no stability enduring over time. (Hume also uses a second metaphor, comparing the mind to "a kind of theatre," such that we are normally aware of what is on the stage without ever being able directly to perceive the theatre itself.) On this view, the notion that the mind has any ongoing "identity" is "only a fictitious one" of the imagination. In a very important passage in the Appendix to his *Treatise*, Hume concedes that there are problems with this phenomenalistic account. If the mind were a mere bundle of perceptions, what ties together my bundle, distinguishing it from yours? What is it that views the action on the stage of my theatre, and what experiences yours? Hume candidly admits that he could not adequately answer such questions. As if throwing up his hands with exasperation, he explains, "For my part, I must plead the privilege of a sceptic, and confess, that this difficulty is too hard for my understanding." But, he modestly adds, others, or even he, "upon more mature reflexions," might some day figure it out. He also confesses that such skeptical reflections sometimes left him melancholic as well as baffled. Yet he finds refreshing diversions therapeutic: "I dine, I play a game of back-gammon, I converse, and am merry with my friends," and the gloomy clouds dissipate, leaving him sufficiently recuperated to return to his philosophical inquiries (*Treatise*, 176–179, 207, 251–253, 259, 633–636, 269–271).

As he follows Hobbes in deemphasizing the uniqueness and spirituality of human reason, so he agrees with his predecessor in emphasizing the great significance of the passions in our lives and behaviors, devoting the second book of his *Treatise* to the topic. There he distinguishes between "*original* and *secondary*" impressions. The former are sensations, as when I hear you insulting my mother, while the latter are reflections on sensations, as when I become angry as a result. Later, I can recollect the idea of what you said as well as my own angry reaction. Our passions or emotions, as immediately experienced (e.g. my anger when I feel it), are secondary impressions of reflection. They can be either "calm," as when I feel that a sunset I see is beautiful, or "violent," as are "the passions of love and hatred, grief and joy, pride and humility," Hume admitting that this distinction is imprecise. Passions can be either "*direct*" or "*indirect*," the former (e.g. "desire, aversion, grief, joy, hope, fear, despair," etc.) arising immediately from perceptions of good and evil or pleasure and pain, while the latter (e.g. "pride, humility, ambition, vanity, love, hatred, envy, pity, malice, generosity," and so forth) are conjoined with other qualities than those. For instance, we have a direct desire for the company of friends to the extent that we consider it good and pleasant; we have a direct aversion to the company of surly, abusive sadists, because we find them bad and their company painful. By contrast, the indirect passion of pride is pleasant and associated with having considerable self-esteem, whereas shame is painful and associated with a lack of self-approval. A particularly important aspect of human nature is our natural capacity for sympathy: "No quality of human nature is more remarkable, both in itself and in its consequences, than that propensity we have to sympathize with others, and to receive by communication their inclinations and sentiments, however different from, or even contrary to our own." The reason this is so important is that it will provide a non-egoistic foundation for morals and social relationships (allowing Hume to distance himself from Hobbes). This does not keep Hume from acknowledging "*self-love*," which is normally a fact of life; and the two need not be in conflict, though they can be. Our sympathy for another person can engender unselfish love, with a subsequent desire for his happiness and aversion to his misery, while a lack of sympathy can make it easier to hate another person, desiring his unhappiness. Sympathy facilitates pity, while its absence renders malice easier. Sympathy and love promote benevolence, while an unsympathetic hatred renders malevolence more likely, the former normally being a pleasant passion and the latter tending to be unpleasant. The passions of desire and aversion involve the will, which Hume defines as "*the internal impression we feel and are conscious of, when we knowingly give rise to any new motion of our body, or new perceptions of our mind.*" (It seems problematic to define the will as a felt impression rather than as a faculty of the mind, as well as to assume that it must always be so transparent that we are conscious of it.) Even relatively calm passions can motivate the will, and they can be so calm that we mistake them "for the determinations of reason." Also, a relatively calm passion, such as annoyance, can be transmuted into a violent one, such as hatred. Some direct passions – e.g. "hunger, lust, and a few other bodily appetites" – seem to be natural impulses or instincts. An uncertain good arouses hope,

170 | 11 David Hume

while an uncertain evil "gives rise to fear," both of these being potentially powerful psychological motivations. As has already been indicated, Hume rejects Hobbesian egoism: "So far from thinking, that men have no affection for anything beyond themselves, I am of opinion, that tho' it be rare to meet with one, who loves any single person better than himself, yet 'tis as rare to meet with one, in whom all the kind affections, taken together, do not over-balance all the selfish." Given three sorts of goods we value – mental satisfaction, physical pleasures, and the enjoyment of external things – the last category would include friends and other people we love. While sympathy is natural to humans everywhere and we can experience it directly in ourselves, of course we can only infer it of others from their behavior (*Treatise*, 275–277, 286, 316, 329, 367, 369, 382, 387, 399, 417, 437–439, 487, 575–576; cf. "Of the Dignity and Meanness of Human Nature," in *Essays*, 85–86, for another critique of egoism). Because Hume assigns a relatively limited, modest role to reason, the passions assume an even more significant role in human nature and action. Later we shall consider how he handles the controversial issue of the relationship between reason and the passions.

11.7 Freedom

As Hume's skepticism leads him to limit sharply the bounds of knowledge, to hold a phenomenalistic view of reality, to adopt a position of fideistic deism, and to reduce humans to a mass of thoughts, passions, and volitions, all dependent on the body, so it eventuates in causal determinism. Hume holds that there is "no such thing as Chance in the world." For all his skepticism about our being able to *know* of any objective, mind-independent linkage between causes and effects, he *believes* that every event in the universe, including every human action, is causally determined. Yet he wants to maintain a distinction between acts of liberty and acts of extrinsic necessity, if only to try to leave some room for moral responsibility. The *locus classicus* for his views on this topic can be found in the eighth section of his first *Enquiry*. There he reiterates that the constant conjunction of different events, combined with the human perceiver's mind being "determined by custom to infer the one from the appearance of the other," forms the basis for our idea of causal necessity. Human experience universally attests to the fact "that there is a great uniformity among the actions" of all humans, "in all nations and ages, and that human nature" is constant "in its principles and operations. The same motives always produce the same actions." (This may be a bit of an exaggeration; but it at least seems *generally* to be the case.) Indeed, the great value of history, of which he was a dedicated practitioner, presupposes the truth of this claim. Were we to encounter a traveler from distant lands who reported on people so radically different from us as never to be motivated by "avarice, ambition, or revenge," who were purely kind and generous under all circumstances, we would not believe him, as such a tale would run counter to our common experience. However, this does not mean that human behavior is as predictable as that of running water, because human nature and human behavior are so much more complex. He concedes that there are some human actions such that we do not understand the motivation behind them. But we should not conclude from that fact that they are not determined – merely that we are sometimes ignorant of their determining causes. He goes so far as to aver that, to the extent that we understand people's characters, "the conjunction between motives and voluntary actions is as regular and uniform, as that between the cause and effect in any part of nature" and reasonably assumed. The commitments we make in our everyday lives and ordinary expectations we reasonably have – both theoretical and practical – presume "the doctrine of necessity, and this *inference* from motives to voluntary actions; from characters to conduct" in our lives. Hume gives three splendid examples to illustrate his point: (i) a prisoner sentenced to death can be practically certain that his jailer is not likely to let him escape; (ii) a person inviting a best friend over to his house can be practically certain that the latter will not stab him in the back in order to steal his silver service; and (iii) a person leaving a "purse full of gold" unattended on a busy intersection can be practically certain that it will not remain there "untouched an hour later." Now, admittedly, all of these are matters of probability rather than of absolute certainty, and sometimes we are surprised that things do not turn out as reasonably expected. If the only two conditions for saying an action is determined are "the *constant conjunction* of objects and the consequent *inference* of the mind from one to another," and both of these conditions apply to all voluntary human actions, then they all must be determined. This argument is valid. But Hume's premises are false if we adhere to the adjective "constant." What if we reduce that word to "customary," as he occasionally did? The premises would still be disputable, because the case can be one not quite like any other previously experienced or because of some sort of unknown perversity of will on the part of a rebelling agent. At any rate, all this leads Hume to his definition of human freedom: "By liberty, then, we can only mean *a power of acting or not acting, according to the determinations of will*." On this view (sometimes called "compatibilism," because it considers freedom to be compatible with – rather than the opposite of – determinism), an act of freedom is *internally* determined by the will, while an act of necessity is *extrinsically* determined by outside forces. Meanwhile, whenever we imagine an act to be spontaneous, rather than determined, it is allegedly only because we are ignorant of the causation. Hume leaves unaddressed the question of what ultimately causes the will to be so moved; but this theory of universal causation ultimately requires some such necessary causal conditions as a combination of genetic forces and elements of the natural and social environments. Far from acknowledging that this view compromises moral responsibility, rendering all punishment unjust, he, in fact, regards such determinism as "essential to morality" (*Essential*, 85, 104–117; cf. *Treatise*, 312, 404–405, 408–409). Surely, if a person's act were spontaneous and not caused by some aspect of himself, moral responsibility would be lost. But, if it were caused by his will, which he ultimately could not control, the same would seem to be the case.

11.8   Morality

Some of us might wish to object that reason – or the rational faculty of the mind – is self-determined in motivating the will to voluntary actions to which moral value is legitimately attached. But, against this, in the *Treatise*, Hume argues "*first*, that reason alone can never be a motive to any action of the will; and *secondly*, that it can never oppose passion in the direction of the will." The function of human reason is to make judgments – demonstrative judgments regarding relations of ideas and probability judgments regarding matters of fact. The first of these does not motivate action; from the mathematical calculation alone that 7 plus 5 equals 12, we are not motivated to do anything. But what of probability judgments regarding matters of fact? If you have a headache and judge that taking aspirin would probably eliminate the pain, you might very well be motivated to act. But did the rational judgment by itself motivate your action? No, it had to be working in combination with your desire to get rid of the pain. But, also, reason cannot, by itself, move the will against a passion. Suppose you figure out that, by taking the aspirin, you will be contributing to your excessive dependence on pain killers. That rational probability judgment cannot deter you, except in conjunction with some other passion, such as the desire to break rather than aggravate your dependence, which overcomes the earlier one (of eliminating the pain). Hume expresses his view here quite arrestingly: "Reason is, and ought only to be the slave of the passions, and can never pretend to any other office than to serve and obey them." Given passions, such as desires and aversions, reason can be extremely useful in judging effective means to achieving their objects. This claim would prove to be crucial to Hume's radical break from the rationalistic ethics that had dominated Western philosophy since the time of Plato. But, then, we might wonder, what would it mean to determine that a passion is "unreasonable," on Hume's grounds? It means that it is based on a false supposition of fact or motivates us to choose inadequate means to desired ends. For example, it would be unreasonable of you to try to get rid of your headache by slamming your head against a brick wall as hard and as often as you could. So, when we call a passion "unreasonable," we are really referring to a mistaken judgment. Strictly speaking, no passion by itself is unreasonable (or, for that matter, reasonable): "'Tis not contrary to reason to prefer the destruction of the whole world to the scratching of my finger." Of course, that preference might be founded on a mistaken assumption, such as that the destruction of the world will be less harmful than the scratching of my finger. "In short, a passion must be accompany'd with some false judgment, in order to its being unreasonable; and even then 'tis not the passion, properly speaking, which is unreasonable, but the judgment" (*Treatise*, 413–416). Now we shall explore the implications of all this.

Let us start, then, with a commonly experienced fact, which even a mitigated skeptic should be able to acknowledge: each of us makes moral distinctions and can come to realize that others do so as well. The question of interest to Hume is whether these moral distinctions are reason-based or sentiment-based (or some combination of the two). If reason-based, morals could be objective and universal; if sentiment-based, they would seem to be subjective and relative. Arguments can be plausible on each side. Ethical rationalism can say that we only dispute matters of objective truth and not of subjective taste and, obviously, do dispute about morality. Ethical emotivism can say that morals must motivate us but that only our passions (and never reason by itself) can do that. Hume postpones answering the question until he completes an empirical analysis of virtues, starting with the two "social virtues, benevolence and justice." Obviously, we commonly consider benevolence a morally desirable virtue. But why do we feel such approval? An evident part of the answer is its "utility" to the benevolent person as well as to society. But another part of the answer is that it tends to be agreeable both to the benevolent person and to society. By contrast, the moral virtue of justice is allegedly valued only for its "public utility"; it is not necessarily agreeable to anyone or even useful to the just person himself. Hume employs a wonderfully imaginative argument designed to prove his point, utilizing four hypothetical worlds significantly different from our own. First, in a paradise situation, in which everyone automatically enjoys everything desired, the rules of justice would be superfluous, and justice would not be a virtue. Second, in a scenario in which everyone were entirely altruistic, never acting out of self-interest alone, the rules of justice would, again, be superfluous and justice not a virtue. Third, in a world of utter destitution, justice would be counterproductive, conflicting with survival, and therefore no virtue. Fourth, in a human environment in which everyone was completely selfish, cruel, brutal, and insensitive to others, justice would also be counterproductive, conducive to the victimization of the just, and thus not a virtue. Justice is a virtue, relative to the facts of our world and of human nature, as we actually experience them to be, because, *in that context*, it is socially useful. Reason can and does make judgments about what is useful. But why do we allegedly *value* what is useful? Because experience discloses that what is useful is conducive to pleasure, satisfaction, comfort, and security, all of which we feel are agreeable (their opposites tending to be disagreeable). For Hume, as for so many other philosophers, justice is both a moral and a sociopolitical virtue. He makes it clear that he does not identify it with "*perfect* equality," a false ideal which he considers "*impracticable*," in that it could never be thoroughly enforced, given our natural inequality, and "*pernicious*," in that serious attempts at enforcing it would have to violate liberty and privacy and destroy

11.8 Morality | **173**

our incentives to excel – all of which would prove detrimental rather than useful. Hume identifies justice with property rights, in a broad sense, conservatively inclined to maintain whatever property relations already prevailed. However, he is willing to admit that, in extreme circumstances, public utility itself (the basis of justice) could warrant their violation. He defines a person's property as anything "which it is lawful for him, and him alone, to use" (*Essential*, 180-194, 198-201). This presumably includes, in addition to physical possessions, a person's life, liberty, and natural capacities.

We have already seen that Hume rejects the Hobbesian theory of egoism, "which accounts for every moral sentiment by the principle of self-love." He maintains that even the most selfish human would normally have enough natural sympathy for others that he would not want to crush "another's gouty toes, whom he has no quarrel with," unless there be some other reason (the sadist and sociopath seem beyond his ken). Our natural feelings of altruistic sympathy are parts of Hume's theory of moral psychology, as they are not of the Hobbesian alternative. However, he admits that there are limits, insofar as we tend to care for ourselves more than for others and for others who are close to us more than for "persons remote from us." Benevolence, the sympathetic tendency to wish others well, is a complicated virtue, in that it is agreeable to both the benevolent person and to others around her *and* also useful to both. This takes us to Hume's ingenious fourfold taxonomy of the virtues: (i) some qualities, such as "justice, fidelity, honour, allegiance, and chastity," are only considered virtues because they are useful to other members of society; (ii) some qualities, such as "discretion, caution, enterprise, industry, . . . prudence," etc., are considered virtues because they are useful to the person who has them; (iii) some qualities, such as cheerfulness, self-esteem, courage, and tranquility, are considered virtues, primarily because they are agreeable to the person having them; and (iv) some qualities, such as "good manners or politeness," wittiness, modesty, decency, and cleanliness, are considered virtues because they are agreeable to others (Hume sometimes refers to these as the "*companionable*" virtues). So these are the four sorts of virtues: (i) useful to others, (ii) useful to oneself, (iii) agreeable to oneself, and (iv) agreeable to others. And, as we have seen illustrated by benevolence, some virtues are rich enough to be of more than one sort. In a footnote, Hume provides a general definition of virtue that would cover all of these, as "*a quality of the mind agreeable to or approved of by every one, who considers or contemplates it.*" We approve of some virtues, even if they are not immediately agreeable, because of their utility. (We should not take too literally the words "every one" in his definition.) He considers the problem of the "sensible knave," or clever rascal, who wants moral rules, such as "*honesty is the best policy,*" generally to apply, while making an exception of himself. This is, indeed, a problem for Hume, because he rests morality on feelings rather than on reason. He admits that it is difficult to know how to respond to such a "sensible knave" (*Essential*, 216, 221–222, 224–225, 233–234, 239–244, 247–248, 251–252, 263). Perhaps all we can hope to do is control his behavior with the carrot of social rewards and the stick of threatened punishment; we cannot change his feelings by reason alone but must address his desires and aversions.

As what we now call a virtue ethicist, Hume approaches his analysis of morality through the virtues, toward which we have feelings of approval because experience shows them to be either immediately agreeable or useful in ways we feel are desirable. Having laid this foundation of empirical analysis, he is ready to return to the question he has not yet generally answered, as to whether morality is essentially based on reason or on feelings or (somehow) on both combined. It should come as no surprise by now that he opts for ethical emotivism. Though reason has a role to play in making judgments concerning what various qualities and actions tend to produce in the way of effects, sentiments or passions are more fundamental, especially the sentiment the utilitarians would later emphasize, "a feeling for the happiness of mankind, and a resentment

174 | *11 David Hume*

of their misery." Hume gives a second definition of virtue as *"whatever mental action or quality gives to a spectator the pleasing sentiment of approbation."* To the extent that morality is about the virtues, which are here defined in terms of sentiment, his answer is clear enough, that morality is essentially a matter of sentiment. For the approval he is discussing (and, for that matter, also the disapproval of vice) is not a rational judgment but "an active feeling or sentiment." If we ask for what reason a man exercises regularly, he might say to stay healthy; if we ask why he wants to stay healthy, he might say because sickness is a nuisance and/or interferes with his work; if we ask about that, he might say that the nuisance or interference would be painful; but if we ask for what reason *"he hates pain,* it is impossible he can ever give any."* The explanatory chain ends with the natural feelings that we like and tend to seek pleasure and dislike and tend to avoid pain. So morality is ultimately derived from feelings, rather than from reason, which makes Hume an ethical emotivist (rather than an ethical rationalist). We have already seen that he does not limit our basic feelings to those of self-love and is a critic of Hobbesian egoism. Indeed, he characterizes "the selfish system of morals" as "depraved." We commonly experience both "general" and "particular" benevolence – the former for people merely as fellow humans and the latter for those with whom we have some special relationship. Neither sort is a crafty Hobbesian way of camouflaging self-interest. Hume thinks that the commonplace experience of such benevolence is evidence that "the selfish hypothesis" of (Hobbesian) egoism is erroneous. Hume might be considered a proto-utilitarian in that he has morality standing on the two legs of agreeableness and utility, while the classical utilitarians (such as Bentham and Mill) try to support it on the second leg alone. Matters of moral and sociopolitical justice, in particular, for Hume, do stand on the leg of utility alone. While it may be anachronistic to pin a twentieth-century label on an eighteenth-century thinker, Hume seems to adopt, in matters of justice, a view later called rule-utilitarianism, meaning that we should support, enforce, and abide by rules that are beneficial to society, even though, in particular cases, applying them might seem to generate more (immediately) bad than (immediately) good consequences. He considers the issue of whether justice is a "natural" virtue or not: it is so, in the sense of normal rather than unusual; it is so, as opposed to supernatural or miraculous; but it is *"artificial"* in that human beings invent it for their own purposes. Finally, although he fails to develop the idea, he holds that we have duties to ourselves, as well as to others (*Essential*, 264–268, 270–274, 278–281, 292).

A couple of paragraphs from the third book of his *Treatise* have historically proved to be more important than Hume himself seems to have anticipated. The first passage distinguishes between descriptive language regarding what *"is*, and *is not"* and prescriptive language purporting to say what *"ought*, or *ought not"* to be. Hume complains that, all too often, moralists pass without argumentation or any warning from descriptive premises to prescriptive conclusions. Ironically, Hume himself, as an ethical empiricist, tends to cross this is–ought divide without justification; furthermore, for the rest of his career, he proceeds as if he had never written this paragraph, leaving it to his successors (starting with Kant) to take it more seriously. The second passage attacks natural law theories in ethics, maintaining that "nothing can be more unphilosophical than those systems, which assert, that virtue is the same with what is natural, and vice with what is unnatural." He explains that virtue and vice are both natural rather than supernatural, that virtue is often unnatural, meaning unusual, and that virtue and vice are both artificial in that they are contrived by humans to achieve certain desirable results. We might say that cruel brutality is "natural" but ought to be repressed, while sacrificing one's own life for an ideal is "unnatural" but admirable. "'Tis impossible, therefore, that the character of natural and unnatural can ever, in any sense, mark the boundaries of vice and virtue" (*Treatise*, 469, 475). The correct way to distinguish between them, as we have seen, is by our feelings of approval and disapproval, based on our experience of agreeableness and utility. Again, this critique of natural law theory would be better developed by later thinkers (such as John Stuart Mill).

11.9 Society

Hume's skepticism in the area of political society takes the form of striking a balance between opposing views on controversial issues. In his most frequently read political essay, "Of the Original Contract," this amounts to his not decisively taking sides in the dispute between divine right of kings theorists and social contract advocates. Although he does not explicitly deny that the rule of legitimate monarchs is authorized by divine providence, his religious skepticism renders his agreement unlikely. But, even if we could assume this, it would not sanction the absolute political authority that most monarchists demand. Hume (like Hobbes) believes that humans are naturally, overall, virtually equal and that, therefore, their consent is needed to render government legitimate. This is the truth embedded in the myth of the social contract. But social contractarians push this truth too far, and Hume is bent on exposing their myth. He does so, in this essay, first as a historian and then as a philosopher. As a historian, he understandably demands evidence. But there is no evidence that many, if any, political societies were originally "founded on consent and a voluntary compact." Even if they had been, what legitimacy has been inherited over generations, such that people today would be bound by agreements made long ago? In fact, the testimony of historical evidence tells us that almost all existing governments were "founded originally, either on usurpation or conquest, or both, without any pretence of a fair consent, or voluntary subjection of the people." Even the "Glorious Revolution" that put William and Mary on the British throne (and which Locke so eagerly supported) did not affect the legislating part of the government (Parliament) and was ratified by "only the majority of seven hundred, who determined that change for near ten millions." Whether or not the masses of British citizens would have agreed to that change in regal rule, the fact of the matter was that they had no choice. The much vaunted democracy of ancient Athens was just as unrepresentative; with no women, slaves, or resident aliens ever allowed to vote, only about 10% of the population actually had a say politically. Hume does favor government founded on the consent of the people; he just does not think that reality squares with that ideal. Nor can contractarians get around these problems by invoking the notion of "a *tacit* consent" given by the mere fact of "living under the dominion of a prince," because, in reality, most people have very limited options regarding geographical mobility. This, in brief, is Hume's historical critique. Now we shift to the "more philosophical" one in the essay. There are two sorts of moral duties – "those to which men are impelled by a natural instinct," such as love for their own children, gratitude toward their benefactors, and pity for the unfortunate, and those based on "the necessities of human society, and the impossibility of supporting it, if these duties were neglected," such as the duties of justice and fidelity and respect for others' property. The "political or civil duty of *allegiance*" to one's government is obviously of the second sort, which is based entirely on public utility. So, even if we had, at least tacitly, committed our allegiance to our government, the philosophical grounds of duty regarding both allegiance and fidelity to our commitments would be public utility: "If the reason be asked of that obedience, which we are bound to pay the government, I readily answer, *because society could not otherwise subsist*," Hume writes (*Essays*, 466–475, 479–481, 486–487; cf. *History*, V, 192–194, 482, 533, and VI, 389–390, 523, 526–528). This is, arguably, the most powerful critique of the social contract ever published.

Since the allegiance owed to their government by citizens of a political society is based on public utility, it is not absolute but can "be suspended" in extraordinary circumstances, Hume maintains (with Locke and against Berkeley) in his essay "Of Passive Obedience." Fanatical rule-worship, in

176 | *11 David Hume*

the name of some abstract conception of sacred justice, is dangerous to the common good. Resistance against oppression can be justifiable, but where should we reasonably draw the line? Hume's own judgment here is conservative: "I must confess, that I shall always incline to their side, who draw the bond of allegiance very close, and consider an infringement of it, as the last refuge in desperate cases, when the public is in the highest danger, from violence and tyranny." Even in circumstances in which we have voluntarily committed ourselves as political subjects, we do not forfeit our right to fair treatment under just laws. "But as a right without a remedy would be an absurdity, the remedy in this case, is the extraordinary one of resistance, when affairs come to that extremity, that the constitution can be defended by it alone" (*Essays,* 489–492; cf. *History,* V, 544–545). It is difficult to say how the violent execution of a deposed monarch could ever be justified.

Hume is a proponent of political science, and not merely of political theory. In his essay, "That Politics May Be Reduc'd to a Science," he contrasts autocratic, "absolute governments," which require efficient executive administration, with "a republican and free government," which can be guided by constitutional "checks and controls" that should encourage all citizens "to act for the public good." He claims that political science could establish testable empirical conclusions with "almost" as much certainty as we find in "the mathematical sciences." He holds that the best form of monarchy is "*an hereditary prince*," the best form of aristocracy "*a nobility without vassals*," and the best form of democracy "*a people voting by their representatives*." In his essay "Of the First Principles of Government," he maintains that the opinions of the people are crucially important. In any society in which "the many are governed by the few," as in a monarchy or an aristocracy, it is important that the people believe that the government's power is legitimate, that it serves the common good, and that the ruler(s) is (are) entitled to his (their) authority. In "Of the Origin of Government," Hume points out that we are all born to some family and commonly seek social relationships from some combination of need, natural inclination, and habit. We seek political society, in particular, for the sake of peace, security, and justice. Because of our flawed nature and selfish tendencies, we need public officials to enforce rules of justice and normally owe them our allegiance. Every political society must try to strike a reasonable balance "between authority and liberty; and neither of them can ever absolutely prevail," except at the expense of the public good. In his "Idea of a Perfect Commonwealth," Hume proclaims that an "established government" will normally enjoy "an infinite advantage," thanks to its longstanding traditions, "the bulk of mankind being governed by authority, not reason." A wise ruler should respect this fact of human nature, refraining from any unnecessary radical departures from tradition; "and though he may attempt some improvements for the public good, yet will he adjust his innovations, as much as possible to the ancient fabric, and preserve entire the chief pillars and supports of the constitution." Of all forms of government, Hume seems to favor a "limited monarchy," with a balance of power involving officials elected by and representative of the people. While conceding that it is "difficult to form a republican government" on the scale of a nation-state, "such as France or Great Britain," Hume maintains that, once established, it would tend to stability and public utility (*Essential*, 466–467, 469, 477–478, 480–483, 492). His skepticism in this area of his system generates this moderate, balanced perspective that tends to avoid extremes.

11.10   Review

Historically, the most important feature of Hume's philosophical system is the skepticism emphasized here. In the narrative arc of modern European philosophy, most of the great thinkers from Descartes through Berkeley have been unwittingly and, for most of them, unwillingly blazing a trail that would lead to Hume. Calling Kant the pivotal modern philosopher, with everything else being either pre-Kantian or post-Kantian, is fairly commonplace. It is a correct characterization, as far as it goes. But, without Hume, it is difficult to see how Kant's philosophy and German idealism would ever have come to be. It might be better, then, to view Hume and Kant as the paired hinges on which the door of modern philosophy swings from its earlier to its later period. Schopenhauer (whom we shall study later) was, no doubt, exaggerating for effect when he said that more was to be learned from a single page of Hume than from the collected works of Hegel. However, it would have been an even more outrageous statement if any earlier modern philosopher's name had been substituted for Hume's. His skepticism vitally affects every area of philosophy we are considering: on knowledge, it leads him to a severe limitation of what can be certainly known; on reality, it leads him to phenomenalism; on God, it leads him to reject the traditional view of ethical mono-theism; on human nature, it leads him to deemphasize reason and accentuate the role of passions in our lives; on freedom, it leads him to determinism, on morality, to emotivist relativism, and on society, to a very balanced position that avoids political extremes.[2] This skepticism precipitates a crisis in modern philosophy. As we shall see, in responding to it, Kant has to invent a revolutionary new approach, incidentally starting the movement of German idealism and the backlash reactions that would follow in its wake. But, before that, we shall consider another thinker who would profoundly influence Kant – namely, Rousseau.

11.11 Another Perspective

Lady Mary Shepherd (1777–1847), born Lady Mary Primrose on her family's Scottish estate, was privately tutored at home. Her daughter reported that the tutor taught her mathematics, Latin, and history, urging her to study areas of greatest interest to her. At the age of 31, she eloped with a lawyer named Henry John Shepherd, who was six years younger than she. Her two most important published treatises were *An Essay on the Relation of Cause and Effect* (1824) and *Essays on the Perception of an External Universe* (1827). Their primary critique is directed against Hume, although the second one also takes on Berkeley's immaterialism, which, she is convinced, also leads to skepticism. Her daughter wrote that, in her own day, Shepherd was called "an unanswerable logician" by William Whewell, a distinguished philosopher of science at Cambridge University (whose work influenced John Stuart Mill's treatment of inductive logic).

While Shepherd's critique of skepticism is mainly directed at Hume, whose views could undermine both scientific knowledge and religious faith, she is also sharply critical of Berkeley's brand of phenomenalism (as a sort of halfway house on the path to Hume). In the later of her two main works,[3] Shepherd worries that the fact that she agrees with Berkeley that only an idea can resemble an idea and that primary qualities, as well as secondary ones, "are sensations, or ideas, or perceptions," might lead people to think her a follower of his. But, in fact, she disagrees with his view that "*objects* are nothing but what we perceive by sense." To the contrary, she claims that objects of perception are the joint product of sense perception and "*reasoning*," this complex experience being causally triggered by "*an outward object*" that is independent of our minds. When Berkeley

---

2 For more on Hume, see ch. IV of *Twelve Great Philosophers*, by Wayne P. Pomerleau (New York: Ardsley House, 1997), and ch. 5 of *Western Philosophies of Religion*, by Wayne P. Pomerleau (New York: Ardsley House, 1998).
3 References for this work will be to *Women Philosophers of the Early Modern Period*, ed. by Margaret Atherton (Indianapolis: Hackett Publishing Co., 1994).

speaks of objects as ideas imprinted on the senses, this suggests that we have bodies and physical sense organs so that the phrase itself presupposes "the very doctrine he is controverting" (150–151).

She takes him to task for committing the fallacy of equivocation: when he says that material objects are only what we perceive by sense, he refers to things like sticks and stones; but when he says that the only things we can perceive are our own "ideas and sensations," he refers to the mind's own images. His shift in reference is slick but does not withstand close analysis. Shepherd also shows that Berkeley uses "the word *object*" ambiguously to refer, for example, to tables and chairs external to our minds and also to images of them, which, of course, are internal to the mind. She thinks Berkeley should have been able to use an argument such as the one he uses to support belief in "*other minds* than our own" to support belief in substantial material objects: while the knowledge is not immediate, reason can establish their reality based on their operations. Finally, she challenges the intelligibility of Berkeley's claim that spirits are the causes of ideas with a sharp rhetorical question: "Also, what notion can he have of cause at all, if he knows of '*nothing but ideas*'" (152–153, 155, 158).

This takes us to her critique of Hume in the first of her two major treatises.[4] Her principal target here is his theory of causality, which is a fundamental root of his skepticism. She reminds us of his claim that we can establish "that everything which begins to exist must have a cause" neither by intuition nor by demonstration. This principle is not a matter of definition (as "every effect must have a cause" could be an abstract relation of ideas); but neither is it an ordinary matter of fact, discoverable by sense perception. Hume's subjective definition of causality in terms of customary conjunction in the past and expectations for the future overly subjectivizes its interpretation. Her claim is that only "*reason*, not *fancy* and 'custom'," can lead us to such knowledge – that is, reason analyzing the findings of experience. Her own definition is decisively objective: "The very meaning of the word Cause is *Producer* or *Creator*; of Effect, the *Produced* or *Created*" (688–689). While this is not a new and original philosophy, Shepherd exhibits a keen critical ability in taking issue with the skeptical tendencies of two great predecessors.

---

4 References for this work will be to *Modern Philosophy: An Anthology of Primary Sources*, third edition, ed. by Roger Ariew and Eric Watkins (Indianapolis: Hackett Publishing Company, 2019).

12

Jean-Jacques Rousseau

Source: Georgios Kollidas/Adobe Stock

12.1 Overview

Rousseau was, arguably, the most complex (and least emotionally balanced) personality we have studied thus far. His life was fascinating, in part because he refused to accommodate it to others' expectations. His thought was provocative, in part because it was riddled with internal tensions while defying conventional points of view. He was remarkably lacking in formal education, such as might render him a follower of any other thinker; yet he was so successfully self-educated as to enable himself to exploit his genius to rival others' perspectives. He was neither an orthodox rationalist, following Descartes and others, nor an orthodox empiricist, following Hobbes and others. Indeed, he can hardly be said to have been an orthodox anything. Of all the modern thinkers we have studied thus far, he may have agreed most with Pascal, though this is ironic, given that that

Modern European Philosophers, First Edition. Wayne P. Pomerleau.
© 2023 John Wiley & Sons, Inc. Published 2023 by John Wiley & Sons, Inc.

earlier thinker was an orthodox Christian to the marrow of his intellectual bones, while this later one was a freethinker/deist. Neither of them was a distinguished epistemologist or metaphysician; yet both developed insightful theories of human nature, as well as views in other areas (Pascal in the philosophy of religion, Rousseau in sociopolitical philosophy). Both were reacting against the mainstream approaches to philosophy in their times, thinking them ineffectual, and each one blazed his own distinctive path. We have already analyzed the earlier one; now let us consider the other.

12.2   Biography

Jean-Jacques Rousseau was born on June 28, 1712, in the independent city-state of Geneva, which was committed to republican government and Calvinist virtue (it would not join the Swiss Confederacy until the nineteenth century).[1] He was the second son of Isaac Rousseau, a watch-maker descended from French Protestants who had found refuge in Calvin's city, and his wife, Suzanne Bernard, who died, a few days after he was born, from complications connected with childbirth. In his *Confessions*, the greatest autobiography of early modern times, Rousseau wrote: "I was born weak and sickly; I cost my mother her life, and my birth was the first of my misfortunes." By the time he was six years old, he and his father were reading novels his mother had left behind; by 1719, they were reading heroic biographies by Plutarch, who remained Rousseau's favorite author. In 1722, his father quarreled with a man, wounding him with his sword, had to leave Geneva, moving to Nyon, and remarried. His two sons had received no formal education. His brother, seven years older than he, was apprenticed to a watchmaker but left Geneva, never to return; Rousseau lost all contact with him, though occasionally seeing their father over the course of several years. Rousseau himself stayed in Geneva under the guardianship of his maternal uncle, who had a son about his age. The two cousins were sent off to stay with a village minister and his sister, from whom they received a rudimentary education. But then Rousseau, back in Geneva, worked briefly as a notary's clerk before being apprenticed to an engraver in 1725 (for a five-year term). His master was cruel and beat him; he, in turn, developed bad habits, including lying and stealing. He later blamed the corruption of his personality on his hostile environment: "Constant scoldings and beatings on the one hand, continual secret and unsuitable reading on the other, all of this began to have a bad effect on my character and temper, and to make me taciturn and unsociable, a real misanthrope." Then one day, in 1728, "restless and discontented with everything," including himself and his life, he missed the city curfew, so that he was locked outside the city gates of Geneva; rather than return to his master for another beating the next day, he ran away (*Confessions*, 7–9, 11–12, 29–33, 39–41).

He was taken in by a Catholic priest in Savoy, who denounced Calvinism as a heresy and sent him to Annecy and the protection of a Mme de Warens, who had recently converted to Catholicism,

---

1 References to Rousseau's writings will be to *Confessions*, by Jean-Jacques Rousseau, trans. by Angela Scholar (New York: Oxford Univ. Press, 2000), to *The Social Contract and Discourses*, by Jean-Jacques Rousseau (hereafter called *Contract*), trans. by G.D.H. Cole (London: J.M. Dent, 1993), to *Émile*, by Jean-Jacques Rousseau, trans. by Barbara Foxley (London: J.M. Dent, 2000), to *The Reveries of the Solitary Walker*, by Jean-Jacques Rousseau (hereafter called *Reveries*), trans. by Charles E. Butterworth (New York: Harper & Row, 1982), to *The Government of Poland*, by Jean-Jacques Rousseau (hereafter called *Poland*), trans. by Willmoore Kendall (Indianapolis: Bobbs-Merrill, 1972), and to the *The Collected Writings of Rousseau*, 13 volumes (hereafter called *Writings*, followed by volume and page numbers), ed. by Roger D. Masters and Christopher Kelly (Hanover, NH: Univ. Press of New England, 1990–2010).

had left her husband, and was receiving a pension from the King of Sardinia (who controlled Savoy). She was about 14 years older than the teenager, who found her immensely attractive, lovable for both her looks and her personality, "her gentle and loving nature, her concern for the needy, her inexhaustible goodness, her gaiety, her frank and open disposition," etc. She warmly welcomed him before sending him to Turin, Italy, where he renounced his Calvinism and became a Roman Catholic, thus automatically forfeiting his Genevan citizenship. As a servant in the household of a countess, he once stole a ribbon and, when questioned about it, cast the blame on a servant girl named Marion, who was fired as a result of his false accusation. More than a third of a century later, he expressed guilty feelings over his base act, wondering what horrible consequences befell Marion as a result of his hateful lie and attributing his subsequent devotion to truth to the remorse he continued to feel over this shameful incident. In 1729, he returned to Annecy, where he was taken in by Mme de Warens, who, at first, was like his adopted mother. He wrote, "From the very first day we were on terms of the most tender familiarity, and thus we remained for the rest of her life. I was her *little one*, my name for her was *Maman*." Meanwhile, he earned some money through various musical, secretarial, and teaching jobs. He spent a few months at the Cathedral choir school in Annecy, which he described as "one of the periods in my life when I enjoyed the greatest peace of mind and which I remember with the most pleasure." When he was almost 20, he became a music teacher in earnest, though inadequately trained for it. He wrote, "There I was, a singing master who could not decipher the simplest tune." He composed a piece of music which, though wretched, was performed before a live audience. Still he persisted. As he wrote, "Gradually I learned music by teaching it." At the age of 20, he rejoined Mme de Warens, who was living at Les Charmettes near Chambéry. Sometime in 1733, he became her lover. The years from 1735 to 1738 constituted a period of intense self-education, including an absorption in the study of music. He began reading Voltaire, whose work inspired him to pursue the serious study of ideas. This was a particularly happy period of his life. He was studying great philosophers, including Arnauld, Descartes, Locke, Malebranche, and Leibniz (noticing how deeply they disagreed), as well as music history and theory. In 1740, after Mme de Warens took another young lover, Rousseau went to Lyons to work (unsuccessfully) as a tutor to two boys. But, through his connection with this family, he met the Abbé de Condillac, a Lockean philosopher and the brother of his employer; thus started his association with the French *philosophes*. He had invented a new system of musical notation and set off for Paris in hopes of having it accepted there (*Confessions*, 45–49, 67–68, 78–79, 82–85, 104, 119, 144–145, 149, 172, 182–183, 188–195, 209, 220, 231, 240, 260–261, 263, 265–266; see *Reveries*, 43–44, 51–53, for more on the "criminal lie" that got "poor Marion" fired, and 141 for a glowing recollection of his happy years with Mme de Warens).

When he arrived in Paris (in 1742), Rousseau tried to work as a musician and composer. He presented his system of musical notation to the Academy of Sciences, but it was not accepted. He worked at writing an opera called *The Gallant Muses* and accepted a position as secretary to the French ambassador to Venice, in 1743; but they quarreled, and he was dismissed the following year. After returning to Paris, he finished his opera, which was performed in 1745. He met Thérèse Le Vasseur, a young, illiterate washerwoman at a hotel; she soon became his permanent companion, bearing his five children, before (much later) becoming his wife. Despite her shortcomings, he seems to have genuinely cared for her. In Paris, he met Diderot, d'Alembert, and Voltaire, all giants of the French Enlightenment, becoming quite friendly with Diderot, who was about the same age as he. He was supporting himself by doing secretarial and musical work. In 1746, Thérèse gave birth to the first of their five illegitimate children, all of whom Rousseau left at the foundlings' hospital in Paris, rather than raising them himself. His friendship with Condillac deepened, and he claimed to have been the one who introduced him to Diderot. Diderot and

182 | 12 Jean-Jacques Rousseau

d'Alembert (who were also friends of Hume's) were embarking on a huge project of creating the great *Encyclopedia*, for which the former invited Rousseau to write articles on music, which he did in 1749. But Diderot's own writings were being condemned as freethinking. "Work on the proposed *Encyclopaedia* was interrupted by his imprisonment. His *Philosophical Thoughts* had got him into trouble" on account of its professed materialism. Rousseau was appalled that "Diderot was sent to the prison at Vincennes." After being released from prison, Diderot was placed in a looser sort of confinement, where he was allowed visitors. In going to visit him one day, Rousseau had a life-changing experience. In October of 1749, he was walking the distance of some five miles between Paris and Vincennes (an avid walker, at that time, he could not afford to take a carriage) to visit his friend. He had taken a publication to read on his day trip, in which he saw an advertisement for an essay contest sponsored by the Academy of Dijon on the following subject: "*Has the progress of the sciences and the arts contributed to the corruption or the purification of morals?*" The very reading of the question provoked a profound epiphany for Rousseau: "The moment I read these words I saw another universe and I became another man." By the time he reached Vincennes, he wrote, he "was in a state of agitation bordering on delirium." Diderot encouraged him to write an essay on the topic and to enter it in the contest. Rousseau was thrilled at the prospect: "My feelings, with incredible rapidity, had soon risen to the same pitch of favour as my ideas. All my little passions were stifled by my enthusiasm for truth, for liberty, for virtue." The excitement, indeed, "continued unabated" for several years thereafter. He composed the essay on nights when he could not sleep and dictated it to Thérèse's mother. When he had finished, he "showed it to Diderot, who liked it," and then submitted it to the Dijon Academy. The essay boldly argued that the arts and sciences have promoted human corruption rather than moral progress, thus working against the ideals typical of the Enlightenment and advocated by *philosophes*. Rousseau claimed that he had forgotten about the essay when, in 1750, he learned that it had been awarded the prize. Diderot arranged to have it printed in 1751 (which was also the year the first volume of the great *Encyclopedia* was published). This first *Discourse*, as it is now called, did not yield him financial rewards, and he began working as a music copyist, an occupation he would continue to practice, through the years, to earn his living. His literary success, however, did establish his fame, if not his fortune; yet, as he saw things, this was more curse than blessing: "For as long as I was unknown to the public, I was loved by everyone who knew me and had not a single enemy. But as soon as I had a name, I no longer had friends" (*Confessions*, 277, 286, 301–303, 320–323, 335, 337–338, 341–343, 346, 353; for Rousseau's defensive attempt to explain his turning his own children over to a foundling institution, see 347–349, 406, as well as *Reveries*, 123–124). Although he had finally succeeded in casting off his personal dependence on others, this success did not bring him much happiness.

In 1752, a second opera, called *The Village Soothsayer*, was performed for King Louis XV and Mme de Pompadour at Fontainbleu. It was so well received that an offer was extended to Rousseau to be presented to the king the following morning; but Rousseau "pleaded ill health" (he did have a chronic problem with urine retention due to a malformed bladder), thus forfeiting his chance at receiving a royal pension. When Diderot heard of this, he reproached Rousseau and urged him to do whatever he could to get it; but he chose to do nothing about it. In 1753, Rousseau's *Letter on French Music*, favoring Italian over French music, led to his being hanged in effigy by the orchestra of the Paris Opera. In 1754, he wrote an essay on "the *origins of inequality among men*" for another contest sponsored by the Dijon Academy; this great essay, now called his "second *Discourse*," dedicated to the city of Geneva, did not win the prize but added considerably to his notoriety. Rousseau returned to Geneva, reconverting to Calvinist Protestantism and regaining his Genevan citizenship. Four months later, he returned to Paris, where he prepared his second *Discourse* for publication

12.2 Biography | **183**

(1755). Its argument was that men, naturally good and equal, are corrupted by civilization, which introduces the evils of artificial inequality. He sent a copy to Voltaire, who sarcastically thanked him for his attack on the human race which, he remarked wryly, made him want to walk on all fours again. Rousseau was offended, rather than amused, and chose not to live in Geneva, in part because Voltaire had settled there. In 1755, Rousseau's important article on "Political Economy" was published in the fifth volume of the *Encyclopedia*, introducing his now famous concept of the "general will" of a society; this third *Discourse* was separately published three years later. In 1756, he left Paris to go live at the Hermitage "on the edge of the forest of Montmorency." During the next six years, despite nagging health problems, frequent interruption by visitors, and the need to spend time each day copying music in order to make money, he managed to be very productive. In 1757, he antagonized Diderot and other *philosophes*, having already denied the Enlightenment ideal of human progress. He published a letter criticizing d'Alembert, who had previously taken issue with his views on the corrupting influences of civilization. He was working on a *Dictionary of Music*. In 1758, he published *Julie*, a novel about a girl who had a love affair and regained her virtue by becoming a good wife; it was a great success, turning out to be one of the best-selling books of the century. Meanwhile, he was working on *The Social Contract*, his political masterpiece, and *Émile*, a pioneering work on progressive education, both of which were published in Holland in 1762. The month after it was published, *Émile*, containing a deistic "Creed of a Savoyard Priest," which would generate religious controversy, was condemned by the *Parlement* (law court) of Paris with an arrest warrant issued for its author. Mme de Boufflers was so agitated and concerned for him that she urged Rousseau to go to England, where "many friends, among them the famous Hume," would secure him refuge. He was not enthusiastic about her proposal, preferring "to retreat to Geneva." But the imprudence of doing so was soon obvious. Both of his just published books were banned and condemned as subversive in Geneva, with a warrant issued for his arrest. So he sought asylum in the Swiss territory of Berne (*Confessions*, 359, 366–372, 375, 379–380, 382–387, 393–395, 400, 425, 475–478, 483–484, 564–569, 574; cf. Rousseau's four autobiographical letters to Malesherbes, *Writings*, Vol. 5, 572–583).

He was not in Bernese territory very long before realizing that "a storm of protest was gathering" against him there, "which was thought to be the work of religious zealots." He decided to go to Môtiers, in the principality of Neuchâtel, ruled by "the king of Prussia," Frederick the Great. The following year, 1763, Rousseau published his *Letter to Beaumont*, responding to criticisms of some religious ideas in *Émile* by the Archbishop of Paris. That same year, he renounced his Genevan citizenship and completed his *Dictionary of Music*. In 1764, he published his *Letters Written from the Mountain*, responding to attacks on *The Social Contract* and criticizing Genevan institutions as despotic; he placed his personal motto, "to devote one's life to truth," on the title page. (The following year, that publication would be burned in several cities.) He then decided to write his autobiographical *Confessions*. Meanwhile, Church ministers tried (unsuccessfully) to turn the state council against him, and he was repeatedly vilified. The local pastor attempted (again unsuccessfully) to have him excommunicated. As he put it, "I was preached against from the pulpit, denounced as the Antichrist, and pursued across the countryside like some sort of werewolf." In 1765, his house was stoned, driving home the realization that he should move on. He was again encouraged to flee to England with "Hume, who was then in Paris." At that time, Rousseau had a favorable opinion of Hume. He wrote, "The desire to become acquainted with this rare man and to obtain his friendship had greatly increased the temptation to go to England that the solicitations of Mme de Boufflers, an intimate friend of M. Hume, had aroused in me." Still he was reluctant to live in England. Instead, he went to St. Peter's Island, which was under the authority of Berne, hoping to distance himself from his persecutors: "It seemed to me that on this island I would be more isolated from other men than before, more shielded from their insults, more forgotten, more abandoned, in a word, to the joys of idleness and the contemplative life." He was rather happy there and might have been content to spend the rest of his life on the island. But, in fact, he only had about six weeks there, being ordered to leave the island and expelled from all Bernese territory. So where could he safely go? He made up his mind "to go to Berlin." His *Confessions* dramatically ends with his leaving the island, thinking he would settle in Berlin, and not yet aware that he "was in fact leaving for England" (*Confessions,* 578–580, 590–597, 613–614, 616–617, 621–625, 632, 638, 640, 642; cf. *Reveries,* 62–65, for an idyllic description of his brief stay on St. Peter's Island). He next lived in Staffordshire, where he began writing his *Confessions.* As we have already seen, despite Hume's kindness, generosity, and patient indulgence, Rousseau's persecution complex led him to insult and antagonize the Scotsman. Disappointingly little of what he wrote about their relationship is enlightening. In a very strange book, *Rousseau, Judge of Jean-Jacques* (also called the *Dialogues*), he presented a character called "The Frenchman" as his accuser, who spoke favorably of Hume. But what is most perplexing is the triviality of Rousseau's self-defense regarding this unpleasant affair. The most significant passage is an utterly petty diatribe against Hume for having Allan Ramsay paint "a most unflattering portrait" of him, which he thought depicted him as a monster (*Writings,* Vol. 1, 62, 205, 91; surprisingly, the completed part of Rousseau's *Reveries* does not discuss his friction with Hume at all). At any rate, in the spring of 1767, after irreparably offending Hume, Rousseau returned to France under the pseudonym of Jean-Joseph Renou. He lived there incognito for three years. In 1767, his *Dictionary of Music* was published; and, the next year, he married Thérèse.

In 1770, Rousseau returned to Paris; although technically subject to arrest there, he was left alone by the authorities. He copied music for a living and completed the writing of his *Confessions,* from which he started giving private readings. The next year, he was writing his considerations on *The Government of Poland.* His readings from his *Confessions* were banned by the police. In 1772, he finished his work on *The Government of Poland* and began writing *Rousseau, Judge of Jean-Jacques* (the *Dialogues*), a completed copy of which he gave to Condillac four years later. Between 1776 and his death, he was writing his *Reveries of the Solitary Walker,* which he called "the sequel" or "an appendix to my *Confessions.*" There, near the end of his life, he described his own personality as he saw it: "Born sensitive and good, full of pity to the point of weakness, and feeling my soul exalted by everything which relates to generosity, I liked, even passionately liked, being humane, beneficent, and helpful, as long as only my heart was involved." He admitted that he was incapable of acting against his inclinations: "Whether it be men, duty, or even necessity commanding, when my heart is silent, my will remains deaf, and I am unable to obey." In these last few years, he withdrew from public life and social contacts, writing, "I have never been truly suited for civil society where everything is annoyance, obligation, and duty." He seemed to become embittered by his personal history of broken relationships and persecution. He wrote, "I have become solitary or, as they say, unsociable and misanthropic, because to me the most desolate solitude seems preferable to the society of wicked men which is nourished only by betrayals and hatred." He had also developed a fascination for botany (*Reveries,* 5–6, 77, 83, 95, 103) and loved to walk privately through the natural environment, studying and appreciating the variety of specimens he encountered (this love of nature would later endear him to the Romantics). In 1778, he moved to Ermenonville, north of Paris, where he died of apoplexy on July 2. He was buried on an island in a lake there. His writings were sold to the Société Typographique de Genève for the publication of his collected works, beginning in 1780, with the money from the sale going to Thérèse (who died in 1801). In 1782, his main autobiographical works, the *Confessions,* his *Dialogues,* and the *Reveries,* were published, as was *The Government* _of Poland._ In 1794, in the wake of the French Revolution, which his writings had helped inspire, the National Convention transported his ashes to the Panthéon in Paris, where they were laid to rest – ironically, near the remains of his enemy Voltaire.

12.3   Knowledge

As has been said, Rousseau does not have a particularly significant epistemology. However, his "Creed of a Savoyard Priest" does at least indicate the elements of one. He has a character espouse his own "constant devotion to truth." Having experienced the sort of "doubt and uncertainty" that launched Descartes on his quest for truth, being anti-skeptical, he finds that state intolerable, saying that (like Pascal) he "prefers to be deceived rather than to believe nothing" and thinks one must find truth in one's "own heart" rather than in logical argumentation. We know, through introspection, that we want to understand. "The one thing we do not know is the limit of the knowable." Like Pascal, he thinks all philosophical systems to be ultimately lacking in firm foundations, most valuing personal knowledge and subjective truth. Introspectively, he knows that he exists and has sense impressions that are externally caused, so that both radical skepticism and solipsism are unacceptable. There must be material reality, comprising an external environment of bodies. He knows that he perceives bodies through intuitive sensory feelings and makes comparative judgments regarding those objects. While our perceptions are always subjectively accurate, our judgments about them are objectively fallible. Through reflection, we make judgments regarding the nature of bodies, their interrelationships, and their motions and states of rest. A state of rest seems to be the natural state of a body, with motions being either "acquired" by external causation or "spontaneous or voluntary," caused from within. When I voluntarily "move my arm," the causation comes from within me. By contrast, most physical motions of bodies in our universe are externally caused. Later we shall see that the _ultimate_ or "first causes of motion are not to be found in matter" at all, but in a will that transcends the entire universe of bodies. Meanwhile, sticking to this world, it is mysterious how, for example, my mental will can cause my bodily arm to move; yet, somehow, it does. We know _that_ it does, without being able to know _how_ it does so. Likewise, we can value our beliefs regarding, for instance, the origin and destiny of our minds or souls; yet this is beyond the bounds of possible knowledge. We know that "personal identity depends upon memory," as Locke argued, but not whether that will extend beyond bodily death. This is admittedly a very thin epistemology, and we understandably want to know more. But, beyond these limits, all seems "full of perplexity, mystery, and darkness" (_Émile,_ 274–283, 294–295, 309). It is useless to pursue knowledge of the unknowable.

12.4   Reality

Beyond these admittedly narrow limits, our metaphysical urges to know the nature of reality seem mostly doomed to frustration and failure. In attempting to indulge them, we risk becoming enmeshed in foolishness: "The chief source of human error is to be found in general and abstract ideas; the jargon of metaphysics has never led to the discovery of any single truth, and it has filled philosophy with absurdities of which we are ashamed as soon as we strip them of their long words." We might note that Rousseau offers us no argumentation supporting this wholesale generalization on the futility of metaphysics (any more than Pascal did), merely asserting it, as if its truth were obvious. Yet he goes on to make what will look like knowledge claims regarding the nature of God

186 | 12 Jean-Jacques Rousseau

and the nature of humans. In such matters, at least, the Savoyard priest confesses, "This is the unwilling scepticism in which I rest." On the one hand, Rousseau is not an accomplished logician; but, on the other, we have no reason to imagine that he particularly wants to be one. In the second sentence of his profession, the Savoyard priest admits, "I am no great philosopher, nor do I desire to be one" (*Émile*, 283, 326, 274).

12.5 God

He perceives order in the external world, without knowing anything of its purpose. Reason determines that "the visible order of the universe proclaims a supreme intelligence," rather than being the product of mere chance. This, of course, is a version of the argument from design, although the word "supreme" would seem not to have been justified. Rousseau's limited natural theology points to a divine "wise and powerful will" as the ultimate cause of all motion. Even though he speaks of it as a singular "God," he admits that, strictly speaking, he cannot know whether monotheism or polytheism is correct. And, apart from the divine "intelligence, power, will" required to account for intelligent design, the Savoyard priest admits that God is hidden and unknown. Such reasoning leads him "to adore the wise Author who reveals himself" in the book of nature, though he rejects petitionary prayer, which would try to influence the divine will, as superstitious. What we should note here, and what Rousseau's Savoyard priest tries to emphasize, is that all of this is "natural religion" and not revealed religion, which was rejected as conducive to dogmatism, arrogance, and intolerance. This rejection of scriptural revelation, as other than humanly created or a source of theological knowledge, in favor of natural religion, based on human experience and reason alone, constitutes deism and explains why this work was so roundly condemned by the Catholic and Protestant Christianity of that time. But, further, Rousseau makes it sufficiently clear that he sees no good reason to hold that any one religious faith is more correct or true than all others. Two centuries before it became fashionable, he, in effect, was advocating religious pluralism. He refuses to believe that any one religious tradition has a monopoly on the truth, let alone that the failure to adhere to that one could, by itself, constitute adequate grounds for damnation. While people might reasonably follow the religious traditions of their own cultures, healthy religion should unify rather than divide people. We should be tolerant of other religious traditions and not discriminate against others, based on sectarian prejudice. At any rate, true religion should be moral rather than institutional. What ought to matter is not the specific dogmas and ritualistic practices we accept but the moral practices we pursue – especially, the unfailing effort "to love God above all things and to love our neighbour as ourself" (*Émile*, 284–287, 308, 310, 312–316, 318–324, 326–332), as was taught by Jesus of Nazareth (*Matthew* 22:37–39).

As we have seen, like *Émile*, Rousseau's *Social Contract* was also roundly condemned by Protestants and Catholics alike. Why? It was mainly because of a chapter, near the end, on "Civil Religion." There he writes that Jesus tried to establish a spiritual kingdom that would be separate from all political government. Yet, when Christians achieve political power, they use it to oppress others. Rousseau writes that "the humble Christians changed their language, and soon this so-called kingdom of the other world turned, under a visible leader, into the most violent of earthly despotisms." But, in fact, Rousseau himself agrees with Hobbes in favoring a unifying of religious and political authority, with the head of state also being the head of its religion. He analyzes three sorts of religion, all of which, he says, "have their defects." First, there is what he calls "the true theism," which "has neither temples, nor altars, nor rites, and is confined to the purely internal cult of the supreme God and the eternal obligations of morality"; this is "the religion of man," whereby "all men, being children of one God, recognize one another as brothers," and its problem is that it tends to dissociate itself from the practical affairs of civil society. Second, there is a state religion, which "has its dogmas, its rites and its external cult prescribed by law"; while this unity of the political and the religious is good, it is inevitably "founded on lies and error," deceiving people into superstition and tending toward intolerance. Third, there is a religion with its own legislative code and authority structures utterly independent of those of the state; this is bad, in that it renders social unity impossible. The most notorious statement here that could unite Protestants and Catholics in their condemnation of Rousseau alleges that Christianity is incompatible with all republican freedom: "Christianity preaches only servitude and dependence. Its spirit is so favourable to tyranny that it always profits by such a regime. True Christians are made to be slaves." Rousseau thinks it proper for a political Sovereign to prescribe articles of faith to citizens and to banish those who do not accept them, for the sake of social unity. He even advocates the death penalty for citizens who publicly accept such doctrines and then behave in ways incompatible with them. In endorsing civil religion, Rousseau holds that its doctrines "ought to be few, simple, and exactly worded, without explanation or commentary." Its adherents should believe in the "existence of a mighty, intelligent, and beneficent Deity, possessed of foresight and providence, the life to come, the happiness of the just, the punishment of the wicked, the sanctity of the social contract and the laws." All of this is, presumably, associated with citizens' taking morality seriously and consistently practicing it. The only negative doctrine of civil religion is that none should practice intolerance. We should, to put the point ironically, not tolerate the intolerant – i.e. those who proclaim, "Outside the Church is no salvation" (*Contract*, 300–308), as Christians have done.

12.6 Humanity

Unlike Hume (whose greatest book is entitled *A Treatise of Human Nature*), Rousseau never developed a systematic theory of humanity. Nevertheless, his views can be stitched together from what he writes in various works. In his *Reveries*, he is acutely aware of the constant changes in everything, including us. Our pleasures are transitory. Present experiences are temporary; we remember the past, which no longer exists, and anticipate the future, which may or may not ever actually come about as expected or feared or desired. Thus we should not reasonably assume that we shall ever achieve a stable happy state in this life. Human happiness, such as it is, requires a balance of activity and rest. As we are legitimately concerned for our own welfare, we should enjoy what contentment we can achieve. Our "love of self" (*amour de soi*) is natural and appropriate. It should be distinguished from the narcissistic "self-love" (*amour-propre*) that is a bad form of selfishness, the irrational source of unhappiness. He writes that, to the limited extent that he can achieve happiness, "love of myself does all the work; self-love has nothing to do with it" (*Reveries*, 68–69, 122, 116–117). Love of self is a natural affection conducive to our self-preservation and well-being. It is non-envious, content with satisfying its own desires, always good, and the root source of other loving affections, as Rousseau says in *Émile*. By contrast, "selfishness, which is always comparing self with others, is never satisfied and never can be," as it demands that others favor us as we favor ourselves, "which is impossible" and also the source of all "the hateful and angry passions" that alienate us from other people. Love of self can lead us to feel a sympathetic pity for others, while selfishness leads us to a competitive envy of others. As long as we control our passions, they are good; when they control us, they become bad. We are not responsible for being tempted by our passions, but only for succumbing to their temptations. "To feel or not to feel a passion is beyond our control, but we can control ourselves. Every sentiment under our control is lawful; those which control us are criminal" (*Émile*, 207–209, 219–220, 490). So we are essentially creatures driven by feeling (as was also true for Hume).

But this is not to denigrate reason, which is also extremely important in our human nature. The Savoyard priest points out that it is our knowledge that renders us superior to all the beasts. The nature of man involves two competing principles. The first has always "raised him to the study of the eternal truths, to the love of justice and of true morality, to the regions of the world of thought . . .; the other led him downwards to himself, made him the slave of the senses, of the passions which are their instruments, and thus opposed everything suggested to him by the former principle." The first is the active principle of free reason, aligned with a healthy love of self; the second is the passive principle of selfish passions that threaten to enslave us. Already we see Rousseau's yearning for self-control and aversion to being an object of external control. Our active principle and free will indicate (against Hobbes) that we cannot be purely material creatures. As humans, we "have always the power to will," even when we lack the strength to follow reason and succumb to selfish desire. A limit on our freedom (rooted in our natural love of self) is that we must desire our own welfare; but what we choose to do in relation to this desire is the product of free will. And we are responsible for such actions. Our souls, as immaterial substances, may possibly survive the deaths of our bodies, but we cannot know that. Rousseau's reason for believing it does (anticipating Kant's) is the moral demand for a correction of the injustice of "the triumph of the wicked and the oppression of the righteous in this world." At least, his conviction that the soul is a substance independent of the body makes it reasonable for him (as it did for Descartes) to believe in immortality. So we have a kind of dualism suggested here (not found in, say, Hobbes and Hume). A most important aspect of the soul, related to reason and free will, essentially relevant to values, is conscience, called the "infallible judge of good and evil, making man like to God!" Human excellence and morality are functions of conscience (*Émile*, 287–291, 294, 304).

Rousseau's views on the relationship between the sexes are quite controversial. They are equally human: "But for her sex, a woman is a man; she has the same organs, the same needs, the same faculties." However, because of their sex differences, he thinks that man should be dominant. "The man should be strong and active; the woman should be weak and passive." Going still further, he writes that "woman is specially made for man's delight." While they have similar passions, men need to control theirs by reason, while women must resort to a sense of modesty to restrain theirs. Because men depend on women for the satisfaction of natural needs and desires, he thinks they should try to please them and, thus, cultivate their goodwill. This inequality leads to a classical double-standard. While a husband is wrong to commit adultery, it is allegedly "worse" in a wife (as she risks giving her husband children that are not his own). While fidelity is important in both spouses, the appearance of fidelity is supposed to be more important for the wife. (Rousseau even criticizes Plato's more egalitarian treatment of women.) However, he does not call for keeping women ignorant or treating them like slaves. "On the contrary, nature means them to think, to will, to cultivate their minds as well as their persons." He thinks men and women unequally interdependent, women needing men more than the other way around. He considers women's reason to be more practical, while men have a greater facility for theoretical judgment, so that they can complement each other. While women are allegedly more observant and wittier, they are supposedly incapable of grasping either "works of genius" or "the exact sciences" (*Émile*, 384–395, 400–401, 407, 419). Thus, in their differences, they would seem to be naturally made for each other.

Arguably, Rousseau's most important and most influential treatment of humanity is in his second *Discourse*, which argues that an adequate explanation of human inequality requires a general understanding of human nature, which has purportedly been perverted by society from what it was in its original state, in which humans were allegedly "naturally equal among themselves." (Based on what has already been said, we might surmise that he did not apply this natural equality to women in relation to men.) He seems ambiguous about whether this "original condition" of equality ever existed as an historical fact. Of course, people are naturally unequal, for example, in bodily strength, agility, and intelligence. Yet, he claims, "moral or political inequality" is artificial, the result of arbitrary social conventions that are "established, or at least authorized, by the consent of men." He thinks that the problem with earlier social contract thinkers, such as Hobbes and Locke, is that they failed to recognize that people were transformed by the transition from "the state of nature" to that of civil society. It is not merely that our situations and relations changed, but we ourselves supposedly did. Originally, we were mere animals, satisfying our natural desires. Rousseau denies the Hobbesian thesis that this "savage man" must have been fiercely aggressive and hostile, holding that his natural enemies were infirmity, illness, old age, and melancholy, rather than other men. Prior to becoming socialized and a slave to convention, man would have been strong, courageous, independent, with modest needs, not necessarily even including those for housing and clothing. He would have been different "from the brute" not qualitatively but "only in degree." What accounted for this modest difference was not rational understanding but freedom from the tyranny of instinct, which facilitated progressive "self-improvement" of a sort of which brute animals are incapable. At this early stage of human evolution, there may have been no interpersonal communication, as it was unneeded. Primitive man had no moral character, "no moral relations or determinate obligations one with another, could not be either good or bad, virtuous or vicious." This profile of "savage man" as amoral in "the state of nature" might seem somewhat Hobbesian, though Rousseau rejects the view, which he attributed to Hobbes, that man is "naturally wicked." This seems a distortion of Hobbes. But he is correct to distinguish his own view from the Hobbesian rejection of the role of natural compassion in moderating the selfishness of "*amour-propre*," which, unlike the natural "love of self," did not exist "in our primitive condition" but only developed later. As the human population increased, competition for limited resources did as well. Interpersonal interactions would become more frequent and more significant. At this point, people may have begun to value the esteem of others, leading to vanity, shame, envy, and contempt – all products of selfish self-love. They developed tools and methods of cooperating in cultivating the earth, giving up the independence that had previously allowed them to lead "free, healthy, honest and happy lives." Housing and agriculture established a sense of property, and people adopted primitive "rules of justice" regulating property rights. Even with all this, "equality might have been sustained, had the talents of individuals been equal." But, of course, they are not, and inequality became increasingly prevalent. The strong, smart, and wealthy were able to subdue and dominate the less gifted. "Usurpations of the rich, robbery by the poor, and the unbridled passions of both suppressed the cries of natural compassion and the still feeble voice of justice, and filled men with avarice, ambition, and vice." People presumably joined together in civil societies, accepting artificial inequality and rules to which they would be "obliged to conform." Here we have seen the faint suggestion of a social contract – but negatively described as placing "new fetters on the poor" and as having "destroyed natural liberty, eternally fixed the law of property and inequality, converted clever usurpation into unalterable right, and, for the advantage of a few ambitious individuals, subjected all mankind to perpetual labour, slavery, and wretchedness." In an important footnote, he writes that "man is naturally good" but became "depraved" through subjection to the artificial structures of society; yet he denies that he would "destroy society, abolish" private property, or "go back to living in the forests" as primitives, even if that were possible (*Contract*, 43–45, 49–50, 52–61, 64, 71–73, 84–99, 118, 125; see also 169–176, from "The General Society of the Human Race," for a more Hobbesian portrait of the state of nature and natural humanity). Rousseau thus speculates regarding our original condition and how it became perverted by artificial social structures.

12.7 Freedom

The first line of the first chapter of the first book of *The Social Contract*, the most famous sentence that Rousseau ever wrote, poses a paradox, the solution of which would require philosophical analysis: "Man is born free; and everywhere he is in chains." Indeed, the problem of human freedom is an enduring concern to him. Why does he take an anti-Enlightenment stand against the progressive influence of the arts and sciences and regard their influence as, rather, corrupting? Early in the first *Discourse*, he explains that it is because they "stifle in men's breasts that sense of original liberty, for which they seem to have been born; cause them to love their own slavery, and so make of them what is called a civilized people." Granting that the arts and sciences have a civilizing influence on those who study them, why this translates into the undermining of natural freedom seems maddeningly obscure, so that *philosophes* seemed justified in resenting the claim. In the dedication (to the Republic of Geneva) to his second *Discourse*, he expresses his fervent desire "to live and die free" and writes that men must be accustomed to liberty in order to understand how to use it responsibly rather than confusing it with a destructive license that will only forge stronger chains to shackle them to base desires. He calls Geneva "a free city," a republic whose citizens were used to liberty. Later, he contrasts "civilized man," who willingly submits to the fetters of artificial culture, and the "savage man," who "prefers the most turbulent state of liberty to the most peaceful slavery," obviously favoring the latter. He agrees with Locke that no one can so alienate "his liberty as to submit to an arbitrary power which may use him as it likes." One can alienate a piece of physical property, such as a vehicle, without caring how its new owner might use or abuse it, but one cannot do so regarding one's own liberty, which is essential to one's humanity. And, even if we could legitimately alienate our own freedom, surely we have no right to transfer that of our children, as in hereditary slavery, as this would reduce them to mere property. So Rousseau (a few decades before Kant did likewise) presents freedom as essential to humanity and slavery as a fundamental violation of what later thinkers (including Kant) would call human dignity. Despite our being "born free," our natural liberty can be lost as a result of physical force, the threat of violence, the power of political rulers, the pressures of social conventions, and so forth. In the state of nature, man would be "his own master" and have the liberty to provide for his own preservation and satisfaction of desires as he saw fit; such people, "being born free and equal," would only alienate their natural liberty in order somehow to benefit themselves. Where Aristotle thought some people ought to be slaves because they are naturally inferior, Rousseau holds that slaves become inferior as a result of being deprived of their liberty. Sounding like Locke, he claims that consent is the only basis of legitimate political authority and that it would be irrational to renounce one's natural freedom, which would be tantamount to renouncing one's humanity with all its rights. Against Hobbes, he denies that war is a natural human state, whose terrors justify abdicating one's freedom. Nor do the rights of war justify depriving conquered, unarmed foes of their lives or their liberty. Indeed, the relation between a master and a slave is itself a "state of war" rather than a way to end it. A person who deprives another of natural freedom thereby creates no moral authority over him; the person so deprived has, as a consequence, no moral obligations to his oppressor (*Contract*, 181, 5, 33–34, 102–103, 105–106, 182–183, 185–189; see also *Writings*, 9, 260–261). A group of people subdued by force and subjected to the will of others does not constitute a political society and cannot do so as long as they lack the freedom to give their consent.

Earlier we considered Rousseau's bold and novel claim that the transition from the state of nature to that of civil society effects a transformation in man himself. But we were not able to explain this alleged transformation well until we had set up the present focus on freedom, which is at its core. He writes in *The Social Contract*, "What man loses by the social contract is his natural liberty and an unlimited right to everything he tries to get and succeeds in getting; what he gains is civil liberty and the proprietorship of all he possesses." Where natural liberty was limited only by the individual's personal power, civil liberty is supposedly limited by the law that is a consequence of the general will. In the state of nature, one might happen to possess something; but in civil society, he can have a right to own it as property. Rousseau masterfully carries this idea a step further: "We might, over and above all this, add, to what man acquires in the civil state, moral liberty, which alone makes him truly master of himself; for the mere impulse of appetite is slavery, while obedience to a law which we prescribe to ourselves is liberty." This is a truly revolutionary idea. Through the acquisition of "moral liberty," man becomes what he could not be in the state of nature, a moral agent; as such, he develops (what Kant later calls) autonomy, the freedom to subscribe to a law of his own making. On this view, a member of political society is a qualitatively different being from anything that was possible in the state of nature – an autonomous moral agent. Thus, perhaps we should refine our earlier claim that we cannot legitimately alienate our freedom, to say that we can only alienate part of our natural liberty in exchange for the acquisition of civil liberty and moral liberty. (By the way, this concept of alienation will subsequently become very important in the philosophies of Hegel and Marx, as we shall see.) We should acknowledge how this moves Rousseau's version of social contract theory beyond those of Hobbes and Locke: where they thought the transition from a state of nature to one of civil society improved man's lot, he maintains that it also improves man himself (*Contract*, 196, 205, 207). Is it not understandable that leaders of the French Revolution would have been inspired by his analyses of equality and freedom? Nevertheless, it should be pointed out that Rousseau declares himself opposed to any armed revolt, even in defense of freedom (*Confessions*, 211).

12.8 Morality

While Rousseau never systematically develops an ethical theory, he offers us key elements that might have been combined to establish one – namely, those of compassion or pity, conscience, and the equality and freedom of all humans. Like Hume, he maintains that compassion (or pity) moderates selfish self-love (*amour-propre*); the rule of compassion, admittedly "less perfect" than the Golden Rule but "perhaps more useful," commands, "*Do good to yourself with as little evil as possible to others.*" The equality which he advocates is allegedly lost in man's transition from a state of nature to that of civil society, one in which right replaced "violence and nature became subject to law." He thinks Hobbes mistakenly believed all men to be "naturally wicked," just because, in the state of nature, he had "no idea of goodness"; but this would be a non sequitur. Man's natural goodness, indeed, was a function of his compassion for others, which Hobbes failed to respect sufficiently. It can and should lead us to respect all others as morally equal to ourselves. This involves the natural freedom of all persons, which, as we have seen, must never be compromised without their consent. Force can negate this equal freedom; yet we should clearly recognize that "force does not create right," and no adult person has any legitimate natural authority over any other. Like so many of his philosophical predecessors, Rousseau is a proponent of justice. But, unlike them, he defined it in terms of respect for others as moral equals, advocating, more specifically, "equality of rights and the idea of justice which such equality creates." This is arguably the first theory of justice (before Marx and even before Kant) defined in terms of equal rights for all and would later inspire leaders of the French Revolution (*Contract*, 76, 49–50, 71–73, 182, 184–185, 199, 205).

One of the requirements of justice is honesty. Yet he writes in *Reveries* that, in specific situations, fabrications and distortions of the truth can be appropriate: "Particular and individual truth is not always a good; it is sometimes an evil, very often an indifferent thing," depending, it seems, on whether its consequences are beneficial, detrimental, or neutral. We allegedly owe people the truth, as a matter of justice, when it would be useful. But the obligation is purportedly not absolute. "Truth stripped of every kind of possible usefulness cannot therefore be a thing owed, and consequently he who suppresses it or disguises it does not lie at all." In order for the speaking of a falsehood to constitute a lie, it must be motivated by the "intent to deceive" and "an intent to harm." On this view, uttering a falsehood with no selfish wish to profit ourselves or to harm anyone else "is not a lie; it is a fiction" and innocent. (This is an even more cavalier attitude toward dishonesty than we shall see in the rule-utilitarianism of Mill.) Among moral values, he distinguishes between actually doing good, which allegedly confers "the truest happiness the human heart can savor," and merely abstaining from "doing evil," which is sometimes the best our circumstances will permit. He also distinguishes between the naturally good person, who acts spontaneously, and the morally virtuous person, who acts from a sense of duty. The naturally good person follows his inclinations and derives pleasure from doing good. "But virtue consists in overcoming them when duty commands in order to do what duty prescribes." He sees himself as a naturally good person rather than as a man of duty (*Reveries*, 45–46, 48–50, 75–78).

The first sentence of *Émile* famously makes a point we have already considered: "God makes all things good; man meddles with them and they become evil." Thus artificial human conventions supposedly pervert our natural goodness. Yet all values are relative, it would seem: "Absolute good and evil are unknown to us. In this life they are blended together." Within this continuum, Rousseau claims, "freedom, not power, is the greatest good," apparently disagreeing with Hobbes, who was willing to give up freedom to gain the sort of power that would promote security; nevertheless, Hobbes was correct that we naturally want the power needed to satisfy our desires, including that for security. While we are all naturally good, we should use our freedom to become virtuous, which requires that we try to follow our rational conscience and become our "own master" by doing our duty. (This is a point of view that would greatly influence Kant.) The Savoyard priest claims that justice and goodness are ultimately inseparable and, thus, cannot conflict; "for that love of order which creates order we call goodness and that love of order which preserves order we call justice." So our mission as moral agents is to help create and help maintain a moral order. He assures Émile (and us) that conscience, "the voice of the soul," is a true guide that "never deceives us." Our first duty is to ourselves, to choose natural values and pursue virtue, according to conscience. He says, "The decrees of conscience are not judgments but feelings," and "the love of good and the hatred of evil are as natural to us as our self-love." He agrees with Hume in maintaining, "Reason alone is not a sufficient foundation for virtue." The priest's final paragraph includes a straightforward exhortation: "Speak the truth and do the right; the one thing that really matters is to do one's duty in the world." Reason has a role to play in informing conscience; but Rousseau might have been paraphrasing Pascal when he wrote, "The heart is a law to itself." Our most basic sense of good and evil springs from natural "feelings of love and hatred" (*Émile*, 5, 51, 56, 60, 238, 489, 293, 298–303, 305, 332, 234–236). In conclusion, Rousseau's treatment of morality involves an affirmation of our natural goodness, of the importance of compassion and freedom, of respect for others as moral agents, and of the need to follow conscience in doing our duty and achieving virtue. He never pulls these elements together in a systematic ethical theory or carefully argues for much of what he says here; nevertheless, the elements themselves are worthy of our consideration.

12.9 Society

While he is not a great moral philosopher, if we can legitimately separate ethics from sociopolitical philosophy, his theory of political society is great. Without considering it thoroughly, we can use the thesis of his first *Discourse* as a backdrop for this theory. We recall that, against the prevailing view of Enlightenment thought, Rousseau advances the provocative thesis that, far from contributing to human progress and happiness, "the arts and sciences" have actually "corrupted" human beings, spoiling their natural goodness. But, even if we suppose that "savage man" was naturally good, why should we also believe that it is better to be innocent than to be civilized, and how did our becoming civilized purportedly lead to that corruption? His second *Discourse* memorably answers these questions. The "savage man" was, allegedly, not vain or competitive, accepted his equality with others, and was "his own master," with the potential of "human perfectibility." Civilization supposedly ruined all that. How did this cataclysmic change come about, but by the establishment of private property, which precipitated that of civil society. This gave rise to inequality and the abdication of personal freedom. People became envious and competitive, inviting treachery and even violence in order to get ahead. For Rousseau (different from Hobbes), the social contract that generated political society is not unilateral but bilateral between subjects and their rulers, either party being able to revoke it. But the inequalities of "riches, nobility or rank, power and personal merit" gradually led to despotism and the rule of might rather than that of right, in effect, "a new state of nature." In the third *Discourse*, after criticizing Sir Robert Filmer's notion of hereditary political authority not based on consent, he makes the important distinction between "Sovereignty," which alone "has the right of legislation," and government, whose only right is to carry out the execution and enforcement of that legislation. Like Hobbes, Rousseau develops an intricate metaphor to characterize a political social order, which "may be considered as an organized, living body, resembling that of a man"; the sovereign power is its head, laws and customs its brain, the locus of understanding and will, whose organs are judges and magistrates, with "commerce, industry and agriculture" the mouth and stomach, public revenues its lifeblood, and an economy a heart pumping that blood; "the citizens are the body and the members, which make the machine live, move, and work." And now we get to Rousseau's most famous (and perhaps most perplexing) concept: what should move the body politic is a "general will, which tends always to the preservation and welfare of the whole and of every part, and is the source of the laws, constitutes for all the members of the State, in their relations to one another and to it, the rule of what is just or unjust." This is the first appearance of Rousseau's famous concept of the general will in his writings. (That same year, 1755, Diderot also wrote of the "general will" – *volonté generale* – in his *Encyclopedia* article on "Natural Rights.") Here Rousseau speaks more positively of private property than he had in his previous *Discourse*, now calling the right to it "the most sacred of all the rights of citizenship, and even more important in some respects than liberty itself," because it constitutes the very "foundation of civil society" itself, which is no longer being presented as evil. However, some of citizens' property can be legitimately demanded in the form of taxation, since state government and basic civil services must be maintained and paid for. In order for taxation to be just, it must be authorized by the "general will, decided by vote of a majority, and on the basis of a proportional rating which leaves nothing arbitrary in the imposition of the tax." That so-called "proportional rating" could involve taxing citizens with twice as much property twice as much or taxing luxury items at a higher rate than necessities or taxing citizens according to the benefits they receive from society. In any case, more will be exacted from the rich than from the poor. Thus Rousseau's favored "economic system" would be designed to help "bring all fortunes nearer to that middle condition which constitutes the genuine strength of the State," bolstering the middle class rather than ignoring or increasing the gap between rich and poor. By taxing the rich more heavily, he would push the wealthy to be more productive for the common good and less idly extravagant or to contribute significantly to state revenues; in either case, the social order would supposedly benefit (*Contract*, 8, 82, 84, 111, 113–114, 131–132, 151, 158–162, 166–167). So property rights, in general, would be protected, but taxes would be levied to support government services.

We now turn from these highlights from the first three Discourses to those from Rousseau's mature masterpiece on political society, *The Social Contract*, whose alternative title is *Principles of Political Right*. The problem it poses and purports to answer is how it could be possible for citizens to be bound to obey the laws of the state and yet also remain genuinely free. We must start by acknowledging the old truism that might by itself cannot establish any moral authority: "Let us then admit that force does not create right, and that we are obliged to obey only legitimate powers." As we have seen, we are supposed to be naturally free, yet the rule of law and societal mores necessarily constrain that freedom. (Hobbes, by contrast, thought that submission to intimidating force is a source of rightful authority.) It is the social contract that legitimates a sociopolitical order. Prior to choosing a ruler, human beings must unanimously agree to "become a people" and form a "body politic"; anyone who does not join in that agreement is not a part of that political society. Only after thus quitting the state of nature can a people adopt a convention, for example, of majority rule or procedures for selecting leaders. What would motivate them to form society is that the inconveniences and obstacles to self-preservation and satisfaction come to outweigh their resources and favorable prospects, so that they are willing to join forces. In joining, each member allegedly alienates himself, "together with all his rights, to the whole community." It would seem that this "total alienation" would annihilate his freedom. But this supposition would be rash and wrong. Rousseau thinks, paradoxically, that "each man, in giving himself to all, gives himself to nobody" and acquires the same rights against everyone else as he gives up to them; this allegedly yields no loss of right and a gain in power to enforce right. The formula for this fundamental social contract can be expressed thus: "*Each of us puts his person and all his power in common under the supreme direction of the general will, and, in our corporate capacity, we receive each member as an indivisible part of the whole.*" In contrast to the individualistic social contract theories of Hobbes and Locke, Rousseau developed an organic model, whereby the contract "creates a corporate and collective body," which includes individuals but is more than their totality. This "*Republic* or *body politic*," as a passive entity called a "*State*," is referred to as "Sovereign when active." The human beings thus associated "take collectively the name of *people*, and severally are called *citizens*, as sharing in the sovereign authority, and *subjects*, as being under the laws of the State." Each citizen, "as a member of the Sovereign," or active entity, is bound to all others; and, "as a member of the State," or passive collective body, he is bound to the Sovereign. Thus he must respect the interests of all and try to realize the general will. Given this organic model, an injury to any one member of political society is an offense against the entire corporate body. A citizen should be able to distinguish his own selfish, particular will from the general will with which it may conflict and to which it should be subordinated. But what of the member of society who will not do this? In a pronouncement that liberals have found chilling, Rousseau writes that "whoever refuses to obey the general will shall be compelled to do so by the whole body. This means nothing less than that he will be forced to be free." Presumably, the passage from the state of nature into civil society so transformed man that he became a moral agent capable of thus unselfishly acting out of a sense of duty and of subordinating his particular will to the general will. This key concept of the "general will" is almost as opaque as it is important to Rousseau's philosophy. Whereas a person's individual will aims at his own particular good, the general will aims at "the common good" of society. There need not be unanimous agreement regarding the general will, although it can only be discerned after every vote is considered. It is not comprised of any combination of individual wills, which are motivated by self-interest rather than by the common good. It is fallible and can make mistakes, because the citizens' judgment of what is conducive to the common good, however nobly intentioned, can be in error. Citizens must cooperate with one another, "each with all, and all with each," to try to determine the general will as best they can. Since there is no algorithm for determining the general will with certainty, as it is neither the will of any majority or supermajority nor even the will of all, and since it is fallible because it could be ill-informed, the concept, however intriguing, seems hopelessly problematic. Whenever I vote in accordance with what I honestly think will serve the common good, if I am outvoted by fellow citizens, then I presumably should assume that I was wrong: "When therefore the opinion that is contrary to my own prevails, this proves neither more nor less than that I was mistaken, and that what I thought to be the general will was not so" (*Contract*, 185, 190–196, 200–201, 203, 207, 212, 278). But does it? Or isn't this a muddle, since we can never be sure that others were voting for the common good or that they were not ill-informed. (Also it is deeply ironic that Rousseau was such an iconoclastic nonconformist that he could no more have fit comfortably in this regime than Socrates would have been comfortable in Plato's ideal republic!)

Near the beginning of *The Social Contract*, we are assured that in a good society, "justice and utility" will converge. In a just society, the equal rights of all citizens (feminists might demand, what of women?) will be respected. Even though I am bound to obey the law, as a member of the Sovereign, I am involved in making that law. Thus, in being obliged to obey the law of my own making, I remain free, and supposedly my freedom is not compromised. But this is implausible, on any normal interpretation of freedom. If, in good conscience, I vote for what I correctly deem to be the common good but am outvoted by fellow citizens who are mistaken in their assessment of the common good, how am I free in being obliged to obey a bad law (i.e. one contrary to the common good) which I did not support and in being forced to meet that obligation? I am not free to take action in protest, to engage in civil disobedience in the name of conscientious objection. This leads to the question of the relationship between the people and their government. The body of citizens represents the sovereign authority, which is to have "*legislative power,*" and the "*executive power*" of the government is, supposedly, their administrative agent. Rousseau defines the "government" as an "intermediate body set up between the subjects and the Sovereign, to secure their mutual correspondence, charged with the execution of the laws and the maintenance of liberty, both civil and political." The individual members of government, or "*governors,*" are public officials or "magistrates"; they serve at the will of the people, who are not contractually bound to them at all. Thus the whole body of citizens, purportedly serving the general will, has sovereign power to make the laws; government officials execute or administer those laws, enforcing their observance by individual subjects and thus, allegedly, maintaining the liberty of all. When government usurps power and becomes tyrannical, oppressing the people rather than serving them, it becomes illegitimate. There are three general types of government: (i) in a "*democracy,*" all citizens or a majority of them govern; (ii) in an "*aristocracy,*" government is invested in a few citizens; and (iii) in a "*monarchy,*" a single chief executive holds administrative power. No one of these is absolutely best under all possible circumstances; but, as a general rule, the number of government officials "should be in inverse ratio to the number of citizens," so that "democratic government suits small states, aristocratic government those of middle size, and monarchy great ones." The larger a society is, the more concentrated government bureaucracy must be to govern it efficiently. At any rate, government officials are public servants of the people. Since the people are not contractually bound to their government, they are free to change its form or its administrators at will. Rousseau holds, "Every legitimate government is republican," whatever its form of administration, where by a "Republic" he means any "State that is governed by laws," rather than by the caprice of men (*Contract*, 181, 229–230, 237–238, 270–273, 212; see also *Writings*, 9, 301). Law, as reflecting the general will of the people, is a necessary condition of a genuine civil society. Thus Rousseau tries to synthesize justice, equality, freedom, sovereignty, law, and government as elements of a good political society. If the effort falls short of striking a credible balance, it is an impressive failure that would prove inspirational.

12.10 Review

Although Rousseau is not generally admitted into the ranks of first-rate philosophers (such as Descartes, Hume, Kant, and Hegel), the impact of his writings was swift and striking. His "Creed of a Savoyard Priest" presents a deistic embracing of natural religion (and rejection of revealed religion) that drew the immediate ire of orthodox Christians, while his appeals for religious pluralism and tolerance were, sadly, ignored. His view of humans as naturally free and equal and compassionate, with the potential to develop conscience and moral agency, would influence Kant and others. Before the end of the century, early feminist Mary Wollstonecraft was attacking his ideas on the inferiority of women. His views on human freedom as potentially involving man's being his own master would inspire Kant's idea of moral autonomy. Most significant, of course, were his views on political society. If there were a single idea that could be targeted as most valuable, it would be that of moral and political equality, with justice being defined in terms of equal human rights; it deeply influenced Kant and, presumably, Marx. His most famous concept is that of the general will, but it is so enigmatic as to be problematic. His idea that citizens should be forced to conform to it has an antidemocratic edge to it. His inspiring the French Revolution, if originally good, went bad with his follower Robespierre's bloody Reign of Terror.

12.11 Another Perspective

Mary Wollstonecraft (1759–1797) was born in London and was largely self-taught, including in both French and German. She and her two sisters founded a progressive school for girls near London, which failed after about a year. But the experience provided a basis for her first publication, *Thoughts on the Education of Daughters*, published (in 1786) by Joseph Johnson, a radical publisher in London. She took a position as a governess to an aristocratic Irish family; but she did not seem to get along well with the mother of the family, was dismissed after a year, and returned to England. She wrote a novel entitled *Mary, a Fiction*, which Johnson published in 1788. Through Johnson she met other prominent radicals, including Thomas Paine, William Godwin, and William Blake. Her *Vindication of the Rights of Man*, published in 1790, was followed by her most famous book, *A Vindication of the Rights of Woman*, published in 1792, an instantly successful and controversial work that extensively criticized Rousseau's assertions of female inferiority.[2] That same year, she went to Paris, where she fell in love with Gilbert Imlay, an American writer by whom she had a daughter. In 1794, she published *An Historical and Moral View of the Origin and Progress of the French Revolution*. After unsuccessfully attempting suicide twice because of Imlay's infidelity, Wollstonecraft got pregnant by William Godwin, the influential anarchist, in 1796. They married in 1797, but she died of a post-partum infection just a few days after giving birth to Mary Godwin, who later became Mary Shelley, the author of *Frankenstein*. Some might date the feminist movement from the publication of Wollstonecraft's masterpiece, which we shall now consider.

Her *Vindication of the Rights of Woman* is arguably the most influential book of modern European philosophy written by a woman. Anyone studying the history of feminist literature would do well to take it under consideration. (She never uses the word "feminism," as it was not coined until the nineteenth century.) While the book meanders and is somewhat repetitious, its central thesis is

---

2 All references to her work will be to *A Vindication of the Rights of Woman*, by Mary Wollstonecraft (Mineola, NY: Dover Publications, 1996).

that the inferiority of women is not natural but is the consequence of their being denied educational opportunity; this claim runs counter to that advanced by Rousseau in his *Émile*. Though Wollstonecraft lacks the logical acumen of, say, Lady Shepherd, she does offer us an argument to support her call for equal educational opportunity for females. She does not develop a comprehensive philosophical system; her work here is, rather, focused on the area of social ethics.

She holds that "true dignity and human happiness" are a function of strength "both of mind and body," which must be the result of the very sort of education denied to women. Without it, they can only manifest themselves as "a frivolous sex" and can only "rise in the world" by attracting men to marry them. This forces them to be weak, dependent, and submissive. A human being's defining feature is reason; a human's most valuable acquisition is virtue; and a human's best sort of experience involves knowledge of how to moderate the passions. "Consequently the perfection of our nature and capability of happiness must be estimated by the degree of reason, virtue and knowledge that distinguish the individual" (8–11). But women are raised such that their reason is stunted rather than exercised, their minds are given knowledge of only superficial trivialities, and true virtue becomes impossible for them, since they have no significant freedom of choice. Because they are thus denied their rights to develop their capacities as human beings (and children of God), they cannot realize their potential as citizens, wives, and mothers.

She denies that she means "to invert the order of things." Though she grants that men may be capable of "a greater degree of virtue," she opposes the view that male virtue and female virtue differ in nature. The target here is clearly Rousseau, who sees women as naturally inferior to men and needing to be raised to please them by being attractive and even coquettish, "the toy of men." (We might note here that contemporary feminists are not likely to appreciate her "frankly acknowledging the inferiority of women" in her appeal for respect for their rights.) Doing one's duty in life requires virtue, reason, and freedom of choice, all of which Rousseau's views would deny females in any significant way. Thus, to a great extent, it is "Rousseau's wild chimeras" that she means to expose. As human reason is the same in kind in men and women, so "not only the virtue, but the *knowledge* of the two sexes should be the same in nature." But this will require radical reform in how children are educated – and in a direction far removed from that favored by Rousseau. Even if "woman is naturally weaker than man," Rousseau's approach would render her "still weaker than nature intended her to be," which involves a violation of her rights to development as a person (26, 33–36, 38–40, 79).

Wollstonecraft realizes that, with adequate training, women could acquire skills "sufficient to enable them to earn their own subsistence, the true definition of independence." She advocates educating boys and girls together, not only playing together and getting the same exercise, but having access to the same knowledge, use of reason, and ideals of virtue. Then women might be capable of doing their duty as citizens; for she believes that "women ought to have representatives, instead of being arbitrarily governed without having any direct share allowed them in the deliberations of government." She thinks women should be doctors as well as nurses, which, of course, requires education and specialized knowledge. If given a fair chance, they could make valuable contributions to society in the business world. Education is the key. Young children, "from five to nine years of age," should all have a free education, regardless of class. After the age of nine, those with more ability might be separated from less gifted students. But equality of ability should entail equality of access regardless of gender. Respecting females' natural rights will help them to develop as rational agents and "free citizens, and they will quickly become good wives and mothers," more valuable members of society (87, 151–152, 174, 184). Wollstonecraft was considerably ahead of her time here; and it is little wonder that her views both inspired the desire for social change in some and generated a reaction of resistance in others.

13

Immanuel Kant

Source: vodolej/Adobe Stock

13.1 Overview

In this study of modern European philosophers, there is no thinker more revolutionary than Kant. The division of modern European philosophy between its pre-Kantian period and its post-Kantian one is clearly warranted. As we have seen, before Kant, it largely amounted to a clash between two

Modern European Philosophers, First Edition. Wayne P. Pomerleau.
© 2023 John Wiley & Sons, Inc. Published 2023 by John Wiley & Sons, Inc.

great rival movements – continental rationalism, from Descartes through Leibniz, and British empiricism, from Hobbes through Hume. Academically trained in a kind of Leibnizian rationalism and then jolted out of that by Hume's radical empiricism, Kant devised an entirely original synthesis that would spawn a third movement of German idealism. Like Hume before him (and Hegel afterwards), he put together a complete and comprehensive philosophical system that hangs together coherently and each of whose major parts is impressively well developed. We shall see how he used the transcendental method he invented as a foundation for constructing his critical philosophy in all the various areas we are considering.

13.2 Biography

Immanuel Kant spent all of his life within 75 miles of the city of his birth, Königsberg (now Kaliningrad, Russia), then capital of East Prussia. He was the son of Johann Georg Kant, an honest, industrious master harness maker, and Anna Regina Reuter Kant, the pious, morally earnest daughter of another local harness maker, the fourth of their nine children.[1] Born April 22, 1724, Kant appreciated his home city (*Anthropology*, 4–5n.). At the age of eight, he was enrolled in a Pietist school directed by the Kant family's pastor, where he got excellent training in Latin but was repulsed by the enforced piety. In 1737, his mother died of a disease contracted while nursing a sick friend. In 1740, with his pastor's support, he was enrolled in the Albertus University of Königsberg, just a couple of months after Frederick II, who came to be called Frederick the Great, was inaugurated as King of Prussia in Kant's home city. Frederick, who loved philosophy and literature and introduced freedom of the press and freedom of worship, encouraged enlightened thought, leading Kant to write, in 1784, that he lived in "the age of enlightenment, the century of *Frederick*" (*Political*, 58). At the university, Kant came under the influence of a Leibnizian-Wolffian Pietist philosopher named Martin Knutzen, with whom he also studied Newton's scientific writings. The young man started publishing in modern philosophy and science by 1747. But, by then, his father had died, necessitating his leaving the university to earn a living. He worked as a

---

1 References to Kant's works will be to *Anthropology from a Pragmatic Point of View*, by Immanuel Kant (hereafter called *Anthropology*), trans. by Victor Lyle Dowdell, ed. by Hans H. Rudnick (Carbondale, IL: Southern Illinois Univ. Press, 1978), to *Correspondence*, by Immanuel Kant, trans. and ed. by Arnulf Zweig (New York: Cambridge Univ. Press, 1999), to *Critique of Judgment*, by Immanuel Kant (hereafter called "third" *Critique*), trans. by J.H. Bernard (New York: Hafner Publishing Co., 1968), to *Critique of Practical Reason*, by Immanuel Kant (hereafter called "second" *Critique*), trans. by Lewis White Beck (Indianapolis: Bobbs-Merrill, 1956), to *Critique of Pure Reason*, by Immanuel Kant (hereafter called "first" *Critique*), trans. by Norman Kemp Smith (New York: St. Martin's Press, 1965), to *Education*, by Immanuel Kant, trans. by Annette Churton (Ann Arbor: Univ. of Michigan Press, 1960), to *Ethical Philosophy*, by Immanuel Kant, second edition (hereafter called *Ethical*), trans. by James W. Ellington (Indianapolis: Hackett, 1994), to *Lectures on Ethics*, by Immanuel Kant (hereafter called *Ethics*), trans. by Louis Infield (Indianapolis: Hackett, 1981), to *Lectures on Philosophical Theology*, by Immanuel Kant (hereafter called *Theology*), trans. by Allen W. Wood and Gertrude M. Clark (Ithaca: Cornell Univ. Press, 1978), to *Logic*, by Immanuel Kant, trans. by Robert Hartman and Wolfgang Schwarz (Indianapolis: Bobbs-Merrill, 1974), to *Metaphysical Elements of Justice*, by Immanuel Kant, second edition (hereafter called *Justice*), trans. by John Ladd (Indianapolis: Hackett, 1999), to *Political Writings*, by Immanuel Kant, second edition (hereafter called *Political*), trans. by H.B. Nisbet, ed. by Hans Reiss (Cambridge: Cambridge Univ. Press, 1991), to *Prolegomena to Any Future Metaphysics*, by Immanuel Kant (hereafter called *Prolegomena*), trans. by Paul Carus, revised by James W. Ellington (Indianapolis: Hackett, 1977), to *Religion within the Limits of Reason Alone*, by Immanuel Kant (hereafter called *Religion*), trans. by Theodore M. Greene and Hoyt H. Hudson (New York: Harper & Row, 1960), and to *What Real Progress Has Metaphysics Made in Germany since the Time of Leibniz and Wolff?*, by Immanuel Kant (hereafter called *Metaphysics*), trans. by Ted Humphrey (New York: Abaris Books, 1983).

children's tutor for several families outside the city, developing habits of fine dress and refined manners. (He was a small, frail man, never more than five feet, two inches tall or weighing more than a hundred pounds, narrow-chested, with one shoulder a bit higher than the other.) These tutorial positions afforded him ample time for scholarly reading and writing.

In 1754, ending his employment as a domestic tutor in provincial households, Kant returned to the city to work on his graduate dissertation and to write for publication. All of this was successful; he published several scientific papers, was awarded a doctorate, and qualified for university teaching. In 1755, he started teaching at the university as a *Privatdozent*, or private lecturer, with no guaranteed salary but collecting fees from students attending his lectures. Though a popular teacher, for the 15 years he taught in this capacity, he was poor and had to live quite modestly. He taught mathematics, physics, logic, and metaphysics, later expanding his repertoire to include geography and ethics. It was hard work, lecturing between 16 and 24 hours a week. In 1759, he wrote to a friend, complaining about the brutal routine (*Correspondence*, 56). He applied unsuccessfully for the philosophy chair left vacant by Knutzen's death. He then applied for another philosophy chair at the university, but the position went to a senior *Privatdozent* named Buck. During the 1760s, Kant was studying the works of Hume and Rousseau, which had a profound influence on his intellectual orientation, leading him to shift the emphasis of his own writings from natural science to pure philosophy and helping to wean him away from the Leibnizian-Wolffian rationalism in which he was raised. He wrote that Hume's writings "first interrupted" his "dogmatic slumber" (*Prolegomena*, 5; see also second *Critique*, 54) and that Rousseau helped him to get over the illusion of superiority and to learn to respect common people (*Justice*, xxiii–xxiv). Between 1763 and 1768, he published a series of works. In 1769, he was finally offered a philosophy professorship; but it was at Erlangen rather than at Königsberg, and he declined the offer on account of his abiding "aversion to change" (*Correspondence*, 101). At any rate, it was clear that his reputation was growing and spreading.

In 1770, he was offered a professorship at the University of Jena (where J.G. Fichte and G.W.F. Hegel would later teach) but again declined to move. A couple of months later, a chair in mathematics became vacant at Königsberg. Professor Buck moved into that, with Kant assuming the chair in logic and metaphysics. The position for which he had patiently waited was finally his. In August of 1770, he presented and defended his inaugural dissertation. This was a watershed work in Kant's philosophical career, separating all his precritical writings from the critical philosophy for which he is justly famous. Indeed, in 1797, when a publisher wanted to put out a collection of Kant's writings, he agreed, but with the proviso, "I would not want you to start the collection with anything before 1770, that is, my Dissertation" (*Correspondence*, 528). His critical writings render his precritical works largely obsolete. The next 10 years are sometimes called Kant's silent decade, because he published nothing of great importance. He was trying to develop his own original philosophy, which would be a kind of synthesis of modern rationalism and modern empiricism. He was able to cut back his exhausting teaching schedule to facilitate that. As a teacher, he tried to challenge his students to develop and exercise critical thinking skills instead of merely memorizing what they heard from him. We have testimonials to the excellence of his teaching, including one from Herder that says, "He incited and gently forced others to think for themselves; despotism was foreign to his mind" (second *Critique*, xxii). He served as dean of the university's philosophy faculty in 1776 and again in 1779–1780 and was appointed a member of the university senate in 1778, the year he declined a professorship at Halle.

But, most tellingly, he was trying to work out how he would establish the foundational book for his own original system that would steer a middle path between the dogmatism of classical rationalism and the skepticism of radical empiricism. This book, his *Critique of Pure Reason*, the first of

13.2 Biography | 201

his three great Critiques, was finally published in 1781. His hopes for its immediate success were quickly dashed, as it was too long, too abstract, too technical, and too revolutionary to be understood, let alone appreciated. As he later admitted, "the work is dry, obscure, opposed to all ordinary notions, and moreover long-winded"; he sadly expressed the wish that, as a writer, he had been "gifted with the subtlety and, at the same time, with the grace of David Hume" (*Prolegomena*, 6–7). In 1783, he published his *Prolegomena to Any Future Metaphysics*, which might serve as a gentler introduction to the more daunting and more rigorous first *Critique*. Having taken over a decade to lay the foundation of his system, for the next decade, one great work followed another in staggeringly rapid succession: in 1784, his manifesto "What Is Enlightenment?", in 1785, his *Grounding for the Metaphysics of Morals*, in 1786, his *Metaphysical Foundations of Natural Science*, in 1787, a significantly revised second edition of the first *Critique*, in 1788, his second *Critique*, the *Critique of Practical Reason*, in 1790, his third *Critique*, the *Critique of Judgment*, and, in 1791, his essay "On the Failure of All Attempted Philosophical Theodicies."

In 1786, the enlightened, tolerant Frederick the Great died and was succeeded by his illiberal nephew, Frederick William II, who imposed on Prussia a strict, conservatively Christian censorship policy in 1788, cracking down even harder in 1792. Meanwhile, Kant was at work on what would become his controversial and groundbreaking *Religion within the Limits of Reason Alone*. Having been denied permission to publish what would become its Book II by the Berlin censor, Kant sent the manuscript for the entire book to Jena, where the whole work was granted publication approval. When Wöllner, the king's reactionary minister, found out about it, he was furious, writing Kant a nasty letter, accusing him of undermining orthodox Christianity and threatening him with "unpleasant measures" should he repeat such offenses in the future. In reply, Kant wrote the king a letter, denying that his *Religion* in any way disparaged Christianity but promising, "as Your Majesty's loyal subject," that he would "refrain altogether from discoursing publicly, in lectures or writings, on religion." Kant intended that qualifying phrase to limit his commitment to the king's lifetime. He later included these documents in the Preface to his *Conflict of the Faculties*, explaining in a note that he used the qualifying expression to avoid renouncing his freedom to publish his views "*forever*, but only during His Majesty's lifetime" (*Correspondence*, 485–489). He kept his word, publishing nothing on religion until after Frederick William II had died (in 1797).

In 1795, his *Perpetual Peace* was published, and he reduced his teaching to the daily public lectures on logic and metaphysics, delivering his last lecture at the university in July of 1796. The following year, his *Metaphysics of Morals* was published in two parts, *Metaphysical Elements of Justice* and *Metaphysical Principles of Virtue*, as was his essay "On a Supposed Right to Lie Because of Philanthropic Concerns." When Frederick William II died, his son and successor, Frederick William III, dismissed Wöllner and abolished the censorship program. So, in 1798, Kant published *The Conflict of the Faculties*, which does deal with religion, as well as his *Anthropology from a Pragmatic Point of View*. During the period from 1784 to 1798, Kant was remarkably prolific and became the most significant living philosopher in Germany. But, by the end of this period, his mental and physical decline had clearly begun.

Near the end of 1797, Kant wrote a letter to Fichte, saying that "for the past year and a half, my poor health and the frailties of age had forced me to give up all my lecturing," that his writing had become "slow going and effortful," that he was no longer up to "the subtlety of theoretical speculation," and that he had "no idea how much longer" he would be "able to work at all." In 1798, he joked, "It is a great sin to have grown old, but no one is spared the punishment for it: death." That same year, he wrote, "I am as it were mentally paralyzed even though physically I am reasonably well," adding that he was anxious to complete his philosophical system, by bridging the "gap" between metaphysics and physics. He hyperbolically continued, "My health, as others will have

202 | *13 Immanuel Kant*

informed you, is less that of a scholar than that of a vegetable – capable of eating, moving about, and sleeping," but not much more. He had become a self-professed "invalid." In 1799, he issued a public declaration, disavowing Fichte's philosophy as "a totally indefensible system" not truly in line with his own "critical philosophy" (*Correspondence*, 534–535, 543, 551–553, 559–560).

By this time, he was becoming alarmingly forgetful; by 1800, he was losing his short-term memory. That year, his *Logic* was published, edited by someone else. By 1801, his vision was failing badly, and he needed to have a friend assume custody of the keys to his household. Early in 1802, Martin Lampe, his servant for 40 years, had to be dismissed. Yet Kant needed help with even small, routine tasks. He lost weight and began having trouble walking. In 1803, his *Education* was published, edited by someone else. He wrote his last letter in April of that year. By the fall of 1803, his youngest sister, a widow, moved in to take care of him. By the beginning of 1804, he was unable to recognize his friends. He was having trouble eating and sleeping and was rarely coherent. After uttering his last words, "*Es ist gut*" ("It is good") the day before, he died on February 12, 1804. For the next 16 days, crowds came to pay their respects; his funeral was well attended, and he was buried on February 28. On April 23, the day after his eightieth birthday, there was a memorial service at the university. In May of 1804, his *What Real Progress Has Metaphysics Made in Germany since the Time of Leibniz and Wolff?* (written in 1790 and edited by someone else) was published. Starting the following year, a Kant Club annually convened to honor his birthday. His *Lectures on Philosophical Theology* was published in 1817. A statue of Kant walking was erected in Königsberg in 1864. In 1924, his *Lectures on Ethics* were finally published. Now, more than two centuries after his death, he remains the watershed figure of modern philosophy, separating his predecessors from his successors by his own monumental critical system, which challenged the former while inevitably influencing the latter.

13.3 Knowledge

In the wake of Hume's skepticism, Kant inherited a major problem that represented a crisis in and a threat to modern philosophy: unless we have innate ideas, how is it possible for us to achieve universal and necessary factual knowledge? The innate ideas which rationalists had dogmatically embraced seemed unsupported and insupportable. But the factual findings of concrete experience were only particular, and generalizing from them could only yield probable, contingent conclusions, indicative of an uncertain skepticism. Either the old doctrine of innate ideas would need to be rehabilitated or the notion that all factual truth is particular, contingent, and merely probable would have to be accepted or some new explanation would have to be found. Kant became famous for utilizing that third option, as we are about to see. Regarding his reaching his own original solution to this problem of epistemology, five observations might be made. First, in thinking for himself rather than following in the footsteps of others, he takes his own advice from the first paragraph of "What Is Enlightenment?" – that one should dare to "use one's own understanding without the guidance of another" (*Political*, 54). Second, this requires a new philosophical method never employed before, the transcendental method, which seeks to identify the necessary conditions of some aspect(s) of human experience – in this case, the fact that we do have some necessary factual knowledge. Third, he is quite aware that his work here involves "an intellectual revolution" and compares it to that of Copernicus in astronomy (first *Critique*, 20, 22, and 25n.). Fourth, he is consciously trying to avoid the extremes of both the modern rationalists and the modern empiricists; writing, "Weary therefore of dogmatism, which teaches us nothing, and of scepticism, which does not even promise us anything," he was hoping to steer a middle path between them (*Prolegomena*, 19). Fifth, in constructing his epistemology, he tries to move toward answering the first of his central, pivotal philosophical questions. The first three of these were, "What can I know?," "What ought I to do?," and "What may I hope?" (first *Critique, 635*). He later added a fourth core question, "What is man?" (*Logic*, 29, and *Correspondence*, 458). By analyzing the nature and necessary conditions of knowledge, Kant was able to determine its limits. In order for "mere *judgments of perception*," which are "only subjectively valid," to become "*judgments of experience*," which "have objective validity," they must be grounded in concrete sensible experience, as the empiricists insisted. Yet, in order for the latter both to be factual and to have "apodeictical certainty," as universally and necessarily so, they must have a priori elements, even if these do not take the form of the rationalists' discredited innate ideas (*Prolegomena*, 41, 25). Kant's transcendental method of inquiry was designed to expose the necessary conditions of knowledge.

In trying to identify the nature of knowledge, Kant concurs with the traditional notion that knowing anything requires believing it to be true, its actually being true, and one having sufficient justification for thinking it to be true. He distinguishes among three levels at which one can think something true. The justification for holding a mere opinion is insufficient for anyone. Thus, for example, our opinion that there is intelligent, personal extraterrestrial life in the physical universe is not yet based on evidence that is either objectively or even subjectively sufficient. Second, one's personal belief in God, for example, can be based on subjectively sufficient justification that is nevertheless objectively insufficient to persuade others. And, third, "when the holding of a thing to be true is sufficient both subjectively and objectively, it is *knowledge*." For example, the truth of the Pythagorean theorem goes beyond subjective "*conviction* (for myself)" to objective "*certainty* (for everyone)," being truly knowable (first *Critique*, 646). But the question facing us now is the transcendental one – what are the necessary conditions of our knowing any general matters of fact (as opposed to mere relations of ideas, such as that no bachelors are married, and particular facts, such as that my car is currently white) – for example, that all mammals that permanently stop breathing die? This is what Kant calls a judgment that is both "*a priori* and synthetic" (first *Critique*, 61); that is to say, it is both universally and necessarily so, on the one hand, and informative about reality, rather than merely explaining the use of concepts, on the other. Let us now consider this more deeply.

Prior to Kant, the truth of a judgment was thought to be an implication of the fact that it conformed to some state of affairs. This traditional "correspondence theory" held that, because the belief that all animals ultimately die corresponds to the facts of biology, it is therefore "true." But there is a problem with this, revealed by Locke in the seventeenth century and not yet adequately answered, leading to the triumph of skepticism: if our ideas are the only direct, immediate objects of our minds, how can we ever possibly get outside our own ideas to determine whether they correspond to external factual reality or not? What Kant does that constitutes a bold new "experiment" is turn the needed conformity upside down. Instead of maintaining that the knowing mind must conform to the reality of the known object, we should "make trial whether we may not have more success . . . , if we suppose that objects must conform to our knowledge" (first *Critique*, 22). In other words, why not suppose that, in order to be an object of human knowledge, a thing must meet certain specifiable requirements of the knowing mind. We would still have a correspondence; but, instead of the object being known being the independent variable and the knowing mind the dependent variable, it would be the other way around. This gives primacy to the mind, in the knowing process, opening the path to some sort of idealism. But, we might object, do we not have the same problem of ascertaining whether the independent reality of our objects does or does not conform to the mind's requirements? After all, Kant is a good modernist in that he does not think we ever have direct, immediate experience of anything external to the mind. We experience our own sensible intuitions (e.g. of white, hard, sweet cubes), whose objects are never things in themselves

13 Immanuel Kant

(e.g. sugar cubes) but only clusters of phenomenal appearances. It is these, objects as we experience them, that must conform to the conditions required by the knowing mind. While we cannot know things as they are in themselves, we must "*think* them" as transcendental conditions of the phenomena we experience and can know; "otherwise we should be landed in the absurd conclusion that there can be appearance without anything that appears." (We might mention at this point that this inference toward things in themselves will prove a serious bone of contention in later German idealism.) So Kant's dualism views reality "from two different points of view," so that an object like a sugar cube "is to be taken *in a twofold sense*, namely as appearance and as thing in itself" (first *Critique*, 27, 23n., 28). Notice how this is already carving out a middle ground between the dogmatic assumption that, of course, we know at least some things as they are independent of our experience of them, on the one hand, and the skeptical conclusion that we can never have any knowledge of factual reality at all.

Kant agrees with the empiricists when he writes, "There can be no doubt that all our knowledge begins with experience." We must start with our own intuitions; and, unlike the rationalists, Kant holds that all human intuition is sensible rather than intellectual. "But though all our knowledge begins with experience," he teasingly adds, "it does not follow that it all arises out of experience." In addition to sensible intuitions providing us with objects to be known, as the rationalists recognized, we must bring some a priori concepts to the knowing process. Both content and concepts are essential: "Thoughts without content are empty, intuitions without concepts are blind." Further, only the senses, and not the understanding, can intuit objects; only the understanding, and not the senses, can think (first *Critique*, 41, 92–93). In order to make sense of our sensible intuitions, the mind must arrange them in some sort of order and does so by means of the a priori forms of sensibility, time and space. But that only gives us coherent experience, which might be capable of being thought. In order to move beyond this to the level of understanding and knowledge, more is needed. Consider Kant's own example: "when the sun shines on the stone, it grows warm." This is a matter of sensible intuition and "is a mere judgment of perception." It expresses a spatiotemporal correlation, but no understanding. But now suppose we say that "the sun warms the stone." We have now employed the a priori concept of causality to explain why we experience such a correlation (*Prolegomena*, 44n.).

So far, so good. However, we must now try to penetrate more deeply, at this point subjecting ourselves to a bit of Kant's rather technical terminology. "Analytic judgments" are "explicative," in that the predicate term merely explains something already conceptually contained in the subject term. For example, in the proposition, "All bachelors are unmarried," the concept of being unmarried is part of the very meaning of a "bachelor," so that the proposition is true by definition; conversely, it would be necessarily false (by definition) to say that some bachelor is currently married. We do not need to interview any bachelors to see whether or not they are married; we only have to understand the meaning of the concept. Every analytic judgment is also a priori, universally and necessarily so, with no need for empirical confirmation. By contrast, there are synthetic a posteriori judgments, whose predicate concepts are not implicitly contained in their subject concepts, so that they are not true or false by definition; rather, their truth or falsehood can only be determined by experience – for example, "All bachelors are narcissistic." These two types of judgments correspond, respectively, to Hume's "relations of ideas" and "matters of fact." Now no analytic judgment could possibly be a posteriori. But Kant breaks with tradition by explicitly raising the issue of judgments that are both synthetic (that is, factually informative), on the one hand, and a priori (that is, universally and necessarily so), on the other. He maintains, for example, that the laws of Newtonian physics are both, so that natural science can be a body of certain knowledge. By contrast, Hume's skepticism ought to have extended beyond metaphysics (and theology), his intended target(s), to physics, reducing it to a system of mere empirical generalizations. Kant ends up defending not only the value of metaphysical speculation against Hume's skepticism, but also the knowledge of Newtonian science as well. This requires that he raise, and try to answer, a radical question never previously asked, let alone answered: "How are *a priori* synthetic judgments possible?" (first *Critique*, 48–55). The answer would come in the form of innate, a priori structures of the human mind, which are not innate ideas because they are pure form and have no content – one of the most strikingly original insights in the history of philosophy.

Just as the "two pure forms of sensible intuition, . . . namely space and time," are the transcendental conditions of any coherent perception, yet are merely the forms under which we humans organize our experiences of phenomenal appearances, so we must have and be able to use innate, a priori concepts of the understanding in order to gain knowledge. There are 12 of these, which Kant organizes into four groups of three each. For example, having experienced, through sensible intuition, the chair on which I am sitting, I can understand it as one single piece of furniture (the concept of *unity*), which is real and actually existing (*reality* and *existence*), a wooden *substance* that was *caused* to be by humans operating woodcrafting machinery, and designed to be in *community* with tables or desks. These six of the 12 "categories" (he sometimes adopts Aristotle's word for them) have been employed to constitute knowledge and understanding (first *Critique*, 67, 113). All of that goes into the judgment that the object of my perceptual experience is an actual chair. To say that a chair on which I am sitting is *one really existing substance caused* to be in *community* with other objects is to state a matter of objective knowledge and need not be merely subjectively believed. But these innate a priori structures of the mind – space, time, and the 12 categories – can only be known to apply to phenomenal appearances and not to our ideas of things in themselves. In order for something to be known, it must (i) be given to us in sensible intuition; (ii) be capable of being experienced temporally and, if it is external to the mind, spatially; and (iii) be thinkable in terms of one or more of the 12 categories, which we only know legitimately apply to phenomenal appearances. None of these three conditions applies to things in themselves.

The 14 mental structures we have been discussing here have a "constitutive" function, in that they help the mind constitute knowledge. Dogmatic rationalists were guilty of assuming that they can be legitimately applied to things in themselves, such as the mind and God. Skeptical empiricists were guilty of assuming that concepts can only be valuable if they serve such a constitutive function. By contrast, Kant maintains that our concepts can also serve a valuable "regulative" function of helping to regulate or direct human thought and action without ever constituting knowledge (first *Critique*, 210–211; *Prolegomena*, 90), as in areas of metaphysical (including theological) speculation. This will take us to a third level of transcendental inquiry (in our next section). In order to speculate about the nature of reality in itself, the mind needs a priori ideas of pure reason, of which there are three, all of which have regulative, but not constitutive, value. These are the idea of the soul (the central idea of philosophical psychology), the idea of the cosmos (the central idea of philosophical cosmology), and the idea of God (the central idea of philosophical theology). Despite the warnings of Kantian epistemology, we shall always remain vulnerable to the "*natural* and inevitable" danger of the "*transcendental illusion*" that these ideas might be put to a constitutive, rather than merely a regulative, use, thereby generating a body of metaphysical knowledge. Kant speaks of a "*logic of illusion*" as "a natural and unavoidable dialectic of pure reason," which pulls reason from a metaphysical "thesis" to its opposing "antithesis," with plausible supporting arguments for each side and no way of resolving the logical conflict, precisely because reason has transcended its legitimate bounds, approaching the supersensible ideas of metaphysics as if they could be used to constitute knowledge

13.4 Reality

Given the three conditions of knowledge mandated by Kant's epistemology, it follows that we cannot have knowledge of the noumenal reality of metaphysical things in themselves. Those who reduce reality to that would claim that Kant is therefore a skeptic. Phenomenalists like the early Hume, who go to the opposite extreme and reduce reality to phenomenal appearances, could also hold that, in maintaining unknowable things-in-themselves, Kant must be a dogmatist. But Kant's dualism allows him to dodge both traps. He believes in a dual aspect theory of reality: a level of phenomenal appearances and an underlying level of noumenal things in themselves; the former is the level at which knowledge is possible, and the latter is that of rational faith. Indeed, for better or for worse, what sets Kant apart from later German idealists is that he combines his transcendental idealism with empirical realism. He bends over backwards to dissociate himself from the sort of idealism that "consists in the assertion that there are none but thinking beings." Against Berkeley, for example, he writes that "it never came into my head to doubt" the independent, external "existence of things" (*Prolegomena*, 32, 37). The second edition of his first *Critique* contains a "Refutation of Idealism," and it is "the *dogmatic* idealism of Berkeley" that is its primary target (first *Critique*, 244). That sort of monistic idealism, of course, is inconsistent with belief in physical reality outside the mind. "The transcendental idealist, on the other hand, may be an empirical realist or, as he is called, a *dualist*." Actually, in Kant's case, it is more than "may be." He commits himself to an "empirical realism" that considers the objects of our outer intuitions to be real apart from any perception of them. Yet he combines this with a "transcendental idealism" that maintains that time, space, and the concepts we use to think about reality are in our minds – or mind-dependent (first *Critique*, 346–349).

If we defy the cautions of Kantian epistemology and try to gain knowledge of noumenal reality, we encounter the "dialectical illusion" of metaphysical puzzles, regarding the psychological idea of the soul or mind or self, the cosmological idea of the cosmos, the world as an organized whole, and the theological idea of God. In each case, reason is seeking to transcend the limits of experience and to achieve complete understanding by grasping the unconditioned condition of a given series. Yet, since metaphysical knowledge is impossible for us, the project is doomed, from the outset, to frustration and failure. Particularly interesting are the four antinomies concerning the cosmological idea, each of which has a thesis and an opposing antithesis (the first having to do with whether the world, as a whole, had a beginning in time and space or is infinite; the second having to do with whether everything in the world is made up of atomic, monadic simples or whether everything is irreducibly composite; the third having to do with whether there are free causes in the world or whether everything happens by natural necessity; and the fourth having to do with whether there is some necessary being in the series of world causes or whether everything that happens in the world is contingent). Reason is impotent to resolve any of these because the issues themselves, as metaphysical, are unknowable. However, speculating about such matters is natural to the human mind and leads us away from the stagnant reductionism of materialism, naturalism, and fatalism, having a spiritually salutary effect (*Prolegomena*, 89, 80–81, 103). Metaphysical speculation, though dangerous, invites us to expand our intellectual horizons. Believing in the possibility of the soul (or mind or self) helps us get past the lazy assumption that the material world we see is all that is real. Believing in the possibility of a supernatural order helps us get past the lazy assumption that the natural order is all there is. And believing in the possibility of free causal efficacy helps us get past the lazy assumption that nothing could ever have been otherwise than, in fact, it is. (Regarding Kant's purely negative treatment of dialectical reason, we might note that it will play a more positive role in subsequent German idealism, with Hegel elevating it to the status of a superior logic in which higher, more inclusive syntheses allegedly emerge from the conflicts between theses and antitheses.)

13.5 God

The third of Kant's four core philosophical questions, for what may I (reasonably) hope?, leads us into his philosophy of religion. His answer, briefly put, is a God, who is a just Judge, and an immortal human soul whose natural life will be succeeded by a supernatural afterlife. But we must consider the development of this excessively short response. On this topic, yet again, Kant carves out an original new position midway between his predecessors. He believes in the same God of orthodox Judeo-Christianity as the early modern rationalists, Locke, Berkeley, and Butler, rather than in the deistic God of Hume. On the other hand, like Hume, he does not think God's existence could be conclusively demonstrated, he thinks the argument from design to be the most effective of the traditional arguments for God, and he takes the problem of evil very seriously as posing an obstacle for rationally justifying belief in an infinitely perfect Deity. We must recall here that, for Kant, God is a regulative, metaphysical idea of pure reason never capable of constituting knowledge, because God would, as such, have to transcend any and all possible natural human experience. The Kantian epistemology rules out any chance of speculatively proving or knowing God for us (at least in this life).

In a very famous part of the first *Critique*, Kant organizes all previous speculative attempts to prove God's existence philosophically into three sorts. First, "the *physico-theological*" argument from design starts with our "determinate experience and the specific constitution of the world of sense" as both complex and orderly. Second, there is *"cosmological"* reasoning based on "experience which is purely indeterminate, that is, from experience of existence in general." And, third, there are attempts at *"ontological"* argumentation, which "abstract from all experience and argue completely *a priori* from mere concepts, to the existence" of a supreme Being. Kant claims, not only that these are the only three possible approaches of speculative reason, but also that the first tends to involve the second and the second, the third. Yet all fail to be logically cogent. First, the argument from design, though respectable and psychologically powerful, is a probability argument, based on analogy, yielding no certain conclusion. Second, even if we accepted it, it would only give us an enduring (not necessarily eternal), intelligent (not necessarily omniscient), powerful (not necessarily omnipotent) *"architect* of the world" and not a necessarily existing, infinitely perfect God. For that, other arguments would have to be employed: "Thus the physico-theological proof of the existence of an original or supreme being rests upon the cosmological proof, and the cosmological upon the ontological." If cosmological arguments worked, they would give us a necessarily existing (and thus eternal) first Cause of the universe. But, in order to make them work, we would have to apply the category of causality to the cosmos, or world as a whole, which would transcend the legitimate bounds of Kantian epistemology: we have no experiences of the world as a whole and no reason to assume that such a concept of the understanding could legitimately apply to a noumenal idea. So cosmological reasoning must fail. But, even if it worked, it would only give us an abstract metaphysical principle, a necessarily existing first Cause, and not an infinitely perfect, personal God of religion – for which we need ontological reasoning. But the ontological argument (so named by Kant himself), long favored by rationalists, tries to treat existence, a concept of the human understanding, as an attribute or "predicate" or perfection of an "absolutely necessary being" (note that necessity and reality are also mere categories of our thinking). This is the only speculative argument which, if it worked, could rationally establish the perfect, personal God of religion. But it also fails (first *Critique*, 499–500, 522, 524, 509–511, 502–506). Yet this is not the end of the matter.

Although speculative theology fails to establish knowledge of God, Kant turns to moral theology to establish God as a postulate of practical reason to which our moral experience rationally leads us, as he insists immediately after concluding his critique of traditional arguments. If *"logical"* certainty regarding God proves impossible to establish, he thinks it essential to establish *"moral* certainty" regarding both it and human immortality (first *Critique*, 526–527, 650). For this moral argumentation we must now turn to his *Critique of Practical Reason*. It is a curious but original approach. Kant thinks that we, as moral agents, have a responsibility to work to bring about "the highest good, i.e., happiness proportional to that morality" toward which we are rationally bound. Yet, since we cannot have any obligation that would be impossible (since "ought" implies "can") and since we lack sufficient ability ever to bring about that end by ourselves, we "must postulate the existence of God as necessarily belonging to the possibility of the highest good," this being a matter of practical faith. "Therefore, it is morally necessary to assume the existence of God," given our alleged moral obligation, "this moral necessity" being a "subjective" rational belief that can never constitute knowledge. Religion, then, represents a bond between God and us, acting as we believe a perfectly good Deity would have us behave: "Religion is the recognition of all duties as divine commands." Similar reasoning purportedly can establish belief in our own immortality of spirit as a credible, but not knowable, postulate of practical reason: we are allegedly obliged to strive to bring about the highest good, which we could never do in the brief span of this life; but, since "ought" implies "can," we must have an afterlife in which we could accomplish this (second *Critique*, 126–134). People can decide for themselves whether this moral argument for God and human immortality has any psychological force at all. (See also third *Critique*, 301, 306–307, 321–324, 338; see also *Metaphysics*, 131, for the three basic articles of Kant's moral faith.) But, surely, from a logical point of view, it is unconvincing, because it is based on an unjustified and doubtful assumption that we are morally obliged to help bring about the highest good of happiness proportional to moral desert. Even if we do have an obligation to try to help bring about such a just state of affairs, that is not to say that the ideal will ever be fully reached or, if it is, that that requires either Kant's perfect God or our own personal immortality. The best Kant could claim for these two postulates of practical reason is that they represent reasonable hopes we can meaningfully harbor.

Kant's God has the standard metaphysical attributes associated with the orthodox Judeo-Christian conception of God – "*omniscient, omnipotent, eternal.*" But even more important in his moral theology were "the moral perfections of *holiness, benevolence,* and *justice,*" three aspects of God's moral nature "as a *holy lawgiver,* a *benevolent sustainer of the world,* and a *just judge.*" The reality of evil in the world may very well, as Hume thought, call into question all three of these. Yet it is by the freedom, autonomous choice, and responsibility for their own development that rational creatures such as humans make possible "the incompleteness" that is evil (*Theology*, 111–112, 115–117). Kant's *Religion within the Limits of Reason Alone*, arguably his most underrated great work, is also his most mature treatment of religion. Even though the postulate of God "arises out of morality," it is not the foundation of moral obligation. "Morality thus leads ineluctably to religion, through which it extends itself to the idea of a powerful moral Lawgiver." A moral religion, of the sort Kant advocated, must essentially consist in "the heart's disposition to fulfill all human duties as divine commands" and never be reduced to dogmas and rituals. Thus the only "true religion" is a moral religion, one which sees all moral duties as commanded by God. Kant boldly concludes, "There is only *one* (true) *religion*; but there can be *faiths* of several kinds." Judaism, Catholic Christianity, Islam, and Protestant Christianity, on this progressively pluralistic view, are all various faiths within the one true moral religion, which believes in a God that is a "*holy* Legislator," a "*benevolent* Ruler," and a "*righteous* Judge." Kant condemns as religious "pseudo-service" mere statutory outward displays of sacrifices, cultic rituals, penances, and so forth. What matters is a truly religious person cultivating a morally good will. Enlightened religion should serve God through moral choices and virtuous conduct. Pious ceremonies without good character are worthless (*Religion*, 5, 79, 95, 142, 98, 131, 156–157, 167, 189). It is not difficult to see why a conservative eighteenth-century Christian censor might have been unwilling to authorize the publication of such revolutionary religious ideas.

13.6 Humanity

The fourth of Kant's core philosophical questions, What is a human being?, takes us into his philosophy of human nature, which reflects his dualistic theory of reality. A human being ("man" in the generic sense) is an animal body in the world of phenomenal appearances and, as such, scientifically knowable. But a human is also a mind or self or soul in the realm of noumenal reality and, as such, not knowable but merely an object of rational faith. So, on this dualistic view, we can have knowledge of man as a physical being in the sensible world but only rational belief regarding man as a person. The third (final) section of Kant's *Grounding for the Metaphysics of Morals* presents an excellent, brief exposition of his dualism as applied to human nature. It reminds us of his distinction "between a world of sense and a world of understanding," the former being a knowable realm of phenomenal appearances, including the human body, and the latter a noumenal realm of things in themselves, including the human mind. Thus, in this dual aspect theory, considered from "one point of view," our actions are extrinsically caused, while, from "another point of view," some of our actions are self-determined or freely chosen. Thus, we are complex beings inhabiting both worlds. Man is rightly a citizen of both. "Therefore he has two standpoints from which he can regard himself" legitimately and is subject to two sets of laws, the empirical laws of nature and the rational moral law. (We shall consider this complex dynamic between "human freedom and natural necessity" in our next section.) However, like the rationalists, he tends to identify man's "proper self" with his mind, rational will, and personality, which involves membership in "a universal kingdom of ends in themselves (rational beings)" of a spiritual nature (*Ethical*, 52–62).

In his *Anthropology*, Kant focuses more on the physical dimension of human nature, trying to discuss it scientifically. A human being is born "as an animal endowed with the capability of reason"; by developing that potentiality, he "can make himself a rational animal," but this requires effort. This capacity for developing reason is the root of "his technical gift for manipulating things (mechanically connected with consciousness), his pragmatic gift (being clever in the use of others for his own purposes), and his moral gift of character (so that he can act toward himself and others according to the principle of freedom under the law)," rendering him unique among the animals. Kant recognizes that our biology influences our empirical psychology, analyzing four types of temperaments, the "sanguine person," who tends to be "carefree and full of expectation" but superficial and lacking in seriousness, the melancholic person, who "thinks deeply" and takes commitments very seriously, "the choleric person," who tends to be "hot-tempered," easily offended, interested in appearances and formalities, and motivated keenly by pride, and the phlegmatic person, who has a "tendency to inactivity" and "insensitivity" but also to coolness and persistence. Such psychological temperaments are determined by our biological natures; but our moral character depends on our own free choices in the context of given circumstances, including such empirical tendencies. Also parts of our animal nature are our passions and emotions. "The inclination which can hardly, or not at all, be controlled by reason is passion," which is therefore dangerous. "On the other hand, emotion is the feeling of a pleasure or displeasure at a particular moment," which can be quite independent of reason. Although both emotion and passion can be beyond the control of reason, the former tends to be so valuable that there seems to be something miserably unfortunate about a person devoid of emotion. "Passion, on the other hand, no man wishes for himself. Who wants to have himself put in chains when he can be free?" Kant distinguishes between two sorts of passions, "those of natural inclination (innate) and those arising from the culture of mankind (acquired)"; sexual passion is an example of the former, as "ambition, lust of power, and avarice" are examples of the latter. Both sorts are seen as dangerous and undesirable. So Kant acknowledges as significant the physical dimension of human nature. Although he does not use the phrase, he seemed to regard a human being as essentially a personal animal, his personality being rooted in reason: "The fact that man is aware of an ego-concept raises him infinitely above all other creatures living on earth. Because of this, he is a person; and by virtue of this oneness of consciousness, he remains one and the same person" throughout the many physical changes of his natural life (*Anthropology*, 238–241, 198–200, 203, 155–157, 175, 9; cf. *Education*, 71, 79).

We still need to explore further this concept of personhood, as it becomes foundational to Kant's ethics and theory of society. In the first *Critique*, he writes, "That which is conscious of the numerical identity of itself at different times is in so far a *person*." Thus personhood is rooted in rational self-consciousness over time. Kant's dualism is such that we experience ourselves at the level of physical phenomena through "outer sense" and as persons through "inner sense." We are aware of our bodies through passive sense experience and aware of ourselves as minds through our active intellectual faculties of "understanding and reason." Our reason is shown to be causally active in the imperatives it generates for itself. "'Ought' expresses a kind of necessity and of connection with grounds which is found nowhere else in the whole of nature," being producible by reason alone. As Hume recognized, the phenomenal world of nature is purely a realm of fact, impervious to values. For Kant, our undeniable experience of values signifies that reason, their only possible source, must transcend that realm. This is also indicative of human "*freewill*," which is determined by rational motives "independently of sensuous impulses," as opposed to a merely "*animal*" will that can only be physiologically determined (first *Critique*, 341, 351, 472–473, 633).

In his *Religion*, Kant analyzes three dimensions of human nature: "(1) The predisposition to *animality* in man, taken as a *living* being; (2) The predisposition to *humanity* in man, taken as a living being and at the same time a *rational* being; (3) The predisposition to *personality* in man, taken as a rational and at the same time an *accountable* being." As animals, we are subject to such "*beastly* vices" as gluttony, drunkenness, and lasciviousness, like other animals. As humans, we are subject to excessive pride and jealousy, as well as such "*diabolical* vices" as spitefulness, envy, and ingratitude that tend to put us at odds with other humans. But it is as persons that we are moral agents, with a responsibility to resist such negative inclinations, to exercise "respect for the moral law within us," and to try to develop virtuous character. Kant makes it clear that all three of these predispositions are good in themselves and quite natural. "Man can indeed use the first two contrary to their ends, but he can extirpate none of them." Human nature does involve a propensity toward evil, which he analyzes in terms of its "*frailty*" or weakness of will, its "*impurity*" or selfish motives, and its "wickedness" or tendency to spurn our duty. Nevertheless, it is worth observing that Kant does not think that our "*sensuous nature* and natural inclinations" are at all to blame in these tendencies; only our free will, which can choose well or badly, can be legitimately imputed. There must be some good even in an evil person, whether or not others can detect it, and moral transformation or reform is always possible, so long as there is rational choice; but self-love can become the root of evil, when it becomes our uncontrolled driving force. Although some of our animal and human tendencies are dangerous and need to be controlled by reason, none is intrinsically evil. "Natural inclinations, *considered in themselves*, are *good*, that is, not a matter of reproach, and it is not only futile to want to extirpate them but to do so would also be harmful and blameworthy. Rather, let them be tamed" by reason (*Religion*, 21–25, 30, 32, 41, 43, 51).

In discussing natural teleology in his third *Critique*, Kant writes that we naturally desire happiness, but that our development as persons is "the ultimate purpose of nature here on earth," to which "all other natural things" are subordinate. (Some fault this anthropocentrism in Kant.) Such development can only be achieved within "a *civil community*," involving peaceful international relations, and culminating in "a *cosmopolitan* whole, i.e. a system of all states that are in danger of acting injuriously upon one another." Otherwise, conflict and the constant threat of war will jeopardize the achieving of human culture. It is only as a moral agent, rational, free, and responsible, that "man is the final purpose of creation," to which all the rest of the natural order is and should be "teleologically subordinated" (third *Critique*, 279–286; cf. *Ethics*, 252–253). The source of man's dignity and moral and cultural development is his rational freedom.

13.7 Freedom

As God and human immortality were postulates of practical reason in Kant's system, so was human freedom. All three can be transcendentally argued for: as God and our own immortality are allegedly necessary conditions of our ever being able to achieve the highest good, so our own freedom is a necessary condition of our moral responsibility. To a great extent, Kant's entire system revolves around the seminal value of human freedom. More than any other thinker included in these studies, he emphasizes freedom as a fundamental fact of our nature and experience as persons, as well as the root of all our involvement with values. In his view, rational freedom distinguishes the human person from all other earthly creatures. As a Newtonian scientist, Kant thinks it a universal law of nature that "everything which happens has a cause," as he says in his first *Critique*; but, as a Christian, he was also committed to the view that some human actions are freely chosen. The dialectic of metaphysical reason presents this conflict as one of contradictories, with good arguments available to support each side. Kant's dualism allows him to have it both ways, without any logical contradiction, because the first view, of mechanistic determinism, embraced by Hobbes and Hume, applies to the physical realm of phenomenal appearances, while the second, the view of Descartes and Malebranche, applies, at the level of noumenal reality, to the mind or soul. Kant defines freedom positively as "the power of beginning a state *spontaneously*" and negatively as "the will's independence of coercion through sensuous impulses." When someone chooses to get to work, her rational will, spontaneously (on its own) and without being necessarily compelled by any external forces, causes her body to move and act in certain ways, so that her will freely determines her body's behavior. "There is in man a power of self-determination, independently of any coercion through sensuous impulses." This capacity of self-determination makes possible the autonomy and moral responsibility emphasized by Kantian ethics, without compromising the determinism of physical phenomena at all. "In this way freedom and nature, in the full sense of these terms, can exist together, without any conflict, in the same actions, according as the actions are referred to their intelligible or to their sensible cause" (first *Critique*, 464–465; cf.

Prolegomena, 84–87). Before Kant, no philosopher had ever adequately laid the epistemological and metaphysical groundwork that could render such a dualistic account credible.

In the second *Critique*, he explicitly draws out the ethical implications of this, in discussing human "personality, i.e. the freedom and independence from the mechanism of nature regarded as a capacity of a being which is subject to special laws" of a moral sort. Because of this capacity for autonomy, the human person, thus defined with reference to freedom, like "every rational creature," is intrinsically valuable and must always be respected as having dignity (more of this in our next section). The human person is free both "in the negative sense" of being independent of all extrinsic causal determination and "in the positive sense" of being self-determined and autonomous in making choices in relation to the moral law. There is no empirical evidence that could verify or falsify our free choice in such a way as to establish scientific knowledge. "Thus the concept of freedom is made the regulative principle of reason." Freedom in both the negative and the positive senses must remain scientifically unknowable. It is one of the three "postulates of pure practical reason," which are rational "presuppositions" to which we are led by reflecting on our moral experience; though they can never constitute knowledge, they are regulative of meaningful human thought and action. "These postulates are those of immortality, of freedom . . . , and of the existence of God" (second *Critique*, 89–90, 33, 49–50, 137). Yet, as Kant observes in his *Logic*, freedom is unlike the other two postulates in that it can be proved by transcendental (though not by empirical) reasoning (he may have realized the dubious status of his assumption of the "highest good" in his moral argumentation for God and immortality). At times we do experience ourselves as morally obliged to do our duty. Let us, then, ask the transcendental question, "what is the necessary condition without which we could not experience any such obligation?" Since there cannot be any duty without the capacity to meet it, the answer is that we must be free to meet that obligation or not: "One cannot provide nor prove objective reality for any idea [of pure reason] but for the idea of freedom; and this is the case because freedom is the condition of the *moral law*, whose reality is an axiom" (*Logic*, 98). If we did not have free, rational will, all values, including moral ones, would be either nonexistent or irrelevant to us.

13.8 Morality

The third of Kant's core philosophical questions, "What ought I to do?", shifts us from the speculative to the practical portion of his system in two dimensions. First (in this section), we shall consider how a person should behave as an individual moral agent; then, second (in our next section), we shall consider how we should structure our communities as social beings. Although his ethical theory is extremely famous and his sociopolitical philosophy far less so, it is too little recognized that he explicitly maintains "the primacy" of "practical reason" over "speculative reason" (second *Critique*, 124–126). In other words, for Kant, philosophy has an essentially pragmatic function – it is not abstract knowledge and speculation merely for their own sake but, rather, reasoning oriented toward choosing and acting well. Even the *Critique of Pure Reason*, the theoretical keystone of his entire system, aims to move us beyond what is and what may be to what *should* be. There he uses Hume's "is" versus "ought" distinction to repudiate the very sort of empirical approach to ethics that Hume represented: "Nothing is more reprehensible than to derive the laws prescribing what *ought to be done* from what *is done*." Our experience of phenomenal fact is always and necessarily contingent and limited; thus it is hopelessly inadequate as a basis for the moral law, which must be universal and unconditional. The world, seen from the "ought" perspective, is "a *moral world*," subject to the laws of morality, as "the sensible world," viewed from the "is" perspective of physical fact, is amoral and subject to the laws of natural science. The one world we humans inhabit can be legitimately regarded from two distinct perspectives, according to Kant's dual aspect theory. Thus, even if it were true, as a matter of fact, that humans naturally desire happiness above all other goods, that would only summarize the way the world actually *is*, and not establish anything about how it *ought* to be, which can only be established rationally, and not empirically. Because Leibniz subscribed to a dichotomy between "*the kingdom of grace*" and the "*kingdom of nature*," he was vulnerable to Hume's criticism as to how the former, a realm of the *ought*, could ever be derived from or clearly related to the latter, a realm of what empirically *is*, despite the claim that humans somehow have a foot in each world. But Kant does not have that problem because he thinks them two dimensions of one and the same world, with the moral laws of what morally *ought* to be and natural laws explaining what empirically *is* being independent of each other (first *Critique*, 313, 636–641). Thus he does not make the mistake, which ethical empiricists cannot help making, of trying to derive what *ought* to be from what *is*.

Nevertheless, this is not to say that all facts are empirical and that there are no moral facts. As Kant explicitly holds, "the moral law is given" as a non-sensible "fact, as it were, of reason." It is not a mere hypothesis or even a mere "postulate," but the object of our moral, as opposed to sensible, experience. Objects of external sensibility are outside us, while our sense of duty can only be experienced in our own minds. Yet both can be continuously astonishing, as he famously writes (in words that would later serve as his epitaph): "Two things fill the mind with ever new and increasing admiration and awe, the oftener and more steadily we reflect on them: the starry heaven above me and the moral law within me" (second *Critique*, 48, 166). Somehow, mysteriously, our freedom allows us rationally to determine how our bodies will act, against inclination and passionate desire – contrary to Hume's deterministic view that reason can only serve the passions. Nor are Kant's critics correct when they attribute to him the outrageous view that moral action utterly divorces reason from all feelings, including pleasurable ones, whatsoever. He explicitly writes that it is "a mark" of genuine moral virtue that a person should have a "happy" heart in doing his or her duty and that the moral resolution "to do better in the future" than we have done in the past should "beget a joyous frame of mind" in good people. Even if we could eliminate all feelings from the moral life, it would be unnatural and undesirable. But it is impossible. And, since "ought" implies "can," it is absurd to suppose that, as moral agents, we should be purely rational and devoid of all feeling. Morality cannot ever require the impossible, as "duty demands nothing of us which we cannot do." For example, we are morally required to improve our characters, which can be quite difficult; but "when the moral law commands that we *ought* now to be better men, it follows inevitably that we must *be able* to be better men" (*Religion*, 19n., 43, 46). The autonomy of human reason is such that it can resist the temptations of inclination and passionate desire and also achieve an integrated balance with feelings.

We now turn to Kant's most famous and influential treatment of ethics, his *Grounding for the Metaphysics of Morals*. He immediately explains why he opposes the empirical approach of, say, Hobbes and Hume: if any ethical principle "is to be morally valid, i.e., is to be valid as a ground of obligation, then it must carry with it absolute necessity" and certainty. But any empirical approach, as such, "is only very contingent and uncertain." Therefore every empirical approach to ethics must be inadequate. Promising someday in the future to publish a complete "metaphysics of morals" built on this *Grounding* (which he did 12 years later), he makes it clear that here he is sharply focused on "establishing the supreme principle of morality," which is the categorical imperative. He argues that the only "good without qualification" is "a *good* will." Any combination of other values – including "talents of the mind," such as intelligence and cleverness, "qualities of temperament," such as courage and perseverance, and "gifts of fortune," such as wealth and power – can be dangerous if divorced from a good will and even pernicious if connected with ill will. By contrast, a good will, like a unique "jewel," that shines by its own internal light, is intrinsically good and needs nothing else to make it valuable. So what is a "good will"? It is one which habitually tries to do its duty out of respect for the moral law. Thus, deliberately doing one's duty is a necessary, but not a sufficient, condition of being a person of good will. One must do it for the right motive, out of a sense of duty or respect for the moral law. It is a matter of dispute whether this motive must be pure with no presence of inclination assisting in order for an act to be one of good will. And it must be admitted that Kant occasionally – as in his example of the unsympathetic philanthropist – does indicate that an act of good will must be done "solely from duty." But he is merely highlighting those sorts of actions that are most *obviously* acts of good will – namely, those done out of a sense of duty against our inclinations. It would be better to say that an act of good will must be motivated, at least in part, by a sense of duty. Thus the charitable person whose beneficence is motivated by both compassion and a sense of duty would be acting out of good will. So what is duty? "Duty is the necessity of an action done out of respect for the law" of morality. This is, of course, a moral – rather than a physical or metaphysical – "necessity." Kant next provides his first statement of his ultimate principle of moral duty: "I should never act except in such a way that I can also will that my maxim should become a universal law" of morality. (By a "maxim" he means the subjective principle of will that explains why one chooses to act in a particular way.) The idea here is that we should be able rationally to universalize any action in accordance with moral duty. This provides us with a test we can use to show that certain sorts of action are morally wrong. For example, we know that "a false promise" cannot be rationally universalized, because doing so would render promises unbelievable, defeating the very purposes for attempting false promises, so that it fails the test, showing that "a false promise" must be wrong (*Ethical*, 2–5, 7–11, 13–15). This rationalistic approach to ethics has come to be called "deontology," because it is duty-based rather than consequentialist.

Kant realizes that egoists like Hobbes ascribe everything we voluntarily do to "a more or less refined self-love," rather than a concern for others for their own sakes or a sense of duty for duty's sake. And, more than a century before Freud, he recognizes that we can never "completely plumb the depths of the secret incentives of our actions," since we so often tend "to flatter ourselves" as operating under "a more noble motive" than mere self-interest. So we should be cautious about assuming that we have certain knowledge of anyone's motives, including even our own. What Kant thinks we can claim with certainty is that some actions are intrinsically obligatory and others morally wrong, regardless of what people think, feel, and say. Thus, for instance, we are morally obliged to try to be sincere with friends, even if nobody has ever fully lived up to that ideal (the "ought" being independent of the "is"). Moral laws hold true for all rational beings, human or otherwise. For, by their nature, they can come to grasp the ultimate principle of morality, which Kant calls the "categorical imperative." As an "imperative," it is a rational command expressible in terms of concepts like "ought" and "should"; it is "categorical" in the sense of being unconditional. Unlike "hypothetical" imperatives, which are conditioned by what is actually desired ("assertoric" ones) or by what might be desired ("problematic" ones), categorical imperatives are binding on moral agents, no matter what. Kant holds that, while there are innumerable hypothetical imperatives, "there is only one categorical imperative," although it can be stated in various ways, which may be more or less helpful, depending on the sort of moral judgment to be made. The first formulation of it, which we can call the principle of universalizability (already considered above), says, "Act only according to that maxim whereby you can at the same time will that it should become a universal law." If an action is morally permissible, then we could rationally will that it be universalized. Another way of putting it is, "Act as if the maxim of your action were to become through your will a universal law of nature." In other words, we should consider an action wrong unless it establishes a moral precedent which we could reasonably will that everyone else should follow. Moral duties can be analyzed as "perfect" or "imperfect," where a perfect one "permits no exception in the interest of inclination" and an imperfect one allows for discretion regarding under what circumstances we can try to meet it. We can also distinguish between duties to oneself and duties to other persons, so that there are four possible combinations. Kant shows how we can use the principle of universalizability to see that four different sorts of actions, each representing a violation of one of the four different kinds of duties, are morally wrong: (i) suicide is a violation of the perfect obligation to self not to try to destroy one's own life; (ii) a false promise is a violation of the perfect obligation to other persons not to try to deceive them; (iii) a life of intentionally undeveloped talents is a violation of an imperfect obligation to oneself to try, at least some of the time, to develop at least some of our talents (we can pick and choose which ones and when); and (iv) a life of social apathy, never trying to help anyone who is in need, even when we are in a position to do so, is a violation of the imperfect obligation to others of beneficence (again, it is an imperfect duty in the sense that we can exercise discretion regarding whom to try to help and when) (*Ethical*, 19–20, 23–32). These examples are helpful illustrations of how the principle can be applied.

One of the most remarkable features of Kant's ethics is that the categorical imperative applies to "all rational beings" as moral agents, regardless of gender, ethnic origin, socioeconomic status, and so forth. Even rational beings that are not human, such as extraterrestrial intelligent life or God, would be subject to morality and covered by it as persons having "absolute worth" as "ends in themselves." As opposed to mere "things," which are properly treated as objects to be used "merely as means" to the ends of persons, the latter must always be treated with respect. This leads us to a second formulation of the categorical imperative: "Act in such a way that you treat humanity, whether in your own person or in the person of another, always at the same time as an end and never simply as a means." The qualifier "simply" is important here; of course, we must use other people as means to our ends to some extent, and this is morally legitimate so long as we do not treat them *merely* thus. Also we should remember that, though Kant calls this a "principle of humanity," it would apply even to nonhuman persons, if we ever had dealings with any. Kant shows how this second formulation can be used as an ethical test by applying it to his same four examples of suicide, false promises, a life of intentionally undeveloped talents, and a life of never trying to help anyone else. In setting up "the third practical principle" or formulation of the categorical imperative, Kant observes that in making truly moral decisions a rational being or person must act autonomously, as if casting a vote to help in the "legislation of universal law." The "ethical commonwealth" to which all moral agents, as such, belong is now called "a kingdom of ends"; it is a free and equal association of all persons as rational beings and autonomous agents, a spiritual society governed by moral law, analogous to a political society governed by civil law. Kant considers God its "sovereign," while every other person (again, regardless of gender, ethnic origin, socioeconomic status, and even species) belongs to it "as a member." As such, every person has "dignity, i.e., unconditional and incomparable worth" (above all possible price), intrinsically valuable and worthy of respect; indeed, Kant's principle of humanity is sometimes called a "respect for persons" principle, though not by Kant himself. It is because we belong to a species that comprises autonomous persons that we are members of the kingdom of ends: "Hence autonomy is the ground of the dignity of human nature and of every rational nature" (*Ethical*, 35–43).

A person is autonomous to the extent that she thinks for herself, makes her own decisions, and is responsible for her own actions. Exercising her autonomy is comparable to casting a vote to help determine what the moral law should be, as applying to all rational beings. This leads us to Kant's third formulation of the categorical imperative: "Act in accordance with the maxims of a member legislating universal laws for a merely possible kingdom of ends." Kant calls this third formulation "the principle of autonomy." No previous ethical theorist had ever so emphasized the centrality of human autonomy. This theory holds that we must rationally determine our duty for ourselves and try to do it regardless of any and all consequences. By contrast, every previous one attempted to tell us how we ought to act and be, in order to realize certain desirable consequences and avoid undesirable ones, making them more or less heteronomous and rendering their principles merely hypothetical, conditioned by a regard for alleged consequences (e.g. if you want to save your soul, or be happy, or go to heaven, or minimize conflict with others, or fulfill your human nature, or have others like you, act thus). Only Kant so clearly maintains that you must use your own reason to judge for yourself what is right and your own autonomous will to choose it, just because it is the right thing to do, regardless of consequences. For this theory, the end can never justify the means, in the sense that no end, regardless how desirable it may be, can justify our use of means we believe to be immoral. By contrast, every form of consequentialism, as such, allows some "wiggle room" for flexibility. Finally, Kant recognizes that his entire ethical theory presupposes that we are rational beings with free will (*Ethical*, 43–51), as he tries to show in his philosophy of human nature. Kant's ethical system becomes more detailed and elaborate in his two-volume *Metaphysics of Morals*, where he distinguishes between strict duties of justice (the first volume) and "broad" or "imperfect" duties of virtue (the second volume). We should also briefly consider his notorious treatment of honesty in "On a Supposed Right to Lie Because of Philanthropic Concerns." We might recall that honesty is a perfect duty that we must try to meet toward all other people all the time. But what if the only way we can help innocent people avoid severe harm is to lie on their behalf? Here the perfect duty of honesty conflicts with the imperfect duty of beneficence. Kant's highly controversial claim is that the perfect duty must take precedence over the imperfect one, and good ends can never justify evil means, so that we may not morally lie. (These later ideas of Kant's ethics are also contained in *Ethical*.)

13.9 Society

Interpreting Kant's "What ought I to do?" question more broadly gets us into his theory of sociopolitical ethics. We have seen how several great early modern philosophers (i.e. Hobbes, Locke, and Rousseau) employed the social contract theory, as well as how Hume trenchantly attacked it. In his work "On the Common Saying: 'This May be True in Theory, but it does not Apply in Practice,'" Kant presents a new version of the social contract theory. Unlike his predecessors, he holds that social union with others is not merely instrumentally valuable as a means to other ends (like survival and security), but is "an end in itself" that we have a moral duty to pursue and that requires "a civil state, i.e. a commonwealth." A social order is essential to protect "the *right* of men *under coercive public laws* by which each can be given what is due to him and secured against attack from any others." Justice requires the protection of everyone's freedom: "*Right* is the restriction of each individual's freedom so that it harmonizes with the freedom of everyone else." Civil laws and their enforcement are necessary to ensure public right. In a just civil constitution, as Rousseau recognized, citizens' freedom is protected, rather than threatened, by coercive external laws. In a republican commonwealth, citizens will help determine such laws in accordance with three a priori principles: "1. The *freedom* of every member of society as a *human being*. 2. The *equality* of each with all others as a *subject*. 3. The *independence* of each member of a commonwealth as a *citizen*." The first of these would call for a liberal tolerance of others. The second would mandate equality under the law for all citizens, including a measure of equal opportunity, but not a socialistic equality of possessions. The third would involve all fully vested citizens, directly or indirectly, in the legislating process. Kant holds that any adult male who both is "his *own master*" and has "some *property*" (which can include any skill, trade, artistic ability, or technical expertise that allows him "to support himself") should qualify as a citizen. We should not expect unanimous agreement but should make legislation a function of majority rule. A way Kant avoids Hume's critique is by clearly specifying that the social contract is "an *idea* of reason" rather than a historical fact. By belonging to society and benefiting from it, we implicitly and tacitly obligate ourselves to obey its laws and respect its established authorities. We are duty bound to contribute to "the public welfare," allowing others to pursue their own happiness in their own way, so long as "the lawful freedom and rights" of others are not violated. Rebellion against the social order is criminal, even in the face of tyrannical government. For if a subject is at odds with his sovereign, who can arbitrate between them? There would have to be an arbitrating power superior to the sovereign, which Kant thinks absurd. So he agrees with Hobbes and disagrees with Locke about citizens' right to revolt against tyranny. Even though he admits that they "have inalienable rights against the head of state," he denies that they can have any coercive authority to enforce them. For example, citizens should have freedom of expression, and it is wrong for a political sovereign to deny it; but revolutionary force can never legitimately be employed against him, even in defense of it (*Political*, 73–81, 84–86). Kant may well be wrong in denying a right to revolution, if, as many of us believe, a social contract is bilateral and imposes enforceable obligations on both citizens and their government officials alike.

In his "Idea for a Universal History with a Cosmopolitan Purpose," Kant writes, "*The greatest problem for the human species, the solution of which nature compels him to seek, is that of attaining a civil society which can administer justice universally.*" What makes this so very difficult is that people are both naturally drawn to establish social relations and divided by a natural "antagonism" toward one another. This "*unsocial sociability*" (to use his splendid phrase) makes it a delicate task to establish lawful order among them without nullifying their freedom. How can people submit to a governing master without abdicating their freedom? (This was Rousseau's problem as well, and Kant's answer generally agrees with his.) Through the social contract, we become our own masters collectively, each submitting to a lawful order he himself has helped establish. But this problem of a good society cannot be isolated from the need for just international relations as well. No society, regardless how internally harmonious, can be truly fulfilling if it is in conflict with its neighbors, involved in war and the preparation for war. Hence Kant calls for an international league of nations, "a federation of peoples," designed to resolve differences peacefully. Anticipating a point Hegel would make famous, Kant holds that nature is teleologically ordered so that human history pursues "the realization of a hidden plan" for gradual enlightenment, so that we cannot help caring about the future of our species (*Political*, 44–51).

"Perpetual Peace" is arguably Kant's best known social essay, as relevant today in explaining how we might minimize human conflict as it was more than two centuries ago. First, he helps us understand that "a mere truce" or temporary cessation of hostilities is not equivalent to a treaty designed to establish lasting peace. Second, states are human societies and not merely plots of land; as such, they should not be taken over by other states. "Standing armies," third, threaten war and should, therefore, be abolished. Fourth, states should not go into debt in order to accumulate weapons of war. Fifth, no state should interfere with any other sovereign state's government. And, sixth, states should not employ disreputable practices internationally, such as political assassinations, genocidal extermination campaigns, and deceptive spying. Governments should be constitutional republics, based on principles of freedom, acceptance of lawful authority, and equality, adopting a separation of political powers, and representing the people's will. For this sort of government gives its people a vested interest in maintaining peace and avoiding war, except as a last resort. By a republic, he was not committing himself to democracy; and the opposite of republicanism was held to be despotism. A "*federation of peoples*" in an international league of nations could protect the peace and liberties of free peoples. Our cosmopolitan status as citizens of the world should promote the ideal of "Universal Hospitality" toward visiting foreigners. This cosmopolitan "universal community" should help us realize that "a violation of rights in *one* part of the world is felt *everywhere*." Nature seems to contrive to push us toward increasing international harmony, and certainly the terrors of war become more and more horrifying. These ideals, needless to say, could never easily be realized, but it is our duty to try to approach them. Kant condemns three cynical political maxims as immoral and destructive of peace and justice. The first would hold that people should act as they please and then be prepared to make necessary excuses for their misbehavior. The second would maintain that if they have done something wrong, they should just deny it. And the third is the old "divide and conquer" notion of pitting people against each other so that they can be weakened and more easily subjugated. These are the unjust principles of a political moralist, pragmatic and utilitarian, resorting to whatever means necessary to achieve desired ends. By contrast, Kant advocates moral politics, whereby public policy is ultimately directed by what is morally right. He thinks that, in the final analysis, there should be "no conflict whatever between morality and politics" that is truly good. All human rights should be respected as "sacred," never to be violated for selfish purposes. Kant also advocates a principle of publicity: "All actions affecting the rights of other human beings are wrong if their maxim is not compatible with their being made public." Thus, for example, he thinks armed revolution could only succeed if it were done surreptitiously and, thus, must be wrong. He realizes that so-called realists could dismiss these as empty ideals but insists that, in fact, human history has us gradually approaching their realization (*Political*, 93–97, 99–102, 105–108, 114, 120–126, 130).

Perhaps Kant's most systematic work of sociopolitical philosophy is his *Metaphysical Elements of Justice* (the first volume of his *Metaphysics of Morals*). In his theory of justice, as on so many topics, he breaks fresh ground – in this case, by essentially connecting matters of justice to the only fundamental innate right that all persons, as such, have the right to free choice and action (within reasonable limits, of course). The social virtue of justice, properly analyzed, (i) only has to do with external, practical interpersonal relations, (ii) only pertains to the relationships between one person's will and another's (not to mere wishes or desires or even needs), and (iii) does not significantly involve specific ends that people mean to bring about. Given these specifications, he writes, "Justice is therefore the aggregate of those conditions under which the will of one person can be conjoined with the will of another in accordance with a universal law of freedom." It is that last word that was new in the history of justice theory. "Hence the universal law of justice is: act externally in such a way that the free use of your will is compatible with the freedom of everyone according to a universal law." The ethical idea of universalizability has obviously been incorporated here. Justice would respect persons' freedom to do anything compatible with the freedom of all other persons in morally similar circumstances. I should be free to tear around in all sorts of ridiculous ways, so long as my doing so does not violate the freedom of anyone else. But Kant also argues that justice is compatible with coercion, when the latter is necessary to prevent violations of or severe threats against the freedom of others. Restraint and punishment limit others' freedom but can be justified as retribution for the abuse of freedom by a criminal. The social virtue of justice has to do with both "*Natural Law*" and "*positive (statutory) Law*," and we can legitimately speak of both innate rights and acquired rights. Kant maintains that "the one sole and original right belonging to every person by virtue of his humanity" – i.e. the only innate human right – is the right to freedom or "independence from the constraint of another person's will." Despite this talk of rights, we should recall that Kant's practical philosophy is essentially deontological or duty-based and not fundamentally rights-based. Rights are derivative from duties, and the reason we have an innate human right to freedom is that that is a transcendental condition of our ability to choose to act in accordance with duty. All other rights either follow from this one or are derived from civil law. Kant interestingly analyzes this innate right to freedom in three dimensions: (i) it involves an element of "innate *equality*," with no person bound to others in ways that could not be reciprocal; (ii) it involves an element of autonomy, with each person "his own master" as long as he has not committed an injustice calling for punishment; and (iii) it involves an element of political liberty "to do anything to others that does not of itself derogate from what is [properly] theirs" (*Justice*, 29–31, 37–38). On this theory, justice is essentially about freedom rather than, as for Hume, about property rights.

Nevertheless, Kant does include property rights in his discussion, defining my property as anything that belongs to me that nobody else can use without my consent without thus injuring me. If you were to take and use my car without my permission, you would deprive me of the freedom to use my own car while it was in your possession. If an external object does not belong to anyone, you might be free to appropriate it; if it does already belong to someone else, a just transaction could transfer ownership to you. People have a natural right to property (related to freedom), even apart from the arrangements of civil society, that is, even in a "*state of nature*." In a state of nature, Kant claims (against Hobbes), "there can be legitimate societies (for example, conjugal, paternal, domestic groups in general, and many others)" other than civil society. But Kant holds that we have a moral duty, independent of all pragmatic self-interest, to enter into juridical relations. A true civil society does require "coequal partnership" so that a relationship between master and servant does not qualify. Justice, as an alternative to violence, calls for a "postulate of public Law," which demands, "If you are so situated as to be unavoidably side by side with others, you ought to abandon the state of nature and enter, with all others, a juridical state of affairs, that is, a state of distributive legal justice." So, ethically speaking, we are morally obliged to enter into civil society with others, if we cannot avoid them; here Kant is saying something no previous social contract theorist had said. Our behavior toward other members of civil society should be governed by reciprocally binding rules, and coercion against others can be justifiable for purposes of self-defense or to protect society against those who would violate persons' rights (*Justice*, 42–43, 54, 114–115).

A "group of persons" united "under laws of justice" (which cannot exist in a state of nature, where there would be no competent, disinterested judge to settle disputes) is called a state. Any political state must include three sorts of authorities, however they be united or separated. "The sovereign authority resides in the person of the legislator; the executive authority resides in the person of the ruler (in conformity to law), and the judicial authority (which assigns to everyone what is his own by law) resides in the person of the judge." In our own country, these three are held by the separate powers of the houses of Congress, the President, and the judiciary system. Legislative authority should reflect the "general united Will of the people" – namely, the citizens. A citizen can be identified by these attributes: "first, the lawful *freedom* to obey no law other than one to which he has given his consent," at least indirectly by committing himself to abide by majority rule; "second, the civil *equality* of having among the people no superior" other than one over whom he can have reciprocal rights, as by the holding of political office; and, "third, the attribute of civil *self-sufficiency*," such that he owes "his existence and support, not to the arbitrary will of another person in the society, but rather to his own rights and powers as a member of the commonwealth." Since citizens ought to have voting rights, which requires that they be "independent," rather than physically or economically or legally under another's control, Kant thinks women "lack civil personality" and are "passive citizens." That is, because they depend on men (their fathers, husbands, sons, and so on) for their "support (subsistence and protection)," they should not vote, serve on juries, or hold public office. Now Kant did say that "everyone" ought to be "able to work up" from passive citizenship to active citizenship, as male children typically do by becoming independent (*Justice*, 118–121); but he did not explicitly say that women could do this (making this part of his theory odious to many contemporary feminists).

The social contract constituting the moral foundation of a civil society need not be interpreted as "a historical fact," for Kant. Whether or not there ever was a time when people, by mutual agreement, actually passed from a state of nature to a state of civil society, as we have seen, they allegedly never have a moral right to violent rebellion against the state, Kant calling it "high treason," deserving of "no lesser punishment than death." A sovereign has rights over his subjects but no duties that he can be violently coerced into fulfilling, Kant holds (agreeing with Hobbes). A tyrant might be nonviolently removed from power, but not justly punished; and the idea of executing a deposed monarch, like "Charles I [of England] or Louis XVI [of France]" filled Kant with moral revulsion. He did allow that the "negative resistance" of a Parliament or Congress to a ruler's demands can be morally legitimate, as when a legislature refuses to fund a chief executive's war. Also, if a past revolution succeeded and generated a new constitution (as in America), its illegitimate beginnings cannot excuse its "subjects from being bound to accept the new order of things as good citizens." A chief executive, Kant thinks, has the right to "levy taxes" on his subjects "for their conservation" – for example, "for the relief of the poor, foundling hospitals and churches," the rich being legitimately taxed to help support the poor (*Justice*, 123–128, 131–132).

Magistrates have a duty to punish convicted criminals, who, in turn, can forfeit their citizenship rights. As public crimes are brought before a criminal court, private crimes are brought before a civil court. Some crimes, like assault and battery, are violent, while others, such as embezzlement, are merely base. We should never try to justify punishing a person on utilitarian grounds, for that would be using him merely as a means to desirable consequences. Rather a criminal should be punished because his crime merits punishment. "The law concerning punishment is a categorical imperative," Kant wrote, adding, "and woe to him who rummages around in the winding paths of a theory of happiness looking for some advantage to be gained." (Whether or not he had read it, Jeremy Bentham's seminal work of utilitarian theory, which we shall consider in the next chapter, had been published eight years earlier.) The "principle of equality" must govern the handing out of punishments to prevent one criminal getting an extremely harsh punishment while another gets very little for the same crime. It is appropriate to require mandatory labor from criminals to pay for their own upkeep. And Kant holds that the death penalty is the only morally equitable punishment for convicted, premeditated murderers, as "there is no substitute" that will satisfy the requirements of legal justice. Yet Kant disapproves of mistreating, as with torture, even the worst offenders (*Justice*, 137–140). The only legitimate justification for any sort of punishment is purportedly retribution – never utilitarian restraint.

Like so many political philosophers before him, Kant distinguishes three basic sorts of government: "a single person in the state has command over all, or several persons who are equal and united have command over all the rest, or all the people together have command over each person, including themselves." He calls these types of government, respectively, "*autocractic, aristocratic*, or *democratic*." He considers democracy "the most complex" and the least efficient; autocracy is the simplest and most efficient, though also "the most dangerous" in being susceptible to oppressive despotism. No matter what form of government is preferred, a good society requires a republican constitution, "in which the law is self-governing and does not depend on any particular Person" for its maintenance. Any of the three forms of government could be compatible with such a republican constitution, where "every true republic is and can be nothing else than a representative system of the people if it is to protect the rights of its citizens." Such a constitution will protect the rights of all, whether the chief executive power lie in one, some, or all citizens (*Justice*, 146–149).

As a cosmopolitan, Kant recognized sooner than most the need for peaceful international relations among free states. "A league of nations in accordance with the Idea of an original social contract is necessary" for mutual security against hostile aggression. But this alliance should take the form of a confederation of equal states rather than one of dictatorial domination. They should work together to promote peace and minimize the threats of war. Yet countries have a right to go to war to protect themselves from attack and injury and to maintain "a balance of power" needed for purposes of security. But even in a just war, people's rights must be respected, and there are reasonable limits that cannot rightly be transgressed. Even when fought with just cause, a merely punitive war or a war bent on extermination or a war of subjugation would be unjust. Spies, assassins, guerrillas, and rumor-mongers all strike Kant as wrong means of waging war, as are treachery and the plundering of the vanquished. A just treaty should never deprive conquered peoples of their civil freedom or establish any form of "hereditary slavery" and should include "a general amnesty." The rights of neutrality, security, and reciprocal defensive alliances must be respected (*Justice*, 152, 154–157).

The ideal of "perpetual peace" is, of course, a hypothetical "Idea" toward which we should aim, even if it will never be fully realized. This ideal of "a universal union of states" must be freely accepted rather than coercive. Kant realizes that, with advancing human capacities, the idea of a world community would come closer to a reality, so that even oceans would no longer so separate nations that they could safely ignore each other. As we discover new lands, it can be permissible to appropriate them, but not by forcibly taking them from their inhabitants. (Kant interestingly uses those of "the American Indians" as an example.) So peace and justice ought to be our constant goals in our dealings with all other persons. This may best be achieved by promoting free societies living under republican constitutions and the rule of law (*Justice*, 158–163). These were remarkably progressive views on international relations.

13.10   Review

As premodern Western philosophers have long been measured against the twin giants Plato and Aristotle, so modern (and contemporary) ones must find the two titans Hume and Kant to be most powerful figures for comparison. In many ways, they represent a dividing point in modern philosophy – the pre-Humean portion generally leading up to the crisis that Hume's skepticism precipitated and the post-Kantian portion having to come to terms with the revolutionary approach of Kant himself to responding to that crisis. It was the transcendental method that allowed Kant to break new ground in developing a middle ground between traditional rationalism and traditional empiricism. Future rationalists (such as Hegel) and future empiricists (such as Mill) would have to take Kant into consideration in formulating their views. So what was it that was so new here? In the area of knowledge, it was the untried combination of transcendental or critical idealism, on the one hand, and empirical realism, on the other. In the area of reality, it was Kant's unique sort of dualism that viewed the realm of phenomenal appearances and that of noumenal reality (or things in themselves) as two dimensions of the same reality. On the topic of God, it was a commitment to the infinitely perfect Deity, whose reality cannot be speculatively proved but can allegedly be argued for on the basis of our moral experience. In the area of humanity, it was his analysis of the human person as essentially a free and rational moral agent. In the area of freedom, it was his artful use of his dualism to show that we are determined as physical beings but self-determined as minds, the two not representing any contradiction. In the area of morality, it was his use of the categorical imperative as a basis for establishing an ethical "ought" that is not a function of any empirical "is." In the area of society, it was his fresh and internationally extended use of the social contract to establish our obligations of justice to others at all levels of sociopolitical relations.[2] Not only did he contribute something importantly new in all these areas, but he weaved these contributions together into a unified, coherent philosophical system against which ideological opponents would contend and from which the movement of German idealism would emerge.

13.11 Another Perspective

Gabrielle Émilie Le Tonnelier de Breteuil (1706–1749) was born in Paris to an aristocratic family. At the age of 18, she married the Marquis Florent-Claude de Châtelet-Lamont, becoming the Marquise du Châtelet; they had three children. In 1733, she met Voltaire, with whom she had a serious romantic and intellectual relationship. Having learned several languages (including Latin, German, English, Greek, and Italian) in her youth, under his influence she studied philosophy, mathematics, and physical science. She translated Newton's *Principia Mathematica* and wrote a commentary on it, helping to facilitate the move of French scientists from Cartesian to Newtonian physics. In 1740, she published her *Foundations of Physics*, with a second edition being published a couple of years later. She also wrote a "Discourse on Happiness."[3] In 1748, she became pregnant by her lover and died of a pulmonary embolism six days after giving birth. Frederick the Great of Prussia admired her work and corresponded with her. Some of her ideas appeared in several sections of the great *Encyclopedia* of Diderot and D'Alembert.

Du Châtelet is a pre-Kantian philosopher. Although their lives overlapped, it is doubtful that she ever read or even heard of Kant, as she died a couple of years after his first publication. (For his part, Kant was somewhat familiar with her work, and one of his critics even accused him of taking over some of her ideas.) While there is nothing novel in her views to be considered here that might stretch already current canonical positions, Du Châtelet's philosophy is far more typical of mainstream eighteenth-century philosophy than Kant's. Thus, an examination of some of her views can help emphasize how radical and revolutionary his ideas were.

Let us start with her most important philosophical work, *The Foundations of Physics*, in which she adopts a surprisingly Leibnizian position. All philosophical and scientific knowledge must allegedly be grounded in self-evident principles, which can be held with certainty and can be applied in a rationally certain way (unlike Descartes's principle of clarity and distinctness, which misled him into the false conviction that the essence of bodies consists "only of extension"). The most basic of these principles, as Leibniz showed us, are those of noncontradiction, which is the foundation of all necessary truths, and of sufficient reason, the foundation of "all contingent truths." Whatever violates the principle of noncontradiction is impossible, and whatever does not do so is possible; but for a possibility to be actual, there must also be a sufficient reason for its actuality. This even extends beyond matters of theoretical speculation: "The principle of sufficient reason is also the foundation of the rules and customs founded only on what is called propriety" (718–723). Because Kant was so

---

2 For more on Kant, see ch. IV of *Twelve Great Philosophers*, by Wayne P. Pomerleau (New York: Ardsley House, 1997), and ch. 6 of *Western Philosophies of Religion*, by Wayne P. Pomerleau (New York: Ardsley House, 1998).
3 All references in this section will be to *Early Modern Philosophy: An Anthology*, ed. by Lisa Shapiro and Marcy P. Lascano (Peterborough, Canada: Broadview Press, 2022).

13.11 Another Perspective | **223**

influenced by the Leibnizian-Wolffian philosophy, this is compatible with his thinking. But it never occurs to Du Châtelet (or to anyone else prior to Kant's revolutionary first *Critique*) that possibility, contingent existence, and necessity might be a priori structures of the mind itself.

The same is true of the concept of substance, which she defines as *"that which conserves the essential determinations and the constant attributes, while the modes in it vary and succeed one another"*; though this definition of substance as "a durable and modifiable subject" is a serviceable one, it does not escape Locke's epistemological misgivings. She also adopts the Leibnizian view that space is "nothing but the order of coexisting things"; she never suspects that it might be a transcendental concept innate to the human mind rather than objectively independent. Du Châtelet also endorses Leibniz's view that the ontological building blocks of reality are monads, "simple beings having no extension," and thus "indivisible." These monads are not material and have no shape or physical dimensions; they are essentially psychic centers of force, "the real substances." She advocates the Leibnizian view that souls are like mirrors representing the entire universe, however obscurely (729–730, 736, 739, 743–747). She does not succeed, any more than Leibniz himself did, in explaining how bodies, entirely comprised of non-extended monads, can only be perceived as extended or why this does not make the Creator a deceiver. At any rate, her epistemology is such that, unlike Kant, she cannot find a middle ground between such dogmatic metaphysical claims and skepticism.

Let us now turn to her "Discourse on Happiness," which, while not Leibnizian, again breaks no new ground and is at loggerheads with Kant's position, being more popularly acceptable than his view. Early on, in reading her essay, one suspects that she is a eudaemonist, seeing the pursuit of happiness as ultimate, a hedonist, measuring human happiness in terms of pleasure and the absence of pain, and an egoist, seeing one's goal of securing one's own happiness as paramount. When these suspicions get verified by her text, we might very well identify her position with Hobbes's, though she presents it in more attractive language. She analyzes five requirements for happiness: "In order to be happy, one must have freed oneself of prejudices, one must be virtuous, healthy, have tastes and passions, and be susceptible to illusions." Uncritically held prejudices lead to trouble, particularly when provoking our choices; however, she is not opposed to observing conventional "proprieties," as they help us to get along better with others in our culture. Without a virtuous regard for the well-being of our own society, we are likely to miss out on our own happiness. Being healthy and having good taste and reasonable passions are, perhaps, self-explanatory. Finally, illusions provide an agreeable basis for hope and effort in the face of adversity and failure. A key sentence supporting the characterizations of hedonism and egoism is this: "One must begin by saying to oneself, and by convincing oneself, that we have nothing to do in the world but to obtain for ourselves some agreeable sensations and feelings." All of this, needless to say, is contrary to the Kantian position, which is opposed to egoism, to hedonism, and even to eudaimonism (though not, of course, to happiness itself). One area where she diverges from the Hobbesian position, however, is that she thinks the most pleasurable passion and the one most conducive to our own happiness is the love of others. Where she can agree with both Hobbes and Kant is in thinking that our surest path to happiness is that directed by reason (749–752, 755–756, 758).

14

Jeremy Bentham

Source: C. Fox, 1838, after H. W. Pickersgill./Wellcome Collection/Public Domain

14.1 Overview

Before we turn to the two most important German idealists following Kant, we shall now consider a thinker who represents a striking alternative. In the distinguished line of British empiricists, Jeremy Bentham was the most significant one between Hume and Mill; as he was significantly influenced by the former, so he significantly influenced the latter. He was among the most practical

Modern European Philosophers, First Edition. Wayne P. Pomerleau.
© 2023 John Wiley & Sons, Inc. Published 2023 by John Wiley & Sons, Inc.

philosophers we are studying here, being little interested in abstract thought for its own sake. Though he is best known as the founder of the utilitarian movement, there is more to his philosophy than that would suggest.

14.2 Biography

Jeremy Bentham was born on February 15, 1748, in Houndsditch, London. His father, Jeremiah Bentham, was a wealthy lawyer who intended that he also become a lawyer and, perhaps, move into a successful political career. The boy was a prodigy, allegedly reading English history while still a toddler, studying Latin at the age of three, learning to play a violin, attending the Westminster school at the age of seven, and then being sent to Queen's College, Oxford, in 1760. There, at the age of 12, he was required to sign the Thirty-nine Articles of faith for the Church of England,[1] despite his hesitant doubts about doing so (*Works*, x, 37). After graduating in 1763, he started studying law, before taking a Master's degree in 1766. However, despite his father's wishes, he chose the life of a writer, dedicated to reforming the law, rather than actively practicing law or seeking political office. He had heard lectures by the famous William Blackstone and been unimpressed by their uncritical allegiance to the *status quo*. In 1776, he published (anonymously) *A Fragment on Government*, a critique of Blackstone's *Commentaries on the Laws of England*, arguing that laws should be socially useful, following Hume, whose writings on practical philosophy had left him feeling "as if scales had fallen" from his eyes and as having offered sufficient reason to dismiss the social contract theory. In this first great work of Bentham's, an old idea of public utility as a criterion of moral value (which we have seen in Hume) became irretrievably publicized: "*It is the greatest happiness of the greatest number that is the measure of right and wrong*" (*Reader*, 62–63, 45).

Although his father had raised him as a Tory, even as a young man, he desired a reform of the *status quo*. But, failing to realize that those in power opposed reform, he mistakenly supposed that they only needed to be instructed in what reforms would be good for society to embrace them. In 1789, his masterpiece, *An Introduction to the Principles of Morals and Legislation* (first printed in 1781), was published. This great book is generally regarded as the seminal text of the utilitarian movement. In 1791, his *Panopticon* appeared, presenting a blueprint for a model prison, featuring central heating, running water, and clean spaces, devoted to the humane reform of criminals; as he said, it was to be "a mill for grinding rogues honest, and idle men industrious" (*Works*, x, 66, 185, 226); there guards could constantly monitor their prisoners, without themselves being seen, and convicts would be paid for their labor. Bentham's 20-year effort to promote this plan never led to the British government's accepting it, though, in 1813, he was given 23,000 pounds as compensation for his efforts.

---

1 References to Bentham's writings will be to *The Works of Jeremy Bentham* (hereafter called *Works*, followed by volume and page numbers), ed. by John Bowring, 11 volumes (Edinburgh: William Tait, 1838–1843; reprinted in New York in 1962), to *A Bentham Reader* (hereafter called *Reader*), ed. by Mary Peter Mack (New York: Pegasus, 1969), to *Bentham's Theory of Fictions* (hereafter called *Fictions*), by C.K. Ogden (Paterson, NJ: Littlefield, Adams, 1959), to *Jeremy Bentham* (hereafter called *Bentham*), by Charles W. Everett (New York: Dell, 1966), to *An Introduction to the Principles of Morals and Legislation* (hereafter called *Principles*), by Jeremy Bentham (New York: Hafner Press, 1948), to *Selected Writings* (hereafter called *Writings*), by Jeremy Bentham, ed. by Stephen G. Englemann (New Haven: Yale Univ. Press, 2011), to *The Influence of Natural Religion on the Temporal Happiness of Mankind* (hereafter called *Religion*), by Jeremy Bentham (Amherst, NY: Prometheus, 2003), and to *The Panopticon Writings* (hereafter called *Panopticon*), by Jeremy Bentham (London: Verso, 1995).

226 | *14 Jeremy Bentham*

In 1792, Bentham's father died, leaving him independently well-off. That same year, three years after the French Revolution, he was made an honorary French citizen. For almost all of his last 40 years, he led a quiet life of writing at home but attracted a circle of followers. In 1808, he met James Mill, who was to become an important disciple, and, through him, Mill's son, John Stuart Mill, who would become the most famous philosophical proponent of classical utilitarianism. For a while, the Mill family leased a house on Bentham's property. These last four decades of his life were largely devoted to writings designed to reform legislation in such a way as to yield progressive utilitarian consequences. He was pursuing the ideal of creating a "Pannomion," or comprehensive legal code. In 1823, he cofounded with the senior Mill the *Westminster Review*, a journal for philosophical radicals, devoted to progressive reform, edited by his disciple, John Bowring, whom he later called "the most intimate friend I have" (*Works*, x, 591). Bentham inspired the founding of University College in London in 1826, the first nonsectarian college in England; his utilitarian follower John Austin, a distinguished legal theorist, was appointed its first professor of jurisprudence in 1829. Bentham died peacefully, in the company of Bowring, on June 6, 1832, the day before the great Reform Bill, calling for significant progressive legislation, would receive royal approval. After he died, as he had instructed, his body was dissected, with the skeleton reconstructed, with a wax head replacing his own mummified head, dressed in his own clothes, and displayed sitting in a wooden case with a glass front in University College, London.

14.3 Knowledge

In addition to being influenced by Hume's psychology and practical philosophy, Bentham was also influenced by Locke's empirical method, seeing all knowledge as derived from sensation. His goal was to apply this approach to moral, political, and legal knowledge. He employs a method of reductive analysis, reducing complexes to the simpler elements comprising them and wholes to their constituent parts. This leads to the sort of individualism we have already seen in earlier British philosophers. Bentham is a nominalist, considering all real entities to be particulars – particular humans, particular values, particular laws, particular punishments, etc. The only universals are fictitious universal terms – e.g. humanity, value in general, the law, and punishment generally. They are fictions in that they masquerade as real entities without being perceptible objects of possible sensation. These fictions can be useful; but they can also prove dangerously misleading.

Even before his *Fragment on Government* was published, Bentham wrote about this in his *Commonplace Book*, holding that such fictions are seductive falsehoods used to give the mask of objectivity to our judgments. After repeated use of such concepts (saying, for example, that justice requires defiance of the law), familiarity can psychologically incline us to treat them as if they were real entities (*Works*, x, 74–75). So long as we can believe what we are saying and, thus, be credible, it is more impressive to say, "I have to do that because justice requires it" than to say, "I want to do that because I imagine that doing it will benefit me." In the Preface to the first edition of *A Fragment on Government*, Bentham complains of lawyers (including Blackstone) employing such tactics for their own purposes, writing that "the pestilential breath of Fiction poisons" the law (*Works*, i, 235).

His theory of fictions is his most significant contribution (however negative) to his analysis of knowledge, in general, and of the deceptions leading to false claims of knowledge, in particular. The psychology of belief (we might recall that Hume had discussed the relationship between believing in something and merely entertaining a fiction) and the power of language converge to lead us to mistake the "names of fictitious entities" for the "names of real entities." Here is where Bentham's technique of "paraphrasis" comes into play. "By the word *paraphrasis* may be designated that sort of exposition which may be afforded to transmuting into a proposition, having for its subject some real entity, a proposition which has not for its subject any other than a fictitious entity." If one says, "Duty requires that we miss class today," it will be difficult to refute the claim. By contrast, if the desire for clarity leads us to convert that subject referring to a fictitious entity (Bentham points out that propositions typically comprise three parts – subjects, predicates, and the copula verbs linguistically linking them) into one whose subject is empirically verifiable or falsifiable, we might say, "The third provision of the institution's attendance policy requires that we miss class today." Successful paraphrasis converts an obscure proposition into one that can be related to perception – including to the sensations of pleasure and pain (we shall soon consider Bentham's hedonism). Thus, we have read and/or heard the third provision of the attendance policy and can imagine our being punished for violating it. Notice that "Duty" is a "noun-substantive" as is the "attendance policy"; but the first refers to "a fictitious entity," while the second refers to "a real entity" (*Fictions*, 15–16, 86–89, 114), which can be empirically consulted. The replacement of the first by the second helps protect us from mistaken assumptions of knowledge.

14.4 Reality

Just as Bentham's explorations of epistemology were motivated by their possible practical implications, the same is true of his explorations of metaphysics; as the former could help inoculate us against mistaking fictitious beliefs for knowledge, so the latter could help us to differentiate myth from reality. Thus it is revealing that his most important contributions to ontology, the general theory of being that comprises physical and mental science, are contained in his theory of fictions. Bentham's basic ontological concept is that of an "entity," which is a subject of discourse referred to by "a noun-substantive." (This basic concept corresponds to that of "*substance*," used by metaphysicians.) Entities can be either "*perceptible*," such as the chairs on which we are sitting, or "*inferential*," such as God is for believers. Both of these sorts of entities can be "either real or fictitious." We know perceptible entities through sense experience, while we are led to think of inferential ones through reasoning. "A perceptible real entity is, in one word, a body." Bodies are of three sorts, "viz. animal, vegetable, and mineral" (e.g. horses, flowers, and rocks). Bodies are either animate or inanimate, and a living one can be sensitive or not; a living sensitive one is an animal, a living one that is not sensitive is a vegetable, and a nonliving one is a mineral. The inferential entities we think about tend to be either human or superhuman – a disembodied soul being an example of the first and God an example of the second. An entity we believe to be real is one to which we ascribe existence. Our own ideas are perceptible realities, while those of other people are inferred realities. An inferred entity could be real, like atoms, or fictitious, like wookies, or either, such as ghosts (*Fictions*, 7–11, 16).

Interestingly enough, physical entities that are inferred rather than perceptible can be fictitious yet still practically useful. Such are (Aristotelian) categories, such as substance, quantity, quality, relation, time, and place. Yet some of those predicates, such as the first four, can be applied to mental entities also, both human and superhuman. "The word *matter* is but the name of a class of fictitious entities, springing out of the sort of real entity" that is physical and perceptible, or a body. All perceptible bodies are physical, limited, "real entities" in time and occupying space, while perceptions are "real psychical entities" – i.e. mental. Relations, including those of "diversity" and "identity," which is but "the negation of diversity," though fictitious entities, are very useful. "Whatsoever two entities, real or fictitious, come to receive names, and thus to receive their nominal existence," they can be related to each other as different or identical. Thus we can say that

Socrates's wife was a shrew, while Berkeley's wife was not. A particularly valuable relation between fictitious entities is that "between cause and effect." The idea of causation is derived from relating time and place, two fictitious ideas; physical causation involves one body somehow affecting the motion of another in time and space. Particularly useful to us is the distinction between voluntary causation, such as animals are capable of manifesting, and nonvoluntary causation, such as non-sentient entities can generate; voluntary actions can be productive or unproductive. When the agent is sentient, we can speak of its voluntary acts in terms of final causation, referring to "the *end* which the agent had in view"; this, in turn, can be conceived in terms of some good to be attained, which can be interpreted in terms of some pleasure(s) to be attained and/or some pain(s) to be reduced or avoided. This notion of final causality is meaningful "only in so far as the effect is the result of design on the part of a sensitive being – a being susceptible of pains and pleasures." Thus, for example, the (Aristotelian) notion of an acorn's final cause being to grow into an oak tree is mere nonsense, assuming that an acorn is insentient. We should note one last point regarding Bentham's theory of reality: all words referring to immaterial reality are meaningful only insofar as they are derived from physical reality – "the root of the *immaterial* will be found in the *material*" (*Fictions*, 19–21, 23–27, 29, 39, 41, 49, 137). We can anticipate that this ontology will find little need for God, immaterial souls, or freedom of the will.

14.5 God

It is telling that Bentham worked on a book on religion without clearly affirming or denying the existence of God. This book, *The Influence of Natural Religion on the Temporal Happiness of Mankind*, is a peculiar book, relative to the Christian culture in which it was published in 1822. Its contents were so controversial that it was published under a pseudonym, that of "Philip Beauchamp." But, furthermore, Bentham seems to have written it with a scholar named George Grote (a founding father of the secular University College in London); and we do not know how much (or which parts) of the book each of the coauthors wrote. The book is not patently atheistic, in that it does not explicitly deny the existence of God. It does eschew revealed religion in favor of natural religion, avoiding the issue of whether God is myth or reality; one might say that it is simply agnostic regarding the existence of God (and the reality of a human afterlife). Instead of considering whether religious beliefs are true, the book focuses on whether they tend to make people happy (in this life). And its findings turn out to be strikingly negative.

In the Preface, there appears the controversial utilitarian claim that the advantages and disadvantages of religious beliefs should be calculated before we bother to consider whether or not they are true; this subordination of truth to utility will strike many of us as problematic. We are also told that "whenever the general term *religion* is used" in the book, what is meant is "*mere Natural* Religion, apart from Revelation"; this seems appropriate, given the epistemological background of radical empiricism. The practical consequences of natural religion, over the millennia of human history, have involved a mixture of "bad effects" and "good effects." The issue, then, has to do with their relative balance. Natural religion purports to establish "the existence of an almighty Being, by whom pains and pleasures will be dispensed to mankind, during an infinite and future state of existence." This characterization of God as an administrator of carrot and stick, of rewards and punishments, in the afterlife allows us to consider whether believing in such a deity tends to make us happier or more miserable in this life. Given that the afterlife involves the unknown and that we naturally fear the unknown, it seems obvious that the primary consequence is worry over the "impending pain and misery" to which we may be subjected in the hereafter. Of course, it would be possible for a believer in the afterlife to be confident that it will hold permanent "blissful" joy; but most believers seem to suffer from expecting the worst. Adding to the terror is the fact that natural (as opposed to revealed) religion gives us no guidance as to how we ought to behave in order to escape damnation. It is no wonder that our imaginations run wild and torment us (*Religion*, 19–21, 29–33, 36, 38, 41).

Who would most stand to benefit if such belief were correct? It would be those who most actively advocate the belief – which means priests and ministers, who devote their lives to such advocacy, providing them with motivation to remain active in the cause. Who would most stand to lose if such belief were correct? It would be atheists and others who critically question religious belief – in other words, skeptical philosophers. Next to priests and ministers, believers who flatter the deity and humiliate themselves could hope for rewards; next to atheists and skeptics, those who are irreverent would be targets of divine wrath. Our alleged "*duty to God*" would lead us to prostitute our autonomy, which would be "detrimental to human felicity in this life." Thus, it would seem that the consequence of religious faith, in this life, at least, tends to be "injurious to an extent incalculably greater than it is beneficial." Then there are specific religious deprivations – including fasting, celibacy, and the gratuitous renunciation of time, labor, and property – that, by their very nature, involve a systematic denial of pleasure. So the fears and anxieties accompanying religious belief tend to render our lives less satisfying and our coming death more terrifying. Priests and ministers profit from this, in that gullible believers can be dominated by them. The former get to dictate to the latter what are the rules of divine law that must be obeyed, as well as the remedies that are necessary for violators to be forgiven (*Religion*, 57–58, 67, 93, 99, 156–157). Obviously, this is a distinctly one-sided assessment, placing no emphasis whatsoever on love, charity, kindness, joy, and transcendent purposefulness; and it seems distinctly Humean.

14.6 Humanity

As Bentham's theory of reality inclines him toward religious skepticism, so it inclines him toward a naturalistic philosophy of human nature – tending to materialism rather than to taking seriously the notion of humans being or having immaterial souls. Indeed, we shall not find much here that we have not already seen in Hobbes and/or Hume. Nevertheless, the first five chapters of Bentham's *Principles* have proved very influential.

From the outset, he establishes an uncompromising position of universal human hedonism: "Nature has placed mankind under the governance of two sovereign masters, *pain* and *pleasure*." It may or may not be telling how he places these two motivating forces in the order given. At any rate, he continues, "It is for them alone to point out what we ought to do" (this is a clear statement of ethical hedonism) as also "to determine what we shall do" (this clearly expresses his psychological hedonism). No exception is allowed for reason choosing to follow duty or to pursue abstract good apart from all hedonistic goals having to do with pleasures and pains. "They govern us in all we do, in all we say, in all we think." Bentham's fundamental teaching, his "*principle of utility*" (also called "the *greatest happiness* or *greatest felicity* principle"), is irrevocably based on this hedonism. But happiness (and pleasure), as well as unhappiness (and pain), can only be experienced by individuals; while we do sometimes speak of collective happiness and unhappiness, that is merely a figure of speech. "The community is a fictitious *body*, composed of the individual persons who are considered as constituting as it were its *members*." Thus, whenever we refer to "the interest of the community," we really mean the collective interests of the various individual members comprising it. Now people generally tend to pursue their own perceived self-interest; yet they

14 Jeremy Bentham

sometimes are motivated to act for the good of others, even, at times, at the expense of self-interest. Indeed, we can come to identify our own perceived good with that of others. The explanation for this has to do with the vast range of possible human pleasures (and pains), including "the pleasures of good-will, the pleasures of sympathy, or the pleasures of the benevolent or social affections." These are the only pleasures (and pains) Bentham considers "*extra-regarding*," all the others being "*self-regarding*"; nevertheless, these are quite important. Because we find benevolence pleasurable, we can use associationist psychology to explain our coming to identify with others' good (*Principles*, 1–3, 33–36, 41).

We can use reason to calculate whether one course of action is likely to prove more or less pleasurable than another in its consequences. But this process of setting up a hedonic calculus that will allow us to know which is the better action can turn out to be a seriously complex affair. Bentham maintains that we should consider seven different component characteristics of the pleasure to be achieved. First, its "*intensity*" – how deeply felt is it likely to be? Second, its "*duration*" – how long is it likely to last? Third, its "*certainty*" – how sure of it can we be before the fact? Fourth, its "*propinquity*" – how soon will it likely occur? Fifth, its "*fecundity*" – how fruitful is it likely to be in generating similar pleasures down the road? Sixth, its "*purity*" – how unlikely is it to generate painful consequences as well as the pleasurable ones intended? And, seventh, its "*extent*" – how many people are likely to be affected (pleasurably and/or painfully) by the consequences of the action? Notice two things concerning these seven measures of pleasures (*Principles*, 29–30): that they are all quantitative and that no discrimination is made based on who enjoys the pleasurable consequences. First, Bentham is infamously insistent that, quantitative considerations being equal, there is no reason to prefer one kind of pleasure over another kind: "Prejudice apart, the game of push-pin" [a simplistic, trivial children's game] "is of equal value with the arts and sciences of music and poetry" (*Works*, ii, 253). What we naturally and reasonably desire is whatever seems likely to maximize pleasure and minimize pain. But, then, pleasure and pain for whom? Here we get to the second point: in theory, it should make no difference whether the beneficiary of the pleasure (or the victim of the pain) is me or my mother or my best friend or a casual acquaintance or a complete stranger – as they all count equally. But now let us consider a third point, relative to the vast array of pleasures and pains possible in the wide range of our experience. The general types of pleasures and pains to which humans are susceptible do not vary from one culture to another – "in this point at least human nature may be pronounced to be every where the same." Nevertheless, we know that different people, people of different times in history, and people from different societies find different sorts of things pleasurable and painful. The explanation is a function of two variables – "the state and condition of the person" experiencing a potentially pleasurable or painful phenomenon and "the state and condition of the external object" being experienced (*Writings*, 155). At any rate, in theory, our desire for pleasure and aversion to pain provide us with the motivating force causing all voluntary action.

14.7 Freedom

Bentham's radical empiricism and materialistic ontology also leave no room for freedom in the sense of self-determined will. He says that he tries to "purposely abstain from" using "the words *voluntary* and *involuntary*" because of their ambiguity. Nevertheless, certain actions and/or their consequences are consciously intended. An intentional act is the product of the understanding, forming ideas regarding the circumstances, and the will, intending the act itself. Physical and psychological pain can be used to coerce a person's will – positive coercion being "*compulsion*" and negative coercion being "*restraint*" (*Principles*, 82n., 82, 71, 243). We have already seen that (perhaps despite himself) Bentham does distinguish between actions caused by "*volition*" occurring "in the mind of a sentient and self-moving being," such as an animal or human, and "those in the production of which volition is not seen to have place." Whenever volition plays a role, it is proper to expect will to be involved in the agent's actions (*Fictions*, 41).

But, we want to ask, is that will ever free to make its own choices? It would seem the answer is negative for Bentham as it was for Hobbes and Hume, although there appear to be few passages in which he explicitly discusses the matter. He is willing to speak of a person's civil "*liberty*" as a member of a state; but this is merely a political recognition that the person can act in certain ways without risking legal punishment, servitude being a severe curtailment of such liberty and slavery its annihilation (*Principles*, 263). On this view, as he says, "No law can be made that does not take something from liberty"; social order requires restraints on liberty, and law is the mechanism civil society uses to maintain social restraints. Bentham attacked the abstract values of the French Declaration of Rights of 1791, including its invocation of the alleged natural rights of freedom and equality. He thinks it factually erroneous to imagine that people are born free and equal, and that mere political rhetoric will never succeed in establishing that they should live as such (*Works*, ii, 493, 497–498). Still, we notice that Bentham has not even raised, let alone answered, the question posed at the beginning of this paragraph. And the failure to do so will have implications for moral and sociopolitical responsibility.

14.8 Morality

Given that we are limited altruists who are always fundamentally motivated by the hedonistic desire for pleasure and aversion to pain, yet (apparently) not free to make autonomous choices, independent of extrinsic causation, we are prepared to consider Bentham's view of how we ought to act. Part of the simplicity of his ethical system is that it boils down to a single empirical moral principle: "By the principle of utility is meant that principle which approves or disapproves of every action whatsoever, according to the tendency which it appears to have to augment or diminish the happiness of the party whose interest is in question; or, what is the same thing in other words, to promote or to oppose that happiness." This is so pivotal to his system that a few comments are in order. First, this (like Kant's categorical imperative) is not one moral rule among others but the single basic ethical principle, from which the multitude of moral rules allegedly can be derived. Second, it (like Hume's theory) purports to explain the legitimate basis for moral approval and disapproval. Third, it is primarily used to morally evaluate human actions and only secondarily human agents. Fourth, it looks to the consequences those actions appear to tend to have (rather than always can be certain to have). Fifth, it is all about consequences likely to increase or decrease the happiness of the sentient beings that might be affected by those actions. And, sixth, these include the public actions of governments as well as the private ones of individuals. "By utility is meant that property in any object, whereby it tends to produce benefit, advantage, pleasure, good, or happiness (all this in the present case comes to the same things) or (what comes again to the same thing) to prevent the happening of mischief, pain, evil, or unhappiness to the party whose interest is considered," whether that party be a group or an individual (*Principles*, 2). We might observe that this is a form of ethical consequentialism (indeed, the most popular one in the world today), rendering morality relative to contingent empirical circumstances and likely consequences, rather than absolute. On this view, any action which is likely to increase the ratio of happiness over unhappiness is therefore the right action and, thus, morally obligatory. Any that tends to increase the ratio of unhappiness over happiness is wrong and,

14 Jeremy Bentham

thus, morally impermissible. And any that will likely produce an even balance of happiness and unhappiness is morally permissible to be done or not done.

Bentham makes it quite clear that there is no "direct proof" of the principle of utility, since it is a fundamental principle and, thus, the basis for proving other ethical matters. At the same time, he points out what he takes to be the folly of attempting to argue for any ethical conclusions without resorting to utility considerations. In the second chapter, he tries to show that the viable alternatives to the principle of utility are unacceptable. He takes the main two to be "the principle of *asceticism*," which turns utility upside down by approving of pain and disapproving of pleasure, and "the principle of *sympathy* and *antipathy*," which involves intuiting our own subjective feelings of approval and disapproval and using them as our criteria. A third derivative alternative that he calls "the *theological* principle" is a synthetic blend of some combination of the other three. Briefly, what is wrong with the principle of asceticism is that consistently putting it into practice on a large scale would have the effect of turning "this earth . . . into a hell." What is wrong with the principle of sympathy and antipathy is that it is so subjective and unstable, being based on fleeting feelings, that putting it into practice on a large scale would result in chaos, to the detriment of all (reminiscent of a Hobbesian state of nature). The problem with the theological principle is that it requires that we conform to the will of God; yet we have no way of knowing what that is. So, by a process of elimination, we are allegedly left with Bentham's principle of utility as the only viable one (*Principles*, 4–9, 13, 16, 21–23). From a critical perspective, what is wrong here is that more attractive alternatives have been left out of consideration – e.g. Kant's deontological one of the categorical imperative.

The third chapter covers the question of sanctions: if we violate the principle of utility, what sort of consequences should we reasonably worry about, which might prove a deterrent? Bentham claims that there are four of them and that "they may be termed the *physical*, the *political*, the *moral*, and the *religious*." Physical pain and suffering sometimes result from bad actions. Second, what he calls "political" sanctions particularly involve *legal* punishments. Third, what he calls "the *moral* or *popular sanction*" concerns the social responses of other people. And, fourth, for people of religious faith, the conviction that God will punish them can be a deterrent, even if they are not worried about any of the first three (*Principles*, 24–25). Let us take an example to illustrate how the four sanctions could apply, using one of an action that would have been considered morally wrong by most people in Christian England during Bentham's lifetime. Suppose that an Englishman, two hundred years ago, was deciding whether to cheat on his wife and commit adultery with a prostitute. What could he reasonably fear that might deter him from violating utilitarian rules against adultery and prostitution? First, there is the physical sanction of venereal disease (with no antibiotics developed yet); second, there is the political or legal sanction of being arrested, incarcerated, and fined for criminal activity; third, there is the popular or social sanction of humiliating disgrace, including his wife finding out and being fit to be tied over it; and, fourth, even if he should get away with all those, he may believe in the sort of God who misses nothing and will make sure that he is implacably punished and forever sorry.

Let us now return to Bentham's fourth chapter and its seven dimensions of the purely quantitative hedonic calculus. The idea is exclusively to use criteria that, in principle, can be quantified and will, therefore, be scientifically objective (*Principles*, 29–30). But let us invent an example to illustrate how the calculus might work and then use that example as a basis for generating a critique of this approach to ethics. Suppose that an ethics teacher is calculating final grades for her course and realizes that two of her students – Alpha, whom she likes, and Omega, whom she dislikes – both barely missed the passing mark. She feels tempted to pass Alpha and fail Omega. She knows that her university would regard as unjust her doing that and, thus, disapprove, perhaps with severe

14.8 Morality | **233**

penalties. But, she reasons, justice is merely an abstract concept, and the odds are nobody else will ever know what she has done. Let us now calculate. Alpha, who is worried about his final grade, is certain to experience intense pleasure, immediately upon finding out that he has passed, and it will endure a good while; his pleasure will be fruitful in relation to further studies and uncontaminated by any pain at all. Omega, by contrast, who is also worried about his prospects in this course, will surely feel the pain of having his fears realized, and that pain will last quite a while, beginning as soon as he gets the bad news. His pain will be fruitful, in that it will affect his attitude toward related coursework in the future. But the pain is "impure" in that Omega will learn a lesson, buckle down, and start studying, giving him a sense of accomplishment and better grades in the future – maybe. Then there is the teacher herself. She can be proud that she gave Omega the grade he deserved but ashamed that her personal animus against him was a determining reason. She can be pleased to think that she contributed to Alpha's happiness but suffer some remorse over treating him differently for unprofessional reasons. She knows herself well enough to predict that those bad feelings will last longer than the good ones; both sorts will be felt from the beginning of her acting, and both involve a mixture of pleasure and pain for her. But implications for her self-image as a professor going forward will be more lastingly negative, as she will get over the good feelings but be haunted for the rest of her career by worry that she will be found out and punished. Assuming these are the only three persons who will be affected by her decision, what should she do?

Now let us use these two hypothetical examples to develop a critique of Bentham's ethical model. First, his four sanctions may or may not be effective in deterring the would-be adulterer from violating the rules, as he may not believe in God and have circumstantial reasons to think he can be cautious enough to avoid the other sanctions as well. There is no internal sanction of conscience that might support the rules anyhow. So here we encounter a problem comparable to that of the one of the "sensible knave" that Hume faced; like his predecessor, Bentham needs to find a solution to it (more of this later). Second, regarding the tempted teacher, notice that we have not actually quantified the factors with units of pleasure and pain; to do so would seem ludicrously artificial, for what is a "unit" here anyway, how do we measure intensity, and so forth? Third, ultimately, there is no way of predicting what consequences will and will not ensue in the future, given that circumstances are never identical to those of past situations we use as our basis for judgment; our hypothetical teacher, like us, can only guess and hope for the best. Fourth, granted that we may be motivated by sympathy for others in our moral actions, why *should* we ever be, and, more pointedly, why *ought* we ever to sacrifice our own (perceived) self-interest for the (apparent) well-being of others? Here we find ourselves running headlong into Hume's is–ought problem with no basis for solving it. Fifth, by denying anything like natural rights – an idea he dismisses as "nonsense upon stilts" (*Works*, ii, 501) – Bentham leaves no room for justice except as what Hume called "public utility"; both of our hypothetical examples involve issues of justice, but it's hard to get any traction. And, sixth, why should we accept the counterintuitive idea that one person's happiness should be regarded as of equal value to any other's (Bentham attacks the abstract idea of equality)? The virtue of Bentham's theory is that it seems simple, nontechnical, and readily understandable; but, as these criticisms might suggest, its fatal flaw is that it is too simplistic.

Later, John Stuart Mill will adapt this ethical theory into a more sophisticated form. Yet his too will be an ethic that sees right and wrong as relative to circumstances and likely consequences. On this view, it would seem that no conceivable action can be categorically ruled out as absolutely wrong. Indeed, Bentham accepts the saying, "The End Justifies the Means," so long as "three conditions" are all jointly met: (i) the end sought must be good; (ii) to the extent that the means chosen is evil, that evil must be outweighed by the good to be achieved by the end; and (iii) the means must contain more good or less evil than any other means that might have been used to attain that end (*Bentham*, 194–195). Thus, to invoke a now banal hypothetical case, if the only way to save

14 Jeremy Bentham

19 innocent hostages is deliberately to kill one innocent hostage, then, on this utilitarian view, it would seem that might be not merely morally permissible, but even morally obligatory, which strikes many of us as ethically dubious.

14.9 Society

If all of us consistently acted in accord with the principle of utility, if we would curb our selfish tendencies to act against the interests of others and civil society, if we could always subordinate our individual desires to the good of the community, then we might have no need for political society. But, for Bentham, these are too many ifs contrary to factual reality. We do need political society, including law, government, and enforcement powers to manage and limit interpersonal conflict. These were his abiding, dominant interests, even if most of his pursuit of them were nonphilosophical. His assault on abstract concepts such as natural rights, the state of nature, the social contract, natural liberty, innate equality, natural law, etc., as pernicious "fictions" placed him closer to Hume's skepticism than to these ideas as they appeared in Hobbes (or Locke, for that matter). Not only does he consider them unfounded fancies, but they are counterproductive in that they are readily used to buttress up the *status quo* and impede progressive reform.

Bentham agrees with Hume that society of some sort (family, tribe, clan, etc.) is necessary for humans to survive. But human nature is such that a larger political society is also necessary. The first principle of morality also is that of politics: "The right and proper end of government in every political community, is the greatest happiness of the greatest number." As we have seen, self-interest usually motivates most of our voluntary actions: "In the general tenor of life, in every human breast, self-regarding interest is predominant." This leads to a second principle of political society, "the principle of self-preference." This suggests a permanent possibility of competition for limited desirable resources, without which we would not need to manage and limit interpersonal conflict. As the first principle indicates "what *ought to be*" and the second "what *is*," so a third indicates "the *means*" to bringing about what ought to be. Bentham calls this one the "*junction-of-interests-prescribing* principle." Peace, civil order, decency, and fair treatment are consequences of a society of people serving their own interests by acting in accordance with the principle of utility. By doing what is in their own enlightened self-interest, they serve the general interests of society as well (*Works*, ix, 5–6).

While the notions of natural rights and absolute duties are "fictions," for Bentham, rights and obligations are functions of constitutional, criminal, and civil law. As he writes, "The law prohibits me from killing you – it imposes upon me the *obligation* not to kill you – it grants you the *right* not to be killed by me – it converts into an *offence* the positive act of killing you – it requires of me the negative *service* of abstaining from killing you." This theory later came to be called legal positivism. Where the law neither requires nor prohibits, people are free – i.e. unrestrained – to act or not as they prefer. In practice, the universal happiness prescribed by the principle of utility often translates into "a *maximum* . . . of comfort and security" for as many people as possible, even though that may seem a passive sort of pleasure (*Works*, iii, 159, 452). Another principle that he thinks government should try to abide by is one whereby it avoids disappointing people's reasonable expectations; he calls this (notice how he has a penchant for making up names for principles) "the *disappointment-preventing principle*" (*Works*, v, 416). If the powers-that-be took away your car to give it to your socially more popular neighbor, the odds are that your resentment would outweigh his joy.

As people bound by law, then, we have duties and rights. As Bentham writes in *Principles*, our "duties, therefore, may be either *extra-regarding* or *self-regarding*: extra-regarding have rights to correspond to them: self-regarding, none." When we violate our extra-regarding duties, we are liable to be also violating rights and become subject to punishment. If we do not have freedom of will, such that we can sometimes exercise autonomous choice independent of extrinsic causal determination, it is problematic how we can ever be sufficiently responsible for anything we do so that we can be justly punished. But another way of looking at it, putting aside issues of justice, is that a well-administered penal system can cause a serious decrease in criminal activity by way of negative conditioning. The law would be toothless in preventing violations of rights and duties without a system of enforcement mechanisms. Every law, as a restriction of liberty, can be seen as evil designed to minimize the evil of "mischief." Yet "all punishment is mischief: all punishment in itself is evil." The mischief or evil of arresting, trying, sentencing, and punishing assumed criminals, however, is justifiable to the extent that the good it does outweighs the mischief it involves. Punishment should never be inflicted in any combination of four cases: (i) where it is "*groundless*," because there is no harm it is deterring; (ii) where it is "*inefficacious*" or incapable of deterring the mischief there is; (iii) where is it "*unprofitable*, or too *expensive*," because it causes more harm than it prevents; and (iv) where it is "*needless*," in that the mischief being deterred would cease anyhow. While we cannot afford to explore them, Bentham works out a series of rules that should govern good utilitarian punishment (*Principles*, 225n., 170–171, 179–185). As the chief function of constitutional, criminal, and civil law is thought to be protection, so the fundamental utilitarian purpose of punishment is to deter future crime rather than to exact retribution (as for Kant). Without a system of punishment, we would not have stable government; and without stable government, there could be no civil society. Of particular interest in his day, as in ours, was capital punishment. Early on, Bentham wrote on this topic, leaning in favor of its abolition, as it tends to be ineffective in deterring people other than the convicted criminal from committing further crimes and inevitably involves the risk of excessively harsh and irremediable error; but, further, paradoxically, it can be counterproductive in encouraging crimes by fostering a culture of death in which the state is killing its own citizens (*Works*, i, 525–532). But also, as we have seen, given that we need to punish criminals in order to deter crime and that society must be protected, even prisons need to be reformed so that criminals are treated humanely, which could help generate the good consequence of rehabilitation, as well as that of deterrence (*Panopticon*, 33–35, 50). This is a plausible theory of punishment that coherently follows from the application of utility.

Let us conclude this section by briefly considering a few more key social pieces of Bentham's utilitarian agenda: equality, broader voting rights, freedom of expression, sexism, slavery, the treatment of animals, and sexual behavior. Even though he spurned the idea of innate equality as a fiction, he does value equality under the law, viewing it in terms of a balanced "*distribution*" of "*benefits*" and/ or of "*burdens*." In general, equality under the law is good in that it makes most people happy (*Works*, ii, 271–272). Bentham calls for "*virtual universality of suffrage*," meaning that rational adult citizens should be given voting rights – his justification again being public utility (*Works*, iii, 452–453). He defends freedom of expression, including "the liberty of the press," as conducive to good order and social tranquility, providing an effective "check upon the conduct of the ruling few" in government who might be tempted to abuse their power (*Works*, ii, 277–279). His "principle of equality" should extend to females as well as to males, including the area of voting rights (*Works*, ix, 108). In an interesting footnote in his *Principles*, he castigates the "tyranny" of both sexism and slavery. In another (more famous) footnote, he indicates that it is sentience, rather than rationality, that ought to give animals moral standing, saying that "the question is not, can they *reason*? Nor, can they *talk*? But, can they *suffer*?" Because nonhuman animals suffer pain, they matter. He even speculates that, at some time in the future, they may acquire rights against cruel treatment, as Black people were then starting to do (*Principles*, 268n., 311n.). Another area in which Bentham is remarkably progressive concerns a tolerance for sexual behavior deviating from the norms of Judeo-Christian society. He analyzes eight different sorts of sex acts in which humans can engage and the five types of offense that "irregular" ones can cause, maintaining that adultery and rape are the worst, because they involve, respectively, injury to the spouse and the violent use of force. But where mutually willing adults enjoy pleasure, while harming nobody, utility points in the direction of tolerance, including regarding homosexual sex (*Writings*, 37–42, 70, 74, 78–79, 83, 85). These are all steps in the direction of progressive reform, aimed at maximizing human happiness and well-being.

14.10 Review

We have seen how Bentham's radical empiricism and materialistic ontology lead him to skepticism regarding God and to a hedonistic view of humans as limited altruists, determined in their actions. The principle of utility is his central, seminal moral principle; he hopes it can be used to generate and apply a concrete hedonistic calculus for distinguishing right from wrong actions. He is intent on applying this to matters of law, government, and political society, avoiding the mesmerizing fictions of abstract concepts. Opinions regarding his work have proved very varied. Karl Marx is quite unfair in calling him an insipid, pedantic philistine who was nothing more than a spokesman for the mentality of bourgeois shopkeepers. John Stuart Mill was closer to the mark in calling him, not a great philosopher, but a great philosophical reformer. For all of his limitations as a thinker, probably more good has been done under the influence of the movement he founded than due to that of any other modern secular ethic.

15

Johann Gottlieb Fichte

Source: R. F. Jones & G. H. Turnbull/Wikimedia Commons/Public Domain

15.1 Overview

Fichte, who took it upon himself to transform Kant's critical philosophy into a metaphysical idealism, is often regarded as the most important transitional German philosopher between Kant and Hegel but is significant in his own right.[1] As these are the three greatest German idealists, as Fichte was influenced by Kant and influenced Hegel, perhaps something should be said about their seminal similarity and their distinguishing differences. To say that all three are idealists of some sort is

---

1 References to Fichte's writings will be to *The Popular Works of Johann Gottlieb Fichte* (hereafter called *Popular*, followed by volume and page numbers), trans. by William Smith, fourth edition, 2 volumes (London: Trübner & Co., 1889), to *Johann Gottlieb Fichte's Popular Works* (hereafter called *Works*), trans. by William Smith (London:

Modern European Philosophers, First Edition. Wayne P. Pomerleau.
© 2023 John Wiley & Sons, Inc. Published 2023 by John Wiley & Sons, Inc.

15 Johann Gottlieb Fichte

to attribute to them the view that the nature of reality is fundamentally mental or spiritual; in this respect, they are opposed to all naturalistic views, such as that of materialism, which would reduce mind or spirit to naturalistic processes or material things. (Thus, Hobbes was a materialistic naturalist and Berkeley an idealist.) We have seen that Kant characterized his position as "critical" idealism and also as "transcendental" idealism and what those characterizations meant. (Hegel, as we shall see, will label his own position "absolute" idealism.) Now the early Fichte (through 1800 at least) adopts both of Kant's labels to describe his own philosophy; and he sees himself as the legitimate successor to Kant (*Knowledge*, 21–22, 24, 4–5; *Wissenschaftslehre*, 26–27). However, at least three points importantly separate the two: first, Fichte rejects Kant's empirical realism; second, he also rejects any unknowable thing-in-itself; and, third, he accepts intellectual intuition, as opposed to his predecessor's claim that our only form of intuition is sensible. These differences will create a problem, for Fichte, of establishing any sort of objectivity outside the subjective mind – indeed, the early Fichte, at least, has been accused of being a subjective idealist, ever since Hegel raised the charge. Fichte's position can also be called an ethical idealism, as he pushes Kant's view of the primacy of practical reason over speculative reason even further than the earlier thinker did; indeed, in at least one place, he speaks of his own idealism as a "practical" one (*Knowledge*, 147). From a historical perspective, it is interesting how Fichte not only radicalized Kant's philosophy but also represented a catalyst for Hegel's subsequent radical form of idealism.

15.2   Biography

Johann Gottlieb Fichte was born on May 19, 1762, in Saxony, the oldest son of a poor ribbon weaver and head of a pious family. A local baron took an interest in him and funded his education. The story goes that the baron arrived at the church too late to hear the sermon but was told that a local boy would be able to recite it almost verbatim from memory, which the young Fichte did, earning the patronage of the baron. He was sent to a celebrated boarding school at Pforta (where Nietzsche also later studied), which prepared its pupils for the university and where the young Fichte received a good grounding in the classics. In 1780, he became a theology student at the University of Jena, later moving to the University of Leipzig. But when his patron died (in 1784), he had to end his education, without obtaining a degree. He then became a tutor for a prosperous family in Zurich, during which time he read Rousseau, became an enthusiast for the French Revolution (of 1789), and, most importantly, started studying Kant's philosophy around 1790. Under the influence of Spinoza, he had been flirting with becoming a determinist, but Kant's writings cured him of that. In 1790, he also became engaged to Johanna Rahn (*Works*, 4–5, 12–13).

Trübner & Co., 1873; reprinted by Forgotten Books, 2012), to *Attempt at a Critique of All Revelation*, by Johann Gottlieb Fichte (hereafter called *Revelation*), trans. by Garrett Green (Cambridge: Cambridge Univ. Press, 1978), to *Fichte: Early Philosophical Writings* (hereafter called *Writings*), trans. by Daniel Breazeale (Ithaca: Cornell Univ. Press, 1988), to *The Vocation of Man*, by Johann Gottlieb Fichte (hereafter called *Vocation*), trans. by Peter Preuss (Indianapolis: Hackett, 1987), to *Fichte: Science of Knowledge with the First and Second Introductions* (hereafter called *Knowledge*), ed. and trans. by Peter Heath and John Lachs (New York: Appleton-Century-Crofts, 1970), to *Introductions to the Wissenschaftslehre and Other Writings* (hereafter called *Wissenschaftslehre*), by J.G. Fichte, ed. and trans. by Daniel Breazeale (Indianapolis: Hackett, 1994), to *Fichte: Foundations of Transcendental Philosophy* (hereafter called *Foundations*), trans. and ed. by Daniel Breazeale (Ithaca: Cornell Univ. Press, 1992), to *The System of Ethics*, by Johann Gottlieb Fichte (hereafter called *Ethics*), trans. and ed. by Daniel Breazeale and Günter Zöller (Cambridge: Cambridge Univ. Press, 2005), to *Addresses to the German Nation*, by Johann Gottlieb Fichte (hereafter called *Addresses*), trans. by R.F. Jones and G.H. Turnbull, ed. by George Armstrong Kelly (New York: Harper & Row, 1968), and to *The Science of Rights*, by J.G. Fichte (hereafter called *Rights*), trans. by A.E. Kroeger (London: Routledge & Kegan Paul, 1970).

The following year, he moved to Warsaw, becoming a tutor in the house of a Polish nobleman. But this position turned out to be a bad experience, which ended rather abruptly. Returning to Germany, from Poland, Fichte decided to travel to Königsberg, in hopes of meeting Kant himself. Their first meeting, on July 4, 1791, went poorly, and Kant seemed unimpressed with the young man. In hopes of proving himself worthy, Fichte quickly produced a monograph relating Kant's philosophy to divine revelation (*Works*, 37–38). The great man was quite favorably impressed with the manuscript, and it was published under the title *Attempt at a Critique of All Revelation* in 1792. Because of some sort of oversight, the author's name was left off the published book. Because of the title, the content, and the Königsberg publisher, some reviewers jumped to the conclusion that it was a fourth *Critique* written by Kant. In setting the record straight, Kant praised the work, and Fichte quickly became famous.

Fichte had to support himself for a while longer as a tutor but was also publishing political writings, gaining himself a reputation as a democratic supporter of the French Revolution (a "Jacobin"). In 1793, he returned to Zurich and married Johanna Rahn. In December, partly on the recommendation of Goethe, he was invited to fill a philosophy chair at the University of Jena, replacing the Kantian Reinhold; he started teaching there in 1794 (*Works*, 51, 73–74). At first this appointment might have looked like a dream realized. That year, he published his *Science of Knowledge* (*Wissenschaftslehre*, a word he coined), his own idealistic version of Kant's critical philosophy, followed by a couple of introductions to it three years later. He remained dissatisfied with this early work, trying to rework it. In 1794, he also delivered five lectures published as *The Vocation of the Scholar*. In 1796, he published his *Science of Rights* (before Kant published his comparable work). In 1798, he published *The System of Ethics*, as well as "On the Basis of Our Belief in a Divine Governance of the World." The essay triggered charges of atheism and nihilism against him; his attempts to defend himself proved unsuccessful, and he had to resign his position at Jena, fleeing to Berlin in the summer of 1799. That same year, Kant publicly disavowed Fichte's *Science of Knowledge* as truly Kantian. The following year, Fichte published *The Vocation of Man*, which would become the most popular version of his philosophical system.

In 1805, after delivering his lectures on *The Characteristics of the Present Age* in Berlin, he taught for a semester at the University of Erlangen, before returning to Berlin. In 1806, his *Characteristics* was published, as was his *The Way towards the Blessed Life, or the Doctrine of Religion*. When the French army occupied Berlin that same year, he fled to Königsberg, Kant's city. Returning to French-occupied Berlin in 1807, he delivered his *Addresses to the German Nation*, published the following year. When the University of Berlin opened in 1810, Fichte was appointed its first dean of the philosophical faculty; he also was elected university rector for 1811–1812. In 1812, he published on ethics and political philosophy. In 1813, he canceled his lectures at the university, so that students could join the War of Liberation against Napoleon; and he himself joined the militia. His wife, Johanna, while serving as a volunteer nurse in a military hospital, caught typhus; although she recovered, Fichte also caught it and died of it (*Works*, 109–113, 117, 125–127, 129–130) on January 29, 1814. Their son, Immanuel Hermann Fichte, was himself a philosophy professor at the University of Tübingen. Fichte's chair in philosophy at Berlin remained vacant until 1818, when it was filled by Hegel.

15.3 Knowledge

Let us begin our analysis of Fichte's epistemology by considering his famous First Introduction to his *Science of Knowledge*; we shall quickly see that, while he adopts Kant's labels to describe his own philosophical system, their presentations are strikingly different, even if he insists, "my system is nothing other than the *Kantian*." He calls for us to begin (in rationalist fashion) with introspection: "Our concern is not with anything that lies outside you, but only with yourself." What we directly and immediately experience are our own states of consciousness, some of which are "accompanied by the feeling of freedom, others by the feeling of necessity." Philosophically, we must seek the ground of all experience, which, as such, cannot itself be empirical. "*The thing*" that is the object of typical experience is determined independently of our free will, while "*the intelligence*" that is the subject of our experience is also the subject of freedom. A philosophy that focuses on the subject in its freedom "is called *idealism*," while one that focuses on the object in its necessity he calls "*dogmatism*," adding that "these two are the only philosophical systems possible." While dogmatism purports to emphasize knowledge of the external "thing-in-itself," idealism begins with knowledge of the "self-in-itself." While Fichte favors the latter, he warns us that neither of these mutually opposed philosophies can refute the other. Experience requires some relationship between subject and object, idealism viewing the subject as the independent variable and dogmatism making the subject dependent on the determined object. What determines which of these two antithetical philosophies a thinker will embrace, given that neither is provable? Is it purely a matter of arbitrary whimsy? No, it is, rather, a function of that thinker's temperament and character: "what sort of philosophy one chooses depends, therefore, on what sort of man one is." While the dogmatic materialist views empirical things as fundamental, Fichte, the idealist, regards intellect as basic; while things are essentially passive, intellect is essentially active. "The intellect, for idealism, is an *act*." (Goethe famously wrote, in *Faust*, in the beginning was the act.) For example, the "law of causality," rather than being "a primordial law" of things, "is merely one of several ways of connecting the manifold" of experience, by intellect. While it may be disappointing that idealism must remain "unproved and unprovable," Fichte is convinced that "perfected transcendental idealism" can only be established by his *Wissenschaftslehre* or Science of Knowledge (*Knowledge*, 4–6, 8–10, 12–14, 16–17, 21–22, 24, 28).

In the Second Introduction to his *Science of Knowledge*, Fichte explores the sort of "*intellectual intuition*" his system requires on account of his anti-empiricism. This is what allegedly gives me "immediate consciousness that I act, and what I enact: it is that whereby I know something because I do it." We might notice here that its object is one's own actions. This intuition, like sensible intuition, "must be *brought under concepts*" in order to be known. It is the most reliable foundation we can have for constructing a philosophical system. Fichte insists that this approach to knowledge "is perfectly in accordance with the teaching of Kant, and is nothing other than Kantianism properly understood," although it would seem to be contrary to Kant's explicit claim that our only intuition is sensory, as Fichte admits. Without intellectual intuition, we must either give up on the thing-in-itself altogether or at least resign ourselves to the notion that it is unknowable. But Fichte maintains that its object is not existence but action. For example, the mandate to act in accordance with "the categorical imperative" is a matter of practical, rather than speculative, reason, which Kant failed to consider (*Knowledge*, 38, 41, 43–46).

Moving to the body of the *Science of Knowledge*, as has already been indicated, at one point Fichte characterizes his own brand of idealism as "practical" and explains that it "does not determine what *is*, but what *ought* to be." Now another significant departure from Kant has to do with dialectical reason, which the earlier thinker warned is nothing but a logic of illusion, reaching the insuperable dead end of antitheses that cannot be cognitively overcome. By contrast, Fichte (anticipating Hegel, who may have gotten the idea from him) sees dialectical reason as productively leading to knowledge: "Just as there can be no antithesis without synthesis, no synthesis without antithesis, so there can be neither without a thesis." So Kant was correct in recognizing that metaphysical thinking leads us from a thesis to opposition with its antithesis but incorrect in denying

15.3 Knowledge | **241**

that any reliable synthesis can ever emerge from that opposition. The "interplay" of antitheses is purportedly such that "a synthetic unity" can emerge as "*an absolute conjoining and holding fast of opposites.*" If they are adequately considered, neither a thesis nor its antithesis is possible without the other. Not only is there a necessity to their relationship, but in that relationship, he claims, they "are mutually determinable by each other." Needless to say, we are dealing here with logic, and the dynamics of dialectical reason involves "three logical principles" of critical value to our thinking: first, "that of *identity*, which is the foundation of all others" (e.g. every thesis is identical to itself); second, "the principle of *opposition*" (e.g. every thesis can involve an antithesis); and, third, "the *grounding* principle" (e.g. there must be some adequate basis for every relation). Here Fichte is plowing new epistemological ground (*Knowledge*, 147, 113, 85–86, 120, 145), moving beyond Kant (and in the direction of Hegel).

At this point, we can turn to Fichte's best known book, *The Vocation of Man*, to critically explore the implications of all this. (By the way, the "I" of narration here represents any person philosophizing, such as the reader, and not merely Fichte himself.) This book is divided into three major parts: Book One, on "Doubt," can be seen as representing a naturalistic skepticism rather like Hume's; Book Two, on "Knowledge," can be seen as representing a transcendental idealism, such as Kant's, that denies metaphysical knowledge; and Book Three, on intersubjective "Faith," can be seen as representing Fichte's own position. From an empirical standpoint, we imagine we know a great deal about objects and how they are related by causal determination. In a way, I think of myself as part of this chain of natural necessity; but I also think of myself as independent and free. My regret over some of what has been and my worry about some of what may come to be both presuppose the sort of freedom that would allow things to be otherwise. But, then, is the perspective of freedom or that of universal determinism correct? At the empirical level, I find it "impossible for me to decide; I simply have no sufficient reason for deciding one way or another," leaving me in skeptical doubt. After moving from empirical skepticism to the knowledge of transcendental idealism, Fichte changes the format to that of a dialogue between the narrating thinker and the voice of Spirit. All sense experience, even if doubtful, implies the possibility of self-awareness. As I think that I am sensing a tree, I can become aware of myself sensing it as well as of the tree – a subject experiencing that object. All perception, whether veridical or hallucinatory, implies the possibility of self-awareness. Indeed, strictly speaking, we directly experience only our own mental states, and not external objects at all. I "assume" that there is some substantial reality outside my mind somehow corresponding to ideas of the tree in my mind; but that substance of the tree is never directly experienced, only properties attributed to the tree. So, paradoxically, our direct consciousness is only of our own consciousness and never of external things, such as trees. Thus dogmatic empiricism must take a back seat to idealism. We should distinguish between "*immediate* knowledge," as of my own mental states, and "*mediated* knowledge," as of the colors and shapes I attribute to trees; and the latter must presuppose the former. While sensation, which gives me mediated awareness, is passive, productive reflection, which gives me immediate awareness, is active self-awareness. But this yields a merely subjective sort of idealism. As Spirit explains, "You realize that all knowledge is only knowledge of yourself, that your consciousness never goes beyond yourself, and that what you take to be a consciousness of the object is nothing but a consciousness of your *positing of an object*" (*Vocation*, 2–7, 11–12, 14–15, 20–22, 24, 26–29, 32–33, 36, 40–41, 44–45).

So far we have no grounds for transpersonal objectivity; if I can know anything at all at this level, it is only of my own subjective states and nothing objective about the tree. As we move into the section on "Faith," we realize that we want to believe we know all sorts of things about trees but have reason to worry about self-deception. Our purported knowledge of reality outside our own minds could all be illusory; we simply cannot tell. All alleged objective knowledge presupposes and is based on subjective faith, which is a product of the will. Thus faith turns out to be volitional rather than intellectual, generating a commitment to belief that transcends mere presentations of intellect (*Vocation*, 69–72). This is a subjective idealism, at least implicit in Fichte's early (i.e. pre-nineteenth-century) writings. The challenge will be to see if he can succeed in getting past it to some genuine extramental objectivity.

15.4 Reality

This, of course, opens up the issue with which Kant wrestled – namely, what, if anything, can we know of objective reality? His dualism allowed him to distinguish the reality of phenomenal appearances, which we can objectively know, from that of noumenal things-in-themselves, which we cannot. But, now, what about Fichte? Let us return to Book Three of his *Vocation of Man*. He realizes that, unless he can gain access to some objective reality to which his subjective presentations can correspond, then the latter will remain groundless. But, perhaps, what is needed is a move from speculative to practical reason. As Spirit exclaims, "Your vocation is not merely to know, but *to act* according to your knowledge." Whatever "I" may be, through intellectual intuition, I experience myself as existing. But one exists not for the sake of abstract reflection alone. "No, you exist for activity. Your activity, and your activity alone, determines your worth." Not only is action "the final purpose of knowledge" for us as subjects. "When I act I will without doubt know that I act and how I act." Here we have a synthesis of the "I" as acting subject and my actions as object. "Who am I? Subject and object in one," to the extent that I identify with my actions, so that there is a synthesis of the antitheses of subject and object. "My thinking and originating of a purpose," to be objectified in action, "is in its nature absolutely free and brings forth something from nothing." I know myself as subject and my actions as objects, experiencing these not merely as antithetical but as synthesized. This "real power of mind to act" is authenticated in experience that is intuitively certain. But have we reached the extramental reality of objective knowledge? Fichte seems to acknowledge a negative answer when he writes "let things be as they may with the reality of a sensible world outside of me. I have reality and I apprehend it. It lies in me and is native to myself" (*Vocation*, 67–69). From a critical perspective, we must wonder how this improves upon Kant, who gives us objective knowledge of phenomenal reality. But the "acting" at which Fichte arrives is still subjective, since the "activity" I intuitively know is that of my own free choices and not that of causal impact on the outside world. Is this not still the sort of solipsism that would seem to justify (Hegel's later) identifying Fichte's view as a subjective idealism? And can he not do better?

Let us consider a later work, *The Way towards the Blessed Life, or the Doctrine of Religion* (1806). On the surface, it would seem that it is making objective claims about reality, talking, as it does, about "Life, Love, and Blessedness." And, to be sure, he does try to distinguish "the True Life from the mere Apparent Life." The former is supposedly identified with "Being" and, ultimately, with "Absolute Being." By contrast, merely "Apparent Life" is identified with the "Nothingness" of death. The ultimate "object of the Love of the True Life" is Absolute Being or God, "the Infinite and Eternal," our unity with which constitutes "Blessedness." But will this get us out of the subjective realm of our own conceptions? Fichte himself admits that "the Eternal can be apprehended only by Thought, and is in no way approachable by us." Nor does it help to stipulate that the state of "Blessedness" consists in "unwavering repose in the One Eternal" Absolute Being and that "the condition of *becoming* blessed is the return of our love from the Many to the One." Unity with God is presumably through intellectual intuition, as "the Divine Existence" is essentially "nothing else than pure Thought." Fichte acknowledges (and resents the fact) that all this will be dismissed as "Mysticism" (*Works*, 389–395, 397–399, 404–406, 413–415). Be that as it may, this still does not get us out of the sphere of subjectivity. Fichte has hung on to Kant's subject–object dichotomy but denied his empirical realism. Unlike Kant, he maintains that we have intellectual intuition. But its only object so far is that of the "I" or ego and its ideas. This is solipsism, and it explains why Fichte's critics, starting with Hegel (who will use the dialectic to show that the subject–object dichotomy is bogus), have characterized his position as subjective idealism. Unless he can do what Descartes thought he had done, using intellectual intuition to prove the objective reality of something outside and independent of his own mind, he is stuck in solipsism. But, even then, a problem with claims to intellectual intuition is that they do not appear to be verifiable or falsifiable.

Let us, however, try to refocus on Fichte's characterization of his own philosophy as "practical" idealism, applying it to his approach here. He says that it is only through action, not abstract reflection, that the self achieves self-awareness. His analysis of "*intellectual intuition*" was in terms of "the immediate consciousness that I act, and what I enact: it is that whereby I know something because I do it." This might provide a helpful clue to how he proceeds. "The self's own positing of itself is thus its own pure activity. The *self posits itself*, and by virtue of this mere self-assertion it *exists*." This self-positing is an act of self-awareness, whereby the self functions as a self. "It is at once the agent and the product of action." The act of self-awareness is such that the self is both acting and realizing itself as a self. Not only are subject and object identical, but "action and deed are one and the same, and hence the 'I am' expresses an Act." This leads directly to a first principle: "*That whose being as essence consists simply in the fact that it posits itself as existing, is the self as absolute subject.*" There is an identity between the self-aware self and the self existing as fully realized. This first principle of self-identity relates to the logical law of identity, "A=A" (*Knowledge*, 147, 34, 38, 97–99).

But we have not yet burst the bounds of subjectivism. To do that, we must move to Fichte's second principle. The self-aware self is driven to act. But, sooner or later, in acting, it encounters the opposition of resistance by some other. "But that which is opposed to the self = the *not-self*." Since the self is not opposed to itself, it has encountered something other than itself, thus allegedly overcoming solipsism; "*so surely is a not-self opposed absolutely to the self.*" In terms of logic, "~A is not equal to A." If the self-positing self is viewed as a thesis, this not-self, whatever its nature, is its antithesis. "And with this we have also discovered the second basic principle of all human knowledge." We have generated negation (*Knowledge*, 104–105), allegedly moving beyond solipsistic subjectivism. But dialectical reason being what it is for Fichte (as opposed to what it was for Kant), a higher synthesis ought to emerge from these antitheses, which could constitute a third principle.

Both the not-self and the self to which it is opposed are posited as limited or divisible. But they are synthesized as parts of a more encompassing whole; and, ultimately, an "absolute self is posited as indivisible" or unlimited. Thus "the absolute self" includes both the limited self and the not-self; yet both of these can be differentiated from "the absolute self" in addition to being antithetically opposed to each other. Fichte calls his third principle "the *grounding* principle: A in part = ~A, and *vice versa*." The absolute self is identical in part with the limited self and in part with the not-self. That third principle holds, "*In the self I oppose a divisible not-self to the divisible self.*" While it remains cryptic what is the nature of that "absolute self," Fichte has supposedly established that something other than the subjective self is real, while also using his dialectical logic to analyze relations. Elsewhere, he speaks of the not-self that resists the activity of the subjective self as "a check" (*Knowledge*, 109–110, 191).

But does this completely and necessarily exonerate Fichte from the charge of subjectivism? It only does so to the extent that we can be confident that the "not-self" from which the subjective

244 | *15 Johann Gottlieb Fichte*

self feels opposition is not itself a part of that subjective self. It may be the case that Fichte did not imagine opposition internal to the subjective self (Hegel would soon write of a divided soul, alienated from itself). But might such an option not be a problem here? Finally, if the "absolute self" is, indeed, transcendent to the subjective self, is the former divine or, if not, what is its nature?

15.5 God

While the "absolute self" discussed in our previous section could be interpreted as referring to God, Fichte's *Science of Knowledge* makes no case for its system requiring a deity. Indeed, it may be revealing that he writes in a footnote that "the Science of Knowledge is not atheistic" (*Knowledge*, 245n.). Let us look elsewhere to see what he does say about this matter. In his *Attempt at a Critique of All Revelation*, following Kant, he argues for postulating a God, as we should postulate a moral law. This God would be needed to "produce that complete congruency between the morality and the happiness of finite rational beings," so that "he must be *totally just*"; Fichte also conceives of God here as omnipotent, omniscient, and eternal, although offering no good argument to show that God's being extremely powerful, extremely knowledgeable, and enduring for an extremely long duration would not suffice. So far, he acknowledges, we have only "a *theology*" but "no *religion*." The morality of our actions need not be a function of the divine will, although the Kantian perfect good would seem to be. Indeed, rendering the moral law a function of God's will would seem to make it transcendently alien, he says (anticipating Feuerbach), "and this alienation is the real *principle of religion*, insofar as it is to be used for determining the will." He writes, "God is to be thought of, in accordance with the postulates of reason, as that being who determines nature in conformity with the moral law." On this view, God freely causes the entire world of phenomenal appearances. But, of course, morality is a matter of freedom rather than of determination. Regarding divine revelation itself, it seems to be "merely problematic that anything at all could be a revelation," although Fichte does not categorically rule out the possibility. Before we start encouraging belief in revelation, at any rate, we should focus on trying to make people morally good (*Revelation*, 60–61, 63, 70, 73, 119–120, 151, 172). The influence of Kant is utterly evident here.

Let us next consider "On the Basis of Our Belief in a Divine Governance of the World," the essay that got Fichte in so much trouble. He again invokes "the so-called moral proof of a divine governance of the world," recognizing the importance of appealing to reason rather than settling for "an arbitrary assumption." The naturalistic perspective will inevitably dismiss transcendence as nonsense; but "the transcendental standpoint" must take it seriously. A "moral world order" requires a realm of freedom that is irreducible to the materialistic, deterministic processes of naturalism. I intuit freedom in myself, thus establishing the reality of "a supersensible world." To the extent that we could be mistaken in that intuition, we are operating at the level of rational faith rather than at that of certain knowledge. So far, so Kantian. But now comes the controversial part. Not content with the Kantian idea that the moral law and our own freedom lead us to a rational faith, Fichte claims, "This moral order is what we take to be *divine*. It is constituted by right action." This is a denial of any transcendent God and reduces religion to morality. He maintains that meaningful atheism simply consists in disobeying "one's own conscience." He does conceive of the moral order as dynamic and transcendent, acted upon by living persons like us. "This living and efficaciously acting moral order is itself God. We require no other God, nor can we grasp any other." In particular, the reality of God as a divine substance is dismissed as "impossible and contradictory," and a life of "joyful right action," stripping away superstition, should be regarded as "the true religion"

15.6 Humanity | **245**

(*Wissenschaftslehre*, 143–147, 150–152). This blatant reduction of religion to morality goes beyond any of the views of Kant published during his lifetime.

Turning to *The Vocation of Man*, we find Fichte becoming more cautious. Here he not only speaks of a higher "supersensible world" that is already present, rather than yet to come. But now he accepts an "infinite reason" living in a "purely spiritual order." This spiritual world has its own nonphysical law, whose source must be a free and "sublime will," with which we "finite rational beings" have "a spiritual bond," which is that of religion. This "infinite will," which he sometimes (in neo-Platonic fashion) calls "the One," is also "the voice of conscience within me." He both harks back to something like the occasionalism of Malebranche (in maintaining that we can only know and act on each other through the mediation of the One) and anticipates Hegel's panentheism (in suggesting that our reality is in the One rather than separate from it). Yet he does not entirely abandon the controversial views of his 1798 essay, as he claims that belief in our moral duty is itself faith in "the One Eternal Infinite Will." Our finite reason is depicted as existing and functioning in and through "infinite reason" rather than being independent. Not only are there suggestions of panentheism here, but there are also elements of mysticism, as when he writes of the "Sublime living Will, which no name can name and no concept encompass." Wanting to avoid anthropomorphism, Fichte accepts the fact that the infinite is humanly incomprehensible (*Vocation*, 99, 106–112) – which may or may not be why he so seldom uses the word "God" here.

Fichte's *Doctrine of Religion* (of 1806) still identifies "True Religion" with "right moral action." Its key doctrinal commitment seems to be that "God actually lives, moves, and perfects his work in us." This would seem to point to an immanent deity. What is being ruled out is a transcendent God separate from a world of creation: "There is absolutely no Being and no Life beyond the immediate Divine Life." It may be ambiguous, but this does not sound that far removed from Spinoza's panentheism. Human "Blessedness" (which Spinoza also emphasized) requires a willing acceptance of our dependence on the Divine (*Works*, 461, 464, 520). This would presumably be "True Religion," stripped of superstitious anthropomorphism. In a little essay from 1810, called "Outlines of the Doctrine of Knowledge," Fichte seems to return to comfortably speaking of "God," seeing our knowledge of divine Power as coming through "*Intuition*." We can learn that the "*One*" that is God can come to be "broken up into *Many*" (*Popular*, II, 501, 506, 511). Again this is ambiguous, but it would seem to intimate panentheism. Fichte does not seem to take very seriously the orthodox Christian view of a transcendent God.

15.6 Humanity

The most important source for Fichte's philosophy of human nature is, arguably, *The Vocation of Man*. Through intellectual intuition (which we have questioned), he is directly and immediately aware of his identity as a self contrasted with all external things; he is a subject, a knower of objects. In self-knowledge, he experiences an identity of subject and object. But every act of his consciousness implies at least a potential self-awareness. Also, he can use "the principle of causality" to go beyond intuition by means of inference. But, beyond our representations of things, there is no "thing in itself" to which we can ever have access. He writes that "*the consciousness of a thing outside of us is absolutely nothing more than the product of our own presentative capacity*." This is one of those jarring statements that gets (the early) Fichte branded as a subjective idealist; and he adds that "we know nothing more about the thing . . . than we posit through our consciousness." So what can he make of the mind–body relation, without slipping into Berkeleyan immaterialism? He seems to adopt a dual aspect theory: "I, the mental being, the pure intelligence, and I, this body in the physical world, are one and the same thing, only seen from two

15 Johann Gottlieb Fichte

sides, only apprehended in two different ways, the first by pure thinking, the second by external intuition." While we might form "*images*" of the self, strictly speaking, it is never given as a substantial object of experience, merely as a process of thinking. The voice of Spirit, speaking to the human interlocutor, utters the thesis statement of the book: "Your vocation is not merely to know, but *to act* according to your knowledge." The "dignity of human nature" is rooted in practical reason, and our thinking is anchored in our drives. By means of my thinking, choosing, and acting, in some sense, I produce the person I become. Perhaps exaggerating in his use of the adverb, Fichte adds, "I am thoroughly my own creation." I will to believe and act on my faith. Determined neither by chance nor by necessity, I am self-determined or free. Thus can arise the meaningful "ought" of duty or moral obligation. My vocation is to obey the dictates of conscience, and the natural world is my arena for action. Fichte indicates that it is reasonable to believe in some form of afterlife, as providing a more ultimate justification for what we experience here and now, so that, in some sense, "I *am* immortal." However, it is unclear what is to be the relationship between our "future life" and "infinite reason" (*Vocation*, 47–48, 53, 56, 59, 61, 63, 67, 73–75, 96–99, 123; for more on "Human Dignity," see *Writings*, 83–86, 145–151).

In *The System of Ethics*, Fichte articulates the flip side of human dignity after reiterating the importance of free action. As our dignity consists in our thinking and acting as autonomous moral agents, we lose respect and legitimate self-respect by denying our own freedom and succumbing to some deterministic "series of natural causality." Only the mind or spirit is capable of dignity and worthy of respect. "There can never be respect for what is empirical." This might seem to reflect a more negative attitude toward the body and the natural world than we saw in the empirical realist, Kant. Fichte tries to insist that their views are "compatible" and that his "does not diminish the dignity of humanity" (*Ethics*, 99–101, 135–136, 138, 244–245). Yet the attitude expressed toward our bodies and physical environment seems less than positive.

In *The Characteristics of the Present Age*, Fichte portrays humans as part of "a *World-plan*," as applied to "the progressive Life of the [human] *Race*, not of the Individual" human. On this view, the story of history is that of the greater realization of "the Freedom of Mankind," as developing "*according to Reason*." The two principal epochs of human history are that in which human relations are not primarily ordered according to rational freedom and that in which, for the most part, they are; this is the difference between reason functioning instinctively on our drives and reason operating through free choice. (We shall see something like this again in Hegel.) More analytically, Fichte lays out five periods of humanity's earthly existence: first, "*the State of Innocence of the Human Race*" living instinctively; second, "*the State of progressive Sin*," arising from disobeying external authority; third, "*the State of completed Sinfulness*" by means of a liberation from both instinct and external authority; fourth, "*the State of progressive Justification*" through rational knowledge; and, fifth, "*the State of completed Justification and Sanctification*" through autonomous practical reason. Different periods can coexist at any particular time; so it is a question of predominance. Fichte thinks his own culture, in the first decade of the nineteenth century, is mostly in the third period, liberating itself from the shackles of instinct and external authority, but not yet enlightened (*Popular*, 4–12, 16–18).

15.7 Freedom

Much of what should be said about Fichte's theory of freedom is covered in other sections of this chapter; but let us begin this one with a look at portions of *The Vocation of Man* that we have not yet considered. From the limited perspective of the sensible world, every physical event seems to be mechanistically determined, such that freedom "and the good will would be quite superfluous." Yet intuition reveals our freedom to us. Thus it is reasonable to view our dignity as consisting in the good will of freely following "the inner voice of conscience," as we can because we are *not* merely "dead mechanisms." Thus we already inhabit "the supersensible world," in addition to the sensible one (maintaining a Kantian dualism). As he puts the point, "I will not gain entry into the supernatural world only after I have been severed from connection with the earthly one. I already am and live in it now, far more truly than in the earthly." I am not only a being in the natural world, but also "a citizen of the realm of freedom," whose will can function as an efficient cause producing effects in the physical world. By freely choosing to raise my arm, I somehow make it happen; my will (somehow) can cause bodily effects. As there are physical laws of nature governing actions in the sensible world of causal determination, so there are moral laws governing actions in "the spiritual world" of freedom. Just as my will is not the author of the physical laws of nature, neither is it the source of the moral laws of freedom. Our moral free will is a self-determined rational response to laws of the spiritual realm, which could only have come from some other will, with which we can establish some sort of "spiritual bond." Somehow that "sublime will," different from my own, "is the voice of conscience within me." Fichte jumps to the conclusion that this is the "infinite will" of "the One," which is the original source of both my will and the rest of the "spiritual world" and mediates between me and it. This spiritual world, encompassing me, the One, and all other persons in a moral community, a "*union and direct interaction of a number of autonomous and independent wills with each other*" (*Vocation*, 93–95, 104–108; see also *Foundations*, 68, 92–93, 145–147), is similar to Kant's spiritual "kingdom of ends." Our freedom rationally to respond to the dictates of the moral law is the bond among us.

Like Kant, Fichte emphasizes the critical link between freedom and morality, as the duties of morality are laws of freedom. In *The System of Ethics*, he argues that being bound by moral law and being free to obey it are mutually implicative, even though neither of them causes the other. The intuitive conviction of my own freedom provides me with a "first article of faith" that is a transcendental condition of moral duty; my experiencing dictates of moral conscience reveals my awareness of my own freedom. Without human freedom, there could be no "*categorical imperative*," at least for us; and our experience of the "*ought*" renders rational our postulating of freedom. This can even take the form of an "imperative to suppress every inclination," difficult though that may be. Doing so strikingly reveals the capacity for "*autonomy*" on which our dignity is founded. By contrast, our violating our duty in order to satisfy inclinations is an embracing of "*heteronomy*." Unlike empiricists, who have trouble accepting the "*absoluteness*" of human autonomy, Fichte thinks we experience it "through intuition" and, like Kant, makes human dignity a function of it. Because he rashly identifies this absoluteness with reason itself, Fichte suggests that determinism is incompatible with philosophy itself: "Either all philosophy has to be abandoned, or the absolute autonomy of reason must be conceded." Granted that we must be rational to do philosophy. But why should we grant Fichte's notion that "*absolute self-sufficiency*" is a transcendental condition of reason itself (*Ethics*, 55–61)? This would dismiss the work of Hobbes, Spinoza, Hume, and Bentham as bogus philosophy.

15.8 Morality

In an early work, Fichte embraces Kant's categorical imperative in formulating "the principle of morality" as fundamentally mandating, "Act so that you could consider the maxims of your willing to be eternal laws for yourself" (*Writings*, 149). In *The System of Ethics*, a few years later, he writes that "I posit myself" as both "a knowing subject" and an "active" being; thus theoretical and practical reason are synthesized in my self-consciousness. As I know myself as limited by that which is other (the not-I), so I experience my own activity as "*determinate.*" The resistance to my will of that which is other than me requires that my activity be determinate. Subject and resisting objects must be synthesized for ordinary action to occur. The only absolute activity I experience is my own act of subjective will prior to the "resistance" of objects. Only by acting "autonomously," responding to the dictates of practical reason, rather than heteronomously, responding to the demands of inclination, can we be moral. Regardless how we respond, the moral law "commands categorically" how we ought to act. It is through rational intuition that we know what "conscience," which is "*the immediate consciousness of our determinate duty,*" requires of us. No external verification or falsification of this can be found in the sensible world. Of course, as Kant indicated, whatever is morally required of us must be possible: "Something impossible is never a duty, and a duty is never impossible." Because freedom is essential to personhood, morality requires that we always try to respect human freedom. Fichte wishes to distinguish between "*immediate . . .* and *unconditioned* duties," including some I owe to other persons, and "*mediate* and *conditioned* duties," such as some we have in relation to ourselves. Because practical reason "demands that I believe that every human being can improve himself," and because moral improvement requires remaining alive, it is prima facie wrong to commit either "premeditated suicide" or the "premeditated murder of someone else." This leaves open the possibility of justifying, for example, the executions of some convicted felons and "the killing of an armed enemy during warfare." The integrity and healthy functioning of the human body are helpful for achieving the rational end of moral improvement. We must try to respect them, in the case of others every bit as much as in our own case. Whether or not our normal drive toward self-preservation and our weaker drive toward sympathy toward others are in force, such respect is a matter of moral duty (*Ethics*, 10–15, 75, 145, 164, 168, 197, 222, 246, 266–269, 288).

We have already seen the thesis statement of *The Vocation of Man*, which is that our vocation, as rational moral agents, is "not merely to know, but *to act* according to your knowledge." Let us now explore the implications of this claim for *what* we should know about morality and *how* we ought morally to act. First, we should know that we live in a social environment of other persons, that conscience requires us to respect them, their freedom, and their rational purposes. They are not to be treated as "things" or mere objects of our own "need, desire, and enjoyment." As we would reasonably be angrily resentful of being ill-treated by others, so we should expect them to react the same way to our disrespect for them. This indicates positive and negative duties we have toward one another. Thus, he writes, "I ought to will in conformity with the law" of morality, regardless of inclination and likely (utilitarian) consequences. The primacy of practical reason is such that our knowledge should be oriented toward discerning our moral duty. Regardless of adverse circumstances, he says, I "ought to be concerned only to do my duty." No matter how we might feel about other persons, we should always try to "respect their freedom." Here moral knowledge is allegedly possible. "I care to know only one thing: what I ought to do, and this I always know infallibly." Here Fichte's explicit adoption of intellectual intuition (for which he offers no argument) allows him to be more dogmatically certain than Kant. But can he achieve this certainty objectively, or is it incorrigibly subjective? What ultimately matters, Fichte writes (in the spirit of the Enlightenment at the end of the eighteenth century), is the progress of reason and morality; to this end, I am an instrumental means. Thus I may try to subordinate my own ego to this overarching greater good (*Vocation*, 67, 76–79, 100, 116–118). This does not merely reveal the influence of Kantian ethics; but Fichte's controversial claim to intellectual intuition provides him with a basis for dogmatic moral certainty to which his predecessor could not so confidently lay claim. Perhaps this is why the earlier thinker places greater emphasis on the categorical imperative as an ethical litmus test for distinguishing right from wrong.

15.9 Society

As we have already seen, practical reason involves sociopolitical philosophy as well as ethics. But Fichte wants to separate them more than Kant was willing to do. Like Kant, he sees the progress of humanity as a function of a move toward social unity. But, unlike Kant, who regards this as contingent on our free choices, Fichte seems (dogmatically) to see it as necessary: "We have already come a long way on the road to this goal, which is the condition of further common progress, and we may surely count on reaching it." Anticipating Marx, he foresees mass "resistance aroused by . . . subjugation," with the oppressed rising up against exploitative inequality. He predicts a move to greater international cooperation and the eventual elimination of war as the way of solving international conflicts. He even thinks that, increasingly, nations will become committed to positively assisting one another, helping them move in the direction of "universal peace," which "will gradually encompass the whole earth." He sees the human race, more and more, as taking seriously the requirements of international justice, with the use of force becoming increasingly unattractive. This, he maintains, will allow us to turn from fighting one another to cooperating in the "common purpose" of cultivating nature for our common good (*Vocation*, 85–90). While Kant would share the hope that all this might come to pass, Fichte seems more confident that it will.

Let us now glean some pertinent ideas from Fichte's first four lectures on the scholar's vocation. While man's goal, as a rational moral agent, must be "to perfect himself without end," this cannot be in isolation from others, as we live and function in society. Fichte explains, "By 'society' I mean the relationship in which rational beings stand to each other." Our identity as persons is a function of interpersonal relationships with other persons; "the social drive is one of man's fundamental drives," the isolated human being incomplete. Like Kant, Fichte thinks we have an obligation to be part of "purposeful community." The political state, however, is "only a *means for establishing a perfect society*." If this could ever be achieved, the means would no longer be desirable. Thus, Fichte concludes (anticipating Marx), "the state aims at abolishing itself. *The goal of all government is to make government superfluous.*" The hallmark of a healthy society is "*free interaction*," and the state should facilitate, rather than hinder, this goal. Ethically speaking, we should try to cultivate greater sociability with others. "The social drive aims at *interaction, reciprocal* influence, *mutual* give and take," seeking out other "*free, rational* beings" and trying to "enter into community with them." Ideally, our goal of sociability would involve people becoming "totally equal to each other," increasing the likelihood of social "harmony." While our physical inequalities may be naturally given, social inequality is man-made. Of course, each individual person is unique. But as our personal integrity requires harmony with others, which, in turn, requires social equality, "the final aim of all society is *the complete equality of all of its members*." Our ongoing "*struggle with nature*" is more effectively waged through widespread social cooperation. We have some choice regarding how we shall develop and use our talents in this enterprise; and our social class is likely to be a function of the roles we take on. But each of us must do his or her part to contribute to the common good. Nobody should be forced to join any particular social class or barred from trying to do so. Our common goal, to which all of us can contribute, should be "the constant improvement of the human species – liberating it more and more from natural compulsion, and making it ever more independent and autonomous." We need and should respect all productive established social classes. This includes the class of scholars, who should be the teachers of mankind, not merely analyzing present conditions, but envisioning a better future for all. The true scholar should be "a priest of truth" working on behalf of future generations and their intellectual and moral progress (*Writings*, 152–169, 174–176).

Fichte's most important work of political philosophy is, arguably, *The Science of Rights*. Reason's conception of right is held there to be "a necessary condition of self-consciousness," as this has a social dimension. I "posit" myself as rational and free in relation to other free and rational beings. I must respect the freedom of others, which requires that I limit my own. "The conception of Rights is, therefore, the conception of the necessary relation of free beings to each other," without which true community is impossible. This is facilitated by the "rule of law" – speaking now of civil and criminal law, rather than the moral law. A person may invoke rights protected by law or not, as he chooses. But, if he does, the law must be enforced, which is the responsibility of the executive power of government. The function of the law should be to protect people's freedom from violation by others. Without such protection, true community becomes impossible, precluded by coercion and threats of violence. I surrender my rights to protect my own freedom to government in return for the assurance that the law will be enforced for the protection of all, rather than used for their oppression. The central problem here is put in the form of a question: "*How may a community of free beings, as such, be possible?*" In reply, echoing both Rousseau and Kant, Fichte calls for "the freedom of each to be restricted by the freedom of all others." Like Bentham, Fichte does not believe in natural, "original" human rights, agreeing that rights arise only in the context of community and that the concept of "original rights" is only "a pure *fiction*," even if it can be a useful fiction. Certainly, we have a natural instinct of self-preservation; and, to the extent that we want to be able to function as free beings, we must adopt and enforce a system of rights, which will tell us what political society can require that we do, as well as what we shall be allowed to do, if we so choose. If we were perfectly moral, then we could dispense with this system of rights; but, as things actually are, it is needed for the sake of social security (*Rights*, 17–22, 26, 77–79, 126, 137, 153–156, 159–162, 199–202, 205).

Fichte speaks of a "property-compact," whereby members of society agree not to violate one another's property rights, as well as a "protection-compact," whereby they commit themselves to mutual protection. A momentarily exciting passage channels the call for equal rights for women in the wake of the French Revolution: "The question, whether the female sex has really a claim to all the rights of men and of citizens which belong to the male sex, could be raised only by persons who doubt whether women are complete human beings. We do not doubt it." However, Fichte goes on to undermine the promise of this general statement in a way that is sadly disappointing. In the area of international relations, he maintains that a state can rightfully compel a stateless person to either submit to its laws or get out of its territory; and people who are stateless can unite to found a state. Different states that have no reciprocal influence on each other can have no legal relationship. When states wish to establish a relationship with each other, they should agree on a mutual contract whereby they pledge to protect the security of each other's citizens, thus reciprocally recognizing each other. A people with no established government is not a state and, thus, has "no rights at all," since there are no innate human rights. (This is different from Kant's view that all persons have an original right to freedom.) Treaty agreements that are to ensure a lasting peace should treat the parties involved as equal, even if most actual treaties fail to do this. States at war with one another have no rights against one another, and "the natural end of war is always the *annihilation of the opponent*," through death and/or subjugation, though a peace treaty might short-circuit that end result. But war should only be waged against combatants and "not the unarmed citizens" of the enemy state. A state cannot give its soldiers a right to kill the enemy; yet each soldier does have "the right of self-defense" against hostile forces. Curiously, Fichte considers the killing of enemy troops by snipers to be dishonorable and murder. Following Kant, he imagines a future time in which a worldwide "confederation of states" will be established, bringing about "*eternal peace*" all over our planet (*Rights*, 218–219, 440 ff., 473–479, 482–484, 488–489).

We need not spend much time dealing with Fichte's *Addresses to the German Nation*, as it is not really philosophical. But, as a seminal document of German nationalism, which later led to Otto Bismarck and Adolf Hitler, it has gained considerable notoriety. We should recognize that these addresses were originally delivered in Berlin at a time when it was occupied by Napoleon's French troops. Fichte calls for the German people, who comprised several states rather than constituting a fully united nation, to serve as a model for future progress for the rest of humanity. By leading other peoples, Germans can allegedly help bring about international relations that would be "universal and cosmopolitan." But before this can occur, the German people must be educated in love of the "fatherland," extending this program of education to all. This will develop German character and pride, facilitating German unity. It can then be spread over all of humanity, leading to "a regeneration of the human race." Thus the German people will presumably become planetary leaders (*Addresses*, 40, 99, 132, 166, 177, 187, 215–216). To us today (living after the two world wars), this has an ominous tone of world domination that would not have bothered many members of Fichte's audience to any significant extent.

15.10   Review

Although he is legitimately seen as the greatest German philosopher between Kant and Hegel, it is unfair to Fichte to reduce him to a mere link between them. He develops a complete system that has its roots in Kant but moves beyond him, paving the road to Hegel without becoming so extreme. There is a problem with Fichte's philosophy which a label of Hegel's can help us analyze. Hegel accuses both Kant and Fichte of "subjective idealism," which, in contrast to his own "absolute idealism," he thinks incapable of establishing any objective knowledge of reality outside one's own mind. This accusation seems unfair in relation to Kant but fair with reference to Fichte. From a Hegelian perspective, any idealist – basing a philosophical system on the mind of the thinking subject and its ideas – who also accepts a subject–object dichotomy (as almost all great Western philosophers before Hegel do) will have trouble establishing any objective reality outside the mind. Hegel himself solves the problem by dialectically showing an identity between subject and object. What can save Kant is his empirical realism, which, from the start, insists on the givenness of objects outside the mind. What of Fichte? Like Kant, he believes in a subject–object antithesis (although there is some sort of synthesis between ego and non-ego); unlike Kant, he rejects empirical realism; yet he believes that our intellectual intuition, denied by Kant, gives us access to objective as well as subjective reality. But this is itself a subjective conviction asserted without argumentation – as dogmatic as the pre-Kantian rationalists. Even if this "subjective idealism" becomes less pronounced in Fichte's nineteenth-century writings, it never quite disappears. The stage is thus set for Hegel's grand entrance.

16

Georg Wilhelm Friedrich Hegel

Source: Sophus Williams/The Library of Congress/Public Domain

Modern European Philosophers, First Edition. Wayne P. Pomerleau.
© 2023 John Wiley & Sons, Inc. Published 2023 by John Wiley & Sons, Inc.

16.1 Overview

Hegel's absolute idealism was influenced by the philosophies of other German idealists, Kant, Fichte, and Schelling, while being distinctly different. Hegel is, arguably, the last great revolutionary thinker (after Descartes, Locke, Hume, and Kant) in modern European philosophy – such that his successors have to come to terms with his system. While he is a radically original thinker, he can also be regarded as the first great historian of Western philosophy and can mine this expertise to strengthen the development of his own system.[1] He is unusual, up to his time, in being both a numerical monist, like Spinoza (as opposed to a generic monist like Hobbes or Berkeley), and an idealist – believing that all reality is one and spiritual in nature. And, perhaps most striking of all, recognizing the inadequacies of the old Aristotelian logic for coming to know ultimate reality, he invented a new dialectical logic.

16.2 Biography

Georg Wilhelm Friedrich Hegel was born on August 27, 1770, in Stuttgart, in southwest Germany, the son of Georg Ludwig Hegel, a civil servant in the department of finance, and Maria Magdalena Louisa Hegel, the daughter of a lawyer in the high court of justice. His only sister, Christiane, born in 1773, never married and suffered mental problems. Their brother, Georg Ludwig Hegel, born in 1776, died fighting for Napoleon in the Russian campaign of 1812. They seem to have enjoyed a comfortable, stable family life in that Protestant enclave in Catholic Swabia in what was then still part of the "Holy Roman Empire."

Hegel started school in 1773 and seems to have been an earnest, diligent student who was, however, not considered gifted. While he was still a schoolboy, his mother, who had already taught him some Latin, died of a fever. In 1784, his father sent him to the *Gymnasium Illustre*, a college preparatory school where he was exposed to Enlightenment ideas and ideals and from which he graduated in 1788. He then left Stuttgart to attend the Protestant seminary in Tübingen, where he befriended and roomed with Friedrich Hölderlin, who would become an important German Romantic poet, and the precocious (five years younger) Friedrich Wilhelm Josef Schelling, who

---

1 References to Hegel's writings will be to *Hegel: The Letters* (hereafter called *Letters*), trans. by Clark Butler and Christiane Seiler (Bloomington: Indiana Univ. Press, 1984), to *Hegel's Logic* (hereafter called *Logic*), trans. by William Wallace (London: Oxford Univ. Press, 1975), to *Phenomenology of Spirit*, by G.W.F. Hegel (hereafter called *Phenomenology*), trans. by A.V. Miller (New York: Oxford Univ. Press, 1979), to *Hegel's Lectures on the History of Philosophy* (hereafter called *Lectures*), trans. by E.S. Haldane and Frances H. Simson, abridged by Tom Rockmore (Atlantic Highlands, NJ: Humanities Press, 1996), to *Hegel's Science of Logic* (hereafter called *Science*), trans. by A.V. Miller (Amherst, NY: Humanity Books, 1998), to *Hegel's Philosophy of Nature* (hereafter called *Nature*), trans. by A.V. Miller (London: Oxford Univ. Press, 1970), to *Hegel's Philosophy of Mind* (hereafter called *Mind*), trans. by William Wallace and A.V. Miller (London: Oxford Univ. Press, 1971), to *Three Essays, 1793–1795*, by G.W.F. Hegel (hereafter called *Three*), ed. and trans. by Peter Fuss and John Dobbins (Notre Dame: Univ. of Notre Dame Press, 1984), to *Early Theological Writings*, by G.W.F. Hegel (hereafter called *Early*), trans. by T.M. Knox (Philadelphia: Univ. of Pennsylvania Press, 1971), to *The Difference Between Fichte's and Schelling's Systems of Philosophy*, by G.W.F. Hegel (hereafter called *Difference*), trans. by H.S. Harris and Walter Cerf (Albany: State Univ. of New York Press, 1977), to *Faith and Knowledge*, by G.W.F. Hegel (hereafter called *Knowledge*), trans. by Walter Cerf and H.S. Harris (Albany: State Univ. of New York Press, 1977), to *Lectures on the Philosophy of Religion*, by Georg Wilhelm Friedrich Hegel, in three volumes (hereafter called *Religion*), trans. by E.B. Speirs and J. Burdon Sanderson (London: Routledge & Kegan Paul, 1968), to *Introduction to The Philosophy of History*, by G.W.F. Hegel (hereafter called *History*), trans. by Leo Rauch (Indianapolis: Hackett Publishing Co., 1988), and to *Hegel's Philosophy of Right* (hereafter called *Right*), trans. by T.M. Knox (New York: Oxford Univ. Press, 1967).

would achieve philosophical eminence long before Hegel would do so. The three friends shared an enthusiasm for the French Revolution, and there is an apocryphal story that they erected a "liberty tree" to commemorate it. Hegel, nicknamed "the old man" for his seriousness, studied Rousseau with considerable excitement but, unlike his two friends, held back from joining the Kant club at the seminary. In 1790, Hegel received his Master of Philosophy degree and started preparing for his theology exams, though (like his two friends) he had decided against becoming a Protestant pastor. After Kant's *Religion within the Limits of Reason Alone* was published in 1793, Hegel became more sympathetic to Kant's ideas. That same year, Hegel passed his exams and left the seminary, needing to find a job.

Like Kant and Fichte, he became a family tutor, his first such position, from 1793 to 1796, being in Berne, Switzerland, where he wrote *The Positivity of the Christian Religion*, which reflects the influence of Kant. In letters to Schelling, he revealed his discontentment with his place and position. He told his friend that he had resumed studying Kant and that Hölderlin was attending Fichte's lectures at Jena, closing with an Enlightenment slogan, "Reason and Freedom remain our password, and the Invisible Church our rallying point." He wrote, "From the Kantian system and its highest completion I expect a revolution in Germany." He praised Schelling's writings for already having "illuminated" the Kantian "postulate according to which practical reason governs the world of appearances" and for having done so "in a most splendid and satisfying manner." But it was his other friend, Hölderlin, living in Frankfurt, who found him a position as a family tutor there. After a brief visit with his family in Stuttgart, in January of 1797, he began his new job in Frankfurt. In 1798, he wrote *The Spirit of Christianity and Its Fate*, in which he started to put some critical distance between Kant and himself. That same year, Schelling joined Fichte as a professor at Jena, though Fichte had to leave the year after that under suspicions of pantheism and charges of atheism. In 1799, Hegel's father died, leaving him enough of an inheritance that he could quit working as a family tutor (*Letters*, 30–32, 35, 41).

In 1800, Hölderlin left Frankfurt, and Hegel wrote to Schelling, "I am looking for inexpensive provisions, a good beer for the sake of my physical condition, [and] a few acquaintances." He expressed great admiration for the rapid accomplishments of his friend and eagerness for their reunion. Schelling, whose scholarly record was already becoming brilliant, helped him become a *Privatdozent* (unsalaried lecturer) at the University of Jena, starting in early 1801. Later that year, Hegel's first published work appeared, *The Difference Between Fichte's and Schelling's Systems of Philosophy*, defending the latter against the former. By the end of that year, Hegel wrote of "the first issue of a *Critical Journal of Philosophy*, which I am editing with Schelling – with whom I am lodging." Hegel's essay on *Natural Law* and his *Faith and Knowledge* were published in that journal in 1803. But that same year, Schelling left Jena to become a professor at Würtzburg. By 1804, Hegel, who was developing an unwelcome reputation as a follower of Schelling's, was attracting more students. The next year, he was promoted and began lecturing on the history of philosophy. He had used up his inheritance and, needing money, signed a contract for the *Phenomenology of Spirit*, his "voyage of discovery" that would launch his own original philosophical system. He wrote at the time, just as "Luther made the Bible speak German," so "I wish to try to teach philosophy to speak German." His contract for the *Phenomenology* threatened severe financial penalties if he failed to get a completed manuscript to the publisher by October 18, 1806. On October 9, he mailed "half a manuscript," intending to send the rest a few days later. But, on October 12, Napoleon's French troops bombarded Jena, invading it the next day. Hegel wrote, "I saw the Emperor – this world-soul – riding . . . It is indeed a wonderful sensation to see such an individual, who, . . . astride a horse, reaches out over the world and masters it." Hegel had been a Francophile since his Tübingen days and admired Napoleon. But the disruption caused Hegel to miss his deadline. The university was shut down, and Hegel's lodgings were ransacked. He left Jena, having impregnated his landlord's wife, who, in February of 1807, gave birth to Ludwig Fischer, Hegel's son, in Jena (*Letters*, 64, 89, 107, 114, 116, 423).

The following month, Hegel moved to Bamberg, in Catholic Bavaria, to edit a French-controlled daily political newspaper. Soon thereafter his *Phenomenology* was published. He tried to warn Schelling that its Preface attacked "the shallowness" of some of Schelling's followers. In fact, it was tantamount to a declaration of independence from Schelling himself, who was understandably hurt and so angered by "the polemical part of the Preface" by his former protégé that their friendship was broken. Meanwhile Hegel, while earning a living with the newspaper, had begun writing his *Science of Logic*. By the summer of 1808, he was sick of the newspaper job, saying he was "looking forward to my deliverance from the yoke of journalism," which had become "even more oppressive" due to tensions with the censors. He appealed to a friend, who was reorganizing schools in Bavaria, to help him return to academic life (*Letters*, 80, 130, 134, 166–167, 169).

His friend did help him get a position as rector (headmaster) and philosophy teacher at the classical humanistic *Gymnasium* in Nuremberg in 1808. Though it paid less than the newspaper job, it better complemented the writing of his *Logic*. By early 1811, he was courting the aristocratic Marie von Tucher, who was about half his age, with romantic poetry he composed. They married later that year. Early in 1812, the first volume of his *Logic* was published. That summer, Marie gave birth to a daughter who died a few weeks later. In 1813, their son Karl was born, and a second part of his *Logic* was published. In 1814, a second son, Immanuel, was born. And in 1816, the third volume of his *Logic* was published (*Letters*, 178, 236–238, 261, 269–270, 296, 310, 312, 327).

Though somewhat defensive about the quality of his teaching, with the publication of his *Logic*, Hegel had become attractive as a candidate for a university professorship. In August of 1816, he got a letter from a Prussian official saying he was being considered for Fichte's chair at Berlin that had been left vacant since his death in 1814 and that the only reservation had to do with his teaching abilities. He tried to assure the man that his teaching had improved while at the *Gymnasium* in Nuremberg but that he had already accepted an offer from Heidelberg and would honor that commitment. Hegel and his wife decided to have his 10-year-old (illegitimate) son, Ludwig, whose mother had died, come live with them in Heidelberg. Meanwhile, Hegel was developing lecture series on philosophy of mind, political philosophy, and the history of philosophy, as well as adding aesthetics to his repertoire. That same year, he published the first edition of his *Encyclopedia of the Philosophical Sciences* in three parts (a logic, a philosophy of nature, and a philosophy of mind). This led to his receiving and accepting an offer to fill Fichte's chair at Berlin in 1818 (*Letters*, 431, 332, 411, 433–434, 367, 381).

Although a relatively new university, Berlin was quickly becoming an important center of German academics. In 1821, Hegel's *Philosophy of Right* was published, leading to accusations that he had become an apologist for the Prussian state. We have a draft of a letter he wrote to a Prussian official (in 1820), proclaiming that his writings "aim at showing agreement with the principle which the Prussian state – belonging to which necessarily gives me great satisfaction – has had the good fortune of having upheld and of still upholding under the enlightened Government of His Majesty the King and Your Highness's wise leadership." In 1821, Hegel started lecturing on the philosophy of religion, and on the philosophy of history after that. His lectures had begun attracting large audiences from all over Germany. He also became dean of the philosophical faculty for a one-year term. But, by 1825, accusations of Hegelian "pantheism" (often identified with atheism) were spreading. (Among the students attending his lectures was Ludwig Feuerbach, who actually

256 | *16 Georg Wilhelm Friedrich Hegel*

would develop philosophy in an atheistic direction.) In 1826, Hegel protested, "I am a Lutheran, and through philosophy have been at once completely confirmed in Lutheranism" (*Letters*, 413, 459–460, 470, 437–438, 467, 520). About this time, his son Ludwig left the family and joined the Dutch military, being assigned to the East Indies.

In 1826, the journal *Yearbooks for Scientific Criticism*, a vehicle for Hegelian philosophy, was founded. The following year, a second edition of the *Encyclopedia* was published. In 1828, reacting to attacks on his alleged religious heterodoxy, Hegel wrote Georg Andreas Gabler, a former student at Jena, concerning "the twaddle about pantheism," saying, "It is likewise necessary to attack this rubbish head-on." But the following year, he was elected university rector for a one-year term. However, by then his health was becoming a problem, with chest pains interfering with his work. He visited a spa at Karlsbad, where he unexpectedly encountered Schelling. In 1830, a revised third edition of his *Encyclopedia* was published, and he was revising his *Science of Logic* for a new edition. Though a long-time Francophile, he reacted negatively to the July Revolution in France, writing, "It is a crisis in which everything that formerly was valid appears to be made problematic." He wrote his sister, expressing his nervous anxiety regarding political instability, on the one hand, and his pride at having his likeness sculpted, on the other. In 1831, he worried that repercussions of the July Revolution were threatening trouble in Germany (*Letters*, 525, 556, 535, 396–398, 544, 422, 675). Because of his failing health, he had to cut back on his lectures. Yet he managed to publish three of the four parts of his critical essay "On the English Reform Bill." He was decorated by King Frederick William III of Prussia for service to the Prussian state. A cholera epidemic had spread into Prussia, sweeping through Berlin. On November 13, he became violently ill; the following afternoon, he died peacefully in his sleep. (He never learned that his son Ludwig had died a bit earlier in the East Indies.) There was a massive turnout for his funeral two days later. A few weeks after his death, his sister, Christiane, distraught, committed suicide by drowning herself. Four of Hegel's lecture series – on the philosophy of history, on the philosophy of art, on the history of philosophy, and on the philosophy of religion – were published posthumously.

Hegelianism soon split into factions, with a conservative right wing, represented by his former student Gabler, who succeeded to his chair at the university, a reform-minded center, and a radical left wing, represented by his former student Feuerbach. In 1841, his one-time friend Schelling, who had become very conservative, was appointed to take Hegel's chair at Berlin, being urged to destroy remnants of Hegelian "pantheism" there. Attending Schelling's inaugural lecture were Friedrich Engels (later the collaborator of Karl Marx), Søren Kierkegaard (the founder of existentialism), and Michael Bakunin (the famous theorist of anarchism). Schelling lived until 1854 (it is curious that Fichte, Hegel, and Schelling all ended their teaching careers holding the same chair at Berlin). Hegel's wife, Marie, died the year after that, after becoming extremely pious. Both of her sons, Karl and Immanuel, had long, successful lives.

16.3 Knowledge

As we have done when dealing with earlier modern philosophers, we shall begin our study of Hegel's system by considering his epistemology, which is, arguably, its most revolutionary component. He is in critical dialogue with many of them, including, especially, Kant. He criticizes his "critical idealism" as "subjective idealism," the same phrase he uses to describe Fichte's theory, indicating that objectivity gets absorbed in the subjective (which seems fair to Fichte but not to Kant, on account of the "empirical realism" that sets Kant apart from the other famous German idealists). We might mention here that Schelling's philosophy of nature can be accused of being

16.3 Knowledge | **257**

"objective idealism," in that subjectivity gets absorbed in the murky fog of objective nature. By contrast, Hegel says his own system "should be termed absolute idealism," as representing a synthesis of subject and object in absolute reality. Because Kant and Fichte allegedly subjectivize the objects of the mind, even the former's "empirical realism" does not, in Hegel's mind, prevent him from subjectivizing the objects of sense experience. He tries to retain the "thing in itself" but renders it "empty," devoid of cognitive content. He allegedly treats human thought as a mere subjective "instrument of philosophic knowledge," reinforcing the subject–object dichotomy that has haunted all of modern philosophy (except, perhaps, Spinoza) and for which Hegel's own method of dialectical reasoning will supposedly provide the cure. It will only be in the highest synthesis of ultimate reality that reason will fully grasp a key Hegelian insight, that "Truth, then, is only possible as a universe or totality of thought." The problem, however, is that Kant's logic of the understanding can only lead to irresolvable antitheses when dealing with absolute Truth, for which only the dialectical logic of reason will purportedly prove capable of rising to increasingly comprehensive syntheses. Hegel thus proposes to mend the "divorce between thought and thing," which the critical philosophy allegedly encourages, though this will require a radical new logic that *"coincides with metaphysics,"* incorporating (synthesizing) both content and form (*Logic*, 70–71, 73, 188, 65–68, 70–74, 14–15, 20, 35–36, 40; famous alternative statements of the critique of thought as a mere instrument, the claim, "The True is the Whole," and the proclamation of "the identity of Thought and Being" can be found in the *Phenomenology*, 46–47, 11, 33, respectively).

The relationship between subjective thought and objective reality is not only the crucial divide between Kant and Hegel but, in the latter's opinion, the central philosophical issue: "The task of modern German philosophy is, however, summed up in taking as its object the unity of thought and Being, which is the fundamental idea of philosophy generally, and comprehending it." Hegel does give Kant credit for being the first clearly "to distinguish understanding and reason." But the handicap of his (Aristotelian) logic of understanding (as we have seen) cannot get him beyond the stage of antithetical contradictions when applied to ultimate reality. It works well enough at the levels of common sense and natural science, but a new logic of reason is needed for metaphysical knowledge of the transcendent. Kant sees the dialectic as nothing more than "a logic of illusion" and cannot get to more comprehensive synthetic truth. Thus Kant's dualism supposedly represents merely a "philosophy of the Understanding, which renounces Reason" as providing any knowledge of ultimate reality. Nevertheless, Hegel grants, Kant has led us to the use of dialectical reason by exhibiting the possible cognitive pattern of "thesis, antithesis and synthesis," even though he himself did not take that final step. Without that step of synthesis, Kant can never reach a true unity of thought and reality, so that his theory can only be considered "a good introduction to Philosophy" (*Lectures*, 573, 595–597, 627–629). After abortive attempts by Fichte (and Schelling) to complete the product of "critical idealism," it is only Hegel's own "absolute idealism" that presumably will succeed. So let us see.

The Introduction of his *Science of Logic* criticizes the traditional logic, first systematized by Aristotle, for emphasizing "the *mere form*" of thought to the exclusion of "all *content*." Hegel's rationalism commits him to the view that "things and the thinking of them" ultimately have "one and the same content." The problem is that (Kant's) *"reflective* understanding," limited to the abstract traditional logic, cannot adequately access this content, leaving philosophers to despair of knowing things-in-themselves. Thus reason denies itself and abdicates its role of knowing absolute truth, having to fall back on opinion and belief. The understanding shies away from the contradictions encountered as a result of restricting itself to traditional logic. The mind must find a way to do better. A logic of pure reason is needed to penetrate absolute reality, leading us, ultimately, to "God as he is in his eternal essence before the creation of nature and a finite mind." While other areas of human thought have progressed over the centuries, Hegel holds that logic has undergone no transformation since Aristotle and desperately needs one. Whereas Aristotelian logic's basic laws of thought – such as the principles of identity, of noncontradiction, and of the excluded middle – force us to think in terms of mutually exclusive alternatives, the Hegelian dialectic pushes us to "the recognition of the logical principle that the negative is just as much positive, or that what is self-contradictory does not resolve itself into a nullity, into abstract nothingness, but essentially into the negation of its *particular* content." The negation of any particular thesis by its particular antithesis can then be overcome by a more adequate (i.e. more inclusive) synthesis, which relates the two antitheses to one another. Hegel has a very powerful word in German to represent this activity of dialectical reason. The thesis, brought into opposition with its antithesis, is "superseded" or "sublated" (*aufgehoben*) by the synthesis. Thus, "to supersede" or "to sublate" (*aufheben*) simultaneously means nullifying, preserving in some sense, and elevating to a higher level. This represents a more positive and productive use of the dialectic than was ever achieved, for example, by Plato or Kant, though the latter at least recognized it as "a *necessary function of reason*" (*Science*, 43, 45–46, 50–51, 54–56). We might also observe here that Hegel almost never uses the concepts of "thesis," "antithesis," and "synthesis" together.

In the Introduction to his *Encyclopedia Logic*, Hegel quotes his own catchy slogan (from his *Philosophy of Right*) to the effect that "What is reasonable is actual" and "What is actual is reasonable." He particularly wants to use this double-barreled claim as the edge of the wedge against any empirical prejudice that "Ideas and ideals are nothing but chimeras, and philosophy a mere system of such phantasms." But, without dialectical reasoning, skepticism and subjectivism will always prevail due to the separating of thought from reality. Only the true dialectic will be able to justify the seminal claim of Hegel's idealism, that Reason rules the world. Kant's epistemology, like all empirical ones, tries to place absolute limits on the human mind and its capacity to know. But Hegel maintains that to know a limit is already (at least implicitly) to transcend it. He thinks (as did Descartes) that we could not even grasp the finite without having at least some implicit awareness of the infinite. Life itself involves the dialectical movement of opposition and its overcoming; and our logic must reflect that rather than ignoring or denying it. As an illustrative example, Hegel asks us to consider "Pure **Being**," which is "simple and indeterminate"; as such, it is inconceivable and dialectically experienced as "**Nothing**" at all, pure negativity, not a thing, the antithesis of pure Being. The understanding, using the limited traditional (Aristotelian) logic, can only vacillate fruitlessly between these two opposites. By contrast, reason, utilizing the logic of the dialectic, transcends the opposition. "The truth of Being and of Nothing is accordingly the unity of the two: and this unity is **Becoming**." Hegel points out that such dialectical sublation involves both annulment of each antithesis by the other and the preservation of each. The process of becoming involves movement away from what something initially just appeared to be to what it appeared not to be at all with a partial incorporation of both of them in a newly revealed unity. Thus the old "Laws of Thought" have been found only to hold at the lower levels of common sense and physical science. Things are not merely static and self-identical but in a process of dynamic change. "Contradiction is the very moving principle of the world" (*Logic*, 9, 37, 91–92, 116, 118, 124–130, 142, 167, 172–174). The logic of reason must be rich and bold enough to reflect the complexity of reality if it is to facilitate adequate knowledge. Hegel's epistemology is difficult on account of a combination of the same two attributes as characterized Kant's – its being abstract and its being revolutionary. Whether it is an improvement hinges on whether there is, indeed, a unity of thought and Being and whether the logic of the dialectic can provide us with its knowledge. It does not appear that either theory will conclusively disprove the other, so that we must consider which, if either, we find more convincing for illuminating our experience.

16.4 Reality

Moving from the first volume of Hegel's *Encyclopedia*, the *Logic*, to the second, on *Philosophy of Nature*, we shift in focus from his methodology to his metaphysics. From the perspective of idealism, which views reality as essentially spiritual, Nature is problematic, Hegel admits – both attractive, as a context in which human spirit develops, and repellent, as other than spirit. Absolute Spirit, the ultimate reality that religion considers "God," he maintains, "is that Being in whom Spirit and Nature are united," so that the latter is quite important. It is the nature of the Absolute to be self-revealing, and this allegedly requires a natural order: "God reveals Himself in two different ways: as Nature and as Spirit . . . God, as an abstraction, is not the true God, but only as the living process of positing His Other, the world." Without his using the jargon of the dialectic, we see him referring to the Absolute as a synthesis of antitheses. The natural order, including us humans, is the Absolute as revealed in space and time. "Nature is Spirit estranged from itself" and no longer abstract. (We shall see a good deal more of his concept of estrangement.) A dynamic God must transcend the realm of abstract idea and be related to its antithesis. "Nature is the Idea in the form of otherness," our world. Because it is the self-manifestation of God, in principle the natural order is itself divine, though in all its finite limitations, it falls short of divine perfection and completeness. So it is with us as natural beings – though essentially spiritual, we are also "*bodies*" and thus "*essentially* spatial and temporal." After all, a human being is an "*animal* organism," representing "one organic system of Life." Indeed, he adds, natural organic life achieves its "most perfect development" in the human body, which is the most exquisite physical "instrument of spirit" in our world (*Nature*, 3, 8, 13–15, 17, 47, 273, 421–422). So Hegel's idealism, far from denying substantial reality to the physical world (as did Berkeley's), embraces it as an essential aspect of the ultimate reality of the Absolute.

If the physical world of nature is the expression of the self-manifestation of the Absolute, the human spirit is even more obviously so. In the third volume of his *Encyclopedia*, his *Philosophy of Mind*, he begins with the ancient Socratic slogan, "Know thyself," which he thinks an "absolute commandment." It is not merely the superficial self-awareness of our physical states that is meant. "The knowledge it commands means that of man's genuine reality – of what is essentially and ultimately true and real – of mind as the true and essential being." The mind experiences an inward spiritual life that is not reducible to physical operations, not necessarily determined but capable of autonomous choices. "The substance of mind is freedom, i.e. the absence of dependence on an Other." This human freedom is best manifested in community with others rather than in isolation from them. Mind or Spirit, like everything else, is dynamic. It evolves "in three stages": first, there is "*Mind Subjective*," as ideal, self-contained reality, then, "*Mind Objective*," related to its sociocultural world, and, finally, "*Mind Absolute*," which is comprehensive and all-inclusive. Subjective mind is represented as consciousness, soul, and independent psychological subject. Objective mind comprises law, morality, and sociopolitical relationships. Absolute mind strives to grasp the ultimate through "art, religion, and philosophy." However, these are not three different minds but three "stages" in the evolution of mind. The mind must come to recognize that it is part of a comprehensive rational order of reality, "that, in short, there is Reason in history." To the extent that it becomes "the wisdom of the world" that it should be, philosophy reveals the truth and gives "governments and nations the wisdom to discern what is essentially and actually right and reasonable in the real world." Ultimately it must grasp God or the Absolute not only as "the one and universal *substance*" underlying everything (this is monism), but also as in spiritual "community" with us and all reality. This idea that God is all-encompassing and immanent in our world rather than merely transcendent, that all things are aspects of God, is called *panentheism* (as opposed to *pantheism*, which simply reduces God to our world); we have already seen another example of it in Spinoza's system. Hegel is also a religious rationalist, considering matters of faith, at least in principle, dialectically knowable, writing that "belief or faith is not opposite to consciousness or knowledge, but rather to a sort of knowledge" (*Mind*, 1, 3, 11, 15, 20–22, 25–28, 277, 281, 285–286, 292); this reference is to the understanding's knowledge of natural science.

Hegel finds Kant's dualisms objectionable, because they lead to his alleged "subjectivism" and skeptical denial of any possible human knowledge of ultimate reality. He thinks the assertion of unknowable things-in-themselves to be incoherent. Against this, he maintains a monistic idealism – there is only one infinite reality, and it is essentially spiritual, but its finite manifestations include human spirits and physical things. As he puts it near the end of his *Lectures on the History of Philosophy*, "In apprehension the spiritual and the natural universe are interpenetrated as one harmonious universe," which "in its various aspects develops the Absolute into a totality" (*Lectures*, 697). Notice that this theory of monistic idealism asserts – against all appearances – the controversial and counterintuitive ontological or metaphysical knowledge claim that all of reality is one and essentially spiritual in nature, while being both spiritual and physical in its manifestations. By contrast, on the "dual-aspect" interpretation of Kant's theory, no ontological or metaphysical knowledge claim whatsoever, regarding things-in-themselves, need be made. The claims made are epistemological – that we experience a world of phenomenal appearances, can reasonably think that they are appearances of some noumenal realities, and can develop diverse beliefs regarding them and their relation to us and the world of our experience. The claim that all reality is integral to Absolute Spirit screams for justification, and that is supposed to be provided by the logic of dialectical reason. But is it? More specifically, have we been given any reason to believe that dialectical logic can synthesize all antitheses and yield metaphysical knowledge of ultimate reality?

16.5 God

We have seen that Hegel adopts a panentheistic concept of God and the conviction that all matters of religious faith are, at least potentially, also knowable. In this section, we explore these ideas in more depth. In his *Lectures on the History of Philosophy*, he takes Kant to task for treating God as merely a matter of "faith, an opinion, which is only subjectively, and not absolutely true." For Hegel, this is an abdication of our efforts to know reality itself. Nor does Kant's moral argument for the reasonableness of belief in God help. If morality is to be pursued for its own sake rather than for the sake of extrinsic rewards, why must we invoke "a holy lawgiver" to motivate our performing acts of good will? (Kant does, in fact, think we ought to do our duty for duty's sake and not merely for selfish desires for reward and fear of punishment; but believing in God helps us to maintain the conviction that, ultimately, justice will prevail, with the virtuous rewarded and the vicious punished.) So, despite the pretense of supporting belief in God, Kant is allegedly stuck at the level of subjective, unjustified faith. Hegel sarcastically compares this God to "some kind of scarecrow" constructed by children to frighten one another into being good. (In fact, Kant's God is more designed to give us hope that justice will be served than instill fear of divine wrath.) Hegel also sarcastically suggests an incoherence in thinking that an utterly unknowable God might be an appropriate object of worship, comparing it to St. Paul's report on the Athenians dedicating an altar "to the Unknown God" (*Acts*: 17:22–23), an idolatrous object of superstition (*Lectures*, 614, 626). True religion should be founded on at least the possibility of knowledge of God, in his view.

Recalling that he was a student of theology, we should not be surprised to find that Hegel has a great deal to say about God and religion, starting with his early theological writings (from the last decade of the eighteenth century) and extending to his lectures on philosophy of religion (from the third decade of the nineteenth). We shall only briefly consider his works before the *Phenomenology*, as they are mainly of interest as revealing his philosophical development. His "Tübingen Essay" (of 1793) starts with the proclamation, "Religion is one of our greatest concerns in life" and reflects the influence of Kant in holding that our performing morally right actions is the way to honor God rather than with superstitious rituals. In his "Berne Fragments" (from 1793 to 1794), he reiterates this Kantian idea that moral conduct is the essence of the religious life, holding that belief in Christ, for example, is not a requirement of practical reason and characterizing Jesus as "a personified ideal." Then, in his "Life of Jesus" (of 1795), he portrays Christ as preaching the Kantian morality of respect for all persons, interprets the kingdom of heaven as a Kantian realm of rational ends governed by the categorical imperative, and concludes his narrative with the burial of the crucified Jesus, not mentioning any resurrection (*Three*, 30, 32–33, 35–36, 42, 45, 70, 72, 81, 93–94, 96, 98–99, 112–115, 127, 141–142, 154, 165).

In *The Positivity of the Christian Religion* (also from 1795), he continues this Kantian perspective, criticizing Christianity as a "positive religion, i.e., a religion which is grounded in authority and puts man's worth not at all, or at least not wholly, in morals," and praises Christ for advocating a non-authoritarian religion of morality. He anticipates his mature philosophy, writing that religion becomes "positive" when human "mediation" is limited to a single person; but he cautions that an adequate analysis of this matter will require "a metaphysical treatment of the relation between the finite and the infinite." In *The Spirit of Christianity and Its Fate* (of 1798), however, Hegel is starting to break away from Kantianism and to exhibit more sympathy for the Christianity of his day. Now he distinguishes between the mission of Christ, as expressed in the Sermon on the Mount, and Kantian ethics, which allegedly reduces love to mere commitment to duty. Now we must find a way to transcend the limitations of "reflective thinking," our awareness of the infinite requiring that we ourselves should be infinite: "Faith in the divine is only possible if in the believer himself there is a divine element." Hegel is committed to our capacity to know God but claims that "only a modification of the Godhead can know the Godhead." Then he establishes a link between his earlier Kantian treatment of Christianity and the more radical anti-Kantian treatment that was to come: "All thought of a difference in essence between Jesus and those in whom faith in him has become life, in whom the divine is present, must be eliminated" (*Early*, 68–69, 71, 86, 91–92, 176, 206, 212–215, 223, 262, 266, 268).

At the beginning of the nineteenth century, having joined Schelling in Jena, Hegel was already starting to see the need for a new way of thinking to overcome (what he would later call) the "subjectivism" of both Kant and Fichte. Healing the breach between the infinite and the finite will require reason's rising above the "rigid antitheses" of reflective understanding. What must be accepted is the fact that "opposition" is an element of reality itself, not to be rejected as a bad sign. "What Reason opposes, rather, is just the absolute fixity which the intellect gives to the dichotomy" (*Difference*, 89–91). But he has yet to figure out how dialectical reasoning will work. His final important work prior to doing so is *Faith and Knowledge* (of 1803), in which he solidifies his critical distance from both Kant and Fichte. In abdicating objective knowledge of God, reason settles for mere belief, slipping back into its medieval role as "the handmaid of a faith," putting philosophy in a subordinate position. If sensible intuition is the only sort we have, then "the antithesis" between the finite and the infinite will remain insuperable. Hegel labels this approach "an idealism of the finite." On this view, philosophical knowledge is of the human and not of the divine. From this subjective perspective, "the absolute identity of thought and being" can never be established. Hegel dramatically calls this tragic renunciation a "speculative Good Friday" in which reason perishes in the "harshness of its Godforsakenness" (*Knowledge*, 55–56, 60, 62, 64–65, 94, 191). What is not yet indicated is how reason can use dialectical logic to achieve knowledge of the ultimate reality of God.

This breakthrough becomes manifest in the *Phenomenology* (of 1807), a brilliant account of the evolution of the human spirit that includes an excellent triadic analysis of natural religion, aesthetic religion, and revealed religion. Natural religion (primarily Asian and Egyptian) comprises the Persian religion of Zoroastrianism, the animistic religions of India, and the creative artifice religions of Egypt. Aesthetic religion (primarily ancient Greek) likewise assumes three progressively developed forms – the abstract work of art (such as religious sculptures), the living work of art (such as ecstatic religious dance), and the spiritual work of art (such as religious literature). Higher than either natural or aesthetic religion is the revealed religion of ethical monotheism. Here the object of reverence is seen neither merely as "*Substance*" (as in natural religion) nor merely as "*Subject*" (as in aesthetic religion), but as infinite "*Spirit*," a synthesis of the two. As the human spirit has evolved, the religious symbols of the distant past have lost their significance. Obsolete conceptions of the divine must be abandoned, so that, in that respect, modern man must cope with "the hard saying that 'God is dead'" (in the words of a Lutheran hymn). With Christianity, the most adequate religion, the idea of a perfect synthesis of the human and the divine provides a higher insight into the relationship between finite and infinite. Because this is the closest that the "*picture-thinking*" of religion can come to grasping the truth, we may consider Christianity "the absolute religion," the one in which the identity of the human and the divine is "*revealed*." In the person of Jesus, at least, the "divine nature is the same as the human." To see that this is symbolic of the universal truth regarding the relation between all spirits and absolute Spirit is to overcome the "picture-thought" that still leaves God as the transcendent Other (*Phenomenology*, 417–421, 424, 427, 430–435, 438–440, 443, 450–451, 453–455, 457–463, 468, 476–477). But this is the work of philosophy.

All three volumes of the *Encyclopedia* develop this philosophical conception of God. Indeed, his *Logic* identifies this as "the highest problem of philosophy." He laments the fact that, in modern times, some prominent thinkers (such as Hume and Kant) have ruled that God's existence is neither provable nor knowable. Using the limited logic of the understanding, these proofs do fail. But, as activities of reason, the proofs help the mind to "leap into the supersensible," involving "an exaltation above the finite, above the senses," above the realm of mere appearances. We should conceive of God not as "*a* Being" but as "*the* Being," all-encompassing. To the extent that we can think this way, we shall "know God as our true and essential self" (*Logic*, 57–58, 81, 104, 164, 261). In his *Philosophy of Nature*, Hegel makes the panentheistic claim that God is "that Being in whom Spirit and Nature are united." Hegel's God is essentially self-revealing and "reveals Himself in two different ways: as Nature and as Spirit." The purely transcendent God of popular monotheism is simply an abstraction. Our world, while "His Other," is not separable from a God that is absolute Spirit. Ultimately, all is one. If it be asked why God, who lacks nothing, should "disclose Himself in a sheer Other of Himself," the answer seems to be that it is required by the divine nature (*Nature*, 8, 13–14). God would not be God without an Other to whom the divine nature is revealed and in whom it becomes manifest.

In the *Philosophy of Mind*, Hegel writes that "*religious* consciousness . . . pierces through the seemingly absolute independence of things to the one, infinite power of God operative in them and holding all together." The function of philosophy is conceptually to grasp one great truth: "*The Absolute is Mind* (Spirit)." The eastern and Jewish religions allegedly see God as abstract, transcendent substance, the Greeks as engaged individual subjects, and Christianity as revealed Spirit.

The final section, on "Absolute Mind," interprets the increasingly adequate paths of art, revealed religion, and philosophy to God, the ultimate object of each of them. Taking issue with Hume, Kant, and Fichte, Hegel holds that "belief or faith is not opposite to . . . knowledge" but, instead, is "only a particular form of the latter." So, here, again, we see him challenging distinctions without providing any argument to support his demolition. But he is not finished establishing a general identity between the human and the divine: "God is God only so far as he knows himself: his self-knowledge is, further, a self-consciousness in man and man's knowledge *of* God, which proceeds to man's self-knowledge *in* God." We should, presumably, embrace this intellectual intimacy. Hegel sets up a dialectic. Its abstract thesis is God "as eternal content, abiding self-centred" Being; its antithesis, in distinction as its manifestation, is "the phenomenal world" of nature and finite spirit; and its synthesis is to be an "infinite return, and reconciliation with the eternal being, of the world it gave away," in self-estrangement, in order to achieve full self-actualization. While religion and philosophy differ in their forms of thinking (i.e. pictorial thought vs. conceptual thought), "the content of religion and philosophy is the same," namely the Absolute or God. Philosophers who consider unorthodox perspectives on God have long been accused of atheism (having "*too little* of God") or pantheism (having "*too much* of him"). While some philosophers are atheistic, Hegel doubts that any serious philosopher is a crude pantheist, maintaining that "God is everything and everything is God" (*Mind*, 12, 18, 20, 292, 298–299, 303–305). However, unless "everything" there means only everything in our finite world of time and space, it seems that Hegel (and, before him, Spinoza) did qualify.

In his *Lectures on the Philosophy of Religion*, Hegel goes into all of this more extensively than we can consider here. Indeed, his whole system revolves around God, as he makes clear: "The object of religion as well as of philosophy is eternal truth in its objectivity, God and nothing but God, and the explication of God . . . Philosophy, therefore, only unfolds itself when it unfolds religion, and in unfolding itself it unfolds religion." Here lies the alleged identity of philosophy and religion, which should not be shocking if outside God there is nothing at all. Their difference is merely one of form, philosophy having to justify its claims rationally as opposed to religion's resting on faith and authority. This requires argumentation, and he is familiar with the critique of traditional arguments for God raised by, for example, Hume and Kant, at the level of reflective understanding. What he seeks is a revolution in our thinking about their proper role at the level of reason. What must be avoided is any suggestion that "the Being of God" is "dependent on the Being of the finite," as if they are separable. The Infinite cannot be deduced from the finite. The function of the proofs is, rather, to show how human reason can rise to the level of the infinite and establish "the implicit unity of the divine and human natures." In demonstrating monistic panentheism, Hegel's system presumably overcomes all the dualisms of thinkers such as Kant. As he writes, "There is only one Being, . . . and things by their very nature form part of it." We finite spirits and all physical objects are part of the Absolute: "Everything is thus included in it, and it is immediately present in everything." This is no "absurd" crude "Pantheism," but a monistic panentheism (*Religion*, I, 2, 19, 168, 170–171; II, 349; III, 315–316, 319, 348). However, despite his protests that he was an orthodox Christian, it is easy to understand his being accused of heterodoxy.

16.6 Humanity

In the Introduction to his lectures on the philosophy of history, Hegel views all of human history as the self-manifestation of absolute Spirit in time. While we are essentially rational beings, the actions of all humans are rooted in "their needs, their passions, their interests, their characters and talents," rather than in pure reason. As we are psycho-physical beings, our needs and interests are physical, emotional, psychological, social, and so on. Our history, of course, is marked by conflict, violence, and grief. Yet, even as we reflect on history as a worldwide "slaughter-bench," we should consider it in the context of an "ultimate goal" and the means necessary to achieve it. On an individual scale, we seek personal satisfaction, requiring a combination of reason and desire. But, on a larger scale, human history (contrary to the views of Bentham) is not a matter of human happiness. Even the most powerful and influential of humans, "the *world-historical* individuals," such as Alexander, Caesar, and Napoleon, achieve little in the way of happiness for themselves or their adherents. Yet they unwittingly and often unwillingly advance the hidden designs of "the World Spirit," so that, despite all their petty selfishness, they "can be called *heroes*." They may lead lives of stress and hardship and often meet with tragic ends. "They die young, like Alexander; they are murdered, like Caesar; they are exiled, like Napoleon." But their happiness does not matter, so long as they serve the plan of absolute Spirit. "This may be called the *Cunning of Reason*," that all of us are used for greater purposes than we can comprehend. Yet this is not to say that we are merely means to extrinsic ends. It is in the area of personal values – "*morality, ethics, religious commitment*" – that persons "are to be regarded as ends in themselves" (as Kant had put it), these being areas of rational freedom and personal dignity. Apart from these areas, the demands of "the World Spirit" must take priority over our wishes. It is our capacity for rational thought and personal freedom that sets us apart from all other animals (*History*, 23–26, 29, 32–33, 35–36, 40, 74). And, as we shall see, the goal of human history is the progressive development of the consciousness of human freedom.

Before we explore some of the most brilliant and famous portions of the *Phenomenology*, we should understand that Hegel views all of reality as dynamic and constantly developing, even God. As he succinctly puts the point, all of Life is "a *process*" of becoming. Thus, more than half a century before Darwin published his views on evolution, Hegel was already theorizing along comparable lines. Human self-consciousness is motivated to change and to act by desire. Among our universal human desires is that for personal recognition. But this can only come from another personal subject and never from a mere object. Yet, until we learn to respect others as persons, we inevitably treat them as mere objects, demanding from them the recognition we desire while refusing to reciprocate. Each person may encounter the other as alien to itself, conflict which leads each to want "to supersede the *other*." Each recognizes the other as representing a radically different perspective and set of conflicting desires, and they are mutually estranged. Each wants to reduce the other to a mere object to eliminate the threat to his own subjectivity, setting up "a life-and-death struggle," psychologically, if not also literally. The simplest solution is for one of them to destroy the other. But if this literally occurs, the loser would be reduced to a lifeless corpse, which would be counterproductive, since a corpse cannot confer recognition. What is needed is for one of them, fearing for his life, to back down and submit to the will of the other, creating the relationship of "lordship" and "servitude," with the "lord" functioning as the independent variable and the "bondsman" as dependent. Thus it would appear that the antithetical opposition has been involved in the synthesis of recognized domination and subordination denied such recognition. But the dialectic is never that simple and easily stabilized. The bondsman learns to master the environment by his labor, achieving a sort of recognition and satisfaction, though still a bondsman, subject to the will of another. Meanwhile, the lord becomes dependent on the expertise, industry, and productivity of the bondsman, whose very recognition becomes worthless, as coming from a servile inferior (*Phenomenology*, 107, 109, 111–119). So the alienation from the other, instead of being genuinely resolved, has been intensified by a dramatic reversal or "counterthrust" of Hegelian dialectic.

What could occur next is that both the lord and the bondsman should come to realize that he is alienated from what is external to himself but free and independent in the areas of his own thinking. Each is master of his own internal thoughts and desires, ideas and ideals, views and values – the arena in which personal satisfaction can be found. So each tends to retreat into the privacy of his own self-consciousness and to withdraw from external relationships, to the extent that this is possible. This is the position of Stoicism, available to all of us, whether lord ("on the throne" like Marcus Aurelius) or slave ("in chains" like Epictetus) or anything in between such extremes. So, once more, we have what initially appears as a synthesis. But, again, it proves illusory. By denying all external relations, Stoicism deprives itself of any adequate criterion of truth and value, introducing a new depth of alienation, this time from our own thinking. With this, consciousness has fallen into Skepticism. Without any independent criteria, it has no basis for delineating true from false beliefs, good from pernicious values. But now, alienated from its own thoughts, the mind finds itself effectively devoid of any stable content at all. It has sunk into the pit of what Hegel calls "the *Unhappy Consciousness*," profoundly alienated from everything, including even itself, a divided soul. "Here, then, we have a struggle against an enemy, to vanquish whom is really to suffer defeat," as we are waging war on ourselves, rather than on others (*Phenomenology*, 119–127). The root of the problem is that, at this stage of development, we are so inclined to self-absorption as to be yet incapable of healthy interpersonal relationships. We must, somehow, move in the direction of community.

This requires a transition from self-centered self-consciousness to the level of Reason and, beyond that, to the level of Spirit. Prior to these transitions, the mind has not grasped the identity of the rational and the actual, of thought and reality. "Reason is the certainty of consciousness that it is all reality." This is the truth of German idealism. Initially, that is allegedly mere subjective idealism (represented by Kant and Fichte); but then it develops into objective idealism (Schelling), and, finally, into (Hegel's own) absolute idealism. Reason "merely *asserts* that it is all reality, but does not itself comprehend" this truth. Coming to do so will require dialectical development. So long as reason remains individualistic, its identification with reality will remain abstract. By contrast, Spirit recognizes itself as essentially social and in community. "Reason is Spirit when its certainty of being all reality has been raised to truth, and it is conscious of itself as its own world, and of the world as itself." With increasing socialization, the alienation of individualism is healed, the self embracing the world as no longer "something alien to it." Spirit is dynamic, "*actual* and *alive*," in us and all around us. All more rudimentary "shapes of consciousness are abstract forms of it." As such, they fall short of the truth. By contrast, "Spirit is the *ethical life* of a nation" capable of genuine community (*Phenomenology*, 139–142, 263–265), the level of life at which freedom, values, rights, and proper social institutions should prove operative. A few decades later, Marx would follow Hegel in diagnosing the alienation of humans and prescribing a cure.

16.7 Freedom

We have already gotten a preview into the thesis of Hegel's philosophy of history, that the "*final goal of the world* . . . is Spirit's consciousness of its freedom, and hence also the actualization of that very freedom." He analyzes this process in three main phases: (i) that of "the ancient Orient," which only recognized that "*one* person is free" – e.g. the emperor; (ii) that of the ancient Greeks and Romans, that "*some* persons are free" – e.g. citizens; and (iii) that of Christian "German peoples" (broadly interpreted to mean northern Europeans) that "*every* human is free by virtue of being human" – e.g. Kantian thought. As we move forward in time, humanity becomes increasingly aware of this expansion as appropriate. "World history is the progress in the consciousness of freedom," which is itself, however, necessarily determined. But here things get complicated: on the one hand, we are free, but, on the other hand, the arc of history is itself determined. So even "the *world-historical individuals*" who are the primary agents of change are surreptitiously directed by "the *Cunning of Reason*," to which they may be oblivious. So where is there room for freedom from the manipulations of cosmic Reason and for meaningful self-determination? It seems that we are truly free only in choosing our own values – that is, in the areas of "*morality, ethics, religious commitment*." We have seen this move made before, asserting that, ultimately, we are only free in and responsible for our internal acts of will and never in our external physical actions. So abstract acts of free will are "self-determining"; but their expression is in the context of potential negative opposition, out of which "negation (*Aufheben*)" there can emerge a synthesis that is "an affirmative, richer, and more concrete determination" of our choices (*History*, 21–23, 32–36, 67).

In his *Philosophy of Right*, Hegel appropriately locates all right as stemming from free will. But it is a mistake to reduce "the will's self-determination" to mere "negative freedom, or freedom as the Understanding conceives it," as was done by such empiricists as Hobbes, Locke, and Hume, when they analyzed liberty. The positive dimension of freedom has to do with "the *self*-determination of the ego," and not merely with negative freedom from restraint. Freedom, properly understood, is freedom *for* determining our own wills and not merely freedom *from* the sort of extrinsic force over which we have no control. Nor should we conceive of freedom in terms of arbitrary whimsy: "If we hear it said that the definition of freedom is ability to do what we please, such an idea can only be taken to reveal an utter immaturity of thought, for it contains not even an inkling of the absolutely free will, of right, of ethical life, and so forth." Unfortunately, this is the way we tend to think of human freedom. Moral freedom consists in choosing as we rationally should rather than merely as we arbitrarily please (*Right*, 20, 22–23, 27, 230).

There is more in the sections on "Mind Practical" and "Free Mind" from Hegel's *Philosophy of Mind*. He writes, "True liberty, in the shape of the moral life, consists in the will finding its purpose in a universal content, not in subjective or selfish interests." Happiness is subjective, while morality is objective. What Hegel calls "*Free Mind*" is a synthetic "unity of theoretical and practical mind." But people from cultures other than those of modern Europe allegedly could not grasp the very idea (with even Plato, Aristotle, and the Stoics insufficiently developed), mistakenly supposing it contingent on accidents of birth. "It was through Christianity that this Idea came into the world," even so needing time to be realized. It was a revolutionary idea that all persons are rightly free and have the sort of "infinite value" that Kant called "dignity" (*Mind*, 228, 238–240). This takes us to the topics of morality and ethical life.

16.8 Morality

We have traced the roots of alienation to excessive individualism and self-absorption. But self-consciousness "is better than it thinks" itself to be, since even its selfish behavior "is at the same time an implicitly universal action." The "cunning" of Reason is such that we, however unwittingly, serve higher purposes than our own. Ironically, moral reason, striving to be categorical, cannot both be practical and ignore circumstantial conditions. For example, using a favorite Kantian duty, to say, "Everyone ought to speak the truth" is to assume knowledge of the truth, which is contingent on circumstances. Kant's categorical imperative, detached from all empirical conditions, allegedly is purely formal and thus impractical. Ethics must be contextual, the content being provided by "the *ethical life* of a nation," the moral "community." At the other extreme, however, Bentham's utilitarian theory would reduce all value to the empirical consideration of "pure utility." The truth of utilitarianism is that it values happiness; and any moral theory of *"pure duty"* that tries to divorce morality altogether from our natural inclination to happiness (as Kant's critics wrongly accuse him of doing) is doomed to a surreal artificiality. The cult of pure duty can lead to an abstracted moral perspective that "flees from contact with the actual world" and which Hegel sarcastically calls the "beautiful soul." The problem is that this would-be moral individual has established an "antithetical" relationship with society; what is needed is the synthesis of genuine community (*Phenomenology*, 235, 254, 256, 265, 267, 342–343, 366, 400, 409).

In his *Philosophy of Right*, Hegel locates the core of ethics "in the law of the land, in the morality of everyday life, and in religion," which might immediately arouse suspicions of moral relativism. He identifies right with the expression of free will, as the rational mind is the locus "of all truth, worth, and dignity." He distinguishes among, first, abstract right derived from contractual agreement, second, private morality, including personal responsibility and individual conscience, and, third, concrete ethical life, which comprises (i) "the *Family*," (ii) "*Civil Society*," and (iii) "the *State*" in its internal relations, international relations, and place in world history. He correctly points out that his distinction between abstract morality and concrete "ethical life" is unusual in modern philosophy. He considers Kant's treatment of morality abstract because it is focused on the universal rather than on concrete ethical life, downplaying the consequences of actions, actual "needs, inclinations, passions," and so forth, as well as the value of human "welfare or happiness" (emphasized by utilitarians). Hegel thinks that Kant, ignoring sociocultural content, holds the preposterous view that we are morally better persons if we do our duty against our own inclinations and disregarding human well-being: "Welfare without right is not a good. Similarly, right without welfare is not a good." If the first of those represents the utilitarian thesis and the second the Kantian antithesis, what is needed is a synthesis of the two, a marriage of welfare and right. Of course, we should try to do our duty; but this should not indicate an insoluble dichotomy between doing what is right and promoting human welfare. To renounce the latter for the sake of the former, as Kant is suspected of having done, is to reduce ethics "to an empty formalism, and the science of morals to the preaching of duty for duty's sake." Nor does he think that Kant's categorical imperative is particularly helpful in resolving concrete moral dilemmas, such as whether we can (or even should) commit theft to save innocent lives or desert our military charge in order to avoid a suicidal mission. But then the opposite extreme of utilitarian consequentialism, popularly summarized by "the notorious maxim: 'The end justifies the means,'" is also "trivial and pointless" when interpreted as a universal ethical principle abstracted from concrete circumstances. What is needed is to transcend the sphere of private, formal morality and to rise to the concrete level of "Ethical Life," at which values are considered in a particular sociocultural context from the real world. Mere abstract morality is inadequate and subjective. Thus we must now turn to consideration of an actual "objective ethical order" (*Right*, 3, 20, 30, 35–36, 80, 83–84, 87, 89–90, 97–98, 103, 105).

16.9 Society

Hegel's sociopolitical theory seems to move from reformist in his youth to conservative in his elder years; for example, he was an enthusiastic supporter of the French Revolution of 1789 but an opponent of the July Revolution (also in France) of 1830. But, even in the *Phenomenology*, there are indications of what today is called communitarianism. He writes, "The wisest men" have "declared that wisdom and virtue consist in living in accordance with the customs of one's nation." This indicates a conformity to a *status quo* that "exists merely as something *given*" in a nation's "customs and laws." Eighteen years after the French Revolution, he says, "The *community*, the superior law whose validity is openly apparent, has its real vitality in the government" as the source of prescriptive behavior, in the context of "the three relationships" of the family, those of "husband and wife, parents and children, brothers and sisters." Although such social relationships may, in fact, be based on "customs and laws," it seems presumptuous of Hegel to assume that they should be. Hegel blames the cult of individualism and utility for the French Revolution's radical pursuit of "*absolute freedom*" and its subsequent reign of terror. "In this absolute freedom, therefore, all social groups or classes which are the spiritual spheres into which the whole is articulated are abolished" in the name of abstract ideals of equality and utility, leading to the destructive negative consequences of the Terror of 1793. The lawless anarchy of absolute freedom spawns a pervasive fear of death that cows people into a submission to social oppression reminiscent of lordship and bondage, but at a more collective level. Under such false ideals as liberty, equality, and fraternity, human beings are butchered in the name of "the Utility of the Enlightenment"; with the guillotine as cold, efficient instrument of dispatch, life becomes cheap, negated by "the death that is without meaning." Liberal values have run amok; and, in the short run, at any rate, "nothing positive" seems to come of it all (*Phenomenology*, 214, 272–273, 356–357, 359–362). Even if Hegel's collectivism is at odds with the individualism that dominates eighteenth- and nineteenth-century European philosophy, it is, at least, consistent with his idealistic monism.

His *Philosophy of History* calls for a synthesis of "the subjective will and the rational will," forming "an ethical totality, the *state*." Genuine ethical freedom is positive commitment to following reason and not negative caprice. If this suggests a call for conforming our personal will to a glorified collective, Hegel boldly adds, "The State is the divine Idea, as it exists on earth." Again, this is consistent with his rationalistic panentheism, even if it raises red flags regarding individual autonomy. He rejects the "state of nature" and the social contract theory that accompanies it. Far from limiting freedom to join society, by conforming to the customs and laws of society, we allegedly realize genuine freedom. He attacks as "a false and dangerous assumption" the democratic notion that sociopolitical legitimacy is a function of popular consent. Of the three forms of government – monarchy, aristocracy, and democracy – he favors constitutional monarchy, as both consolidating power and protecting genuine freedom. He assails the popular "prejudice" in favor of representative government, denouncing it as "malicious" and rooted in a fatuous commitment to "the principle of individuality." Far from valuing a separation of politics and religion, he explicitly holds that "the state rests upon religion" (again, the emphasis is on unity rather than segregation). On this view, religion is "prior" to politics, the latter being properly based on the former. What is needed in all this is to strengthen social bonds that will provide an antidote to "the isolation of individuals from one another." The march of world history, as it progresses toward a healthy society in which genuine freedom is universally realized, "rises in the East," then "goes from East to West," and will, finally, "sink in the West." Thus it purportedly moves from its primitive "childhood" in Asia, through its "adolescence" in ancient Greece and its "manhood" in the Roman culture, to its mature "old age" among Christian Germanic peoples (*History*, 41–43, 46–47, 49–56, 80, 92–97). At any rate, no healthy society can be merely a collection of individuals, regardless how extrinsically interrelated they may be.

Hegel's *Philosophy of Right* is his masterpiece in this area. And, fairly or not, it is the book that most solidified his reputation of having become, in the last dozen years or so of his life, an apologist for the Prussian state. In the Preface, he maintains that philosophy is a public, rather than a private, activity performed "in the service of the state." (This can be placed in some context, however, by remembering that German universities of that time were state institutions and that their professors were civil servants.) Let us now consider the three great organizations of ethical life, starting with the family, which ought to be held together "by love," such that every member functions as an interconnected part of the whole rather than as a separate individual. He writes, in some detail, about three phases of family life – the marriage relationship, which should be based on love, mutual trust, and common sharing, with the husband the "active" partner and the wife the "passive" one; "possessions" or "capital" belonging to the entire family but managed by its head; and the children, who have a right to maintenance and education, at the expense of the family's capital, until they come of independent age, with the family being dissolved with the death of the parents and the passing on of its remaining capital through inheritance (*Right*, 7, 110–114, 116–119).

The second great organization of ethical life is civil society, which is construed as "a system of complete interdependence, wherein the livelihood, happiness, and legal status of one man is interwoven with the livelihood, happiness, and rights of all." Our economic needs are best met through interpersonal cooperation, and the flourishing of our spiritual nature requires the meeting of physical needs. Reminiscent of Adam Smith's "invisible hand" theory, Hegel maintains that "each man in earning, producing, and enjoying on his own account is *eo ipso* producing and earning for the enjoyment of everyone else" (Marx and Engels will reject such economic idealism). "Men are made unequal by nature," Hegel writes, and civil society should not try to create an artificial social equality; nor is there necessarily anything wrong with class divisions (contrary to what Marx and Engels will argue). In addition to meeting economic needs, civil society must administer justice, pursuing and punishing criminals, using "retribution" to uphold civil law and order. Also, civil society should use its public authority to care for the poor, providing opportunities for honest work and maintaining a decent "standard of living" for all citizens (*Right*, 123, 128–132, 141, 148–150).

The third great organization of ethical life is the state, which, insofar as it is rational, "is the actuality of the ethical Idea." As such, the "final end" of collective unity "has supreme right against the individual, whose supreme duty is to be a member of the state." This view (with which Kantians can be seriously troubled) is another statement that may well have bolstered Hegel's popularity with the Prussian state. The state should be responsibly involved in constitutional law, international law, and the process of world history. Hegel sees "a division of powers within the state" as imperative, with the crown, the executive, and the legislature collaborating in ruling; and he favors a "constitutional monarchy." In terms of the ancient (Aristotelian) trichotomy of government by one, by some, and by the many, he sees the monarch as the one, the executive as the few, and the elected legislature as the many. The state should be regarded as "an organism" and not merely as "an aggregate" (as it was by Bentham). While the legislature passes the laws, the monarch should have ultimate decision-making authority and should be advised by the executive, which would be comprised of civil servants drawn from the middle class. Hegel is quite ambivalent about public opinion, which he says "deserves to be as much respected as despised," and about freedom of expression (including both "the press and the spoken word"), which should be both protected by law and have its excesses punished by law. He also refuses categorically to denounce warfare as undertaken by the state: "War is not to be regarded as an absolute evil." He warns that "the product of prolonged, let alone 'perpetual' peace" would likely be national corruption (*Right*, 155–156, 160, 175–176, 180–181, 186, 190–193, 204–207, 209–210).

Finally, let us turn to Hegel's treatment of the state's involvement with international law and world history. Every nation-state has "absolute power" over its own territory and people, is, therefore, "sovereign and autonomous against its neighbors," and should be recognized as such. Different states can always conflict in their interests and policies and should try to resolve their disagreements peacefully; but sometimes these attempts will fail, and the issues between them

16 Georg Wilhelm Friedrich Hegel

"can only be settled by war," despite the Kantian dream of "a League of Nations" that might maintain "perpetual peace" among nation-states. Hegel considers world history to be the final "court of judgement," and he expresses his (unjustified and, probably, unjustifiable) confidence that this will never be merely "the verdict of mere might." He even makes the startling (for an idealist) claim that the verdicts of world history operate at a higher level than all of our moral ideals. In any given period of world history, some nation or other best represents that phase of the Absolute's self-expression and tends to be "dominant" and legitimately exerts its will internationally. "In contrast with this its absolute right of being, . . . the other nations are without rights, and they, along with those whose hour has struck already, count no longer in world history." (One can see how this viewpoint could be used to justify geopolitical domination by force.) Nothing is permanent in human affairs; and every "world-historical nation" will rise in influence, then gradually decline, and, finally, be eclipsed by another. Ordinary people function merely as their "living instruments" for effecting their will, with little or no compensation or recognition. Nor should we expect "civilized nations" to treat "barbarians" with respect as if they were equals. The historical evolution of human beings from "the Oriental" phase, through the Greek and Roman, to the Germanic Christian is pertinent to this (potentially dangerous) idea. Although it is controversial to say so, Hegel's theory of the state seems to conduce to nationalistic exploitation and oppression. We can end with two particularly disturbing statements. First, Hegel says, "The march of God in the world, that is what the state is." And, finally, as one last gift to practitioners of political absolutism, he adds, "Man must therefore venerate the state as a secular deity" (*Right*, 212–214, 216–222, 279, 285).

16.10   Review

Hegel is one of the most complex and influential of all modern European philosophers. Important aspects of his legacy are indisputably great, including (but not limited to) his capacity to make critical use of the history of philosophy, his clear-eyed commitment to working out an epistemology that will open up knowledge of ultimate reality, his pushing of German idealism to its monistic limits, and his robust development of dialectical logic. But there are other dimensions of his thought that are so ambiguous as to be both challenging and frustrating, including (especially) his philosophical theology, which has been interpreted here as a panentheistic alternative to atheism, skepticism, and deism, rather than as the orthodox ethical monotheism that some would say it is, and his sociopolitical philosophy, interpreted here as collectivistic and conservative, rather than the reform-minded liberalism that some would make it out to be. At any rate, Hegel gives us a coherent, comprehensive system to which every one of the philosophical theories we shall study in the following chapters can be viewed as a more or less hostile reaction (i.e. the voluntarism of Schopenhauer, the atheism of Feuerbach, the communism of Marx, the radical utilitarian empiricism of Mill, the Christian existentialism of Kierkegaard, and the atheistic existentialism of Nietzsche), not to mention American and twentieth-century philosophies not considered here. Hegel's impact has been huge.[2]

---

2 For more on Hegel, see ch. V of *Twelve Great Philosophers*, by Wayne P. Pomerleau (New York: Ardsley House, 1997), and ch. 7 of *Western Philosophies of Religion*, by Wayne P. Pomerleau (New York: Ardsley House, 1998).

17

Arthur Schopenhauer

Source: Johann Schäfer/Wikimedia Commons/Public Domain

17.1 Overview

Schopenhauer's philosophy is quite different from most others we have thus far considered. It metaphysically emphasizes will over reason, is distinctly pessimistic rather than optimistic, is irreligious rather than religious, is influenced by Eastern thought as well as by Western philosophy, and develops a system designed to provide both a diagnosis of and therapy for human suffering. He is in the tradition of German idealism but not quite of it, considering himself the legitimate critical heir of Kant and seeing Fichte, Schelling, and Hegel as sophists who were merely Kant's intellectual bastard descendants. While his work was unsuccessful until rather late in his life, his unusual voluntaristic idealism grew in influence toward its end and after his death. It was a series of essays in popular philosophy that attracted an audience to his more rigorous works.[1]

17.2 Biography

Without too outrageous a venture into playing amateur psychologist, one can see how his eccentric personality, strained relationships with other people, and odd life experiences might have contributed to his producing an iconoclastic philosophical system. Arthur Schopenhauer was born on February 22, 1788, in Danzig, a free city on the northern coast of what is now Poland. His father, Heinrich Floris Schopenhauer, a prosperous upper-class merchant, was a cosmopolitan lover of liberty; his mother, Johanna Troisner Schopenhauer, almost a couple of decades younger than his father, was cultured and artistically inclined, later becoming a popular writer. Their republican family motto proclaimed, "no happiness without liberty," and the parents celebrated the news of the French Revolution in 1789. When Arthur was five, the family moved to Hamburg, Germany (a free constitutional republic), because Prussia was annexing Danzig. In 1797, Arthur's sister Adele was born. Between 1797 and 1799, Arthur was living in France with a family connected to his father – this was the most pleasant period of his childhood, and he became fluent in French. After returning to Hamburg, he was sent to a school that educated future merchants. In 1803, in return for Arthur's commitment to become a merchant, his parents took him on a European tour; for 12 weeks he attended a school in Wimbledon, England, where he learned English very well. The following year, he returned to Danzig, where he apprenticed under a friend of his father's; near the end of 1804, he relocated in Hamburg, becoming an apprentice to an associate of his father's. He hated the work and wanted to read and study instead but felt bound by his earlier commitment. Meanwhile, his father's mental health was deteriorating, and he died unexpectedly in the spring of 1805; Arthur was badly affected by the death, while his mother was not, and both of them believed it was suicide. Johanna sold the family business; she and Adele subsequently moved to the cultural center of Weimar, while Arthur continued his apprenticeship in Hamburg. Johanna started her own salon, hosting tea parties for artists and intellectuals, with Goethe being a frequent guest, at about the time Napoleon was invading Germany. Arthur and his mother got along quite badly; but she did support his ending his apprenticeship and starting to prepare for a university education, at a school in Gotha, in the summer of 1807. By the end of that year, he had withdrawn from the school after being chastised for writing a disrespectful poem about one of his teachers; he moved to Weimar but did not choose to live with his family there. In 1808, he was studying classical languages, history, and mathematics, in order to qualify for admission to a university.

---

1 References to Schopenhauer's writings will be to *The World as Will and Representation*, by Arthur Schopenhauer (hereafter called *World*, followed by volume and page numbers), trans. by E.F.J. Payne, 2 volumes (New York: Dover Publications, 1966), to *On the Fourfold Root of the Principle of Sufficient Reason*, by Arthur Schopenhauer (hereafter called *Root*), trans. by E.F.J. Payne (LaSalle, IL: Open Court, 1974), to *Essay on the Freedom of the Will*, by Arthur Schopenhauer (hereafter called *Freedom*), trans. by Konstantin Kolenda (Indianapolis: Liberal Arts Press, 1960), to *On the Basis of Morality*, by Arthur Schopenhauer (hereafter called *Morality*), trans. by E.F.J. Payne (Indianapolis: Bobbs-Merrill, 1965), to *Philosophy of Arthur Schopenhauer* (hereafter called *Philosophy*), trans. by Belfort Bax and Bailey Saunders (New York: Tudor Publishing Co., 1949), to *Philosophical Writings*, by Arthur Schopenhauer (hereafter called *Writings*), trans. by E.F.J. Payne, ed. by Wolfgang Schirmacher (New York: Continuum, 1994), to *On Human Nature*, by Arthur Schopenhauer (hereafter called *Human*), trans. by Thomas Bailey Saunders (London: Swan, Sonnenschein & Co., 1906), and to *Essays and Aphorisms*, by Arthur Schopenhauer (hereafter called *Essays*), trans. and ed. by R.J. Hollingdale (Harmondsworth: Penguin Books, 1970).

In 1809, on his twenty-first birthday, he received a third of his father's estate as his inheritance and then enrolled at the University of Göttingen as a medical student. He also studied metaphysics, psychology, and logic there, his philosophy teacher recommending that he focus on Plato and Kant in his private studies. In 1811, he went to the recently opened University of Berlin to study philosophy, attending Fichte's lectures there (as well as Schleiermacher's); his attitude toward Fichte shifted from reverence to contempt. In 1812, when he was preparing to begin his dissertation, Napoleon's troops moved through Berlin on their way to Russia, Schopenhauer fleeing from the city. He briefly returned to Weimar and then settled in Rudolstadt to write his dissertation *On the Fourfold Root of the Principle of Sufficient Reason*; it was accepted by the University of Jena in 1813 (earning him his doctorate) and published later that same year, after which he returned to Weimar. His mother had recently published a travel memoir, which was a popular success. When she scorned his book as reading attractive only to pharmacists (who are interested in "roots"), he told her his book would be read when there would no longer be any copies of hers, to which she contemptuously replied that his entire edition would go unsold. A bitter break between them was imminent. But, during this unhappy period of living with his mother, he did become friendly with Goethe and met an Orientalist, who introduced him to the Eastern thought of ancient India; he started studying a Latin translation of the Hindu Upanishads. In the spring of 1814, after further quarrels with Johanna, he moved to Dresden, never to visit his mother again. Meanwhile, Goethe had published his (unsuccessful) theory of color, which Schopenhauer openly advocated. Indeed, he wrote a book, *On Vision and Colors*, the manuscript for which he sent to Goethe, telling him it was based on Goethe's ideas. Schopenhauer's work was published in the spring of 1816, and he sent a copy to Goethe.

He began work on *The World as Will and Representation*, the book that would become his *magnum opus*, viewing Plato and the Upanishads, as well as Kant, as his philosophical inspirations, identifying Plato's changing world of transitory things and the Hindu veil of *Maya* with Kant's order of phenomenal appearances. By 1815, he had also begun reading a bit about Buddhism. His book was finished early in 1818 and published near the end of that year; he sent a copy to Goethe. He left Germany for Italy. In the spring of 1819, while he was away, a maid in Dresden gave birth to his daughter, but she died in infancy. That summer he returned to Germany, and near the end of the year, he applied to teach as a *Privatdozent* (private lecturer) at the University of Berlin. He was accepted and, in 1820, deliberately scheduled his classes at the same time as the formidable Hegel's classes, so that students would have to choose between them; hardly any students enrolled in his courses, and he bitterly gave up before the term was completed. Meanwhile, reviews of his book, while generally praising its writing style, dismissed its content. In 1821, he began an affair with Caroline Richter (later called "Medon"), which lasted about a decade. She already had a son. When he later left Berlin, in 1831, to avoid the cholera epidemic, he invited her to accompany him, but without her son; she declined his invitation. In the summer of 1821, he quarreled with a neighbor of his, a seamstress who was loudly gossiping outside his door, calling her a name and pushing her; she fell and was injured. Claiming that he had punched and kicked her, she filed assault charges against him. He ended up being legally required to pay her every year for the rest of her life; when she died (in 1842), he commented, "*obit anus, abit onus*" (meaning, "the old woman died, the burden removed"). In 1822, he left Berlin for another tour of Italy and generally enjoyed it. After returning to Munich in 1823, he was ill and depressed (possibly having contracted syphilis from visiting Italian bordellos). He unsuccessfully tried to get a contract to translate Hume into German. After returning to Berlin, he studied Spanish (in 1825). In 1826, he read the first edition of Kant's first *Critique*, thinking it significantly superior to all subsequent editions. (He owned four different engravings of Kant.) In 1827, he again tried teaching, again at the same time as Hegel, and encountering humiliating failure once more. He unsuccessfully inquired about teaching positions at Würtzburg and Heidelberg. When he left Berlin in 1831, to escape the cholera epidemic that killed Hegel, he moved to Frankfurt. He was so depressed that, in 1832, he isolated himself in his own apartment for a couple of months. He moved to Mannheim, where he lived for about a year, before moving back to Frankfurt, where he lived for the remainder of his life. As an adult, he seemed to have lurched from one failure to another, always anxiety-ridden (he slept with a loaded pistol) and without any genuine friends. (He loved his poodle, named Atma, which children called "Young Schopenhauer.")

In early 1836, he published *On the Will in Nature*. Two years later, his mother died in Bonn; he did not attend the funeral. In June of 1838, he submitted his essay *On the Freedom of the Will* for an essay contest. In early 1839, it won the gold medal from the Royal Norwegian Society of Sciences sponsoring the contest; it was published in 1840. In the summer of 1839, he submitted *On the Basis of Morality* to the Royal Danish Society of Sciences as an entry in its prize essay contest; it did not win even though his was the only entry, partly because of its insulting some recent thinkers. When he learned of this decision in 1840, he was furious; later that year, he published both of these essays together as *The Two Fundamental Problems of Ethics*, in the Preface of which he attacked Fichte and Hegel. In 1841 (the year Frederick Wilhelm IV brought Schelling to Berlin and the year Feuerbach published *The Essence of Christianity*), Schopenhauer was working on essays that would become the second volume of *The World as Will and Representation*. In 1842, he visited his sister in Frankfurt – the first time in a couple of decades he had seen his only sibling. In 1844, the second edition of *The World as Will and Representation* was published. The following year, he started writing his *Parerga and Paralipomena* (Byproducts and Omissions). In 1847, a revised second edition of *On the Fourfold Root of the Principle of Sufficient Reason* was published. In 1848, the year the *Communist Manifesto*, by Marx and Engels, was published, violent revolutionary activity spread to Frankfurt; the conservative Schopenhauer was antidemocratic and, no doubt, relieved that the uprisings failed; indeed, he later amended his will to leave the bulk of his estate for the support of Prussian soldiers. In 1849, he met with Adele for the last time; she died the next month in Bonn, her brother not attending her funeral. In 1851, his *Parerga and Paralipomena*, a series of essays in more popular philosophy, was published; it was his first successful publication, helping to build the small following he had, and, for once, the reviews were, for the most part, positive. In 1854, second editions of *On the Will in Nature* and *On Vision and Colors* were published. In early 1856, he read that the University of Leipzig was sponsoring an essay contest on the Schopenhauerian philosophy; he worried that it would provide an occasion for publicly attacking him, and his anxieties were confirmed when a theology student won the prize. By 1857, lectures on his philosophy were being presented at the Universities of Bonn, Breslau, and Jena; yet no academic school of followers ensued. Near the end of 1859, a third edition of *The World as Will and Representation* was published. In September of 1860, a second edition of *The Two Fundamental Problems of Ethics* was published. But that same month he developed an inflammation of the lungs. On September 20, he fell while getting out of bed and hit his head; and the next day, he died. There was a small private funeral for him on September 26; and, in 1895, a monument to him was erected in Frankfurt.

17.3 Knowledge

Schopenhauer's philosophy selectively but significantly draws from the writings of Kant, Plato, and the Upanishads, as he makes clear in the Preface to the first edition of his masterpiece; but, of these, the most indispensable source of inspiration was Kant. He writes in the Preface to the second edition that his "philosophy starts from Kant's, and therefore presupposes a thorough knowledge of it." Indeed, he can be considered a critical follower of Kant's, who views other German idealists – Fichte, Schelling, and, especially, Hegel – to have distorted and corrupted his perspective. Schopenhauer himself professes to set the record straight in pursuit of truth (*World*, I, xv, xxiii–xxiv, xxi, xxvi; cf. *Philosophy*, 119–122, 195).

Even though we shall not devote much attention to his first book (his doctoral dissertation), *On the Fourfold Root of the Principle of Sufficient Reason*, he plausibly claims that it is necessary epistemological background for his main work (*World*, I, xiv). Like Kant, he distinguishes between the order of phenomenal appearances and the noumenal realm of the thing-in-itself, maintaining that our knowledge of the former involves the principle of sufficient reason, as well as the forms of time and space, though none of these apply to the thing-in-itself. His formulation of this "fundamental principle of all knowledge" of phenomenal appearances is that of Christian Wolff, the follower of Leibniz, that nothing is without a reason why it is rather than is not. He distinguishes four roots of the principle, distinguished by their objects. First, there is a "principle of reason of becoming," applied to the changes in empirical, material things, allowing us to relate causes and their effects. Second, there is a "principle of sufficient reason of knowing," whose objects are concepts, allowing us to establish connections of logical necessity. Third, there is a principle of reason of being, applicable to the constructions of mathematical essence. And, fourth, there is a principle of reason for acting, which identifies psychological motives determining actions. "Accordingly, there is a fourfold necessity corresponding to the four forms of sufficient reason" – physical, logical, mathematical, and moral. Two observations are in order at this point: all cognitive knowledge involves necessity, and the principle of sufficient reason, in all four forms, only applies to the order of phenomenal appearances. One last epistemological point should be mentioned: "All knowledge inevitably presupposes subject and object." This is true of all phenomenal knowledge, as well as of the noumenal knowledge that he will go on to affirm; "even self-consciousness," he claims, "is divided into a known and a knower" (*Root*, 2, 6, 25, 52–53, 156, 194, 214, 226–227, 234, 207–208). So Schopenhauer articulates four different dimensions of the Leibnizian-Wolffian principle of sufficient reason and embraces the subject–object dichotomy Hegel denounced.

Now we should be prepared to explore key epistemological elements of *The World as Will and Representation*, the main body of which comprises four books: the first deals with the world of phenomenal appearances, as subject to the principle of sufficient reason; the second deals with the noumenal world as will; the third deals with the phenomenal world again, but this time from the perspective of art, rather than from that of sufficient reason; and the fourth deals with the world of will again, but this time with a focus on how we can cope with it rather than merely knowing it. The famous first sentence of the first book clearly establishes its idealism: "The world is my representation: this is a truth valid with reference to every living and knowing being, although man alone can bring it into reflective, abstract consciousness." In fact, it applies to inanimate bodies as well. It is presupposed by even time and space, the two (Kantian) forms of sensible intuition, and causality (the only one of Kant's 12 categories that Schopenhauer accepts). The subject of knowledge is a knower, and everything else in our world, including his own body, is a potential object; and all objects of conceptual knowledge are subject to the principle of sufficient reason. A representation or idea involves a relationship between a subject and some object(s), with the principle of sufficient reason applying to all phenomenal objects, with science being systematic knowledge governed by it. In the second book, he observes that a knowing subject's body is a complex phenomenal object in the world of representations. He has sensible experience and knowledge of it and its movements. But, additionally, he experiences it as an object of his will, which can generate its actions. Through our "acts of will" we have *a priori*

17 Arthur Schopenhauer

(non-sensible) knowledge of our bodies, and through willed bodily movements we can know our own will. "Therefore, in a certain sense, it can also be said that the will is knowledge *a priori* of the body, and that the body is knowledge *a posteriori* of the will." I can have immediate knowledge of my own will only through my body's actions, which are phenomena of my will. To assume that this is uniquely true of my body and of no others is a form of "*egoism*." If we are to avoid the egoistic assumption that all bodies other than our own are merely our representations, we must conclude that their inner essence is also will. While this falls short of being a convincing argument, on account of its needed assumptions, it nevertheless yields striking consequences. On this view, Kant was wrong, and the "*thing-in-itself*" is knowable as will, even though it is never given to us as an object of sensible intuition. Because it is not a phenomenal object, the will is not limited by "time and space," which constitute the basis of individuation; it also transcends the principle of sufficient reason (*World*, I, 3, 5–8, 25–26, 28, 99–105, 109–110, 113–115). If a person's own will is the thing-in-itself, how can a human being not be subject to time and still be individually distinct from others? And, for that matter, given that Schopenhauer will adopt a position of determinism, if her will is beyond all causally sufficient reason, why is it not free? These remain nagging critical problems.

The second edition of his major work comprises 50 essays as supplements to the first. Let us now consider a few of the things there added or elaborated. Aligning himself with Kant (and also Berkeley, but not Fichte or Hegel), he writes that "true philosophy must at all costs be *idealistic*," that is, taking as its "starting-point" nothing but "*the subjective*, our *own consciousness*." Like Kant, he commits himself, however, to "*empirical* reality" as well as to "*transcendental* ideality," in that an objective world of experience is given to consciousness. Even though the will, as thing-in-itself, constitutes our true inner nature, he now claims that "in itself it is without consciousness," since the latter only operates under the "forms of knowledge, namely space, time, and causality," while our will is intuitively felt in its influence on our body (*World*, II, 3–5, 12–13, 19, 201–202). Even if we assume that Schopenhauer is correct and Kant incorrect about our having intuitive noumenal knowledge, however, it is problematic how the will can move the body outside of consciousness, time, space, and causality.

17.4 Reality

Schopenhauer's metaphysical theory has already been adumbrated in our consideration of his epistemology and likewise takes its start from Kant's views. The very title of his chief book suggests a Kantian view of reality as comprised of two dimensions – that of phenomenal appearances and that of things-in-themselves. Like his predecessor, he believes in both of these dimensions, that we have conceptual knowledge of the former but not of the latter, and that the latter is somehow the ground of the former. Both thinkers are committed to an empirical realism as well as to a transcendental idealism. But, unlike Kant, he thinks we are capable of non-sensible intuition and a non-conceptual knowledge that noumenal reality is some cosmic will. In *On the World in Nature*, he writes of the "fundamental truth that what Kant set as the *thing-in-itself* over against mere *appearance*, more definitely called by me *representation* [*Vorstellung*], and regarded as absolutely unknowable, that this *thing-in-itself*, I say, this substratum of all appearances and consequently of the whole of nature, is nothing but what we know immediately and very intimately and find ourselves as *will*." Will is the only noumenal reality, intellect being merely a phenomenon of will (*Writings*, 76–77). So let us now explore this metaphysical theory of reality, which will involve implications for his views on God, humanity, freedom, morality, and society.

17.4 Reality | **277**

Everything, including human beings, in the world of phenomenal appearances is individuated by time and space and subject in everything it phenomenally is and does to the principle of sufficient reason. This is all that empirical knowledge derived from sense perception can disclose. But this leaves unsolved "the riddle" of its inner nature, the thing-in-itself. Here a person's twofold experience of her own body is the key to solving that "riddle." From one perspective, she can see and smell her own hand and feel it with the other hand, as she can see, smell, and feel a flower. But, from another perspective altogether, she can experience her will moving that hand when she wants to grasp that flower. But it is only her own body, and no other one, that she can experience in this second way; all other things can be experienced "only as representations." For Schopenhauer, our awareness of will is not merely a matter of belief, even of rational faith, but one of intuitive knowledge of the thing-in-itself that constitutes our own "inner nature." Critically speaking, there are problems here. Allegedly, time, space, and causality do not belong to the thing-in-itself. Yet my will to move my hand seems to act in time and to cause actions in its spatial environment. And, if only phenomena, whose reality is in "time and space," are individuated, then it would seem that my will, which I experience immediately, would be one with anyone else's will, which I cannot. Schopenhauer is moving toward the monistic view that the thing-in-itself underlying all phenomenal representations "is everywhere one and the same" and that, whatever misinterpretations our intellect imposes, it "only strives blindly in a dull, one-sided, and unalterable manner." And, since this will is "groundless," lying totally outside the bounds of sufficient reason, it would seem to be a brute, inexplicable given fact and causally to generate nothing in the phenomenal order. But, in that case, we shall have to ask what function the construct serves. The short answer is that, since all phenomena are merely the surface appearances of this blind, nonrational cosmic will, all life involves "inevitable suffering" with an abundance of "folly and wickedness" and little that is truly "noble and wise." Contrary to a Leibnizian best of all possible worlds, this would seem to be a miserable hell on earth. While rationalists, such as Leibniz and Hegel, try to convince us that reason rules the world, it turns out to be merely an evanescent veneer masking the horrible reality. The notion that "God's in his heaven – All's right with the world" (as Robert Browning put it in the poem "Pippa Passes" in 1841) is merely a fatuous fantasy. Schopenhauer is adopting what would turn out to be the most famous version of pessimism in the history of Western philosophy. He brands "*optimism*" as (worse than absurd, shallow, thoughtless chatter) "a bitter mockery of the unspeakable suffering" endemic in life itself (*World*, I, 99–101, 105, 117, 113, 118, 163, 323–326).

We may well ask why we should subject ourselves to so dark a nightmare vision of reality. How can such reflections generate anything more than gloom and doom and brooding despair? There are two strands to his reasoning here. The theoretical answer is that it is our nature to wonder about ourselves and our world so that we cannot help it. As Plato and Aristotle said more than two millennia earlier, philosophy is born in wonder, which Schopenhauer calls "the mother of metaphysics." Human reason makes us unique in our "*need for metaphysics*," and he famously characterizes man as "an *animal metaphysicum*" (an opinion Kant shared, even though he did not use that descriptive phrase). The great world religions, in their own mythological way, can be seen as responses to that same sense of wonder about ourselves and our world; in trying to solve this "riddle," religions can be "optimistic," like Greco-Roman paganism, or forms of "pessimism," such as Christianity. It is particularly when we suffer hardships that we are led to seek some explanatory account. Not only do we wonder, as Leibniz observed, that there is any world at all, but why "it is such a miserable and melancholy world," in particular, "is the *punctum pruriens* of metaphysics," literally the "itching point" that philosophical (and religious) metaphysics is designed to scratch (*World*, II, 160, 170, 172). But, as we shall see, the practical answer to why we should entertain such

17 Arthur Schopenhauer

a theory is that, by accurately diagnosing the disease of life, we shall become able to discover a temporary cure, as well as a more permanent one.

17.5 God

Since Schopenhauer was an atheist, we can expect him to have more to say about religion than about God. It should come as no surprise that he finds all the traditional arguments for God's existence – the three Kant criticized and the one he invented – to be worthless failures. The ontological argument confuses logical necessity with existential necessity, two different sorts of sufficient reason. The cosmological and teleological arguments mistakenly attempt to apply causality to a noumenal reality transcending the order of phenomenal appearances. (All of that is essentially Kantian critique.) Kant's own moral argument is a pathetically useless attempt to give us hope, comfort, and consolation in our slough of suffering. Indeed, this argument is so poor that he wonders whether Kant "was quite serious about it"; it seems to "make morality rest on" the tantalizing promise of heavenly reward, supplying an egoistic motivation for it – all of which is incompatible with Kantian deontology (*Human*, 29).

In *The World as Will and Representation*, Schopenhauer suggests (what Feuerbach made more explicit) that man created God/gods in his own image and likeness, setting up a variety of ritualistic practices that might allegedly appease the fetishistic object(s) of his superstitious imagination. As has already been suggested, he thinks it more significant whether religions are optimistic, like Greco-Roman paganism, appealing to our hopes, or pessimistic, like Christianity, appealing to our fears, than "whether they are monotheistic, polytheistic, pantheistic, or atheistic." He finds the Old Testament of the Bible to be "optimistic" and its New Testament to be "pessimistic" (*World*, I, 323; II, 170, 620–621; in "Some Words on Pantheism," in *Philosophy*, 263–265, he condemns this conception of God as preposterous) – both of which claims seem quite controversial.

In a couple of his essays on religion (again comparable to Feuerbach's views), Schopenhauer has some more interesting ideas to offer us. He writes, "Religion is the metaphysics of the people," calling it "folk-metaphysics" and explaining that we all need a worldview we can understand, which is easier when expressed metaphorically than philosophically. People tend to cling to the religious beliefs with which they grew up and which divide them from people who cling to alternative doctrines. Some pretend that society and values depend on religion, but this is "*untrue*" propaganda. To say that religion expresses truth allegorically and mythologically (as Hegel did) is like saying that "truth is to be clothed in lies." All religion allegedly involves distortion; thus "a true philosophy is possible, but not a true religion." So, as a champion of truth, Schopenhauer calls for "the euthanasia of religion"! And is it not ironic to hold that virtue can be based on a "pack of lies"? Still, humans are metaphysical animals in need of beliefs that their lives have some sort of ultimate meaning. If only they can become capable of achieving meaning without deception! We should also factor in the long history of "atrocities" perpetrated in the name of religion (a point earlier made by Hume, whose work Schopenhauer admired). The premodern notion that theology is a science is preposterous, since a science "has to do only with what can be *known*" to be true and never with the fantasies of "what should or may be *believed*." To its credit, Christianity does – at least in theory – preach a gospel of love of others and denial of egoistic will, even if it accepts a deity that is often cruel and vengeful. The idea that we can win over any sort of deity by means of religious practices is mere "*idolatry*" (Nietzsche will later write an entire book called *Twilight of the Idols*). Christianity, like Hinduism and Buddhism, is characterized as "pessimistic." Anticipating Nietzsche's striking message of "the death of God" (as well as precursory of Freud), Schopenhauer announces, "Mankind is growing out of religion as out of its childhood clothes" (*Essays*, 96, 99–103, 106–109, 113, 180, 182, 184, 189–190, 195–197). As an atheist denouncing religion, he seems a prophet of the secular thought that would develop in Euro-American cultures in the twentieth century.

17.6 Humanity

Schopenhauer agrees with Buddhism that all of life is suffering, that suffering stems from relentless desire, and that the only way we can be happy would be to extinguish the fires of desire. There are at least three elements involved in our ordinary quest for happiness. "(1) What a man is" has to do with his "personality" in a broad sense comprising "health, strength, beauty, temperament, moral character, intelligence, and education." This is more important that the other two elements. "(2) What a man has," in the sense of every sort of "property and possessions," is significant to some extent. And "(3) How a man stands in the estimation of others" involves his reputation and others' opinions of him. To the extent that we are the slaves of our own desires, suffering is inevitable, satisfaction proving either elusive or transitory. He writes that "the two foes of human happiness are pain and boredom" (*Philosophy*, 3, 12, 18). As if it were not enough that we remain susceptible to pain throughout our lives no matter what, so many of our desires go unfulfilled or only partially satisfied, generating the pain of frustration. To the extent that we get what we want, we sink into boredom.

Turning to *The World as Will and Representation*, we see that reason, which is unique to humans and "a special faculty of knowledge," facilitates greater depths and more dimensions of suffering. Also, our self-conscious reason nurtures the illusion of individuality, complicating sources of pain and animosity, setting up competition with others (of the sort Hobbes identified); thus we encounter "*homo homini lupus*" (man as a wolf toward man). In this regard, Schopenhauer compares man to "the bulldog-ant of Australia," which, when chopped into two pieces, is such that its head enters into mortal combat with its tail. "The head attacks the tail with its teeth, and the tail defends itself bravely by stinging the head," culminating in mutual destruction. Having diagnosed our miserable condition, we may well be ready for treatment. What can be done to cope with the horror of our natural condition? A disinterested engagement with art (such as Kant discussed) – as creative genius and/or as contemplating perceiver – provides a temporary escape. There is a timelessness about the work of art, the contemplation of which removes us from the principle of sufficient reason. As the artist can become absorbed in her creative activity, forgetting or ignoring her aches and pains, her melancholy and frustrations, her disappointments and boredom, so the perceiver can be lifted out of his own selfish, narrow concerns in "the pure contemplation" of (Platonic) Ideas, yielding knowledge of universal truth. To the extent that aesthetic experience is disinterested, we can be "delivered from the miserable self," with all its cravings, if only for a while. While all the other arts use particular representations to give us knowledge of universal Ideas, music uniquely "passes over the Ideas" and transcends "the phenomenal world" to generate intuition of will itself (*World*, I, 83, 118, 147, 184–185, 195, 197, 199, 257, 262, 267; cf. *Essays*, 41–49, where Schopenhauer argues that the world is hell and that we are both torturing devils and tormented victims). But even this greatest of all the arts can offer us only temporary relief, before the demands of desire regain a grip on our consciousness.

Fortunately, there is a more permanent solution to the problem of pandemic suffering; but, to find it, we must look to Eastern thought, rather than to Plato, Kant, or any lesser Western thinker. All knowledge generated by art (other than musical art) reveals individual phenomena and keeps us shackled to the principle of sufficient reason in time and space; while music is an exception to this

17 Arthur Schopenhauer

rule, it still provides only temporary distraction for consciousness. "Willing and striving are its whole essence, and can be fully compared to an unquenchable thirst." The demands of the body, described as "nothing but the objectified will-to-live," seem incessant thus far. Schopenhauer (maybe being autobiographical) identifies sexual desire as a particularly insidious source of suffering. Is there any permanent cure? "True salvation, deliverance from life and suffering, cannot even be imagined without complete denial of the will." We must become resigned to the idea that suffering is inevitable so long as we cling to our own selfish desires. If we can strip away the illusory veil of *Maya*, "seeing through the *principium individuationis*" that leads to our self-image as separate from all others, and achieve a compassionate sympathy for all others, our fellow-sufferers, then we can renounce the will and its egoistic desires. We might note here that he implausibly argues that suicide is not the answer because, ironically, it allegedly involves the embracing of will rather than its renunciation (*World*, I, 311–312, 329–330, 397–398; cf. *World*, II, 201, 209–211, 215, 225, 240).

Again, some of his essays offer interesting elaborations. As if channeling Hobbes, he writes, "Man is at bottom a savage, horrible beast" and that it is terrifying to realize how we are beneath the thin veneer of civilization. In particular, he cites our historical tendency to enslave others to our own selfish will (think of Hegel's master–bondsman dialectic). It isn't merely that we are selfish egoists, ready, willing, and sometimes able to use others merely as means to our own ends (despite Kant's categorical imperative); but we all contain "a fund of hatred, anger, envy, rancor and malice, accumulated like the venom in a serpent's tooth." While Kant identifies these negative tendencies as "the radical evil of human nature," he prefers to speak in terms of a naturally selfish "will to live" indefinitely without suffering, all of which is a phenomenon of blind, nonrational cosmic will, the thing-in-itself. While a person's knowledge can change, leading to a change in motives, causing a change in behavior, according to Schopenhauer, "*a man does not alter*, and his *moral character* remains absolutely the same through his life." (This would strike most of us as an implausible, wild generalization, as his characterization of "the *depravity* of man" seems quite one-sided.) But no sooner than he makes this bold claim, he tries to take it back, saying that it is only "outside of" life and time, "as a result of the self-knowledge which life gives," that "character undergoes alteration." This seems somewhat incoherent, in that a person's character, as phenomenon, is in time and an aspect of an individual's life. But, then, as if reversing himself again, he denies that character can ever "undergo any change under the influence of life" (*Human*, 18–20, 22–23, 27, 31–32, 91–92, 94). What has thus been painted is a dark, problematic portrait of human nature more arresting in its vision than cogent in its argumentation.

17.7 Freedom

Remembering Schopenhauer's view that everything in the phenomenal world, including human beings, is governed by the principle of sufficient reason, which is inapplicable to will, the noumenal thing-in-itself, we can anticipate that his theory of freedom and determinism will introduce tensions into his system. It is reasonable to ask "why?" regarding every decision ever made. Every voluntary action is determined by some motive(s) or other, with motives being determined by a person's character, which he (sometimes) characterizes as unalterable. This is not to say that we – or even he – can always identify the relevant motive(s) or understand the person's character, of course, let alone predict, before the fact, his voluntary actions, since the psychology involved can be quite subtle and complex. At any rate, "the inevitability" of causal "*necessity*" is inescapable here. Given the antecedent conditions, *all* human "action then ensues just as inevitably as does every other effect of a cause" (*Root*, 212, 225, 227). So long as we are referring to the phenomenal realm alone, we might say that this is, therefore, in agreement with Kant's view – except that, for him, moral character is not phenomenal.

But by the time of *The World as Will and Representation*, the Kantian perspective is being modified, with every individual person being a "*phenomenon* of the will" rather than a noumenal reality. From this modified perspective, we see that, no matter how free we may fancy ourselves to be, who we are and what we do are strictly determined. By contrast, the will, as thing-in-itself, allegedly transcends the principle of sufficient reason and is therefore "*free*." But, given that the will is supposed to be blindly irrational, what difference can this possibly make? "The concept of freedom is therefore really a negative one," meaning nothing more than not determined by any principle of sufficient reason. It most emphatically does *not* mean the will could have "chosen" to become manifest in a world in which Schopenhauer, rather than Abraham Lincoln, was a member of the American Congress in 1848. So what, we may ask, is its "freedom" worth? But, getting back to the human phenomenon of will, as if recognizing that this determinism will cause problems of logical consistency in the rest of his system, he suddenly reverses himself to say that (somehow), through our knowledge of insatiable will as constituting our true "inner nature," we can initiate the sort of change that can relieve suffering: "Thus the freedom which in other respects, as belonging to the thing-in-itself, can never show itself in the phenomenon, in such a case appears in this phenomenon." This is a startling self-contradiction, which is rendered even more jaw-dropping by the fact that, before the same (long) paragraph has ended, he flips back to maintaining that "man is never free, although he is the phenomenon of a free will"! He tries to smooth over this troublesome wrinkle in his theory by invoking the Kantian distinction between a lack of any "empirical freedom" and a commitment to "transcendental freedom"; but his distortion of Kantian dualism dooms the effort to failure. He tries to employ the quasi-Platonic notion that increased knowledge can open up alternative motives, altering "the direction of the will's" thrust. But does this move not subject the will to the principle of sufficient reason operating in time? Still, he wants to say that increased rational knowledge can facilitate "a complete *elective decision*" in a human being (*World*, I, 113–114, 286–290, 294, 297–298; cf. "Free-Will and Fatalism," in *Human*, especially 69–70, 75, 80–83, 87). This might take us closer to Kant's position; but the path to getting there seems a logical muddle.

Let us turn to his little book on freedom to see if it more plausibly treats the issue. Repeating the idea that the concept of freedom "turns out to be negative," he proceeds to make some definitional distinctions among "physical, intellectual, and moral freedom." The first of these is (what we saw in Hobbes) merely "the absence of material hindrances of any sort"; thus, if a stream is not dammed up, it can flow freely, and, interestingly, he places "political freedom" in this category. Intellectual freedom is the capacity to think as we will, rather than having thoughts forced upon us by external circumstances. But moral freedom is the sort in which philosophers are largely interested, as personal responsibility hinges on it. To ask whether an act is morally free is to inquire whether the agent could have chosen otherwise or whether it was necessitated by some sufficient reason. This is a helpful threefold analysis. To say that I am free in any of these senses is to say that "I can do what I will." But the nagging question remains as to whether I am ever free to choose what I shall will or whether everything that I will is determined by some sufficient reason(s). This is another way of asking, according to Schopenhauer, whether I could be something other than I am. This presupposes the (dubious) idea that the same person cannot will two alternative outcomes, such as going to work and calling in sick instead. If he were to remain consistent with the claim that the principle of sufficient reason governs all phenomena, he should say that I could not be other than I am and therefore do not have the moral freedom to choose what I shall will. However, he wants to hold that a human can be "relatively free" – relative to additional possible motives that might result from intellectual "deliberation." But this awkward position is still subject to the problems already indicated above: he is trying to have it both ways, as did Kant, but lacks the sort of Kantian dualism that would render that possible. Here he still sees a person's character as the ground of motives, which, in turn, constitute the ground of action; and he still wants to say that one's character is immutable, which should mire him in moral determinism. But again we see a flip-flop, since he needs to carve out a niche for "the true moral freedom" of man, for the legitimate reason of leaving space for "accountability for our actions." He wants to say that a person is morally responsible for "*his character*." Though he expresses admiration for Kant's treatment of the problem of freedom and determinism and seems to want to adopt a comparable perspective, his different take on dualism and noumenal reality renders him unable convincingly to justify his claim that his theory "does not eliminate freedom" of any meaningful sort (*Freedom*, 3–5, 7–8, 16, 21–25, 36–37, 45–46, 51–52, 58, 60, 62, 93–94, 96–99).

17.8 Morality

His problems with freedom, his (Hobbesian) egoistic philosophy of human nature, and his position of voluntarism over rationalism will present a challenge for his ethical theory. Any effective conceptual moral system must be capable of motivating desirable behavior. "But a morality that *does* motivate can do so only by acting on self-love," given that egoism. Further, any behavior derived from our natural self-love is devoid of "moral worth," the conclusion being that no abstract conceptual system (such as Kant's?) is adequate to generate true virtue. So what is needed is sympathetic intuitive awareness that others have "the same inner nature" as our own, which allows us to cross the superficial boundaries of distinguishing individuation. This returns us to the epistemological notion that we have "intuitive knowledge" as well as conceptual "abstract knowledge communicable through words." The path to good will and ill will (as Kant argued) is that of motives. But (as he also thought) it is difficult enough for us intellectually to know our own motives, let alone those of others. What is needed – to the extent that it is achievable – is "direct and intuitive knowledge," which would be verbally inexpressible. It is a sympathetic grasp of what motivates conduct that can allow us to see through the illusory principle of individuation, "the veil of Maya," to recognize that others are essentially the same as we are. This intuitive recognition becomes a foundation for genuine "conscience," allowing us to identify with (rather than to objectify) others, in accordance with the ancient Hindu saying, *Tat tvam asi* ("This art thou!"), opening the door to compassion and love. By identifying with the suffering of others, we can better resign ourselves to the fact that life is that way and, thus, come to renounce the craving, selfish desires that cause suffering. (Suicide is allegedly a bogus solution here, as it is merely one more way of abdicating our lives to will.) The ideal, to the extent that it is feasible, is to liberate ourselves from the domineering enslavement to will and, thus, to move into a state of "empty *nothingness*," an extinction of the self that the Buddhists call "*nirvana*" (*World*, I, 367–370, 372–374, 397–398, 408–409, 411–412; cf. *Writings*, 42, 45–46, 298, and *Human*, 3–5, 28, 97–101).

Stripped of the metaphysical foundations of this ethical theory that have already been questioned (and ignoring the controversial claims about the desirability of nothingness), these views might be considered attractive. In his book *On the Basis of Morality*, Schopenhauer develops this theory. Much of the book is an extended critique of Kant's ethics, for which he exhibits little respect. He faults it for its rationalism, accuses it of being disguised "*egoism*," and thinks its categorical imperative fraudulent. He sets forth his own basic moral principle, which says we should injure no one (justice) and, on the contrary, help everyone, as much as we can (beneficence). If sympathy is the motivating force behind virtuous action, the incentive leading to immoral behavior is the selfish cravings that stem from our natural "*egoism*." To the extent that egoism prevails over sympathy, "*ill will* or *spitefulness*" will undermine the moral motive of "*loving-kindness*." This, at its worst, can extend to "malice and cruelty." The formula for extreme egoism is, help no one; on the contrary, injure everyone if doing so is to your advantage. The formula for malice and cruelty is, injure all people, as much as you are able. Actions that have "moral worth" must be motivated by altruistic kindness and devoid "of all egoistic motivation." (Given that egoism is natural to us and determined by blind will, this would seem to be an impossible goal.) Morality involves our sense of what is beneficial and what is detrimental, helpful and harmful, what affects "*weal and woe*." Egoistic actions focus on "the *weal and woe . . . of the doer himself*." Actions that have "*moral worth*" aim to increase the welfare "*of another*" and/or to decrease his suffering; these are acts of compassion. Acts of malice aim at increasing another's suffering and/or decreasing his well-being; these can extend to "the limits of extreme cruelty." Thus the wrongdoing of "*injustice*" involves aiming at "*injuring* another." As justice is a cardinal virtue in his system, so is "loving-kindness." The compassion which he is advocating should extend to "all living beings" and not merely to fellow humans, so that we should have a concern for the well-being and suffering of nonhuman animals – no one who is cruel to animals should be considered virtuous. As a person with "*good* character" feels a oneness with fellow humans, so he should feel a kinship with all animals; as someone who selfishly regards others merely as his objects is one of "*bad*" character, so is a person who regards other animals in that arrogant manner (*Morality*, 51, 83, 92, 131, 134, 139–145, 164, 152, 162, 167, 172, 175, 179, 211). Again, to the extent that one can overlook the shaky foundations of this ethical theory represented by his metaphysical system (and his unfair characterization of Kantian ethics), Schopenhauer's views on morality seem rather attractive.

17.9 Society

As a loner (some might call him a misanthrope) and a conservative mainly interested in government maintaining order and providing protection, Schopenhauer did not offer us a very well-developed theory of society or politics. Nevertheless, we can splice together some pieces we do have. In *The World as Will and Representation*, he subscribes to the Hobbesian view that people are naturally egoistic, lawless, and hostile, tending toward a war of all against everyone else. This leads them to wrongfully injure one another, as can be seen in acts of deliberate murder, slavery, and even cannibalism. Antisocial wrongdoing can be done "through *violence* or through *cunning*." Deception and broken commitments erode interpersonal trust, if there is any. Violence and deception can be morally justified if necessary for self-protection. Apart from moral considerations, one could agree with Hobbes and "declare right and wrong to be conventional determinations arbitrarily assumed," but this view is short-sighted. Schopenhauer maintains that morality is concerned "with the *doing* of right and wrong," while politics is "concerned solely with the suffering of wrong." While morality is concerned with promoting the well-being of others, politics springs from egoism and serves its narrow interests. In order for a state to be just, its laws must accord with morality. The law should serve to "*deter*" people from violating others' rights. To be effective, it must be sanctioned with just punishment (*World*, I, 333, 335, 337–338, 340, 342, 344–349; for more on slavery, see *Essays*, 138–139). This represents a view of political society that blends a Hobbesian foundation with the Kantian view that politics should be morally legitimate as well as pragmatically effective.

The second edition contains a notoriously controversial essay on "The Metaphysics of Sexual Love" (up to that time a topic few modern philosophers dared touch), in which he maintains that, in humans, sexual desire is second in force only to the will to life as a motivating power and that romantic love is "rooted in the sexual impulse alone" and, indeed, is nothing more than particularized sexual desire. Its power is such that people will sometimes sacrifice "wealth, position, and happiness," even their

17 Arthur Schopenhauer

health or life itself, for its gratification. "Indeed, it robs of all conscience those who were previously honourable and upright, and makes traitors of those who have hitherto been loyal and faithful." In general, he claims, it operates in us "as a malevolent demon, striving to pervert, to confuse, and to overthrow everything." It is a piece of irrational will, promoting reproduction, which produces more future victims of suffering. So-called love matches are actually about procreating more children, even if their participants do not realize it (a sort of cunning of will, as opposed to the Hegelian cunning of reason). It is not difficult to see why this was so controversial in the middle of the nineteenth century. He even discusses the generally taboo topic of pederasty, of which he seems to disapprove on grounds that it is an unnatural perversion; he holds that it is "usually a vice of old men," who are unable to procreate anyhow, but that it still sinks its practitioner into desire and, thus, suffering (*World*, II, 533–534, 545, 557, 561, 565–567; see, also, *Essays*, 80–88, for his infamous, misogynistic "On Women"). If we knew and did what is good for us, we would try to renounce all such selfish desire.

For the sake of liberty and orderly security, we need to strike a balance "between two impulses, two evils in polar opposition, *despotism* and *anarchy*." But they are not equally bad; like Hobbes, he thinks the latter worse than the former, so that we should err on the side of despotism to avoid the horrors of anarchy. Here we get into his theory of politics and turn to his rather long essay on "Government." He begins by criticizing the tendency of Germans to work abstractly, as with the notion of natural right. He claims that right is a merely negative concept, signifying what is the opposite of wrong, which refers to any "injury . . . to a man's person or to his property or to his honour." The state's essential function is to deter wrongdoing. He agrees with Rousseau that the people should be "sovereign" but thinks them childish and always in need of guardians. In practice, might prevails over abstract right, "the problem of statesmanship" being how to use power to minimize wrongdoing. The elimination of wrongdoing is "merely the ideal to be aimed at," but never fully achievable. While freedom of the press can be useful "as a safety-valve" for releasing dangerously pent up anger, because people are so ignorant, gullible, and foolish, the mischief it does tends to outweigh its benefits. For the same reason, he is opposed to democracy and favors monarchy; the sort of republican government that Kantians advocate is allegedly "unnatural," while monarchy is purportedly "natural." Further, he claims, republics are historically built on the backs of slaves and citizens who are not politically active but are subject to the decisions of others. Finally, he writes, "Republics are very easy to found, and very difficult to maintain, while with monarchies it is exactly the reverse" (*Human*, 132, 37–39, 48, 50, 52–54, 57–58, 60). While this relatively unknown aspect of his philosophical system falls short of profundity or originality, it is provocative, particularly by today's sociopolitical standards.

17.10 Review

The strength of this philosophical system is its provocative synthetic power; but its crucial weakness is its logical incoherence and lack of much cogent argumentation. Its epistemological and metaphysical dimensions are its most original and most striking adaptations of German idealism. The combination of this with his voluntarism and pessimism makes for a unique theory. His views on God and religion anticipate Feuerbach, whom he occasionally mentions (*World*, I, 349; *Morality*, 119n.), and Marx. Those on morality constitute a strong alternative to both Kantian deontology and utilitarianism and, in some ways, are reminiscent of Hume. His treatment of society and politics, while scattered and sketchy, can be seen as a reaction against the progressivism and liberalism of Enlightenment thought. Although nobody could have seen it coming during his lifetime, it turned out that Schopenhauer was blazing a trail that would dead-end into Nietzsche's termination of modern European philosophy.

18

Ludwig Feuerbach

Source: Ernst Keil/Wikimedia Commons/Public Domain

18.1 Overview

Feuerbach was quite influential during the 1840s but is nowadays seen mostly as a materialistic critic of religion and an important link between Hegel and Marx. After abandoning Hegel's absolute idealism in favor of a position of humanistic materialism, he developed an empirical atheism which renounced the metaphysical system-building of post-Kantian German philosophers, such as Fichte, Schelling, Hegel, and Schopenhauer. This was a more radical form of criticism than

Modern European Philosophers, First Edition. Wayne P. Pomerleau.
© 2023 John Wiley & Sons, Inc. Published 2023 by John Wiley & Sons, Inc.

18 Ludwig Feuerbach

Kant's and was meant to transform philosophical thinking from theological to anthropological.[1] Its influence on German thought for the remainder of the nineteenth century would prove to be profound.

18.2 Biography

On July 28, 1804 (a few months after Kant's death), Ludwig Andreas Feuerbach was born in Landshut, Bavaria, of a distinguished German family. His father, Anselm Feuerbach, was a prominent jurist who was ennobled in 1813; a professor at Jena, then at Kiel, then at Landshut, he was a liberal Protestant and influenced by the writings of Kant. Anselm's own father and grandfather were also lawyers, as was his mother's father. One of Ludwig's older brothers was a respected archeologist, professor, and author; another was a mathematics teacher, and a third a law professor. Ludwig's younger brother was a philologist and became an advocate of Ludwig's ideas. One of his nephews was a famous painter. In addition to the four sons, Anselm and his wife, Wilhelmine, had three daughters. In 1816, Anselm left his wife to go live with a mistress, who bore him a son; after she died, he went back to his wife and their family. In 1817, Ludwig entered the *Gymnasium* in Ansbach. He was quite religious at the time and went to Heidelberg to study theology in 1828. There he came under the influence of a Hegelian theologian (who had helped to bring Hegel to Heidelberg for a couple of years). Wanting to study under the master himself, Ludwig, in 1824, talked his father into letting him go to Berlin, where the famous theologian Schleiermacher was teaching, to study theology. But he quickly decided that he wanted philosophy's focus on reason rather than theology's on faith, transferring to philosophy in 1825. He attended almost all of Hegel's courses while at Berlin, those on logic more than once. But family money problems pushed him to transfer from Berlin to the less expensive university at Erlangen in 1826. He got his doctoral degree there with a Hegelian thesis, *On Reason: One, Universal, and Infinite*, in 1828. The following year, he started teaching there as a *Privatdozent* (until 1832). He was clearly a Hegelian at this stage of his life, except for his lauding of philosophy at the expense of theology (*Brook*, 266–273).

In 1830, Feuerbach anonymously published his *Thoughts on Death and Immortality*, which, adopting a naturalistic position, denied the Christian doctrine of personal life after death. The identity of its author was soon known. As a result, he was denied promotion at the university, quit teaching, and would never again secure a stable teaching position. He started publishing on modern philosophy as an independent scholar (*Brook*, 273, 283). In 1834, he met Bertha Löw, who had inherited partial ownership in a porcelain factory in Bruckberg; three years later, they married, living comfortably but not lavishly there for more than two decades. He was developing a bit of a reputation as a Hegelian scholar, while more and more moving from idealism to materialism (*Brook*, 284–286). In 1839, he published "Towards a Critique of Hegel's Philosophy," establishing his break toward intellectual independence.

---

1 References to Feuerbach's writings will be to *The Fiery Brook: Selected Writings of Ludwig Feuerbach* (hereafter called *Brook*), trans. by Zawar Hanfi (Garden City, NY: Doubleday & Co., 1972), to *Thoughts on Death and Immortality*, by Ludwig Feuerbach (hereafter called *Thoughts*), trans. by James A. Massey (Berkeley: Univ. of California Press, 1980), to *The Essence of Christianity*, by Ludwig Feuerbach (hereafter called *Christianity*), trans. by George Eliot (New York: Harper & Brothers, 1957), to *Principles of the Philosophy of the Future*, by Ludwig Feuerbach (hereafter called *Future*), trans. by Manfred H. Vogel (Indianapolis: Bobbs-Merrill, 1966), to *The Essence of Faith According to Luther*, by Ludwig Feuerbach (hereafter called *Faith*), trans. by Melvin Cherno (New York: Harper & Row, 1976), and to *Lectures on the Essence of Religion*, by Ludwig Feuerbach (hereafter called *Lectures*), trans. by Ralph Manheim (New York: Harper & Row, 1967).

Two years later, his very successful masterpiece, *The Essence of Christianity*, was published, viewing religion as merely a projection of the human imagination and quickly marking him as the most prominent member of the left-wing Young Hegelians; this book went through three editions in seven years. In 1842, he published his *Preliminary Theses on the Reform of Philosophy* and, the following year, his *Principles of the Philosophy of the Future*. He signaled the evolution of his thought thus: "God was my first thought, reason the second, and man the third and the last. The subject of the deity is reason, but the subject of reason is man." In 1844, he published *The Essence of Faith According to Luther* (*Brook*, 286–288, 291–292, 295). In 1846, he published *The Essence of Religion* and started publishing his *Collected Works*.

By this time, he had become accepted and respected as a prominent democratic socialist, who was a champion of joining the values of self and society, asking and answering the question of the foundation of his own philosophy: "What do I take as my principle? Ego and alter ego; 'egoism' and 'communism'; for both are as inseparable as *head and heart*. Without egoism, you have *no head*; without communism, you have *no heart*" (*Brook*, 295). Revolution was being advocated; yet he was dubious about the likelihood of its succeeding in Germany. In 1848, when the revolutions did erupt, he was sympathetic but not actively involved. He did attend the democratic congress in Frankfurt that year. That same year, students at Heidelberg invited him to deliver a lecture series on religion, which he did from the end of 1848 to early 1849. But the Frankfurt parliament fell, and conservative reaction was firm. This was the end of his pronounced influence, and he returned to Bruckberg.

In 1851, he published the *Lectures on the Essence of Religion* that he had delivered at Heidelberg. His wife's porcelain factory was ceasing to be successful; in 1859, it went out of business, closing off a major source of family income. He moved to less expensive lodgings in Rechenberg (near Nuremberg). The family was now impoverished and dependent on the financial support of his friends and followers. He continued to publish his *Collected Works* until 1866; but he had been eclipsed by other thinkers (e.g. Marx and Engels), and his work no longer attracted much interest. In 1870, he joined the German Social Democratic Party. He was working on an essay on ethics but never completed it. He had a stroke, never totally recovering his health thereafter. On September 13, 1872, he died in Nuremberg, where he was buried; his wife died 11 years later.

18.3 Knowledge

Feuerbach is not known as a particularly important epistemologist, and his theory of knowledge is neither novel nor profound. His sense-based empiricism and opposition to idealism represent a consistent thread through his mature works. In "Towards a Critique of Hegel's Philosophy," he recognizes that this puts him at odds with his former teacher and identifies Hegel as "the culminating point of all speculative-systematic philosophy," against which he takes his stand. He thinks that even dialectical thought, which he accepts, is misunderstood by idealists: "Dialectics is not a monologue that speculation carries on with itself, but a dialogue between speculation and empirical reality." Indeed, he indicts all of modern rationalism with the charge that it is hopelessly disconnected from "sensuous perception." Compounding the problem, idealists such as Fichte tried to render the world of nature a mere object of the ego. Nor does the Hegelian attempt to bridge the gulf between the antitheses of "nature *and* spirit" in the alleged synthesis of some abstract "Absolute" help at all. What is needed is to start with nature and to give up attempting to reduce it to what it is not, since "the all-inclusive and all-encompassing reality is nature" itself and not some abstract, amorphous Absolute. Elsewhere, he argues that, if philosophy, "the mother of all sciences," is ever to be allied with other sciences, it must be rooted in "empirical knowledge." Indeed, the ego itself should be seen as part of nature rather than as opposed to it. "The ego is corporeal" rather than abstract spirit. The aspect of the ego that is "the will" (as Schopenhauer recognized) is only conceivable in relation to material objects with which it is physically engaged (*Brook*, 68, 72, 74–77, 80–82, 94, 136–138, 142, 144; cf. 285, 295). We have seen earlier forms of empiricism (from British thinkers) already, but not explicitly presented as preferable alternatives to modern idealism.

In his greatest work, *The Essence of Christianity*, Feuerbach declares his opposition to all idealistic speculation and commits himself "only to *realism*, to materialism." This pits him against any system that is "perverted and crippled by a superhuman, i.e., anti-human, anti-natural religion." This renders the focus of his philosophy as "not the Substance of Spinoza, not the *ego* of Kant and Fichte, not the Absolute Identity of Schelling, not the Absolute Mind of Hegel, in short, no abstract, merely conceptual being, but a *real* being, the true *ens realissimum* – man." His work has both a negative goal of exposing the problems of alternative theories and the positive one of uncovering their truth. His most conspicuous theme is that "theology is anthropology." He not only reduces the former to the latter but also tries to "exalt anthropology into theology, very much as Christianity, while lowering God into man, made man into God" – presumably with its doctrine of the Incarnation. But where is real being to be found? "Only in the realm of the senses, only in space and time." The natural, and not the supernatural, is the proper field for philosophy. And only sense experience can give us access to "empirical existence" (*Christianity*, xxxiv–xxxviii, 23, 201).

In his *Principles of the Philosophy of the Future*, Feuerbach, having permanently burned his bridges to mainstream philosophy, is even more blunt about it. In opposition to the many modern philosophers we have already studied who see spirit rather than matter as "the essential object of reason," he holds that this is matter, without which "reason would have no stimulus and substance for thinking and thus no content" at all. The only ultimate object of empirical thought is material nature, the object of sense perception. This is largely the same epistemological position as was adopted by Hobbes almost two centuries earlier but now with the advantage of dialectical thinking that rises above a mere negation of rationalism and idealism. "The new philosophy is the realization of the Hegelian philosophy . . . , a realization, however, which is at the same time the negation, and indeed the negation without contradiction, of this philosophy." The truth of Hegel's idealism is that the "otherness" of thought and being – of subject and object – must be overcome to reveal a distinction that is conceptual rather than ontological. While it may be useful to conceive of them as different, in human experience they are correlative. "The new philosophy is, therefore, the truth of the Hegelian philosophy and of modern philosophy in general." Crude empiricism is correct in holding that, ultimately, all our ideas are derived from sense experience, but incorrect if it ignores the fact that "the most important and essential sense object of man is man himself." Idealism is correct in thinking that all of our ideas originate in the human mind but incorrect in trying to divorce that from material reality. A proper middle ground can be carved out between the two. (We might wonder why Kant cannot be said to have already found it with his transcendental idealism that is also an empirical realism.) Mind apart from empirical reality has "no criterion of truth other than" mere coherence. But several alternative coherent sets of ideas could coexist; we could only know which of them, if any, has "real truth" by employing sense perception. There is a meaningful "unity of thought and being," but it is only grounded in man and not in some abstract Absolute Spirit (*Future*, 26, 28, 31, 44, 49, 58, 60, 63–68). Reality is the proper object of knowledge; and, since reality is essentially corporeal, our only access to it is, ultimately, our human sense perception, according to this perspective.

18.4 Reality

Feuerbach's ontology is thoroughly naturalistic as well as thoroughly materialistic. All intervention of the supernatural must be expunged from human history, if it is to be rationally comprehensible. Human history is irrevocably temporal; but time applies only to natural phenomena; thus the supernatural, being atemporal, must also be forever detached from human history, as he suggests in "Towards a Critique of Hegel's Philosophy." Despite the care with which the Hegelian system was constructed, it failed to recognize this (*Brook*, 57, 58, 61, 68). As Feuerbach says later, in his *Lectures on the Essence of Religion*, to the extent that such a worldview abandons the natural in favor of the supernatural, it gives us a model of "a world upside down." It is the proper business of the new, post-idealistic philosophy to turn the model of reality right side up again. The "upside-down world" is one that encourages a detachment from the real and an attachment to the fanciful – a task for fiction rather than philosophy. We shall need to explore the theocentric model further and to demythologize it in order to grasp its truth; but this must not be done at the expense of the anthropocentric view, which is naturalistic (*Lectures*, 103–104, 114).

Abstract thinking, disconnected from material, natural reality, allegedly "has no conception at all of being, of existence, or of reality," he writes in his *Principles of the Philosophy of the Future* (anticipating Kierkegaard's similar claim by a few years). The "being" of "Hegelian logic" and of "the old metaphysics" is a vacuous concept having no reality whatsoever, Feuerbach maintains, and is merely nothing at all, devoid of content. "Only a sensuous being is a true and real being." What cannot be perceived by the senses is only abstract idea. Nor should we be fooled into believing in dualism's supersensible world as distinguished from the sensuous world – a distinction for which we have no basis. Human beings, in their natural wholeness, rather than some abstract reason or spiritual ego, must take their place as the proper focus of "the new philosophy" of the future (*Future*, 40–42, 51, 59, 66–67).

18.5 God

The intertwined topics of God and religion represent the aspect of Feuerbach's philosophy that is most central to his thought and for which he is most famous. Given his near obsession with these topics and the fact that he published hundreds of pages on them over the years, it is a bit of a challenge to determine which bits to use here and what mass of material not to include. Perhaps the best approach to employ is a highly selective chronological one. In *Thoughts on Death and Immortality*, his first published book, he has not yet completed his break from Hegel or conspicuously embraced atheism. As a recent student of Christian theology, he writes, "God is love. The human loves, but God is love." He is still subscribing to a personal God. He does maintain that the divine attributes also "exist in finite personhood" but that they are in God "infinitely." Yet God, as absolute Spirit, must include the natural order rather than being utterly separate from it. Personhood and nature are antitheses that are synthesized in Spirit. God's infinite love necessarily involves a "being-together, being-in-common" with what we might try to distinguish from God. Here we see a distinctly Hegelian influence and an assertion of what we have called "panentheism" (he does not use the word, which was only coined a couple of years earlier, near the end of Hegel's lifetime). This conception of God is all-inclusive, dissolving the radical otherness of divine transcendence, arguing that our existence as finite persons and that of finite nature are comprehensively contained in infinite Spirit. While we cannot afford to consider them at much length here, the many epigrams Feuerbach attached at the end of the book, which he admits "are bitingly satirical," savagely mock popular religious faith. Speaking of orthodox, conventional believers, he writes, "For centuries they have sucked at the udder of the Bible/So that it is now empty once and for all – even the cow died!" Blind faith, devoid of rational justification, is allegedly defenseless, doomed to being feckless and ineffectual. But even the use of reason by dogmatic rationalists, used merely as religious apologetics, is obnoxious and useless: "What they call reason is only the vapor/Collected from the economical dung of the Kantian philosophy." Finally (for our purposes, anyhow), as if anticipating Nietzsche, he denies that Christianity can solve any of the genuine problems of humanity: "Should we be Christians? It would be better to be healthy;/Only medicine and chemistry can still give us health" (*Thoughts*, 19–30, 45, 173, 175, 178, 188, 192, 231). It is easy to see how this book, without being blatantly atheistic, proved offensive enough to ensure that he would never hold a permanent teaching position.

In *The Essence of Christianity*, having declared his independence from Hegel, Feuerbach develops the views for which he is justly famous. Near its beginning, he makes a claim that could still be interpreted as Hegelian panentheism: "Consciousness of God is self-consciousness, knowledge of God is self-knowledge." He claims that the object of religious worship is essentially human and that the radical distinction between God and man "is altogether illusory." But he soon disabuses us, saying that it is not merely the divine "attributes, the predicates" of God that are human but also "the subject of these predicates." Of course, we cannot avoid "anthropomorphism" in speaking and thinking about God; but we must also come to realize that the very "existence of God, the belief that there is a God," is a myth, a mere "fiction." If anything religious will remain here, it will have to be a humanistic religion: "Man, especially the religious man, is to himself the measure of all things, of all reality." But what does it mean, psychologically, for us to attribute infinite perfection to a mythological transcendent subject in contradistinction to our own finite imperfections? Here the Hegelian concept of alienation (which will also figure prominently into Marxian thought) comes into play: "To enrich God, man must become poor; that God may be all, man must be nothing . . . because what he takes from himself is not lost to him, since it is preserved in God." In thinking of God's omniscience, omnipotence, and infinite goodness, we implicitly indicate our own pathetic ignorance, impotence, and evil. God is a projection of the human imagination and "makes himself an object to this projected image of himself thus converted into a subject in our fancies." God, as an extramundane being, is, however, nothing else than a human fiction that alienates us from our own human nature. On this view, "theology is nothing else than an unconscious, esoteric pathology, anthropology, and psychology." Ultimately, Schleiermacher was correct in locating the essence of religion in "human feeling," which Feuerbach identifies as the feeling of "longing." But that longing turns out to be for an idea that has no independent reality. "The beginning, middle and end of religion is MAN." Here we have a position that can be properly called atheistic. As he writes, "Religion is a dream, in which our own conceptions and emotions appear to us as separate existences, beings out of ourselves." If we are to be mature thinkers, we must awaken from the dream and embrace reality. This is what should come of our understanding that theology reduces to anthropology (*Christianity*, 12–14, 17, 19–22, 25–27, 29–30, 33, 38, 66, 89, 127, 140, 146, 184, 204, 207, 230–231), that the study of God is nothing more than the study of man.

Feuerbach's next important work on these topics is his *Preliminary Theses on the Reform of Philosophy*. It opens with the claim that "the secret of *speculative philosophy*," such as we find in Hegel, "turns out to be *speculative* theology," which, as we have already seen, is essentially "anthropology." Christianity, with its central myths of the Trinity and the Incarnation, synthesizes the antitheses of monotheism's one God and polytheism's many gods and of the human versus the divine. Pantheism merges everything conceived of as natural and divine into one all-encompassing reality. "'Atheism' is reversed 'Pantheism'"; for instead of holding that everything is divine, it maintains that nothing is divine. "The Absolute Spirit" is merely a ghostly residue of theology, "a *specter*" that "haunts the Hegelian philosophy." The failure to recognize that fact makes it possible for philosophers to imagine that they have outgrown the childish picture-thinking of religion, when it has only assumed a disguised form. The problem with this fantasy is that it undermines the possibility of healthy self-affirmation. "The Hegelian philosophy has alienated man *from himself*," as we have seen. The cure is to ground our thinking in sense perception and to adopt a naturalistic theory of reality as materialistic. Philosophy tries to make religion a matter of "the *head*," which leads to idealism. But this is a distortion: "Religion is only emotion, feeling, heart, and love" (as Schleiermacher taught, contrary to the Hegelians). Feuerbach's "new philosophy" is based on these theses (*Brook*, 153–154, 157, 159–164, 166, 170), which are opposed to the views of all the religiously orthodox theories we have studied and not only to the Hegelian view.

In his *Principles of the Philosophy of the Future*, Feuerbach characterizes his project here as the "humanization of God – the transformation and dissolution of theology into anthropology." The anthropomorphism of "ordinary theology" turns out to be "self-contradictory," in that it wants to conceive of God as "a non-human" but can only speak and think of the divine in patently human terms. By contrast, "speculative theology or philosophy," more cognizant of the limits of language, emphasizes the "contradiction" between divine and human ways of being. Yet both involve the alienation of "the negation of all finiteness," such as is essential to humans and their natural environment. Like both ordinary and speculative theology, Hegelian thought fails to address our estrangement as only atheism can do. "So does absolute philosophy externalize and alienate from man his own essence and activity" (Marx would pick up this theme a couple of years later). The longing of religious faith is for bliss and the cessation of human misery (*Future*, 5, 11–12, 24, 37–38, 48).

In his *Lectures on the Essence of Religion*, Feuerbach repeats his famous mantra, "*Theology is anthropology*," by which he means that "man's God is nothing other than the deified essence of man" himself. He realizes that this view will be condemned as "atheism" and accepts Schleiermacher's view that "the foundation of religion is a feeling of dependency," despite Hegel's quip that, on that account, a dog must be religious, since "he feels dependent on his master." Other feelings that stem from this are fear, joy, gratitude, and love. He can feel all of this toward nature itself: "Though I myself am an atheist, I openly profess . . . nature religion," he says, while rejecting all "supernaturalism," whose God is "merely the *hypostatized and objectified essence* of the human imagination." His atheistic naturalism, unlike conventional theism, is firmly grounded in empirical reality. He acknowledges but dismisses (too easily, perhaps) the argument that the human spirit could only have originated in spiritual reality and not in material nature, indicating that it betrays both "too disparaging a conception of nature and too lofty a conception of spirit." Far from denying religion altogether, he advocates a natural religion which, instead of alienating us from our essence, will celebrate it and be committed to working on its behalf. This is a humanistic religion, thoroughly anthropocentric. "For God did not, as the Bible says, make man in His image; on the contrary man . . . made God in his image." The goal of liberating man from the alienation of supernaturalism is "to put nature into the hands of man, to harness it to man's striving for happiness." This would represent a practical transformation in the direction of independence and control. Supernaturalism is not just an erroneous worldview; it stunts our development and impedes human progress. "True atheism," he avers, is not "mere negation" but is "also an affirmation" (*Lectures*, 17, 23, 25, 31, 35, 40, 136, 150, 153–154, 181, 187, 207, 219, 282) of the natural order and of humanity itself.

18.6 Humanity

Let us now examine Feuerbach's theory of human nature independent of attachment to the supernatural. In his *Thoughts on Death and Immortality*, his central position is that, as natural beings, when we die, we cease to be and that there is no reason to cling to the fatuous belief in immortality. Without denying the human soul here, he seems to adopt a position of epiphenomenalism, viewing the soul's reality and functioning as "dependent" on the living body; "in other words, the body is the condition and presupposition of the soul; the soul cannot exist without a body." The individual human comprises body and soul, in working relation to each other, but is not Spirit, as God would be (remember that, at this stage of his career, he had not yet turned to atheism). "Consciousness is the absolute center of humanity"; yet human consciousness is body-dependent (*Thoughts*, 62, 87, 117). The first section of *The Essence of Christianity* is a good text for discerning his philosophy of human nature. It holds that consciousness is what essentially separates man from brute animals. It is human consciousness that allows us to think about species, while other animals can only consider individuals. This allows man to have a rich "inner life" of thought and a richer social life of communication with others. What defines human nature, then? "Reason, Will, Affection." Man is thus unique among the animals. "To will, to love, to think, are the highest powers, are the absolute nature of man as man, and the basis of his existence. Man exists to think, to love, to will." Our consciousness allows for operations of disinterested intellect and passions (such as a commitment to truth). The operations of human consciousness also involve at least an implicit reference to ourselves as conscious ego. It is quite natural to compare ourselves to other members of our species – to such an extent that we can mistakenly ascribe our own limitations to others (*Christianity*, 1–3, 5–7). He seems to agree with some earlier modern philosophers (such as Hobbes, Rousseau, and Kant) that self-consciousness both constitutes our dignity and is the source of many of our problems.

His *Principles of the Philosophy of the Future* tries to turn away from "the philosophy of the absolute" (e.g. Hegelian thought) toward "a philosophy of man" – that is, from theology to anthropology. The upshot should be to replace the alienating supernatural with the natural as object "of love and feeling." By contrast to the mind and its pursuit of speculative thought, "The heart does not want abstract, metaphysical, or theological, objects; it wants real and sensuous objects and beings." It is practical love and not theoretical logic that determines what we shall regard as true and real for us. Through sense perception, we can experience not only other things but ourselves; this self-consciousness achieves an "identity of subject and object" so desired by Hegelian thinkers. Thanks to the power of self-consciousness and the capacity to think in terms of species, rather than merely in particular, individual terms, man can understand "the distinction between I and thou," as well as the relationship between "subject and object," enabling him to do philosophy. Near the end of the book, Feuerbach adopts the famous humanistic statement of Terence (a celebrated Roman author from the second century BC), "I am a man; I consider nothing human alien to me," as an appropriate "motto of the new philosophy" (*Future*, 3, 5, 53–55, 58, 69–70; cf. *Faith*, 14–15).

In his *Lectures on the Essence of Religion*, he lauds – rather than deploring – the fact that humans are natural, rather than spiritual, beings. "For it is in nature that we live, breathe, and are; nature encompasses man on every side; take away nature and man ceases to exist; he subsists through nature and is dependent on nature in all his activities, in every step he takes." This includes the reality of "human egoism," which is not, in itself, bad. For egoistic self-interest is a function of our vulnerability as beings dependent on the natural environment for our very lives. While maintaining that the mind "is the highest part of man," distinguishing him from brute animals, it is the culmination of natural development rather than its origin, not leading logically to the reality of any divine mind. And, given his atheism, Feuerbach thinks that a belief in human immortality is baseless and foolish (*Lectures*, 78–80, 155, 267, 270; cf. *Brook*, 286, 293, 295). At any rate, he sees humans as derived from the natural environment but as having developed to a level of superiority (as if anticipating Darwinian evolutionary theory by a few years).

18.7 Freedom

His comments on human freedom are few, brief, and scattered. He believes that humans, as moral beings, are equally free. In his *Thoughts on Death and Immortality*, when he still seemed to subscribe to Hegelian panentheism, he holds that our particular, individual wills subsist in some "universal element of will," which is vague but reminiscent of Schopenhauer (*Thoughts*, 75). By the time he writes *The Essence of Christianity*, he has dropped this notion and writes that freedom is essential to the reason, will, and affection that are implicated by human nature. He says, "Only he who thinks is free and independent," brute animals being incapable of abstract thought (*Christianity*, 3, 39). In his *Preliminary Theses on the Reform of Philosophy*, he develops the humanistic position that "the existence of freedom" is embodied in man and that man is the touchstone of "the *ground and base* of the Fichtean Ego," of "the Leibnizian Monad," and "of the Absolute" of Hegel. But, unlike predecessors who try to spiritualize freedom, he maintains that "the new philosophy will succeed in *naturalizing* freedom" (*Brook*, 172). Unlike other animals, which are only conscious of individual objects as particulars, we think in general terms. Our capacities for universality, absoluteness, and freedom are inseparable, he claims (*Future*, 69). In his *Lectures on the Essence of Religion*, he anticipates Marx and Engels, holding that we can never be liberated until we have cast off the shackles of religious dependence: "True freedom is present only where man is also free from religion" (*Lectures*, 218).

18.8 Morality

Feuerbach's ethical theory is fairly simple but difficult to classify, apart from calling it humanistic naturalism. In *Thoughts on Death and Immortality*, he condemns as "the most immoral, the most pitiable, the most vain, and the most futile morality in the world" any that hinges on life after death with its enticing promises of reward and terrifying threats of punishment. Eschatological consequentialism of that sort betrays a pathetic blindness to "the reality of the good in and for itself" (*Thoughts*, 126, 135–136). In *The Essence of Christianity*, having turned to atheism, he employs the Kantian "ought" implies "can" principle for his own non-Kantian purposes; the notion that we must behave as God desires is merely "a ludicrous chimera." It is because real people in the natural world commonly suffer here and now that human sympathy is genuine, which, in turn, facilitates interpersonal love. He denies the notion that atheism nullifies morality and holds that it disparages virtue to render it dependent on a superstitious pipedream. Making morality theocentric tends to make it a matter of faith in authority and impervious to "the test of reason." Religious ethics also, he thinks, tends to be correlated with "the most immoral, unjust, infamous things" imaginable (*Christianity*, 28, 54, 202, 274).

In his *Lectures on the Essence of Religion*, he is blunt about it: "But where, the believers cry, do the laws of morality come from if there is no God? Fools! Laws consonant with human nature originate solely with man" (*Lectures*, 257). An interesting sentence in *The Essence of Faith According to Luther* draws a contrast between "the supreme principle" of his humanistic ethics ("Do good for

18 Ludwig Feuerbach

man's sake"), on the one hand, and, on the other, both that of Christian ethics ("Do good for God's sake") and that of deontological ethics ("Do good for the sake of the good"). Faith of any sort always aims at some object somehow associated with the good. But that tends to be an egoistic good related to "my own welfare," as opposed to love, which aims at "the welfare of others" (*Faith*, 62n., 89, 102; cf. *Brook*, 278, 288, 295). We never altogether escape egoistic self-interest; but we can learn to temper it with a concern for other people.

18.9 Society

It is somewhat ironic that in the area of sociopolitical theory, one of the two areas (along with that of religion) where he would prove to be most influential, Feuerbach has so little obviously revolutionary to say. In *The Essence of Christianity*, he contrasts legal requirements, a matter of the understanding (or the head), with moral prescriptions, a matter of love (or the heart). While the law deals with a person "only as an abstract being," love treats him as a particular individual. "The law holds man in bondage" by obliging him to do certain things and refrain from others; but "love makes him free" to act on human sympathy for the welfare of others or not. Rather like Schopenhauer, he maintains that compassion stems from a sensitivity to others as fellow sufferers. He says, "My fellow-man is the bond between me and the world." So much of who we are and what we do is socially constructed, "products of culture." By respecting this we can, to some extent, counterbalance natural tendencies toward egoism (*Christianity*, 47–48, 54, 82–83).

In his *Preliminary Theses on the Reform of Philosophy*, he reveals both the influence of Hegel and his disagreement with Hegelian collectivism: "Man is the fundamental being of the state" expresses a kind of individualism. Yet he also characterizes the state as the full realization of an individual person. Another piece, called "The Necessity of a Reform of Philosophy," is important for establishing links between politics and religion. To transform the former into a humanistic version of the latter, the needed principle "is nothing other than atheism." The shedding of supernatural religion can help generate the realization of man's energized natural potential, a genuine liberation. The hope is that this will move us from authoritarian dependence toward republican independence (*Brook*, 172, 149–152). In his *Principles of the Philosophy of the Future*, he writes that the realization of the human essence can be found "only in the community and unity of man with man." Only liberated society can establish a healthy synthesis between the antitheses of egoistic "being-for-itself" and authentically interpersonal "being-for-others" (*Future*, 71, 52).

But all of this is only achievable in the context of naturalism. On the very first page of his *Lectures on the Essence of Religion*, he boldly asserts that "we are as sick of political as we are of philosophical idealism; we are determined to become political materialists." In another passage that must have pleased secular socialists, he admits, "The principal reason for my interest in religion has always been that, if only in the imagination, it is the foundation of human life, the foundation of ethics and politics." Transforming supernatural religion into a secular religion of humanity will help us to deal with "the oppression of mankind." Rather than our serving the interests of abstract justice, justice should serve interests of natural humans. Unless and until we eliminate the shackles of supernatural religion and liberate humanity, he claims, "all political and social reforms are meaningless and futile." In a sense, what this radical transformation requires, he exclaims, is "a *new religion!*" (*Lectures*, 1–2, 22, 96, 217–218).

18.10 Review

Like some other thinkers we have studied here (e.g. Bentham), Feuerbach has more to offer us than that for which he is most famous – his atheism and anti-idealism. Like some others (e.g. Fichte), he is more than a vital intellectual link between predecessors (e.g. German idealists) and successors (e.g. Marx and Engels). He gives us a fairly complete philosophical system, even if parts of it are underdeveloped. One problem we might mention is a lack of much argumentation to support the alternative point of view he presents; but, to his credit, he was aware of and acknowledged that fact when he wrote, "I am guilty of failing to provide many proofs, explanations, and elucidations of my position" (*Faith*, 21–22). Nevertheless, he does represent an honest commitment to naturalism and an undermining of idealism that would characterize much of European philosophy for the rest of his century. And his radical socialism was to be extremely influential even while he was still alive – particularly in its developing into the communistic theory of Marx and Engels, whose thought we shall consider next.

19

Karl Marx

Source: Olga/Flickr/CC BY-SA 2.0

19.1 Overview

None of Hegel's other successors (including Schopenhauer, Feuerbach, and Kierkegaard) offers us a more influential philosophy than that of Marx (and Engels). Indeed, in terms of its impact on the world beyond the realm of philosophy, no other modern philosophy (including even Locke's and utilitarianism) can equal, let alone surpass, it. It will develop an even more radical materialism and atheism than Feuerbach's to provide the critique of society itself that will generate communist revolutions. We shall focus on Marx here, viewing Engels primarily as his chief collaborator; and we shall emphasize the philosophical writings of the younger Marx more than the economic writings of his later years.

19.2 Biography

Karl Marx was born on May 5, 1818, in Trier, Prussia, the son of Heinrich and Henriette Marx, both of whom were descended from Jewish rabbis. Heinrich, a successful lawyer and a liberal follower of the Kantian Enlightenment, was baptized as a Protestant in the face of anti-Jewish Prussian laws and had his children baptized in 1824. In 1835, Karl enrolled in the faculty of law at the University of Bonn; he went wild there, being imprisoned for disorderly conduct, and transferred to the law faculty at the more serious University of Berlin the following year (five years after Hegel died there).[1] Having become secretly engaged to Jenny von Westphalen (to whom he wrote poetry), he became acutely interested in Hegelian philosophy and history, associating with the radicalized Young Hegelians. His father died in 1838, the year he began his doctoral thesis on the natural philosophy of Democritus and Epicurus. He submitted this thesis to the philosophy faculty at the University of Jena, which granted him a doctorate in 1841. He would have liked to pursue an academic career, but his radicalism and atheism precluded that. So the next year he moved to Cologne, where he became editor of the liberal newspaper, *Rheinische Zeitung* (*Rhineland News*). In that capacity, in 1842, he met Friedrich Engels there; it seems they were mutually unimpressed with each other at that time. Engels (born in Germany in 1820) served in the Prussian army, attended lectures at Berlin, and joined the Young Hegelian radicals. This was upsetting to his father, a successful textile manufacturer, who wanted his son to go into the business and sent him to train for business. Engels attended Schelling's inaugural lecture at Berlin, denouncing it, as well as other anti-Hegel lectures. In March of 1843, Marx relinquished his position due to censorship restrictions; two months later, he married Jenny in a Protestant church. He started work on a critique of Hegel, and he and Jenny moved to Paris, a center of socialist thought (*Writings*, 10–13, 424–426).

In Paris, Marx became coeditor of a new, radical newspaper, the *Deutsch-Französische Jahrbücher* (the *German-French Annals*), in October of 1843. Engels contributed articles to it, including his *Outlines of a Critique of Political Economy*, and the two subsequently began their long correspondence. In that periodical, Marx published his *Critique of Hegel's "Philosophy of Right"* and *On the Jewish Question*, both in 1843; in the former, he was still adhering to a Feuerbachian humanism, while the latter moves toward communism. That turned out to be the only issue of the paper published. Marx was accused of treason by the Prussian government in the spring of 1844 at about the

---

1 References to Marx's writings will be to *Selected Writings*, by Karl Marx (hereafter called *Writings*), ed. by David McLellan, second edition (New York: Oxford Univ. Press, 2000), to *Selected Letters: The Personal Correspondence, 1844–1877*, by Karl Marx and Friedrich Engels (hereafter called *Letters*), ed. by Fritz J. Raddatz, trans. by Ewald Osers (Boston: Little, Brown and Co., 1981), to *The Marx-Engels Reader* (hereafter called *Reader*), ed. by Robert C. Tucker (New York: W.W. Norton & Co., 1972), to *The German Ideology* (hereafter called *Ideology*), by Karl Marx and Frederick Engels, ed. by C.J. Arthur (New York: International Publishers, 1970), to *Economic and Philosophic Manuscripts of 1844*, by Karl Marx, trans. by Martin Milligan, and the *Communist Manifesto* (hereafter called *Manuscripts*), by Karl Marx and Frederick Engels, trans. by Samuel Moore (Amherst, NY: Prometheus Books, 1988), to *Grundrisse*, by Karl Marx, trans. by Martin Nicolaus (New York: Vintage Books, 1973), to *Capital*, by Karl Marx, abridged edition, ed. by David McLellan (Oxford: Oxford Univ. Press, 2008), to *The Poverty of Philosophy* (hereafter called *Poverty*), by Karl Marx, trans. by H. Quelch (Amherst, NY: Prometheus Books, 1995), and to *Ludwig Feuerbach and the Outcome of Classical German Philosophy*, by Frederick Engels (hereafter called *Feuerbach*), ed. by C.P. Dutt (New York: International Publishers, 1941).

time he was writing his *Economic and Philosophic Manuscripts* – but nothing came of it. His first child, Jenny, was born in May. Later that year, he made contact with French socialist Pierre-Joseph Proudhon and Russian anarchist Mikail Bakunin. Marx was writing for the radical newspaper *Vorwärts!* (*Forward!*), which was associated with a utopian socialist secret society called the League of the Just. On August 28, 1844, Marx met with Engels at a café, starting the friendship and collaboration that would endure until Marx's death. Engels, returning to Germany from England, spent several days with Marx there in Paris. They worked together on *The Holy Family*, published in 1845. Meanwhile, Marx was studying political economists, including Adam Smith and James Mill. The French government, at the request of the King of Prussia, shut down *Vorwärts!* and banished Marx from France. So he moved to Brussels, where he was joined by his wife and daughter. A bit later, Engels also moved to Brussels. Marx wrote his "Theses on Feuerbach," moving decisively from his predecessor's humanism to historical materialism, the view that material practice, rather than ideas, drives human change (*Writings*, 426–427).

In the summer of 1845, Marx and Engels went to England and met with the Chartists, a British socialist group already known to Engels from his earlier time spent in Manchester. There they also encountered the League of the Just, which would evolve into the Communist League. They co-wrote *The German Ideology*, solidifying their break from Feuerbach and the other Young Hegelians, all of whom were seen as too idealistic; it was only published in the twentieth century (*Writings*, 426). After Marx returned to Brussels, his daughter Laura was born. Marx, under pressure from the government, relinquished his Prussian citizenship. In 1846, Engels went to Paris to work for the communists. The following year, he attended the first Congress of the Communist League in London (Marx could not afford to go), which authorized the writing of a promotional document. Marx published *The Poverty of Philosophy*, a critique of Proudhon, who had written *The Philosophy of Poverty*. In late 1847, Marx participated in the second Congress of the Communist League in London, which authorized him to draft its manifesto. He wrote the *Manifesto of the Communist Party* with Engels; it was published in London on February 21, 1848. Soon thereafter, a spate of revolutionary uprisings occurred in various European countries, with Marx actively participating in preparations for revolution in Brussels and Cologne. In early March, he was arrested and escorted to the French border, from where he made his way to Paris. He and Engels were both active in the Communist League there. They moved to Cologne, where he organized and edited a daily newspaper, the *Neue Rheinische Zeitung* (the *New Rhineland News*). But a state of emergency was declared, allowing authorities to suspend its publication indefinitely. A month later, the state of emergency was lifted, and the paper resumed publication. But a few months after that, the Cologne government ordered Marx out of the country, and the final issue of the paper there was published, printed in red ink. Marx returned to Paris in June of 1849, leaving for London in August. He would spend the rest of his life living in England, Engels also arriving soon after (*Letters,* 20–22).

In 1850, Marx was working to get support for German refugees in London. But he was without funds: he could not pay his rent, had to pawn possessions, and moved his family into a hotel after being evicted. Engels was living in Manchester, working to support the Marx family, as well as himself. After moving his family out of the hotel into an apartment, Marx secured access to the British Museum Reading Room, where he could study economic theory. Though it never actually happened, Marx was considering moving to America with his family and Engels. He was chairing weekly meetings of the London chapter of the Communist League in 1851. He was invited to write articles for the liberal *New York Daily Tribune* and accepted, with Engels actually writing many articles under Marx's name (*Writings*, 427). In 1852, Marx was working to establish a German workers' association in London. But the family was in dire financial distress. Mrs. Marx, Jenny, and Arlene Demuth, their maid, were all ill, and they had no money for doctors or medicines. Marx was unable to write articles for the *Tribune* because he could not afford to buy any newspapers to get the news. Before the end of 1852, the Communist League was dissolved (*Letters*, 35, 37, 50–51).

In the beginning of 1853, Marx was able briefly to resume his economic studies at the British Museum, before becoming too sick to continue. In early 1855, his daughter Eleanor was born. The following year, Mrs. Marx and her three daughters traveled to Trier to be with her sick mother, who died that summer. In the fall, the Marx family moved into larger quarters. In early 1857, Marx began writing on economics, preparing some manuscripts that would become part of his *Grundrisse*. His *Critique of Political Economy* was published in Berlin in 1859. In 1861, he got some money from an uncle in Germany, which temporarily helped to alleviate his financial problems. He also visited his mother in Trier, who destroyed some IOUs Marx had previously written her. He tried to become renaturalized as a citizen but was rejected. Throughout 1862, he was drafting economic writings that would become part of *Das Kapital* (*Capital*), working on it through 1863 as well. Before the end of 1863, his mother died, and he went to Trier to settle her estate, though he was ill (*Letters*, 78, 89, 99, 108). After receiving his share of an inheritance, he rented new accommodations In England.

In 1864, Marx attended the founding of the International Workers' Association (called the First International), for which he wrote an inaugural address and statutes, reading them to the central committee, which unanimously accepted them. The following year, the central committee appointed him its provisional secretary. Toward the end of 1866, he began sending manuscript portions of *Capital* to a publisher in Hamburg; the following September, its first volume was published. But Marx was indigent and needing to accept money from Engels. In 1868, his daughter Laura married a French socialist. Engels offered to pay all his debts and provide him with an annuity so that he could focus on his work, as he was revising the second volume of *Capital*. In 1870, Engels moved to London, 10 minutes away from Marx and his family; they got together almost every day for the rest of Marx's life. In 1871, Marx played a prominent role in the International Workers' Association's conference in London. He also worked on revising the first volume of *Capital* for a second German edition. The following year, he actively participated in the fifth congress of the International Workers' Association in the Hague. His daughter Jenny married a French socialist the following month. Marx spent the first few months of 1874 working on the second volume of *Capital*. When he applied for British naturalization, he was denied. He and his daughter Eleanor traveled to Karlsbad, where he was under police surveillance (*Letters*, 121–122, 130–131, 133–134, 138, 155). In 1875, he wrote his *Critique of the Gotha Program* before returning to his revisions of the second volume of *Capital*. In 1877, he went to Germany with Eleanor and his wife, who was ill. In early 1879, Mrs. Marx was very sick, and his own health was deteriorating, so that he sometimes could not work. Later he visited his daughter Jenny, who had a baby, and his health began improving. But the following year, he was physically exhausted, so that his doctor forbade his doing any extensive work. He asked Charles Darwin to accept a dedication of the second volume of *Capital*, but Darwin declined.

In 1880, Engels published *Socialism: Utopian and Scientific*, a pamphlet that would prove to be very popular and highly influential. Through most of the first half of 1881, Marx and his wife were both suffering from bad health, on account of which he again fell into debt. Again Engels helped him out financially. On December 2, Mrs. Jenny Marx died of liver cancer. When she was buried three days later, Marx's doctor forbade his attendance, and Engels spoke at the gravesite. The following year was a bad one for him as well, as he suffered from insomnia, a lack of appetite, and depression. He did manage to write a preface to the second Russian edition of the *Communist Manifesto*. By the end of 1882, he was permanently confined to his room and only occasionally able to work. In January of 1883, adding to his misery, his daughter Jenny died. He had bronchitis and

300 | *19 Karl Marx*

laryngitis, could hardly swallow anything, and was developing a tumor in his lung. On March 14, 1883, he died of the lung tumor. Three days later, he was buried, with Engels delivering a speech at the graveside (*Reader*, 603–604). In 1885, the second volume of *Capital*, edited by Engels, was published. The following year, Engels wrote and published *Ludwig Feuerbach and the Outcome of Classical German Philosophy*. In 1887, an English translation of the first volume of *Capital*, edited by Engels, was published. Seven years later, the third volume of *Capital*, edited by Engels, was published. On August 5, 1895, Engels died of cancer of the throat, having left a significant portion of his valuable estate to Marx's two surviving daughters.

19.3 Knowledge

Although Marx was not a great epistemologist, he emphasizes both the use of a dialectical method of analysis and a pragmatic orientation for the discussion of ideas. Starting with the second of these two points, we can observe that the second of his 11 "Theses on Feuerbach" holds that "the truth, i.e. the reality and power" of thinking can only be proved "in practice." The most famous of these "Theses" is the last, which says, "The philosophers have only *interpreted* the world, in various ways; the point is to *change* it." In *The German Ideology*, he maintains that we must turn from the abstract theories of philosophy to sensible reality, employing a provocative analogy: "Philosophy and the study of the actual world have the same relation to one another as masturbation and sexual love" (*Ideology*, 121, 123, 103; that eleventh of his "Theses" was engraved on Marx's tombstone). While his target here is philosophy in general, more particularly he would have in mind that of the German idealists and the "Young Hegelians," especially Feuerbach.

Even though he faults Feuerbach for not adequately recognizing that our thoughts, beliefs, and truths are shaped by socioeconomic forces, he nevertheless exhibits considerable respect for his predecessor. In both the Preface to his *Manuscripts of 1844* and its final section, he expresses his admiration for Feuerbach, saying that "*positive*, humanistic and naturalistic criticism" really begins with him, that he was "the only one" who properly grasped "the Hegelian dialectic," and that he can therefore be considered "the true conqueror of the old philosophy" (*Manuscripts*, 15–16, 143–144; see Marx's letter to Feuerbach in *Writings*, 122). Let us, then, turn to Marx's appropriation of the dialectical method of analysis.

Like Hegel and Feuerbach, Marx sees reality as involving conflict, such that our thinking, if it is adequately to reflect reality, must be dialectical. But analyzing "*theoretical* antitheses" is not sufficient, as their resolution is "*only* possible *in a practical* way" in a social context. More specifically, only "*communism*" can resolve the conflict of interests of one socioeconomic class with those of another, achieving a practical "negation of the negation" among humans. In his "Critique of the Hegelian Dialectic," Marx pays tribute to Hegel for recognizing (decades before Darwin) that our awareness of ourselves *and* our actual development as a species is an evolutionary historical process *and* that the "alienation" of conflict triggers this process. The root of Hegel's shortcomings, however, is that his understanding of reality is idealistic rather than naturalistic. We must start, as Feuerbach does, with "real, corporeal *man*, man with his feet firmly on the solid ground, man exhaling and inhaling all the forces of nature." Yet, unlike Feuerbach, we must recognize that man, "both in his being and in his knowing," is inevitably shaped by the economic forces of his social environment (*Manuscripts*, 109, 114, 149–150, 153, 155–157, 160–162; cf. *Grundrisse*, 88, 101–102).

In Hegel's most brilliant illustration of the dialectical process, the master–slave relation represents an unstable resolution of interpersonal conflict. But, rooted in an idealistic worldview, it fails sufficiently to appreciate the material forces that drive the conflict and must be dealt with in order to achieve a stable resolution. Whereas Hegel sees the material world as a spatiotemporal expression of "the Idea," Marx holds that the ideal is merely the mind's way of thinking of the natural order. As Marx famously comments, Hegel's view has the relation between the real and the ideal "standing on its head. It must be turned right side up again," which is what he sees himself as doing (*Capital*, 11). While Marx does not himself use the phrase "dialectical materialism" to characterize his position, this passage supports its applicability to his theory.

For Marx, because man is essentially a socioeconomic animal, interpersonal conflict must be grounded in material interests. The interests of the laboring class (which he calls the proletariat) are diametrically opposed to those of the owners who employ their paid labor (which he refers to as the bourgeoisie). The laborers are without money (capital) and desperately need it to survive, while the owners have money and desire to increase its amount as much as possible. Laborers try to get the greatest possible compensation in return for the least amount of work, while their employers want to pay the minimum amount possible in return for a maximum amount of labor. What divides the "haves" from the "have nots" is property (or capital) and the lack of it. The resolution can only come from a communist revolution, in which the exploited masses will rise up against their masters, abolish private property, and establish a classless society. This, Marx avers, is how the dialectical method should productively proceed. It would be convenient if Marx used the now familiar categories of thesis, antithesis, and synthesis in his analysis of the dialectic at work. But, in fact, he only does so in *The Poverty of Philosophy* (and that occurs in his ridiculing of Proudhon), where he writes about "the thesis, the antithesis and the synthesis," adding that those unfamiliar with Hegel can employ the "formula, affirmation, negation, and negation of the negation" (*Poverty*, 114–115, 117, 128). At any rate, Marx embraces the dialectic as a method that can give us practical knowledge of how to resolve the conflicts characteristic of reality, so long as that reality is conceived along the lines of materialistic naturalism rather than idealistically.

19.4 Reality

Marx is a consistent, committed materialist, seeing all reality as fundamentally physical, including that of the human mind. Even if his philosophy is anthropocentric (i.e. human-centered), he does not view humans and the natural environment as pitted against each other. In his *Manuscripts*, he writes of both "the coming-to-be of nature for man" and man's "*process* of *coming-to-be*" through labor in the natural environment. There need not be and should not be any alienating opposition between the two (*Manuscripts*, 113). His sort of materialism is not mechanistic like that of Hobbes, since humans' choices, in the context of material nature, purportedly help determine outcomes.

As Marx's position has been aptly called "dialectical materialism" even though he did not do so himself, it has also legitimately been called "historical materialism," though, again, he does not appear to have used the phrase. As he writes in *The Poverty of Philosophy*, changes in our modes of material production trigger corresponding changes in all of our social relations. "The same men who establish social relations conformably with their material productivity, produce also the principles, the ideas, the categories, conformably with their social relations" (*Poverty*, 119). In *Socialism: Utopian and Scientific*, Engels writes about "two great discoveries, the materialistic conception of history and the revelation of the secret of capitalistic production through surplus value," both of which "we owe to Marx" and the convergence of which rendered socialism scientific (*Reader*, 622).

The German Ideology contains a few paragraphs constituting a good early statement of this view: "The first premise of all human history is, of course, the existence of living human individuals. Thus the first fact to be established is the physical organization of these individuals and their

302 | *19 Karl Marx*

consequent relations to the rest of nature." While they are animals, humans are unique among the animals in producing the means of their own subsistence. "By producing their means of subsistence men are indirectly producing their actual material life." It should be obvious that this thoroughgoing materialistic conception of all reality would strike a death-blow to Hegelian idealism. In the first of his "Theses on Feuerbach," Marx tries to distinguish his own form of materialism from all previous forms ("that of Feuerbach included") in being dynamic rather than static, practical rather than theoretical. The tenth of his "Theses" observes that the perspective from which "the old materialism" (e.g. of Hobbes) operates is that of "civil society," which is ideologically attached to the prevailing *status quo*. By contrast, Marx claims, "the standpoint of the new is human society, or social humanity" (*Ideology*, 42, 39, 121, 123). By the way, Marx seems inclined to view all philosophy but his own as "ideology" in a disparaging sense. But if "ideology" is to refer to any set of ideas reflecting the interests of a particular class of people but intended and interpreted as indicative of universal truth, then might we not ask whether his philosophy is not simply another exercise in ideology (on behalf of the laboring class)?

19.5 God

Like Feuerbach, Marx is an atheist who is committed to the view that believing in and adoring God alienates us from our true potential. As he writes in the *Manuscripts*, "atheism, being the annulment of God," generates "the advent of theoretic humanism," such as we have seen represented by Feuerbach. This is a positive step for human emancipation but not enough. We must take the next step to "practical humanism," which will be accomplished by communism's "annulment of private property." Yet both "atheism and communism" should be seen as positive steps toward the realization of our human potential, rather than merely forms of negation. But we must understand why atheism's "annulment of religion" is so necessary (*Manuscripts*, 161).

Let us, then, consider what is probably the most famous passage in Marx's writings on the evils of religion and need for atheism, from "Towards a Critique of Hegel's *Philosophy of Right*: Introduction." He makes the Feuerbachian point that the legitimate basis of atheism is the recognition that "man makes religion, religion does not make man." In other words, systems of religious faith are figments of our imagination rather than reflections of reality – all of which, as we have seen, is material. God is simply a fantasy. But is the fantasy beneficial or detrimental to us? It is an aspect of the human condition that we suffer. We sensibly seek comforting relief from that suffering, imagining that we might find it through belief in God: "Religion is the sigh of the oppressed creature, the feeling of a heartless world, and the soul of soulless circumstances. It is the opium of the people." This powerful metaphor is telling. Like opium, faith in God can distract us from our troubles but proves addictive and undermines our ability to find real-world solutions to real-world problems. It is a toxic, destructive "illusion," from which we must become "disillusioned" (*Writings*, 71–72). Feuerbach's diagnosis was correct, as far as it went: belief in a supernatural God alienates us, as natural beings, from the natural world to which we properly belong.

But Feuerbach, like all the Young Hegelians, fails to take the criticism far enough. In *The German Ideology*, Marx and Engels criticize these other post-Hegelians for never getting beyond the "criticism of *religious* conceptions" to that of the socioeconomic conditions that generate them. Feuerbach, in particular, recognizes that religious alienation must be addressed by the materialistic substitution of a thoroughly secular world in place of "the religious world," as Marx writes in the fourth of his "Theses on Feuerbach." Yet, as he observes in the sixth and seventh of these "Theses," Feuerbach mistakenly sees humanity as merely an "abstraction inherent in each single individual" rather than as the product of an "ensemble of the social relations" in which people find themselves (*Ideology*, 40–41, 122). So, as Marx holds in *Capital*, the entire "religious world is but the reflex of the real world," the supernatural an imaginary projection of what is utterly natural and material. It will only prove disposable "when the practical relations of every-day life offer to man none but perfectly intelligible and reasonable relations with regard to his fellowmen and to Nature" (*Capital*, 49–50). It is the communist revolution that will allegedly transform social relations and precipitate the transformation of humanity itself.

19.6 Humanity

Real human beings – as opposed to those imagined by philosophers and theologians – are allegedly nothing but sensuous animals in a material environment, there being no mind or soul that is any sort of spiritual substance. All of our mental activities are the products of this material reality, as Marx and Engels argue in *The German Ideology*: "In direct contrast to German philosophy which descends from heaven to earth, here we ascend from earth to heaven." All of our ideas are grounded in our flesh-and-blood material reality: "Morality, religion, metaphysics, all the rest of ideology and their corresponding forms of consciousness thus no longer retain the semblance of independence" that they have in idealistic philosophy. Our lives are a complex set of physiological processes. "Life is not determined by consciousness," as for Hegel, "but consciousness by life." We have needs that motivate our actions and can only be satisfied by objects in our environment. Feuerbach got that right; but he failed to appreciate the fact that humans are also historical animals – we make history and, in turn, are shaped by it. In an incomplete "Introduction to a Critique of Political Economy," Marx insists that we are also essentially social animals, the atomistic individual, such as is found in British political economists like Adam Smith and David Ricardo, being a mere myth. Swept under the umbrella of this myth is the fictitious social contract theory of Rousseau (and, we might add, of Hobbes, Locke, and Kant also). As Hume already observed, humans would never have survived without being nurtured by family members or some other people. "Man is a *zoon politikon* in the most literal sense: he is not only a social animal, but an animal that can individualise himself only within society" (*Ideology*, 42, 47, 59, 64, 124–125).

Some of Marx's most important ideas on human nature can be found in his *Manuscripts*. Even though he consistently maintains that all substantial reality is physical, he regards his own naturalistic anthropology as a middle ground between "idealism and materialism" of the Hobbesian sort. "*Man* is directly a *natural being*" – a "living" and "*active* natural being," with physical needs, impulses, and desires, whose life is forever susceptible to "*suffering*." Human history itself "is a *real* part of *natural history*," rather than being otherwise. Everything about us is ultimately "of a sensuous nature," with no separable spirituality. A deservedly famous section of the *Manuscripts* is the one on alienation or "Estranged Labor." Capitalism divides society "into two classes – the property-*owners* and the propertyless *workers*." Workers are expected to produce as much through their labor as possible in return for minimum compensation that is hardly above the level of subsistence. Not only are the products of a worker's labor "commodities," but his labor is itself "a *commodity*," as is the worker himself. This leads to a profound sense of alienation on the part of the worker, who is estranged from his labor, its products, and even himself. Where Hegel wrote of alienation in a psychological sense and Feuerbach in relation to religion, Marx does so socioeconomically. He analyzes four dimensions of the worker's alienation: (i) from the products of his labor; (ii) from his own acts of production; (iii) from his "*species being*" or sense of what it is to live and act as a free human seeking to realize his potential; and (iv) from other people, by whom he is exploited or with whom he must compete for employment. The dialectical relation between the worker and his labor is such that he is made to produce more and more wealth for others but gets less and less for himself. He is enriching the owners who employ him and slowly impoverishing himself. The capitalist employer becomes the worker's "master," and the worker becomes "the servant of the wage." Here we see Hegel's master–servant relation generalized to apply to socioeconomic classes. This also purportedly carries over to the commodification of women, who must either find ways of supporting themselves or find others – most likely men – who will support them; either way, they are liable to experience and have to endure sexual exploitation (*Manuscripts*, 154, 111, 106, 69, 71–83, 101; cf. *Grundrisse*, 266, 307, 458, 470–471, 496, 500).

In a note "On James Mill" (John Stuart Mill's father), Marx sets out his vision for the future of a humanity that has overcome class conflict and alienation. Everyone could affirm "himself and his fellow men" through his labor in a fourfold way: (i) his individuality would be maintained and expressed in his activity; (ii) a person would enjoy helping others meet their needs through work; (iii) each might help rather than hinder others in consciously relating to our shared species life; and (iv) each of us would reciprocally realize his potential in relation to our shared "communal essence." Elsewhere, he explains that such a transformation is possible on account of the relative flexibility of our needs and our capacity to postpone seeking their gratification and even to "repress" them altogether, when necessary. In one of his final writings, Marx says that, like other animals, humans must adapt to their environment to continually meet their own needs but that human needs expand over time. "At a certain point in their evolution, after the multiplication and development of their needs and of the activities to assuage them," humans transform both themselves and their environment (*Writings*, 132, 560, 629).

19.7 Freedom

All of this invites the question of the extent to which we are free in our actions and in control of our own future. Given his materialism, we might expect Marx's position on human freedom to be as problematic as those of some of his predecessors (e.g. Leibniz and Hegel). The claim that life determines consciousness, rather than the other way around, could be interpreted as leaning toward determinism. But, in fact, Marx did not seem very interested in the metaphysical issue of free will, does seem to need room for human choices, and is not bothered to try to hammer out a coherent position here. He is more focused on the emancipation of people from subjection to and exploitation by others. As he writes in his *Manuscripts*, "A *being* only considers himself independent when he stands on his own feet; and he only stands on his own feet when he owes his *existence* to himself." Subservience and independence are antithetical conditions. The *Communist Manifesto* attacks the false "freedom" of bourgeois society, at one point indicating that it boils down to the "free trade" that benefits the rich and powerful. The objective of a classless society should be to build the sort of community "in which the free development of each is the condition for the free development of all." The emancipation at which Marx and Engels aim would overthrow the domination of the privileged few over the disadvantaged many and move in the direction of equality. Their words still ring strong today: "Let the ruling classes tremble at a communistic revolution. The proletarians have nothing to lose but their chains. They have a world to win" (*Manuscripts*, 112, 211–212, 225, 231, 243).

In *The German Ideology*, they distinguish between the "illusory community" of bourgeois society, in which "the ruling class" achieves freedom through the slavery or economic bondage of others, and "a real community," in which all can "obtain their freedom in and through their association" as equals (*Ideology*, 83, 118). However broad or narrow the scope of what Marx calls (in the third volume of *Capital*) "the realm of freedom" may be, it can only function in the context of a "realm of physical necessity." There is no liberation possible from the needs and demands of nature, even if choices can be made within their parameters. "Men make their own history," Marx writes, indicating some room for choice. But he quickly adds that "they do not make it under circumstances chosen by themselves, but under circumstances directly found, given and transmitted from the past." Engels seems to support this view that we do make choices within limits circumscribed by forces beyond our control. "Man's own social organization," he writes, "becomes the result of his own free action." He can learn to exercise some control over nature itself through cooperation and collaboration. But this will require the transformative evolution "of man from the kingdom of necessity to the kingdom of freedom" (*Reader*, 320, 437, 637–639). This, of course, is where the communist revolution will supposedly take us.

In *On the Jewish Question*, Marx distinguishes between the "political emancipation" of some, as when a Christian country grants freedom of religion to Jews, and "universal human emancipation," for which he is striving; the former, of course, is desirable, but it is incomplete, the latter requiring permanent revolution and not merely the passing of an emancipatory law. The Enlightenment concept of liberty, endorsed by Kant before him (and Mill after him), as the freedom to do anything that does not harm or threaten others, leaves the systemic structures of bourgeois society untouched. Capitalism, by its very nature, requires a subservient laboring class dependent on property owners for survival. As Marx writes in "Towards a Critique of Hegel's *Philosophy of Right*: Introduction," this is "the proletariat," the only class that can dissolve the very structures of bourgeois society. (By the way, this article, published in 1844, seems to mark the first time the proletariat was identified as the agent of human emancipation.) Philosophy must provide the ideas that will generate human emancipation: "The head of this emancipation is philosophy, its heart is the proletariat." As Marx observes, in bourgeois political society, people are more or less "free" to the extent that they have some control over their rulers. Genuine freedom, however, he writes in his "Critique of the Gotha Program," requires that the state be "completely subordinate" to the people rather than "an organ superimposed on society," even with checks and balances. Ironically, this post-revolutionary ideal will supposedly come to be after passing through a phase of the "dictatorship of the proletariat" (*Writings*, 50–51, 54–55, 60, 63, 81–82, 610–611).

19.8 Morality

If we can distinguish between ethics and sociopolitical philosophy, Marx is not among the great ethical theorists of modern times. As we have seen is the case with freedom, he is deeply suspicious of all values that are ideological (that is, represent certain sets of class interests while being presented as if they were universally applicable); that includes moral ones. As Marx and Engels succinctly put the point in the *Communist Manifesto*, speaking of the proletarian, "Law, morality, religion are to him so many bourgeois prejudices, behind which lurk in ambush just as many bourgeois interests." There is no truly human morality in capitalist society, only a more or less deceptive camouflage for the bourgeois interests of the ruling class. As those change over time, so does what passes for conventional morality. Ethicists pretend they are examining "eternal truths," such as that we must always act justly and all must do only what is right. "But communism abolishes eternal truths, it abolishes all religion, and all morality, instead of constituting them on a new basis." The promise of moral reform is just another fraudulent swindle. The reforms (if one insists on using that word) demanded by communism are far more practical and revolutionary – such as abolishing property in land, all inheritance rights, and ownership and management of modes of communication and transportation; they will help bring about the dismantling of the entire system of capitalism (*Manifesto*, 220, 229–231). Why are such radical measures required?

The problem with the entire capitalist system, the rot at its core, if you like, is that, by its very nature, it promotes acquisitive greed and ruthless exploitation. To succeed in the system, people must use others as mere means to their own ends (the sort of thing Kantian ethics purports to condemn). "Each tries to establish over the other an *alien* power, so as thereby to find satisfaction of his own selfish need," as Marx writes in his *Manuscripts*. It is in the interest of the owners to keep their workers as poor, as needy, as powerless, as dependent as possible. But what they fail to foresee is the inevitable explosion that will constitute the revolution and will radically topple all the old moral systems of the past. The hypocritical charade is maintained partly by the lie that ethics will maintain a critical moral check on the bourgeois political economy of Adam Smith, David Ricardo, James Mill, and so forth. In fact, it is money and the lack of it that drives all social values in capitalist society, with overwhelming power: "It transforms fidelity into infidelity, love into hate, hate into love, virtue into vice, vice into virtue, servant into master, master into servant, idiocy into intelligence, and intelligence into idiocy" (*Manuscripts*, 115–116, 121, 140; cf. 198–199 for a similar treatment by Engels). Even if we resist the communist treatment, we would do well to consider whether there is, at least, some truth to this diagnosis.

By the time of Marx and Engels, the two dominant forms of secular ethics in Western Europe were the Kantian and the utilitarian, both of which offer us a single foundational principle designed to replace moral relativism with an objective criterion of right and wrong. But in *The German Ideology*, they make quick work of both systems of bourgeois ethics. Kantian "good will," allegedly intrinsically valuable regardless of consequences, is so ineffectual that all Kant can offer us is the pie-in-the-sky hope that righteousness will be rewarded and wickedness punished at some point in "*the world beyond.*" As for utilitarianism, Hegel has already allegedly exposed it as a "theory of mutual exploitation" which is justified as serving the common good, but, in fact, boils down to "monetary-commercial" relationships that help further enrich the ruling class. Every bourgeois ethical theory must strive to conceal the same dirty little secret (which Nietzsche would later also strive to expose): "The ideas of the ruling class are in every epoch the ruling ideas" of its moral culture. Thus, for example, when "the aristocracy was dominant, the concepts honour, loyalty, etc." prevailed. A structural change in the ruling class ushered in new values, so that "during the dominance of the bourgeoisie the concepts freedom, equality, etc." prevailed (*Ideology*, 97, 109–110, 112–114, 64–65). But this is still sheer, unadulterated ideology.

Engels later distinguishes between all class-based moralities, such as those spawned by "the feudal aristocracy, the bourgeoisie and the proletariat," on the one hand, and a "really human morality," derived from "the future classless society" that will supposedly emerge after the revolution, on the other. However, Marx is quite nebulous regarding details about the latter. Even though equality is a valuable ideal, it can overlook the fact that people themselves are not, in fact, equal, particularly when communist society is just emerging from capitalism. How can we expect equal treatment, benefits, rights, etc. across the board, given the differences in natural ability, age, marital status, number of children, and so forth? There will have to be a period of transition in which rough approximations are to be expected. But, then, what is to be the rule for the moral treatment of all? Marx's famous answer (in his "Critique of the Gotha Program") is drawn from already existing socialist literature and may seem as abstract, idealistic, and utopian as philosophers he himself criticized: "From each according to his ability, to each according to his needs!" (*Reader*, 667–668, 385–388). We might well wonder how humanity could ever realize such an evanescent goal, even if it is worth striving to achieve.

19.9 Society

Money is a key medium of exchange in capitalist society. Hired labor is employed by the owners, who pay their employees in wages in return for the workers surrendering the products of their labor. But how much of a wage in return for what volume of work must be determined through the antagonistic "struggle" between capitalist and worker, as Marx writes in his *Manuscripts* (perhaps thinking of the life-and-death struggle leading to Hegel's master–servant dialectic). Because he has to sell his labor, the worker becomes "a commodity," to be used by others for their own purposes. The deal is rigged in that the more profit owners get and the more impoverished their workers become, the more divided they become and the more at loggerheads their interests become. As long as the capitalistic system endures, "the inevitable result for the worker is overwork and premature death, decline to a mere machine, a bond servant of capital." The capital owned by the bourgeois gives them formidable power over the proletariat. Communism calls for the annulment of such capital and of the power it confers on some over others. Later will follow "the annulment of the state," leading to the transformation of the human person "as a *social* (i.e., human) being," living beyond artificial alienation. Finally, a human being will be free to appropriate "his total essence in a total manner, that is to say, as a whole man" (*Manuscripts*, 19–23, 36, 100, 102, 106).

All of this, of course, will require a societal cataclysm, such that the famous threat posed in the *Communist Manifesto* has a reasonable basis: "A specter is haunting Europe – the specter of communism." The increasingly polarized split between "bourgeoisie and proletariat," as two antagonistic antitheses, makes an explosive revolution seem inevitable to Marx and Engels, even if the time and place are uncertain. The bourgeoisie has allegedly created the proletarian class that it oppresses and exploits, so that it may be said to have "forged the weapons" that will destroy it. Nor is the oppressor merely the owner together with his managers; they are aided and abetted by "the landlord, the shopkeeper, the pawnbroker, etc.," who, like vultures, pick off whatever is left. The proletariat, though not the only class that struggles against the bourgeoisie (there are, for example, the "lower-middle class, the small manufacturer, the shopkeeper"), is the only "really revolutionary class," the others conservatively trying to maintain their standing in the middle class. The revolutionary conflict will initially be national, later becoming international. The key move will be the abolition of all private property that gives some the power to oppress and exploit others. "Abolition of the family" may seem even more radical. But in bourgeois society the relations between man and woman, as well as between parents and children, have become incorrigibly corrupt. Ultimately, communism wants "to abolish countries and nationality" altogether, to achieve global human society. Part of what is so unsettling about Marx and Engels and the communists is that they "disdain to conceal their views and aims. They openly declare that their ends can be attained only by the forcible overthrow of all existing social conditions" that can be altered (*Manuscripts,* 208, 210, 215, 217, 219–221, 223–224, 226–228, 243).

In *The German Ideology*, they paint a lovely utopian picture of what life will be like in their post-revolutionary classless society. Specialized social roles will be abolished, so that a person will no longer be designated "a hunter, a fisherman, a shepherd," and so forth. Now, instead, societal regulation of production will make "it possible for me to do one thing today and another tomorrow, to hunt in the morning, fish in the afternoon, rear cattle in the evening, criticise after dinner, just as

19 Karl Marx

I have a mind, without ever becoming hunter, fisherman, shepherd or critic." This sort of genuine freedom of choice will supposedly allow for meaningful human flourishing of an individual truly socialized in community (*Ideology*, 53, 83). But we should not imagine that we can easily reach such an end without going through the awful conflict of revolution. As Marx writes in *The Poverty of Philosophy*, it is especially delusory to suppose that "*social evolutions*" can render "*political revolutions*" unnecessary (*Poverty*, 190). Given the structures of capitalist society, the latter seem inevitable. Marx sees John Stuart Mill, for example, as trying thus, by means of "a shallow syncretism . . . to reconcile irreconcilables" (*Capital*, 8–9). We shall attempt to discern whether this is a fair characterization of Mill or merely a facile dismissal.

There are numerous other threads of Marxian social theory to be woven into this tapestry, some of which we shall now consider. Not only are we told that communism can only come about through revolution, but Marx contends that capitalism will never allow for any sort of socialistic society "without a revolution." He identifies communism as the most openly revolutionary form of socialism in its "declaration of the permanence of the revolution, the class dictatorship of the proletariat as the necessary transit point to the abolition of class distinctions generally." While denying himself credit for discovering the class struggle, Marx does claim to have made three significant contributions: (i) he sees that the formation of socioeconomic classes is due to developments in modes of production; (ii) he sees the (alleged) inevitability of "the dictatorship of the proletariat"; and (iii) he foresees this as merely a transitional period on the way to "a classless society." Since the ruling classes are armed and organized in defense of their vested interests, it will be important for the proletariat to be likewise. Toward the end of his life, however, Marx did seem to acknowledge the possibility that social reform ("evolution") might avert the need for violent insurrection ("revolution") in England; indeed, in a speech he delivered in Amsterdam (in 1872), he holds out hope that in a few "countries like America, England," and perhaps Holland, workers might be able to wrest tolerable concessions "by peaceful means," even if force will be needed in most places (*Writings*, 137, 323, 371–372, 306, 308–309, 642–643).

19.10   Review

Of all the philosophies considered in this book, none has had a more obviously striking impact on our world than this one. Through communist revolutions in Russia, in China, in Cuba, and elsewhere on our planet, this became one of the most influential political ideologies of the twentieth century. In sociopolitical philosophy, also, this appeal for equality from the perspective of the oppressed peoples of the world has had a significant impact. Engels, his steadfast friend and close collaborator, modestly but accurately wrote that, while he played a valuable role in the development of this philosophy, Marx could have done it without him. There was a group of other interrelated socialists working at about this same time. But, says Engels, "Marx stood higher, saw further, and took a wider and quicker view than all the rest of us. Marx was a genius; we others were at best talented" (*Feuerbach*, 42–43n.). There are, to be sure, problems with this theory, at some of which we have already hinted. It needs free choice; yet the deterministic philosophy of human nature permits no metaphysical foundation for it. Marx asks us to subscribe to his dogmatic materialism, his dogmatic atheism, and his dogmatic relativism, offering no argumentation for their truth but only a narrative of why they might seem preferable. His dialectical analysis of the class struggle between proletariat and bourgeoisie is quite apt in the wake of the Industrial Revolution. But his stepping back from the bold claim that it can only be resolved by violent revolution does not inspire confidence. His call for a dictatorship of the proletariat and forced annulment of the structures of capitalist society is alarming; and it strains credulity that that allegedly temporary, transitional phase would ever pass away and yield to the utopian ideal of a classless society. Still, Engels was correct in saying that "Marx was before all else a revolutionist" (*Reader*, 604). He has also, quite rightly, been called, along with Nietzsche, one of the great nineteenth-century masters in the school of suspicion, having taught us to question even ideologies to which we ourselves are committed.

20

John Stuart Mill

Source: London Stereoscopic Company/Wikimedia Commons/Public Domain

20.1 Overview

The most enduringly popular of Mill's philosophical books were *On Liberty* and *Utilitarianism*, which reflect the influence of the two men who were most important to his development – namely, James Mill, his father, and Jeremy Bentham, the philosopher, respectively. Yet, as we shall see, Mill goes beyond them in these two books. And, as we shall also see, there is a great deal more to Mill's system of thought than these two books can convey.

20.2 Biography

John Stuart Mill, born in London on May 20, 1806, was the first of nine children of James and Harriet Burrow Mill. James was a Scottish intellectual (arguably what we would call a social scientist) who had attended the University of Edinburgh and was licensed to preach by the Presbyterian Church, though he quit the ministry and moved to England; he was a fierce proponent of the Enlightenment ideals of liberal culture. Stern and undemonstrative, he was strict with his children. In 1808 (a year after the British slave trade was abolished), James Mill met Jeremy Bentham, becoming committed to his utilitarian views. The following year, John met Bentham.[1] Also in 1809, James began teaching John at home, starting with Greek. This was the beginning of what Mill's noteworthy *Autobiography* calls his "unusual and remarkable" education. In 1813, he read half a dozen of Plato's dialogues. At the age of eight, his father began teaching him Latin, Euclidean geometry, and algebra, also assigning him to teach some of his siblings some of what he was learning. After reading Hume's history and Newton's physics, he studied the logics of Aristotle and Thomas Hobbes (*Essential*, 11–16, 20–23).

Meanwhile, James Mill was writing a *History of India*, which the boy helped him proofread. After it was published in 1818, he secured a position as assistant examiner of correspondence with the East India Company. James led John through the political economy of Adam Smith and David Ricardo; Ricardo was a personal friend of James and a dedicated utilitarian Benthamite. James was training John, along the same ideological lines, to become a fellow Philosophical Radical. Two distinguishing features of this educational journey were that John was trained to try to solve problems himself rather than immediately being given solutions and that he was taught to think for himself about things, even to the point of being allowed to disagree with his father. This pedagogical regimen was so strict that John was not permitted to play with other boys (*Essential*, 24–30).

In 1820, James Mill's influential essay on "Government" was published, presenting a powerful case for the Philosophical Radicals. As a Benthamite, he argues that the function of good government is to promote the greatest happiness of the greatest number of citizens. He advocates a mixed government, with checks and balances, a representative democracy with the vote expanded to all male citizens who are heads of households and at least 40 years of age. Mill's father had become a religious agnostic and raised his son with no conventional attachment to any organized religion, although knowledgeable about a variety of religious traditions. His role model was more Socrates than any religious figure. In 1820, Mill went to France for an extended stay with Sir Samuel Bentham, the philosopher's brother. There he learned French, studied French literature, and took piano lessons, returning to England in 1821. Making a serious study of Bentham's philosophy, he became an ardent disciple, regarding Benthamism as almost a religion, for which he would become

---

1 References to Mill's writings will be to *Essential Works of John Stuart Mill* (hereafter called *Essential*), ed. by Max Lerner (New York: Bantam Books, 1965), to *An Examination of Sir William Hamilton's Philosophy* (hereafter called *Examination*), by John Stuart Mill (London: Longman, Green, 1865), to *Essays on Politics and Culture* (hereafter called *Essays*), by John Stuart Mill, ed. by Gertrude Himmelfarb (Garden City, NY: Anchor Books, 1963), to *Collected Works of John Stuart Mill* (hereafter called *Collected*), ed. by J.M. Robson (Toronto: Univ. of Toronto Press; eight of these many volumes have been reprinted by the Liberty Fund of Indianapolis), to *Auguste Comte and Positivism* (hereafter called *Positivism*), by John Stuart Mill (Ann Arbor: Univ. of Michigan Press, 1961), to *Theism*, by John Stuart Mill, ed. by Richard Taylor (Indianapolis: Bobbs-Merrill, 1957), to *Considerations on Representative Government* (hereafter called *Considerations*), by John Stuart Mill, ed. by Currin V. Shields (New York: The Liberal Arts Press, 1958), to *Essays on Sex Equality* (hereafter called *Equality*), by John Stuart Mill and Harriet Taylor Mill, ed. by Alice S. Rossi (Chicago: Univ. of Chicago Press, 1970), and to *Principles of Political Economy* and *Chapters on Socialism* (hereafter called *Principles*), by John Stuart Mill, ed. by Jonathan Riley (Oxford: Oxford Univ. Press, 1994).

312 | *20 John Stuart Mill*

an evangelist. In 1822, he was studying law with John Austin, a proponent of utilitarian jurisprudence, as well as beginning to write for periodicals. The next year, he founded a "Utilitarian Society" of like-minded young men who followed Bentham's views (*Essential*, 31–34, 36, 41–42, 44–47, 54). He even got arrested for distributing birth control pamphlets (which the law then classified as obscene) in a working-class London neighborhood and was jailed overnight.

It is curious that the published version of his *Autobiography* never directly mentions his mother. In an early draft, he partly blamed her for his father's older children having no love or affection for him, writing that "a really warm-hearted mother would in the first place have made my father a totally different being and in the second have made the children grow up loving and loved." He then dismisses her as a mere drudge, saying and doing nothing to make his childhood one of love rather than one of fear, abdicating to his father her moral responsibility for her son. In the spring of 1823, his father got him a position in the East India Company, working under himself. He would work for the company for "the next thirty-five years" in a job that was neither very taxing nor particularly time-consuming, giving him ample leisure for his voluminous writings. That same year, Bentham started the *Westminster Review* as a periodical for Philosophical Radicalism, offering its editorship to James Mill, "who declined it as incompatible with his India House appointment." John became a frequent contributor to it during this period of "rapidly rising Liberalism," characterized by growing enthusiasm for both "representative government and complete freedom of discussion." The younger Mill, having been raised by his father to downplay his feelings, was lacking in sympathetic benevolence and functioning more like "a mere reasoning machine" (*Essential*, 3–4, 55, 60, 63–64, 68, 70).

By the beginning of 1825, the younger Mill was editing Bentham's *Rationale of Judicial Evidence*, published in five volumes two years later (with Mill's name on it as editor). Also in 1825, Mill helped found a London debating society. He was learning German and resumed studying logic, including that of Hobbes. Due to a combination of overworking and routinely repressing his feelings, in 1826, he suffered a mental crisis. He asked himself, if all his utilitarian goals were met, whether he would then experience "great joy and happiness." Remarkably, he realized that he would not. This seemed to undermine everything in his life that most mattered to him. He consequently suffered a profound depression. There seemed to be nobody to whom he could turn for help – least of all his father. Though he continued doing his job at India House, it was only done "mechanically, by the mere force of habit." But then, reading an account of someone's father's death, he burst into tears, which helped him realize that he was not altogether devoid of feeling. This gave him hope, and the gloom of depression began lifting. He drew two instructive conclusions – that true happiness requires that we focus on some objects(s) other than our own happiness and that the cultivation of feelings, which had been neglected in his own upbringing, was essential to "human well-being." He turned to romantic poetry, especially that of Wordsworth, as a sort of therapy. In 1828, he was promoted from clerk to assistant examiner at India House, still under his father's supervision, and started making friends who were about his own age. He became exposed to the ideas of the romantic poet Coleridge, who was influenced by German idealism, and studied some early work of Auguste Comte, who was then developing socialist ideas, teaching that human culture evolves from theological explanations to metaphysical ones to a scientific or "positive stage" (*Essential*, 73–74, 76–77, 83–84, 87–88, 90–92, 95, 101).

In 1830, Mill started working out some of his "ideas on Logic," particularly "the problem of Induction," as well as the problem of freedom and determinism that had haunted him during his severe depression. He believed that "though our character is formed by circumstances, our own desires can do much to shape these circumstances" and, thus, our character. The year 1830 was also that of the July Revolution in France; Mill immediately went to Paris, hoping that permanent

20.2 Biography | **313**

progressive reform was taking shape there. Next he started writing five *Essays on Some Unsettled Questions of Political Economy* (not to be published until 1844). In 1831, he published seven articles on "The Spirit of the Age," characterizing his period of history as transitioning from old ideas and institutions to new ones, calling for progressive evolution rather than violent revolution such as Marx and Engels advocated (*Essential*, 97, 103, 105, 109, 105).

Things did seem to be changing. In 1832 (the year Bentham died), the First Reform Bill, supported by progressive liberals, including Benthamites, passed through Parliament and became law. The following year, slavery was abolished in all British territories. In 1835, Mill started and edited the *London Review*, which was the *London and Westminster Review* from 1837 to 1840. Also in 1835, Mill reviewed Alexis de Tocqueville's *Democracy in America*. The following year, James Mill died (*Essential*, 115, 121), and John was promoted at India House. In 1838 (a year after Victoria became Queen of England), his essay on "Bentham" was published, making it clear that he should not be considered as a mere uncritical follower. Mill was invited to assume a chair in moral philosophy at Glasgow but declined the offer. In 1840, he published an essay on "Coleridge," making it obvious that he had accepted some ideas of romantic idealism. He was corresponding with Comte and writing *A System of Logic*, which was published in 1843 and became a surprising success. In 1848, a series of socialist revolutions erupted on the European continent, with Mill hopefully supporting the one in France, which ultimately failed when Louis Napoleon usurped power and became Napoleon III. Also in 1848, Mill published his *Principles of Political Economy*, which turned out to be another great success.

In 1830, Mill met Mrs. John Taylor at a dinner party given by her husband. She would become one of the most important people in Mill's life, along with his father. They were kindred spirits, both committed to democratic, liberal culture and progressive social reform. He describes Harriet Taylor as "the most admirable person" he ever knew and their relationship as the "chief blessing" of his entire life. Though Mr. Taylor was no intellectual, Mill respected him as "a most upright, brave, and honourable man, of liberal opinions and good education." Mr. and Mrs. Taylor had two sons, and their daughter Helen (called Lily) was born in 1831. Mill credits Harriet with inspiring him with valuable ideas, regarding morality and sociopolitical relationships. After a while, she and her husband agreed to live apart (she with Lily) much of the time. With her husband's knowledge, Harriet and Mill spent a good deal of time together; though it is doubtful that they ever did anything wrong, given the customs of Victorian England, they were the targets of cruel gossip. Under her influence, Mill was shifting from being a traditional democrat to having some attraction to socialism. They agreed that the great social problem was how to balance "individual liberty of action" with "a common ownership in the raw material of the globe and an equal participation of all in the benefits of combined labour." They worried about the tendency of most socialistic systems to favor or at least accept the "tyranny of society over the individual." Their relationship lasted for about two decades. In 1849, Mr. Taylor died of cancer. A bit less than two years later, in 1851, Mill and Harriet married. He considered their seven and a half years as a married couple to be the happiest of his life. But in 1858, she suffered "a sudden attack of pulmonary congestion" in Avignon, France, and died of it. Mill bought a cottage near her gravesite, where he and his stepdaughter, Helen, spent about half of each year for the rest of his life (*Essential*, 111–113, 135, 137, 141–143). In his grief, Mill submerged himself in his writings.

In 1859, Mill published two volumes of his *Dissertations and Discussions*, as well as *On Liberty*, on which he and Harriet were working when she died, and "A Few Words on Non-Intervention." In 1860 and 1861, he was writing his *Considerations on Representative Government* (published in 1861), *The Subjection of Women* (published in 1869), and *Utilitarianism*, first published in three installments (in 1861) "and afterwards reprinted in a volume" (in 1863). In 1862, Mill published

"The Contest in America," supporting the North against the South in the Civil War, on account of his fierce opposition to slavery. Between 1863 and 1865, he was writing *An Examination of Sir William Hamilton's Philosophy*, which was published in 1865, as was his *Auguste Comte and Positivism*. Around that time, he voluntarily gave up some author's royalties on some of his books, so that "cheap People's Editions" of works "most likely to find readers among the working classes" might be printed (*Essential*, 153, 155–159, 161–163). In 1865, he was also elected Rector of St. Andrews University.

After he was promoted to chief examiner of India correspondence at India House in 1856, there was a mutiny in India against British rule. It was quashed, and Parliament placed the administration of India under strict government control. Mill was offered a position in the governing of India in 1858 but refused it and retired – leaving him free to be prolific in his subsequent writings. In 1865, however, he was asked "by some electors of Westminster" to run for a seat in Parliament's House of Commons. He refused to campaign or spend any of his own money to get himself elected and announced that, if elected, he would work for larger issues he considered important, rather than devoting "time and labour" to merely local interests. He warned the electors that he wanted the vote extended to women and refused to discuss his own "religious opinions." To his surprise, he beat the conservative candidate and won the election, serving a three-year term as a liberal legislator, during which time another Reform Bill passed into law. In 1867 (the year he published the third volume of his *Dissertations and Discussions*), he unsuccessfully campaigned for women's suffrage. His motion to substitute the gender-neutral word "person" for the word "man" in Disraeli's Reform Bill also failed, though the bill itself passed. He supported greater autonomy for Ireland. In 1868, he delivered a famous speech against abolishing capital punishment. He supported a Married Women's Property Bill, though it did not pass until 1870. Tories tried to criticize him for calling the Conservative Party "the stupidest party"; but their attempt backfired, as that characterization had a popular appeal that "stuck to them for a considerable time afterwards." Mill's advocacy of such progressive causes led to his being "thrown out" of office when he ran for reelection in 1868. Although he was invited "to become a candidate for other constituencies," he declined (*Essential*, 163–168, 180, 182).

He returned to his literary work and to the enjoyment of country life with Helen. They made some revisions in *The Subjection of Women* and published it in 1869. They cooperated in establishing a National Society for Women's Suffrage (*Essential*, 182, 177). In 1872, he worked on a new edition of his *System of Logic* (and also, incidentally, became godfather to Bertrand Russell). Near the beginning of May, 1873, he walked 15 miles on a botanical expedition. Four days later, May 7, 1873, he died of a fever in Avignon. His last words, spoken to Helen, were, "You know that I have done my work." Three days later, he was buried in a grave next to his beloved wife. He left half of his estate to charity. Later that year, his *Autobiography*, edited by Helen, was published. In 1874, Helen had his *Three Essays on Religion* (*Nature*, *Utility of Religion*, and *Theism*) published, followed, the next year, by the fourth volume of his *Dissertations and Discussions*. In 1879, his unfinished *Chapters on Socialism*, edited by Helen, was published. In 1910, *The Letters of John Stuart Mill*, edited by Hugh Elliot, was published. Mill was arguably the greatest British philosopher of the nineteenth century.

20.3 Knowledge

Mill is a radical empiricist and a phenomenalist in the tradition of Hume. Not only does he think all ideas must be ultimately derived from sensory experience, but he is radical in that he does not think anything that is not accessible to sense experience of some sort is humanly knowable. As such, he is opposed to the modern rationalism that extends from Descartes through Spinoza and Leibniz, was "temporarily modified" by Kant, but then slipped into the "wrong groove" with Hegel. We can only know objects perceived by the senses. "By those channels and no otherwise do we learn whatever we do learn concerning them. Without the senses we should not know nor suspect that such things existed. We know no more of what they are than the senses tell us, nor does nature afford us any means of knowing more" (*Examination*, 542, 6–7). Though he was positively influenced by Coleridge, Mill disagrees with his notion, inspired by Kant, that we have a capacity for rational intuition, maintaining with "Locke and Bentham" that our only mode of intuition is sensible (*Essays*, 128, 131–132). This position will lead him, as it did Hume, to deny metaphysical knowledge.

But to access Mill's most important contribution to epistemology, we must turn to his *System of Logic*. Logic, "the science of reasoning," should be understood to comprise inductive reasoning (as discussed by Francis Bacon) as well as the deductive syllogisms favored by rationalists. Logic is a tool that should assist us in "the pursuit of truth." Universal premises (asserting "all" or "no"), unless they are true by definition, must ultimately involve inductively inferring from particular experience, as is the case in natural science. All rational discovery of truth that is not intuitively self-evident requires inductive inference, which "proceeds from the known to the unknown." If I know that every human who lived more than five generations ago has died, then I can infer that all the people in my class will probably die, including me. As Hume realized, the axiomatic ground of induction is "our intuitive conviction that the future will resemble the past," at least for the most part. Because fire has always burned in our experience, we believe that it did so before our birth, will do so after we die, and does so in distant, unfamiliar countries on our planet. But to say that the uniformity of nature is axiomatic implies that it is unprovable and must be assumed as long as it pragmatically works (*Collected*, VII, 4, 6, 115–116, 162–163, 203, 283, 288, 303, 306–307).

The phenomenal events of nature occur either simultaneously or successively, the universal law of succession being causal. Every event that "has a beginning has a cause," even if it is unknown to us. Even though night regularly follows day, the latter does not cause the former, as it does not necessitate it. "Invariable sequence, therefore, is not synonymous with causation, unless the sequence, besides being invariable, is unconditional." Mill's definition of the "cause" of any phenomenon is "the antecedent, or the concurrence of antecedents, on which it is invariable and *unconditionally* consequent." This leads us to Mill's justly famous canons of causal reasoning. First is "the Method of Agreement," which holds that, if two (or more) instances of a phenomenon being considered have only a single circumstance in which they agree, that is probably "*the cause (or effect) of the given phenomenon*." If 20 people having nothing else significantly in common all caught a virus after attending a long, wild party, it is probable that they caught it at the party. Second is "the Method of Difference," which holds that if two instances have everything in common but a single point of difference, with one exhibiting a phenomenon and the other not doing so, that point of difference is probably all or part of the cause of the phenomenon. If all the students in a dorm except one attended a long, wild party and all but that one caught a virus, attending the party probably caused the others' infection. Third is "the Joint Method of Agreement and Difference," which holds that if two (or more) instances of an occurrence have only a single circumstance in common and two (or more) instances in which it does not occur agree on nothing but the absence of that circumstance, the circumstance is probably causally related to the occurrence or its absence. If all the students who attended a long, wild party who had nothing in common except that they had not been vaccinated against a virus caught it and all those attending the party and not getting the virus had nothing in common except that they were vaccinated, the vaccination is probably the causal difference. Fourth is "the Method of Residues," which holds that, if

316 | *20 John Stuart Mill*

you remove from any phenomenon that portion known to be the effect of certain antecedents, the remainder of the phenomenon is probably the effect of the remaining antecedents. If students attending a party and subsequently being hospitalized with a severe case of a virus stayed the whole time unmasked and unvaccinated and those who got only a mild case stayed the whole time unvaccinated but masked and those not getting the virus at all stayed the whole time, some masked and some unmasked, having all been vaccinated within the previous few months, then their not getting ill is probably an effect of the vaccine (and the severity of the illness for those infected was probably affected by the use of masks). Fifth is "the Method of Concomitant Variations," which holds that whenever a phenomenon varies whenever another phenomenon does so, they are probably causally related. If everyone attending a wild party got ill but the duration of their illness varied with the amount of time spent at the party, the duration of their stay is probably the causal explanation for the severity of illnesses (*Collected*, VII, 323, 325, 338–340, 390–392, 396–398, 401). These methods of causal reasoning effectively take us beyond Hume's skepticism; however, being examples of inductive logic, they only yield more or less probable conclusions.

If these inductive methods provide legitimate grounds for reasonable belief (as they do), what about reasons for disbelief? Mill considers this also. To believe something is to regard it as true. It can be pragmatically important what we believe; but sometimes it is better to believe that something is false and, at other times, it is better to suspend belief until further evidence is attained. Disbelief is stronger than "the mere absence of belief"; it is a state of mind in which a person is convinced that something is "not true." Sometimes available evidence leads us to conclude that something is "improbable, and is to be disbelieved provisionally," pending further evidence. At other times, we can infer that something is "impossible, and is to be disbelieved totally." An alleged truth cannot "contradict any known fact." As Hume argued (in his essay on miracles), a law of nature cannot permit any exceptions: "We cannot admit a proposition as a law of nature, and yet believe a fact in real contradiction to it. We must disbelieve the alleged fact, or believe that we were mistaken" about the supposed law. If it is a law of nature that once a human being is dead for three days, he cannot be revived, then there should be no exceptions allowed. Of course, we might conclude that he was only in a coma and was brought out of it. Or we might revise our formulation of the law to say that such a person cannot be revived by merely natural means. Mill agrees with Hume that alleged miracles rationally prove nothing regarding the supernatural, as there might always be some unknown natural cause. Mill himself (like Hume) seems not to believe in the interposition of supernatural agents in our natural world. "Suspension of judgment" one way or the other is often the most judicious option for an intellectually responsible inquirer (*Collected,* VII, 622–626, 629). After all, inductive causal reasoning will sometimes not provide adequate grounds for belief or disbelief. Such may be the case regarding some metaphysical matters.

20.4 Reality

The reality we can experience and, to some extent, know is the world of nature. In his essay on "Nature," Mill observes that the nature of any object is a collection of its properties and powers and that, likewise, "Nature in the abstract is the aggregate of the powers and properties of all things," the totality of all phenomena and their causal relationships. Science is valuable for helping us to know and understand the laws of nature (*Essential*, 368–369). We believe in an external world of perceivable objects outside our own minds, most of which we never actually perceive. When I perceive "a piece of white paper on a table," I am convinced that it is real. But what if I leave the room and am no longer perceiving it? I reasonably believe that it continues to exist as a material object or body. This means that even when I no longer perceive it, I could do so again under certain conditions, as it exists independently of my sensations and will. "Matter, then, may be defined, a Permanent Possibility of Sensation," Mill concludes, "permanent" in the sense of enduring through time. A body's secondary qualities (such as color, smell, and taste) can vary considerably from one perceiver to another, while its primary qualities (such as its shape) are more constant, leading us to consider the former more subjective and the latter more objective (*Examination*, 191–203). As an epistemological phenomenalist, Mill thinks we can only experience (and, thus, also know) the phenomenal appearances of bodies, and never the bodies in themselves.

The case is similar regarding minds – our own and those of other persons: "We have no conception of Mind itself, as distinguished from its conscious manifestations" – that is, its fleeting thoughts, feelings, volitions, and other states of consciousness. Yet we think of mind as having an ongoing endurance through time, as something more than "the perpetual flux" of the mental states we experience. But I can only directly experience my own mental states. So why should I believe in "other sentient creatures" that also have minds? I am directly aware of my own body, of mental states within it, and of the behavioral actions to which those states lead. I perceive that others have bodies comparable to mine and exhibit behaviors largely like my own; while I do not directly perceive mental states in them, it is reasonable to believe in them as the unperceived middle links connecting the links I do perceive (*Examination*, 205, 208–209). Thus Mill's phenomenalism extends to mind as well as to matter: "What the Mind is, as well as what Matter is, or any other question respecting Things in themselves, as distinguished from their sensible manifestations," must remain in the realm of metaphysical speculation (*Collected*, VIII, 849). As Mill observes, on this point, not only earlier British empiricists, but even "Kant himself" could agree with this denial of scientific substantial knowledge. "As body is understood to be the mysterious something which excites the mind to feel, so mind is the mysterious something which feels and thinks." The immediate objects of minds are the states of consciousness they feel within. Mill analyzes these as "of four sorts: Sensations, Thoughts, Emotions, and Volitions." Perception generates belief, which is "a kind of thought"; and the effects of our volitions are actions of some sort or other. So what is real in human experience are (i) states of consciousness, (ii) the minds that experience them, (iii) the bodies that can excite mental states, and (iv) the coexistence and successions, similarities and differences, among experienced states of mind (*Collected*, VII, 59, 63–64, 75, 77).

20.5 God

Pursuant to his radical empiricism and phenomenalism, Mill does not believe we can have any knowledge of the supernatural; and he seems to have been unable to believe in the infinitely perfect God of ethical monotheism. In several diary entries of 1854, he expresses some undeveloped thoughts on religion. He observes that in more primitive times religious beliefs were simply assumed, that later people tried to develop elaborate arguments to prove them, but that in more advanced cultures people are encouraged to drop them altogether. This may correspond to Comte's three stages of the theological, the metaphysical, and the scientific. He seems to be attracted to Comte's ideal of a "religion of humanity," if it could become as established and motivating as traditional religions (*Collected,* XXVII, 659, 646). As he indicates in *Auguste Comte and Positivism*, a religion need not be focused on a supernatural God. It must have some sort of creed claiming authority over its believers' lives; it should encompass beliefs about their duty and destiny, to which their actions should be responsive; it should involve a feeling that the creed should influence believers' actual conduct, though that feeling need not involve any specific being as an object of reverence. So Comte's sort of "religion . . . without a God" could qualify (*Positivism*, 132–134); and it would fit well with utilitarianism's ultimate goal of the greatest possible happiness for the greatest possible number of people.

But Mill's most important ideas on this subject are developed in his posthumously published *Three Essays on Religion*. In *Nature*, he warns us of the "sophistry" that is needed to argue from our limited, imperfect world to a perfect and unlimited deity. Like Hume, he points to the evil that is widespread in the world of nature – pain, suffering, cruelty, and so forth. If our natural environment indicates a deity of any sort, either it must be one that is finite in some respects or we must somehow try "denying that misery is an evil." The latter option is clearly unacceptable to Mill. He rather imagines that the Designer of the natural world is limited in power. In *The Utility of Religion*, he points out that it is when people start doubting religious doctrines and arguments propping them up prove unconvincing, that appeals are made to the pragmatic value of religion in human life. Proponents of religion promise eternal rewards for those who believe even without understanding. Even accepting the notion that religious faith has generated some beneficial results (and trying to ignore the evil perpetrated in its name), we might well ask "whether the benefits which it yields might not be obtained otherwise" without the mythology. Let us consider the consequences of religious commitment to both society and the individual. With the evolution of civilization, social progress has occurred. This is largely due to moral education and the power of public opinion, whether or not those be tied to religious commitments. It is only the ignorant who will be adequately motivated by the uncertain and remotely distant prospects of rewards and punishments in the hereafter. Mill thinks it incredible that a good God would condemn even "the worst malefactor" to eternal damnation. The "very real evil" attached to any divine command theory of morality is that its maxims tend to become socially entrenched and above all rational criticism. We should grant that some individuals benefit from the hope and comfort of their religious views. But even that might be achieved without the crutch of supernatural mythology. An active commitment to human happiness, liberty, and progress can produce the same sort of effects, as in a "Religion of Humanity" (*Essential*, 385–386, 396, 402–406, 410–414, 418–419, 421–425). All in all, then, the benefits of religion for both society and individuals do not obviously favor its adoption.

Mill's discussion of God that is best developed is in *Theism*. He begins by asserting that polytheism "is immeasurably more natural" for us to believe in than monotheism and that there is no need to expect the former to evolve into the latter. But because monotheism so often lays claim to supporting reasoning, it more clearly admits of philosophical analysis. Mill asks whether the theory that nature is the work of a creator is consistent with available experiential findings and, assuming that it is, what sort of supporting arguments can stand up to the standards of scientific evidence. The answer to the first part of the question is yes, so long as the theory consistently preserves all natural operations as occurring "by invariable laws." The answer to the second part is that theistic arguments must be empirical or *a posteriori* in order to be scientifically respectable. He evaluates four arguments. First, the "First Cause" argument only works if the origin of the natural world is assumed to be an event involving change. But there is no reason to imagine that the world as a whole is not permanent. Second, the argument from general consent (as Hume argued) "has little weight," as the opinions of the masses are so often false or distortions of reality. Third, what he calls the "argument from consciousness" (attributed to Descartes), moving from an alleged clear and distinct idea of God to God's necessary existence (ontological reasoning), has been definitively exploded by Kant. And, fourth, the argument from design is the most scientifically respectable because it is the most empirically in line with "established canons of induction." But, as Hume showed, it reduces to a rather weak analogy involving the inductive causal method of agreement, where (Darwinian) natural selection or "the survival of the fittest" is at least as plausible an explanation of the order of our world as the hypothesis of intelligent design, which can therefore be regarded as "no more than a probability" of some sort (*Theism*, 6–14, 18, 20–21, 24–25, 27–32). It is curious that Mill, like the two most powerful critics of the argument from design, Hume and Kant, nevertheless thinks it the most respectable reasoning for divine existence.

To the extent that we find any reasoning for God to be compelling, we may ask what we can reasonably say about the divine nature. If God is seen as the Designer (or Creator) of our natural world, "the power, if not the intelligence," of God "must be so far superior to that of man as to surpass all human estimate." But that in no way indicates omnipotence or omniscience, let alone that this is the best possible world God could have designed (or created). There is no reason to assume that "matter and force" were not eternal, God's power thus being limited by the materials available for use. If God's power is seen as limited, then omniscience could be assumed; but there is no evidence supporting such a conjecture, especially given the flaws and evils of the world. And, as Hume argued, there is even less reason to predicate moral attributes of any cosmic Designer (or Creator). The world seems adapted for the temporary endurance of sentient creatures, but less obviously for their well-being. While pleasure is experienced, pain and suffering are also paramount. "If the motive of the Deity for creating sentient beings was the happiness" they would experience, then that project, "in our corner of the universe at least, must be pronounced . . . an ignominious failure." Even the blessing we humans enjoy of being able to improve ourselves and our environment comes at the "frightful cost" of painful struggle, hardship, and ongoing suffering. Other moral attributes, such as divine justice and mercy, lack any shred of evidential support at all. So, if we have any rational basis for believing in a theistic deity, it cannot be safely assumed that it is anything like the infinitely perfect God of Descartes, Locke, and Kant. Indeed, reason cannot cogently provide any evidence that theism is more likely reality-based than a "Religion of Humanity" (*Theism*, 33–34, 36–37, 42–45, 86).

So, even though Mill does consider "the Design argument" to be "the best" argument for theism and "by far the most persuasive," it does not get us very far. If it cannot establish anything regarding God's moral attributes, of what practical value is it to us? Nor does it help to suggest that God's goodness, justice, and mercy are so exponentially different from anything experienced by us here that, of course, we should not expect evidence legitimating belief in them. Mill is fierce in denouncing such a hypocritical dodge: "I will call no being good, who is not what I mean when I apply that epithet to my fellow-creatures; and if such a being can sentence me to hell for not so calling him, to hell I will go" (*Examination*, 491, 103).

20.6 Humanity

Given Mill's phenomenalism, every science must be limited to pursuing knowledge of phenomena and their relationships. This includes the social sciences, and he was a pioneer in their development. What he calls "the science of Human Nature," studying "the thoughts, feelings, and actions of human beings," need not be "an exact science," like physics or chemistry, capable of quantitative precision and certainty. It might be inexact; and, if so, it might someday become exact as did astronomy. We do empirically observe facts about human behavior – both external and internal. "Any facts are fitted, in themselves, to be a subject of science, which follow one another according to constant laws." Mill is confident that there are such laws governing our psychological, social, and political behavior. A science of "Psychology, or Mental Philosophy," studies "Thoughts, Emotions, Volitions, and Sensations" – that is, the "phenomena of mind." Not being a mechanistic materialist (like Hobbes), Mill rejects Comte's notion that psychology can be reduced to physiology. Psychology must be a science in its own right, studying the uniform laws "according to which one mental state succeeds another – is caused by, or at least is caused to follow, another." Consider a few such laws of psychology (inspired by Hume and Mill's father). The first is that mental impressions are associated with ideas. The second is that these ideas are "secondary mental states" derived from our impressions according to certain "Laws of Association." Here are three such laws: (i) "similar ideas tend to excite one another"; (ii) whenever we experience any two impressions together, then when one of them or its corresponding idea occurs, "it tends to excite the idea of the other"; and (iii) the more intense associated impressions are, the less frequently we need them conjoined to associate them with one another. These are empirical laws of the science of psychology, accounting for the ways in which our minds function. Mill also believes "there exist universal laws of the Formation of Character" that can be derived from the laws of mind and can establish another social science of "Ethology, or the Science of Character" (*Collected*, VIII, 844–852, 864, 869, 872–873).

As a classical utilitarian, Mill agrees with Bentham that our ultimate goal should be maximum human happiness; and, like Bentham, he is a hedonist, in that his standard is pleasure and the absence of pain. As he maintains in *Utilitarianism*, other objects of desire are seen as valuable either because they are inherently pleasurable or because we think they will promote pleasure and/or prevent pain. Our willing, he says, "is the child of desire"; but our will can become habitual, so that we will from habit what we no longer desire for itself. If we want to do what is right on account of thinking it will promote some pleasure we desire, so that we develop that as a settled habit, then we can continue wanting it even when we no longer desire that particular pleasure (*Essential*, 194, 225–226). Mill favors "the active" over "the passive type" of character as more conducive to "three varieties of mental excellence, intellectual, practical, and moral." These serve both "selfish and unselfish interests," both immediately and remotely (*Considerations*, 47–49, 51, 96). A point of convergence between widespread human desire and religious beliefs for both passive characters (who merely try not to do wrong) and active characters (who try to do good) is a longing for immortality – selfishly for themselves and unselfishly for others they care about. Mill discusses this in *Theism*. While he is not opposed to people's hope for a future existence after death, he sees no convincing reasons – either religious or nonreligious – that support such hope (*Theism*, 46–55). And it does not appear that he himself believed that any aspects of our personal humanity will survive the death of our bodies.

20.7 Freedom

Mill wrestled with the problem of freedom and determinism, adopting a position of compatibilism comparable to Hume's – our free acts of will are determined by psychical forces, including our own character. In a diary entry of 1854, he writes: "The doctrines of free will and of necessity rightly understood are both true. It is necessary, that is, it was inevitable from the beginning of things, that I should freely will whatever things I do will" (*Collected*, XXVII, 657).

Mill's *System of Logic* contains a chapter entitled "Of Liberty and Necessity" in which he tries to lay out his position. Like Hume (and unlike Kant), he subscribes to "the doctrine called Philosophical Necessity," which considers all "human volitions and actions to be necessary and inevitable." Even free actions are necessary, given the agent's motives, character, and disposition at the time of the action. He admits that we have a "feeling of freedom" from their causal determination. Nevertheless, he maintains that, if we had perfect knowledge of a person and all the factors motivating him, "we could foretell his conduct with as much certainty as we can predict any physical event." Every human action, whether willed or not, is subject to an "invariable, certain, and unconditional sequence" of causal determinants. So far, this sounds like straightforward determinism. But things get more complex when Mill asserts, "When we say that all human actions take place of necessity, we only mean that it will certainly happen if nothing prevents." Those last three words represent a complicating proviso. Our will can causally affect our behavior, so that we are not merely automata. He tries to distinguish his determinism from fatalism, which holds, regarding whatever is happening, "that it will happen however we may strive to prevent it," so that "there is no use in struggling against it." Although our actions are caused by a convergence of motives, aspects of our character, and circumstances, we can cultivate different motives, and we can "modify our own character *if we wish.*" This capacity for willed development accounts for our "feeling of moral freedom." This is presumably why the sort of progressive change to which Mill is so committed is possible (*Collected*, VIII, 836–841, 913–914).

Mill also considers the topic of freedom of the will in a key chapter of his *Examination of Sir William Hamilton's Philosophy*. While we experience "an invariable sequence" between antecedent conditions and voluntary actions, as Hume held, we never can perceive a causal "*nexus*" between them. But that is true of purely physical events as well. As he maintains, our "volitions do, in point of fact, follow determinate moral antecedents with the same uniformity, and (when we have sufficient knowledge of the circumstances) with the same certainty, as physical effects follow their physical causes." We might well wonder about the nature of those "moral antecedents." Mill says they include our "desires, aversions, habits, and dispositions." But they also are causally determined. If the ultimate causes are purely extrinsic (e.g. some combination of hereditary and environmental factors), then it is difficult to see how the will can be truly free. Granting that I sometimes "feel (or am convinced) that I could have chosen the other course *if I had preferred it,*" could I – given all the pertinent circumstances – have actually preferred it? It is difficult to see how Mill can have it both ways here: either everything occurs as it must, given all antecedent conditions, or some events could have gone otherwise, given the same conditions and a genuinely free will. Even though he criticizes Kant's dualistic solution to the problem of freedom and determinism, the position of "the philosopher of Königsberg" seems more coherent than his own (*Examination*, 500, 504, 517). One might also question whether the soft determinism of Mill (and, for that matter, of Hume) is not more problematic than the bold hard determinism of Hobbes. What is at stake for all of them, of course, is the viability of moral responsibility.

20.8 Morality

According to Mill, we human beings naturally desire happiness, measured in terms of pleasure and the absence of pain. Since we are not naturally egoists, we can desire happiness for others as well as for ourselves. For Mill, this represents the ultimate value to be pursued; and virtually all of his writings considered here can be seen as – directly or indirectly – serving this end. "The only true or definite rule of conduct or standard of morality," he writes in his diary of 1854, "is the greatest happiness" (*Collected*, XXVII, 663). Since morality uses the "imperative mood" characteristic of art, rather than the indicative mood characteristic of science (remember Hume's "is" vs. "ought" distinction), morality must be the subject of an art rather than scientific (*Collected*, VIII, 943); thus we should not expect the sort of precision and certainty of an exact science (toward which Bentham's quantitative utilitarianism seemed directed). Mill's own ethical theory is heavily influenced by Bentham's. Mill credits him with having swept away from ethics "the rubbish of pretended natural law, natural justice, and the like" to establish a truly empirical approach to moral

20 *John Stuart Mill*

philosophy (*Collected*, X, 498). Mill agrees with Bentham's consequentialist theory, though the older philosopher needed a better understanding of human nature to appreciate the moral significance of character formation. While Mill started out as a Benthamite, as we have seen, he evolved to develop his own version of utilitarianism. In his essay on "Bentham," he faults his predecessor for only viewing human action from "the *moral*" perspective, neglecting "its *aesthetic* aspect," which concerns our imagination, as well as "its *sympathetic* aspect," which relates to our concern for others. This "one-sidedness" has led people to regard utilitarianism as cold, calculating, and mechanical (*Essays*, 114–117).

One of the most important texts in ethical theory in the entire history of philosophy is Mill's *Utilitarianism*, a short work comprising five chapters. In its first chapter, he does two main things. First, he distinguishes between two approaches to ethical theory. "The intuitive" way is rationalistic, claiming to use rational intuition to determine *a priori* moral principles and apply them for moral decision-making; Kant was arguably the most important proponent of this approach by the nineteenth century. The alternative is "the inductive" approach favored by Bentham and other empiricists, based on experience and observation, from which general principles – such as "the principle of utility" or "the greatest happiness" principle – are inductively inferred. Mill thinks that Kant's categorical imperative is a principle that can justify even "the most outrageously immoral rules of conduct" unless we make it the very sort of consequentialist principle Mill favors and Kant wanted to avoid. (Mill does not seem to appreciate that Kant's categorical imperative does not hold any action to be wrong *because* it leads to unacceptable consequences but only uses them to *show* that it is wrong in itself.) The second thing Mill does in this first chapter is admit that he will not be able to give us a knock-down, drag-out formal proof of the principle of utility, which, as an ultimate principle, can be used to argue that certain actions are wrong or permissible but cannot itself be directly proved. Yet he promises to provide an argument for it, representing rational considerations supporting its acceptance (*Essential*, 190–192).

In the second chapter, Mill again does two main things. To begin, he states and analyzes the principle of utility, also called "the Greatest Happiness Principle," and its hedonistic foundation in human nature. This is short (a single paragraph) and remarkably straightforward: "The creed which accepts as the foundation of morals, Utility, or the Greatest Happiness Principle, holds that actions are right in proportion as they tend to promote happiness, wrong as they tend to produce the reverse of happiness." So the morality of an action is a function of its likely consequences. And, like Bentham before him, Mill is a hedonist in determining the relevant criterion: "By happiness is intended pleasure and the absence of pain; by unhappiness, pain and the privation of pleasure." It is allegedly only pleasure and the absence of pain that are intrinsically desirable ends; other things such as knowledge can be desired for the pleasure they provide or as a means to pleasure and the avoidance of pain (*Essential*, 194).

After this, Mill considers and answers several standard objections raised against this view of morality. First, some regard any sort of hedonism as an insult to human dignity and "a doctrine worthy only of swine." But this is because they rashly and wrongly suppose that we are only concerned with physical pleasures. In fact, there are many other sorts – including aesthetic, social, and intellectual. Against Bentham's entirely quantitative approach, Mill adopts a qualitative version of utilitarianism, holding that "some *kinds* of pleasure are more desirable and more valuable than others," regardless of quantitative considerations, because they are more conducive to progressive development and our "sense of dignity." This allows Mill to hold that it is "better to be a human being dissatisfied than a pig satisfied" or a displeased Socrates than a pleased fool; the human is capable of so much more than other animals, and a wise person has more to offer than a fool. The pleasure that matters is that for all people affected by an action and not merely the agent. Second, some object that the principle of utility is either unattainable or unnecessary. But, so long as we do not adopt an unrealistically exalted sense of happiness, some people actually do achieve it; and, even though people can survive without happiness, there is no reason they should not strive for the balance of "tranquility" and "excitement" that provides it. Third, some think utilitarianism asks too much of us by requiring that we always want to act for the common good. But, in fact, it asks only that we do what will generate good consequences regardless of our motive (which, however, is relevant to the character of the agent). Fourth, some hold that "utilitarianism renders men cold and unsympathizing" calculators of consequences. But, while that impression may be given by Benthamism, Mill thinks the utilitarian ethic to be quite compatible with genuine feeling for others. Fifth, some criticize utilitarianism "as a *godless* doctrine"; but he sees no reason to assume that God desires anything other than "the happiness of His creatures." Sixth, some see the utilitarian ethic as boiling down to a crass allegiance to mere "Expediency"; but if this means acting to achieve merely short-term, narrowly defined consequences, this is not the case. For example, while the rule against lying is not absolute, we must factor in the social value of the rule itself and the long-term effect on it an "immediately useful" lie might have in our judgments (this has come to be called "rule-utilitarianism"). Seventh, some think that we often do not have time to calculate all the likely consequences when making an urgent moral decision; but Mill holds that we can and should then use our knowledge of past experience (our own, that of others, even of people throughout history) as our guide. Finally, some might think that the utilitarian will find ways to rationalize exceptions to moral rules in his or her own favor; but, Mill responds, all moral principles are subject to prejudicial, selfish distortions of interpretation and application (*Essential*, 195–212). In general, Mill does a very good job of confronting and answering these objections to the utilitarian ethic.

In the third chapter, Mill again does two main things. First, he considers the sanctions utilitarianism should recognize as motivating people to try to do the right thing, which can be "either external or internal." He accepts the obvious external ones that Bentham invoked (physical, political or legal, social, and religious). "The internal sanction of duty," in addition, is the sort of feeling constituting "the essence of Conscience." For those of us who were morally well educated, it is the "ultimate sanction," in that we might be able to (or, at least, think we are able to) escape all the external sanctions, but there is no escaping our own internal, cultivated sense of conscience. The second topic is whether the moral "feeling of duty is innate or implanted" (nature or nurture, as we would say). He believes that it is "not innate but acquired" from our experience and social environment but that it is "natural" for humans to develop a sense of duty (*Essential*, 212–216).

We can also highlight two main issues discussed in the fourth chapter. First, there is the unfinished business of providing an indirect (nondeductive) argument for the principle of utility that might prove to be psychologically persuasive, even if not logically coercive. It operates in two stages. First, as we know that something is visible because people actually see it and that something is audible because people actually hear it, so we know that something is desirable because people do desire it. But it is a verifiable, empirical fact that people do desire happiness. Therefore happiness must be desirable. Second, we must specify whose happiness is desirable; since each individual person desires his own happiness, therefore any group of persons must desire "the general happiness." Each of the two stages has been said to rely on a logical fallacy: the first stage, using a dubious analogy, invokes the word "desirable" in a premise, meaning able to be desired, but then in the conclusion uses it to mean worthy of being desired (the fallacy of equivocation); the second stage seems to commit the fallacy of composition, assuming that what is true of all the parts of a whole must also be true of the whole itself. The second issue in Mill's fourth chapter tries to reconcile the claim that happiness is our only intrinsic, ultimate end with the fact that some people (like Kant) sincerely value virtue for its own sake. His psychological solution holds that "naturally and originally" virtue was desired as a means to happiness but that it got to be so intimately associated with happiness in some people's imaginations as to become identified, by them, as a part of happiness itself (*Essential*, 220–224). Again this is less than convincing, in that someone as self-discerning and honest as Kant would credibly maintain that his desire for virtue was totally independent of any pursuit of happiness.

The fifth (and last) chapter can also be analyzed as comprising two (unequal) parts: a statement of the justice objection against utilitarianism and an attempt to meet it. Mill recognizes that problems of justice have perpetually been among "the strongest obstacles" to the acceptance of the utilitarian ethic. Put succinctly, the problem asks what should we do when justice and utility conflict, when the best or only way to serve general utility is wittingly to commit an injustice? If the vast majority of a population can be rendered blissfully happy by unfairly targeting and enslaving some minority group, it seems that utilitarianism would have to condone it. But such an injustice would understandably strike us as morally problematic. Having already explained what "utility" means, Mill now sets out to define the essential nature of justice. What do people mean when they speak of justice (or injustice) or call something just (or unjust)? In the best part of the chapter, Mill analyzes five key dimensions of meaning. First, respecting legal rights is just, and violating them unjust. Second, respecting a person's moral rights is just, and violating them unjust. Third, justice involves giving everyone what he or she deserves, and depriving people of what they deserve is unjust. Fourth, keeping faith with people tends to be just, and breaking faith unjust. And, fifth, in some circumstances, justice requires impartiality, and it is unjust to be partial. Mill also briefly considers the Enlightenment ideal of equality, but he snidely writes, "Each person maintains that equality is the dictate of justice, except where he thinks that expediency requires inequality." At any rate, Mill thinks "the sentiment of justice" involves both a belief that someone has been wronged or harmed and a sense that the wrongdoer deserves to be punished. In such cases, rights have been violated. "When we call anything a person's right, we mean that he has a valid claim on society to protect him in the possession of it, either by the force of law, or by that of education and opinion." Mill considers three problems of social ethics that are as prickly today as they were over a century and a half ago: (i) what should be the rationale of a penal system that is just? (ii) how can we determine a just order of compensation, so that different sorts of workers are fairly compensated? (iii) what constitutes a just scheme of taxation? Mill imagines that this analysis of justice leads to its definition as "certain social utilities which are vastly more important, and therefore more absolute and imperative, than any others are as a class" (*Essential*, 226–238, 240–248). Unfortunately, by defining justice in terms of the most important social utilities, he has not so much solved the problem of justice as dissolved it by defining it away.

For centuries, some moralists have attempted to identify what is morally good and right with what is natural. What can be branded as "unnatural" can readily be considered bad and/or wrong. But this is to confuse what is with what ought to be (a rash step against which Hume tried to caution us). Mill (in *Nature*) considers it preposterous that we should assume that our voluntary actions morally ought to follow the course of physical nature. "If the natural course of things were perfectly right and satisfactory, to act at all would be a gratuitous meddling, which as it could not make things better, must make them worse." In order to survive, let alone thrive, we must interfere with the natural order; we are creatures of the natural world and must adapt the environment to our own purposes. Further, nature is strikingly cruel and murderous much of the time, and there is no reason to believe we ought to follow its example. Almost every admirable, even respectable, human quality results not from following our natural animal instincts but from rationally controlling – and even at times resisting – them. The truth, then, seems to be that our moral duty in relation to nature – both nature in general and human nature in particular – is "not to follow but amend it" (*Essential*, 371–377, 381–382, 390–391, 395).

20.9 Society

While Mill believes the basic unit of humanity is the individual person, as an agent of liberal change, he also recognizes the importance of stable social bonds. As he writes in "Civilization," "There is not a more accurate test of the progress of civilization than the progress of the power of co-operation." This, in turn, requires that the individual be willing to "compromise" in service of the common good. We need government that supports this cause by protecting citizens from "force and fraud." But, beyond this, while "the free agency of individuals" should be encouraged, within the limits of law, it is also legitimate for government to be "promoting the public welfare," as he says in his essay on "Coleridge." In his review of Tocqueville's work, he writes that, while all human governments remain imperfect, democracy, despite its dangers (such as that of the tyranny of the majority over minorities), is most likely to maximize the common good (*Essays*, 48, 164, 210–211). The proof of such a claim will have to be found in consequences regarding people's well-being and not in some alleged account of how we arrived at any given political order; for example, as he writes in *Utilitarianism*, the social contract theory (of Hobbes, Locke, and Rousseau) is not only "a mere fiction," but also less effective at justifying social cooperation than utilitarian considerations (*Essential*, 241).

But let us now turn to *On Liberty*, Mill's political masterpiece and a classic statement of philosophical liberalism. He begins by saying that his focus will be on "Civil, or Social Liberty: the nature and limits of the power which can be legitimately exercised by society over the individual." There was a time when the potential conflict was between individual subjects' freedom and government authority; but this tension has been ameliorated by a combination of a recognition of inviolable rights and "the establishment of constitutional checks" on government authority. But, with the rise of democracy, government officials increasingly represent the people and are answerable to them. So the problem of political liberty has shifted. Yet it has not disappeared. Increasingly, it has taken the form of (what Tocqueville called) "the tyranny of the majority." How can the choices of minority members be protected from the abuse of majority rule, through which a majority can use the law and/or public opinion to stifle personal preferences (*Essential*, 255–258)? Clearly some criterion is required.

The standard Mill proposes is his "very simple principle" of liberty, expressed in two related ways. The "self-protection" version holds, "That principle is, that the sole end for which mankind are warranted, individually or collectively, in interfering with the liberty of action of any of their number, is self-protection." The other formulation, in terms of preventing harm, maintains, "That the only purpose for which power can be rightfully exercised over any member of a civilized community, against his will, is to prevent harm to others." What this rules out is society preventing a responsible, civilized adult from doing what he wants merely for his own good. Exceptions to the rule, then, are children, the insane, and primitive peoples (the first two of these make sense to us, while the third seems more dubious). Interestingly, Mill bases his argument on utility alone and will make no appeals to claims of "abstract right." He provides three areas where he thinks his principle of liberty should be absolute: (i) freedom of thought and expression; (ii) freedom of personal lifestyles, so long as they do not harm others; and (iii) freedom of association for peaceful purposes. A free society must respect these zones of liberty, and none in which they are not absolutely respected can be completely free. "The only freedom which deserves the name, is that of pursuing our own good in our own way, so long as we do not attempt to deprive others of theirs, or impede their efforts to obtain it" (*Essential*, 263–266). So, while utility remains Mill's fundamental value (with justice measured in terms of the most important social utilities), civil liberty is necessary as a means to that end.

Mill's second chapter defends absolute freedom of expression on strictly utilitarian grounds. "If all mankind minus one, were of one opinion, and only one person were of the contrary opinion, mankind would be no more justified in silencing that one person, than he, if he had the power, would be justified in silencing mankind." Regarding any unpopular opinion, given human fallibility, it may possibly be true, or it might be utterly false, or it could be some mix of true and false. First, if it is true, then suppressing it denies people access to the good of its truth. We must not imagine that an unchallenged popular view must be correct. "There is the greatest difference between presuming an opinion to be true, because, with every opportunity for contesting it, it has not been refuted, and assuming its truth for the purposes of not permitting its refutation." Mill also rejects, as "a piece of idle sentimentality," the assumption that a suppressed truth will continually resurface until it is accepted. As truth is a great good, so is its extinction an evil. Second, even if the unpopular opinion is false, if the majority view, though correct, is not subjected to questioning or possible criticism, "it will be held as a dead dogma, not a living truth." Without ever being challenged, the majority believer lacks sufficient warrant for holding a popular opinion. Nor is it enough to concoct artificial, "devil's advocate" objections; what is needed is the reasoning of someone who honestly believes in the unpopular view. And, third, as is often the case, an unpopular opinion may be neither purely correct nor purely incorrect, but partially true and partially false. In this case, preventing the portion that is true from increasing is a "formidable evil" obstructing the greater good of more complete truth. Thus Mill defends the utility of freely expressing unpopular views, whether they be true or false or mixed (*Essential*, 269, 271, 280, 285, 287, 295, 301–302).

Mill's third chapter involves a powerful defense of human individuality, arguing (again on utilitarian grounds) that people should be free to embrace even eccentric lifestyles "without hindrance, either physical or moral, from their fellow-men, so long as it is at their own risk and peril" and does not endanger others. This does not excuse a person's become a public nuisance. "But if he refrains from molesting others in what concerns them, and merely acts according to his own inclination and judgment in things which concern himself" alone, society should respect his freedom. Tolerating alternative lifestyles has the utilitarian value of allowing people to test out what might work best for them and to promote spontaneity, producing not only "human happiness" but both "individual and social progress." Human nature is more like a dynamically growing organism (such as "a tree") than like a programmed machine and needs the soil of freedom. How can genius flourish without it? How can we ever expect "exceptional individuals" to emerge from the barren landscape of "collective mediocrity"? So here again Mill argues against the detrimental "despotism of custom" (*Essential*, 304–305, 308, 313–315, 318).

In his fourth chapter, Mill tries to go beyond defending individual freedom of expression and liberty of personal lifestyles. He states his general position straight away: "To individuality should belong the part of life in which it is chiefly the individual that is interested; to society, the part which chiefly interests society." Violating the rights of others is wrong and legally punishable, as is refusing to bear our fair share of the responsibility for the protection of society. Beyond this, we can hurt or endanger others in ways that do not violate their legal rights, which may be "justly punished by opinion, though not by law." (Of course, we can legitimately avoid people whose conduct we find personally offensive.) One might object that nothing a member of society does can completely fail to affect anyone else, if only by setting a bad example. So Mill's position relies on a controversial distinction between "self-regarding conduct," which should be tolerated, and other-regarding actions, which can be legitimately prevented. For example, he writes, "No person ought to be punished simply for being drunk; but a soldier or a policeman should be punished for being drunk on duty," as he thus endangers the public he is employed to protect. But in dubious, borderline cases, interference with voluntary actions of mature, rational agents runs the risk of doing more harm than good (*Essential*, 322–325, 327–330).

In the last chapter of *On Liberty*, Mill explores some "applications" of his "two maxims," which maintain that people are not accountable to society for their purely self-regarding actions and that they are accountable for other-regarding actions that threaten the interests of others. There are circumstances in which utility can dictate that society should not interfere with some actions even if they harm, or may harm, others – for example, in competition leading to one person getting a job and another remaining unemployed. While adult people should normally be allowed to be privately drunk, the violent drunk, who physically abuses others when under the influence, can legitimately be restricted from getting drunk. While lazy idleness can be purely self-regarding, if it leads to neglecting supporting one's own children, compulsory labor might be permissible. While some vices, such as fornication, should usually be tolerated by the law, if done publicly, they can constitute punishable "offenses against decency." Even when government interference does not unnecessarily restrict liberty, it may be objectionable for other reasons: (i) if what is needed can be better done by individuals, (ii) if individuals acting on their own behalf can thus beneficially learn, or (iii) if the government's interfering unnecessarily increases its power over the people. Mill ends the book with a warning that unnecessarily sacrificing individual liberty to enhance state power will, in the long run, prove counterproductive to public utility (*Essential*, 340, 343–344, 354–356, 360). But, then, so much of Mill's case depends on his assumption that the value of liberty is ultimately instrumental as a means to the axiological end of utility.

As Mill recognizes in his *Considerations on Representative Government*, a good society rightly values both order and progress. By Mill's day, democratic societies had a conservative party that emphasized order and a liberal party that emphasized progress. Mill, a liberal, says, "Progress includes Order, but Order does not include Progress." Good political institutions promote a community's development "in intellect, in virtue, and in practical activity and efficiency." He argues that "the ideally best form of government" must be representative and answerable to an actively participating citizenry. A good political society will not only protect its people but also promote their independence. Still, it should be considered "an open question" what political functions the people themselves should exercise, so long as they are ultimately in control. In a pure democracy, the government is "of the whole people by the whole people, equally represented." But, in practice, democracies tend to have the entire people governed by "a mere majority." Mill believes, however, that minorities should themselves have proportional representation, even if they are outvoted by majority interests. In a developed "and civilized nation," no citizens should be without representation, although Mill does believe that a literacy requirement for voting is appropriate. "But though everyone ought to have a voice – that everyone should have an equal voice is a totally different proposition." Mill would like for the votes of citizens who are superior in knowledge, intelligence, and virtue to count for more than those inferior in those respects. We could determine this by level of education or the voter's occupation. Yet he admits that it may not yet be a practical idea. Also (unlike his father), he thinks it important that women be allowed to vote (*Considerations*, 17, 21, 28, 42–44, 46–47, 55, 70, 102-103, 131–132, 135–140, 143–144, 146).

This leads us to another great work of his (influenced by his wife), *The Subjection of Women*, in which he argues for equality of the sexes on utilitarian grounds. He states his thesis in the first paragraph of its first chapter: "That the principle which regulates the existing social relations between the two sexes – the legal subordination of one sex to the other – is wrong in itself, and now one of the chief hindrances to human improvement; and that it ought to be replaced by a principle of perfect equality, admitting no power or privilege on the one side, nor disability on the other." This calls for equal educational, vocational, and political opportunities. The burden of proof should

328 | *20 John Stuart Mill*

be imposed on those who would stifle liberty along those lines. Those who object that the subordination of women is "natural" are presumptuously making an unknowable claim. It is also unconvincing to say that women accept their subordinate positions in society, as the movement toward gender equality is already underway, and the present inequality keeps women dependent and fearful of complaining. Equal opportunity, regardless of gender, is a matter of both "justice and expediency" and would prove "most advantageous to humanity in general." As things are, what passes for women's "nature" is extremely "artificial"; and we shall not know what women are capable of contributing unless and until equal opportunity is available. We should also note that Mill is not advocating what today is called "affirmative action" or criticized as "preferential treatment." But, as things are, gender discrimination is harmful not only to women but to society in general (*Equality*, 125–127, 137–142, 147–148, 154, 242; see also 67–84 for an earlier essay of Mill's).

In his *Principles of Political Economy*, Mill holds that, while the goods available to us will always be limited, it is "the Distribution of Wealth" that varies with social custom and government policy. Our system of private property, defensible on utilitarian grounds, could also be replaced by a socialistic system in which people hold land and the means of production in common. Some critics of private property favor "absolute equality in the distribution" of goods, while others would allow inequality as long as it is not based on accidental circumstances, such as one's parents. Mill would prefer a socialistic arrangement over the continuation of a social order in which wealth is so inequitably distributed relative to labor. Nevertheless, he hopes that our system of private property might gradually evolve toward a more just arrangement. Ultimately he would favor whatever system is more just and more conducive to human liberty and happiness. He distinguishes between "authoritative interference of government" in people's actions and a non-authoritative form consisting of public information and advice, the second alternative being considerably easier to justify than the first. The burden of proof should always fall on those who favor legal prohibitions. On the other hand, informing and advising does not impinge on liberty of choice. Yet people should beware of becoming too dependent on government even for that. "*Laissez-faire*, in short, should be the general practice: every departure from it, unless required by some great good, is a certain evil," as it can compromise personal autonomy. So people must be educated, public education being one option (*Principles*, 5–16, 325–327, 335, 341; see also Mill's *Essays on Some Unsettled Questions of Political Economy*, in *Collected*, IV, 263–266, 300–301, 318–319, 323).

In his posthumously published *Chapters on Socialism*, after praising "the Reform Act of 1867" for increasing the "electoral power" of working people, Mill expresses confidence that laborers will use it, peacefully but effectively, to protect themselves against the vested interests of established institutions and the ruling class, without recourse to violent revolution (such as Marx thought necessary). The capitalist system itself may require critical reexamination, which might push society toward some sort of socialism. Surely the system then in place involved the social ills of poverty, crime and vice, and greedy competition, which are all deplorable. But socialist propagandists tend to exaggerate the extent of such evils as well as capitalism's responsibility for causing them. "The present system is not, as many Socialists believe, hurrying us into a state of general indigence and slavery from which only Socialism can save us," grave though our social problems may be. Indeed, Mill thinks that, far from getting worse, they are tending to grow less severe. He believes that such "evils and injustices" are decreasing due to the adoption of a series of political reforms without the need to give up on "private property and individual competition" (*Principles*, 373–376, 378–381, 384–385, 403–404, 412–414, 421). It is telling that, through a process of political evolution, Great Britain was able to avoid the sort of communist revolution called for by Marx and Engels.

Mill's famous 1868 Parliamentary speech on "Capital Punishment" counts against the stereotypical generalization that classical liberals have to be soft on crime. Though he makes it clear that he would like to be able to support the motion that the death penalty should be abolished, for utilitarian reasons, he cannot join those who are against it: "I defend this penalty, when confined to atrocious cases, on the very ground on which it is commonly attacked – on that of humanity to the criminal; as beyond comparison the least cruel mode in which it is possible adequately to deter from the crime." While this may strike some as implausible, he maintains that capital punishment is more humane a deterrent against murder than life imprisonment at hard labor. He holds that the death penalty not only prevents convicted felons from further heinous offenses against society, but also deters others from following their bad example. However, such a punishment should be strictly reserved for felons convicted of "the most atrocious crimes," such as first-degree murder; otherwise, the public will cease to support it, possibly rendering it an "idle threat." Mill concedes that the most worrisome implication of his position is the possibility of a wrongful conviction; but he is confident that our sophisticated legal procedures (such as the adversarial court system, the presumption of innocence, rules of evidence, and a strong appeals process) insure that such gross errors can "be made extremely rare." The idea of the state executing one of its citizens is so "shocking" to most civilized people that courts are likely to be cautious. So, while Mill supports limiting the use of capital punishment (in accordance with the Reform Bill of 1867), he opposes its "total abolition" (*Collected*, XXVIII, 266–272; see also "On Punishment," in *Collected*, XXI, 77–79). What we see here is a utilitarian argument based on a cost–benefit analysis.

We cannot explore all the significant writings of Mill applying his seminal views on utility and liberty to social issues. But let us briefly consider just a few. His commitment to liberty and equal opportunity for all places him firmly in the antislavery camp. In 1807 (the year after his birth), the slave trade was outlawed in Great Britain; and in 1833, slavery itself was abolished throughout the British Empire. His article on "The Negro Question" (1850) celebrates the progressive process of human emancipation, though he also acknowledges that it still needs further development. The fight against slavery is characterized as serving "the cause of justice" and as a matter of "moral obligation," the very idea of any human enslaving another person being utterly "detestable." Even if "whites" were born "superior in intelligence to the blacks," which he does not believe is the case, the forced enslavement of the latter by the former would still be "monstrous." He does not think the British will ever revert to slavery but anticipates a "decisive conflict between right and iniquity" in America and announces that he is squarely in "the abolitionist camp." Twelve years later (in 1862), he published "The Contest in America," in which he expresses his satisfaction that England had not taken sides with the South in the American Civil War, which would have been disgraceful. At that point, the North had not banned slavery altogether, which would have been unconstitutional, but could outlaw its spreading into new states and territories. Mill thinks doing so will gradually lead to the extinction of slavery throughout America, which ought to occur as soon as possible, as the slaves are "human beings, entitled to human rights." Even though war is horrible, the Union was fighting "in a good cause," Mill claims, "a war for justice" (*Collected*, XXI, 87–88, 93, 95, 127–128, 132–134, 138–139, 141–142; see also "The Slave Power," in *Collected*, XXI, 145–164).

Let us next consider a couple of essays in the area of international justice. "Treaty Obligations" (1870) criticizes countries that fail to live up to commitments made in international agreements, when they think reneging will benefit them, holding that, among European nations, only England consistently lives up to its treaty obligations. He seeks a reasonable middle ground between the view that treaties are inviolable no matter what (which would be contrary to utility) and the position that countries can break their word whenever it seems advantageous to do so (which is contrary to justice). He rules that countries should not impose on other nations conditions they cannot fairly be expected to keep and that all treaties should be in effect only for a limited number of years. What must be avoided is requiring respect for strong countries' rights and denying respect for the same rights of weak ones. He says, "The community of nations is essentially a republic of

20 John Stuart Mill

equals . . . Whatever rights belong to one belong to all" (*Collected*, XXI, 343–346). As good as this may sound, we might well remember that Mill does distinguish between how civilized nations and barbarian societies can be legitimately treated and that his notion of "rights" is relative to utility.

In "A Few Words on Non-Intervention" (1859), after praising England for generally leaving "other nations alone" and not exhibiting "any aggressive designs" on them, Mill says when it does try to influence other societies, it does so for their welfare rather than for selfish purposes, respecting their liberty and not forcing them into disadvantageous treaty commitments. He cites the example of Great Britain's abolishing slavery and a lucrative slave trade. In general, forced interference is *prima facie* unjust, so that wars of aggression are wrong, while defensive ones can be justifiable. Yet, he admits, there are less clear "cases in which it is allowable to go to war, without having been ourselves attacked, or threatened with attack." The rules that should apply among civilized countries need not be required "between civilized nations and barbarians." The latter have rights as individual humans but (allegedly) not as societies. For example, Mill defends Great Britain's taking over India in order to help civilize it and protect its people from tyranny. He also considers the legitimacy of a civilized nation participating in another country's civil war, to help a people struggling for liberty. Where the despotism is "purely native," it is harder to justify intervention than if it is despotism by a foreign power. However, even here, Mill is reluctant to deny that there may be utilitarian exceptions to the rule (*Essays*, 368–370, 374–384). So here again we see Mill's wish to defend human liberty so long as it does not run contrary to utility. Indeed, a major problem with Mill's philosophy is its subordination of everything else to utility: his epistemology and metaphysical theory are designed to serve his utilitarian moral and sociopolitical causes; justice is seen as a subset of utility; and liberty is assumed to be a necessary means to the ultimate end of utility.

20.10   Review

Nevertheless, if we can accept this view of the fundamental centrality of utility, then his wide-ranging system is coherent. Two of his books – *On Liberty* and *Utilitarianism* – are philosophical masterpieces, while parts of his *System of Logic* (especially on induction and causality) are excellent, *The Subjection of Women* is well ahead of its time, and his *Three Essays on Religion* are valuable contributions to the philosophy of religion. While Mill is not a great original thinker (like Hume or Kant or Hegel), his greatness lies in developing the most lucid and compelling empirical philosophy after Hume. As such, he represents (as do Schopenhauer and Marx) a powerful modern alternative to German idealism.[2]

20.11   Another Perspective

Harriet Hardy was born in October of 1807 in London, England, the daughter of a surgeon and a midwife, and was educated at home. In 1826, she married John Taylor, a pharmacist who was about a generation older than she. Their two sons were born in 1827 and 1830. In 1830, she met John Stuart Mill, their initial meeting apparently being arranged by the head of her Unitarian congregation. They were clearly kindred spirits, and the attraction between them was significant.

---

2 For more on Mill, see ch. V of *Twelve Great Philosophers*, by Wayne P. Pomerleau (New York: Ardsley House, 1997).

However, she was pregnant with a third child, Helen Taylor, who was born in the summer of 1831. Mill was a frequent visitor to the Taylor residence, even when Mr. Taylor was away at his club; but he knew about it and accepted it in return for her remaining his wife and living in his household. But in 1833, the Taylors agreed on a six-month separation; she got a separate residence, living apart from her husband for most of the rest of his life. Their two sons lived with him and Helen with her. The public morals of Victorian England being what they were, the relationship between Mrs. Taylor and Mill became ripe for malicious gossip. Mill wanted to dedicate his *Principles of Political Economy* to her, but Mr. Taylor forbade it for fear of increasing the scandal. Mr. Taylor got cancer; and when it got significantly worse, she cared for him until he died in 1849. In 1851, she and Mill married. They largely avoided socializing in order not to be subjected to hurtful gossip. Mill was even estranged from his mother and siblings, who disapproved of their premarital relationship. Both Mill and Taylor Mill suffered from tuberculosis. After Mill retired from the East India Company in 1858, the two of them were heading to southern France when she got very ill. She soon died of respiratory failure in a hotel in Avignon, France. Mill bought a cottage in Avignon, near the cemetery where she was buried, and lived there with Helen, who helped him with his writings.

Although there is some uncertainty about how much of Taylor Mill's writings were collaborations with her husband, we are practically certain that the two essays on which we shall focus here (both in the area of social ethics) were her own work. The first of these (1832) expresses her thoughts on marriage and divorce; it shows her to be quite progressive relative to her culture and far ahead of her times. "Whether nature made a difference in the nature of men and women or not," she writes, their differences in upbringing and education can account for the apparent fact that "all men, with the exception of a few lofty minded, are sensualists more or less – women on the contrary are quite exempt from this trait." Thus men and women tend to have different motives for getting married. "Women are educated for one single object, to gain their living by marrying." But social structures are such that, once women are married, their husbands wield the power in their relationship. Even when divorce is a possibility, the woman is at an extreme disadvantage legally and in terms of property rights and financial support. Taylor Mill advocates what we call no-fault divorce "at small expense, but which could only be finally pronounced after a long period" of no less than two years from the time of suing for divorce. Women should be granted complete "equality with men, as to all rights and privileges, civil and political." Once this is achieved, she advocates "doing away with all laws whatever relating to marriage." Employment opportunities and public offices should be open to women, so they could support themselves and their children. Then, rather than thinking it in a woman's interest "to have children as so many ties to the man who feeds her," it would be in her interest not to have more children than she could support (*Equality*, 84–86). In some respects (no laws regulating marriage and no requirements that men pay child support for their own children), this position is even radical by today's standards.

Taylor Mill's most influential writing was *Enfranchisement of Women*, published in the *Westminster Review* in 1851. Its first paragraph refers to an American women's convention, which advocated their rights to vote, hold public office, gain "honorable and useful employment," derive advantages from their education, and hold their own property. She cites the Declaration of Independence's claim that "all men are created equal" with "inalienable rights" as applying to all "human beings," so that it is "men" in the generic sense. She regards this convention as a legitimate "collective protest against the aristocracy of sex" and an overdue call for social change. Thus, she writes, "In all things the presumption ought to be" in favor of gender equality. Standing in the way of this, in addition to men having the power and a vested interest in keeping it, is the historical and transcultural force of custom. Only a few great male thinkers, "from Plato to Condorcet" (see Book V of Plato's *Republic* and Condorcet's article "On the Admission of Women to the Rights of Citizenship," published in 1790), have dared publicly to challenge custom in defense of "the equality of women." As things actually were, women

332 | 20 John Stuart Mill

were socially, politically, legally, and economically subject to the tyranny of men in being assigned their allegedly proper sphere of condition and conduct. Her denunciation of this situation is powerful: "We deny the right of any portion of the species to decide for another portion, or any individual for another individual, what is and what is not their 'proper sphere.'" What women can decide for themselves if given all the requisite opportunities should not be presumed and can only be discerned if they are allowed "complete liberty of choice" on par with that of men (*Equality*, 93–100).

Taylor Mill points out the irony of women being systematically denied all other political offices while proving themselves quite capable of ruling effectively as queens, empresses, and regents. But three reasons are typically given why political life is unfit for women: "first, the incompatibility of active life with maternity and with the cares of a household; secondly, its alleged hardening effect on the character; and thirdly, the inexpediency of making an addition to the already excessive pressure of competition in every kind of professional or lucrative employment." If the first reason had any force at all, however, it would only apply to mothers, and there is no reason to think women should only be able to choose between maternity and no social position at all. But why should we assume that women cannot be good mothers and also "practice a profession or be elected to parliament"? The reality is that many women become wives and mothers only because they are denied other occupations. Regarding the third reason (she does not consider the three in the order initially presented), allowing women employment opportunities would only create competition for men in that area. "It gives no excuse for withholding from women the rights of citizenship," such as suffrage, serving on juries, and holding public office. But competition is a dynamic fact of life, and there is no good reason to forbid women's engaging in it. Further, even if women were financially cared for all their lives by men, it would be better for them to be able to earn something on their own, which might help liberate them from the tyranny of those men. Also, why not let women hold jobs that will reduce the need for child labor, allowing children more time for education? Regarding the second reason, there are already "hardening influences" on women as well as on men as is. However, none of these frail reasons for maintaining the unequal *status quo*, based on possible inconveniences of changing it, gets to the heart of the matter: "The real question is, whether it is right and expedient that one-half of the human race should pass through life in a state of forced subordination to the other half." The negative answer is obvious (*Equality*, 102–107). We should notice that Taylor Mill's appeal is to both rightness and expedience and not merely either one of the two, for they converge to lead us to the same negative verdict.

21

Søren Kierkegaard

Source: Niels Christian Kierkegaard/Wikimedia Commons/Public Domain

21.1 Overview

As the first thinker in the movement of existential philosophy, Kierkegaard[1] emphasizes themes of human individuality, freedom of choice, and personal commitment. Like Schopenhauer, Feuerbach, Marx, and Mill, he develops a philosophy opposed to Hegel's; like the first three of those (but unlike Mill), he was directly influenced by the Hegelian system.

---

1 References to Kierkegaard's writings will be to *Papers and Journals: A Selection* (hereafter called *Selection*), by Søren Kierkegaard, trans. by Alastair Hannay (London: Penguin Books, 1996), to *The Point of View for My Work as an Author* (hereafter called *Point*), by Søren Kierkegaard, trans. by Walter Lowrie (New York: Harper & Row, 1962), to *Concluding Unscientific Postscript* (hereafter called *Postscript*), by Søren Kierkegaard, trans. by David F. Swenson and completed by Walter Lowrie (Princeton: Princeton Univ. Press, 1941), to *Johannes Climacus or, De Omnibus*

Modern European Philosophers, First Edition. Wayne P. Pomerleau.
© 2023 John Wiley & Sons, Inc. Published 2023 by John Wiley & Sons, Inc.

334 | *21 Søren Kierkegaard*

21.2 Biography

One of the two most important figures in his life was his father, Michael Pederson Kierkegaard, who was born in poverty in West Jutland but was released from serfdom and brought to Copenhagen by a prosperous uncle at about the age of 12. While still a boy herding sheep in Jutland, he had cursed God over what looked to be his miserable fate, and he seemed to be racked with feelings of guilt over it for the rest of his life (*Selection*, 204). Yet he prospered remarkably well. After his uncle died, he inherited his fortune and went into business for himself, doing so well financially – through a combination of hard work and shrewd investments – that he was able to retire at the age of 40. When his wife of two years died (childless), he got her maid, Ane Lund, pregnant and had to marry her. They had seven children together.

The last of these, Søren Aabye, was born on May 5, 1813. He inherited his father's melancholy and was convinced that God would punish the family for the sins of the father (that is, for cursing God and/or impregnating his first wife's maid); and, as it happened, Kierkegaard himself died young, five of his siblings preceded him in death, and only his brother Peter (who became a bishop) outlived him – and then only to go insane. After retiring, the father committed himself to studying Christian theology and German philosophy, particularly admiring the Leibnizian Christian Wolff. Kierkegaard himself was a clever child, called "the fork" for his sharp, penetrating wit. On the other hand, he was physically misshapen and sensitive to his being a misfit (*Selection*, 117–118, 593–594; *Point*, 76, 81).

In 1821, he entered the School of Civic Virtue; its rector considered him smart but frivolous. In 1828, his father's friend and pastor, J.P. Mynster (who would become Copenhagen's bishop and Primate of the Danish Church) confirmed him. A couple of years later, Kierkegaard (17 years old) joined the Royal Lifeguards but, a few days later, was discharged as physically unfit. He enrolled at the University of Copenhagen as a theology student, his brother Peter having already moved on from there to Germany for graduate studies. Kierkegaard did well in his preliminary language exams, as well as in those in history, philosophy, physics, and mathematics. In 1834, he

---

Dubitandum Est and A Sermon (hereafter called *Climacus*), by Søren Kierkegaard, trans. by T.H. Croxall (Stanford: Stanford Univ. Press, 1967), to *Philosophical Fragments or A Fragment of Philosophy* (hereafter called *Fragments*), by Søren Kierkegaard, trans. by David F. Swenson and Howard V. Hong (Princeton: Princeton Univ. Press, 1967), to *The Concept of Irony* (hereafter called *Irony*), by Søren Kierkegaard, trans. by Lee M. Capel (Bloomington: Indiana Univ. Press, 1968), to The *Present Age and Of the Difference between a Genius and an Apostle* (hereafter called *Age*), by Søren Kierkegaard, trans. by Alexander Dru (New York: Harper & Row, 1962), to *Fear and Trembling and The Sickness unto Death* (hereafter called *Fear*), by Søren Kierkegaard, trans. by Walter Lowrie (Garden City, NY: Doubleday & Co., 1954), to *For Self-Examination and Judge for Yourselves! and Three Discourses* (hereafter called *Judge*), by Søren Kierkegaard, trans. by Walter Lowrie (Princeton: Princeton Univ. Press, 1974), to *Stages on Life's Way* (hereafter called *Stages*), by Søren Kierkegaard, trans. by Walter Lowrie (New York: Schocken Books, 1967), to *Training in Christianity* (hereafter called *Training*), by Søren Kierkegaard, trans. by Walter Lowrie (Princeton: Princeton Univ. Press, 1967), to *Attack upon "Christendom"* (hereafter called *Attack*), by Søren Kierkegaard, trans. by Walter Lowrie (Princeton: Princeton Univ. Press, 1968), to *On Authority and Revelation* (hereafter called *Authority*), by Søren Kierkegaard, trans. by Walter Lowrie (New York: Harper & Row, 1966), to *Purity of Heart Is to Will One Thing* (hereafter called *Purity*), by Søren Kierkegaard, trans. by Douglas V. Steers (New York: Harper & Row, 1956), to *Either/Or* in two volumes (hereafter called *Either/Or*, followed by volume number), by Søren Kierkegaard, Vol. I trans. by David F. and Lillian Marvin Swenson, Vol. II trans. by Walter Lowrie, and both volumes revised by Howard A. Johnson (Garden City, NY: Doubleday & Co., 1959), to *The Concept of Dread* (hereafter called *Dread*), by Søren Kierkegaard, trans. by Walter Lowrie (Princeton: Princeton Univ. Press, 1969), and to *Works of Love* (hereafter called *Love*), by Søren Kierkegaard, trans. by Howard and Edna Hong (New York: Harper & Row, 1962).

took as his theology tutor a young Hegelian named Hans L. Martensen. But he ceased to focus seriously on his studies in theology, instead taking up literature and philosophy. In 1835, he acknowledged that he was behaving like a dilettante, had no deep interest in studying theology, and was doing so to please his father. He wrote, "What I really need is to be clear about *what I am to do*, not what I must know, except in the way knowledge must precede all action. It is a question of understanding my destiny, of seeing what the Deity really wants *me* to do; the thing is to find a truth which is truth *for me*, to find *the idea for which I am willing to live and die*." In these two sentences, we see the seeds of his existential thought and his theory of subjective truth. Outwardly, he seemed to be enjoying life enormously; but, inwardly, he was in despair. He wrote in his journal, "I have just come back from a party where I was the life and soul. Witticisms flowed from my lips. Everyone laughed and admired me – but I left, yes, that dash should be as long as the radii of the earth's orbit – and wanted to shoot myself." His father had revealed something very troubling to him – probably about having cursed God and/or getting his mother pregnant before they married; whatever the revelation was, Kierkegaard experienced it as a "great earthquake" which cast the whole family in guilt, for which divine punishment must occur (*Selection*, 32, 50, 117).

In 1838, he had some sort of religious experience that made him actually joyful. He ceased his profligate ways and reestablished a good relationship with his father, who, however, died a few months later. Kierkegaard regretted that he did not "live a few years more" (*Selection*, 98), presumably to see his son finish his theology degree, which he did in 1840. He inherited the family home and enough financial assets to live on for most of the rest of his life.

Meanwhile, in 1837, he had met Regine Olsen, the other most important figure in his life, who was 10 years younger than he. He fell in love with her but waited a few years for her to grow up, writing in his journal that she was "stored in the deepest recesses of my heart." He saw her often. A couple of months after finishing his degree, he passionately proposed marriage, and she accepted him. Yet, racked with melancholic self-doubt, he writes, "The very next day I saw that I had made a mistake" (*Selection*, 100, 412–413). He entered a seminary, as if training for the clergy, although he never was ordained, and he prepared his academic dissertation, *The Concept of Irony*. In early 1841, he preached his first sermon. A few months later, he submitted his dissertation for a Master's degree; it was accepted by the philosophy faculty at the university, and he made a successful seven-hour defense of it.

The following month (October of 1841), he broke off his engagement in an unusual manner, contriving to convince Regine that he was a cad so that she would not want to marry him, rather than leaving her feeling rejected and dejected. There can be no doubt that he loved her for the rest of his life. So why not go through with his commitment and marry her? The answer is not clear. It may be that he was convinced that his melancholic temperament would make her unhappy. It may be that he didn't think he could love both her and God with all his heart. At any rate, he enigmatically wrote, "If I had had faith, I would have stayed with Regine." If he married her, he would feel obliged, in all honesty, "to initiate her into terrible things, my relationship to father, his melancholy, the eternal night brooding deep inside me, my going astray, my desires and excesses" (*Selection*, 158–159) – all of which would upset her. Yet he never got over her, even though she later married a respectable man who would become governor of the Danish West Indies.

A couple of weeks after breaking off his engagement, Kierkegaard visited Berlin, where he attended some of Schelling's lectures. The latter had been appointed to establish a strong antidote to Hegelian thought; and, while Denmark had become attracted to it, Kierkegaard himself had already become opposed. Yet he was disappointed and cut short his visit. As he wrote to his brother, Peter, who was ordained that same year (1842), "Schelling talks quite insufferable nonsense"; he

21 Søren Kierkegaard

added that he was "too old to attend lectures" and that Schelling (at the age of 67) was "too old to give them" (*Selection*, 121).

At this point, he began a prolific series of writings. *Either/Or* was published early in 1843 and was impressively successful. Even before that, he had begun *Johannes Climacus*, his first work written under the pseudonym of the philosophical Johannes Climacus; however, he never completed it, and it was only published posthumously. In 1843, he also published *Fear and Trembling* (the phrase is from Paul's epistle to the Philippians, 2:12), which he thought would solidify his reputation, and *Repetition*. The next year, he published *Philosophical Fragments*, his second work written under the Johannes Climacus pseudonym, as well as *The Concept of Dread*. In 1845, he published *Stages on Life's Way* and delivered to the printer his *Concluding Unscientific Postscript*, the third work written under the pseudonym of Johannes Climacus, which was published early in the following year. This last book's title is ironic: it is a 550-page "postscript" to the smaller *Philosophical Fragments*; it is deliberately unsystematic as opposed to being "scientific" in any Hegelian sense; and he expected it to conclude his authorship, because he wrongly believed that he would die that year. All of these works were done under a variety of pseudonyms, which he acknowledged as his own in "A First and Last Declaration," appended to the *Postscript*. During this same three-year period, he published many so-called "edifying discourses" under his own name.

The last decade of his life was marked by polemical controversy – first with the press and then with the Danish Church. *The Corsair* was a much read newspaper that dealt in humor, caricature, and gossip. It subjected many to ridicule but praised some of Kierkegaard's writings. Perversely, he challenged it to treat him as it did others, and it savagely met that challenge, mocking him, his appearance, his manner of dress, even his broken romance. Children in the street taunted him, calling him "Old Either/Or." He felt (rightly or wrongly) that a wide range of strangers was making fun of him, enjoying themselves at his expense (*Selection*, 216, 223–224). Thus he came to despise both the press and the crowd, as is evident in *The Present Age*, which he published in 1846. Still, he kept writing, publishing *Works of Love*, *Two Minor Ethico-Religious Essays*, *Sickness unto Death*, and *Training in Christianity* between 1847 and 1850.

Even more galling than his bad experience with *The Corsair* and the public was his soured relationship with the established Danish Church, which he criticized in articles collected in his *Attack upon "Christendom."* He had refrained from criticizing Bishop Mynster for his father's sake, even though he seemed a paradigm example of the sort of complacent man of religion he found objectionably insincere. But Mynster died in 1854 and was succeeded by Hans Martensen, freeing Kierkegaard from his restraint. Kierkegaard regretted that he had died without acknowledging "that what he had represented was not really Christianity" but a cheap and easy pretense. What Kierkegaard despised was the bad faith of Christendom masquerading as true Christianity. He wrote, "Being a Christian in Christendom in plain conformity is as impossible as doing gymnastics in a straitjacket" (*Selection*, 568, 640). When he published such views, he was denounced as an enemy of Christianity. He quit attending church services.

Meanwhile, he had used up almost all of his inheritance. In October of 1855, he withdrew from the bank what was left. On his way home, he lost consciousness and collapsed in the street, his legs paralyzed. In the hospital, he received very few visitors (and not his brother, Peter). Refusing to take communion from any priest, he died on November 11. There was only enough money left to pay the hospital bills and funeral expenses. He had wanted to leave his possessions to Regine, but her husband apparently declined the offer for her. Kierkegaard's brother, Peter, inherited his large library of books, as well as his author's rights to his works. Peter delivered the eulogy at his funeral, and he was buried in the family plot next to their father. There was a disturbance at the cemetery, as Henrik Lund, his nephew and a young physician, raised a protest against the Church's attempt to co-opt its fierce critic, as if he were one of their own. His three-word epithet, "the single individual" (*Selection*, 654, 657–658, 277) aptly describes him. And no thinker considered here more informed his writings with his own personality than he.

A couple of cautions are in order here, as we move from a focus on biography to an emphasis on key ideas. We shall have to deal with two problems that are not issues in considering other great modern thinkers. First, Kierkegaard employs humor and sarcasm and irony to a degree we have not seen in any of our previous chapters, sometimes deliberately writing the very opposite of what we are supposed to believe. And, second, many of his most important writings employ pseudonyms, so that we cannot just assume they simply speak for their author but had best view them as multiple personae, each representing a facet of his thought. Indeed, the most philosophical of his writings – to which we shall devote serious attention – are the three (*Johannes Climacus, Philosophical Fragments*, and *Concluding Unscientific Postscript*) written under the name of Johannes Climacus. These will best connect with the history of modern philosophy as we have discussed it up to this point. In thus proceeding, however, we should acknowledge that Kierkegaard tried to distance himself from his pseudonyms, saying that "in the pseudonymous works there is not a single word which is mine" and asking that quotes from these books be identified with the pseudonyms rather than with him, while expressing the wish that scholars not even try to "lay a dialectical hand upon this work" written pseudonymously (*Postscript*, 551–552, 554).

21.3 Knowledge

Johannes Climacus does not present himself as a philosopher or as a Christian, let alone as a Christian philosopher; yet he uses philosophy to try to analyze what becoming a Christian entails. He is clearly engaging modern thought, considering the method of Descartes – "*De omnibus dubitandum est*: 'Everything must be doubted'" – as his starting point. This is in contrast to ancient Greeks, such as Plato and Aristotle, who "taught that philosophy begins with Wonder." Yet Climacus raises the existential question of how an individual can establish a personal relationship with the truth of Christianity. Modern philosophy seems to culminate in Hegelian thought, whose system has little, if any, room for individuality. An objective truth is "just as true in the mouth of a child or madman as in the mouth of Pythagoras," Climacus observes. But is it subjectively meaningful to the speaker? If doubt is to be existentially significant, it must be more than a methodological exercise – and the same is the case with "doubt's opposite – faith." So objective, disinterested knowledge that does not personally concern the knower is of questionable existential value (*Climacus*, 109, 115–116, 123–124, 128, 130, 132, 135, 146, 152). Here we see a challenging of the very foundations of modern epistemology.

The second of the three books written under the pseudonym of Johannes Climacus is *Philosophical Fragments*, which pursues the learning and knowing of Truth. Climacus sees the passage from "a state of Error" to one of knowing the Truth as potentially personally transformative. As if channeling Plato, he says, "Let us call this change *Conversion*," as the knower turns away from error to truth. But what if the ultimate Truth, worthy of being embraced with greatest passion, involves a "supreme paradox" with which Reason can only collide and which, by its very nature, "thought cannot think" (*Fragments*, 11, 16, 22–23, 46), no matter what philosophical method it may adopt?

The third book attributed to Climacus, *Concluding Unscientific Postscript*, carries this critique of modern epistemology to more definitive conclusions. As modern philosophy culminated in the Hegelian system, it promises that "everything will become clear" when the system is complete but admits that such completion has yet to be achieved. It is alleged to be presuppositionless, yet it presupposes faith in reason and "an interest in understanding" the truth about everything. Despite Hegel's dialectical effort to transcend the subject–object dichotomy, there remains a serious distinction between the "objective problem" of whether Christianity is true and the "subjective problem" of how the individual should relate to it (to which the division between Book One and Book Two of the *Postscript* corresponds). A deficiency of modern philosophy is that it focuses on the objective problem with little or no concern for the existential issue of how an individual might be "infinitely, personally, and passionately" related to the Truth, diverting us from the pursuit of "an eternal happiness." If Christianity essentially involves the ultimate Truth, then this objective, rational approach misses the point: "Christianity is spirit, spirit is inwardness, inwardness is subjectivity, subjectivity is essentially passion, and in its maximum an infinite, personal, passionate interest in one's eternal happiness" (*Postscript*, 16, 18, 20, 28, 32–33, 49). It is difficult to think of any modern philosopher before Kierkegaard (other, perhaps, than Pascal) who shared this emphasis.

So let us now turn to the discussion of the subjective problem of how we might be personally related to the Truth of Christianity (considered in some of the most famous passages of the *Postscript*). Here Climacus reveals the influence of Gotthold Lessing. In subjective thinking, the thinker – far from being disinterested – is passionately interested. The sort of truth that is personally meaningful "exists only in the process of becoming, in the process of appropriation," rather than having to do with abstract, static being. This takes issue with Hegel's analysis of becoming as an abstract synthesis of "being and non-being." Descartes was correct in starting his epistemology with self-certainty; but existence essentially involves change: "An existing individual is constantly in process of becoming." Existence is, to be sure, a synthesis – "of the infinite and the finite, the eternal and the temporal." But its truth is subjective. Climacus is not denying the truth of objective thought; but it is irrelevant to what gives meaning and value to our lives. That cannot be rationally inferred but is accessible only through "a leap" of faith such as Lessing advocated. Such a leap requires decisive personal commitment. Hegel proposed to work out an all-inclusive, comprehensive system without gaps and requiring no leaps. Climacus sarcastically comments that he would be willing to genuflect in worship before it if it were ever completed but finds the notion of an incomplete system oxymoronic (*Postscript*, 67, 72, 74–75, 79, 85, 90–91, 97–98).

He asserts "two theses: (A), a logical system is possible; (B), an existential system is impossible." The first of these is noncontroversial, as has been obvious since Aristotle. But Hegel mistook his metaphysical system for a logical one, despite its blatant incompleteness. In fact, existence is personal and extraneous to logic. As we lose ourselves in abstract thought, we, the thinkers, Climacus alleges, forget that we are existing human beings. In denying the possibility of an "existential system," he means for us humans, not denying that reality itself is a system for God, but only that it can be for existing individuals involved in the ongoing process of developmental and constant becoming. Because ethics essentially involves values of existing persons, it defies efforts of systematization, which may explain why Hegel treats it as social rather than as personal. Ethical truth and religious truth must be subjective, involving the personal commitment of faith. Subjective truth has to do with the dynamic process of existence, and to imagine that it is an Hegelian "identity of thought and being is a chimera of abstraction." Unlike objective truth, which can be systematized, only the subjective truth of "ethico-religious knowledge has an essential relationship to the existence of the knower." Objective truth focuses on *what* is said or believed, while subjective truth is concerned with *how* it is appropriated. We can inquire whether it is objectively always true that sadistic cruelty is morally wrong or that God requires our unfailing obedience to divine commandments; but, from a subjective perspective, the issue is whether we choose to avoid the former

21.4 Reality | **339**

and practice the latter – a matter of personal commitment. This leads us to the famous definition of subjective truth: "*An objective uncertainty held fast in an appropriation-process of the most passionate inwardness.*" This is the most meaningful truth available to "an *existing* individual." But, Climacus adds, this definition also defines faith, which is impossible without risk: "Faith is precisely the contradiction between the infinite passion of the individual's inwardness and the objective uncertainty." Truth is the proper object of both knowledge and belief. In contrast to Hegel's view of the identity of thought and being, Climacus holds, "Subjectivity is truth, subjectivity is reality" (*Postscript*, 99–100, 104, 107–108, 110, 117–119, 176–182, 306; cf. *Love*, 111, 218). Without denying objective truth and reality, this emphasizes what is personally meaningful to us as existing and thinking individuals.

21.4 Reality

Kierkegaard's disinterest in abstract metaphysical speculation is such that he does not commit much time or space to discussions of reality in general – for example, to whether it is essentially material (as with Hobbes) or spiritual (as for Berkeley) or dualistic (for example, according to Descartes). Indeed, in the first volume of *Either/Or*, he has his pseudonym sarcastically denounce the notion that existing philosophers can step outside of reality to analyze it objectively: "What the philosophers say about Reality is often as disappointing as a sign you see in a shop window, which reads: Pressing Done Here. If you brought your clothes to be pressed, you would be fooled; for the sign is only for sale" (*Either/Or*, I, 31). In *The Concept of Irony*, he agreed with Hegel that Kant compromised the plausibility of his system by including the thing-in-itself as distinguishable from the reality of phenomena. "It even became a problem whether the ego itself was not a *Ding an sich*. This problem was raised and resolved by Fichte" (*Irony*, 289–290). But, from an existential perspective, one might ask, what possible difference could it make to real people in the real world? But, again, let us consider what Kierkegaard has Johannes Climacus say about reality. We employ speech to express whatever we immediately experience, so that "immediacy is reality and speech is ideality." Whatever we say about "the actual world" must be distinguished from what we immediately experience of it. Speech mediates our immediate experience. Consciousness requires this duality of reality and ideality, though neither of them essentially is consciousness itself (*Climacus*, 148–150).

But the richest text for a Kierkegaardian treatment of reality is again the *Postscript*. Climacus says, "Whether truth is defined more empirically, as the conformity of thought and being [e.g. by Locke], or more idealistically, as the conformity of being with thought [e.g. by Kant], it is, in either case, important carefully to note what is meant by being." Thought abstractly conceives of being as complete. Only in the arena of concrete reality must becoming be considered. The actual human who philosophizes "is himself existentially in process of becoming" and cannot live and always think in some abstract realm. Only God can transcend the temporal phenomenal world. Thus the notion of our grasping some Hegelian "identity of thought and being is a chimera of abstraction" from the process of change that is characteristic of the becoming of existence. Climacus sees this delusion as typical of modern philosophy. But it is precisely existential knowledge that is "essential" in the sense of being personally meaningful, while the "abstract thought" of philosophers like Hegel is not. This is not to denigrate the greatness of Hegelian thought, but only to point out its limitations. "Existence constitutes the highest interest of the existing individual, and his interest in his existence constitutes his reality." By contrast, abstract thought's disinterested conception of reality is, for us humans, "a phantom." In a sense, modern philosophy has allegedly involved the

21.5 God

So, without ever denying our ability to achieve objective knowledge, Kierkegaard seems to hold that the most meaningful objects of thought are matters of faith rather than of rational understanding and that reality involves spirit more importantly than physical things. This will involve the divine Spirit as well as human spirit – as well as the religious relation between the two. Indeed, he maintains that the most definitive truth of Christianity – that of the incarnation of God in Jesus of Nazareth – defies all rational understanding and can only be held through a leap of faith. Paraphrasing what Kant said about himself, we might say that Kierkegaard limits the objects of rational knowledge in order to make room for faith.

Since almost all of Kierkegaard's writings deal with God and/or religion, it is advisable that we use his *Point of View for My Work as an Author* as a guide for how we might proceed without letting this discussion get unmanageable. He says that "the whole of my work as an author is related to Christianity, to the problem 'of becoming a Christian,' with a direct or indirect polemic against the monstrous illusion we call Christendom." He divides his work into three groups: first, there are "aesthetic" writings, everything from *Either/Or* to *Stages on Life's Way*; second, his *Concluding Unscientific Postscript* is in a class by itself and is transitional, being identified as "the turning-point" in his entire authorship; and, third, there are the strictly "religious" writings, including *Works of Love, Sickness unto Death, Training in Christianity*, and the articles collected under the title of *Attack upon "Christendom"* (*Point*, 5–6, 10n., 13). Climacus, who does not claim to be a Christian but is considering the problem of becoming one, holds that faith in Christianity is "a stumbling block" to Jews, who require the evidence of signs, and "foolishness" to Greeks, who demand rational argumentation as proof (*Climacus*, 167–168, 170; the scriptural reference here is to 1 Corinthians 1:23).

In *Philosophical Fragments*, he confronts the "supreme paradox" of Christianity, that, in the person of Jesus of Nazareth, God, who is infinite, eternal, and immutable, became a finite, temporal, constantly becoming man without abdicating his divinity; this paradoxical mystery (of the incarnation) is "something that thought cannot think." He considers it impossible even to prove that God exists, which, of course, must be presupposed to even try to make any sense of the paradox at all. "Generally speaking, it is a difficult matter to prove that anything exists." We know that something exists by directly or indirectly encountering it and then use reason to determine its essence – moving from the perceived fact *that* it is to the inferred determination of *what* it is. "I do not, for example, prove that a stone exists, but that some existing thing is a stone." If we try to prove God from the order, goodness, and governance of the world, we proceed from our own doubtful "ideal interpretation" of the world, which is highly unreliable. Such proof necessarily requires "a *leap*." The truth seems to be that the God of faith is "the Unknown," which reason should consider to be "absolutely different" from everything it can understand. Reason resists and tends to reject this as "absurd." This is even more obviously the case with the paradox of Christianity, which can only be believed and never rationally known. While faith can be subjectively certain for the believer, "belief is not a form of knowledge, but a free act, an expression of will." (This voluntaristic element in his thought might remind us of Schopenhauer.) One is not logically forced to believe but chooses to do so; or, to the contrary, one can persist in doubt. Nor can such faith be justified by calculating probabilities, as we have no way to reckon them (*Fragments*, 46, 49–57, 59, 65, 76, 101, 103, 105, 118). One must believe or doubt with no definitive rational justification either way.

Unsurprisingly, the *Postscript*, which marks Kierkegaard's turning from a consideration of becoming a Christian to writing from a distinctive position of Christian commitment, explores this relationship between faith and reason more thoroughly, reason proceeding logically, as opposed to by a "leap of faith." The definition of faith given earlier does not characterize logical reasoning; and, as such, it can even accommodate belief in the absurd. "What now is the absurd? The absurd is – that the eternal truth has come into being in time, that God has come into being, has been born, has grown up, and so forth." This central Christian belief of the incarnation is what Climacus describes as "an offense to the Jews and a folly to the Greeks – and an absurdity to the understanding." Unlike humans, whose temporal existence (despite Hegel) separates thought from being, God's eternal being involves no such separation. But all of this, which is essential to Christian faith, surpasses all possible human understanding, accounting for the conspicuous difficulty of truly becoming a Christian, as it "requires a man to give up his reason" – at least in this area. To venture everything against all reason is so extreme a risk that Climacus calls it a kind of "madness," indeed even "a crucifixion of the understanding." Here we have gone beyond the ordinary (and Hegelian) religion of immanence that Climacus calls "religiousness A" and leaped into "the paradox-religious sphere, the sphere of faith" (*Postscript*, 15, 182, 188, 191, 194–196, 290, 296, 337, 380–381, 384, 500–505, 513). Climacus appreciates the challenge of becoming a Christian without accepting it himself.

Accentuating the challenge is that Kierkegaard's transcendent God is radically other than us (and all other creatures). As he writes in "Of the Difference between a Genius and an Apostle" (from 1847), "Between God and man, then, there is and remains an eternal, essential, qualitative difference" (*Age*, 99; cf. *Fear*, 257). His discourse on "The Unchangeableness of God" (first delivered as a sermon in 1851) also emphasizes this radical difference. Thus the threat of anthropomorphism is avoided, but at the cost of our having to wonder, in "sheer fear and trembling," almost to the point of "despair," how a relation between us could be possible (*Judge*, 232–233, 235, 237). And yet this is what authentic religion requires. Reacting against this radical difference, we have an enduring tendency to slip back into anthropomorphism. Sounding like Feuerbach, *Stages on Life's Way* fancifully says, "God created man in His own image, and in requital man created God in his, . . . and it is true that a man's conception of God is essentially determined by the kind of man he is" (*Stages*, 217, 415–416). Reason has no solution, and only the rationally unjustifiable commitment of faith can break the impasse. Kierkegaard eloquently writes in *The Present Age* that "the abyss of eternity opens before you, the sharp scythe of the leveller makes it possible for every one individually to leap over the blade – and behold, it is God who waits. Leap, then, into the arms of God" (*Age*, 82).

Kierkegaard published *Training in Christianity* under the pseudonym of Anti-Climacus; unlike Climacus, who has not committed to Christian faith, he has done so. As a believer, he sees Christ "as contemporary with His presence" and not merely the historical figure of 18 centuries earlier. While history might be able to shed some light on the life of Jesus of Nazareth, it is useless in teaching us anything about the paradoxical nature of his unique identity. It cannot possibly prove that he was God in a literal and unique sense. "At the most it might prove that Jesus Christ was a great man, perhaps the greatest of all; but that He was . . . God – nay." This requires a leap of faith surpassing all empirical evidence. Sensible, rational "Christendom" no longer takes this challenge seriously, so that "one must try again to introduce Christianity into Christendom." History tells us Jesus was a remarkable man in the distant past. But true Christian faith – embracing the "endless yawning differences between God and man" – must be committed to the paradoxical idea of being "contemporary with Christ" today and going forward. This requires a transformative commitment

21 Søren Kierkegaard

that is more existentially life-changing than the abstract faith of such Christian philosophers as, for example, Descartes and Kant: "What the modern philosophy understands by faith is what properly is called an opinion, or what is loosely called in everyday speech believing." But religious faith "in a pregnant sense" calls for a nonrational view of reality that translates into action; and "in relation to action the right understanding is like the spring-board from which the jumper makes his leap" (*Training*, 9, 28–29, 36, 39, 67, 131, 134n., 140, 158).

Let us briefly consider Kierkegaard's polemical *Attack upon "Christendom,"* which is not really philosophical but develops some of the key ideas we have just been discussing. "Christendom" (including the established Lutheran Church of Denmark) has tried to make it comfortably easy for its followers to think themselves Christian by glossing over the difficulties of paradoxical faith. At least pretending to be Christian is requisite to cultural conformity and social acceptance. It is as easy as wearing a white hat in order to be fashionable. "On the other hand, where all are Christians, the situation is this: to call oneself a Christian is the means whereby one secures oneself against all sort of inconveniences and discomforts, and the means whereby one secures worldly goods, comforts, profit, etc." Thus religious orthodoxy prevails as a matter of course; but it is "the orthodoxy which consists in playing the game of Christianity." We join together to create this illusion, and it is to the advantage of religious leaders (such as Bishop Mynster) to collaborate in, or at least to overlook, such hypocrisy. Kierkegaard rhetorically asks, "What do I want?" He immediately answers, "Quite simply: I want honesty." And he accuses his own Church of being unwilling to be so honest. The massive spread of hypocritical "Christendom" is a direct threat to the survival of true Christianity. But this also constitutes a threat to what true Christian faith makes possible – namely, "a total transformation in a man" (*Attack*, 25, 27–28, 30, 37, 39, 167, 221). This will lead us to a study of Kierkegaard's view of human nature.

But first we should take account of his treatment of authority. Modern philosophy from Descartes through Mill has mostly refused to rest any of its case on religious, political, or philosophical authority, accepting only the "authority" of experience and reason. By contrast, Kierkegaard takes seriously the authority of revelation. Christian theologians are misguided in their attempts to use authority "to make *Christianity plausible*." Such a failure to understand that it is essentially paradoxical undermines genuine faith. "Every defense of Christianity which understands what it would accomplish must behave exactly conversely, maintaining with might and main by qualitative dialectic that Christianity is *implausible*" and requires the leap of faith we have discussed. It is rather God's "*divine authority*" to which a person of faith should submit; and that authority is revealed in the Scriptures. This is quite different from the authority of human apologists. "Philosophy, and with that the theology which caricatures philosophy" are simply useless here. What Kierkegaard (perhaps mocking Hegel) calls "the dialectic of authority" springs from the pivotal antithesis of "the paradox-religious sphere" – namely, the "*eternal, essential, qualitative difference*" that there is "*between God and man*." The merely human authority of reason can never synthesize these polar opposites. Hence the need for a nonlogical leap of faith in the acceptance of the authority of biblical revelation. Only this can do justice to the authority of "Christ as the God-Man" (*Authority*, 59–60, 25–27, 111–114; cf. *Age*, 104, for the claim that all of modern philosophy tries to abolish authority).

21.6 Humanity

Kierkegaard subscribes to the Socratic view that, among all desirable sorts of knowledge, self-knowledge is particularly important. Sometimes, through no fault of our own, we are ignorant regarding certain information about ourselves. But, as he writes in his *Purity of Heart Is to Will One*

Thing, "an ignorance about one's own life" that is both tragic and blameworthy is that which is due to "self-deception" (*Purity*, 52). Here we see a precursor of Sartre's famous treatment of what he calls "bad faith." So it is particularly appropriate that we try to understand our own humanity.

Either/Or explores, in considerable depth, two fundamental ways of humanly existing, the first volume the aesthetic way and the second the ethical way. From an aesthetic perspective, the modern age seems "paltry" because it is so lacking in passion. People may mostly do what is expected of them, but so mechanically! By contrast, Shakespeare's characters are fascinating because they vigorously behave like authentic "human beings: they hate, they love, they murder their enemies, and curse their descendants throughout all generations; they sin." The aesthete tends to view things through the lens of what is interesting (and pleasant) as opposed to what is boring (and painful). "Boredom is the root of all evil," for the aesthete; and so much of life is an ongoing battle against being bored. Most people live boring lives. "Those who bore others are the mob, the crowd, the infinite multitude of men in general." It is natural to try to escape boredom by seeking beauty, excitement, adventure, variety, and change (*Either/Or*, I, 27, 281–282, 284–287, 423). Yet even when we achieve what is interesting, boredom always lurks around the corner, waiting to infect us.

By contrast, there is the ethical mode of existence. Consider the difference between aesthetically being romantically in love, "based upon beauty" of some sort and free to stay or leave as one pleases, on the one hand, and being ethically committed to a life of marital love, on the other. The former is fickle, while the latter "is faithful." The latter, unlike the former, requires constancy of character and a sense of duty, generating a kind of stability. By the way, there is a brief acknowledgment of a third way of existence, when mention is made of "the aesthetical, the ethical and the religious." At any rate, once we recognize any alternative to the aesthetic, we can choose to commit or not. "The choice itself is decisive for the content of the personality." By neglecting to choose, we simply remain in the aesthetic. "The only absolute either/or is the choice between good and evil, but that is also absolutely ethical." These are categories that are alien to a merely aesthetic mode of existence. Once an aesthete becomes aware of the ethical alternative but does not choose it, the existential emotion of "melancholy ensues." This is different from sadness, which is a reaction to someone or something or some situation or some occurrence. Why is a person sad? Because his wife left him or he got fired from his job or the world seems infected with violence, hatred, and warfare. "If a melancholy man is asked . . . what it is that weighs on him, he will reply, 'I know not, I cannot explain it.'" It is a reaction to his own manner of existing. A second existential emotion is that of self-aware despair; "everyone who lives aesthetically is in despair, whether he knows it or not." Again, this is not the sort of hopelessness over something external; it is rather reflexively focused on a sense of one's own way of existing as hopeless. Despair is related to a deep and genuine sort of formidable doubt: "Doubt is a despair of thought, despair is a doubt of the personality." If we realize that we are free to choose but fail to exercise that choice, we are open to melancholy and despair. This adversely affects our very self – which essentially "is freedom." Human "dignity" (as Kant argued) consists in one's freedom of choice and the transforming exercising of it (*Either/Or*, II, 21, 140, 142, 148–150, 167–173, 193, 197, 215, 218, 229, 254–255).

Only humans have the sort of spirit that is capable of the existential emotions of melancholy and despair. *The Concept of Dread* analyzes a third such emotion unique to existing human spirits. Experiencing our self as nothing (no thing) with the capacity for free choice "begets dread." It is not the same as fear, which is of "something definite." It is rather a reaction to the possibilities presented by the use of one's own freedom. Consider someone seeking the thrill of doing something dangerous, such as committing a crime. He is attracted to the possibility yet finds the prospect horrifying. "Dread is a *sympathetic antipathy and an antipathetic sympathy*." Eliminate choice, and the dread evaporates. It is possible on account of the complexity of human nature. A human being is "a synthesis of the soulish and the bodily." However, a synthesis requires the unity of antitheses in a third element (notice the playing with Hegelian dialectic here). "This third factor is the spirit." It is spirit that is free, and the awareness of one's own possible choices that underlies dread. "Dread is the possibility of freedom," unique to existing spirits and impossible for beasts or angels (*Dread*, 38–40, 139).

The shallow, superficial aesthete does not exercise his freedom to commit to anything that might make his life meaningful. But, as Kierkegaard's pseudonym says in *Stages on Life's Way*, "I cannot endure that my life should have no meaning at all." The search for meaning is a typical feature of the existential analysis of the human person. It is the ethico-religious life that involves the sort of commitment that can make life meaningful. But now we encounter a distinction between the ethical and the religious. "There are three existence-spheres: the aesthetic, the ethical, the religious." Remember that this was already suggested in *Either/Or*. Now we are led to identify the aesthetic with mere fleeting "immediacy," the ethical with the requirements of moral duty, and the religious with ultimate "fulfillment" (*Stages*, 238, 430). And, as we are about to see, the analysis becomes even more detailed in Kierkegaard's next major work.

In the *Postscript*, Climacus says that "man is a synthesis of the temporal and the eternal." It is this synthesis that conditions human existence, and "the highest stage" possible "for an existing individual" is that of religious faith. Climacus refers back to the "three stages" of existence of which we are capable, the aesthetic, the ethical, and the religious. The object of Christian faith is the God-man, "the fact that God has existed as an individual human being." If Jesus is fully human and fully divine, then he is both finite and infinite; but then our spirits are infinite, while our bodies are finite. (In addition to the three possible spheres of human existence, there are also a couple of "boundary zones" between them: "irony, constituting the boundary between the aesthetic and the ethical; humor, as the boundary that separates the ethical from the religious." However, these are not particularly important for our purposes.) We can identify aesthetes and ethical persons well enough. But the person of religious faith is not so easily identifiable, existing as a "knight of hidden inwardness." Thus we cannot know how many of the people we encounter are truly religious. Climacus interestingly sometimes refers to the three "spheres" of existence as "stages"; for while the word "spheres" does not suggest a hierarchy, the word "stages" clearly does. But, either way, toward the end of the *Postscript*, Climacus distinguishes between two sorts of religion – "religiousness A," a religion of immanence that includes that of philosophers like Hegel, and "religiousness B," which is "the paradoxical religiousness" of genuine Christianity. (Again, it is not particularly important for our purposes, but each of these forms of religion has its own way of being "edifying.") Despite Hegel's best efforts, speculative philosophy cannot dialectically do justice to Christianity as paradoxical (*Postscript*, 54, 85, 259, 261, 290, 350, 448, 452–453, 457, 463, 473n., 494–498, 506–507).

While *The Sickness unto Death*, written under the pseudonym of Anti-Climacus, is not particularly philosophical, in its analysis of despair, it is a masterful exploration of religious psychology that provides more depth regarding human existence. A fascinating paragraph early on seems a satirical takeoff on Hegelian dialectic: "Man is spirit. But what is spirit? Spirit is the self. But what is the self? The self is a relation which relates itself to its own self." To say that the spiritual self is a relation may suggest that it is nothing more than reflective self-awareness. But then things get more complex: "Man is a synthesis of the infinite and the finite, of the temporal and the eternal, of freedom and necessity." Before we can work out what, precisely, this means, Anti-Climacus yanks us out of our Hegelian comfort zone by saying, "So regarded, man is not yet a self." Why is he being so contrary? Because this analysis indicates a "unity" that is fractured by existence, which defies the would-be integration of Hegelian speculation. This disunity is essential to the human condition; and when it is qualified by freedom of choice, it opens the gates to "the sickness unto death" of despair. It is on account of our complexity that despair inheres in us. Despair does not literally kill the spirit; to the contrary, the suffering of despair is compounded by the spirit's inability to die, despite the anguish of being incapable of achieving true integration. The object of despair is oneself, and fighting it is a battle against oneself (this is reminiscent of what Hegel said of the "Unhappy Consciousness"). The only way of escaping despair is, allegedly, to "be a true Christian," and merely being unaware of one's own despair does not negate it. The only way in which hope is possible is through faith in God, for whom "all things are possible" (*Sickness*, 146–147, 149–156, 177, 205, 213; cf. *Love*, 54–55). Without going into the various forms of despair laid out by Anti-Climacus, we can see that human existence is positioned between God, our ultimate source, and God, our ultimate goal. (We can also note, without elaboration, that Kierkegaard's treatments of both dread and despair are religiously related to sin.)

21.7 Freedom

We have already considered enough of Kierkegaard's treatment of freedom to realize that it is central to his existential philosophy of human nature. But let us now try to supplement that with reference to other passages. In *Either/Or*, his aesthetic pseudonym recommends the choice of "arbitrariness" as a key to keeping life interesting and satisfying: "You go to see the middle of a play, you read the third part of a book. By this means you insure yourself a very different kind of enjoyment from that which the author has been so kind as to plan for you" (*Either/Or*, I, 295). But this is a shallow, childish sort of freedom. In *Philosophical Fragments*, Climacus says that "to be what one is by one's own act is freedom" (*Fragments*, 19). This runs deeper and is a good expression of the existentialist idea that freedom concerns not only what we choose to *do* but, even more importantly, what we choose to *be*.

As we have seen, *The Concept of Dread* locates the root of dread in our awareness of possible options. "Possibility means *I can*." The feeling of dread is uncomfortably disconcerting. "Thus dread is the dizziness of freedom when the spirit . . . gazes down into its own possibility." It is only because the human spirit has free choice that it feels dread. The realization that the future is, to some extent, determined by free choice can generate a "dizziness" whereby "freedom swoons." Human freedom also opens the door to the guilt that springs from bad choices (*Dread*, 44, 55, 59–60, 82, 97, 109, 139).

In the *Postscript*, Climacus compares human freedom to a magical lamp, out of which, "when it is rubbed, a spirit appears." Spirit becomes manifest through the exercising of free choice. Distinctively human action is the product of free decision-making. Yet we are so dependent on our Creator that even our free choices are impossible without God (*Postscript*, 124, 302–303, 434–435). *Works of Love* cautions us against the illusion that law limits or blocks freedom, when, in fact, "it is the opposite; without law freedom does not exist at all, and it is law which gives freedom" (*Love*, 53). This is the old (going back to the ancient Greeks) idea that genuine freedom is not license or arbitrary whimsy (as for the aesthete), but orderly, reasonable, responsible decision-making. In *The Sickness unto Death*, Anti-Climacus makes an intriguing statement: "Personality is a synthesis of possibility and necessity" (*Sickness*, 173). As we have seen, possibility is a function of freedom. Yet human freedom is never absolute and can only be exercised within the parameters of conditions beyond our control.

21.8 Morality

Moral responsibility is a function of free choice. Ethics strives to provide us with standards by which we can morally judge choices and behaviors. Unlike Kant and Mill, Kierkegaard is not an ethicist of the first order. Nevertheless, he does offer us an unusual modern version of the controversial divine command theory, which, roughly, holds that it is our duty to obey God's orders. But, before we analyze this position presented in *Fear and Trembling*, let us consider some other contributions to be found in his writings. Remembering that the second volume of *Either/Or* is devoted to the ethical stage of existence, we note that its pseudonym, Judge William, advocates the sort of commitment typical of the ethical life over the arbitrariness of the aesthetic. Like Kant, he maintains that the "ethical is the universal," so that "it appears as law" – namely, the moral law. But he also maintains that moral choices define one's character rather than merely determining right actions, which is typically existentialist. As he puts it, "I have deliberately preferred to use the expression 'choose oneself' instead of know thyself" (which was a Socratic dictum). As we have seen, truth that is personally relevant must be subjectively meaningful and must at least appear to be fulfilling. As the final words of the book put it, "only the truth which edifies is truth for you" (*Either/Or*, II, 259–261, 263, 286–287, 356).

Stages on Life's Way identifies moral commitment with resolution. The ethical person is resolved to make choices in line with moral duty. Again, the example offered is that of a sincere and serious marriage commitment, with a firm resolve to be faithful to it. "The act of resolution is the ethical act, it is freedom." This is radically different from the choice of the aesthete. To make ethical choices as to how one will behave is also "to choose oneself." This is a matter of personal commitment. Perhaps the reason the Hegelian system has no ethics (as opposed to a theory of society) is that it cannot accommodate the existing individual (*Stages*, 113–115, 120, 124, 219). Kierkegaard's *Purity of Heart Is to Will One Thing* is dedicated to "That Solitary Individual," the subject of ethical responsibility. The "one thing" worth willing is the Good. A leap from the ethical to the religious will identify "the Good without condition and without qualification" with God. Whether identified with God or not, everything short of the Good – including all worldly goods – will prove to be manifold and transitory (*Purity*, 53–54, 59–60, 66).

Fear and Trembling, written under the pseudonym of Johannes de Silentio, is a meditation on "the beautiful story about how God tempted Abraham, and how he endured temptation," proving himself to be an exemplar of faith. (Some of us might well find the story more disturbing than "beautiful.") If we remove Abraham's faith in and commitment to God, from an ethical perspective, he sets out to murder his son, Isaac (the biblical reference is Genesis 22). Abraham's faith in God in this situation is maintained "by virtue of the absurd," in that there is no rational accounting for or justification of it. Only in his personal commitment to God can Abraham be a "knight of faith." Outwardly, he appears as a normal man like others. By contrast, a "tragic hero," committed to "infinite resignation" to his moral duty, can be identifiable. "The infinite resignation is the last stage prior to faith, so that one who has not made the movement has not faith." This indicates that the ethical stage is a necessary step to having religious commitment but does not yet confront a person with "the absurd" or "the paradoxical movement of faith." Whereas the ethical is committed to universal values, paradoxical faith is committed to the particular God-relationship as "higher than the universal." The Abraham story does not recommend an abrogation of moral duty but only its "suspension" as overridden in a particular situation in response to a mandate from God. This is famously referred to as "a teleological suspension of the ethical." It is as if it constitutes a singular exception to a moral rule. Thus, for example, Abraham could not take it upon himself to sacrifice his wife, Sarah, to prove his love for God; that was not required of him, so that it would be a simple act of murder, as one ethical principle is not superseded by another or by divine command. (Notice that this is not patently the sort of divine command theory that views all moral duty as derived from God's will.) By contrast, Agamemnon is "a tragic hero" who thinks that his sacrifice of his daughter, Iphigenia, is morally required by a higher duty to his country and who remains in the ethical stage. If Abraham is neither insane nor a sincere "knight of faith," then, in setting out to kill Isaac, he is an appalling murderer. His behavior cannot be justified within the ethical sphere, so that his situation is dreadfully tragic and rationally understandable to nobody. Yet, paradoxically, he supposedly believes that, somehow, what he is doing is justified and will work out for the best (*Fear*, 26, 39, 41, 46–51, 56–59, 62, 65–71, 77, 80, 89–90, 121–122, 124, 129; cf. *Postscript*, 235).

21.9   Society

Given his emphasis on individuality, it should not be too surprising that Kierkegaard does not develop a particularly robust theory of society. However, there are elements scattered about that might be put together to paint a small but coherent picture. He seems to have been a social (and religious) conservative but not to discuss political government much. In an Appendix to the *Postscript*, Climacus says, "Of all forms of government the monarchical is the best." He also condemns democracy as "the most tyrannical form of government" (*Postscript*, 548). Whether or not this is fairly indicative of Kierkegaard's own views, we do know that he visited his king, Christian VIII, a couple of times in 1847.

Like Descartes, Kierkegaard sees Christian love as a glue holding a good society together, referencing the commandment of Jesus, "You shall love your neighbor as yourself" (Matthew 22:39) in his *Works of Love*. Thus love of others is seen as a "duty." Meeting this duty takes us beyond the sort of egocentric selfishness that is socially toxic. It also takes us beyond mere justice, which discriminates between "mine" and "yours" and "gives to each his own." As the title of the book indicates, love that is more than idle sentimentality is expressed in altruistic "works." As he puts it so concisely and pointedly, "What love does, it is; what it is, it does" (*Works*, 34, 36–37, 40, 98, 248, 261).

But Kierkegaard's most remarkable treatment of this topic of society is his denunciation of modern society's conformity and suppression of individuality in *The Present Age*. It begins with his frequent complaint that his culture is too given to intellectual "reflection without passion." He characterizes antiquity as geared toward leadership and Christendom toward representation, but "the present age" as committed to equality and having a "levelling" effect at the expense of individuality. Individuals are seen, and view themselves, as belonging in all things to an abstraction – namely that of "*humanity pure and unalloyed.*" Another name for this "monstrous abstraction," to which individuals have placed themselves in thrall, is "*the public.*" (We might compare his concern for the surviving and thriving of individuality to that expressed by Mill.) He also characterizes the press as the public's amusing pet "dog," which it releases on nonconformists (no doubt with *The Corsair* in mind so soon after it lampooned him). "Mere gossip" and scandalmongering are the weapons of the public's "dog," entertaining subscribers through an invasion of victims' privacy. Religious faith (that has not been corrupted), however, will preserve and nurture individuality, telling each of us, in effect, that "the abyss of eternity opens before you, the sharp scythe of the leveller makes it possible for every one individually to leap over the blade – and behold, it is God who waits. Leap, then, into the arms of God" (*Age*, 33, 52–55, 59–63, 65–67, 69, 72, 82).

The Point of View refers to the abstraction of the public as "the crowd." Many believe the comforting affirmation of the crowd to provide an assurance of correctness, but certainly not Kierkegaard, who succinctly writes, "For a 'crowd' is the untruth." He finds individuality decisively important, both religiously and intellectually. It may be fashionable to try to blend in with the crowd. "And yet," he writes, "if I were to desire an inscription for my tombstone, I should desire none other than 'That Individual.'" He boasts that he has been able to use that category to aim a blow at the Hegelian system (*Point*, 110, 122, 128–129, 134, 149). One can easily see how this aspect of his philosophy might render Kierkegaard's works attractive to other existentialists.

21.10 Review

Relative to all the other thinkers we have considered here, Kierkegaard is unique in content, as well as in style of presentation. The one who comes the closest to him is, arguably, Pascal. But Kierkegaard is the better philosopher, perhaps in part because he had the advantage of studying the German idealists. If Descartes made the subjective turn definitive of modern philosophy (to be followed by the skeptical turn of Hume, then the transcendental turn of Kant, then the dialectical turn of Hegel), Kierkegaard's existential turn lands him in a more subjective position than Descartes, the rationalist, would have tolerated. But, in addition to being intellectually exciting, it is also problematic. For example, what criterion do we have to discriminate between subjective truth and illusion? Why should we assume that famous leap of faith is not into the arms of fanaticism? How is the so-called teleological suspension of the ethical (which can allegedly justify our willingness to kill an innocent young person, who happens to be our own child, because God supposedly ordered it) anything short of either wicked or crazy? Despite such unsettling queries, it should come as no surprise that more recent existentialists, such as Jean-Paul Sartre and Karl Jaspers, should regard Kierkegaard as a spokesperson for our own troubled times, perhaps even more than for his own. And, as we are about to see, the same can be said of Nietzsche.[2]

---

2 For more on Kierkegaard, see ch. 8 of *Western Philosophies of Religion*, by Wayne P. Pomerleau (New York: Ardsley House, 1998).

22

Friedrich Nietzsche

Source: Wikimedia Commons/Public Domain

22.1 Overview

As Kierkegaard was the first great theistic existential philosopher, so Nietzsche[1] was the first great atheistic one. Both were deliberately non-systematic opponents of Hegelian idealism, although neither read the other. As the former focused on the existential significance of subjective truth and

---

1 References to Nietzsche's writings will be to *The Philosophy of Nietzsche: Thus Spake Zarathustra* [trans. by Thomas Common], *Beyond Good and Evil* [trans. by Helen Zimmern], *The Genealogy of Morals* [trans. by Horace B. Samuel], *Ecce Homo* [trans. by Clifton P. Fadiman], [and] *The Birth of Tragedy* [trans. by Clifton P. Fadiman] (hereafter called *Philosophy*), by Friedrich Nietzsche (New York: The Modern Library, 1954), to *Selected Letters of Friedrich Nietzsche* (hereafter called *Letters*), ed. and trans. by Christopher Middleton (Indianapolis: Hackett, 1996), to *The Will to Power* (hereafter called *Power*), by Friedrich Nietzsche, trans. by Walter Kaufmann and R.J. Hollingdale, ed. by Walter Kaufmann (New York: Vintage Books, 1968), to *The Gay Science* (hereafter called

Modern European Philosophers, First Edition. Wayne P. Pomerleau.
© 2023 John Wiley & Sons, Inc. Published 2023 by John Wiley & Sons, Inc.

22 Friedrich Nietzsche

faith, the latter is skeptical regarding any universal truth or value. And, as was said at the end of a previous chapter, Nietzsche, along with Marx, is rightly considered one of the great nineteenth-century masters in the school of suspicion, questioning and doubting conventional ideas and ideals and calling for a culture-transforming "transvaluation of all values" (*Philosophy*, 911, 923).

22.2 Biography

Friedrich Wilhelm Nietzsche was born on October 15, 1844, in Röcken, Saxony (in Prussia), to Karl Ludwig Nietzsche, a Lutheran pastor and a Prussian loyalist, and Franziska Oehler Nietzsche, being named after King Friedrich Wilhelm IV of Prussia (*Philosophy*, 822). His sister, Elisabeth, was born in 1846 and outlived him; his brother, Joseph, was born in 1849. Later in 1849, Ludwig died, supposedly of a brain disease. Soon after that, Joseph died, and the family moved to Naumberg, where Nietzsche lived with his mother, sister, and three elderly female relatives. From 1858 to 1864, he studied on a scholarship at a prestigious boarding school at Pforta (which Fichte had attended), which was strong in languages (Latin, Greek, Hebrew, and French). There was some thought of his becoming a Lutheran cleric like his father, and he excelled in Christian theology (*Letters*, 47). He also began suffering the migraines that would haunt him for the rest of his life.

In 1864, he began studying classical philology (classical languages and literature) and theology at the University of Bonn. He came under the influence of a well-respected philologist named Friedrich Ritschl and, in 1865, followed him to the University of Leipzig. There he studied Feuerbach, lost his faith, quit theology, and discovered Schopenhauer's *World as Will and Idea*, which he found largely persuasive and which moved him toward the study of philosophy. The following year, he read a book on the history of materialism that also proved to be quite influential. In 1867–1868, he was in military service until a riding accident led to his withdrawing and returning to studies at Leipzig. In 1868, he met Richard Wagner at a party in Leipzig, and they discussed Schopenhauer together. Their relationship would, in time, become crucial to the young philologist (*Letters*, 10, 18, 31–32, 34, 39, 53, 65, 294).

In 1869, as a result of an enthusiastic recommendation from Ritschl, he was appointed as a philology professor at the University of Basel in Switzerland before even completing his doctoral requirements, and he renounced his Prussian citizenship. The next year, he was promoted to full professor. But the Franco-Prussian War broke out, and he served at the front as a medical orderly. This harrowing experience, of tending to the wounded, seems to have affected his previous pro-Prussian attitude and sympathetic view of war (*Letters*, 293, 67, 69). He soon contracted dysentery and diphtheria and had to be hospitalized. He returned to Basel, where he unsuccessfully applied for a chair in philosophy. In 1871, Germany was unified, and the Second German Reich was formed, Wilhelm I being crowned as its Kaiser and Otto von Bismarck becoming its first Chancellor; Germany defeated France the following month.

Meanwhile, Nietzsche was working on *The Birth of Tragedy*, which was published at the beginning of 1872. It was generally condemned by philologists (probably cementing his turn from philology

---

Science), by Friedrich Nietzsche, trans. by Walter Kaufmann (New York: Vintage Books, 1974), to *The Portable Nietzsche* (hereafter called *Portable*), trans. and ed. by Walter Kaufmann (New York: Viking Press, 1954), to *Daybreak*, by Friedrich Nietzsche, trans. by R.J. Hollingdale (Cambridge: Cambridge Univ. Press, 1982), to *Human, All Too Human* (hereafter called *Human*), by Friedrich Nietzsche, trans. by R.J. Hollingdale (Cambridge: Cambridge Univ. Press, 1986), and to *Untimely Meditations* (hereafter called *Meditations*), by Friedrich Nietzsche, trans. by R.J. Hollingdale, ed. by Daniel Breazeale (Cambridge: Cambridge Univ. Press, 1997).

to philosophy), though defended by Wagner. He became increasingly close to both Richard and Cosima Wagner, a devoted follower who referred to the great musician as his "Master" and "Father," running errands for them. In 1873 and 1874, he published the first three of his *Untimely Meditations* (on *David Strauss, the Confessor and the Writer*, *On the Uses and Disadvantages of History for Life*, and on *Schopenhauer as Educator*). In 1873, he wrote "On Truth and Lying in a Non-Moral Sense." In 1874, he was appointed dean of Basel's humanities faculty, but his relationship with Wagner was starting to deteriorate. In 1876, he published the fourth (final) one of his *Untimely Meditations* (called *Richard Wagner in Bayreuth*), which led to his break with Wagner (with whom he met for the last time that year). He was ill with severe migraines, eye pain, and serious stomach troubles, taking sick leave from his teaching. In 1877, he resumed teaching. The following year, he published *Human, All Too Human*, which finalized his split with Wagner, who publicly attacked him. In 1879, he resigned from the university for health reasons, being granted a small pension, allowing him to focus on his writings (*Letters*, 146, 149, 156, 188).

Near the end of 1879, he published *The Wanderer and His Shadow*, which would later become part of *Human, All Too Human*. In 1881, he published *Daybreak*, studied Spinoza, whom he admired, and began his seasonal moves back and forth between warm and cool climates. His eyesight got so bad that his handwriting became virtually illegible, and so, in 1882, he acquired a typewriter. It was about that time that he became attached to the idea of an eternal return. He met the highly intelligent Lou Andreas-Salomé, with whom he became infatuated and who rejected his proposals of marriage. That was also the year he published *The Gay Science*, announcing the death of God. He split with his mother and sister, who were scandalized by impressions of his relationship with Lou Salomé. In 1883 (the year Wagner died), he unsuccessfully sought a lectureship at Leipzig. That same year, he wrote and published the first part of *Thus Spake Zarathustra*, in 1884 the second and third parts, and in 1885 the fourth part. That last year, he met for the final time while sane with his sister Elisabeth. She married Bernhard Förster, an anti-Semitic nationalist whom Nietzsche disliked and who committed suicide in 1889. In 1886, Nietzsche published *Beyond Good and Evil* and announced *The Will to Power* as forthcoming, though it never was completed in his lifetime. In 1887, he discovered and admired the work of Russian novelist Fyodor Dostoyevsky and published *The Genealogy of Morals*. He prepared a second edition of *The Gay Science*, adding a fifth book and an appendix of poems to it. In 1888, he published *The Case of Wagner*. Georg Brandes, a professor at Copenhagen, gave a series of lectures on Nietzsche's philosophy; he also got Nietzsche interested in studying the works of Kierkegaard, although madness preempted the execution of that resolution. Also in 1888, Nietzsche wrote *The Twilight of the Idols*, *The Antichrist*, *Nietzsche contra Wagner*, and *Ecce Homo*. Toward the end of that productive year, however, his landlord became concerned about his bizarre behavior, and children were cruelly mocking him in the streets. Among other things, he was identifying himself with Caesar, with Christ, and with the god Dionysus (*Letters*, 239, 242, 194, 199, 283, 256, 260, 269, 327, 295, 297, 299, 302, 285, 315, 319, 324, 326, 344–346).

Then, at the beginning of 1889, he collapsed in the streets of Turin, where he was living, suffering a complete mental breakdown. There has been considerable (inconclusive) speculation about what caused his madness: perhaps manic depression turned psychotic, perhaps a brain tumor on or near his right optic nerve, or perhaps untreated syphilis. At any rate, there would be no recovery. He was committed to an insane asylum in Jena for over a year before being released. From May of 1890 he was with his mother in Naumberg until she died in April of 1897. Meanwhile, *Twilight of the Idols* and *Nietzsche contra Wagner* were published in 1889 and *The Antichrist* in 1894. Elisabeth, his sister, took it upon herself to establish a Nietzsche Archive in Naumberg in 1894, relocating it in Weimar a couple of years later. After their mother died, she moved him to Weimar as well. He

352 | *22 Friedrich Nietzsche*

died there, of pneumonia, on August 25, 1900; no autopsy was performed, and he was buried with his parents in Röcken. The following year, Elisabeth published some of his notes under the title of *The Will to Power*; three years later, she published a significantly expanded edition of it, as well as her biographical *Life of Friedrich Nietzsche*. In 1908, *Ecce Homo* was published. She lived until 1935.

Before we consider his philosophical ideas, a couple of observations are appropriate, in order to short-circuit cheap ways of dismissing them. While there is no doubt that he was insane from 1889 until he died, the writings of 1888 and earlier are not themselves insane. However, sometimes the rhetoric (e.g. of *The Antichrist* and *Ecce Homo*) is extreme enough to make us take notice; and the ideas themselves can be iconoclastic and potentially offensive. The second cheap way of dismissing his philosophy is to brand it as proto-Nazi. He was neither a nationalist nor a socialist; and he was outspokenly opposed to anti-Semitism. There is an infamous photograph of Adolf Hitler with Elisabeth and another of Hitler gently placing his hand on a bust of Nietzsche. In the animosity of world war, he became known as a "Nazi philosopher" in England and the United States. But all this is simply unfair to a fine philosopher, whose ideas should be considered for the imaginative and controversial explosion that they represent.

22.3 Knowledge

As we have repeatedly seen, modern philosophers tend to regard the theory of knowledge as foundational to any philosophical system. While Nietzsche is as opposed to systematizing his thoughts as was Kierkegaard, they, like those of their predecessors, can be cast into a system. But what makes Nietzsche more radical than Kierkegaard – or, for that matter, than any of the modern thinkers we have considered – is his cynical attitude toward truth itself. The very first sentence of the first part of *Beyond Good and Evil* calls into question "the famous Truthfulness of which all philosophers have hitherto spoken with respect." He admits that we naturally seek truth but raises doubts about whether we should be guided by this old prejudice: "Granted that we want the truth: *why not rather* untruth?" Why should we not acknowledge that falsehoods can, in certain circumstances, be more beneficial than truth? Nietzsche urges us to "*recognize untruth as a condition of life*" and thus valuable. So from the outset we see this iconoclast anticipating both postmodernism's refusal to revere the truth and pragmatism's emphasis on meaningfulness and practical value. So many modern philosophers have tried to press us into subscribing to their alleged "immediate certainties" – including Descartes with his "I think," Kant with his "Table of Categories," and Schopenhauer with his "I will." But, in Nietzsche's opinion, none of them makes a compelling case. Rather, such claims to indubitable knowledge are monstrous exaggerations that tend to precipitate the cognitive vacuity of skepticism regarding everything. Nietzsche realizes that he too must beware of adopting the sort of dogmatism that invites nihilism: "He who fights with monsters should be careful lest he thereby become a monster. And if thou gaze long into an abyss, the abyss will also gaze into thee." Nevertheless, he is unrestrained and blunt in castigating his modern predecessors, who are obsessed with epistemology: "Philosophy reduced to a 'theory of knowledge' is no more in fact than a diffident science . . . that is, philosophy in its last throes, . . . something that awakens pity." (As we shall see, he does not admire pity.) Like Kierkegaard, he has little regard for objectivity and "disinterested knowledge." But neither should true philosophy be reduced to mere criticism, as he thinks Kant, "the great Chinaman of Königsberg," tried to do. Rather it should be expressing the "*Will to Power*" by serving to create a better future (*Philosophy*, 381, 384, 391, 397, 466, 500–501, 504, 513–515).

If there is a single sentence from all of Nietzsche's writings that best reflects postmodern thought rather than modernism, it is this one from *The Will to Power* (a compilation of entries from his notebooks) in response to positivism's claim that nothing exists but facts: "No, facts is precisely what there is not, only interpretations." It is one thing for him to deny objective truth as the agreement of beliefs or statements with the facts of reality; after all, how could we even know that such agreement obtains? But it is even more radical to deny that there are any facts for our beliefs and statements possibly to agree with. Nietzsche denies that reality has any objective "meaning," holding that it only has "countless meanings" that are subjective. He calls this view of his "Perspectivism" (*Power*, 267). In *The Genealogy of Morals*, he writes, "There is only a seeing from a perspective, only a 'knowing' from a perspective" (*Philosophy*, 745). The modern philosophers we have studied would be appalled by this.

In *The Gay Science*, Nietzsche speculates that, over time, useful beliefs emerged and were preserved out of an ongoing series of errors, many of which proved useless. "Such erroneous articles of faith" which proved beneficial and thus have stood the test of time "include the following: that there are enduring things; that there are equal things; that there are things, substances, bodies; that a thing is what it appears to be; that our will is free; that what is good for me is also good in itself," etc. We come to embrace such beliefs as our truths and claim to know them. Philosophers and scientists tend to anoint them as objective certainties; but when they no longer seem to further life and power, we tend to modify or abandon them in favor of those that appear to serve us better. The same sort of genealogy allegedly applies to what we regard as logical and illogical, as well as to claims of causal connection. Also, what is familiar is comfortable and, thus, more likely to be regarded as true (*Science*, 169–173, 301–302; see also *Portable*, 46–47, for more on this view that "truths are illusions about which one has forgotten that this is what they are").

But in *Daybreak*, he raises the suspicion that accepting a belief merely because we are used to it can "be dishonest, cowardly, lazy" (*Daybreak*, 59). In *Human, All Too Human*, he warns us, "Convictions are more dangerous enemies of truth than lies" (*Human*, 179). After all, beliefs we have embraced seductively invite ongoing attachment despite counterevidence. Historical knowledge of the past, as he says in his *Untimely Meditations*, may or may not be valuable, depending on how we can use it to improve the present and the future. Something comparable can be said for any philosophical theory: "The only critique of a philosophy that is possible and that proves something" consists of "trying to see whether one can live in accordance with it" (*Meditations*, 77, 116, 187).

In *Twilight of the Idols*, Nietzsche challenges the assumption that all knowledge is good and, thus, also desirable: "I want, once and for all, *not* to know many things. Wisdom sets limits to knowledge too." He is also suspicious of people – philosophers and otherwise – who insist on systematizing knowledge. Likewise, the commitment to "rationality at any price," even to the point of denying natural instinct, is diagnosed as a disease. Our intellectual claims to causal knowledge are particularly susceptible to various sorts of errors, which he analyzes (*Portable*, 467, 470, 479, 492, 494, 496, 499). In all of this exploration of his "perspectivism," we see a deep, critical distrust of epistemology as it has been developed by modern philosophers, including those we have been studying.

22.4 Reality

Nietzsche's ontology is consonant with his epistemology but fairly thin. He does not generally hold that we can know reality as it is in itself. Like Kant, he tends to think that our views on reality are functions of the phenomenal appearances we experience. In *The Gay Science*, he criticizes even the presumption "that the universe is a machine," as attributing such order and purpose to it "does it far too much honor." The world rather seems ultimately to be chaos, despite our anthropomorphic characterizations of it. Trying to make sense of the chaos, we posit interacting bodies, causal connections, content and form, etc. as "articles of faith" that help us to cope. Even consciousness itself, which "is in the main *superfluous*" may well have no purpose in itself. He describes his position here as "phenomenalism and perspectivism." Even Kant's distinction between "thing-in-itself" and phenomenal appearances presupposes too much. Nevertheless, he does attempt a curious thought experiment designed to ask us, if we had a chance to live our same lives innumerable times more, would we be willing to do so, thus affirming our existence? Here we have an anticipation of his theory of eternal recurrence (*Science*, 167–168, 177, 297, 299–300, 273–274; for a critique of Kant's dualism of "appearance" and "thing-in-itself," see *Power*, 300 and 451; for more on eternal recurrence, see *Power*, 549).

In *Thus Spake Zarathustra*, Nietzsche floats the idea that all of life expresses itself as "Will to Power" – a modification of Schopenhauer's "Will to Life." He also renews his advocacy of a theory that all reality might "eternally return." Ultimately, as he posits in *Beyond Good and Evil*, he holds that the touchstone of all "reality" is revealed by our own impulses, passions, and desires. And he hopes to be able to show that these ultimately reduce to the *"Will to Power"* as fundamental (*Philosophy*, 124–125, 174, 247–248, 421–423). Like so many philosophers before him, in *Twilight of the Idols*, he distinguishes between being and becoming, maintaining that we only have access to the latter and not to the former. He agrees with the pre-Socratic Heraclitus that "being is an empty fiction. The 'apparent' world is the only one," and it is one of perpetual becoming. He traces the development of the error that a world of being is the "true world" in six stages: first, Platonism assures us that the sage actually inhabits that world; second, Christianity promises access to it in the afterlife; third, Kantians say it is unattainable but gives rise to the imperatives of moral duty; fourth, positivism holds that, being unattainable, it cannot be the source of any obligation; fifth, anti-metaphysicians aver that it is a "useless and superfluous" idea that should be abolished; and, sixth, his own realistic view is that with the abolition of a world of stable being, the very idea of an apparent world itself becomes meaningless (*Portable*, 479–481, 484–486). By the end of his career, Nietzsche has not only become anti-metaphysical but repudiates all metaphysics as useless.

22.5   God

Not only is Nietzsche an atheist, but his atheism is important to his philosophy, as it removes a basis for the absolute truths and values of which he is so wary. In *The Gay Science*, he proclaims (in his most famous three words) that "God is dead." However, he warns, God's shadow survives in the form of churches, dogmas, and believers, and "we still have to vanquish his shadow." And, indeed, he is committed to that mission. He tells a story of a "madman" who is searching high and low for God, to the amusement of those around him. The madman nevertheless cries out, "God is dead. God remains dead. And we have killed him." But how could we possibly kill God? By ceasing to believe in or to have any use for him. But the madman concludes that the time is not yet ripe for delivering his message. He forces his way "into several churches" lamenting the loss of God and is heard to say, "What after all are these churches now if they are not the tombs and sepulchers of God?" (*Science*, 167, 181–182). How should we interpret this parable, except that the symbol of God has increasingly become meaningless? As a historical note, we might recall that, even though Nietzsche is famous for this claim that God is dead, Hegel used the same phrase (taken from a Lutheran hymn) in an attempt to bury obsolete anthropomorphic conceptions of God.

Likewise, Zarathustra bears witness "that *God is dead!*" The idea of God is a mere "conjecture," but one that is not even "conceivable." A very bad argument is presented to support atheism: "*if* there were gods, how could I endure it to be no God! *Therefore* there are no gods." This non sequitur is probably Nietzsche being playful. As someone who has little use for pity, he claims (perhaps, again, playfully) that God died "of his pity for man." Nietzsche's hostility against idealism targets not only philosophers such as Plato and Kant, but also Christianity, which he considers Platonism for the masses. The notions of a God who is "father," "judge," and "rewarder" have allegedly been debunked. *Beyond Good and Evil* holds that modern philosophy itself, while not necessarily opposed to all religion, skeptically undermines Christianity. Nietzsche's animus against religion in general and Christianity in particular has to do with the vetoing of natural desires and joys, with the call for self-denial and even self-stultification, as we see in *The Genealogy of Morals*. Truthfulness, which is required by Christian ethics, forces us to recognize that Christian doctrine is nonsense. But that same "Christian truthfulness" will also force us to abandon Christian morality itself as bankrupt (*Philosophy*, 6, 90–91, 96, 378, 439, 759, 791–792; cf. *Power*, 117, 126).

Nietzsche saves his most blistering and sustained attack, however, for *The Antichrist*. He believes that both Christian religion and Christian ethics are utterly out of touch with reality. They deal in such sheer illusions as "God," "spirit," "souls," "free will," "sin," "grace," "redemption," and so forth. Even our dream worlds reflect our waking reality, while Christianity creates and peddles a *"world of pure fiction"* to systematically deceive us. It denigrates and disparages the natural world of the body, as if making a "declaration of war against life, against nature, against the will to live!" It tries to tame and civilize us by condemning our natural desires and weakening our instincts. The entire Judeo-Christian ethic is a slave "morality of *ressentiment*" – resentful hostility against whatever is strong and noble. Priests are cunning parasites, enlarging their own power by poisoning all that is natural. Nietzsche maintains that Christ himself was the only true Christian, his presumptive followers deviating from the lifestyle he practiced for their own selfish ends. He denies not only the existence of God but even the worthiness of the Judeo-Christian conception of God. He concludes his own declaration of war thus: "I call Christianity the one great curse, the one great innermost corruption, the one great instinct of revenge, for which no means is poisonous, stealthy, subterranean, *small* enough – I call it the one immortal blemish of mankind" (*Portable*, 581–582, 585–586, 590, 593–594, 597, 612, 627, 656).

22.6 Humanity

Even though Nietzsche's first important publication, *The Birth of Tragedy*, is a work in aesthetics or the philosophy of art rather than one of the philosophy of human nature, its key distinction between the rationally ordered Apollonian dimension of art and a spontaneous, ecstatic Dionysian dimension of will reflects a duality in the human person. (This distinction exhibits the influence of Schopenhauer's dualism of the world as representation and the world as will on Nietzsche.) Ancient Greek sculpture represents the former, Greek music represents the latter, and Greek tragedy represents a coherent synthesis of the two (*Philosophy*, 951, 978, 990, 1033–1034). A successful human being must find a way to balance Apollonian reason and Dionysian will. A life of either extreme at the expense of the other would be either sterile or chaotic. While modern philosophy generally encourages a systematic, rationally ordered lifestyle, in *The Gay Science*, Nietzsche encourages us "to *live dangerously*." But our thinking is important to protect us against self-destructive impulses. He holds that we are continually thinking "without knowing it; the thinking that rises to *consciousness* is only the smallest part of all this – the most superficial" part, indeed (*Science*, 228, 298–299). Here he seems to anticipate Freud's emphasis on the importance of the subconscious.

22 Friedrich Nietzsche

In *Beyond Good and Evil*, we read that psychologists (as well as Schopenhauer) are mistaken in viewing self-preservation as any organism's root concern: "A living thing seeks above all to *discharge* its strength – life itself is *Will to Power*; self-preservation is only one of the indirect and most frequent *results* thereof." Another of its consequences is the drive to be in charge of our own lives. However, few living things can be truly "independent; it is a privilege of the strong." Nietzsche does not seem to need the agreement of others to such unorthodox views. Indeed, he seems to exhibit some pride in being out of the mainstream, writing, "My opinion is *my* opinion: another person has not easily a right to it." He embraces the iconoclastic heterodoxy of "free spirits" or what he also designates as "philosophers of the future." He is willing to defend violence, slavery, predation, and other things commonly considered "wicked" as potentially elevating humanity – or, at least, a portion of it – to a superior level. On the other hand, he warns against the "*universal degeneracy of mankind*" called for by egalitarians, "socialistic fools and shallow-pates," reducing us all to the same stunted, inferior level. Like Kierkegaard (and, for that matter, like Mill), he opposes our becoming like sheep, forever bleating with the rest of the flock. Nor does he favor equality for women; indeed, he is quite negative in viewing woman as disingenuous and superficial, saying that "her great art is falsehood, her chief concern is appearance and beauty." He favors a hierarchical set of interpersonal relations, often advocating what he calls "the *pathos of distance*." Superior people should utilize and even exploit their superiority without being held back by conventional values, recognizing what is natural – namely, that "life itself is *essentially* appropriation, injury, conquest of the strange and weak, suppression," and so forth. The values of superior people *ought* to differ from those of the inferior. "There is *master-morality* and *slave-morality*" (as will be further discussed below), and "egoism" is appropriate for those who are superior (*Philosophy*, 395, 414, 422–423, 427–430, 497, 540–541, 575–582, 590).

Against most Western philosophers before him, Nietzsche insists that human nature is not fixed and an eternal given but exists in a natural process of constant change; "there are *no eternal facts*, just as there are no absolute truths," he writes (*Human*, 12–13). And, ultimately, the goal toward which we should be directing this change is not what now passes as humanity, but rather the "*overman*" (Übermensch) that is yet to be (*Power*, 519). This takes us to Zarathustra, a sort of prophet preparing the way. Mankind as it is must "be surpassed" by the overman, who is called "the meaning of the earth." Present-day man is seen as intermediate between brute animals and the overman. The naturally superior person must use that superiority to realize his potential, answering the personal mandate, "Become what thou art" (*Philosophy*, 6, 8, 265). Thus far, it may seem that Nietzsche is influenced by Darwinian evolutionary theory.

It is obvious that strength – not so much physical as intellectual and psychological – is important to Nietzsche. One of his most famous aphorisms (from *Twilight of the Idols*) avers, "What does not destroy me makes me stronger." From this perspective, challenge and even adversity represent positive opportunities for self-development. Life should be all about a sense of purpose (as for Kierkegaard) and certainly not about the mere pursuit of pleasure or the denial of one's own natural instincts and passions. There is no reason for our existence, which is merely a given matter of brute facticity. Nor is there any predetermined purpose for life, no meaning other than that we ourselves create. Against Darwin, Nietzsche holds that the weak tend to gang up on the strong and subdue them, rather than the fittest prevailing. The strong must pursue their own self-interest and not be gulled by pity or the bogus values of altruism (*Portable*, 467–468, 479, 486–487, 489–490, 500, 522–523, 533–536, 540). All of this, of course, runs counter to the mainstream of modern philosophy since at least the Enlightenment.

22.7 Freedom

According to Nietzsche, human thought and action are determined by will. But the distinction between free and unfree will is phony, as both allegedly are mere fictions. The relevant distinction is, rather, between strong and weak will. He believes in the sort of individuality and autonomy that might allow us to "*become those we are*" – that is, to realize our potential, as is made clear in *The Gay Science*. He admires and supports superior "human beings who are new, unique, incomparable, who give themselves laws, who create themselves," as opposed to the mediocre masses that merely conform to the lifestyle of some herd. But he has no use whatsoever for "the superstition of free will" (*Science*, 266, 285). What we call "freedom of the will," as he explains in *Beyond Good and Evil*, is nothing more than a feeling of being in command and the delight we tend to derive from that feeling, whether or not it is anchored in reality. But the notion that the will could ever be self-caused (or what Kant called self-determined) is preposterous. Likewise, the contrary idea of a "non-free will" is nothing more than "mythology; in real life it is only a question of *strong* and *weak* wills" (*Philosophy*, 400–401, 403–404). *Twilight of the Idols* contains a short subsection, "*The error of free will*," which maintains that the concept and doctrine were created by theologians and religious leaders to saddle the masses with a sense of responsibility and feelings of guilt, "*dependent upon them*" for forgiveness: "Men were considered 'free' so that they might be judged and punished – so that they might become *guilty*" (*Portable*, 499). Here we see the will to power over others in action.

Not only is the notion of something's being self-caused nonsense. But Nietzsche (more radically than Hume) denies causality itself. As he writes in *The Will to Power*, "There is no such thing as 'cause'; some cases in which it seemed to be given to us, and in which we have projected it out of ourselves in order to understand an event, have been shown to be self-deceptions." We do not understand why something occurs; but we want to understand, being driven to concoct some cause, either outside or within ourselves. But he rejects determinism as well as free will as just another myth camouflaging our ignorance: "Necessity is not a fact but an interpretation," and a groundless one at that. So moralists who claim that happiness is a function of virtue, which is a function of the use of free will, have purportedly missed the mark. Nietzsche does not deny that we desire freedom but holds that this desire is merely one of the "*disguised* forms of the will to power." This desire for freedom is particularly blatant "among the oppressed, among slaves of all kinds" – those who are forced to obey and try to please others. He writes, "One desires *freedom* so long as one does not possess power. Once one does possess it, one desires to overpower; if one cannot do that (if one is still too weak to do so), one desires '*justice*,' i.e., *equal power*" (*Power*, 295–297, 375, 406–407, 412). But if we strip away the veneer of superficial appearances, it is all about the will to power.

22.8 Morality

Nietzsche's ethics of two opposed moralities stems from his denial of objective absolutes. Among the most controversial (indeed, for many of us, even shocking) features of his ethical theory is this idea that, instead of there being a single universal, absolute morality, there are two mutually opposed moralities that are relative to the power people can exercise. We have already seen pieces of this theory and can now put them together to constitute a more complete picture. As we proceed, we might well notice how it is fundamentally at odds with earlier modern ethical theories we have already considered.

As early as *Human, All Too Human*, Nietzsche was trying to track the evolution of popular morality. A first stage was the use of "*fear* and *hope*" to enforce codes of behavior that will promote the stability and security of the community (this may be reminiscent of Hobbes). A further stage attributes prescriptions and prohibitions to the divine (as with the Mosaic law). A stage beyond this places the source of "unconditional duty" in alleged rational imperatives (Kant is an example of this). Finally comes a morality of genuine "*insight*," which would presumably be Nietzsche's own theory (*Human*, 321–322). All of this is exploratory, with a more settled view yet to come. In *Daybreak*, he presents his own alternative to the four Platonic "cardinal virtues." The ones he advocates are (i) honesty toward ourselves and our friends; (ii) courage in dealing with enemies; (iii) magnanimity toward those who have been defeated; and (iv) politeness toward everyone (*Daybreak*, 224). In *The Gay Science*, he observes that instincts condemned as "evil" by conventional morality, such as British utilitarianism, "are expedient, species-preserving, and indispensable." But these qualities should be interpreted in a thoroughgoing naturalistic manner; as such, unlike Kant's categorical imperative, they will not lead to fantastic notions, such as God, free souls, and immortality (*Science*, 79, 264). Thus we stay firmly grounded rather than embarking on metaphysical flights of fancy as so many others have done.

As Nietzsche indicates in *Thus Spake Zarathustra*, in order to create a new set of values, the established, conventional one of "good and evil" must first be undermined, which is his agenda. "Nothing is true," Zarathustra observes, so that "all is permitted," opening the door to a radically new set of values. But this is not merely a matter of seeking one's own well-being. Zarathustra advocates working for a cause as preferable; and his cause is the rise of the overman, the superior person of the future. Nor should we be seduced by the Stoic's ideal of living "according to Nature," as Nietzsche argues in *Beyond Good and Evil*. Meaningful living involves exercising the will to power by striving against Nature, which must be conquered. We should feel free to create our own values, since there are no "moral phenomena, but only a moral interpretation of phenomena." European morality near the end of the nineteenth century is allegedly nothing more than "*herding-morality*"; and it pretends to be universally applicable as the only genuine morality. "Free spirits" who are opposed to it, from a conventional perspective, are considered "Immoralists." Nevertheless, they are "men of duty," obliged to fight for their own ideals (*Philosophy*, 125–126, 305, 368, 388–389, 459, 494, 530–531).

These various jabs at conventional ethics and exploratory moves toward a "transvaluation of all values" lead us to the striking theory of *The Genealogy of Morals*. Powerful, aristocratic people, purportedly aware of the "pathos of distance" between themselves and the masses, "arrogated the right to create values for their own profit, and to coin the names of such values," establishing the "antithesis of good and bad." Whatever was characteristic of superiority, nobility, and aristocracy was labeled "good"; whatever was characteristic of inferiority, mediocrity, and vulgarity was labeled "bad." Inferior people, resentful over their subordination to the powerful, launched "a radical transvaluation of values," calling "good" whatever was characteristic of themselves and what was characteristic of aristocrats "evil." Thus, when Nietzsche identifies himself and "free spirits" as "beyond good and evil," he is referring to a revolt against mass morality and a return to an aristocratic ethic. Certain religions, such as Judaism and Christianity, preach against this initiative and attempt to squelch it. This is what Nietzsche calls "slave-morality," as opposed to master-morality. "The revolt of the slaves in morals begins in the very principle of *resentment* becoming creative and giving birth to values," he claims. Where masters naturally exploit the weak, slaves, oppressed as they realize they are, advocate sympathy and pity for the downtrodden, such as themselves. "It is not surprising that the lambs should bear a grudge against the great birds of prey, but that is no reason for blaming the great birds of prey for taking the little lambs." Notice that, for this analogy to be credible, the denial of free will is needed, leaving instinct as our motivating force. So these two sets of values – "good and bad" versus "good and evil" – are mutually opposed to each other. Slave-morality also "invented the 'bad conscience'" as an indoctrinated tool for repressing whatever it regards as "evil." But it is pathological, a sickness of the spirit, spread and fed by popular religion, as a result of which the world has become "a mad-house" (*Philosophy*, 911, 923, 634–637, 643–647, 651, 655–657, 663, 701–703, 706, 712) of topsy-turvy, artificial, toxic values.

Twilight of the Idols and *The Antichrist* carry this full frontal attack to an increasingly vehement level. The first of these books, which Nietzsche calls "a great declaration of war," lambastes ancient Greek ethics, which argues that happiness results from virtue, which is achieved by following reason against our natural instincts. By contrast, his own "naturalism" respects our natural instincts and advocates living accordingly. It is foolish to imagine that there is a single pattern that all good people must adopt, and "immoralists" do well to argue for a diversity of lifestyles. But, of course, this requires their taking a stand "*beyond* good and evil" and recognizing that "*there are altogether no moral facts*" that are already given as objective. The worth of a morality for any individual is relative to its facilitating his or her will to power in a productive manner; "in itself, no morality has any value," he claims. For example, one based on the equality of all persons or on Kant's dignity of all or Schopenhauer's "morality of pity" might serve the vested interests of the weak; but, from Nietzsche's perspective, that sort of thing is indicative of sheer "decadence" (*Portable*, 466, 478, 489–491, 501, 539–540).

He, of course, is committed to the master-morality based on the distinction between good and bad, in which "good" is what enhances power and feeling powerful, and "bad" is what is rooted in weakness, as he notes in *The Antichrist*. Thus happiness is not what moralists from Plato through Mill have thought but is, rather, the sustained feeling of increasing power and the overcoming of resistance. All of this, needless to say, is opposed to popular religion, in general, and to Christianity, in particular. Kantian ethics, with its trumpeting of an alleged "categorical imperative," merely expresses Christian ethics in philosophical form. Nietzsche ends this "eternal indictment of Christianity" and slave-morality by crying out for what he is espousing, "Revaluation of all values" (*Portable*, 570, 572–575, 577, 642, 656).

Let us conclude this section by briefly examining a few passages from *The Will to Power*. There Nietzsche observes that other philosophers, whether "in the Kantian or in the Hegelian" tradition or otherwise, all "*believe* in morality" and use their philosophical systems to try to justify it. By contrast, he uses philosophy to attack any supposedly objective, universal morality. It is not just that no human actions can be conclusively demonstrated to be moral (as even Kant seems to acknowledge). "*There are no moral actions whatsoever*: they are completely imaginary," he claims. Second, the illusion that there is a real distinction between "moral" and "immoral" human actions presupposes another false assumption, that we are capable of acts of "free spontaneity," without which responsibility would be nullified. So Nietzsche's ethical relativism views all moral values as functions of our natural will to power. This puts him at odds with the modern philosophers we have studied and, perhaps, closer to Machiavelli, with whom he seems to identify to some extent (*Power*, 223, 413, 407, 488).

22.9 Society

Whereas his philosophy addresses issues of morality extensively, his views on society tend to be brief and scattered. We may recall that, due to his short involvement in the Franco-Prussian War, he went from being a German nationalist who supported Bismarck to being a European transnationalist opposed to Bismarck's bellicose international policies. In *Human, All Too Human*, he writes that "one should not be afraid to proclaim oneself simply a *good European* and actively to work for the amalgamation of nations." This idea of merging nations to form a

22 Friedrich Nietzsche

pan-European supernation is one we have not previously encountered here. Nietzsche does not discuss politics much in his writings. But he was politically conservative, opposed to both socialism and democracy. Nations with armies pitted against each other, even when not actively fighting, are braced for war, and Nietzsche seems to favor mutual disarmament as "the means to *real* peace." He favors the preservation of private property and opposes both enforced egalitarianism and the transition to community ownership (*Human*, 174–175, 380–381, 384). All of this, of course, is a reaction against socialistic and democratic movements and increasing nationalism and international aggression.

Thus Spake Zarathustra expresses contempt for states that pretend they are representing "the people" in their policies, institutions, and programs. Where state power stops, individual excellence can emerge. Also modern "preachers of equality" lie about our natural condition and threaten the rise of the overman with their attempts at social leveling. "For men are *not* equal," Zarathustra proclaims (*Philosophy*, 49, 52, 108, 138, 320). It is easier to identify what Nietzsche opposes in political society than to get a very developed theory he advocates. Among his favorite targets is socialism, which his *Will to Power* brands as "the *tyranny* of the least and the dumbest, i.e., those who are superficial, envious" levelers. He attacks the doctrines of "equal rights and universal suffrage," which were threatening to gain traction. But what alternative does he favor and support? He answers in a single word, "aristocracy" (*Power*, 77, 396, 493), the rule of the best people, those superior in power.

A passage in *Twilight of the Idols* condemns liberalism of the sort advocated by Bentham and Mill, branding it "herd-animalization," leveling members of society in pursuit of equality. It fraudulently passes itself off as a driver of freedom but forces its own values on others. "Liberal institutions cease to be liberal as soon as they are attained," he complains. They also try to pass themselves off as engines of social progress; but, needless to say, their conception of progress differs widely from Nietzsche's. Christianity is characterized as an ally of liberalism's in advocating "equal rights for all," according to *The Antichrist*, catering to "the *ressentiment* of the masses" and constantly threatening to erode the natural "*pathos of distance*" among people. Nietzsche thinks every society can be analyzed as comprising three unequal classes (reminiscent of Plato): the highest and smallest class consists of those who are spiritually preeminent; second, there are "those who are preeminently strong in muscle and temperament"; and, third, there are the mediocre masses who excel in nothing but their numbers. These three classes constitute "a pyramid" (as for Plato), with a huge base as the lowest class, a much smaller intermediate class, and a tiny upper class of aristocrats, who are fit to rule (*Portable*, 541, 552–553, 619, 645–646). So Nietzsche's critique of actual Western society and the alternative of which he is a champion are consonant with his critique of Western morality and the alternative he favors.

22.10 Review

Nietzsche has exerted considerable influence on contemporary philosophy, particularly on such existentialists as Martin Heidegger and Karl Jaspers. From the perspective of modern philosophy, he is important for the combination of his unsparing critique of modernism and its values, on the one hand, and his strikingly imaginative trailblazing, on the other. The aspects of his philosophy that are particularly exciting and controversial also undercut basic commitments of modernists – to fact and objective truth, to some stable dimension of reality, to something more than a dogmatic atheism, to humanity as essentially rational, to some sense of freedom and responsibility that is more than an illusory feeling, to a single morality or at least ground of morality, and to an ideal of a healthy society that treats all its citizens with decent respect rather than institutionalizing power relationships. Perhaps the greatest philosophical flaw in his thought, however, is that he offers us virtually nothing in the way of cogent argumentation for any of his contrarian views. So, while it is understandable that his ideas represent a bold and potentially fascinating perspective, he gives us no good reason to believe them. Yet he lived and worked in the modern period and was in critical dialogue with modern predecessors. Thus he belongs in our study of modern European philosophers, even if he is the last of the great ones.

Conclusion

The European philosophies of these three centuries (from Descartes's early writings in the 1620s to Nietzsche's death in 1900) constitute a rich canon of texts defining a dialectical development of thought. The seventeenth century and first eight decades of the eighteenth feature an ongoing antithetical dialogue between rationalists and empiricists. With Kant's attempt at synthesizing those opposing systems, a third movement of German idealism gets underway in the late eighteenth and early nineteenth centuries. Finally, following Hegel's death, we see a wide-ranging number of anti-idealist alternatives arising during the last seven decades of the nineteenth century. The glue that holds all this together and makes it modern (in contrast to earlier periods) is its focus on the individual thinker as the subject of experience, belief, knowledge, and action.

For all 21 thinkers we have considered in depth (seven from each of the three centuries), we have set forth their positions and reasoning regarding seven most important, recurring central topics: knowledge, reality, God, humanity, freedom, morality, and society. These common seven planks in each philosopher's platform represent significant facets of their systems of thought and allow for both a study of influence and comparative analysis. In addition to these giants of modern philosophy, there were women philosophers in Europe, who are generally less famous and influential, whose work was largely ignored or even lost, and who (as far as we know) did not create comprehensive systems of thought, but who are nevertheless worthy of our recognition. Nine such have been considered here, in concluding sections of chapters on philosophers with whom they can be compared and/or contrasted.

While these 21 major philosophers have not proved to be all equally significant, each one individually has had some impact on contemporary theories; and collectively they represent a monumental intellectual legacy. This constitutes the background out of which such recent philosophies as existentialism, pragmatism, phenomenology, analytic philosophy, postmodernism, and process philosophy have emerged. By coming to understand these roots, we can better grasp the fruits. Just as the history of philosophy does not begin with Descartes, so it does not end with Nietzsche. Like all human thought, it is constantly developing. Presumably, this will remain the case for as long as we continue to wonder about ourselves, our origin, our destiny, our beliefs, our values, our social structures, and our world. By studying such systems of thought, we can avoid having to start from scratch in our own thinking. Thus we can see further than we would otherwise be able to do, in the words of Isaac Newton, "by standing upon the shoulders of giants."

Modern European Philosophers, First Edition. Wayne P. Pomerleau.
© 2023 John Wiley & Sons, Inc. Published 2023 by John Wiley & Sons, Inc.

Index

a

Abraham story 346–347
"Abridgement of the Argument Reduced to Syllogistic Form" (Leibniz) 116, 123–124
Act, intentional 230
Actuality, principle of 8
Addresses to the German Nation (Fichte) 239, 251
"Affirmative action" 328
Afterlife, religious belief and 228–229
Agent(s)
  of liberal change 325
  "Necessary Agent" 152
  sentient 228
  supernatural 316
Agnosticism 11, 56, 135
Agreements
  international 329
  society and 47
Albert the Great 15
Alexander the Great 10, 17
Alienation 303
  in Feuerbach 290
  Hegelian concept of 290
  in Marx 303–304
The Analogy of Religion (Butler) 146, 147, 148, 149, 151, 152, 154
Anarchism, theorist of 256
Anarchy 48
Anaxagoras 6
Ancient philosophy 4–12
Animal instincts 150, 324

Anselm 12, 14–15, 27
Anthropology from a Pragmatic Point of View (Kant) 199, 201, 209–210
Anti-Cartesianism 95, 102
The Antichrist (Nietzsche) 351, 352, 355, 359, 360
Anti-Climacus (pseudonym) 341, 344, 345
Anti-idealism 295
Anti-idealist alternatives 1
Antiphon 6
Antisocial wrongdoing 283
Aphorisms 55, 59, 356
Apology for the Christian Religion (Pascal) 53
Apperception 120, 121
Aquinas, Thomas 15–16, 42
  "just war" 16
  "natural law" 16
  virtue ethics 16
Aristes (the student) 81, 82, 85, 87
Aristocracy 9, 48, 76
Aristotelian–Thomistic scholasticism 22, 25
Aristotle 5, 8–9, 42
  acorn's final cause 228
  god and 9
  primary and secondary substances 8
  Sophists and 6
  speculative philosophy of 8
  in triumvirate 5
Arnauld, Antoine 53, 59, 80, 81, 115, 116, 119, 125, 181
The Art of War (Machiavelli) 17
"Asceticism, principle of" 232
The Assayer (Galileo) 19

Modern European Philosophers, First Edition. Wayne P. Pomerleau.
© 2023 John Wiley & Sons, Inc. Published 2023 by John Wiley & Sons, Inc.

364 | *Index*

Ataraxia (tranquility)   10, 18
  skepticism and   11
Atheism   85, 87, 142, 270, 289, 354–355
  charges of   239, 254, 263
  empirical   285
  Feuerbach and   292, 293, 294, 295
  Hobbes and   42–43
  irreligion referred to as   138
  Marx and   296, 297, 302, 308
  materialism and   135
  meaningful   244
  need for   302
  pantheism and   255, 291
  Spinozism and   56
  "true atheism"   291
Atomism, corpuscularianism   19
Atomists   6
Attack upon "Christendom." (Kierkegaard)   336,
  340, 342
Attempt at a Critique of All Revelation
  (Fichte)   239
Auguste Comte and Positivism (Mill)   317–318
Augustine   13
Augustinianism   80
Austin, John   226
Autobiography (Mill)   312, 314
"Automatons"   31, 321
Autonomy, principle of   215–216, 247
Avicenna   12
Awareness, perception and   65

b

Bacon, Francis   18–19
  "end of knowledge is power"   39
  "idols"   19
  inductive reasoning and   315
Bakunin, Michael   256
"Barbarians"   12, 17
"Bear and forbear" rule   10
Becoming, unity and   258
Behemoth (Hobbes)   38
Being, pure   258
Belief, disbelief and   316
Benevolence   150
Bentham, Jeremy   224–236, 310
  biography   225–226
  "disappointment-preventing principle"   234

ethical model, critique of   233–234
  freedom   230–231
  God   228–229
  hedonism and   227
  humanity   229–230
  "junction-of-interests-prescribing
    principle"   234
  knowledge   226–227
  morality   231–234
  as nominalist   226
  "paraphrasis" technique of   226–227
  "principle of utility"   229
  pseudonym of   228
  reality   227–228
  sanctions   232, 233
  society   234–236
  theory of fictions   227
  utilitarianism of   235–236, 321
  utilitarian movement founder   225
  utilitarian theory   220, 267
Benthamism   311, 323
Benthamites   311, 313, 322
Berkeley, George   130–144, 138, 139
  biography   131–132
  freedom   141
  God   138–140
  humanity   140–141
  idealism   131
  immaterialism of   133, 134, 136, 137, 143
  knowledge   132–134
  morality   142–143
  reality   134–138
  society   143
  writings of   131, 132
"Berne Fragments" (Hegel)   261
Bérulle (Cardinal)   80
Beyond Good and Evil (Nietzsche)   351, 352,
  354, 355, 356, 357, 358
The Birth of Tragedy (Nietzsche)   350, 355
Bismarck, Otto   251
Blackstone, William   225, 226
Blake, William   196
Boethius, Anicius Manlius Severinus   14
Bourgeoisie society   301, 304, 305, 307, 308
Bowring, John   226
Brain. *See also* Human mind, pineal gland in
  29–30, 49, 89

Index | 365

Bramhall (Bishop)   38, 43, 45
Browning, Robert   277
Buddhism   273, 277, 278
Butler, Joseph   145–154
  biography   146
  freedom   152
  God   148–149
  humanity   149–151
  knowledge   147
  morality   152–153
  reality   147
  society   153–154

C

Caesar, Julius   11, 119, 125, 137
Candide (Voltaire)   122
Capitalism   303, 305
  problem with   306
Capitalist system   328
Capital punishment   235, 314, 328–329
"Capital Punishment" speech (Mill)   328
Cartesian dualism   89
Cartesianism   64, 80, 95
Cartesian metaphysical theory   101, 111
Cartesian pineal gland account   89
Cartesian rationalism   40
Cartesian substance dualism   89
Categorical imperative   214–215
Causal argument. *See* Cosmological
  argumentation
Causal conditions   45
Causal determination   320–321
Causal interactionism   89, 90
Causality, theory of   178
Causal *"necessity"*   280
Causal reasoning, famous canons of
  315–316
Causal relations, God and   85
Causation   162. *See also* Occasionalism
  billiard balls example   162
  external   185, 231
  idea of   162, 163, 228
  occasionalist theory of   93, 128
  theocentric theory of   83, 85
  universal, theory of   171
  voluntary/nonvoluntary   228
Cause, "occasional," "natural," "true"   86

Cause and effect   102, 117, 170, 228
  fictitious entities and   228
  ignorance of cause   73
Cavendish, Margaret Lucas   49–50
Chapters on Socialism (Mill)   314, 328
Character   312
  formation of   320
  "good character"   283
The Characteristics of the Present Age (Fichte)
  239, 246
Christianity/Christians. *See also* Jesus of
  Nazareth
  Catholic   53, 55, 63, 209
  central myths of   290
  Christendom and   336, 341, 342, 347
  "eternal indictment of"   359
  fideism and   18
  God of   24
  Jansenist   52–53
  paradox of   340
  Protestants   186, 187, 209
  revelation and   148
  truth of   338–339
  virtues of   42
Church's Index of Forbidden Books   59, 80, 81
Cicero   10, 11, 108
Circular reasoning   27
"Civilization" (Mill)   325
Civil liberty   11, 48, 190–191, 231, 325
Civil War, American   314, 329
Civil War, English   63
Class distinctions, abolition of   308
Classless society   301, 304, 306, 307, 308, 309
Class struggle, dialectical analysis of   308
Climacus, Johannes (pseudonym)   336, 337, 339
Cockburn, Catharine Trotter   112–113
Cogito   28, 66, 89, 340
"Coleridge" (Mill)   313
Coleridge, Samuel Taylor   314
Collected Works (Feuerbach)   287
Collected Works of John Stuart Mill (Robson)
  328, 329
The Collected Writings of Rousseau (Rousseau)
"Collective mediocrity"   326
"Collegiants"   63
Commentaries on the Laws of England
  (Blackstone)   225

366 | *Index*

Commonplace Book (Bentham)   226

Communism, morality and   305

Communist Manifesto (Marx and Engels)   274, 298, 299, 304, 305

   famous threat posed in   307

Communist revolutions   308

Communitarianism   267

Community, aristocratic rule and   7

"Compatibilism"   45, 171, 320

Comte, Auguste   317–318, 319–320

The Concept of Dread (Climacus)   336, 343–344, 345

The Concept of Irony (Kierkegaard)   335, 339

Concluding Unscientific Postscript (Climacus)   336, 337–338, 340, 341, 344, 345

   Appendix to   347

"Concupiscence"   60, 91

Conduct of the Understanding (Locke)   106

Confessions (Rousseau)   180, 184

Conflict of the Faculties (Kant)   201

Conscience. *See also* Human mind

   atheism and   244

   freedom and   91, 152

   God and   105

   humanity and   149–151, 188

   "inner voice of"   247

   intuitive recognition and   282

   "liberty of"   50

   morality and   152–153, 192, 267, 282, 323, 359

   rational intuition and   248

   society and   92, 153, 284

   "voice of"   245, 246, 247

Consciousness

   of God, self-consciousness and   290

   identity and   105

   "Unhappy Consciousness"   345

Consequentialism   216, 231, 267, 293

Consequentialist theory   322

Considerations on Representative Government (Mill)   313, 327

Constitution, republican   220–221

"The Contest in America" (Mill)   313, 329

Continental rationalism   199

Conway, Lady Anne Finch   77–78

Copernican model of universe   19

Corpuscularianism   19

Correspondence (Kant)   200, 201, 202, 203

"Correspondence theory"   203

Corsair   336, 347

Cosmological argumentation   9, 15, 26, 42, 122, 139, 164, 207, 278

Cosmological idea   206

Cosmological speculation   5, 6–7

"Creed of a Savoyard Priest"   183, 184, 185

Critical Journal of Philosophy   254

Critique of Hegel's "Philosophy of Right" (Marx)   297

Critique of Judgment (Kant)   199, 201, 208, 211

Critique of Political Economy (Marx)   299

Critique of Practical Reason (Kant)   199, 200, 201, 212, 213

Critique of Pure Reason (Kant)   2, 199, 200, 201, 202, 203, 204, 205, 206, 207, 208, 210, 212, 213, 223, 273

"Critique of the Gotha Program" (Marx)   299, 305, 306

"Critique of the Hegelian Dialectic" (Marx)   300

Cudworth, Damaris   127–129

Cudworth, Ralph   96, 97, 112, 127

d

D'Alembert, Jean le Rond   158, 182, 183, 222

Darwin, Charles   299, 356

Darwinian evolutionary theory   264, 318–319, 356

Darwinian natural selection   318–319

Das Kapital (Capital) (Marx)   299, 300, 303, 305

Daybreak (Nietzsche)   353, 358

Deception   283

De Cive (Hobbes)   37, 38, 42, 44, 46, 48, 74

De Corpore Politico (Hobbes)   37–38, 39, 41, 45, 46

Deduction   23

Deductive syllogisms   315

Defense of Mr. Locke's Essay of Human Understanding (Cockburn)   112–113

De Homine (Hobbes)   38, 42, 45

Deism   56, 135, 146, 148, 149, 157, 163, 165, 167, 186, 270

Delphic oracle   7, 58

Democracy   48, 76, 243

   Aristotle and   9

   pure   327

Democracy in America (de Tocqueville)   313

Democritus   6
Deontological ethics   294
Descartes, René   21–35
  biography   22–23
  cogito   28, 66, 89, 340
  freedom   30–31
  God   26–27
  humanity   27–30
  knowledge   23–25
  morality   31–32
  rationalist   21, 23
  reality   25
  society   32–33
de Silentio, Johannes (pseudonym)   346
Despair
  object of   345
  self-aware   343
Despotism   193, 200, 218
  anarchy and   284
  "of custom"   326
  earthly   186
  oppressive   220
  "purely native"   330
Determinism   321
  morality and   171
de Tocqueville, Alexis   313, 325
Deutsch-Französische Jahrbücher (the *German-French Annals*)   297
"Devil's advocate" objections   326
De vita beata (Seneca)   34
Dialectic, master-bondsman, master–servant   280, 307
"Dialectic of authority"   342
"Dialectical illusion"   206
"Dialectical materialism"   301
Dialectical reason
  absolute Truth and   257
  activity of   258
  dynamics of   241
  knowledge and   240
  logic of   258, 260, 262, 270
  Subject–object dichotomy and   243
  "thesis, antithesis and synthesis"   257
Dialectical sublation   258
Dialectical thought   253
  advantage of   288
  development of   362

Hegelian dialectic   264, 344
  idealists and   287
  interpersonal conflict and   300
  master–bondsman dialectic   280
  negative treatment of   207
  reality and   300, 301
Dialogues (Berkeley)   142
Dialogues (Rousseau)   184
Dialogues concerning Natural Religion (Hume)   158, 163, 164, 165, 166, 167
Dialogues Concerning the Two Chief World Systems (Galileo)   19
Dialogues on Metaphysics and Religion (Malebranche), Theodore, spokesman in   81, 82, 84, 85, 87, 89
Diderot, Denis   158, 181–182, 193, 222
The Difference Between Fichte's and Schelling's Systems of Philosophy (Hegel)   254
Dilemma   30, 135
  moral   267
"Disappointment-preventing principle"   234
Discourse of Miracles (Locke)   106
"Discourse on Happiness" (Du Châtelet)   223
Discourse on Inequality (Rousseau)   182–183, 190, 193
Discourse on Metaphysics (Leibniz)   116, 118, 119, 122, 124, 125, 126
Discourse on Method (Descartes)   22, 24, 28–29, 31
Discourse on the Arts and Sciences (Rousseau)   182, 192–193
The Discourses (Machiavelli)   17
Dissertations and Discussions (Mill)   313, 314
"Dissertation upon the Nature of Virtue" (Butler)   153
Divine revelation. *See* Revelation
Doctrine of Religion (Fichte)   245
Dogmatism   26, 52, 101, 167, 186, 200, 202
  idealism and   240
  nihilism and   352
Dogmatists   54, 55, 117
Dostoyevsky, Fyodor   351
Dread   335, 343–344
Drunkenness   326–327
Dual aspect theory   77, 167, 206, 209, 213, 245
Dualism(s)   27–28, 260, 263
  Cartesian   89
  substance   71, 89, 134, 137

368 | *Index*

Dualistic interactionism 29, 34, 61, 89
Dualist(s) 7, 133
Du Châtelet (Marquise) 222–223
Duty/duties
  cult of pure 267
  extra-regarding or self-regarding
    234–235
  to God 229
  internal sanction of 323
  moral 142, 175
  morality 245
  "moral" precepts and 148
  sense of 214
  types of, trichotomy 46

e

Early modern empiricism 1
Early modern rationalism 1
Ecce Homo (Nietzsche) 351, 352
Eclecticism 10
Economic and Philosophic Manuscripts
  (Marx) 298, 302, 303, 304, 306, 307
Education (Kant) 202, 210
Egalitarians 356
Ego, pure 340
Egoism 47, 223
  Hobbesian 170, 174
Either/Or (Kierkegaard) 335, 336, 339, 340,
  344, 345
Elements of Law (Hobbes) 37–38
Elizabeth (Princess) 23, 30, 32, 33–35, 116
Elliot, Hugh 314
Émile (Rousseau) 183, 185, 186, 187–188,
  192, 197
Emotions 43–44. *See also* Happiness
Emotivism, ethical 172
Empedocles 6
Empiricism 8, 23, 38, 44, 48, 61, 63, 82, 112,
  118, 127, 131, 132, 135, 143, 155, 159,
  161–162, 199, 200, 221, 228, 230, 236, 240,
  241, 270, 287, 288, 317
Encyclopedia (Diderot and D'Alembert)
  182, 222
Encyclopedia of the Philosophical Sciences
  (Hegel) 255, 256, 259, 262
End justifies the means, maxim 233, 267
"End of knowledge is power" 39

Enfranchisement of Women (Mill) 331
Engels, Friedrich
  class-based moralities and 306
  collaborator role 308
  economic idealism and 269
  freedom and 305
  at Schelling's inaugural lecture 256
Enlightenment 199, 248, 253, 356
Enlightenment, French 181
Enlightenment slogan 254
Enlightenment thought 95, 131, 147, 165, 182,
  183, 193, 284, 305, 311, 324
Enquiry concerning Human Understanding
  ("first *Enquiry*") (Hume) 157, 159, 161,
  163, 164, 165, 168, 170
Enquiry concerning the Principles of
  Morals ("second *Enquiry*") (Hume)
  157, 168
"Entelechies," (Leibniz) 120
"Enthusiasm" 103–104, 149
"Entity/entities"
  concept of 227–228
  perceptible, real 227
Epictetus 10–11
Epicureanism 11
Epicurus 10
Epiphenomenalism 177
Epistemology 1, 2. *See also* Knowledge
  "moral epistemology" 65
  Vision in God doctrine 82, 84, 85, 93
Equal opportunity 328
Eschatological consequentialism 293
Essay Concerning Human Understanding
  (Locke) 95, 96, 97–101
  Book III of 99–100
  Book II of 106
  Book I of 97–98
  Book IV of 100, 102
  chapters in 103
  Cockburn's defense of 112–113
An Essay on the Relation of Cause and Effect
  (Shepherd) 177
Essays (Montaigne) 18
Essays, Moral and Political (Hume) 157
Essays and Aphorisms (Schopenhauer) 284
Essays on Some Unsettled Questions of Political
  Economy (Mill) 313, 328

Essays on the Law of Nature (Locke) 95, 108
Essays on the Perception of an External Universe
  (Shepherd) 177
Essay towards a New Theory of Vision (Berkeley)
  131, 141
The Essence of Christianity (Feuerbach) 274,
  287, 288, 290, 292, 293, 294
The Essence of Faith According to Luther
  (Feuerbach) 287, 293
Essence of Religion (Feuerbach) 287
Ethical consequentialism 231
Ethical emotivism 172, 173
Ethical Philosophy (Kant) 199
Ethical rationalism 172
Ethical theory, important text on 322
Ethics, social 324
The Ethics (Spinoza) 2, 64–65, 66, 67, 68, 70,
  72, 73, 74
Euclidean geometry 52, 65, 161, 311
Eudaimonia. See also Happiness
  Definition 9
Eudaimonism 223
Euthyphro problem 126
Evil
  choice between good and 343
  "privation theory" 122
  three types of 122–123
  truth and 326
An Examination of Sir William Hamilton's
  Philosophy, (Mill) 314, 321
Existence
  reality and 339
  as a synthesis 338
Existentialism, founder of 256
Expression, freedom of 326
"Extra-regarding" pleasures/pains 230, 234

f
Faith
  "bad" 343
  doing good and 293–294
  paradoxical 346
Faith and Knowledge (Hegel) 261
Fatalism 125, 206, 281, 321
Fear and Trembling (Kierkegaard) 336, 346
Female philosophers. *See* Women
  philosophers

Feuerbach, Ludwig 285–295
  atheism and 292, 293, 294, 295
  biography 286–287
  freedom 293
  God 289–291
  humanity 292–293
  knowledge 287–288
  morality 293–294
  reality 289
  society 294
"A Few Words on Non-Intervention" (Mill)
  313, 330
Fichte, Johann Gottlieb 237–251
  biography 238–239
  freedom 246–247
  God 244–245
  humanity 245–246
  idealism and 238, 240, 242, 243, 251
  intellectual intuition and 248
  knowledge 239–242
  morality 247–251
  reality 242–244
  society 249–251
  writings of 239
Fictions, theory of 227
Fideism 18, 56, 57, 58, 61, 166, 167
  key points of 53–54
  radical 52
Fideistic deism 170
Fideists 57
Fifteen Sermons (Butler) 146, 149
  preface to 147, 152, 154
Filmer, Robert (Sir) 108–109, 193
Forbidden Books, Church's Index of 59, 80, 81
Foundations of Physics (Du Châtelet) 222
Fragment on Government (Bentham) 225, 226
Franco-Prussian War 359
Freedom. *See also* Liberty
  Bentham 230–231
  Berkeley 141
  Butler 152
  definition of 90
  Descartes 30–31
  dread and 343
  of expression 326
  Feuerbach 293
  Fichte 246–247

370 | *Index*

Freedom. *See also* Liberty (*cont'd*)
  Hegel 265–266
  Hobbes 45–46
  Hume 170–171
  idealism and 240
  Kant 211–212
  Kierkegaard 345
  Leibniz 125
  Locke 106–107
  Malebranche 90–91
  Marx 304–305
  Mill 320–321
  naturalizing 293
  Nietzsche 357
  Pascal 58–59
  Rousseau 190–191
  "savage man" and 190
  Schopenhauer 280–282
  Spinoza 73–74
  "of the will" 357
"Free Mind" 266
Free-thinkers 139, 140
Free will 45
  as illusion 39
  self-determination and 266
  superstition of 357
French Revolution 185, 191, 196, 226, 238, 239, 250, 254, 267, 268
Freud, Sigmund 214, 278, 355
Friendship, love and 32

g

Gabler, Georg Andreas 256
Galileo Galilei 19
The Gay Science (Nietzsche) 351, 353–354, 355, 358
  "God is dead." 354
The Genealogy of Morals (Nietzsche) 353, 355, 358
"General will" 193, 194
Genius 6, 20, 23, 52, 63, 84, 102, 114, 179, 188, 308, 326
German idealism 1, 265, 270, 271, 284, 312, 330, 362
German idealists 224, 237, 253, 275, 295, 300, 348
The German Ideology (Marx and Engels) 298, 300, 301, 302, 303, 304, 306, 307

German nationalism 251
Glorious Revolution 109
God. *See also* "Ontological" argumentation
  Abraham story and 346–347
  Aristotle and 9
  Author of Nature 90, 136, 148, 165
  Bentham 228–229
  Berkeley 138–140
  Butler 148–149
  carrot and stick, as administrator of 228
  clockmaker, the 120
  cosmological argument for 9, 15, 26, 42, 122, 139, 164, 207, 278
  Descartes 26–27
  "duty to" 229
  existence of 16, 42, 43, 88, 137, 208, 212, 228, 290, 319, 356
  Feuerbach 289–291
  Fichte 244–245
  "God is dead." 262, 277, 351, 354
  "God is love." 289
  grace of 53, 58, 59, 60, 91, 121
  Hegel 260–263
  Hobbes 41–43
  Hume 163–167
  Kant 207–209
  Kierkegaard 340–342
  Leibniz 121–124
  Locke 103–105
  Malebranche 87–88
  "malicious demon" and 24, 26, 28
  Marx 302–303
  Mill 317–319
  "new" argument for 27
  Nietzsche 354–355
  Pascal 55–57
  perfect nature of 29, 124
  Rousseau 186–187
  Schopenhauer 278–279
  Spinoza 69–71
  as Substance 25, 66–67, 69
  "wager argument" 56–57
  wisdom of 128
  worship of 42
Godwin, William 196
Goethe, Johann Wolfgang von 273
"Golden Age," ancient Greece 2, 5, 10

Index **371**

Golden Rule 43, 46, 127, 151, 154, 191
Good
  choice between evil and 343
  three kinds of 126
"Good-will" 150, 214
Gorgias 6
Government(s)
  allegiance to one's 175
  interference, liberty and 327, 328
  punishment and 235
  Two Treatises of Government 108–111
  types of 48, 76, 110, 195, 220
The Government of Poland (Rousseau) 184–185
Government powers 110
"Greatest happiness or greatest felicity
    principle" 229
Greco-Roman paganism 277, 278
Greece, "Golden Age" of ancient 2, 5, 10
Grote, George 228
Grounding for the Metaphysics of Morals (Kant)
    201, 209, 213
Grundrisse (Marx) 299

h

"Handmaiden of religion," philosophy as 12
Happiness. *See also Eudaimonia*
  described 44
  "Greatest Happiness Principle" 322
  hedonism and 229
  morality and 107, 321
  principle of utility and 322–324
  "three sorts of people" 56
  "true happiness" 34
Hardy, Harriet 330
Hedonism
  egoistic 149, 154
  ethical 229
  hedonic calculus 230
  human dignity and 322
  opposition to 223
  suspicion of 10
  universal human 229
Hegel, Georg Wilhelm Friedrich 252–270
  "absolute idealism" of 251, 253, 258, 259, 265
  biography 253–256
  freedom 265–266
  God 260–263

humanity 263–265
"idealism of the finite" 261
knowledge 256–258
master–bondsman dialectic 280
morality 266–267
reality 259–260
society 267–270
"Unhappy Consciousness" 345
utilitarianism 306
Hegelian collectivism 294
Hegelian concept of alienation 290
"Hegelian dialectic" 258, 264, 300, 344
Hegelian idealism 302, 349
"Hegelian logic" 289
Hegelian "pantheism" 255
Hegelian philosophy 288, 291, 297
Hegelians, Young 287, 297, 298, 300, 302, 335
Hegelian system 289, 333, 337, 340, 348
Hegelian thought 291, 292, 335, 339
Heidegger, Martin 360
Hegelian panentheism 290, 293
"Hellenistic" period 10
Heraclitus 5
Hesiod 5
"Historical materialism" 301
History (Thucydides) 37
History of England (Hume) 158
History of India (Mill) 311
Hitler, Adolf 251, 352
Hobbes, Thomas 29, 36–50
  biography 37–38
  determinist 45
  freedom 45–46
  God 41–43
  greatest book of 39
  hedonism and 107, 151, 154
  humanity 43–45
  knowledge 38–40
  materialist 30
  "mental discourse" 39
  morality 46–47
  reality 40–41
  society 47–48
Hobbesian egoism 170, 174
"Hobbist" 97
The Holy Family (Marx and Engels) 298
Homer 5

Index

Human, All Too Human (Nietzsche) 351, 353, 358, 359
Human beings
 modes and 71
 superior people 356
Human "dignity" 343
"Human emancipation" 305
Human individuality 326
Humanity
 Bentham 229–230
 Berkeley 140–141
 Butler 149–151
 Descartes 27–30
 Feuerbach 292–293
 Fichte 245–246
 Hegel 263–265
 Hobbes 43–45
 Hume 167–170
 Kant 209–211
 Kierkegaard 342–345
 Leibniz 124
 Locke 105–106
 Malebranche 89–90
 Marx 303–304
 Mill 319–320
 Nietzsche 355–356
 Pascal 57–58
 Rousseau 187–189
 "savage man" and 189
 Schopenhauer 279–280
 Spinoza 71–73
Human mind. *See also* Brain; Conscience
 dimensions of 28
 powers of 99
 as a thinking thing 29
Human nature
 duality of 58
 fulfillment of 56
 political society and 234
 social structures and 44
Human Nature (Hobbes) 37, 40
Human psychology 72–73
Hume, David 155–178
 biography 156–159
 "empirical test" of 160, 162, 168
 freedom 170–171
 God 163–167

humanity 167–170
 induction and 315
 knowledge 159–161
 morality 171–178
 reality 161–163
 Rousseau and 158, 183–184
 skepticism of 40, 159, 160, 161, 175, 177, 178, 316
 society 171–176
"Hylomorphism" 8, 16, 119
"Hypothesis of concomitance" 117

i

"I am thinking, therefore I exist" 28
"Idea for a Universal History with a Cosmopolitan Purpose" (Kant) 217
Idealism 135, 330, 349
 "absolute" 251, 253, 257, 258, 259, 265, 285
 "critical" 238, 256
 dogmatism and 240
 economic 269
 father of 131
 "of the finite" 261
 freedom and 240
 German 265, 270, 271, 284, 312, 330, 362
 Hegelian 302, 349
 materialism and 303
 modern 288
 monistic 260
 "objective" 257
 objective 265
 philosophical 294
 "practical" 243
 romantic 313
 "subjective" 241, 242, 251, 256, 265
 "thing-in-itself" 240
 transcendental 206, 238, 241, 276, 288
 voluntaristic 272
Idealists 76, 143, 256, 287. *See also* German idealists
Idea(s)
 Cartesian definition of 117
 categories of 98–99
 cosmological 206
 "ideas on Logic" 312
 mind-independent 131, 136

no innate   27
  perceptions, impressions and   162
"Idea of a Perfect Commonwealth" (Hume)   176
"Identity, personal"   105
"Idols," (Bacon) 19
Ignorance   45, 141, 290
  camouflaging our   46, 106, 357
  determining causes and   73
  one's own life and   343
  superstition   149
  vice and   32
"Ill-will"   150
Imagination   23
  real things and   136
Immaterial, root of   228
Immaterialism   133, 134, 136, 138, 139, 143
"Immediate certainties"   352
"Immoralists"   358
Incorporeal substance   40–41
Individualism   226, 265, 266, 268, 294
Individuality, human   326
Inductive reasoning   315, 316
Infinity, idea of   99, 102
Influence of Natural Religion on the Temporal Happiness of Mankind (Bentham)   228, 229
Injustice   47
Intellect, as phenomenon of will   276
"Intellect, the"   28
Intellectual intuition, controversial claim to   248
Intelligent design, hypothesis of   140, 163, 165, 186, 319
Interactionism   29, 34, 61, 66, 85, 89
International relations   217, 221, 250, 251, 267
"Introduction to a Critique of Political Economy" (Marx)   303
An Introduction to the Principles of Morals and Legislation (Bentham)   1, 225, 231, 232, 234–235, 235
"Intuition"   23
"Invisible hand" theory, (Smith) 269

j

Jansenists/Jansenism   52–53, 59, 81, 88, 91
Jaspers, Karl   348, 360
Jesus of Nazareth   91, 92, 104, 105, 153, 165, 186, 340, 341
Johannes Climacus (Climacus)   336, 337–338

Johnson, Joseph   196
Johnson, Samuel   132
Judaism   71, 209, 358
Judeo-Christian tradition   148, 149
Julie (Rousseau)   183
"Junction-of-interests-prescribing principle"   234
Justice
  and freedom (Kant)   216–221
  and utility (Mill)   324
  appearance of   33
  international   329–330
  "sentiment of"   324
"Just war"   16

k

Kant, Immanuel   198–223
  biography   199–202
  categorical imperative of   322
  freedom   211–212
  God   207–209
  humanity   209–211
  knowledge   202–206
  "League of Nations"   218, 221, 269, 270
  morality   212–216
  ontological argument   207–208
  philosophical questions of   203, 207, 209, 212
  "principle of humanity"   215
  reality   206–207
  society   216–221
  "thing-in-itself"   238, 275, 276, 354
  writings of   199, 201, 202
Kierkegaard, Michael Pederson   334
Kierkegaard, Peter   336
Kierkegaard, Søren   333–348, 344
  biography   334–337
  existentialism, founder of   256
  freedom   345
  God   340–342
  humanity   342–345
  knowledge   337–339
  morality   346–347
  pseudonyms of   336, 337, 339, 341, 344, 345, 346
  reality   339–340
  society   347–348
  temperament of   335
  writings of   336

374 | *Index*

Knowledge
  Bentham   226–227
  Berkeley   132–134
  Butler   147
  conceptual "abstract"   282
  degrees of   66
  Descartes   23–25
  "direct and intuitive"   282
  "end of knowledge is power"   39
  Feuerbach   287–288
  Fichte   239–242
  God's   87
  Hegel   256–258
  Hobbes   38–40
  Hume   159–161
  "idols" and   19
  "immediate"   241
  Kant   202–206
  Kierkegaard   337–339
  Leibniz   117–119
  Locke   97–101
  Malebranche   81–84
  Marx   300–301
  "mediated"   241
  Mill   314–316
  Nietzsche   352–353
  noumenal   275
  Pascal   53–55
  phenomenal   275
  a priori (non-sensible)   275–276
  reliable   65
  Rousseau   185
  Schopenhauer   274–276
  self-   290
  Spinoza   64–65
  subject, object and   275
  three degrees of   101
  types of   100–101
"Know thyself" motto   7, 58
Knutzen, Martin   199

l

Laboring class   301
Lampe, Martin   202
Law(s)
  morality   214
  Mosaic   358
  of motion   41, 140

  natural   46, 47, 88, 109, 127, 142, 316
  physics, Newtonian   204
  types of   107–108
  universal   211, 214, 215, 216, 218, 315, 320
Law of Identity   97, 243
Law of Non-Contradiction   97
"League of Nations"   218, 221, 269, 270
Lectures on Ethics (Kant)   202, 211
Lectures on Philosophical Theology (Kant)   199
Lectures on the Essence of Religion (Feuerbach)
    287, 291, 292, 293, 294
Lectures on the History of Philosophy
    (Hegel)   260
Lectures on the Philosophy of Religion
    (Hegel)   263
Leibniz, Gottfried Wilhelm   135, 164
  biography   115–116
  freedom   125
  God   121–124
  humanity   124
  knowledge   117–119
  metaphysical works of   119
  monads and   119–120
  morality   126
  notions, analysis of   118
  "pre-established harmony"   120
  reality   119–121
  society   126–127
  Sophie Charlotte and   116, 118, 122
  Spinoza and   64
  sufficient reason, principle of   67–68, 69, 117,
    118, 119, 121, 122, 222
  writings, most important   116
Leibnizian-Wolffian philosophy   200, 223, 275
Lessing, Gotthold   338
A Letter Concerning Toleration
    (Locke)   96, 104–105
Letter on French Music (Rousseau)   182
Letters of John Stuart Mill (Elliot)   314
Leviathan (Hobbes)   38, 39, 40, 41, 42–43, 44,
    45, 46, 47, 48
Liberalism   284
Liberty. *See also* Freedom
  civil   11, 48, 190–191, 231, 325
  government interference and   327
  natural   45
Life of Friedrich Nietzsche (E. Nietzsche)   352
"Life of Jesus" (Hegel)   261

Locke, John   94–113
  biography   95–96
  freedom   106–107
  God   103–105
  humanity   105–106
  knowledge   97–101
  morality   107–108
  pseudonym of   96
  reality   101–103
  society   108–111
  writings of   96
Logic (Kant)   202, 203, 212
Love. *See also* Self-love
  of our neighbor   153
  types of   32
"Loving-kindness"   283
Ludwig Feuerbach and the Outcome of Classical German Philosophy (Engels)   300

m
Machiavelli, Niccolo   17–18
Maimonides, Moses   12
Malebranche, Nicolas   79–93
  Aristes (the student)   81, 82, 85, 87
  billiard balls example   162
  biography   80–81
  freedom   90–91
  God   87–88
  humanity   89–90
  knowledge   81–84
  morality   91
  occasionalism, theory of   81, 85, 86, 89, 128, 245
  reality   84–87
  society   92
  Vision in God doctrine   82, 84, 85, 93
"Malicious demon"   24, 26, 28
Manifesto of the Communist Party (Marx and Engels)   274, 298, 299, 304, 305
Married Women's Property Bill   314
Martensen, Hans L.   335, 336
Marx, Karl   296–309
  atheism and   296, 297, 302, 308
  biography   297–300
  classless society   301, 304, 307, 308, 309
  "dialectical materialism"   301
  economic idealism and   269
  freedom   304–305

God   302–303
  humanity   303–304
  knowledge   300–301
  morality   305–307
  reality   301–302
  society   307–308
Marxian social theory   308
Masham (Lady)   127–129
Master–bondsman dialectic   280
Master–servant relation   304, 307
Master-slave relation   300
Materialism   41
  "dialectical materialism"   301
Materialistic monism   41, 43, 61
Maxims
  cynical political   218
  end justifies the means   267
  moral code and   31, 318
  nothing can come from nothing   25
  society, "two maxims"   327
  universal law and   214, 215–216
Mechanistic materialists   6
Medici court   19
Medici family   17
Medieval philosophy   12–16
Meditations on First Philosophy (Descartes)   22, 24, 25, 26–27, 28, 29, 64, 87, 88
"Meditations on Knowledge, Truth, and Ideas" (Leibniz)   116, 117, 121–122
"Mental discourse"   39
Mersenne, Marin   22, 37, 38, 52, 53, 65
Metaphysical duality   27
Metaphysical Elements of Justice (Kant)   201, 218
Metaphysical Elements of Justice and Metaphysical Principles of Virtue (Kant)   201
Metaphysical Foundations of Natural Science (Kant)   201
Metaphysical theory of reality   276–278
Metaphysics
  areas of   1
  "need for," human reason and   277
  question, profound   121
  ultimate reality and   5
Metaphysics of Morals (Kant)   201
"The Metaphysics of Sexual Love" (Schopenhauer)   283–284

376 | *Index*

Middle Ages   13, 14
Milesians   5
Mill, Harriet Taylor   330–332
Mill, James   306, 310
Mill, John Stuart   310–332
  on Bentham   321–322
  Benthamite   311, 313, 322
  biography   311–314
  canons of causal reasoning   315–316
  "Capital Punishment" speech   328–329
  ethical theory and   233
  freedom   320–321
  God   317–319
  humanity   319–320
  knowledge   314–316
  Marx on   308
  morality   321–324
  phenomenalism of   314, 317, 319
  reality   316–317
  society   325–330
  Taylor Mill and   330–332
  "two maxims" of   327
  utilitarian, classical   320
  writings of   313–314
Mind-body problem, "dual aspect"
    solution   71
Mind-body relation   34, 111, 120
Miracles   56, 70, 88, 89, 106, 128, 148, 149, 157,
    158, 163, 165, 166, 316
Modern philosophy
  deficiency of   338
  "father" of   4
  "immediate certainties"   352
"Molyneux's problem"   134
"The Monadology" (Leibniz)   116, 118, 119,
    120, 124, 126
Monads   223
  introduction of term   119–120
  theory of   118
  three levels of   120
Monarchy   48, 76
Monas   121
Monism   63, 66, 67, 78, 259, 268
  materialistic   41, 43, 61
  numerical   66–67, 68
Monistic idealism   260
Monologion (Anselm)   14

Monotheism   164, 186
Montaigne, Michel de   18, 54
"Moral antecedents"   321
Moral code, provisional   31
Moral duty   142, 175, 245
"Moral epistemology"   65
Morality
  Bentham   231–234
  Berkeley   142–143
  Butler   152–153
  Descartes   31–32
  divine command theory of   318
  divine theory command   318
  Feuerbach   293–294
  Fichte   247–251
  Hegel   266–267
  "herding-morality"   358
  Hobbes   46–47
  Hume   171–178
  "imperative mood" and   321
  Kant   212–216
  Kierkegaard   346–347
  Leibniz   126
  Locke   107–108
  Malebranche   91
  Marx   305–307
  Mill   321–324
  Nietzsche   357–359
  Pascal   59–60
  Rousseau   191–192
  Schopenhauer   282–283
  Spinoza   74
  "unnatural," branding of   324
  "weal and woe"   283
Moral laws   214
"Moral nature"   152
Moral relativists   16, 46, 74, 152
More, Henry   77
Mosaic law   358
Murder
  biblical reference   346, 347
  capital punishment and   329
  deliberate   283
  of enemies   342
  premeditated   220
  snipers, enemy troops and   250
My Own Life (Hume)   159

Index 377

n

Napoleon 239, 251, 253, 254, 255, 264, 272, 273, 313
Natural History of Religion (Hume) 158, 163, 164
Naturalism 294
Natural law 46, 47
Natural Law and *Faith and Knowledge* (Hegel) 254
Natural Theology (Sebond) 18
Nature
  Author of (God) 90, 136, 148, 165
  laws of 142
  phenomenal events of 315
  "unnatural," branding of 324
"Nature" (Mill) 316, 324
"Nature abhors a vacuum" 52
"The Nature of Truth" (Leibniz) 117
"The Necessity of a Reform of Philosophy" (Feuerbach) 294
"The Negro Question" (Mill) 329
Neo-Platonism 10, 13
Neo-Platonists 12
Neue Rheinische Zeitung (the New Rhineland News) 298
New Essays on Human Understanding (Leibniz) 116
The New Organon (Bacon) 19
"A New System of Nature" (Leibniz) 119, 124
Newton, Isaac 41, 87, 92, 96, 106, 116, 140, 156, 168, 199, 362
Newtonian physics 204, 205, 222, 311
Newtonians 121, 211
Nietzsche, Friedrich 349–361, 354
  atheism and 354–355
  biography 350–352
  freedom 357
  God 354–355
  "God is dead" 277, 354
  humanity 355–356
  knowledge 352–353
  morality 357–359
  "perspectivism" 353
  reality 353–354
  society 359–360
Nietzsche Archive 351
Nietzsche contra Wagner (Nietzsche) 351

Nihilism 239, 352
"*Nirvana*" 282
"Nominalism" 39, 133
Nominalist 226
"Non-free will" 357
Nothingness 55, 92, 243, 258, 282
  desirability of 282
  negativity, pure 258
  "*nirvana*" 282
  "why is there something rather than nothing?" 121
Notions
  analysis of 118
  of spirit 140
  use of 137, 138
Noumenal knowledge 275
Noumenal reality 281, 282
  appearances of 260
  causality and 278
  "dialectical illusion" and 206
  of metaphysical things 206
  phenomenal appearances and 11, 211, 221, 275
  "phenomenon of the will" and 281
  realm of 209
  will as the only 276
Noumenal things-in-themselves 242, 278
Nullifying/nullity 258
Numerical monism 66–67, 68

o

Observations upon Experimental Philosophy (Cavendish) 50
Occasionalism 81, 85, 86, 89, 121, 128, 245
Occasionalists 93, 120, 128, 136
Ockham's razor 48
Of Liberty and Necessity (Hobbes) 38, 45
"*Of the Difference between a Genius and an Apostle*" (Kierkegaard) 341
"Of the Original Contract" (Hume) 175
"Of the Origin of Government" (Hume) 176
Oligarchy 48
"*On a Supposed Right to Lie Because of Philanthropic Concerns*" (Kant) 201
"On Contingency" (Leibniz) 125
On Free Choice of the Will (Augustine) 13, 26

378 | Index

"On Freedom and Possibility" (Leibniz) 116, 125

On Human Nature (Schopenhauer) 281, 284

"On James Mill" (Marx) 304

On Liberty (Mill) 310, 313, 325, 327, 330

On Natural Law (Hegel) 234

"On Natural Law" (Leibniz) 126

"On Nature Itself" (Leibniz) 119

"On Perplexing Cases in Law" (Leibniz) 115

On Reason: One, Universal, and Infinite (Feuerbach) 286

"On Suicide" (Hume) 159

On the Basis of Morality (Schopenhauer) 274, 282, 284

"On the Basis of Our Belief in a Divine Governance of the World" (Fichte) 239, 244

On the Body. See De Corpore Politico

On the Citizen. See De Cive

"On the Common Saying: 'This May be True in Theory, but it does not Apply in Practice'" (Kant) 216

"On the English Reform Bill" (Hegel) 256

"On the Failure of All Attempted Philosophical Theodicies" (Kant) 201

On the Fourfold Root of the Principle of Sufficient Reason (Schopenhauer) 273, 274, 275

On the Freedom of the Will (Schopenhauer) 274

On the Happy Life (Seneca) 34

"On the Immortality of the Soul" (Hume) 159

On the Improvement of the Understanding (Spinoza) 64, 74

On the Jewish Question (Marx) 297, 305

"On the Ultimate Origination of Things" (Leibniz) 116, 122

On the Will in Nature (Schopenhauer) 274

On the World in Nature (Schopenhauer) 276

"Ontological" argumentation 15, 16, 27, 69, 88, 121–122, 168, 278

  form of 69

  God's necessary existence 318

  Idea of God 139

  indivisibility 66, 68

  as nonempirical 164

  rationalists and 207–208

Ontology

  "entities" and 227–228

  theory of fictions 227

"On Truth and Lying in a Non-Moral Sense" (Nietzsche) 351

On Vision and Colors (Schopenhauer) 273, 274

"On Women" (Schopenhauer) 284

"Optimism" 277

Organon (Aristotle) 19

p

Paganism 277, 278

Paine, Thomas 196

Pandemic suffering 279

Panentheism 68, 87, 260, 289

  Hegelian 290, 293

  monistic 70, 77, 263

  rationalistic 268

  Spinozistic 88, 245

Panentheistic monism 68

Panopticon Writings (Bentham) 225, 235

Pantheism 260

Parallelism 71, 89, 117, 124

Paraphrasis, technique of 226–227

Parerga and Paralipomena (Schopenhauer) 274

Parmenides 5–6

Pascal, Blaise 57–60

  aphorisms of 55, 59

  biography 52–53

  fideism of 52, 53–54, 56, 58, 61

  freedom 58–59

  God 55–57

  humanity 57–58

  knowledge 53–55

  morality 59–60

  reality 55

  society 60–61

Passions

  direct or indirect 169

  "unreasonable" 172

The Passions of the Soul (Descartes) 23, 29, 32, 34

"Passive Obedience" (Berkeley) 131, 142, 143, 175

Pauline principle 142–143

Pelagians/Pelagianism 59, 91

Pensées (Pascal) 53, 54, 59, 60, 61

Perceptible real entities 227

Perception(s)

  "apperception" 120, 121

  awareness and 65

Index | **379**

belief generated by 317
  primacy of 98
  substances and 162
  tiny 118
"Perpetual peace" 217, 269, 270
Perpetual Peace (Kant) 201, 217
Personality 345
"Perspectivism" 353
"Phantasms" 41, 258
Phenomenalism 159, 162, 168, 177, 317,
  319, 354
Phenomenology of Spirit (Hegel) 254, 255, 257,
  261, 262, 264, 265, 267
Phenomenon
  canons of causal reasoning 315–316
  "of the will" 276, 281
Philosophical Commentaries (Berkeley) 131,
  134, 138, 139, 141, 142
Philosophical Fragments (Climacus) 336, 337,
  340, 345
Philosophical Letters (Cavendish) 49
Philosophical questions 203, 207, 209, 212
Philosophical Radicalism 312
Philosophical Radicals 311
Philosophical relation, kinds of 161
Philosophical Thoughts (Rousseau) 182
Philosophy. *See also* Modern philosophy
  ancient 5
  ethical theory, important text on 322
  as "handmaiden of religion" 12
  medieval 12–16
Philosophy of History (Hegel) 267
Philosophy of Mind (Hegel) 259, 266
Philosophy of Nature (Hegel) 259, 262
The Philosophy of Poverty (Proudhon) 298
Philosophy of Right (Hegel) 255, 258, 266,
  267, 268–269
Pineal gland 29–30, 49, 89
Plato
  aristocracy and 9
  Euthyphro problem of 126
  Socrates and 6–8
  Sophists and 6
  theory of ideas 7
  in triumvirate 5
Platonic vitalism 77
Platonism 14, 15, 90, 102, 141, 154, 354, 355
Plotinus 12

Point of View for My Work as an Author
  (Kierkegaard) 340, 348
Political Discourses (Hume) 158
"Political Economy" (Rousseau) 183
"Political emancipation" 305
"Political revolutions" 308
Political society, human nature and 234
Political Treatise (Spinoza) 64, 76
Political Writings (Kant) 199, 202
Polytheism 164, 186
The Positivity of the Christian Religion (Hegel)
  254, 261
Post-Aristotelians 4, 10–12
Potentiality, principle of 8
The Poverty of Philosophy (Marx) 298, 301, 308
Power(s)
  "end of knowledge is power" 39
  freedom and 106
  government 110
  of human mind 99
  sovereign 92
  value of 44
"Pre-established harmony" 120
Preliminary Theses on the Reform of Philosophy
  (Feuerbach) 287, 290, 293, 294
The Present Age (Kierkegaard) 336, 341, 347
Pre-Socratics 5–6
"Primary notion" 25
"Primary Truths" (Leibniz) 117
The Prince (Machiavelli) 17–18, 33, 35, 74
Principia Mathematica (Newton) 222
"Principle of asceticism" 232
"Principle of humanity" 215
"Principle of sympathy and antipathy" 232
"Principle of utility" 229
Principles of Cartesian Philosophy (Spinoza) 64
"Principles of Nature and Grace"
  (Leibniz) 119, 121, 124
Principles of Philosophy (Descartes) 23, 24,
  25, 31, 34
Principles of Political Economy (Mill) 328, 331
*The Principles of the Most Ancient and Modern
  Philosophy* (Conway) 77
Principles of the Philosophy of the Future
  (Feuerbach) 287, 288, 291, 292, 294
Progressivism 284
Prolegomena to Any Future Metaphysics (Kant)
  200, 201, 202, 203, 204, 205, 206, 212

380 | Index

Proletariat 301, 307, 308
Property rights 219
  private property 328
  "property-compact" 250
Proslogion (Anselm) 14, 15
Protagoras 6
Proudhon, Pierre-Joseph 298, 301
Provincial Letters (Pascal) 53, 59
Pseudonym 96, 184, 228, 336, 337, 339, 341,
  344, 345, 346
Psychology
  human 72–73
  laws of 320
Punishment
  capital punishment 235, 314, 328–329
  government and 235
"Pure ego" 340
Pure reason 27, 38, 41, 48, 82, 83, 205, 207, 212,
  257, 264
"Pure utility" 267
Purity of Heart Is to Will One Thing (Kierkegaard)
  342–343, 346
Pyrrhonian skepticism 26
Pyrrhonism 11, 86, 129, 161
Pyrrho of Elis 11
Pythagoras/ Pythagoreans 5, 337
Pythagorean Theorem 100, 161, 203

q

The Querist (Berkeley) 132, 141, 143

r

Radical empiricism 38, 44
Radical materialism 41
Radical skepticism 26, 185
"Rational animal" 8
Rationale of Judicial Evidence (Bentham) 312
Rationalism 135
  continental 199
  ethical 172
Rationalists 7
  dogmatism of 101
"Rational matter" 49, 50
Reality. *See also* Noumenal reality; Substances
  Bentham 227–228
  Berkeley 134–138
  Butler 147
  Cartesian metaphysical theory of 101, 111

Descartes 25
  dialectic thought and 301
  existence and 339
  Feuerbach 289
  Fichte 242–244
  Hegel 259–260
  Hobbes 40–41
  Hume 161–163
  Kant 206–207
  Kierkegaard 339–340
  Leibniz 119–121
  Locke 101–103
  Malebranche 84–87
  Marx 301–302
  metaphysical theory of 276–278
  Mill 316–317
  Nietzsche 353–354
  only one infinity 260
  Pascal 55
  Rousseau 185–186
  Schopenhauer 276–278
  Spinoza 66–69
  three sorts of 102
  ultimate 7
Reason
  aphorisms and 55
  basic operations of 23
  "Cunning of Reason" 264, 266
  dialectic 240
  dialectic of metaphysical 211
  as "handmaiden of faith" 261
  infinite 87, 88, 245, 246
  as natural revelation 104
  "need for metaphysics" and 277
  pure 27, 38, 41, 48, 82, 83, 205, 207, 212,
    257, 264
  revelation and 104
  ruling the world 277
  suffering and 279
  sufficient reason principle 67–68, 117,
    118, 119, 121, 122, 164, 222, 275, 276,
    279, 280
  "truths of" 122
  virtue and 192
Reasonableness of Christianity (Locke) 106
Reasoning. *See also* Ontological argument
  circular 27
  inductive 154, 315, 316

Index | **381**

"*reckoning*" 39
"science of" 315
"Reflections on the Common Concept of Justice"
  (Leibniz) 126, 127
"*Reflective thinking*" 261
"Reform Act of 1867" 328
Reform Bill, Disraeli's 314
Relativism 6, 61, 86, 177, 308, 359
  moral 46, 48, 63, 267, 306
Religion. *See also* God; Revelation
  aesthetic 262
  afterlife and 228–229
  "handmaiden of religion" 12
  "metaphysics of the people" 277
  natural 228–229, 262
  supernatural 294
  True Religion 42, 104, 167, 186, 244–245,
    261, 278
Religion within the Limits of Reason Alone
  (Kant) 201, 210, 254
Religious skepticism 175, 229
Renaissance 4, 12, 14, 20, 22, 75
Renaissance thinkers 17–18
Repetition (Kierkegaard) 336
Representation [Vorstellung] 276
Republican constitution 220–221
Revelation
  authority of 27, 342
  belief in 244
  Christian teachings and 148, 149
  "enthusiasm" and 103–104
  interpretations of 43
  private/personal 103, 104, 146
  reason and 104
  scriptural 149, 186
  supernatural/divine 42, 85, 86, 122,
    239, 244
The Reveries of the Solitary Walker
  (Rousseau) 184, 187, 191–192
Rheinische Zeitung (*Rhineland News*) 297
Ricardo, David 303, 306, 311
Richard Wagner in Bayreuth (Nietzsche) 351
Rights 216
  "abstract right" 325
  ethical 222
  international agreements and 329–330
  obligations and 234
  "original rights" 250

property 219
  violation of 326
Romantics 71, 184
Rousseau, Jean-Jacques 179–197
  biography 180–185
  Calvinism and 180, 181
  freedom 190–191
  God 186–187
  humanity 187–189
  Hume and 158, 184–185
  knowledge 185
  morality 191–192
  operas of 181, 182
  pseudonym of 184
  reality 185–186
  Savoyard priest and 183, 185, 186, 188,
    192, 196
  society 192–195
Rousseau, Judge of Jean-Jacques
  (Rousseau) 184
Rulers, appearance of justice and 33
Rules. *See also* Golden Rule
  civilized countries and 330
  divine law and 229
  for living, maxims and 31
  moral 142, 323
  reciprocally binding 219
  ruling the world 258, 277
  society and 18
  utilitarian punishment and 235
Rules for the Direction of the Mind
  (Descartes) 1, 22, 23
"Rules of justice," primitive 189
Rule-utilitarianism 131, 142, 143, 174, 192, 323

S
Sanction(s)
  duty as internal 323
  question of 232, 233
Sartre, Jean-Paul 343, 348
"Savage man" 189, 190, 193
Savoyard priest 183, 185, 186, 188, 192, 196
Scandalmongering 347
Schelling, Friedrich Wilhelm Josef 253–254,
    256, 261, 335–336
Schopenhauer, Arthur 271–284
  biography 272–274
  dualism of 355

Index

Schopenhauer, Arthur (*cont'd*)
 freedom 280–282
 God 278–279
 humanity 279–280
 knowledge 274–276
 morality 282–283
 reality 276–278
 society 283–284
 sufficient reason principle 275, 276, 277, 279, 280, 281
 writings of 274
Science of Knowledge (Fichte) 239, 240, 244
Science of Logic (Hegel) 255, 256, 257, 262
Science of Mind (Hegel) 262
Science of Rights (Fichte) 239, 250
The Search after Truth (Malebranche) 81, 82, 86, 88, 89–90, 91
The Search for Truth (Descartes) 23
Sebond, Raymond 18
Selected Writings (Bentham) 230, 235
Self, consciousness and 105
Self-aware despair 343
Self-consciousness 290
Self-determination 211
 free will and 266
Self-interest 234
 camouflaging 174
Self-knowledge 290
Self-love 150–151
 humanity and 187
 products of 189
 sympathy and 169
Self-preservation 44, 72, 74, 90, 187, 194, 248, 250, 356
"Self-protection" 325
"Self-regarding conduct" 326
Self-satisfaction 44
Seneca 34
"Sensitive matter" 49, 50
Sextus Empiricus 10, 11, 18, 40
Sexual behavior 235, 283–284, 300
 homosexual sex 236
 sexual desire/passion 210, 280, 283, 283–284
 sexual exploitation 304
Shakespeare, characters of 343
Shame 150–151, 169, 189
Shelley, Mary 196

Shepherd, Lady Mary 177–178
Short Treatise on God, Man, and His Well-Being (Spinoza) 64
Sickness unto Death (Kierkegaard) 336, 340, 344, 345
Skepticism
 ataraxia and 11
 as Hellenistic philosophy 11
 Humean 144
 partial 83
 radical (Pyrrhonian) 26, 185
 religious 175, 229
 Sophists and 6
Skeptics 54
"Slave-morality" 358–359
"The Slave Power" (Mill) 329
Slavery
 abolishing 330
 fight against 329
Smith, Adam 158, 303, 306, 311
 "invisible hand" theory of 269
Social contract
 civil society and 47, 220
 voluntary 110
The Social Contract (Rousseau) 183, 185, 190–191, 194, 195
 alternative title 194
Social ethics 324
"Social evolutions" 308
Socialism: Utopian and Scientific (Engels) 299, 301
Socialists 328
Social progress 326
Social reform 308
Society, 32–33. *See also* Political society
 Bentham 234–236
 Berkeley 143
 Butler 153–154
 Descartes 32–33
 Feuerbach 294
 Fichte 249–251
 "general will" of 183, 194
 Hegel 267–270
 Hobbes 47–48
 Hume 171–176
 international relations and 221, 250, 267
 Kant 216–221

Kierkegaard 347–348
Leibniz 126–127
Locke 108–111
Malebranche 92
Marx 307–308
Mill 325–330
Nietzsche 359–360
Pascal 60–61
Rousseau 192–195
"savage man" and 193
Schopenhauer 283–284
Spinoza 74–76
Socioeconomic classes 304
master–servant relation 307
Sociopolitical philosophy 305
Socrates 40
"know thyself" motto 7
Plato and 6–8
Sophists and 6
in triumvirate 5
Solipsism 26, 185, 242, 243
"Some Words on Pantheism"
(Schopenhauer) 277
Sophie Charlotte (Queen) 116, 118, 122
"Sophistry" 318
Sophists 6, 7
Soul. *See also* Spirit
immateriality of 112
monads and 119–120
"The Source of Contingent Truths"
(Leibniz) 125
Sovereign(s)
social contract and 194
subjects and 48
Sovereign powers 92
Spinoza, Baruch 62–78
biography 63–64
"dual aspect" solution 71
Ethics 2
freedom 73–74
God 69–71
humanity 71–73
human psychology 72–73
knowledge 64–65
Leibniz and 64
monism of 66–67, 68, 77, 78
morality 74

reality 66–69
society 74–76
writings of 64
Spinozism 77
Spirit. *See also* Soul
analysis of 136–137
"free spirits" 358
notions of 140
voice of the 246
The Spirit of Christianity and Its Fate
(Hegel) 254, 261
Stages on Life's Way (Kierkegaard) 336, 340,
341, 344, 346
Stoicism 265
"bear and forbear" 10
skepticism and 11
Stoics 34
The Subjection of Women (Mill) 313, 314,
327–328, 330
Subjectivity 339
Subject–object dichotomy 275, 338
dialectical effort and 338
dialectic and 243
Sublation, dialectical 258
Substance dualism 28, 66, 71, 89, 134, 137
Substances. *See also* Reality
complete 121
"corporeal" 133
created, causal relations and 85
definition of 68
divine 70, 72, 73, 87, 244
"entities" and 227
God as only 66–67, 69, 73
incorporeal 40–41
infinite and independent 25
innumerable 40
"material substance" 136
mind-independent 133, 134, 136
natural religion and 262
nonextended 129
numerical monism and 66–67
perception and 162
physical 99, 101, 162
primary and secondary 8
spiritual 28, 34, 36, 99, 101, 136, 138, 162,
168, 303
"unthinking" 135

384 | *Index*

Suffering
 identifying with 282
 reason and 279
 true salvation and 280
Sufficient reason, principle of 67–68, 117, 118, 119, 121, 122, 164, 222, 275, 276, 279, 280, 281
Suicide 159, 196, 256, 272, 351
 humanity and 280
 morality and 215, 282
 premeditated 248
Summa contra Gentiles (Aquinas) 15
Summa Theologica (Aquinas) 15
Superior people/superiority 356
Superstition 42, 70, 149, 167, 187, 244, 260, 357
"Suspension of judgement" 316
Syllogism 135–136, 315
Sympathy 169
"Sympathy and antipathy, principle of" 232
The System of Ethics (Fichte) 239, 246, 247
A System of Logic (Mill) 313, 314, 315, 320–321, 330

t

Tabula rasa theory 98, 118
Taylor, John 330
Teleological argumentation 278
Thales 5, 10
"That Politics May Be Reduc'd to a Science" (Hume) 176
Theism (Mill) 318–319, 320
Theodicy 88, 122
Theodicy (Leibniz) 116, 117, 124, 125, 126
Theologico-Political Treatise (Spinoza) 64, 70, 75, 76
Theoretical questions, areas of 2
Theoretic humanism 302
Theory of fictions 227
The Theory of Vision Vindicated and Explained (Berkeley) 134
"*Theses on Feuerbach*" (Marx) 300, 302
"Thesis, antithesis and synthesis" 257, 258
"Thing-in-itself" 276, 278
 idealism 240, 257
 inner nature and 277
 mere appearance and 276
 noumenal 242

phenomenal appearances and 275
 unknowable 238
 the will as 276
Thoughts on Death and Immortality (Feuerbach) 286, 289, 292, 293
Thoughts on the Education of Daughters (Wollstonecraft) 196
Three Dialogues between Hylas and Philonous (Berkeley) 131, 137, 138, 139, 142
 Philonous and Hylas 137–138
Three Essays on Religion (Nature, Utility of Religion, and Theism) (Mill) 314, 318, 330
Thucydides 37
Thus Spake Zarathustra (Nietzsche) 351, 354, 356, 358, 360
Torricelli 52
"Towards a Critique of Hegel's Philosophy" (Feuerbach) 286, 287, 289, 302, 305
"*Towards a Critique of Hegel's Philosophy of Right: Introduction*" (Marx) 302, 305
Training in Christianity (Kierkegaard) 336, 340, 341
Tranquility. *See* Ataraxia
Transcendental idealism 206, 238, 241, 276
Transmutation of creatures 78
Treatise (Locke) 108
Treatise concerning the Principles of Human Knowledge (Berkeley) 131, 132, 133, 135, 136–137, 139, 140, 141, 142
 "spirit," analysis of 136–137
A Treatise of Human Nature (Hume) 157, 159, 160, 161, 168–169, 169, 171, 174, 187
Treatise on Ethics (Malebranche) 81, 91, 92
Treatise on Man (Descartes) 23, 29, 80, 85
Treatise on Nature and Grace (Malebranche) 81
"Treaty Obligations" (Mill) 329
True cause 86
"True happiness" 34
True Religion 42, 104, 167, 186, 244–245, 261, 278
Truth(s)
 freedom of expression and 326
 "of reason" 122
 subjective 339
 types of 118, 338–339
"Tübingen Essay" (Hegel) 261

The Twilight of the Idols (Nietzsche)   278, 351, 352, 353, 354, 356, 357, 359, 360
The Two Fundamental Problems of Ethics (Schopenhauer)   274
Two Minor Ethico-Religious Essays (Kierkegaard)   336
Two Treatises of Government (Locke)   95, 96, 108–111

u

"The Unchangeableness of God" (Kierkegaard)   341
"Understanding, the"   86, 90
Universal laws   211, 214, 215, 216, 218, 315, 320
Untimely Meditations (Nietzsche)   351, 353
Untruth   348, 353
Upanishads   274
Utilitarian consequentialism   267
Utilitarianism   267. *See also* Rule-utilitarianism
   approaches to   322–324
   classical   142
      "theory of mutual exploitation"   306
Utilitarianism (Mill)   310, 313, 320, 322, 325, 330
Utilitarian movement   225
"Utilitarian Society," founding of   312
Utilitarian theory   220, 267
Utility
   general   324
   no "direct proof" of   232, 322, 323–324
   principle of   229, 234, 322
Utility of Religion (Mill)   318

v

Van den Ende, Francis   63
Vindication of the Rights of Man (Wollstonecraft)   196
A Vindication of the Rights of Woman (Wollstonecraft)   196–197
Violence   283
Virtue ethicist   173
Virtue ethics   16
Virtues
   cardinal   13, 46, 283, 358
   Christian   42
   definition of   174
   pivotal   7
   reason and   192

Vision in God doctrine   82, 84, 85, 93
The Vocation of Man (Fichte)   239, 241, 245, 248
Voltaire   122, 181–183
Volition   141, 231, 317
Voluntary actions   44, 107, 125, 170, 171, 228, 234, 280, 321, 327
Vorwärts! (Forward!)   298
Voting rights   219, 235, 327

w

"Wager argument"   56–57
Wagner, Richard   350, 351
Wanderer and His Shadow (Nietzsche)   351
War/warfare
   of aggression   330
   "just war"   16
   "self-defense, right of"   250
   undertaken by state   269
The Way towards the Blessed Life, or the Doctrine of Religion (Fichte)   239, 242
Well-being   153
Westminster Review   312
"What is Enlightenment?" (Kant)   201, 202
What Real Progress Has Metaphysics Made in Germany since the Time of Leibniz and Wolff? (Kant)   202
Whitehead, Alfred North   8
"Will, the"   28, 44, 86, 90
   "acts of will"   275–276
   freedom of   357
   intentional act and   230
   "phenomenon of the will"   276, 281
   as "thing-in-itself"   276
   Volition and   141
   voluntary acts and   44
The Will to Power (Nietzsche)   351, 352, 353, 354, 356, 357, 359, 360
Wissenschaftslehre (Fichte)   239, 240
Wolff, Christian   116, 275
   Leibnizian-Wolffian philosophy   200, 223, 275
Wollstonecraft, Mary   196–197
Women
   equality of   331–332
   Rousseau on   188
   subordination of   327–328

386 | *Index*

Women philosophers
    Cavendish, Margaret Lucas 49–50
    Cockburn, Catharine Trotter 112–113
    Conway, Lady Anne Finch 77–78
    Cudworth, Damaris 127–129
    Du Châtelet (Marquise) 222–223
    Elisabeth of Bohemia (Princess) 33–35
    Masham (Lady) 127–129
    Mill, Harriet Taylor 330–332
    Shepherd, Lady Mary 177–178
    Wollstonecraft, Mary 196–197
Wordsworth, William 312
The Works of Jeremy Bentham (Bentham) 225, 233, 234, 235

Works of Love (Kierkegaard) 336, 340, 345, 347
The World as Will and Representation (Schopenhauer) 273, 274, 275, 278, 279, 281, 283, 284, 350
Wretchedness 58, 60, 189
Writings (Marx) 300

y

Yearbooks for Scientific Criticism 256
Young Hegelians 287, 297, 298, 300, 302, 335

z

Zeno of Citium 10, 11, 34
Zoroastrianism 262